ANNALS

OF THE

ARMY OF THE CUMBERLAND

W. S. Rosecrans

ANNALS

of the ARMY of the

CUMBERLAND.

Drawn by T. Taylor

Engraved by Illman Bros.

STACKPOLE
BOOKS

Published by
STACKPOLE BOOKS
5067 Ritter Road
Mechanicsburg, PA 17055
www.stackpolebooks.com

Printed in the United States of America

10   9   8   7   6   5   4   3   2   1

Cover design by Wendy A. Reynolds
Indexed 2003 by Al Austin, member, American Society of Indexers

Library of Congress Cataloging-in-Publication Data

Fitch, John, fl. 1864.
    Annals of the Army of the Cumberland : 1861–1863 / by
John Fitch.—5th ed.
        p. cm.
    Originally published: Philadelphia : J.B. Lippincott, 1864.
    Includes bibliographical references.
    ISBN 0-8117-2627-4 (alk. paper)
        1. United States. Army of the Cumberland. 2. United States—
History—Civil War, 1861–1865—Regimental histories. 3. United
States—History—Civil War, 1861–1865—Campaigns. 4. Stones
River, Battle of, Murfreesboro, Tenn., 1862–1863. 5. Chickamauga,
Battle of, Ga., 1863. I. Title.

    E470.5 .F55 2003
    973.7'41—dc   2002075948

ANNALS

OF THE

ARMY OF THE CUMBERLAND:

COMPRISING

BIOGRAPHIES, DESCRIPTIONS OF DEPARTMENTS, ACCOUNTS OF
EXPEDITIONS, SKIRMISHES, AND BATTLES;

ALSO ITS

POLICE RECORD

OF

SPIES, SMUGGLERS, AND PROMINENT REBEL EMISSARIES.

TOGETHER WITH

Anecdotes, Incidents, Poetry, Reminiscences, etc.

AND

OFFICIAL REPORTS OF THE BATTLE OF STONE RIVER AND OF THE
CHICKAMAUGA CAMPAIGN.

By JOHN FITCH,
ATTORNEY AT LAW, ALTON, ILLINOIS, AND PROVOST JUDGE, ARMY OF THE CUMBERLAND.

Illustrated with Steel Portraits, Wood Engravings, and Maps.

FIFTH EDITION:

PHILADELPHIA:
J. B. LIPPINCOTT & CO.
1864.

STEREOTYPED BY L. JOHNSON & CO.

PRINTED BY LIPPINCOTT & CO.

PREFACE.

To the soldiers of the Army of the Cumberland, and to their friends at home, the author presents this volume of portraits, sketches, and incidents,—a work undertaken at the solicitation of many friends, with the view of affording pleasure to our soldiers and imparting information to the people, and, if it may be, to secure a fund for the erection of a monument to overlook the battle-field of Stone River, Tennessee, where rest, "unknelled, uncoffined, and unknown," hundreds of American citizens.

This work is not intended as a history of the Rebellion, in a general sense, nor even as a detailed account of events occurring in the history of the Army of the Cumberland. It is simply a collection of sketches and portraits of many of its representative men, and a narration of many interesting events which have transpired within its lines. The more important of its military operations are given up to the time of going to press. The various departments are sufficiently described to illustrate their practical operation, at every fireside; and in the grouping together of incident and anecdote, and of spy and smuggling events, the author has aimed to give life and zest to the volume. The work is issued almost regardless of cost, and is intended as a souvenir that shall remain when this army shall have been disbanded and these stirring times and scenes have passed away,—one which, it is hoped, the soldiers of the Cumberland will prize as *their book*, to be preserved by succeeding generations as a household treasure, its pages to be scanned by the descendant, while glorying in the deeds of a patriot sire during the dark days of the Great Rebellion.

The author has endeavored to be modest and impartial in his meed of praise,—a most difficult task, where so much can be truly said of so many. The thousands of noble men in the Army of the Cumberland, who have left home, friends, fortunes, and high position, to brave the perils of camp and battle-field, all merit mention in such a work. Especially was it desirable that many particularly daring deeds of our officers and privates should find record within these pages; but the original limit of the work has already been greatly exceeded, and prudence restrains from a further advance.

Although intended as a picture of our army, it is far from being complete. We have used but a small portion of attainable matter and portraits; and many of our best and most notable generals—as Crittenden, Reynolds, Wood, Granger, Mitchell, Morgan, Turchin, and other high officers—we are unable to properly present in this volume. Ample material is left for a second volume of the "Annals," should its publication prove desirable.

To many friends in the army the author is indebted for assistance in collecting material, and with them any credit arising from the work is duly shared. The composition of such a volume amid the incidents and excitement of the camp will, we trust, constitute some apology for literary deficiencies. All responsibility respecting misstatement of fact in military movements, or of dulness or exaggeration in estimating individual character, rests with the author. Brief outlines were furnished, in some instances: for the rest, we have garnered here and there, with these pages as the result.

This volume is published under peculiar circumstances; and, in behalf of the officers of our army,—whom it represents,—the author tenders acknowledgment for its successful presentation to the public, as a work of art, to Messrs. ILLMAN BROTHERS, the contracting engravers, for the surprisingly faithful likenesses of the portraits,—to MESSRS. L. JOHNSON & CO., and to their admirable proof-reader and critic, for elegance of typography and correctness of diction,—to our publishers; MESSRS. J. B. LIPPINCOTT & CO., for their encouragement, enterprise, and generous expenditure of capital,—and to all connected with the work, for despatch, it being issued within a period of ninety days from the commencement.

Should the work prove sufficiently successful, the monumental idea will be carried out, and a shaft will be erected upon the battle-field, similar in design to that upon our title-page,—not of a boastful and vainglorious character, but simply to proclaim the story of the conflict and to transmit to posterity the moral of civil war.

TULLAHOMA, TENN., AUGUST 10, 1863.

PREFACE TO THE FOURTH EDITION.

THE author, in behalf of the officers of the Army of the Cumberland, makes his grateful acknowledgments for the flattering reception given thus far to this volume. To the public press of the country he is especially grateful for their most liberal, and to himself gratifying, mention of the work.

The present edition contains additional matter of much value, viz.: an account of the campaign of Chattanooga and the consequent battle of Chickamauga, with a map exhibiting the strategic operations of our army. With this addition the work is complete as a history of the Army of the Cumberland under Major-General W. S. Rosecrans.

This work having attracted unexpected attention, and its authorship having been questioned, and attributed to various persons in order to injure them by an implication of self-praise, the author, in justice to those gentlemen, appends his name to the title-page of this edition. His only motive for withholding it was a desire to avoid any notoriety in the connection, as book-making is not his trade.

The author desires to assure the public that the work originated solely in the desire *to do good*,—to cheer and encourage the army, to enlighten the people at home, to advance the Union cause, and to erect a stone upon the first great battle-field of our army. This latter idea will be faithfully carried out if the work be sufficiently successful. If, however, the scheme shall prove inexpedient, owing to unquiet times in Tennessee in the future, or from other cause, the fund accruing from the sale of the volume will be directed to some charitable purpose or channel for the benefit of the invalid or crippled soldier of the Union, his widow or orphans.

THE AUTHOR.

CHATTANOOGA, TENN., NOV. 25, 1863.

ILLUSTRATIONS.

Steel Plates.

Wood Cuts.

Lithographs.

6

CONTENTS.

𝕭𝖎𝖔𝖌𝖗𝖆𝖕𝖍𝖎𝖈𝖆𝖑 𝕾𝖐𝖊𝖙𝖈𝖍𝖊𝖘.

7

Army Departments.

Expeditions, Battles, and Skirmishes

Army Police Record

Miscellaneous.

Appendix.

ARMY OF THE CUMBERLAND.

Major-General William S. Rosecrans and Staff.

WILLIAM STARK ROSECRANS was born in Kingston, Delaware county, Ohio, on the 6th of September, 1819. His mother, the daughter of Stephen and Mary Hopkins, of Wyoming, Luzerne county, Pennsylvania, and his father, the eldest son of Daniel Rosecrans and a Miss Crandell, were married in Luzerne county, Pennsylvania, and in 1808 emigrated to Ohio. The lineal ancestors of the family, about whom much discussion and inquiry have arisen of late, originally came from Brandenburg, whence they removed to Amsterdam, and subsequently, about the year 1660, emigrated to North River, in what was then the Dutch colony of New Amsterdam, and now the State of New York. His name is a peculiar one, and has been variously written and pronounced. The correct spelling, however, as given above, is the same now as it has always been, and the proper, though not the popular, pronunciation is "Rosakrontz."* The father of the subject of this sketch was a prosperous business man, a farmer, and also engaged in mercantile pursuits. In the War of 1812 he served as adjutant to a light-horse company under General Harrison, thus practically exhibiting that self-sacrificing patriotism which was through life one of his most marked characteristics. His intelligence, energy, and determination gave him a wide influence among his neighbors and friends. Though

---

* The derivation is from " Rose," a rose, and " Kranz," a wreath,—making the signification " a wreath of roses," a beautiful idea imparted to nomenclature by a race noted for their appreciation of the poetical and musical.

quiet and unassuming, it was the general opinion that he was possessed of an iron will and a hot temper. His honesty was proverbial, and in those days of early pioneer life he was the arbiter of many disputes and controversies, which were referred to "Captain Rosecrans" with the confident assurance that his decision would be just and impartial. Thus as a friend and adviser of the surrounding people, who often came to him with their trials and difficulties and vexations, he lived as a patriarch in the land, honored and respected by all.

Although his parents were in comfortable circumstances, his father being owner of a store, a farm, and a number of town lots and houses, young William was early taught habits of industry, attending school in winter and working in the garden and upon the farm in summer. At thirteen he had become quite a man upon the farm, and at fourteen was sent to the store of one David Messenger, seven miles from his home, to close up the business, which he did successfully. At times he acted as book-keeper in the store, collected debts; and for some months in 1837 was clerk in a clothing-store. At the age of sixteen he made a trip down the Mississippi River for the purpose of seeing the country, and had proceeded as far as Vicksburg when he was taken ill and compelled to return. In 1837, when in his eighteenth year, he applied to the Secretary of War for an appointment to the Military Academy at West Point, and through the influence of Judge Alexander Harper, member of Congress from his district, and his home friends, obtained the position. The class which he entered numbered one hundred and twelve at the beginning of the course, but at the time he graduated, in June, 1842, it had decreased to fifty-six. In the generality of the studies he stood third, fourth, and fifth in rank. After graduating he entered the Engineer Corps as second lieutenant, and was ordered to report for duty to Colonel R. E. De Russey, at Fortress Monroe, Virginia. Here he remained until the 20th of August, 1843, acting most of the time as First Assistant Engineer, having been promoted to a first lieutenancy in the preceding April. On leaving Fortress Monroe, he was ordered to West Point, as

Assistant Professor in the Engineering Department, which position he held until the next year, when he was detailed as Assistant Professor of Philosophy. In this department he remained one year, and for two years thereafter was First Assistant Professor of Engineering, during a portion of which time he also served, by request, as Post Commissary and Quartermaster, besides having for nine months entire charge of the erection of the cadet barracks then building at that place.

In August, 1847, Lieutenant Rosecrans was detailed to relieve Lieutenant H. L. Eustis, engineer in charge of the fortifications in Newport harbor, Rhode Island. Here five years were spent in constructing a military wharf and completing the batteries and interior arrangements of the forts. Here also he designed a general system of permanent barracks, which was submitted to the War Department, and by it referred to a select committee, who reported favorably upon it. In 1852, a special appropriation was made to survey Taunton and New Bedford harbors, with a view to permanent improvements. Lieutenant Rosecrans was detailed to take the survey, and in three weeks made thirty thousand soundings. In the spring of 1853 he was ordered on detached service to report to the Secretary of the Navy at Washington, by whom he was assigned to the Chief of the Bureau of Docks and Yards, and detailed by the latter as constructing engineer at the Washington Navy Yard. Here he constructed a marine railway, built a large saw-mill, and remodelled and improved the Dahlgren ordnance buildings, which were found to be in a bad condition. He also made plans for an immense machine-shop, a block of buildings 450 by 288 feet. These were to be so constructed that one engine would drive the machinery of the establishment. Plans were also submitted for the blacksmith-shop, it being so arranged that the smoke from the forges would pass off from one stack. He also designed shops for the manufacture of anchors, cables, and blocks, to take the place of the old ones. These plans were submitted to the proper authorities, and approved, and the estimates for construction made. They were much admired at the time by all

who saw them; and the general himself yet takes pride in them
as among his best scientific efforts. Before steps were taken
towards carrying them out, however, his health failed him, and
he was told by his physician that he must have a rest of at least
three months. Applying for leave of absence, he was told by
the chief engineer that he could not be spared. He then resolved to leave the service, and sent in his resignation to Jefferson
Davis, at that time Secretary of War. The latter remonstrated,
and reiterated the decision of the chief engineer, but finally
gave him three months' leave of absence, telling him that at
the expiration of that time he would probably change his mind,
but if not his resignation would be accepted.

His health not improving, he was obliged to persist in his
resignation, which took effect April 1, 1854. He then went to
Cincinnati, and engaged in business as an architect and consulting engineer. His health was still feeble for several months; but
he continued in that profession until June, 1855, when the agent
of an English and American coal company invited him to take
charge of the company's mining-interests on Coal River, Kanawha county, Virginia. One or two veins had been worked
and exhausted, and the geology of the country was not then
sufficiently known to enable the company to open new ones
with any certainty. His first business in his new position was
to examine and report upon the condition of the mines, and the
next to make a geological survey of the country. This he did,
and, by a series of scientific explorations, became so well acquainted with the topographical aspect of the vicinity that he
was able to point out with an almost marvellous certainty the
localities where new and profitable veins could be opened. Satisfied
with the result of his survey, he submitted to the company plans
for the development of the mines. To transport the coal from
the mines to the river, it was necessary to construct a canal; and
he became the president of the Coal River Slack-Water Navigation Company, formed for that purpose, of the stock in which
three-fifths was owned by the State and two-fifths by private
individuals. The company now desiring to engage in the manu-

facture of coal oil, a practical engineer was employed to devise the plans. The result was a report that the oil could be made, but that a certain amount of capital must be furnished in advance. The sum stated was thought to be extravagantly large, and the disagreement which arose upon this point prevented further operations in that direction.

General Rosecrans then determined to engage in the business himself, at Cincinnati. In company with a man who claimed to be experienced in the manufacture, he began the erection of a small establishment; but before it was finished he associated with him two other partners, and constructed largely increased works, capable of producing five hundred gallons per day. His first partner failing to make a marketable article, General Rosecrans determined to try it himself, and accordingly entered the laboratory and began a series of experiments with a view to the manufacture of a pure and odorless oil. After sixteen days' labor, he had about succeeded in his efforts, when he was terribly burned by the combustion of benzole gas, caused by using what was then supposed to be a patent safety-lamp. Although his clothes and flesh were badly burned, he had the presence of mind to make such dispositions that the fire was extinguished without injury to the works. He then walked home,—a mile and a half,—and took to his bed, where he lay nearly eighteen months, and for a time it was doubtful whether he could recover. The scars left by this accident have not yet disappeared, one upon his forehead being visible in his published portraits. During this time of illness his business languished and nearly ceased. His partners were honorable men, but inexperienced in chemistry and therefore not successful. Upon recovering, he again prosecuted the business, and was getting his establishment into good working-order, when the rebellion broke out.

The results of his investigations in the laboratory were numerous and valuable. He believes he was the first to obtain a good article of odorless oil from petroleum. Directing his attention to the chemical composition of soaps, he made some valuable discoveries, among which was the finding of a cheap and sure process of manufacturing a soap with chlorine properties. He also experimented in the construction of lamps, was the first to successfully use the round wick in burning coal oil, and invented a lamp upon which short chimneys could be used with a satisfactory result.

At the beginning of the rebellion General Rosecrans was a private citizen, pursuing the even tenor of his way, his time and attention being occupied with his business and his family affairs. He had never been a politician. He had no taste for the publicity of political life, preferring the ease and quiet of home. But he was known as a military man of experience and judgment, and petitions soon came thronging in upon him from the different wards to assist in drilling the Home Guards. In response to them, he gave his services to the 14th Ward Company, called the "Marion Rifles." When it became evident that military measures must be taken to crush the rebellion, the patriotism inherited from his sire would not permit of his remaining an idle spectator of the scenes about to transpire, and he immediately offered his services to Governor Dennison of Ohio. They were at once accepted, and he was requested to act as engineer and lay out Camp Dennison, which he did. He was next sent to Philadelphia to confer with gun-manufacturers, with a view to procuring a supply for the Ohio troops, and thence proceeded to Washington, to make arrangements for their clothing and pay. While at the capital, he presented to the War Department an application, endorsed by Generals Scott, McClellan, Totten, Mansfield, and others, for an appointment as a brigadier-general of volunteers. Returning to Cincinnati, he found awaiting him there the Governor's commission as Chief Engineer of Ohio, with the rank of colonel, it being intended that he should serve upon the staff of General McClellan. The latter, however, having been appointed a major-general in the Regular Army of the United States, it became obvious to Colonel Rosecrans that he could not serve in that position; and he concluded to enter upon active service in the field. He was accordingly commissioned colonel of the 23d Ohio Regiment, and repaired to Camp Jackson, at Columbus, which he named Camp Chase. Here he prepared a permanent camp for the 23d, 24th, 25th, and 26th Ohio Regiments. Three days afterwards he received the appointment of brigadier-general in the Regular Army, with orders to report to General McClellan, which he did the same night at Cincinnati.

General Rosecrans was ordered immediately to Western Virginia. Arriving at Parkersburg, he assumed command of a brigade composed of the 8th, 10th, 17th, and 19th Indiana Regiments. McClellan having himself reached Grafton soon after, General Rosecrans was ordered to proceed by rail with his brigade to Clarksburg as fast as possible. Advancing from that place, he entered the town of Buckhannon without resistance, and proceeded twenty miles farther, in the direction of Beverly, camping at Roaring Creek within three and a half miles of the enemy, who were intrenched in a forest near the western base of Rich Mountain. The rebel force was then estimated to number from five to ten thousand, but has since been ascertained to have been less. Their position was a gap in the Alleghany Mountains, ten miles from Beverly, through which the road to the latter town ran, and which was the only crossing over those mountains on what was known as the Central Road. The remainder of their force was intrenched on Laurel Hill, on the main road running north to Grafton, Beverly being the centre at which both these roads met and crossed each other. On the 8th of July, 1861, General McClellan made an armed reconnoissance of the enemy's position, supported by General Rosecrans's brigade, which was left in the advance to lead the attack to be made the next morning. Returning to camp, General Rosecrans found there a young man for whom he had been searching some three days, and who was well acquainted with the country, his father living at the top of the mountain. From him he ascertained that there was a by-path by which he could reach the summit of the mountain without advancing on the road in which the rebels were encamped. This fact was at once reported to General McClellan by General Rosecrans, who proposed to take advan-

tage of it, surprising and seizing the rebel position. The plan
was approved, it being arranged that General Rosecrans should
move at three o'clock in the morning, enter the woods, reach
the summit of the mountain, and attack the enemy, while
McClellan, so soon as he should hear Rosecrans's guns, was to
move upon their front. That portion of the work allotted to
General Rosecrans was faithfully performed. Starting in the
midst of a rainstorm, he reached the enemy's position after a
severe march of ten hours through a rough and trackless forest.
It was still raining heavily as he encountered the rebel advance-
guard; but, after a brief reconnoissance, he began the attack, at
half-past three in the afternoon.

At five the battle was over. The gap had been carried, and
two pieces of artillery and a number of prisoners were captured,
the enemy retreating to their camp near the base of the mountain. McClellan failed to co-operate as was expected, and with
his seventeen hundred men General Rosecrans prepared to hold
the gap and advance upon the rear of the enemy's camp. At
this juncture some of the scouts captured and brought in a
rebel officer, Colonel Scott, of the 44th Virginia Infantry, who
said that his regiment was marching to reinforce the troops holding the gap when that point was attacked and carried by the Federal troops, and that it had retreated with the rest to the camp
below. It was now six o'clock in the evening; the men were
weary with their day's work, the one day's rations which they
had brought with them were exhausted, and a heavy rebel force
was in their front. The situation was now dangerous; but the
general determined to hold his position at all hazards, and began
preparations to that end. A portion of the 19th Ohio was posted
on the ridge, covering his rear. One of the captured guns and
a body of troops were posted on the road looking towards Beverly,
and the other gun and a portion of the 8th Indiana placed in
position looking towards the rebel camp. By this time it was
quite dark, and the rain coming down in torrents. The pickets
kept up a constant firing through the night, but, with this exception, nothing occurred to disturb its stillness. At three in the

morning a prisoner was captured, who stated that the enemy, alarmed at the dangerous position he occupied between the two bodies of our forces, was preparing to withdraw from it. Upon receipt of this intelligence, General Rosecrans immediately moved upon their camp and captured it, with two hundred and eight tents, all their artillery, tools, axes, stores, and equipage of every kind, eighty wagons, and some eleven hundred prisoners. The dispersion and capture of this force compelled the rebel General Garnett to retreat from his position at Laurel Hill towards the Northwestern Virginia Road.   General McClellan now pushed on to Beverly, when, learning of Garnett's retreat, he advanced to Cheat Mountain, from whence he was summoned, immediately after the battle of Bull Run, to Washington.

The command in Western Virginia now devolved upon General Rosecrans. Thus far success had attended the Federal arms in every important movement within his department; but the prospects for the immediate future were not bright. The term of his three-months men was just expiring, and he was faced by a rebel army flushed with their recent victory at Bull Run. His orders were simply to hold Western Virginia as best he could. His three-months troops were soon gone, and all he could do was to occupy the Northwestern Virginia Road, Cheat Mountain, and other strong positions, and await reinforcements from the new levy of three hundred thousand men which had been ordered. These began to arrive in due season; and, learning soon after that Floyd was attempting to cross the river at Carnifex Ferry, thus threatening General Cox's command at Gauley, General Rosecrans, with seven regiments of raw troops with arms just put into their hands, marched to attack Floyd and relieve Cox. When within seventeen and a half miles of the enemy's position, he learned that Floyd was strongly intrenched at Carnifex Ferry. Advancing immediately, he reached the vicinity of the ferry that afternoon, and, after reconnoitring the position, began the attack at three o'clock.   Night set in before any decisive result had been achieved, and our troops lay upon their guns, ready to renew the contest in the morning.   When morning came, however, it was

2

found that Floyd had evacuated his position and retreated under cover of night, destroying the ferry-boat as he left. As soon as the necessary preparations could be made, General Rosecrans crossed the river and began the pursuit, in the direction of Cheat Mountain. Floyd was joined in his retreat by Wise, and their united commands—numbering five thousand three hundred men —strongly intrenched themselves upon the top of the mountain. The roads were in an almost impassable condition and the weather stormy and inclement, and further operations against the enemy in their present position were deemed inadvisable. Many of our troops were nearly destitute of clothing; and General Rosecrans determined to fall back twenty-three miles, in order to be nearer his base of supplies.

While thus waiting, General Lee, who had assumed command of the rebel forces in Western Virginia, prepared a plan to attack him in front while Floyd was to come down in his rear, hoping thus between the two forces to crush him, capturing or dispersing his army. General Rosecrans's knowledge of the country now served him to good purpose. He knew that Floyd must come in at Gauley, and accordingly made preparations to meet and capture him there. For some reason—owing to the bad roads, it was said—Lee failed to make his promised attack in front; but Floyd came up in the rear, as arranged, and was repulsed. Through the negligence of subordinate officers, the plan laid for his capture failed, and he escaped. This defeat of Floyd, however, and the subsequent retreat of the enemy to Eastern Virginia, practically ended the campaign, and Western Virginia was virtually cleared of rebel troops. For the service thus rendered, General Rosecrans was presented by the Legislature of Western Virginia with a vote of thanks.

The winter season was approaching; active campaigning in the field was at an end; but General Rosecrans, as commander of the department, still found work for his troops in hunting up and dispersing the numerous guerrilla bands with which the country was infested. This done, he established his outposts on the Kanawha River, concentrated his spare troops at New Creek

Station and Romney, and on the 6th of December, 1861, himself returned to Wheeling, making that city his winter head-quarters. In the latter part of that month he solicited and received permission to go to Washington to lay before General McClellan a plan of operations which he had devised. This was to concentrate the troops in Western Virginia, and to obtain from Ohio and Indiana sufficient new ones to bring the entire number up to twenty-five thousand effective men. This force he would gather secretly at Romney, and with it advance rapidly upon Winchester, which place he would seize and strongly fortify, thus flanking the rebel position at Manassas. Waiting in Washington nearly three weeks for his plans to be received and considered by General McClellan, he learned meanwhile that General Lander had been ordered to occupy the line of the Baltimore & Ohio Railroad, and that all the troops in his own department, with the exception of seventeen hundred, had been sent to that general. With his hands tied, he accordingly returned to Wheeling, there to witness the dissipation of the military power of his command and to contemplate the ignoble results for which the lives of our soldiers were being wasted. Meantime he perfected a long-cherished plan of a train of three hundred pack-mules, which he was the first to suggest and maintain as practicable, demonstrating its superiority in point of effectiveness over the ordinary transportation trains during the winter season, by drawing up and submitting to the Quartermaster's Department tables of the comparative cost of two-, four-, and six-horse or mule teams, and of the pack-mule train. He next formed the plan of a spring campaign, having for its object the possession of the Virginia & Tennessee Railroad, and the penetration of East Tennessee as far as Bonsell's Station, or farther, if practicable, towards Lynchburg, Virginia. This plan was approved by the Secretary of War and General McClellan, each writing him an autograph letter in relation to the matter. Meanwhile, however, the clamor of politicians and the necessities of military rank compelled the administration to create the Mountain Department for the benefit of other generals and their friends. The new arrangement absorbed General Rosecrans's command, and he was ordered to report to the Secretary of War for further orders. Thus, to satisfy outside demands and please a political faction, a practical plan of operations, which promised a highly successful termination and would have proved of immense advantage to the Federal arms, was thrown aside, and the season frittered away in a widely different campaign, barren of results, and, on the whole, not over-creditable to those by whom it was conducted.

Upon General Rosecrans reporting to the War Department, the Secretary expressed much regret at the necessities preventing his assignment to the command of the Mountain Department, and deputed him to find General Blenker's command, of whose whereabouts no definite information could be ascertained. Strange, and even ludicrous, as the fact may seem, the division was actually lost, and an extended and systematic search had to be made for it. General Rosecrans was directed to confer with General Banks, and, after finding the troops of Blenker, to put them in serviceable condition and get them to Frémont as soon as possible. Proceeding to Winchester, he sent out messengers and scouts, and through them learned that General Blenker had reached Berry's Ferry, and, in attempting to cross the Shenandoah at that point, had swamped the ferry-boat and lost a number of men. Blenker was immediately directed to proceed to Snicker's Ferry, cross the river, and come to Winchester. While awaiting the arrival of this division, General Rosecrans occupied the time in conferring with General Banks upon the state of military affairs and planning for the coming campaign.

The situation at that time was thus: General Banks, with thirty thousand men, was advancing up the Shenandoah Valley, and was then sixty miles distant from his base of operations at Harper's Ferry. General Milroy, with five thousand eight hundred men, was at Huttonsville. The centre of Frémont's force, under General Schenck, and numbering about four thousand five hundred effective men, was at New Creek Station. On the rebel side, Stonewall Jackson and Ewell were in the vicinity of Mount Jackson with a light column of from six thousand to eight thousand men. To make the rebels feel the weight of their heavy force, the following plan was agreed upon, after consultation with Generals Banks, Shields, and others, and telegraphed to the Secretary of War. Blenker, without crossing the Shenandoah, was to move rapidly to Sperryville, thus cutting off Jackson's retreat through Luray Gap and compelling him to go southward to Brown's or Rockfish Gap. Banks was to advance immediately to Harrisonburg. The force at New Creek Station was to move up South Branch by way of Franklin, being no longer menaced by the rebels, and join Milroy, who was to come across Cheat Mountain to Middleburg. There the senior officer would take command of the whole force, and move on to Staunton and Charlottesville, while Blenker moved south along the Piedmont, with McDowell's force in échélon to support him. This disposition would bring the weight of a heavy army corps on the left of the enemy's position at Gordonsville, while it would facilitate the taking of the East Virginia Road by Cox. The Secretary acknowledged the receipt of the plan, and submitted it to the President. The latter determined that it was too late to consult all the generals interested, and the whole plan came to naught.

Thus a second opportunity to make an effective campaign was neglected, and a whole season lost. Perhaps its value may be best determined by the disastrous results which followed its non-adoption. The enemy made a raid northward, which this plan would have prevented. McDowell's plan of operations was rendered inoperative. Our magnificent opportunities were wasted. The enemy was relieved of all apprehension of danger from our forces in the Valley. The crushing blow which McDowell, in aid of McClellan, had prepared to deal Jackson was averted, and the rebel general, making good his escape from the Shenandoah, was permitted to fall upon the right of our army on the Peninsula, and thus turn the scale of conflict. Such was the actual result. What would it have been had the plan agreed upon by Generals Banks, Shields, and Rosecrans been adopted and carried into effect? Jackson would have been forced southward, and his junction with Lee prevented. McClellan would have crushed the rebel army on the Peninsula, and McDowell, going in on McClellan's right, would have occupied Richmond. To sum up all in a word, the campaign would have been illustrious, and the rebels have been driven from Virginia.

About the 1st of April, General Blenker's division arrived, hungry and destitute, and went into camp. Their condition was wretched, resulting from neglect and incompetency. General Rosecrans at once inspected the corps and reported their condition to the War Department. His whole attention was devoted to the supplying of their wants and equipping them for the spring and summer campaign. A rise in the Potomac River delayed him somewhat, but he finally succeeded in getting them into serviceable condition, and marched with them to the vicinity of Moorefield, where he reported to General Frémont in person, on the 9th of May, 1862. This duty performed, the general proceeded to Washington, arriving there on the 15th of May, and the same day was ordered to report to General Halleck at Corinth, Mississippi, then the great centre of public interest in the West as the probable field of an impending battle. Leaving his staff, horses, &c. behind, he hastened forward, and reached Corinth on the 23d, when General Halleck ordered him to report to General Pope, by whom he was placed in command of Colonel Jefferson C. Davis's division, which had just arrived from Pea Ridge, Arkansas. Four days afterwards, he was assigned to the command of the right wing of the Army of the Mississippi, just as it had advanced from its camp to the last line of trenches. While thus in the advance, sounds of constantly occurring explosions were heard within the enemy's lines; and he immediately sent to General Pope information that the rebels were undoubtedly preparing to evacuate, and himself sent out two squadrons to reconnoitre. They advanced to Corinth, and, finding it evacuated, poured in with other troops. His command was then ordered to take five days' rations and march in pursuit. He followed the enemy until eleven o'clock that night, by which time our cavalry had arrived and engaged their rear at Tuscumbia. Passing through their deserted camps, in which many tents and much camp-equipage had been left, General Rosecrans pushed on to Booneville, and stationed his outposts beyond that town.

General Halleck followed Beauregard's forces thirty-three miles, and General Rosecrans pushed on twelve miles farther, reconnoitring with infantry and cavalry. At Twenty-Mile Creek he touched the main body of the enemy, in strong force, at several points. Two or three hundred prisoners were captured, and many stragglers released. General Buell's force now reinforced him preparatory to an attack on the rebels; but they hastily retreated; and on the 13th of June General Rosecrans returned to Camp Clear Creek, seven miles from Corinth. On the 17th General Pope left for Virginia, and General Rosecrans assumed command of the Army of the Mississippi, consisting of four small divisions. Of these, two were ordered to reinforce General Buell, and marched to Tuscumbia, while General Mitchel crossed at Eastport. This done, the remainder of the army returned to Corinth,—two and a half regiments having been left at Iuka.

General Bragg's forces had now gone, leaving Price and Van Dorn on their front. Two days after General Stanley's division left Iuka Price advanced and took possession of the place. A reconnoissance made by Colonel Mowry having established the fact that Price was really there, with a force variously estimated at from twenty to thirty thousand men, General Rosecrans devised a plan to attack and capture or totally rout him. With this view, he proposed to General Grant that the latter should advance his forces on one road directly to Iuka, while he himself would march his two divisions by way of Jacinto, get in Price's rear, and cut off his retreat southward. This was agreed to by General Grant; and on the 18th of September General Rosecrans concentrated at Jacinto two divisions of infantry and artillery and two regiments of cavalry. Starting at four o'clock on the afternoon of the 19th, and marching eighteen and a half miles, he arrived within a mile and a half of Iuka. Here the advance-guard of our forces, having skirmished for the last seven miles with the enemy's cavalry, encountered his infantry. Their camps being close by, a heavy force was rapidly pushed out to meet Rosecrans, who was obliged to deploy skirmishers on a narrow, wooded point, where there was room for only seven regiments. The enemy now opened with a heavy fire of canister and musketry, and the battle soon became very hotly contested. But two of General Rosecrans's batteries could be used, and one of these was in a cramped, unwieldy position. Over this battery a fierce contest raged, the enemy seeming determined to capture it at all hazards. Thrice was it taken and retaken, and, a fourth time falling into the hands of the rebels, remained there until the next morning, when it was again recovered. Night put an end to the struggle, as yet undecided; and the wearied combatants rested upon their arms almost within whispering distance of each other.

During the whole engagement General Rosecrans eagerly listened for Grant's answering guns, supposing that he was rapidly advancing in front; but, to his surprise, none were heard. Thus left in suspense as to the other column, he prepared to renew, unaided, the battle against the enemy's whole force. About midnight, however, he found that they had begun to retreat, and were already gone from his immediate front. Pursuit was at once made with cavalry and infantry, and the retreating column overtaken. The cavalry hung upon their flanks, and annoyed them to the extent of their power; but General Rosecrans's force was too small to cope with the rebels, and, having followed them to Bay Springs, a distance of twenty-five miles, he desisted from the chase. Returning to Jacinto, he moved thence to Corinth, and there established his headquarters, having been placed in command of that district by General Grant, who had himself moved to Jackson, Tennessee. This was on the 21st of September. Rumors, various and indefinite, followed the battle, and the movements of the enemy were closely scrutinized. It was finally ascertained that Price, marching rapidly in a southwesterly direction for thirty miles, had struck Baldwin; thence, making a detour to the northwest, he passed Dumas Post Office, fifteen miles from Baldwin, where he was joined by Van Dorn, who assumed chief command. The force now moved to Pocahontas, thirty miles, leaving Ripley a little on the left; and here it was joined by Lovell, whence they were reported to be about moving down to Chewalla, and thence to Corinth.

To meet the emergency, General Rosecrans, upon learning the first movements of the enemy, on the 29th ordered in the troops from Rienzi and Jacinto, and they arrived at Corinth on the 30th and 31st. On the 1st of October it was definitely ascertained, from strong cavalry scouting-parties sent out for that purpose, that the rebels were moving from Ripley via Ruckersville, and that the main body was at Pocahontas. They evidently meant work; but where would the blow fall? From their position it was equally easy to strike Bolivar, Bethel, Jackson, or Corinth; and the question was, which would it be? No map of the country northwest of Corinth could be found; and it was not easy to determine whether the threatened attack upon Corinth was a feint to cover a movement upon some other point, or whether the feint would be made elsewhere and the blow struck there.

Rumors that the attack was to take the direction of Jackson or Bolivar via Bethel were so rife, and the fortifications of Corinth were so well known to the rebels, that General Rosecrans had hopes they would undertake to mask him, and, passing north, give him an opportunity to beat the masking force and cut off their retreat. This hope gained some strength from the supposed difficulties of the country lying in the triangle formed by the Memphis & Charleston and Mobile & Ohio Railroads and Cypress Creek. To be prepared for eventualities, Hamilton's and Stanley's divisions were placed just beyond Bridge Creek, the infantry outposts were called in from Iuka,

Burnsville, Rienzi, and Danville, and the outpost at Chewalla retired to New Alexander, and strengthened by another regiment and a battery, early on the morning of the 2d. During that day it was ascertained that the country to the northwest was practicable, and that there were two good roads eastward from Chewalla, one leading directly into the old rebel intrenchments, and the other crossing over into the Pittsburg Landing road.

Accordingly, at half-past one on the morning of the 3d, General Rosecrans ordered the following disposition of the forces for that day :—

" There being indications of a possible attack on Corinth, immediately the following disposition of troops will be made. General McKean with his division will occupy the present position ; General Davies will occupy the line between the Memphis & Columbus road ; General Hamilton with his division will take position between the rebel works on the Purdy and on the Hamburg roads ; and General Stanley will hold his division in reserve at or near the old head-quarters of Major-General Grant.

" The respective divisions will be formed in two lines, the second line being either in line of battle or close column by division, as their circumstances may require.

" The troops will move towards their positions, with one hundred rounds of ammunition and three days' rations per man, by three o'clock A.M."

The troops at nine o'clock on the morning of the 3d occupied positions as follows :—Hamilton on the right, Davidson the centre, McKean on the left, with an advance of three regiments of infantry and a section of artillery under Colonel Oliver on the Chewalla road, at or near Alexander's, beyond the rebel breastworks. The cavalry were disposed as follows :—a battalion at Burnsville, one at Roney's Mill on the Jacinto and Corinth road. Colonel Lee, with the 7th Kansas and a part of the 7th Illinois, at Kossuth and Boneyard, watching the rebels' right flank ; Colonel Hatch and Captain Wilcox on the east and north fronts, covering and reconnoitring.

These dispositions are said by General Rosecrans, in his detailed report, to have been made because of the fully explained difficulties of the northwesterly approach, and of the possibility that the rebels might threaten on the Chewalla road and attack by the Smith's Bridge road, on his left, or go round and try him with their main force on the Purdy or even on the Pittsburg Landing road. The general plan to be pursued was verbally explained to the division commanders on the morning, and was in effect this :—to hold the rebels at a distance by approaching them strongly from our assumed position, and, when their force became fully developed and they had formed their lines, to take a position which would give us the use of our batteries and the open ground in front of Corinth, that position to be exactly determined by events and by the movements of the enemy.

Early in the morning the advance under Colonel Oliver perceived indications that the pressure under which he had retired on the 2d came from the advancing foe, and accordingly took a strong position on the hill near the angle of the rebel breastworks, with his three regiments and a section of artillery. By eight o'clock there was sharp fighting at this point; but it was still by no means certain that the main attack of the enemy would be on Corinth. By nine o'clock the enemy began to press them sharply and outflank them. An officer sent to the front reported wide-spread but slack skirmishing, and said that the position of our advance-guard was an advantageous one and would be of great benefit to the attacking force. With this view, it was ordered to be firmly held. At ten o'clock word came that the enemy were pressing the point hotly, and that unless reinforced the position must be yielded. General Davies was ordered to send up from his division two regiments; but it was found that General McArthur had taken four more regiments from McKean's division, and was stoutly contesting the ground. General Davies now asked permission to rest his right on the rebel intrenchments; and it was granted, with the verbal instruction that he might use his own judgment about leaving his present position for that, but in no event was he to cease touching, if possible, the left on McArthur's right. Davies accordingly advanced to the breastwork, but leaving an interval between his own and McArthur's left. The rebels, seizing the opportunity, developed their force along that line as McArthur retired from his position, and advanced behind Davies's left, and forced it, after an obstinate resistance, to fall back about a thousand yards, with the loss of two heavy guns.

Our troops were fighting with great determination, firing low and very steadily. At one o'clock in the afternoon, Davies had resumed the position he occupied in the morning, and McArthur's brigade had fought a heavy force. The enemy were evidently in full strength and meant desperate work. There were no signs of any movement on our left, and only a few cavalry skirmishers on our right. It seemed certain that the attack in force would be made on our centre. Orders were accordingly given to McKean to fall back to the next ridge beyond our intrenchments, to touch his right on Davies's left, and Stanley to move northward and eastward, to stand in close échelon, but nearer town. General Hamilton was ordered to face towards Chewalla, and move down until his left reached Davies's right. Davies was informed of these dispositions, told to hold his ground obstinately, and then, when he had drawn them in strongly, Hamilton would swing in on their front and rear and close the day. Owing to a loss of time in conveying the orders to Generals McKean and Davies, they were less perfectly conformed to than was wished, and the movement did not begin until about five o'clock. The enemy pressed Davies back with tremendous force; and Stanley, with his division and his batteries held in reserve, was called upon, and sent a brigade under Colonel Mower to support Davies, whose right had at last become hotly engaged. Mower came up while Davies was contesting a position near the White House, and Hamilton began to swing in on the enemy's flank, across the Columbus Railroad, through a very impracticable thicket, when night closed in and put an end to the operations for the day.

General Rosecrans now had opposed to him the entire army which the rebels could muster in Northern Mississippi, composed of Price's and Van Dorn's armies, Villepigue's and Lovell's commands, and the remnants of Breckinridge's corps, all under the command of Van Dorn. They were in an angle between the Memphis and Columbus Railroads, a position which rendered his left comparatively free but made his right very assailable. They undoubtedly outnumbered us two to one, and were now advised of our intended movements. New dispositions accordingly became necessary. The plan adopted was to rest our left on the batteries extending from battery Robinette, our centre on the slight ridge north of the houses, and our right on the high ground, covering both the Pittsburg and Purdy roads, while it also covered the ridge roads between them, leading to their old camps. McKean had the extreme left; Stanley, with his well-tried division batteries, Williams and Robinette, the Memphis Railroad and the Chewalla road extending nearly to the Columbus road; Davies's sure division was placed in the centre, which was retired, reaching to battery Powell; Hamilton's staunch fighting division was on the right, with Dillon's battery, supported by two regiments posted on the prolongation of Davies's line.

Early in the evening, General Rosecrans called his division commanders together and explained to them the plans. By three o'clock in the morning, these dispositions were completed, and officers and troops, alike exhausted by fatigue, endeavored to obtain some rest. In a short time, however, and before daybreak, they were awakened by the enemy's artillery—four batteries—firing upon battery Robinette, within six hundred yards of which they had planted their guns. Shells flew thick and fast, perforating the Tishemingo House at Corinth, the telegraph-office, and the ordnance building. Our heavy batteries and the 10th Ohio, placed north of General Halleck's old head-quarters, silenced them by seven o'clock, one piece being captured and the rest withdrawn. The skirmishers and sharpshooters were sent forward into the woods on our front, and found the enemy in force, evidently preparing for an assault. No movement took place, however, until about nine o'clock, when the heads of their columns emerged from the woods and bore straight down upon our centre, attacking first Davies, then Stanley, and Hamilton

last. The rebels came on in gallant style; and our troops purposely yielded and fell back, scattering among the houses. Retreating some two hundred and fifty yards, they rallied, and were
reinforced by reserves from Hamilton's division. At the head
of Price's right, storming columns advanced to near the houses
on the north side of the square, in front of General Halleck's
head-quarters, when they were greeted with a storm of grape from
a section of Immell's battery, soon reinforced by the 10th Ohio,
which sent them reeling back, pursued by the 5th Minnesota,
which advanced to them from their position near the depot.
General Sullivan was ordered and promptly moved to the
support of General Davies's centre. His right rallied, and retook
battery Powell, into which a few of the storming column had
penetrated; while Hamilton, having played upon the rebels on
his right, over the opening, very effectively with his artillery,
advanced towards them, and they fled. The battle was over on
the right.

During this time the skirmishers of the left were moving in our
front. A line of battle was formed on the bridge. About twenty
minutes after the attack on the right, the enemy advanced in
four columns on battery Robinette, and were treated to grape
and canister until within fifty yards, when the Ohio brigade
arose and gave them a murderous fire of musketry, before which
they broke and fell back to the woods.

General Van Dorn's attack was to have been simultaneous with
that of Price. The generals had arranged to carry Corinth by
one grand assault. But in their reconnoissance on Friday evening they entirely overlooked Fort Robinette,—a fatal oversight.
When they drove their wedge towards Corinth, one flange on
the Bolivar road, the other on a branch of the Chewalla, they
intended that both wings should move together. Topographical
and artificial obstructions interrupted Van Dorn. He was
obliged to sweep over a rugged ravine, through dense thickets,
up hill over a heavy abatis, with his left; it was necessary for
his centre to dip down hill under the fire of Fort Williams,
Captain Gau's siege-guns in the rear of the town, and under

heavy musketry; while his right had to girdle a ridge and move over almost insurmountable abatis under the point-blank fire of both Fort Williams and Fort Robinette, supported by a splendid division of veteran troops. The latter fort had three ten-pounder Parrotts, and the former, thirty-pounder Parrotts. Price had nothing to delay him, and was in time. Van Dorn was too late,—a few moments only, but long enough to seal the fate of Price, who was overwhelmed and driven back.

Van Dorn's situation was desperate. Nothing but a feat of daring whose success would be little short of a miracle could save his army from total rout. Battery Robinette must be carried by storm; and audaciously enough he attempted it. His men obeyed magnificently. Gallantly they were reformed and led to the charge by Colonel Rogers, of the 2d Texas, acting brigadier-general. The troops most relied on were those from Texas and Mississippi. Two brigades, one supporting the front at close distance, moved up solidly towards the face of the fort. The Parrotts of both redoubts poured a constant stream of shot and shell, grape and canister, into their close ranks, from the moment they began their advance; and at every discharge great gaps were made in their columns. But there was no faltering. The ranks were promptly closed, and steadily they moved to the front, bending their heads to the storm. Scores were slaughtered while thrusting themselves through the rugged timber, but no man wavered. Onward, onward they came, steady and unyielding as fate, their leader in front. The edge of the ditch is reached, and they pause to take breath for a final onset. It is a fatal pause. It gave our men time to recover from the surprise into which the boldness and audacity of the movement had thrown them, and they were now ready for the assailants. Rogers, the brave Texan, with the rebel flag in his left and a revolver in his right, advanced, firing, leaped the ditch, scaled the parapet, waved his banner aloft, and tumbled head-long to its base. And now the deadly musketry fire of the infantry supports staggered and broke the ranks of his followers, and at the word "Charge!" the 11th Missouri and 27th Ohio sprang up and forward at them, chasing their broken fragments back to the woods. Thus by noon ended the battle of the 4th of October.

The day was extremely warm, and our troops were nearly exhausted. Water and ammunition were sent to them as they rested on the field, and they patiently awaited another advance of the enemy. No signs of their reappearance occurring, skirmishers were sent out, who soon found and reported that their skirmishers had gone from the field, leaving their dead and wounded. By four o'clock it was known that the enemy were retreating, at least to Chewalla. Having satisfied himself of this, General Rosecrans rode over our lines, announcing the result of the fight in person, and notified his victorious troops that after two days' fighting and two sleepless nights of preparation, movements, and march, he wished them to replenish their cartridge-boxes, haversacks, and stomachs, take an early sleep, and start in pursuit by daylight.

The results of the battle are thus briefly stated by the general in his official report :—

"We fought the combined rebel force of Mississippi, commanded by Van Dorn, Price, Lovell, Villepigue, and Rust, in person, numbering, according to their own authority, thirty-eight thousand men.

"We signally defeated them, with little more than half their numbers, and they fled, leaving their dead and wounded on the field.

"The enemy's loss in killed was one thousand four hundred and twenty-three, officers and men ; their loss in wounded, taking the general average, amounts to five thousand six hundred and ninety-two. We took two thousand two hundred and forty-eight prisoners, among whom are one hundred and thirty-seven field-officers, captains, and subalterns, representing fifty-three regiments of infantry, sixteen regiments of cavalry, thirteen batteries of artillery, and seven battalions, making sixty-nine regiments, six battalions, and thirteen batteries, besides separate companies.

"We took also fourteen stands of colors, two pieces of artillery, three thousand three hundred stand of arms, four thousand five hundred rounds of ammunition, and a large lot of accoutrements. The enemy blew up several wagons between Corinth and Chewalla, and beyond Chewalla many ammunition-wagons and carriages were destroyed, and the ground was strewn with tents, officers' mess-chests, and small arms. We pursued them forty miles in force, and sixty miles with cavalry."

Something additional may be said in reference to the pursuit. It began early the next morning, and their rear-guard was over-taken at Chewalla. Pressing on, they made a short stand at Tuscumbia Hill, but were driven from it after a short struggle. As our forces advanced, they found innumerable marks of a precipitate and disordered retreat. Tents, camp-equipage, wagons, &c. had been abandoned, and lay thickly scattered along by the roadside. The pursuit was still vigorously kept up. Upon reaching the Hatchie River, the bridge was found to be destroyed; but McPherson's engineers repaired it, and by dark our forces were crossing over and in hot pursuit. On our first day's advance, General Hurlbut had met the rebels and driven them back towards Rosecrans; and now word came from Jonesborough that General Ord's command had fought them and driven them on to the route by which he was so rapidly pursuing them. Upon this intelligence, General Rosecrans requested General Hurlbut to support him, and also asked General Grant to send General Sherman to his assistance. The enemy were thoroughly beaten. Our own men were in the best of spirits, and eager for a rapid, effective, and uninterrupted pursuit until the rebels were captured or destroyed It was explained to General Grant that if Sherman would come in on the west the enemy could be kept moving south, and thus be effectually scattered or driven to the wall. Sixty thousand rations were issued to his own troops, thirty thousand were sent to Hurlbut, and eighty wagon-loads followed immediately from Corinth. But General Grant decided that further pursuit was inadvisable; and the army was recalled, greatly to its chagrin and mortification. Thus we failed to realize the full results of this magnificent victory. The rebels were demoralized and badly frightened, even going so far as to burn their stores at Tupelo. General Rosecrans is confident that had he been allowed to continue the pursuit he would easily have gone to Vicksburg, which was then but feebly defended, and have captured that important stronghold with but a tithe of the blood and treasure which have since been expended in its reduction.

3

Returning from the pursuit, General Rosecrans re-established his head-quarters at Corinth, remaining there until October 26, when, in pursuance of an order from the War Department, dated October 24, creating the Department of the Cumberland and the 14th Army Corps, and assigning him to its direction, he left Corinth, arriving at Louisville on the 30th, and at once assumed command. From that time his military career is inseparably connected with that of the Army of the Cumberland, and is related in other pages of this volume. To them the reader is referred, with the confident assurance that he will there find a record no less bright in all that goes to make his previous life one of usefulness to his country and of honor to himself.

Not only has General Rosecrans excelled as a military leader, but as a far-seeing statesman with military power, located in the midst of a rebellious and socially diseased community. During his several weeks' stay in Nashville, Tennessee, last winter, he was especially mindful of the social condition of that people, and labored with them in every possible direction,—with words of kindness and acts of favor, and at times with force and severity, as occasion demanded. He devised a system of oaths and bonds as one medium of reconciling and persuading, and even forcing, a stiff-necked people to be loyal. Facilities of trade were afforded only to Union men, and passes to and fro were rigorously denied to rebels and traitors. Protection-papers were granted only where parties placed themselves in a proper attitude of loyalty to that power to which appeal was made for protection. He paid much personal attention to his scout and spy system, in connection with his Chief of Army Police, Colonel William Truesdail, with, at times, remarkably beneficial results. He heard complaints, and investigated serious personal charges, daily, restoring property here, condemning it there, and constantly dealing out righteous, even-handed justice, with a quickness, sagacity, and prudence which were universally appreciated. After the memorable tragedy of Stone River, and during the past four or five months, General Rosecrans has been daily called upon to adjudicate in the manner of a magistrate and with the power and responsibility of a military autocrat. Through it all shine forth, daily and hourly, his native, inherent love of truth and justice, and its attendant modesty, simplicity, and gentle kindness. As a rule, his action is in constant conformity to high principle. Recently he ordered the seizure of all serviceable horses in Murfreesborough, Nashville, and the adjacent country, for military necessities; and some seven hundred were thus gathered in and about the city of Nashville. A remarkable sensation ensued: prayers and petitions flooded in upon him for restoration, upon innumerable strenuous pleas, but in vain. He excepted but three cases,—one, of a team owned by and necessary to the manager of the State Insane Asylum, six miles in the interior; one horse owned by the aged Major Lewis, once an aide to General Andrew Jackson; and the carriage-horses of Mrs. Ex-President James K. Polk. "No, sir," said he to one persistent in his claims for restoration: "the Government needs your horses, and will pay you for them. I cannot restore them to you: I could not restore those of my old friend Bishop Whalen, the Catholic Bishop of Nashville, nor can I yours."

As is well known, General Rosecrans is a firm and consistent member of the Roman Catholic Church. His religious duties are a matter of daily thought and practice, whether at home or abroad, at the house of prayer or upon the field of battle. Night and morning find him a suppliant before the throne of the Eternal One, and the life of to-day seems a lesson impressive of the life to come. So believe those who during many months past have often witnessed his heartfelt, unostentatious attention to sacred things. Especially in times of peril is this faith and confidence attended with happiest results. During the battles of Stone River, while riding over the fields through the fiery hail, the general's calm courage was remarked by all. He is truly a hero upon the battle-field. In Western Virginia, and at Iuka and Corinth, he was personally present at each conflict, and at times in its very midst. His record as a general is no brighter than is his record as a soldier. During those momentous hours of undecided contest at Stone River, he was everywhere amidst battle-dangers, cheering and reviving his scattered columns, while his adversary, the rebel General Bragg, is said to have been safely seated in the cupola of the court-house at Murfreesborough, overlooking the field, and from thence momentarily despatching orders. Sustained by his religious faith, and therefore truly fearless of personal consequences, death for him had no terrors. When told that the lamented Colonel Garesché, his chief of staff, had been killed, he remarked to his companions, " Brave men die in battle. Let us push on." Upon learning of the death of the gallant General Sill, and the reported death of Major-General McCook, he paid a brief tribute to their courage, and cheered those about him with words somewhat as just related. When the tremendous battle of Friday evening was won, and Breckinridge and his rebel legions were so signally repulsed, the general remarked, in response to the congratulations of the author, " Yes, God has truly blessed us."

This faith in God and His goodness is the result of many years' belief in the doctrines of the Catholic Church, and of participation in its rites. His parents were Episcopalians, and he was bred to that faith, but embraced Catholicism while a student at West Point,—as was also done about the same time by his brother, now Bishop of Cincinnati, and one of the pillars of that Church in the West. While thus a devoted and earnest Catholic, the general is no bigot. His religion is a personal matter, and is not intruded upon others, he respecting the reasonable views of all, while adhering strictly to his own. His staff embraces religionists of various denominations and creeds, there being upon it but a single Catholic. In the walks of home life he inclines to associates of pure mind and refined understanding, as most congenial to his taste. In time of war he wisely extends this preference, and, while he has due regard for intelligence and purity, is not unmindful of the brightness and beauty of the rough diamond, and delights to call around him the bold and daring.

Another of the general's characteristics is his pride in young men. Of such his staff is mainly composed; and many of his generals have not yet seen the midsummer of life. As with his officers, so with the masses of his soldiery, youth is their marked peculiarity and crowning glory. In this rebellion the general recognizes a contest in which the young and giant mind of the nineteenth century is battling against old systems of social and moral barbarism, and by which a new life and a higher civilization will be developed. He believes it to be a struggle of liberty, Heaven's choicest blessing to man, with human bondage,—a struggle in which the chains of the latter shall be broken, and idleness and the grovelling vices of a serfdom equally degrading to master and slave give place to labor and its concomitant virtues.

Previous to the rebellion, no man's history was complete without the record of his political and partisan life. General Rosecrans has no such record. Party machinery was always uncongenial to him, and he thoroughly avoided it. His aversion to, and even contempt of, professed politicians, the managers of political clubs and caucuses, the connivers at election tricks and the winkers at ballot-box frauds, is refreshingly hearty. He participates in no party caucuses, but votes for such men and measures as seem at the time to be best. Until quite recently, his political views and votes were not generally known beyond the circle of his more intimate friends. He believes that the strict adherence to party in times past, and the consequent party excesses, have been a bane to our national prosperity, and that it is this partyism which, lending strength to ambitious and dissolute leaders, has involved the country in all the calamities of civil war. At the last election he voted for Stephen A. Douglas for President, persuaded that the views of that statesman upon the all-absorbing slavery question, fairly and fully carried out, would best tend to avert the impending storm. When the first gun was fired at Sumter, with Douglas he came to the rescue, believing, with him, that the preservation or

destruction of the Government was now the only issue before
the people.

Upon the question of slavery General Rosecrans is decided,
almost to radicalism. What he would not have forced upon the
South he is now confident they have accomplished for themselves. While he would have left their peculiar system to
wrestle with the steady advance of free labor and thus through
a gradual decline reach at last its inevitable end, he is now
earnest in the belief that its days are numbered with the present
century. The evils of slavery are with him a pregnant text.
In the desolated fields and deserted homes of Virginia and Tennessee he witnesses the vengeance of Heaven upon the iniquities
of man, and in the suffering and sorrow which war produces he
recognizes a just retribution for the wrongs our nation has perpetrated upon a weak and lowly race. Especially is he severe
in his comments upon the assumed superiority and aristocracy
of the slaveholding portion of the South. The author has often
heard him declare that " of all aristocracies upon earth, that of
the slaveholder is the most meaningless, the most contemptible,
and the most damnable." The following extract from a letter
written by General Rosecrans, dated at the head-quarters of the
Army of the Mississippi, July 20, 1862, most forcibly portrays
his sentiments respecting the rebellion, and the institution of
slavery :—

"For more than a year we have engaged in this struggle, into which an
arrogant and dictatorial slave-oligarchy has driven a free, happy, and peaceful people, fighting for the rights of all. With true bravery and invincible
patience our citizen soldiers have stood on this ground to the present moment,
against violators of the laws of war and humanity. Remaining true to their
principles, they have said, by words and actions, to their fellow-citizens in the
South, We fight for common rights. If we win, you win. If the Government is maintained, you will dwell under the protecting shadow as freely
as we. And there we stand, and thus we say, to-day.

" But if the Confederates prevail, farewell peace and safety to us ; farewell
freedom, forever! Their principles and leaders are known to us. They
cheated us, crying out, No coercion ; holding out false hopes and deceitful
assurances of friendly regard, while, assassin-like, they were preparing to
destroy our Government and reduce us to anarchy or servitude. The past
year's experience renders it certain that if they triumph, blood and desola-

tion, fire and sword, or arbitrary subjection to their will, *awaits every white man who has manhood enough to dislike their system of slavery.*

"They will omit no means, honest or dishonest, to insure success. Misrepresenting, calumniating our motives, ridiculing our honest efforts to mitigate the horrors of war, and inflaming the passions of the populace by low epithets, are among the milder and more ordinary means resorted to by this pseudo 'chivalry,' *the meanest aristocracy that ever stood at the head of a civilized society.*"

An incident is related which illustrates his disregard of popular and local prejudices. While in charge of the Government works at Washington, he was for some time superintendent of a Sabbath-school connected with his Church, where some seven hundred little negro children were taught their only lesson of Christianity,—an act creditable to the manliness that will thus rise above prejudices, and due to that true religion which teaches that all nations, all classes, all races, have an equal part and claim in the blood of Christ.

Lest the author should be accused of partiality, which will, at times, mislead the judgment of the most cautious biographer, he appends the following testimony of ability and worth, from an enemy. A correspondent of the Atlanta (Ga.) "Commonwealth," in a letter published some two months after the battle of Stone River, thus speaks of him:—

"General Rosecrans is a man of more than ordinary ability. In all the various positions in which he has been placed, he has exhibited the most untiring industry and indomitable energy. He is an accomplished engineer, a wily strategist, and a brave and prudent leader. He is undoubtedly the ablest general now in the Federal army. He is very different from the native Yankee, being bold, frank, outspoken, and possessing the dash and manner of the Western people. He is the idol of his officers and men, and possesses their entire confidence to an eminent degree. He will fight; and he impresses it upon those about him that hard licks alone will end the war.

"Socially, General Rosecrans is modest, refined, polite, and affable. He would command respect and confidence in any community. In person he is five feet ten inches, and in weight about one hundred and sixty pounds. He stands very erect, with military dash and bearing strongly depicted in his person. His features are mild, but there is a striking expression in his clear gray eyes. His complexion is florid, hair slightly tinged with gray, and his features and person would be called handsome. General Rosecrans is a devoted member of the Roman Catholic Church."

In conclusion, we may add, the friends of General Rosecrans claim for him no Napoleonic attributes, nor do they attempt to clothe him with the Tyrian purple of a Cæsar. Every age has its hero; and the boast of one century may be the curse of another. All that we claim for him is that he is an honest, practical man, a shrewd, patient, skilful general, and an ardent, self-sacrificing patriot. The foregoing pages show that his life has been one of eminent usefulness to society and to his country. As a citizen, as a teacher, as a public servant, as a soldier, and as a commander, we may well regard him as a beaming light in the pathway of virtue, honor, and integrity. His genial countenance, pleasing smile, and easy, unaffected manners, everywhere the same, have kindled in all his friends an affection as lasting as it is warm; and many a soldier and citizen will in after-years remember with feelings of admiration and love the present commander of the Army of the Cumberland.

THE STAFF.

THE staff of General Rosecrans is composed as follows. The biographies of such as we have been able to obtain will be found following the list.

Brig.-Gen. J. A. GARFIELD.................*Chief of Staff.*
Brig.-Gen. J. ST. C. MORTON.............*Chief of Eng'rs, com'd'g Pioneer Brigade.*
Col. JAMES BARNETT, 1st O. V. Art'y...*Chief of Artillery.*
Col. JOS. C. McKIBBIN.......................*Add'l A. D. C., A. A. I. Gen'l.*
Lieut.-Col. C. GODDARD......................*A. A. Gen'l.*
Lieut.-Col. A. C. DUCAT.....................*A. I. Gen'l.*
Lieut.-Col. JNO. W. TAYLOR.................*Qr. M., Chief Quartermaster.*
Lieut.-Col. SAM'L SIMMONS..................*C. S., Chief Commissary.*
Lieut.-Col. WM. P. HEPBURN, 2d Iowa
  Cavalry ....*Insp. Cavalry.*
Major WM. McMICHAEL........................*A. A. Gen'l.*
Major RALSTON SKINNER.....................*Judge-Advocate.*
Surgeon G. PERRIN, U.S.A..................*Medical Director.*
Surgeon A. H. THURSTON, U.S.V.........*Ass't Medical Director.*
Asst.-Surg. DALLAS BACHE, U.S.A.......*Staff Surgeon.*
Asst.-Surg. JAS. F. WEEDS, U.S.A......*Medical Inspector.*

MAJ. GEN. ROSECRANS'

LIEUT. COL. C. GODDARD

LIEUT. COL. JOHN W. TAYLOR

LIEUT. COL. SAMUEL SIMMONS

BRIG. GEN. JAMES A. GARFIELD

COL. J. BARNETT

MAJOR W. H. SIDELL

LIEUT. COL. A. C. DUCAT.   Eng'd by J. C. Buttre   MAJ. W. M. WILES

CHIEF OFFICERS OF STAFF.

J. B. LIPPINCOTT & CO PHILAD^A

Major W. H. SIDELL, 16th Inf. U.S.A...*Must'g and Disb'g Officer.*
Major W. M. WILES, 44th Ind. Vols....*Provost-Marshal General.*
Major FRANK S. BOND........................*Senior Aide-de-Camp.*
Capt. J. H. YOUNG, 15th Inf. U.S.A.....*Mustering Officer.*
Capt. J. C. PETERSON, 15th Inf. U.S.A...*A. A. I. G.*
Capt. HENRY THRALL......................*A. A. G.*
Capt. J. BATES DICKSON..................*A. A. Gen'l.*
Capt. JAMES CURTIS, 15th Inf. U.S.A...*A. A. I. G.*
Capt. A. S. BURT........................*Add'l A. D. C., A. A. I. G.*
Capt. HUNTER BROOKE.....................*Add'l A. D. C., Acting Judge-Advocate.*
Capt. W. M. WARREN.....................*A.Q.M., In charge of Army Supply Trains.*
Capt. ELIAS COSPER, 74th Ill. Vols......*1st Ass't Provost-Marshal Gen'l.*
Capt. R. M. GOODWIN, 37th Ind. Vols...*2d Ass't Provost-Marshal Gen'l.*
Capt. G. S. HUBBARD, 88th Ill. Vols....*Acting Ass't Inspector-General.*
Capt. C. R. THOMPSON....................*Add'l A. D. C., A. D. C.*
Capt. HORACE PORTER.....................*Ordnance U. S. A., Chief Ord. Officer.*
Capt. DAVID G. SWAIM...................*A. A. G.*
1st Lieut. BYRON KIRBY, 6th U.S. Inf...*A. D. C.*
1st Lieut. W. H. GREENWOOD, 51st Ill.
  Vols ....*Ass't Topographical Engineer.*
1st Lieut. HENRY STONE, 1st Wis. Vols.*A. A. A. G.*
1st Lieut. C. M. BRAZEE, 74th Ill. Vols.*A. A. Q. M.*
1st Lieut. H. L. NEWBERRY, 1st Middle
  Tenn. Cav.........................*Chief of Courier Lines.*
1st Lieut. W. L. PORTER, 56th O. Vols..*A. A. D. C.*
1st Lieut. JAS. K. REYNOLDS, 6th Ohio
  Vols ....*A. A. D. C.*

BRIGADIER-GENERAL GARFIÉLD.

JAMES ABRAM GARFIELD was born November 19, 1831, in Cuyahoga county, Ohio. His parents were natives of the New England States. By the death of his father he was, while yet a small boy, thrown upon his own energies and resources for a livelihood. At the age of sixteen he drove horses on the Ohio & Pennsylvania Canal, and in various other employments he " paddled his own canoe" successfully over the waters of varied fortune, and entered Williams College, Massachusetts, where he graduated in 1856. His plan of supporting himself while attending college was ingenious. He insured his life for a considerable amount, and borrowed the necessary funds by pledging the policy as security.   After graduating, he returned to the West, and during a period of three years was President of a Collegiate Seminary at Hiram, Portage county, Ohio.   In 1859 he was elected to the State Senate for the term of two years, and in 1860 was admitted to the bar as a practising attorney.

Upon the breaking out of the rebellion, General Garfield was among the first to lay aside the ease and enjoyment of private life and the attractions of personal and political popularity and enter upon the arduous duties of the soldier.   He set about raising a regiment among his pupils and friends and fellow-citizens; and mainly by his efforts the 42d Ohio Regiment was formed, of which he was appointed colonel, by Governor Dennison, in August, 1861.

On December 17 of that year he left Camp Chase, Ohio, with his regiment, under orders for the Big Sandy Valley region, in Eastern Kentucky, reporting in person to General Buell at Louisville.   Upon arriving in that city he was invited by General Buell to arrange his campaign; and he accordingly worked out a plan, which was submitted to and approved by the commanding general.   The next day he started for his field of operations with a little army of four regiments and about six hundred cavalry.   The Big Sandy was reached, and followed up for some sixty miles, through a rough, mountainous region, his force driving the outposts of General Humphrey Marshall before them for a considerable distance.   On the 7th of January, 1862, he drove the enemy's cavalry from Paintville, after a severe skirmish, killing and wounding twenty-five of them.   At a strong point, three miles above Paintville, Marshall had prepared to make a stand, with two batteries of six guns each, four thousand five hundred infantry, and seven hundred cavalry; but when his cavalry were thus unexpectedly driven in, his courage failed, and he hastily evacuated his works, retreating up the river.

The rapid marching, thus far, had much exhausted General Garfield's forces: still he resolved to pursue, and, picking out eleven hundred of his ablest troops, continued on to Prestonburg, a distance of fifteen miles.   There he found the rebels strongly posted upon the crest of a hill, at once attacked them, and maintained the battle during five hours, the enemy's cannon meanwhile playing briskly. Although they were now under fire for the first time, the daring valor of the Union troops swept all before them: the rebels were driven from every position, and, after destroying their stores, wagons, and camp-equipage, they precipitately retreated to Pound Gap, in the Cumberland Mountains, sixty miles above. This was the first brilliant achievement of the war in the West, and a most complete and humiliating defeat to the rebels, their loss in killed and wounded amounting to two hundred and fifty, in addition to forty taken prisoners, while that of the Federals was but thirty-two, all told. It is related of General Garfield that at the time of this battle he had in his possession a letter written a short time before by Humphrey Marshall to his wife, but intercepted by General Buell and sent to General Garfield, in which he stated that he had five thousand effective men in his command. This letter the general refrained from showing to his officers and men until after the victory. His commission as brigadier dates from the day of the battle at Prestonburg.

General Garfield now moved his force to Piketon, Kentucky, one hundred and twenty miles above the mouth of Big Sandy. Here he remained several weeks, sending out, meanwhile, expeditions in every direction wherever he could hear of a rebel camp or band, and at length completely clearing that whole country of the enemy. While thus employed, his provisions gave out, and, instead of sending, he went himself to the Ohio River for a new supply. The provisions were obtained, and a small steamer seized and loaded therewith. But now a serious difficulty presented itself. The river was swollen by an unprecedented freshet, and its navigation was extremely perilous. No captain or pilot would take charge of the boat: it was an impossibility to navigate the Big Sandy with any thing in the shape of a boat; and they would not go. General Garfield, however, was not to be balked in this way. Determined that the provisions should go through to his starving men, he took com-

mand of the boat himself, and piloted her up the river, standing
at the wheel one day and two nights. It was a perilous voyage,
up an untried stream full of eddies and currents, in which the
little boat quivered and turned, at times threatening to make
instant wreck of itself and all on board; but the indomitable
energy of the general carried him safely through all these difficulties, and in due season himself and his cargo arrived safely
at the camp, greatly to the joy of his suffering soldiery.

About the middle of March he made his famous Pound Gap
expedition, for a proper understanding of which a few words
descriptive of the locality will be necessary. Pound Gap is a
zigzag opening through the Cumberland Mountains into Virginia,
leading into a track of fertile meadow-land lying between the
base of the mountains and a stream called Pound Fork, which
bends around the opening of the gap at some little distance from
it, forming what is called " the Pound." These names originated
in this wise. This mountain locality was for a long time the
home of certain predatory Indians, from which they would make
periodical forays into Virginia for plunder, and to which they
would retreat as rapidly as they came, carrying with them the
stolen cattle, which they would pasture in the meadow-land just
mentioned. Hence among the settlers it became known as
" the Pound," and from it the gap and stream took their names.
After his defeat at Prestonburg, as has been stated, Humphrey
Marshall retreated with his scattered forces through this gap
into Virginia. A force of five hundred rebels was left to guard
the pass against any sudden incursion of General Garfield's force,
who, to make assurance doubly sure, had built directly across
the gap a formidable breastwork, completely blocking up the
way, and behind which five hundred men could resist the attack of
as many thousand. Behind these works, and on the southeastern
slope of the mountains, they had erected commodious cabins for
winter quarters, where they spent their time in ease and comfort, occasionally—by way of variety, and in imitation of their
Indian predecessors—descending from their stronghold into Kentucky, greatly to the damage of the stock-yards and larders of

the well-to-do farmers of that vicinity, and to the fright of their wives and children.

General Garfield determined to dislodge them from their position and so put an end to their marauding expeditions. He accordingly set out with a sufficient force, and, after two days' forced march, reached the base of the mountains a short distance above the gap. Of the strength of the rebels and their position he had been well informed by the spies he had sent out, who had penetrated to their very camp, in the absence of the usual pickets, which were never thrown out by them, so secure did they feel in their mountain-fortress. It would have been madness to enter the gap and attack them in front; and the general did not propose or attempt it. Halting at the foot of the mountains for the night, he sent his cavalry early next morning to the mouth of the gap, to menace the rebels and draw them from behind their defences. This they did, arriving at a given time and threatening an attack. The rebels jumped at the bait, and at once came out to meet them, our men rapidly retreating, and the rebels following until the latter were some distance in front of their breastworks instead of behind them. Meantime, General Garfield with his infantry had scaled the mountain-side, in the face of a blinding snow-storm, and, marching along a narrow ridge on the summit, had reached the enemy's camp in the rear of his fortifications. A vigorous attack was now made, resulting in the complete rout of the rebels, many of whom were killed, wounded, or taken prisoners, and the remainder dispersed through the mountains. The general now reassembled his forces and spent a comfortable night in the enemy's quarters, faring sumptuously upon the viands there found. The next morning the cabins, sixty in number, were burned, the breastworks destroyed, and the general set out on his return to Piketon, which he reached the following night, having been absent four days, and having marched in that time about one hundred miles over a rough and broken country.

On his return, he received orders from General Buell, at Nashville, to report to him in person. Arriving at that place, he found

that Buell had already begun his march towards Pittsburg
Landing, and pushed on after him. Overtaking the army, he
was placed in command of the 20th Brigade, and with his
command participated in the second day's fight at Shiloh.
He was present through all the operations in front of Corinth,
and, after the evacuation of that place, rebuilt with his brigade
the bridges on the Memphis & Charleston Railroad and erected
fortifications at Stevenson. Throughout the months of July and
August he was prostrated by a severe sickness, and, consequently,
was not in the retreat to Kentucky or the battles fought in that
State. During his illness he was assigned to the command of
the forces at Cumberland Gap, but could not assume it. Upon
his recovery he was ordered to Washington and detailed as a
member of the Fitz-John Porter court-martial, which occupied
forty-five days, and in which his great abilities as a lawyer and
a soldier were called forth and freely recognized. When the
court adjourned, he was ordered to report to General Rosecrans,
and by him was placed in the responsible position of chief of
staff, though at first it had been intended to give him only the
command of a division in the field. With the selection thus made
universal satisfaction is everywhere expressed. Possessed of
sound natural sense, an excellent judgment, a highly-cultivated
intellect, and the deserved reputation of a successful military
leader, he is not only the Mentor of the staff, but his opinions
are sought and his counsels heeded by many who are older and
not less distinguished than himself.

In September, 1861, General Garfield was nominated by the
Union Convention of the Nineteenth Congressional District of
Ohio as its candidate for member of the Thirty-Eighth Congress,
and at the election in October was chosen by a majority of over
six thousand votes.

Thus, at the age of thirty-one, the poor orphan boy, without
the aid of wealth or of influential relatives, has achieved a
position of which any American citizen might well be proud.
The record of his life and labors fitly tells the story of his
worth. What the author could truly say in addition is perhaps

better said by his friends of longer acquaintance. The editor of the Xenia "Torchlight," a paper published in his Ohio home, thus speaks of him upon the occasion of his assignment to the Army of the Cumberland and his selection by General Rosecrans as his chief of staff:—

"We have known General JAMES A. GARFIELD for several years, and entertain for him the highest personal regard. He is one of the most eloquent men in Ohio, as well as one of the ripest scholars. Socially and morally he has no superior. He is popular with all, as the attachment of his scholars, as well as his soldiers, for him demonstrates.

"In respect to abilities, nature has by no means been unfriendly to him; and he has neither despised nor slighted her gifts. A severe course of mental training, combined with the mental practice obtained by presiding over one of the colleges of Ohio, has fully developed his natural endowments.

"Above all these considerations, every one respects General Garfield for his stern, unyielding, uncompromising patriotism. The permanent good of his country, the restoration of its unity, and the perpetuation of the national power and glory through all coming time, are the objects which he keeps steadily in view."

LIEUTENANT-COLONEL C. GODDARD, *Assistant Adjutant-General*, was born at Norwich, Connecticut, February 9, 1838. In 1851 he removed to Cleveland, Ohio, where he engaged in commercial pursuits. Soon after the attack on Fort Sumter, he went to Columbus, to assist in organizing the State troops, and remained engaged in that duty and in paying troops in the service of the State until December, 1861. He then received a commission as first lieutenant in the 12th Ohio Volunteer Infantry, and was detailed as aide-de-camp upon the staff of General Rosecrans in Western Virginia. Lieutenant Goddard afterwards accompanied the general to Mississippi, and there served as acting assistant adjutant-general, participating in the battles of Iuka and Corinth. Following General Rosecrans to the Department of the Cumberland, he was appointed major and aide-de-camp, and served until subsequent to the battle of Stone River as acting assistant adjutant-general. Soon after this battle he was appointed, upon the special recommendation of General Rosecrans, assistant adjutant-general, with the rank of lieutenant-colonel.

COLONEL JAMES BARNETT, *Chief of Artillery.* See "The Artillery Service," *post.*

ARTHUR CHARLES DUCAT, *Lieutenant-Colonel, and Inspector-General of the Department of the Cumberland,* is a native of Dublin, Ireland, born in February, 1832, and is the youngest son of the late M. M. Ducat, Esq., of Newlawn, county Dublin. In 1851 he came to New York and engaged in civil engineering, which profession he pursued, until about seven years ago, throughout the Northwest. He was then appointed Secretary and Chief Surveyor of the Board of Underwriters at Chicago, which position he held until the breaking out of the war, when he raised an engineer corps, which was not accepted by the Government. He thereupon entered the service as a private in the 12th Illinois Regiment, which was raised as a three-months regiment under the first call for troops. His regiment was one of those which first occupied Cairo under General Prentiss. In May, 1861, he was appointed second lieutenant and adjutant, and August 1, became captain of Co. A in the same regiment. During this period he served in the occupation of Cairo, Bird's Point, and the reinforcement of Cape Girardeau. He afterwards went to Paducah, and was engaged in the demonstration upon Columbus made by General C. F. Smith at the time of the battle of Belmont. In November, 1861, he was appointed major of his regiment. Participating in the battles of Fort Henry and Fort Donelson, he was promoted to a lieutenant-colonelcy for meritorious services at the latter. and, though severely injured by a shell, he advanced with his regiment upon Clarksville and Nashville, and thence down the Cumberland and up the Tennessee to Pittsburg Landing, where he was taken dangerously ill, and was sent down the river to hospital at Paducah, where he lay for months. Upon his recovery he was appointed chief of grand guards and outposts for the army. In the battle of Iuka he was attached to General Ord's column, and was senior officer on his staff, and afterwards took part in the battle of Corinth and the pursuit of the enemy. Soon after this he was assigned to General Rosecrans as chief of staff, and upon the subsequent assignment of Colonel Garesché to the same position was appointed inspector-general. When General Rosecrans was ordered to Kentucky, he accompanied him to Bowling Green, and thence to Nashville. At this place he was attacked by a severe sickness in December, 1862, and compelled to return home on indefinite leave of absence. Recovering partially, he rejoined the army at Murfreesborough, about the 1st of April, 1863, still in a delicate state of health, but performing his military duties with commendable ardor and alacrity.

LIEUTENANT-COLONEL JOHN W. TAYLOR, *Chief Quartermaster.* See " Quartermaster's Department," *post.*

LIEUTENANT-COLONEL SAMUEL SIMMONS, *Chief Commissary.* See " Commissary Department," *post.*

LIEUTENANT-COLONEL WILLIAM P. HEPBURN, *Inspector of Cavalry*, was born in Columbiana county, Ohio, November 24, 1833, and emigrated to Iowa in 1840. In May, 1861, he entered the service of the State of Iowa as a second lieutenant, and in August of the same year was mustered into the service of the United States as a captain in the 2d Iowa Cavalry. In September, 1861, he was promoted major, and lieutenant-colonel in November, 1862. With the army of the Mississippi he was present during the operations at New Madrid, Island No. 10, Tiptonville, and Fort Pillow, and participated in the battles of Farmington, Blackland, Booneville, Iuka, and Corinth. In June, 1862, he was appointed inspector of cavalry for the Army of the Mississippi, and during November and a part of December of the same year he was acting judge-advocate of the Army of the Cumberland. In the latter part of December he was appointed inspector of cavalry for the department.

SURGEON GROVER PERRIN, *Medical Director*, was born in Clermont county, Ohio, in November, 1823. He was educated at

4

the Woodward High School in Cincinnati, and graduated at the Ohio Medical College, in the same city, in 1846. In 1847 he entered the Regular Army as a surgeon, and served during the Mexican War, and subsequently upon the frontier until the beginning of the rebellion. He was assigned and reported to General Rosecrans as medical director of the Department of the Cumberland, February 21, 1863.

MAJOR W. H. SIDELL, *Mustering and Disbursing Officer*, is a native of New York City, and a graduate of West Point of the class of 1833. He graduated with high honor, but soon resigned from the army to adopt the profession of civil engineer, in which capacity he has been engaged on many important works. When the Mexican War broke out, he volunteered in the 4th New York Regiment, and held the commission of captain; but the regiment, though fully recruited and ready to move at a day's notice, was not called upon. At the opening of the rebellion he received and accepted the commission of major in the 15th Regular United States Infantry. When stationed at Newport Barracks in Kentucky, while the regiment was recruiting, Major Sidell was ordered to Louisville, to receive into the service of the United States the small force of loyal Kentuckians raised by General Rousseau, and accompanied that force to the field when called out from its camp of rendezvous to repel the invasion of the rebel General Buckner in September, 1861. After this he was made chief mustering and disbursing officer of the department, and subsequently general superintendent of volunteer recruiting for Kentucky. From the latter position he was relieved in March, 1862, and ordered to join General Buell on his staff as mustering officer, which he did. In July he was detailed by him as his acting assistant adjutant-general, and was ordered to take post at Nashville, where he remained on that duty as long as General Buell retained command of the army, during which time the city was closely invested by the enemy, remaining so until the advance-guard of the army then under General Rosecrans's command entered the city.

General Rosecrans renewed the detail, retaining him to act as assistant adjutant-general until March 19, 1863, when he was relieved as such, but continued as chief mustering and disbursing officer. As adjutant-general at Nashville, his position was one of great trust and responsibility, the city being beleaguered and incessantly threatened, and for a long time cut off from all communication. The adjutant of a general commanding is always an important officer, especially when separated from his commander; for then he must himself do for him whatever, under the regulations, he believes the general himself would order done, were he present, in all things not immediately under the control of the commander of the post or garrison. In the discharge of these onerous duties, Major Sidell was discreet and zealous, ready to co-operate with and aid the efforts of others.

By the mustering officer all the complicated conditions in regard to the terms on which officers and men are received into the United States service have to be adjudicated. As these terms affect the rank, immunities, and obligations of volunteers in their relations towards each other, as well as towards the Government, the decisions require knowledge of the laws and orders and discretion in applying them. Major Sidell is regarded at Nashville as chief authority in all these matters, and his decisions are rarely reversed in Washington.

Quite recently Major Sidell has received the appointment of assistant provost-marshal general for the State of Kentucky, a position he is eminently qualified to fill, from his long experience as a mustering officer, coupled with his energy, literary attainment, and business tact.

Major and Aide-de-Camp FRANK S. BOND is a native of Massachusetts, and was born in February, 1830. His youth was spent in Connecticut, and he early engaged in business connected with the railroads. For four or five years he was secretary and treasurer of the Cincinnati, Hamilton & Dayton Railroad, and afterwards went to New York in a similar capacity for several Pennsylvania roads. When the war began, he was secretary of the

Almaden Quicksilver Mining Company. In March, 1862, he was appointed a first lieutenant in the 10th Connecticut Volunteers, but never served with the regiment, the commission having been given him that he might occupy a position on the staff of Brigadier-General Tyler, with whom he went West. He was present at the siege of Corinth, and engaged in the battle of Farmington. December 15, 1862, he was assigned to General Rosecrans as acting aide-de camp, and went with him to Bowling Green and Nashville. In the battle of Stone River, as a member of the general's staff, he was present on the field during the entire contest, discharging his perilous duties in the most gallant manner. After this battle he was promoted to his present position.

MAJOR WILLIAM M. WILES, *Provost-Marshal General.* See "Provost-Marshal General's Department," *post.*

CAPTAIN ELIAS COSPER, *First Assistant Provost-Marshal General.* See "Provost-Marshal General's Department," *post.*

CAPTAIN ROBERT M. GOODWIN, *Second Assistant Provost-Marshal General.* See "Provost-Marshal General's Department," *post.*

CAPTAIN HUNTER BROOKE, *Acting Judge-Advocate of the Department,* was born in the District of Columbia, is thirty-two years of age, and has resided for twenty-five years in Cincinnati, Ohio. He is a practising lawyer, which profession he entered in 1851, and has spent several years in political life, in the State Legislature and other public capacities.

At the breaking out of the war, he was temporarily residing in St. Paul, Minnesota, where he had gone on account of the health of his family, and entered the army as a private in the 2d Regiment of Minnesota Volunteers. After serving three months at Fort Ridgely, Minnesota, in November, 1861, he joined his regiment at Lebanon Junction, Kentucky. In December, 1861, he was selected by General Robert L. McCook, and by special permission acted as "volunteer aide-de-camp" upon the general's staff, which position he held during the winter campaign in Kentucky, and at the battle of Mill Spring. After this battle, he was appointed, by the President, additional aide-de-camp to Major-General Halleck, and assigned to duty with General R. L. McCook, with whom he remained during the spring and summer campaign in Kentucky, Tennessee, Mississippi, and Alabama.

On the 5th day of August, 1862, he was riding with General McCook in an ambulance, engaged in nursing him, and was by his side when he was brutally murdered by guerrillas near New Market, Madison county, Alabama. Captain Brooke was taken prisoner, and was released upon parole about the last of August. He reported to General Buell, and by him was ordered to report at Camp Chase, Ohio. In December, 1862, he was exchanged, and reported to Major-General Wright, at Cincinnati. In February he was ordered to report to Major-General Rosecrans for staff duty, and was assigned as aide-de-camp. Major Skinner, deputy judge-advocate, having soon afterwards been temporarily relieved from duty on account of ill health, Captain Brooke was detailed to the position, and is still acting in that capacity.

Captain and Aide-de-Camp CHARLES R. THOMPSON was born in Bath, Maine, February 24, 1840. For several years he resided in California, when, returning East as far as St. Louis, he engaged in mercantile pursuits in that city. He volunteered, October 1, 1861, as a private, in the Engineer Regiment of the West, Missouri Volunteers. Under General Frémont, he accompanied the army to Warsaw, Missouri, and was appointed first lieutenant November 1. He was afterwards present at the battle of New Madrid and the siege of Island No. 10, assisting in cutting the famous canal which led to the capture of the entire rebel force. He accompanied Pope's command up the Tennessee River and in the advance upon Corinth. June 1, 1862, he was appointed post quartermaster at Hamburg, Tennessee, where he remained until August 15, when he was relieved and appointed ordnance officer of the Army of the Mississippi, then under the command of General Rosecrans. At the battle of Corinth he was present in his capacity of ordnance officer, and acted as aide-de-camp to General Rosecrans. For meritorious service in this battle he was, upon the recommendation of the general, appointed captain and aide upon his staff. He accompanied General Rosecrans to the Army of the Cumberland, and, in the performance of his duty, acted a gallant and conspicuous part at the battle of Stone River.

CAPTAIN JAMES P. DROUILLARD, *Aide-de-Camp*, was born in Gallipolis, Gallia county, Ohio, and entered the U. S. Military Academy in June, 1857, graduating July 1, 1861. He chose the infantry corps, on account of more rapid promotion during the war, and was assigned as second lieutenant to the 6th Regiment United States Infantry. Ordered to report to the Secretary of War, he was placed on duty under General Mansfield, commanding the Department of Washington, as instructor of volunteers. Desiring to participate in the active operations then about to be initiated, he was ordered to report to General McDowell, commanding the Army of the Potomac, and was assigned by him to the battalion of regulars under command of Major Sykes, and remained in this position during the campaign which terminated in the memorable battle of Bull Run.

After the concentration of all the regular troops in Washington as a city guard, he was made adjutant of the 3d United States Infantry, which position he held until the promotion of Major Sykes to a brigadier-generalship of volunteers, when he was appointed assistant adjutant-general of the infantry of the city guard. In this capacity he served until December 20, 1861, when, upon the solicitation of General McDowell, he was made aide-de-camp upon the staff of that general. While acting thus, he accompanied, as a volunteer, the expedition of General Augur, which resulted in the capture of Falmouth and Fredericksburg. On the 25th of May, 1862, upon the recommendation of General McDowell, he received from the War Department the appointment of additional aide-de-camp, with the rank of captain.

He remained with General McDowell throughout his campaign with the Army of the Rappahannock, and subsequently with the Army of Virginia, under General Pope. When General McDowell was relieved of command, Captain Drouillard did not abandon him, but remained by his side until the termination of the court of inquiry, resulting in an honorable acquittal of all charges; when, desiring active service in the field, the captain was, upon the request of General Rosecrans, commanding the Department of the Cumberland, transferred to his staff as aide-de-camp.

CAPTAIN HORACE PORTER, *Chief Ordnance Officer.* See " The Artillery Service," *post.*

LIEUTENANT C. M. BRAZEE, *Acting Assistant Quartermaster,* was born in the State of New York, March 10, 1832. In 1857 he settled in Rockford, Illinois. Soon after he commenced the study of law, and was admitted to practice December 29, 1859. August 2, 1862, he entered the service, and on the 9th of the same month was promoted to a first lieutenancy in Company C, 74th Illinois Volunteers. Serving with his regiment in Buell's North Alabama campaign, he was detailed from the regiment with twenty-two men into the Pioneer Brigade, 2d Battalion, November 30, 1862. Here he was constantly on duty until after the battle of Stone River, when he was sick for some weeks, the result of exposure. On the 8th of February, 1863, he was ordered to report to department head-quarters, and assigned to duty upon the staff of General Rosecrans as acting assistant quartermaster.

Major-General George H. Thomas and Staff.

George H. Thomas, Major-General of Volunteers, and Colonel of the 5th United States Regular Cavalry, commanding the 14th Army Corps, was born in Southampton county, Virginia, July 31, 1816. His father, John Thomas, was of English, and his mother, Elizabeth Rochelle, of Huguenot, descent,—both of respectable and wealthy families. Receiving a fair education, he accepted the position of deputy to his uncle, James Rochelle, clerk of the county, and soon after began the study of the law. Through the influence of family friends, he received, in the spring of 1836, an appointment as cadet, and entered the U. S. Military Academy at West Point the following June. Continuing through the entire course, he graduated twelfth in a class of forty-five, June 20, 1840, and on the 1st of July was appointed second lieutenant in the 3d Artillery. In November of the same year he joined his regiment in Florida, eighteen months previous to the termination of the First Florida War. November 6, 1841, he was brevetted first lieutenant "for gallant conduct in the war against the Florida Indians." The regiment having been ordered from Florida in January, 1842, Lieutenant Thomas went with his company to New Orleans barracks, and in June of the same year to Fort Moultrie, in Charleston harbor. Remaining there until December, 1843, he was ordered to duty with Company C, 3d Light Artillery, then stationed at Fort McHenry, Maryland. May 17, 1843, he was promoted first lieutenant of artillery, and in the spring of 1844 joined Company E, 3d Artillery, at Fort Moultrie.

War with Mexico being now threatened, Lieutenant Thomas was ordered with his company to Texas, in July, 1845, to report for duty to General Zachary Taylor. The company arrived at

MAJ. GENERAL THOMAS

LT. COL. GEO. E. FLYNT

LT. COL. A. J. MACK.

MAJOR O. A. MACK.

MAJ. GEN. GEO. H. THOMAS.

LT. COL. J. H. PAUL.

LT. COL. A. VON SCHRADER.

AND OFFICERS OF STAFF.

Eng.d by R. Whitechurch

J. B. LIPPINCOTT & CO. PHILAD.A

Corpus Christi the same month, in company with the 3d and 4th regiments of infantry, they being the first United States troops that occupied the soil of Texas. With the army of occupation his company marched from Corpus Christi to the Rio Grande, and, with one company of the 1st Artillery and six companies of the 7th United States Infantry, was left to garrison Fort Brown, opposite Matamoras, while General Taylor, with the main body of his army, fell back to Point Isabel, there to establish a depot of supplies. On the 2d of May, Fort Brown was invested by the Mexicans, and the garrison sustained a bombardment until the afternoon of the 8th, when the enemy withdrew to Resaca de la Palma to reinforce General Ampudia, who had the same day been driven from his position at Palo Alto by General Taylor while marching to the relief of Fort Brown. On the 9th, General Taylor repulsed the Mexicans at Resaca de la Palma, and drove them across the Rio Grande, the garrison at Fort Brown contributing to this decisive victory by pouring an unintermitted fire of shot and shell into the disordered masses of the retreating enemy as they rushed in hopeless confusion to the river to escape our advancing columns. After the evacuation of Matamoras, Lieutenant Thomas was detached from his company with a section of his battery and assigned to temporary duty with the advance-guard, and remained stationed at Reynosa from early in June until the latter part of July, when he was ordered with his section, still in the advance-guard, and the 7th Infantry, to Camargo. In September, the main body having reached Camargo, he rejoined his command and marched to Monterey. September 23, 1846, he was brevetted captain "for gallant conduct at the battle of Monterey," and about the 1st of November, on the promotion of Lieutenant Bragg to the captaincy of Company C, took command of Company E, as senior lieutenant, which position he retained until February 14, 1847. In December, 1846, he was again placed in the advance, with the brigade of General Quitman, and entered Victoria about the 1st of January, 1847, General Taylor having started for the interior by way of Tampico.

General Scott, having assumed command of the army in the field at Camargo, ordered General Taylor to select a division and with it occupy the country he had conquered. In accordance with these instructions, the latter general, with a squadron of the 2d Dragoons, Companies C and E 3d Artillery, the 1st Mississippi and the 1st Georgia Infantry, and General Wool's brigade, then stationed at Saltillo, returned to Monterey about the last of January. Soon afterwards Santa Anna advanced from San Luis Potosi, with a force outnumbering General Taylor's four to one. General Taylor pushed all his troops, except four regiments, towards Saltillo, and eventually took a strong position about five miles south of that place. Here, on the 21st of February, was fought the bloody and decisive battle of Buena Vista, resulting in the overwhelming defeat of Santa Anna and the dispersion of his army. In this battle Lieutenant Thomas actively participated, and for gallant and meritorious services therein was brevetted major, February 23, 1847. He remained in Mexico on duty until August 20, 1848, when his company recrossed the Rio Grande into Texas, among the last to leave, as it had been among the first to enter, the Mexican territory. About the 1st of September he was ordered to Brazos Santiago, to take charge of the commissary depot at that place, and remained there until December, when his company was ordered to Fort Adams, Rhode Island, and he was relieved in order to join it at that place, which he did, at the expiration of a six-months leave of absence. July 31, 1849, he was placed in command of Company B, 3d Artillery, and in September of the same year was ordered to Florida with his company, hostilities having again broken out between the Indians and settlers in the southern part of that State. Remaining on duty in Florida until December, 1850, he received orders for Texas, but on arriving at New Orleans, on his way thither, found awaiting him there later orders for Boston harbor. He reached Fort Independence January 1, 1851, where he remained until March 28, when he was relieved by Captain Ord, and assigned to duty at West Point as Instructor of

Artillery and Cavalry. This position he retained from April 1, 1851, until May 31, 1854, having been promoted, meanwhile, December 24, 1853, to a captaincy in the 3d Artillery.

Captain Thomas, on leaving West Point, took command of a battalion of artillery, and conducted it to California by way of Panama. Arriving at Benicia Barracks June 1, 1854, he was assigned to Fort Yuma, in Lower California, and, reaching that place July 15, with two companies of artillery, relieved Major Heintzelman of the command. Congress having increased the army by four regiments, two of infantry and two of cavalry, Captain Thomas received the appointment of junior major of the 2d Cavalry, and, leaving Fort Yuma July 18, 1855, joined his regiment at Jefferson Barracks, Missouri, early in the following September. The regiment was ordered to Texas, and Major Thomas remained on duty there from May 1, 1856, to November 1, 1860, when he left Camp Cooper on a leave of absence. During this time he was for three years in command of the regiment, and in August, 1859, headed the escort which accompanied the Texas Reserve Indians from that State to their new home in the Indian Territory. Immediately after this he was ordered to examine the country on the head-waters of the Canadian and Red Rivers. He was absent on this service several months, and collected much valuable information concerning the geography of that region, having passed over a route north of the Canadian which previously had been entirely unknown. In the summer of 1860 he commanded another expedition to the head-waters of the Conchas, on which, besides obtaining much geographical knowledge, he fell in with a party of predatory Indians, and recaptured from them all the animals they had stolen from the settlements. In the skirmish on this occasion, August 26, 1860, he was slightly wounded in the face.

In April, 1861, Major Thomas was ordered to Carlisle Barracks, Pa., to remount the 2d Cavalry, which had been dismounted and ordered out of Texas by General Twiggs. Four companies were equipped at once and sent to Washington to join the two that had preceded them thither. The remaining four were assigned to the

Department of Pennsylvania, and Major Thomas was ordered to report to its commander, which he did on the 1st of May, 1861, at Greencastle, Pennsylvania.   April 25, 1861, he was promoted lieutenant-colonel, and colonel May 3.   From May until July he commanded the first brigade of Major-General Patterson's army in Northern Virginia, and subsequently under Major-General Banks until August 26.   August 17 he was appointed a brigadier-general of volunteers, and on the 26th was relieved from duty in the Army of Northern Virginia, and ordered to report to Brigadier-General Robert Anderson, commanding the Department of the Cumberland.   Arriving at Louisville, Kentucky, September 6, General Thomas was assigned to the command of Camp Dick Robinson, fifteen miles southeast of Nicholasville, Kentucky, which he reached September 15, and relieved Lieutenant Nelson, U.S.N. (subsequently Major-General Nelson, U.S.V.), who had organized the camp and by his energy and boldness had assembled there over six thousand Kentucky and Tennessee troops.   Zollicoffer had invaded Kentucky by way of Cumberland Gap; and General Thomas began making vigorous preparations to meet him and thwart his designs.   Four regiments of infantry, a battalion of artillery, and Woolford's cavalry, under the command of Brigadier-General Schoepf, were sent to Rockcastle Hills, thirty miles southeast of Camp Dick Robinson, where was established Camp Wildcat.   Brigadier-General W. T. Sherman, having been appointed to the command of the department in place of General Anderson, who was relieved at his own request on account of ill health, visited Camp Dick Robinson soon after, and expressed much satisfaction with the dispositions made to resist the advance of the rebels.   The result of these movements was the battle of Wildcat, fought October 26, in which Zollicoffer was completely routed and driven back to Cumberland Gap by our troops, under the personal command of General Schoepf.

Immediately after the battle of Wildcat, General Thomas moved his head-quarters to Crab Orchard and began preparations for an advance into East Tennessee; but, the enemy having

assembled a large force at Bowling Green, the department commander ordered General Thomas to move with his force, except
one Kentucky regiment and the two East Tennessee regiments,
to Lebanon, Kentucky, and be in readiness for an active campaign. Under these orders, General Thomas marched to Lebanon
and there organized the first division of the Army of the Cumberland. Immediately on the arrival of the troops at that place,
it being reported that Zollicoffer had advanced to Monticello,
Wayne county, and was threatening Somerset, General Schoepf
was ordered to the latter place with a battery of artillery and two
regiments of infantry, to prevent him from crossing the Cumberland. Two days afterwards two additional regiments and another battery were ordered to reinforce Schoepf; but Zollicoffer
had succeeded in crossing the Cumberland with about eight
thousand men, and established himself on the north side, opposite
Mill Spring. General Thomas had his command in readiness to
take the field by December 31, and on that day left Lebanon
under orders from Brigadier-General Buell to march against Zollicoffer and dislodge him from his intrenchments if he should not
come out to meet the combined forces of Schoepf and Thomas.
After a most laborious march of nineteen days, over roads made
almost impassable by heavy rains, General Thomas reached a
point ten miles north of Mill Spring, called Logan's Cross-Roads,
with the 9th Ohio, 2d Minnesota, 10th Indiana, and 4th Kentucky Regiments of infantry, Kenny's battery of the 1st Ohio
Artillery, Woolford's regiment of Kentucky Cavalry, and four
companies of the 1st Michigan Engineers. Here he halted to
await the arrival of the 14th Ohio and the 10th Kentucky, and
to communicate with General Schoepf at Somerset and arrange
for a combined movement upon the enemy's intrenchments.

The preliminary arrangements were made on Saturday, and
the troops were to move on Monday, the 20th. But the enemy,
having received information that only two regiments had
succeeded in reaching Logan's Cross-Roads, and that the remainder were still behind, exhausted and discouraged by the
difficulties which they had encountered left his intrenchments

on the evening of Saturday, the 18th, with the evident intention
of surprising and overwhelming the small force at Logan's, and
encountered the Federal pickets at daylight on the morning of
the 19th, driving them in rapidly. Two regiments—the 10th
Indiana and 4th Kentucky—were quickly formed, and advanced
into a wood about half a mile in front of Logan's. This position
was held against a desperate assault of the enemy's advance
until the arrival of the 9th Ohio and 2d Minnesota, when the
battle was renewed by these two fresh regiments attacking
the rebels in front, while the 12th Kentucky and 1st and 2d East
Tennessee advanced on their right and rear. The contest raged
violently for half an hour, until the 9th Ohio routed the enemy's
left at the point of the bayonet, their right being simultaneously
attacked by the 12th Kentucky. The advance fell back in confusion behind their reserves, and the rebels began a rapid and
disorderly retreat towards their intrenchments. As soon as our
troops could refill their cartridge-boxes, the enemy were pursued
to their intrenchments, and preparations were made to storm
them the following morning. But when morning came it was
found that they had fled during the night, abandoning their provisions, artillery, ammunition, wagons, cavalry, horse and camp
equipage of every kind. The rout was complete, and its
demoralizing effect so great that many men of wealth in Middle
Tennessee removed their slaves and household effects to Alabama
and Mississippi, without waiting to hear of new disasters. The
enemy's loss in killed and wounded in the battle and during the
retreat was very heavy, including among the former Brigadier-
General Zollicoffer.

Immediately after the battle of Logan's Cross-Roads, or, as it
is more generally called, Mill Spring, General Thomas concentrated his command at Somerset and entered upon active preparations for a move into East Tennessee, and had nearly
accumulated a sufficient amount of subsistence for that expedition when he received orders to move with all possible
despatch to Lebanon, and thence to Munfordsville, General
Buell intending to concentrate his forces at that place and move

immediately upon Bowling Green. Before the troops could be assembled, however, the enemy had lost Forts Henry and Donelson, and evacuated Bowling Green and Nashville, retreating by different routes through Tennessee, and eventually reassembling in front of Corinth, Mississippi. On the march to Munfordsville, General Thomas received orders to proceed with his division to Louisville, there to take steamers and go to Nashville, which he did, reaching the latter city on the 2d of March, with his division in readiness to take the field. But it constituted the reserve of the Army of the Cumberland, and remained as such until May 1, when the advance from Pittsburg Landing upon Corinth began. As soon as the troops could be supplied with clothing, and the trains fitted up, General Buell began his march to Pittsburg Landing, a portion of his army reaching that place in time to participate in the battle of Shiloh. General Thomas's division, being in reserve, did not reach the battle-ground until after the retreat of the enemy.

April 25, 1862, Brigadier-General Thomas was appointed and confirmed major-general of volunteers, and on the 1st of May his division was transferred to the Army of Tennessee, he being assigned by General Halleck to the command of the right wing of that army, consisting of Brigadier-General T. W. Sherman's division (the old 1st Division), Brigadier-General W. T. Sherman's division, Brigadier-General S. A. Hurlbut's division, Brigadier-General T. J. McKean's division, and Brigadier-General Thomas A. Davies's division. He continued in command until the evacuation of Corinth by the rebels, when his division was stationed along the Memphis & Charleston Railroad, from Iuka, Mississippi, to Tuscumbia, Alabama, for its protection. On the 10th of June he was re-transferred to the Army of the Ohio (the first Army of the Cumberland), and about the 1st of August was ordered to concentrate his command at Dechard, Tennessee, at which place he arrived about the 6th and remained with his division several days. Leaving his command here in temporary charge of General Schoepf, he proceeded to McMinnville, to take charge of the divisions of Generals Nelson and

Hood at that place. September 3, he left McMinnville, having received orders from General Buell to join him with his forces at Murfreesborough, the rebel cavalry having destroyed the Louisville & Nashville Railroad and blown up the tunnels near Gallatin, Tennessee, thus rendering a backward movement necessary. On arriving at Murfreesborough, he found that General Buell had already gone to Nashville, leaving orders for the army to follow him. Reaching Nashville on the 8th, General Thomas was at once put in command of the post. The next day General Buell, having already pushed forward a portion of his troops, set out for Kentucky. On the evening of the 13th, General Thomas received orders to follow, and at four o'clock on the evening of the 15th started with his division, leaving at Nashville the divisions of Generals Negley and Palmer, the whole under command of the former. Joining Buell at Prewitt's Knob, near Cave City, on the 19th, he was made second in command of the entire army. Approaching Munfordsville, it was expected that Bragg would make a stand there, and preparations were made for a battle; but the enemy were soon found to be retreating, and the march was resumed on the 23d, and in three days the army reached Louisville.

On the 29th, the Army of the Ohio was divided into three corps, under Generals McCook, Crittenden, and Gilbert, General Thomas still remaining second in command of the whole. On the 1st of October the army left Louisville for Bardstown, where the rebel army was encamped, their cavalry vedettes extending to within five miles of Louisville. As Buell advanced, Bragg retreated, evacuating Bardstown after a slight skirmish. The rebel forces making a stand at Harrodsburg and Perryville, a severe battle was fought, principally by General McCook, commanding the left wing, the right, under General Thomas, being engaged only in skirmishing. General Thomas accompanied the army in all its movements until it again concentrated at Bowling Green. When the command was assumed by Major-General Rosecrans, its name was again changed to the "Army of the Cumberland," and on the 5th of November General

Thomas was placed in command of the centre, 14th Army Corps, Department of the Cumberland, consisting of the 1st Division, Brigadier-General S. S. Fry commanding, the 3d Division, Major-General L. H. Rousseau commanding, the 8th Division, Brigadier-General J. S. Negley commanding, the 12th Division, Brigadier-General E. Dumont commanding, and the 13th Division, Brigadier-General J. M. Palmer commanding. In charge of his corps, General Thomas reached Nashville early in November, where he remained until the morning of the 26th of December, when the army advanced towards Murfreesborough. In command of Rousseau's and Negley's divisions, he left Nashville on the morning of the 26th, moving on the right of McCook by the Franklin and Wilson pikes and falling in by cross-roads to Nolensville. During the whole of that terrible series of battles on Stone River, he was cool, active, and vigilant, cheering on his men by voice and example, and sharing their dangers, and in the official reports of General Rosecrans is mentioned with especial commendation as "true and prudent, distinguished in council and on many battle-fields for his courage."

Since the occupation of Murfreesborough, the Army of the Cumberland having been divided into three army corps,—the 14th, 20th, and 21st,—General Thomas has been in command of the 14th Army Corps, comprising five divisions, under the command of Major-Generals L. H. Rousseau, Jas. S. Negley, and J. J. Reynolds, and Brigadier-Generals S. S. Fry and R. B. Mitchell.

General Thomas's residence—the place of his birth—is now in possession of the rebels. In 1852 he was married to Miss Frances S. Kellogg, of Troy, New York, and his wife now resides in New York City. Notwithstanding his many years of military service and active campaigning, he is still apparently in the prime of life. In personal appearance dignified and manly, in manners gentle and courteous, in habit temperate and virtuous, none "know him but to praise." His military and personal record is without a blot. Although a Virginian, he never faltered for a moment in his duty to his country to follow after the false gods of his native State and the South; and let it ever be

5

remembered that it was he who won for our arms one of the first and most decisive victories of the present war, in front of Mill Spring, Kentucky.

THE STAFF.

LIEUTENANT-COLONEL GEORGE E. FLYNT, *Assistant Adjutant-General*, was born in Delaware county, New York. He received a mercantile education, and was engaged in trade until the year 1853. In the following year he emigrated to Texas. During his residence in that State he was more or less, socially and in his business relations, connected with the United States Army there on duty. At the commencement of the rebellion he was present at Camp Cooper, on the Clear Fork of the Brazos River, when it was surrendered to the Texas rebels. Having no sympathy with the revolutionists, he left Texas at the earliest moment, and arrived in Western New York in June, 1861. At the request of Brigadier-General George H. Thomas, he was commissioned assistant adjutant-general, with the rank of captain, August 31, 1861, and was assigned to duty on the staff of General Thomas, joining him at Camp Dick Robinson. Captain Flynt was with General Thomas in his Kentucky campaign, being present in the decisive battle of Logan's Cross-Roads (known as the battle of Mill Spring), and for his gallantry on that occasion was honorably mentioned in the official report. At Shiloh, Major-General Thomas was placed in command of the right wing of the Army of Tennessee, and selected Captain Flynt as his chief of staff, he having been promoted major, by commission bearing date June 11, 1862, after the taking of Corinth. Major Flynt accompanied General Thomas when that officer was transferred to the Army of the Cumberland, and with him participated in the battle of Perryville. Major-General Rosecrans having been assigned to the command of the Army of the Cum-

berland, and Major-General Thomas being appointed to the command of the centre, the subject of this sketch, as his assistant
adjutant-general, was present with him at the battle of Stone
River. After the battle, General Thomas was placed at the
head of the 14th Army Corps, and Major Flynt, for his prompt,
efficient, and gallant conduct, was called to the staff of this corps,
with the rank of lieutenant-colonel, which position he now fills.

LIEUTENANT-COLONEL ALEXANDER VON SCHRODER, *Assistant
Inspector-General*, was born at Blankenburg, in the Hartz Mountains, in 1821.   His father, an old soldier, who had fought
his way up from the ranks to a lieutenant-generalship, and for
his bravery had been made a nobleman, thought no profession
so fitting for his son as the one by which he himself had won
honor and position; and accordingly, in 1835, at the early age
of fourteen, the latter entered the Prussian army as a cadet.
Here he remained for two and a half years, when he entered
the service of the Duke of Brunswick, and served three years
as cadet and ensign.   During this time he was either on active
duty with his regiment or hard at study.   In 1841 he was commissioned as second lieutenant in the body-guard of the Duke
of Brunswick.   This regiment was called "the schwarzen
Jaeger," and their dress was black, with a skull and cross-bones
as a distinctive badge.   The organization was maintained in
remembrance of Frederick William, Duke of Brunswick, who
had ten thousand such troops, to raise and equip which he had
sold all his possessions.

In 1852, Lieutenant Von Schroder left Germany for England,
where he remained some months, and then came to America.
The following ten years were spent in various pursuits.   At the
beginning of the present war he was residing in Cincinnati.
Having always been loyal to good government, he was ready
to render his best service.   He accordingly acted for a time
as drill-master to the 18th Ohio Regiment at Camp Dennison, and
afterwards to the 73d Ohio Regiment at Chillicothe.   Subsequently he was appointed major in the latter regiment, and on

the 10th of December, 1861, was commissioned lieutenant-colonel in the 74th Ohio, and was mustered into the service from that date. The regiment was detailed to guard prisoners at Camp Chase for several months, and, Colonel Moody being post commander, Lieutenant-Colonel Von Schroder was in command of it during this time. Thence he proceeded, still commanding officer of the regiment, to Nashville, where he remained for about two months, until Colonel Moody, being relieved as post commander at Camp Chase, rejoined his regiment, which was shortly after attached to the command of Brigadier-General Negley, by whom Lieutenant-Colonel Von Schroder was placed in charge of the troops guarding the railroad between Franklin and Columbia. In this position his soldierly abilities attracted the attention of his commanding general, who made application for his appointment on his own staff as division inspector. Upon General Negley's assuming command at Nashville, Lieutenant-Colonel Von Schroder became inspector of the division and post, and so remained during the investment. He participated in the fight in front of the city, November 5, 1862, and, together with three other of General Negley's staff officers, led the cavalry charge upon the rebels, within four miles of Franklin.

As inspector, Lieutenant-Colonel Von Schroder discharged his important duty with unusual skill and fidelity; for which he was specially complimented in the following order from head-quarters :—

"SPECIAL ORDER No. 2.

"HEAD-QUARTERS 14TH ARMY CORPS, DEPARTMENT OF THE CUMBERLAND.
"NASHVILLE, TENNESSEE, Nov. 19, 1862.

"XII. The general commanding has read with great pleasure the favorable report of Lieutenant-Colonel Ducat, Assistant Inspector-General, upon the condition of the grand guards and pickets of the garrison of Nashville, on the recent inspection ordered from these head-quarters, without any notice to the troops.

"The general compliments Lieutenant-Colonel Von Schroder,

the officer in charge of grand guards, the officers and men of the 21st Ohio and 27th Illinois Infantry, on duty the day of inspection.

*   *   *   *   *   *   *   *   *

"By command of Major-General Rosecrans.

"W. H. SIDELL,

"*Major* 15*th U.S. Infantry, and A.A.A. G.*"

On the 16th of December, 1862, he was assigned to General Thomas as acting assistant inspector-general of the 14th Army Corps, and was with him during the battle of Stone River, remaining by his side during that terrible conflict, exhibiting coolness and courage under most trying circumstances. After the battle, at the request of General Thomas, Lieutenant-Colonel Von Schroder, by a special order from the War Department, was assigned to the staff of General Thomas as assistant inspector-general, which position he now fills. To this office he brings the experience of many years, and the same ability and faithfulness which characterized his labors at Nashville. Only recently he was again complimented by General Rosecrans, in the following note to General Thomas :—

HEAD-QUARTERS, DEPARTMENT OF THE CUMBERLAND, April 19, 1863.

"MAJOR-GENERAL THOMAS, *Commanding* 14*th Army Corps.*

"GENERAL:—Your picket-line, inspected under orders from these head-quarters, has recently been reported as in the best possible condition.

"The major-general commanding desires to express to you his satisfaction, and to compliment Lieutenant-Colonel Von Schroder, A.I.G. of your corps, upon the zeal and energy which he has displayed in the discharge of this duty.

"Very respectfully,

"Your obedient servant,

"WILLIAM McMICHAEL,

"*Major and A. A. G.*"

LIEUTENANT-COLONEL A. J. MACKAY, *Chief Quartermaster*, is a
native of Livingston county, New York, of Scotch descent, and
about thirty-three years of age. At the age of sixteen he emigrated
to Texas while it was yet an independent republic, and remained
there until the breaking out of the rebellion. In June, 1861, he
returned to New York. October 7, 1861, he was appointed
assistant quartermaster, with the rank of captain, and assigned
to duty with General Thomas, then in command of Camp Dick
Robinson. He has since remained upon the staff, and has risen,
gradually and by merit, to his present rank. Possessing rare
business qualifications, he discharges the responsible duties of his
office with general satisfaction.

LIEUTENANT-COLONEL JAMES R. PAUL, *Chief Commissary*, was
born and raised in Franklin county, Ohio, and now resides in
the city of Columbus. Until twenty-eight years of age he was
a farmer, and then engaged in the grain and produce business.
On the 31st of October, 1861, he was appointed by the President a commissary of subsistence, with the rank of captain, and
assigned to duty on the staff of General O. M. Mitchel. In this
position he remained until General Mitchel was ordered East,
when, on the 4th of July, 1862, he was transferred to the staff
of General Rousseau, and remained with him up to the time of
the Stone River battle. Just before the fight began, he was
assigned to General Thomas as chief commissary, and acted as
such during the engagement. During his long service he has
had many remarkable experiences and some narrow escapes.
At the battle of Stone River he saved a large wagon-train by
his presence of mind. He also rode back to Lavergne to find
the trains and get flour for the men, and discovered a small drove
of cattle and a large amount of corn belonging to the rebels,
which was immediately distributed among the soldiers. In this
and other ways he rendered efficient and invaluable service.

January 28, 1863, Colonel Paul was promoted to his present
rank. He is one of the most competent and faithful commissaries in the army. He has a family whom he has not seen since

entering the service, having been constantly at his post without asking for a furlough.

MAJOR OSCAR A. MACK, *Senior Aide-de-Camp*, entered the United States Military Academy at West Point as a cadet from New Hampshire in 1846. He graduated eighth in his class in 1850, was attached as brevet second lieutenant to the 3d Regiment of Artillery, and in 1851 was promoted as full second lieutenant in the 4th Regiment of Artillery. In this regiment he served on the Northern lakes, the Atlantic seaboard, in Florida during the last campaign against "Billy Bowlegs," and on the Western frontier.

On the breaking out of the rebellion he was a first lieutenant, commanding a company of his regiment at Fort Randall, Nebraska Territory. In April, 1861, he was ordered into the States, and reached Cincinnati with his company in May. In June he accompanied Major-General McClellan to Western Virginia, and commanded his body-guard until after the battle of Rich Mountain. About that time he accepted the appointment of senior captain in the 13th Regular Infantry.

Captain Mack was then given a mountain-howitzer battery, manned by his old artillery company, and remained in Western Virginia under General Rosecrans, accompanied him through his campaign on the Gauley, and was present at the battle of Carnifex Ferry and the affairs on New River.

In December, 1861, Captain Mack was ordered to Kentucky to report to General Buell. On arriving in Louisville he was placed in command of the artillery camp of instruction for volunteer batteries. While there, he fitted out his own battery with light field-guns and a section of ten-pounder Parrotts. About the middle of January, 1862, he left Louisville with his new battery and joined General George H. Thomas at Somerset, Kentucky, but too late to be in the fight at Mill Springs. He remained with General Thomas's division, accompanying it to Nashville and Pittsburg Landing, until May, when he relinquished the command of his battery and accepted the position of inspector of artillery on the staff of General Thomas, then assigned to the command of the right wing of the Army of the Mississippi. He served in this capacity with General Thomas through the operations about Corinth, in Northern Alabama, Tennessee, and Kentucky. After the battle of Perryville, he was obliged to go home on sick leave. He rejoined General Thomas at Nashville, and at the battle of Stone River, December 31, 1862, was severely wounded. From the effects of this wound he has not yet sufficiently recovered to take the field.

On the 11th of March, 1863, he was confirmed by the Senate as aide-de-camp, with the rank of major.

CAPTAIN JOHN D. BARKER, *Aide-de-Camp*, and commander of the escort, was born in Marietta, Ohio, February 16, 1832. He was raised a farmer-boy, but at the time the rebellion began was engaged in mercantile pursuits. He entered the service, September 16, 1861, as lieutenant of a company partly enlisted by himself, and belonging to the 1st Ohio Cavalry. For a time he was actively engaged in scouting in Kentucky, and was afterwards at the battle of Shiloh and the siege of Corinth on ordinary cavalry duty. In March, 1862, he was assigned to General Thomas as aide-de-camp and commander of his escort, and has thus remained with him to this time. He participated in the battles of Perryville and Stone River, and soon after the latter was promoted to a captaincy. Captain Barker is especially commended by his associates as a faithful officer and a brave soldier.

J.B. LIPPINCOTT & CO. PHILADA

Major-General Alexander McDowell McCook.

ALEXANDER McDOWELL McCOOK, Major-General of Volunteers, and Captain of the 3d Regiment U.S. Infantry, commanding the 20th Army Corps, was born in Columbiana county, Ohio, April 22, 1831. At the age of sixteen he entered the Military Academy at West Point, and graduated in July, 1852. Upon graduating, he was commissioned brevet second lieutenant in the 3d Regular Infantry, and detailed to duty at Newport Barracks. Remaining there a few months, he was ordered, in April, 1853, to join his regiment, then serving in New Mexico. He continued there nearly five years, constantly on active duty in the field, and participating in several of the Indian campaigns on that remote frontier. His long service and good conduct were mentioned and complimented in general orders by Lieutenant-General Scott. In January, 1858, he was recalled from New Mexico, and assigned to the Military Academy at West Point. as Instructor in Tactics and the Art of War.

At the beginning of the present rebellion he was relieved from duty at West Point, and in April, 1861, ordered to Columbus, Ohio, to act as mustering officer for the volunteers of that State. Before his arrival, however, he was elected colonel of the 1st Ohio Volunteers, a three-months regiment, already on its way to the seat of war in Virginia. Hastening to assume the position to which he had been elected without his knowledge or solicitation, he soon had an opportunity of exhibiting his ability as a field commander. On the 17th of June a train of cars containing a detachment of Ohio troops under command of Brigadier-General Schenck, of which Colonel McCook and his regiment formed a part, and which was on a reconnoitring expedition, was fired upon by a masked rebel battery near Vienna, Virginia. The fire

73

proved very destructive, and threw the troops into confusion, from which they were rallied by the skill and coolness of Colonel McCook, and succeeded in retiring from the place without further casualty. In the battle of Bull Run Colonel McCook was engaged, and won universal commendation for the admirable manner in which he managed his men. At the close of this memorable conflict he marched his regiment back to Centreville in the same good order in which it had left that place, an honorable exception to the wide-spread confusion that prevailed elsewhere among the Union forces.

When the three-months men were mustered out of the service, he received authority from the President to raise the 1st Ohio Volunteers, a three-years regiment; but on the 3d of September, 1861, and before his command was ready to take the field, he was appointed a brigadier-general, and assigned to the command of the advance of the Federal forces in Kentucky, then at Camp Nevin. There, and while lying in camp on Green River, he organized his notable 2d Division, with which he afterwards marched to Nashville, and thence towards the Tennessee River. On the 6th of April, 1862, alarmed by the sullen sound of distant artillery, and aware of the dangerous situation of General Grant's army, he moved his division over wretched roads twenty-two miles to Savannah, there embarked on steamboats for Pittsburg Landing, and, after clearing with the bayonet a road through the army of stragglers that swarmed upon the river's bank, soon after daylight on the morning of the 7th deployed his brave and eager men upon the field of Shiloh. General McCook fought his troops on that day with consummate ability, holding them well in hand. His line of battle was not once broken nor retired, but was steadily and determinedly advanced until the enemy fled, and the reverse of the day before was more than redeemed by the victory which crowned the second day's struggle.

In the movements upon Corinth which followed the battle of Shiloh, General McCook commanded the advance of General Buell's corps, and his skirmishers were among the first to scale the enemy's works. After the evacuation of Corinth, his command was moved through Northern Alabama to Huntsville, thence to Battle Creek, Tennessee, where it remained for nearly two months, confronting Bragg's forces at Chattanooga. On the 17th of July, 1862, he was appointed major-general, in view of his gallant conduct and distinguished services in the battle of Shiloh and the siege of Corinth. Upon the withdrawal of General Buell's army from Alabama and Tennessee, General McCook moved his division, by a march of four hundred miles, back to Louisville. Here the Army of the Ohio, newly equipped and largely reinforced, was divided into three corps, and he was assigned to the command of the first. On the 1st of October he started from Louisville upon a new campaign in pursuit of Bragg. On the 8th the enemy was met and engaged near Perryville; but, owing to accidental causes, two divisions of General McCook's corps—one of them Jackson's, composed entirely of raw recruits —were forced to bear unsustained the assault of nearly the entire rebel army. The unexpected withdrawal of General Gilbert's corps from the right, the early death of those two gallant generals, Jackson and Terrill, and the tardiness with which reinforcements arrived, made the contest a desperate one, and when night settled upon the combatants it was yet undecided. During the night, however, the enemy retreated, leaving the Union forces masters of the field and winners of an honorable but incomplete and dearly-bought victory.

The object of this sudden onslaught by Bragg upon McCook's corps has never been fully determined; but the most plausible presumption is, that, supposing he could completely crush it before the arrival of reinforcements, he hoped thus so to weaken Buell as to prevent further pursuit and enable him safely to make his way from Kentucky into Tennessee. The desperate resistance of General McCook's gallant twelve thousand troops against overwhelming odds, losing in the fight one-fourth of their number in killed and wounded, but inflicting far deadlier injury upon the enemy, frustrated the designs of the rebel leaders. Bragg, however, succeeded so far as to escape from Kentucky without again coming in contact with the Federal forces;

and the march of the latter was now turned towards Nashville. On the 30th of October General Rosecrans assumed command of the Department of the Cumberland, and on the 6th of November General McCook was placed at the head of the forces in the vicinity of Nashville; and upon the organization of the Army of the Cumberland he was assigned to the leadership of the right wing.

On the 26th of December the army moved from Nashville to attack the enemy in position in front of Murfreesborough, General McCook commanding the right. His line of march was by the Nolensville pike to Triune, where he arrived on Saturday, having had a brisk skirmish at Nolensville the day previous, resulting in his capturing one gun, and gaining possession of the town and the hills in front, with a loss of about seventy-five in killed and wounded. On Sunday the troops rested, and on Monday, the 29th, he was ordered to move from Triune to Wilkerson's Cross-Roads, six miles from Murfreesborough, leaving a brigade at Triune. By evening he reached Wilkerson's Cross-Roads, with an advance brigade at Oversall's Creek, and the next day moved steadily forward, meeting with obstinate resistance from Oversall's Creek, and about four o'clock in the afternoon he got position on the Wilkerson pike, joining General Thomas, having lost in the day's contest about one hundred and thirty-five in killed and wounded. It was now the evening of December 30, and the two armies were in line of battle, confronting each other.

General Rosecrans had massed his reserve on the left, to crush the rebel right with heavy columns and turn their position. But Bragg, learning of this disposition during the night, massed the larger portion of his force in front and on the flank of McCook, and in the gray of the following morning, before any attack had been made upon the left, advanced in heavy force and with great fury upon the right wing. Outnumbered and outflanked, the right was forced to give way, but not until its line of battle had been marked with the evidences of a fiercely-contested struggle and of a fearful havoc in the enemy's ranks. To check the advance of the already victory-flushed rebels, the Federal reserve were rapidly moved forward, and by their aid the enemy was held at bay and the right wing and the fortunes of the day were saved. Defeated on the left and in the centre, checked on the right, foiled in every attack, and again defeated on the 2d and 3d of January, the rebels, having lost nearly one-third of their army, abandoned the field on the night of the 3d, and on the 4th the victorious army of the Union passed through their deserted intrenchments and entered the town of Murfreesborough.

General McCook comes from a remarkable family of " fighting-stock,"—several brothers of whom have fought, and some fallen, in defence of their country. As possessors of stalwart and vigorous frames and constitutions, they are notable. The subject of this sketch is the hero of several contests. At Chaplin Hills he displayed great coolness and daring; and during the adversities of the memorable 31st at Stone River he rode to and fro through the fiery storm, narrowly escaping death at every hand, losing his horse, struck dead under him, and his own death being for several hours currently reported upon the battle-field.

A brief allusion to the causes of the first day's discomfiture at Stone River will not in this connection be deemed improper. The smoke of the battle-field has cleared away, and time and reflection and better knowledge are aids to a clearer under-standing of recent momentous events. General McCook's division, composing the right wing of the Army of the Cumberland, led the advance from Nashville to Murfreesborough For three days preceding, this division had followed up the rebel forces, constantly skirmishing with and forcing back their heavy rear-guard of cavalry and artillery. Arrived at the final battle-ground, the lines of our right wing were formed to face the lines of the enemy's left. If our right wing was too far extended, so was theirs. The surface of the country, though not hilly, was very rough, rocky, and broken with clumps of low, scrubby cedars,—very unfavorable ground upon which to manœuvre troops and re-form broken lines. But the ground was ours from necessity, not

choice. When General McCook was questioned by the commander-in-chief as to his ability to maintain that three miles of
battle-line, he replied that he was confident he could do it; and
his grounds for that confidence seem ample. His troops were
flushed with the successes recently obtained, they had been
under fire in Kentucky, and there was mutual confidence and
the best of feeling between officers and men,—which continues
to this day.

The massing of the rebels upon the extreme right of that
wing early in the morning, and their impetuous dash, their
rushing upon one or two batteries at the outset and seizing
them, some of the horses, it is said, being away to be watered (a
very natural and necessary circumstance), and the ground being
so rough and clumpy that large bodies of troops could not be
successfully halted and re-formed or reserves be brought up at
the right time and place,—were among the causes of the misfortunes of that day. History is pregnant with kindred instances,
where many minor and even trifling occurrences have contributed to momentous results. Be the circumstances of this
mishap as they may, the author but repeats the familiar military opinion and criticism of months past, in asserting that
they were such as no ordinary military foresight could have
foreseen, and no individual human skill and bravery have more
speedily resisted.

After the occupation of Murfreesborough, the Army of the Cumberland was divided into three army corps,—the 14th, 20th, and
21st; and Major-General McCook, who fully retains the confidence
and esteem of the commander-in-chief and of his soldiers, was
assigned to the command of the 20th Army Corps, the position he
now holds. On the 29th day of January, 1863, he was married
to Miss Kate Philips, of Dayton, Ohio, a lady whose beauty and
gentleness are appreciated in the Army of the Cumberland, where
she has since been a welcome visitant. In this instance the
saying is indeed trite, that "none but the brave deserve the
fair."

MAJ. GEN. ROUSSEAU.

MAJ. W. P. MC DOWELL

LT. COL. MARION C. TAYLOR

MAJ. GEN.

MAJ. GEN. L. H. ROUSSEAU.

COL. C. O. LOOMIS.

AND

LT. W. M. CARPENTER.

OFFICERS OF STAFF.

Engd by G.R. Hall

J.B. LIPPINCOTT & CO. PHILADA

Major-General Lovell H. Rousseau and Staff.

LOVELL H. ROUSSEAU, Major-General of Volunteers, commanding 1st Division, 14th Army Corps, was born in Lincoln county, Kentucky, August 4, 1818, and is of Huguenot stock, derived through purely Southern channels. His father was descended from one of three brothers who settled in South Carolina shortly after the revocation of the Edict of Nantes. This Huguenot line subsequently allied itself with some of the most noted families of the Old Dominion, the mother of the subject of this sketch being a Gaines, thus connecting him with the Gaineses and Pendletons of Virginia.

Acquiring the rudiments of an English education at a common country school, young Rousseau prosecuted his studies, unassisted, at home, mainly by night; and thus he mastered the French language, the elements of mathematics, &c. The death of his father, and the call upon him to aid in supporting a large and helpless family, now in straitened circumstances, interrupted his studies at this point. Later in life, the study and practice of his profession afforded opportunities, never left unimproved, of largely increasing his general knowledge. On reaching the age of manhood, he began the study of law, in the face of almost insuperable difficulties, without an instructor. First relinquishing to his sisters his interest in a family of negroes, to prevent their being sold apart, he located himself in the country near Louisville. He studied unremittingly until August, 1840, when his laborious application produced its natural result, by prostrating him upon a bed of sickness, from which at times his recovery was despaired of. Late in the autumn, however, he began to mend slowly.

In a few weeks the buoyancy of youth and the vigor of his

constitution asserted their power and restored to him his memory and energy unabated. A location where he could make the future study of his profession self-sustaining by means of practice was with him now a necessity. After due inquiry and deliberation, he chose Bloomfield, Greene county, Indiana, and in the winter of 1840 went to his new home, performing a great portion of the journey on foot with a bundle of clothing at his back. Here, after a hasty review of his previous acquirements, he applied for a license as an attorney, and was admitted to the bar. A remunerative practice soon followed, and he steadily rose in public appreciation.

In the summer of 1843 he was called upon to become a candidate for the Legislature. The Whig party of Greene county, invariably beaten from year to year, had at length become disheartened and disorganized. The Democratic majority varied from two to four hundred, according to the candidate. Rousseau's first canvass against this heavy odds was perhaps never exceeded in vigor and excitement by any ordinary county contest. His competitor—a man of wealth and position, and for twenty-seven years a resident of the county—had been unanimously nominated by the convention of his party. Rousseau—a new-comer, poor, and a Whig—was elected by a majority of forty-three votes, his own township going so strongly for him as to decide the contest. The next summer he was re-elected by a majority of one hundred and forty-three, over a competitor of wealth and ability.

When the Mexican War broke out, Rousseau raised a company of volunteers and became its captain. He was in the battle of Buena Vista; and his conduct upon that occasion received marked commendation in the official reports of Colonel Humphrey Marshall and other superior officers.

In the summer of 1847, while still absent in Mexico, he was brought forward by his friends as a candidate for the Indiana Senate, in the district composed of Greene and Owen counties. His opponent was John F. O'Neal, a well-known and popular gentleman, who, in a long experience of political life and party contests, had never been beaten. Hon. George G. Dunn was a candidate for Congress the same year, Owen and Greene counties being a part of his district. The Congressional race was close; but the success of the Whig ticket in Owen county, where Dunn had a majority of fifty-nine, secured his election by a majority of one vote in the entire district. Rousseau's majority in Owen county was two hundred and twenty-nine, and in Greene and Owen combined four hundred and fifteen.

In 1849, desiring a larger field for the practice of his profession, he determined to return to Louisville. Being still a member of the Indiana Senate, he desired to resign his seat in that body; but, his constituents expressing their wish with much unanimity and fervor that he should continue to represent them until the expiration of the term for which he had been chosen, he consented, and attended the legislative sessions at Indianapolis for two years after he had removed to Louisville.

The Louisville bar at this time was rich in talent and learning. James Guthrie, Preston S. Loughborough, Chas. M. Thurston, Garnett Duncan, W. P. Thomasson, Wm. S. Pilcher, the firm of Page & Fry, James Speed, W. S. Bodley, Hamilton Pope, Henry C. Pindell, W. T. Heaggin, and the firm of the Ballards, one of whom is now a member of the Federal judiciary, were among its most conspicuous and honored members. Hon. S. S. Nicholas was Chancellor, Hon. W. F. Bullock judge of the Circuit Court, and Hon. Nat Wolfe attorney for the commonwealth. Hon. Henry Pirtle—a revered and venerable name—was still a practitioner at the bar, not then having ascended the woolsack, which he has now adorned for so many years. Hon. Peter B. Muir, since known as one of the ablest jurists of the West, removed to Louisville about the same time; and Hon. Robert F. Baird was that summer a candidate to represent the city of Louisville in the State Legislature, where he was subsequently known as "the lone-star emancipationist." As a practitioner, Rousseau's position at the Louisville bar was commanding from the beginning. In jury-trials his success was uniform, he very rarely losing a verdict. He was ever the champion of the poor and

6

lowly, and defended their rights as vigorously as though they had been able to pay him. One striking feature in his experience as a lawyer and throughout life has been his hold upon the good will and the affections of the humbler classes. Among the most interesting and important cases in which he was engaged may be mentioned the trial of Cope for abduction, the Brier Creek murder case, the trial of Preston for killing Reichardt, and the trial of the Allens and Hickses, charged with murdering Paschal D. Craddock, the history of any one of which would fill a volume.

In the spring of 1860, while absent from home, he was elected to the Kentucky Senate without opposition, both political parties voting for him. At the regular and called sessions of the autumn, winter, and following spring he took a prompt and decided stand for the Government. He advocated a coercive policy at the very beginning of the rebellion. When Sumter was bombarded, he wished for "power to sweep out of existence the miscreants who had done that treason," and declared that "a Government worth living under is worth fighting for." These bold utterances were made against earnest remonstrances, and at a time when the stoutest hearts in Kentucky were dumb with fear. He understood the character and extent of the rebellion too well to be influenced by timid counsel, and, in his place in the Senate and before the people, continued to advocate prompt and vigorous measures. He opposed the policy of neutrality which a majority of the Legislature adopted; and, unable to influence his colleagues to take proper action, he resigned his seat in the Senate, and began raising troops for the service of the Government,—a daring step at that time. Applying to the War Department for authority to enlist men in Kentucky, he was commissioned colonel of volunteers in June, 1861, and at once entered upon his difficult and dangerous work. He was somewhat obstructed in this at the beginning by a resolution which was adopted by the leading politicians of the State at a secret meeting, protesting against the establishment of any United States recruiting rendezvous within the limits of Ken-

tucky. Undaunted by these new difficulties, he established
"Camp Joe Holt," an ever-memorable spot on the northern bank
of the Ohio River across from Louisville and adjacent to the
Falls. Many of his oldest Kentucky friends now stood aloof from
him. Few cared to be seen in conversation with him, and none to
share the odium of his course. He encountered only cold words
and averted faces. For loyalty's sake he was become a stranger
in his own home. But there came a day when all this was
changed. The poorer classes of Louisville and of the neighboring
counties approved his action and filled his ranks. By the 1st
of September he had recruited two full regiments of infantry
and a battery of artillery. He then received orders to report to
General Frémont at St. Louis, and was ready to go; but, through
the interposition of the leading citizens of Louisville, fully
awakened to the danger of a rebel invasion, these orders were
countermanded just as his troops were on the point of departure. The threatened rebel invasion followed a few days
afterwards, and Colonel Rousseau, crossing the Ohio with the
utmost celerity and secrecy on the night of September 17,
gained Muldraugh's Hill by rapid marches, thus protecting
Louisville from invasion.

On the 1st of October Colonel Rousseau was promoted to a
brigadier-generalship, and assigned to the command of the 4th
Brigade of the Army of the West, the first of General McCook's
division. This magnificent brigade consisted of three battalions
of regulars,—one each from the 15th, 16th, and 19th Infantry,—
the Louisville Legion, the 1st Ohio and 6th Indiana Volunteers,
and Terrill's Battery H, 5th Regular Artillery. The division
lay in camp, confronting Buckner, and perfecting its drill and
discipline, until February 18, 1862, when it began the march that
led to Shiloh and Corinth. At Columbia, Tennessee, General
Rousseau was attacked by severe sickness; but, determined to
participate in the great events apparently at hand, he rode
for several days in an ambulance at the head of his command.
On the morning of April 6, while the brigade was still on
the march, twenty miles in rear of Savannah, the booming of

cannon announced that the battle of Shiloh had begun. Mounting his horse and urging forward his men, he reached Savannah with his command in time to be transported to Pittsburg Landing by daylight the next morning. His brigade was under the immediate supervision of his department and division commanders, and fought with a bravery and determination that attracted the notice of even the generals of the sister army. It drove the enemy steadily before it, and at the close of the action had gained about two miles of ground in the front. General McCook, in his official report, spoke of General Rousseau as having "won the admiration of the army" by his bearing that day; General Sherman mentioned him as having driven the enemy steadily before him; General McClernand's language was not less commendatory; and General Buell called the attention of the War Department to his services.

The 4th Brigade and its leader took an important part in the operations before Corinth, and when General Buell's army was sent into Northern Alabama, General Rousseau was placed in command of the 3d Division, then stationed at Huntsville. Here his administration of affairs was firm and just; and perhaps no other portion of his life has been more successful than this.

General Buell's march to Kentucky in his campaign against Bragg now ensued. At Munfordsville, where a battle was expected, General Rousseau commanded the right wing. Buell's army, having been supplied and reinforced at Louisville, marched from that city on the 1st of October, in three columns. The left wing, consisting of the divisions of Rousseau, Sill, and Jackson, and commanded by Major-General McCook, marched (except Sill's division) by way of Taylorsville and Bloomfield, and reached Mackville on the night of October 7. Bragg, having concentrated the bulk of his own army, was probably moving to form a junction with Kirby Smith at Harrodsburg, preparatory to giving Buell battle. But, pressed too closely for his own safety, or tempted by the chances which the topography of the country seemed to afford him, or perhaps influenced by both of these considerations, he halted, and made the hills of Chaplin historic. The Perryville and Harrodsburg road, which was his line of march, formed a small angle with the Perryville and Mackville road, over which our left wing was moving. Waiting, therefore, with his forces well in hand until our left came within striking-distance, he fell upon it with an impetuosity and fury never exceeded in the annals of warfare. Jackson's division, composed entirely of raw troops, was overwhelmed and quickly routed, with heavy loss, including that of its gallant commander and two of its brigade commanders, Brigadier-General Terrill and Acting Brigadier-General Webster. The whole weight of the rebel army now fell upon Rousseau's division with redoubled fury. Selecting a new position, and encouraging his men by a fearless exposure of himself, he stemmed the torrent and repulsed the enemy. The battle was terrific, there being scarcely an instant's pause from the beginning to the end. From half-past twelve at mid-day until dark, the battle-field was one unbroken scene of flame and death. General Bragg, who was at Buena Vista and Shiloh, calls it "the severest and most desperately contested engagement within his knowledge." General Rousseau lost one-third of his entire division,—which consisted of three brigades of volunteers, commanded by Colonels Lytle, Harris, and Starkweather, and four batteries of artillery. Opposed to them were three divisions of Bragg's favorite corps, the rebel Army of the Mississippi. The enemy withdrew in great confusion during the night, too badly shattered to give General Buell further battle.

Immediately after the battle General Buell telegraphed to the War Department, recommending the promotion of General Rousseau to a major-generalship "for distinguished gallantry and good service in the battle of Perryville." The promotion was at once made, to date from the day of the battle, the commission accounting for itself in the precise language of General Buell's despatch. Bragg having hastily evacuated Kentucky, Buell directed his march towards Nashville, and at Bowling Green was superseded in command by General Rosecrans. A reorganization of the army now took place, and General Rousseau's division was assigned to the centre corps, commanded by Major-General Thomas. After some time spent in necessary preparations, General Rosecrans advanced from Nashville on the 26th of December.

On the morning of December 31, the battle of Murfreesborough, or Stone River, opened. Colonel Starkweather's brigade having been temporarily detached, and not arriving on the field until evening, General Rousseau's division, composed of one brigade of regulars under command of Colonel Sheppard, two brigades of volunteers under command of Colonels Scribner and Beatty, and two batteries of artillery, was massed in reserve in a cotton-field to the right of the Murfreesborough and Nashville turnpike. The right of the division rested on a dense cedar forest. Half an hour after this disposition had been made, General Thomas ordered the division to move to the support of the right wing, which was drifting around to the rear of the centre before the overwhelming masses of the enemy. Extreme difficulty was experienced in getting the troops and batteries through the cedars; but at length the heads of the brigades, marching by the flank, reached the opposite edge of the forest by two separate roads. It being impossible to make the least use of the batteries, they were sent to the rear again. The infantry were formed and posted as advantageously as the circumstances would allow, and the right was immediately engaged with the enemy. The division of the right wing retired through the line and around its flanks, closely pressed by the enemy. In this manner the right of the division was quickly turned, and its left seriously threatened. To prevent its being taken at such disadvantage, the division was retired to the open ground which it had lately left, the batteries were massed on a commanding knoll, and the infantry posted in skilfully-selected positions. The enemy, following with reckless energy, made a bold dash for the new position. A terrible fire of grape and musketry swept the left and centre of their line, and covered the ground with their dead and wounded. Towards the right of the division, the rebel line, encountering resistance and natural obstructions, did not reach the open ground until the repulse and rout of the rebels on our left. General Rousseau at once ordered his right, consisting of the regulars, to charge, and the enemy were driven precipitately in that quarter also, though not without heavy loss to us. The enemy subsequently made several determined but unsuccessful attempts against the position with artillery, and in this way succeeded in killing many of our men. They also made formidable demonstrations by a heavy massing of infantry, but could not induce their men to make another assault. On Saturday evening a portion of Colonel Beatty's brigade drove the rebels from a wood and a line of temporary works in the front, thus closing the battle. The distinguished service rendered by General Rousseau in this engagement was freely acknowledged by the commanding general, who in his official report returned his thanks to "the gallant and ever-ready Major-General Rousseau."

Athletic and of commanding appearance, few men possess a nobler presence than General Rousseau. Knowing no distinction of classes, and receiving with equal favor the humblest and the proudest, he is noted for the amenity and kindness of his manner. As a legislator, his views have been liberal and statesmanlike. As a commander, he is honored by his compeers and esteemed by his men. In the walks of private life his friends witness the more attractive traits of his character exemplified,—traits to which the sternness and tumult of war give little room for display. His early and determined opposition to the rebellion as a Kentuckian is alone sufficient to make his an honored name. His devotion to the principles he then professed has been demonstrated by nearly two years of active and efficient service.

In 1843, General Rousseau was married to Miss Antoinette Dozier, daughter of James J. Dozier, the law partner of Felix Grundy, of Tennessee. His family consists of his wife and four children; and their present residence is in the city of Louisville.

THE STAFF.

MAJOR WILLIAM PRESTON McDOWELL, *Assistant Adjutant-General*, is, like his general and hundreds of other brave men in this army, a Southerner by birth and education. He was born in Louisville, Kentucky, in the year 1837; and at the outbreak of the rebellion we find him engaged in the study of the law in one of the Clerks' offices in his native city.

No sooner had the President called upon Kentucky for her quota of troops than he enlisted in the 15th Regiment Kentucky Volunteer Infantry. On the 15th of September, 1861, he was commissioned adjutant of the same regiment.

He served with his regiment until August 3, 1862, when he was detailed on the staff of General Rousseau, then commanding the 3d Division of the Army of the Ohio, and at the battle of Chaplin Hills, Kentucky, served as aide, and received much praise for his gallant behavior. After this battle he was appointed acting assistant adjutant-general on the staff, and served in this capacity until after the battle of Stone River. In the first day's engagement he was wounded severely in the left arm; but, although the wound was painful, he refused to leave the field until loss of blood compelled him to retire.

On the 15th of March, 1863, he was commissioned by the President as assistant adjutant-general, with the rank of major. One of our youngest and bravest officers, we bespeak for him a brilliant future.

COLONEL MARION C. TAYLOR, formerly acting assistant adjutant-general, at present commands the 15th Regiment Kentucky Volunteers. He was born in Ohio county, Kentucky, in the year 1822, and at the commencement of the rebellion was enjoying a lucrative practice of the law at Shelbyville. He was among the first in that section of the State to respond to the call of the President, and in a short time recruited a full company for the regiment which he now commands. From September, 1861, to December, 1862, he served as captain in his regiment. He was then detailed upon the staff of Major-General Rousseau. When Major McDowell received his wound at the battle of Stone River, Captain Taylor succeeded him as assistant adjutant-general. During this battle the colonel of his regiment was killed, and in February, 1863, the Governor of Kentucky commissioned Captain Taylor as colonel. The regiment which he now commands has already lost in battle two colonels and every field officer of its original organization.

We have been unable to obtain sketches of—

COLONEL C. O. LOOMIS, *Chief of Artillery.*

CAPTAIN C. K. SMITH, *Quartermaster.*

LIEUTENANT ALFRED PIRTLE, *Ordnance Officer.*

LIEUTENANT W. M. CARPENTER, *Aide-de-Camp.*

LIEUTENANT S. L. HARTMAN, *Aide-de-Camp.*

LIEUTENANT HARRISON MILLARD, *Aide-de-Camp and Division Inspector,* is familiar to many in the musical world; and the past two years have proved him as gallant in battle as he is popular in song. He was born and educated in Boston, Massachusetts, and at an early age evinced a strong passion for art and song, his devotion to which impelled him to go abroad to complete his musical studies. There he remained for upwards of five years, spending most of the time in Italy and Paris. The breaking out of the rebellion found him pursuing his profession in New York City; but, notwithstanding a brilliant career was opening before him, he was one of the first to enlist for his country's defence. Two years before this, he had written and published the widely-known national song " *Viva l'America,*" which has found a place in thousands of homes and hamlets in this country and has warmed thousands of hearts. He was a private in the Light Guard, Company A, 71st New York V. M., and with thirty-six hours' notice he was with his regiment on his way to Washington when danger first menaced our capital. The incidents of that journey were depicted in his extensively-read " *Only Nine Miles to the Junction.*" For three months·he was stationed at the navy yard in that city, cheerfully performing the drudgery and monotonous duty of a common soldier.

A short time before the expiration of his three-months enlistment, he was offered and accepted a first lieutenancy in the Regular Army; and he immediately reported for duty at Indianapolis, Indiana, the head-quarters of the 19th U.S. Infantry. Lieutenant Millard performed a few months' duty with his regiment, when he was called to the staff of General Rousseau, then commanding the brigade; and he has ever since remained with the general. He was with him at the battles of Shiloh, Chaplin Hills (Perryville), Kentucky, and Murfreesborough, Tennessee. During the five days' battle at Stone River he was constantly near the general, having his horse killed under him and his overcoat perforated with bullets. We cannot close this brief sketch better than by appending the following extract from a letter of " W. D. B." to the Cincinnati Commercial, as indicative of the character and traits of Lieutenant Millard :—

" I desire to call the attention of wives and mothers to an exquisite little song that was composed by a soldier the night before the battle of Stone River. Lieutenant H. Millard, 19th U.S.A., and aide-de-camp to Major-General Rousseau, is the author. On the night of the 29th of December, when the division bivouacked on Stewart's Creek, Lieutenant Millard's wife bade him good-bye. We expected to go into battle next morning. Lieutenant Millard reclined on a shock of corn, looking into the blue skies, thinking of his wife,—for soldiers think of wives and little ones at such periods. His comrades were speculating on the chances of battle, now and then expressing amiable envy that Millard could sleep so soundly. Suddenly he sprang from his couch, and, calling Lieutenant Pirtle, he repeated the result of his fancies to him, in verse, which he entitled 'Whisper Good-Night, Love.' Tuesday night (30th of December), while the division was bivouacked in front of Murfreesborough, he composed and arranged the music for the piano. The next day five hundred and eight of Millard's comrades were bleeding on the field of battle. I don't know what our music-loving lady friends may think of our soldier's song; but indeed it touches soldiers' hearts."

MAJ. GEN. NEGLEY

CAPT. JAS A. LOWRIE.

CAPT. & M. L. JOHNSON.

MAJ. GEN.

J. S. NEGLEY.

CAPT. CHAS T. WING.

MAJOR F. H. GROSS.

AND

OFFICERS OF STAFF.

Eng.ᵈ by J. Rogers

J. B. LIPPINCOTT & CO PHILADᴬ

Major-General James S. Negley and Staff.

James S. Negley, Major-General of Volunteers, commanding 2d Division, 14th Army Corps, was born December 26, 1826, in East Liberty, Alleghany county, Pennsylvania. His family is of Swiss descent; and its members are very numerous and among the most respectable and influential in the county. His earlier days were spent in the quiet of home, and employed in obtaining a plain practical education in the English branches as taught in the common schools of Pennsylvania. After passing through the preparatory studies, he entered college, but had left it, and was preparing himself for mercantile pursuits, when the military ardor of his nature, then already attracting comment and attention, was fully aroused by the declaration of war with Mexico and President Polk's call for troops. Though not of age, young Negley enlisted in the Duquesne Grays, at that time one of the finest companies in the State, and thus became a private in the 1st Pennsylvania Infantry. His friends and relatives doubted his physical ability to endure the hardships of the campaign, and endeavored to dissuade him from his purpose. Failing in this, they applied to the legal authorities to prevent his going. With a spirit of determination which later events have shown to be a prominent characteristic of the man, he informed the court that it was his purpose to go at all events. Under such circumstances it was thought useless to restrain him longer; and he was allowed to go with his company. During the campaign under General Scott, Negley participated in the siege of Puebla, the battle of Cerro Gordo, and other minor engagements. During this service his friends heard of his severe illness, which nearly proved fatal, and, on application to the War Department, procured his honorable discharge. This reached him immediately after the siege of Puebla; but he refused to accept it; and, though it could not be cancelled, he remained on duty—having been promoted to be a sergeant—until the close of the war, when he returned home with his company.

Negley now went to Pittsburg, where he engaged in the manufacture of agricultural and railroad machinery; but, this proving unprofitable, he returned to East Liberty and devoted himself to agriculture and horticulture; and in these pursuits he was distinguished for activity and scientific ability. While thus engaged, he was married to Miss Kate Lozey, a niece of the late Commodore Van Voorhies.

Although thus retired to private life, Negley felt an active interest in military affairs. A company was formed in his native village, of which he was elected commander, and, devoting thereto much time and attention, by his labors raised it to a state of the highest efficiency. Several of its old members hold distinguished positions in our army; and the company itself—the Negley Zouaves—is attached to the 77th Regiment Pennsylvania Volunteer Infantry, at present in the Army of the Cumberland.

The interest felt by Captain Negley in military matters was not confined to his own company. As early as 1858 he became generally known by his earnest efforts to induce the executive and legislative powers of his native State to reorganize the State militia, predicting at that early day that a time would soon come when Pennsylvania would regret that her militia was not upon a war-footing. Although Captain Negley's plans and arguments were much in advance of the hour, they were not wholly lost upon the people, and something of a military interest was created in his own county, which gradually extended over the State. In 1858 he was offered the colonelcy of a regiment raised in Alleghany county, but declined, as he subsequently did the proffered major-generalship of the 18th division of the State militia, accepting, however, the brigade-generalship of the troops raised as militia in his own county, believing that he could thus more effectually contribute to the State military service. He early foresaw that the political struggles of 1860 would eventuate in civil 'war, and made earnest preparations to take the field at the head of a brigade, and as early as December 1, 1860, offered the services of the brigade to the Governor of Pennsylvania. At last the war opened, as he had predicted. Governor Curtin, on the 18th of April, telegraphed General Negley that his services and those of his brigade were needed; and the call was immediately responded to by the organization of the brigade, and its appearance in Harrisburg within ten days thereafter.

The organization of all the volunteers in Western Pennsylvania was then placed under General Negley's control, and he soon forwarded several regiments to Washington. In addition to his brigade, he organized forty companies, all of which subsequently took the field. He was then ordered to Harrisburg, York, and Lancaster, where he was placed in charge of the 14th and 15th Pennsylvania Regiments, which he soon brought to an excellent state of discipline. He also, with the assistance of Captain (now Brigadier-General) Charles Campbell, organized the first battery of the famous regiment of Pennsylvania Artillery. During the three-months service, General Negley commanded a brigade in Maryland and Virginia. Previous to its close, however, he was authorized by the War Department to raise a brigade for the three-years service, which was done in an almost incredibly short period. On the 28th of September, 1861, he was ordered to march his brigade, consisting of the 77th, 78th, and 79th Pennsylvania Regiments and Mueller's Pennsylvania Battery, to join General Rosecrans in Western Virginia. Before embarking at Pittsburg, however, the order was countermanded, and he was directed to report to General Sherman at Louisville, Kentucky. Upon arriving there, his brigade was attached to the division of General McCook, and remained with it during the weary waiting at Green River and the advance upon Bowling Green. Subsequently detached from the division at the request of General Negley, it made the overland march to Nashville, and advanced with Buell's army towards Pittsburg Landing, as far as Columbia, Tennessee, where General Negley was left in command.

General Negley assumed command at Columbia, April 1, 1862, with a force of three thousand men, which was gradually increased, as the armies of Buell and Mitchel advanced, to about ten thousand. In his new position he labored under many disadvantages. He had the entire rear of both armies to protect, their communications to keep open, their supplies to forward, and at the same time was expected to be ready at a moment's notice to march to the aid of either. To add to his labors, every thing was in disorder and confusion. The stragglers, convalescents, and sick of Buell's whole army, amounting to some five thousand men, were left at Columbia, with no commander, no rations, no quarters, and, in fact, no one to do any thing for them. His first duty was to attend to these. He immediately cleared out and prepared for their use several of the largest buildings in the town, and by sending those able to do duty to their commands on the march to the Tennessee River, and moving the convalescents back to Nashville, he reduced the number of hospital patients, in less than ten days, to not more than one hundred. In his new command it was his especial duty to guard the posts of Columbia, Shelbyville, Franklin, Tullahoma, Pulaski, Mount Pleasant, and other minor points, besides keeping open at all hazards the railroads to Huntsville and Decatur, Alabama. The country swarmed with guerrillas, who were constantly hovering about our lines, on the alert for every chance that might offer for a dash at an inferior force, or a surprise of some inadequately guarded supply-train. In watching the movements of these roving bodies, and in governing and keeping in order the inhabitants of his district, the period of his command at Columbia was mostly occupied: yet he found time for two important expeditions,—one to Rogersville and Florence, and the other to Chattanooga,—besides various smaller skirmishes and guerrilla-hunts.

On the 8th of May he was ordered by General Mitchel to concentrate at Pulaski, Tennessee, at least two thousand men, infantry and cavalry, and three thousand, if possible, from his own command at Columbia and Colonel Duffield's at Murfreesborough, for a movement upon the enemy's cavalry beyond Elk River and in the vicinity of Rogersville and Florence. On the 10th he left Columbia, with about one thousand men, for Pulaski, ordering about the same number from Mount Pleasant to join him at the rendezvous. On the 13th, at three P.M., his force, consisting of four regiments of infantry, two battalions of cavalry, and two sections of artillery, left Pulaski, and marched twelve miles, where they encamped for a few hours, and then made a forced march of twenty-one miles in six hours. The enemy's pickets were driven in, and gave the alarm to the forces in the town of Rogersville, who fled in every direction. A portion of the cavalry pushed on to Lamb's Ferry, on the Tennessee River, and fired upon a boat-load of the enemy as they were crossing the river, killing several men and horses. Once over the river, the rebels opened fire upon our men, but were soon dispersed by the Federal artillery, and fled hastily beyond the range of our guns. A ferry-boat on the north side of the Tennessee was destroyed, and General Negley pushed on to Florence and to Cheatham's Ferry, fifteen miles below, destroying all the water-craft as he proceeded. He also arrested all the manufacturers of cotton and woollen goods, and all the iron-founders near Florence who had been supplying the rebel army with their products, and exacted of them heavy bonds and their parole of honor not to sell, directly or indirectly, any thing to the enemies of the Federal Government,—a policy then considered of great importance, as immense quantities of goods had been sold there. He also levied taxes upon the prominent secessionists to remunerate Union men for the damages done them by the rebels, and on one occasion ordered his aide-de-camp to ride many miles out of the way to pay, from the funds thus raised, a widow who had been robbed by guerrillas. For his energy and rapidity of movement in this expedition he was highly complimented by Major-General Mitchel.

Returning to Columbia on the 20th, matters remained quiet

for a day or two, when General Negley advised General Mitchel that a large force of rebel cavalry was being concentrated at or near McMinnville, Tennessee, and urged upon Mitchel to allow him to strengthen Colonel Lester at McMinnville. About the same time he reported that Starns's rebel cavalry was said to be moving towards McMinnville. On the 25th of May, General Mitchel, again urged, gave General Negley the requested order, and Murfreesborough was strengthened by forces placed at Shelbyville, Wartrace, and other points. General Mitchel, about the same time, getting important information on the subject, went from Huntsville to Nashville, where on the 26th of May he telegraphed to Negley to meet him.

On the 27th of May, Negley was at Nashville, and had an interview with Mitchel and Lester. Mitchel asked of him an elaboration of the views he had telegraphed. General Negley stated to him briefly his information. The rebel forces threatening Murfreesborough had come from Chattanooga, taking advantage of the Sequatchie Valley. The true way to attack him, he argued, was to do so by the same valley, thus endangering his rear. At the same time, he proposed to attack Starns's force in front and drive it into or across the river, or capture it. By thus threatening Chattanooga, the rebels would be compelled to withdraw from McMinnville, or from some other point, to reinforce Chattanooga. While this plan would be offensive against Starns, it would be strategical also; and, besides, if made by the route named, the railroad brought supplies near at hand. To make Murfreesborough the base would require a force of greater magnitude than both generals could raise. A calculation was made: five thousand men could be spared for the expedition. General Mitchel decided that it should be made, and placed General Negley in command of it. "When can you put your troops in motion?" asked Mitchel. "To-night," replied Negley. "Then I will go to bed," said Mitchel; and the interview ended, Lester, however, being dissatisfied with the plan.

At four o'clock the next morning the troops of General Negley were in motion at Columbia, on the way to Pulaski.

By a special train the general reached Columbia the same day. From there he telegraphed to Governor Johnson and General Morgan, in front of Cumberland Gap, the purpose of the expedition. He said to Morgan that he should be in front of Chattanooga on the 6th of June, and that it was his belief that the movement would result in the evacuation of Cumberland Gap; that the rebels laid more stress on the position at McMinnville, and the result it promised, than they did on the gap. He pushed forward, assumed the command, and entered Pulaski on the 29th. On the 31st he was at Fayetteville, where he received further intimations of danger at Murfreesborough, and was required by Mitchel to look to that place and reinforce it. Mitchel in this despatch said that he was at a loss to understand Beauregard's movements,—the evacuation of Corinth taking place at that time. Negley's reply was to the effect that if the expedition were pushed forward and the road cut at Chattanooga, the evacuation of Corinth would be in vain, and that in his opinion Beauregard was passing East via Chattanooga. On the 3d of June, the march having been resumed, Negley entered Winchester, dispersing a small force of the enemy and capturing several prisoners. On the 4th, General Morgan thanked General Negley for his advice, and desired to know what force was moving against Chattanooga.

On the same day (June 4), having made a forced march of twenty miles over a rugged and almost impassable mountain-road, he captured the enemy's pickets at Sweeden's Cove, completely surprising General Adams's rebel cavalry encamped at the foot of the mountain. After a hand-to-hand fight in a narrow lane and upon broken ground, the enemy was routed, with a loss of twenty killed and twice as many wounded. Thus dispersed, they fled in wild disorder, strewing the ground for miles with guns, swords, and pistols, and not once stopping until they reached Chattanooga, forty-three miles distant. Their ammunition and commissary wagons, filled with supplies, were also captured by our forces. On the 5th of June, General Negley arrived at Jasper, beyond his new base of supplies, and he

7

began to look to the safety of his flanks. He put Colonel Sill's brigade at Shell Mound to protect his right, and stationed a regiment at Battle Creek to protect the left and to hold the pontoon bridge over the creek. He then ordered Turchin's brigade by one road, and Colonel Hambright's by the Anderson road, to Chattanooga. On the 6th of June he was opposite that place. On the 7th the battle occurred, consisting principally of a heavy cannonade lasting an hour and a half, during which the enemy was driven from his guns and three of them seriously damaged ; and on the evening of the 8th he began his retreat.

Why did he withdraw? Why did he not occupy and hold the place after he had silenced the enemy's fire and driven them from the city? Simply because he had not force enough to cross the river in the face of the enemy with safety, or to hold the place when once within it. The moment Adams was defeated at Sweeden's Cove, Kirby Smith with five thousand men withdrew from Cumberland Gap, and on the 8th was actually in Chattanooga. This decided Negley to withdraw. It also decided Morgan to enter Cumberland Gap; and in that and in the dispersal of the guerrillas we have the legitimate results of the expedition, and all that Negley had expected of it. On the 7th Negley knew that Chattanooga was occupied by only a small force under John Morgan. He telegraphed to Mitchel and Buell, "I can take Chattanooga without loss. Will you give me enough men to hold it?" Not receiving from them any assurance of the needed reinforcements, he telegraphed on the 8th, "It is almost impossible to construct sufficient pontoons to cross the river in force. I do not consider the capture of Chattanooga as very difficult or hazardous, if we were prepared to do it and then to hold the place. But, taking into consideration the exposed condition of both front and rear of our lines to Pittsburg Landing, the long line of communication over a hardly passable road, the liability of a rise in the streams we have to ford,—some of them being now three feet deep, with rough bottoms,—our limited supplies, and the fact that our expedition has accomplished all we expected to do, have determined me to retire, the forces taking different routes, so as to drive Starns to Knoxville. I shall make another demonstration against Chattanooga this morning, during which time the trains will be ascending the mountain, which is almost impassable for artillery and loaded wagons." During the evening of the 7th the enemy threatened to cross the river opposite Chattanooga and at Shell Mound; but the dispositions made by General Negley prevented them from carrying out their object.

At nine o'clock on the morning of the 8th, Colonel Scribner's command took position before Chattanooga. His artillery immediately opened fire upon the enemy's works, while the infantry approached to within six hundred yards and drove the rebel sharpshooters from their places of shelter. Having again silenced the enemy and driven him from the town, Colonel Scribner marched for the Sequatchie Valley; and this was the end of the Chattanooga expedition. The forces were withdrawn with rapidity and divided, General Turchin's brigade being stationed at Battle Creek, and General Negley with the remainder of the force pursuing Starns via the Altamont and Thierman road.

Returning to Shelbyville by way of Manchester, he resumed command at Columbia, where he remained until its evacuation on the 31st of August following.

General Negley ruled with an iron hand at Columbia. The country, under former commanders, had been infested with guerrillas. Men suspected of belonging to these bands were arrested, and the guilty were punished. The new ruler soon became distasteful to the citizens. His manners and kindly mode of doing his duty prevented their hating him; but they feared him. With a small force, a good deal of energy, and the daily illustrated determination to punish the guilty, he kept the country quiet and free of guerrillas. He instituted a military prison, into which many rabid rebels found their way. If drunken soldiers committed outrages, he made the man who sold the liquor pay the damages.

Even those who had once been advocates of the tender, considerate, and forgiving policy which has since been designated as the "rose-water" system were at length compelled to acknowledge the correctness of General Negley's conclusions. Many who had thought that severity could do no good, and who were sorry when General Buell passed through the State and left it to the not over-tender mercies of Generals Negley and Mitchel, soon found their mistake; and when General Buell returned and reinstated his "rose-water" policy it was made thoroughly manifest. The rebels flew to General Buell for protection from the iron rule of Negley. The screws were taken off; and the natural result followed. The country was overrun with guerrillas. The citizens formed guerrilla bands in every county, giving an almost inconceivable amount of trouble. So great was it, in one way, that it kept Buell's army on half-rations. The guerrillas organized in such force that they actually captured whole regiments, as at Murfreesborough. A short time before the evacuation of Columbia, General Negley received information that sixty guerrillas had attacked eight of his men in a log house within five miles of his head-quarters, and had demanded their surrender. The men refused. Reinforcements were sent; but the guerrillas had disappeared. It afterwards appeared in proof that these guerrillas were citizens, and that they had demanded the surrender of the eight men by a flag of truce carried by a lone woman.

The general was no respecter of rebel rights or property. He was the first officer in General Buell's department to use slaves as teamsters. He levied taxes upon the Secessionists, and in all his district guarded the property of but two men, one John Morgan, and General Gideon Pillow. The premises of the first were guarded to protect the horses of Mr. Morgan, who was an ardent, uncompromising Union man. The guard over the property of General Pillow was instructed to take care of four hundred head of United States horses which were quartered there for some four months. These horses were broken-down animals left behind by General Buell's army, and were collected together and recruited upon rebel pastures. Towards rebel sympathizers, as well as those actively engaged in guerrilla or regular warfare, he was unrelentingly severe. He also struck a blow at the States' Rights doctrine by requiring of every one who applied for a pass, oaths of allegiance, fortified by heavy bonds.

On the 11th of August, 1862, General Negley planned an expedition against a guerrilla band of about five hundred men who were constantly hovering about Mount Pleasant, Williamson, and Hillsborough. He sent by the way of Spring Hill to Hillsborough a cavalry force of about three hundred, and by way of Williamson one of about one hundred and fifty troops. The detachment sent to Spring Hill met a party of the guerrillas, about three hundred strong, a few miles beyond that place; and a sharp skirmish ensued, resulting in the total rout of the enemy, with a loss of thirty killed and wounded and forty-five prisoners. The remainder, retreating towards Hillsborough, came in contact with the force sent by way of Williamson, when a hand-to-hand engagement occurred, and the rebels, again completely routed, took to the woods and hills. Some of them were found concealed in hollow logs, others under jutting rocks, having thrown their arms into the creek. A number, when caught, declared, with a fine show of innocence, that they were "only out squirrel-hunting."

It having been determined to abandon Northern Alabama and Southern Tennessee in order to be able to cope with Bragg in Kentucky, a gradual withdrawal of the forces began in the latter part of August. The evacuation of the line of railroad under General Negley's command took place under very peculiar circumstances, involving danger to a large amount of rolling stock and Government property. The commandant at Nashville withdrew the guard of the railroad bridges at Elk River and Richland Creek, while four trains and two regiments of infantry were between the two. The bridges were destroyed by Biffles's regiment of rebel cavalry, thus rendering retreat by rail impossible; and the officer in command of the trains would have burned them and the Government property but for the timely

interference of General Negley, who started from Columbia on
the 27th of August, with a force of two hundred infantry and
his cavalry escort, leaving Captain Lowrie, his adjutant-general, with but ninety men, to guard Columbia. He marched to
Reynolds's Station, got the trains under way, and arrived with
them at Richland Creek. Here he impressed all the negroes in
the vicinity, and constructed a bridge by means of timber and
cotton-bales, over which he passed the entire force and trains,
running them safely to Nashville.

Soon after his return, General Negley was ordered to evacuate
Columbia with his command. The evacuation was admirably
accomplished, all the beef-cattle in the surrounding country
being collected and driven to Nashville, and one hundred thousand bushels of corn, together with all the commissary, quartermaster's, and ordnance stores, the sick, and even the hospital
furniture, being shipped safely to that city.

The occupation of Nashville during the two months when
the city was isolated and cut off from communication with
the North constitutes a feature in this war as novel as it is
interesting. In the space to which we are confined, it is hardly
possible to present as graphically as we desire the strange and
novel picture. Assuming command on the 6th of September,
with two small divisions as a garrison, General Negley found
himself shut up with but five days' provisions in a city weakly
fortified and strongly menaced, with a hostile people within his
besieged lines to rule and to watch. With the aid of Captain
Morton, chief engineer, he pushed forward to early completion
the forts which subsequently became known as " Forts Negley,"
"Andrew Johnson," "Confiscation," and "Casino," and established a complete and thorough picket-line, strengthened by
rifle-pits and heavy abatis, soon making the city one of the best-
fortified in the country. At the same time he reorganized the
8th Division, composed of fractions of brigades and regiments
left, by reason of non-organization, to add to the garrison at
Nashville. He also formed a regiment out of the convalescents
of various regiments left by Buell's army in the rear. He

made new laws for the regulation and control of the hostile citizens within his lines, and soon began at Nashville the process of government which had produced such happy results at Columbia. Perhaps in no city in the South had our army met with so bitter a reception as at Nashville. The intense hatred of the Secessionists of Nashville for the Union troops displayed itself in the most contemptuous expressions and incidents. As an instance, we transcribe the following inscription, written in a female hand on the window-shutter of a house in Nashville then used by us as a hospital :—

" I hope that every officer who enters this house may depart this life in double-quick time; that they may suffer the torture of ten thousand deaths before they die. And paralyzed be the hand that would alleviate their sufferings; and may the tongue of him who would speak words of comfort cleave to the roof of his mouth. And as for the Yankee women who are hungry for the spoils, may——but cursed are they already. God bless the Southern cause! curse the Northern, and all that fight for it !"

General Negley did not confine his operations to the government of the rebel citizens or the fortification of the city. Repeated sallies were made upon the guerrilla bands, and foraging-parties went many miles into the country, invariably meeting with success. Shortly after assuming command, he surprised Bennett's rebel cavalry at Goodlettsville, and, after a short but sharp contest, completely routed him, capturing forty prisoners and most of their horses and entirely destroying the regiment as an organization.

One of the most complete and successful expeditions of the whole war was carried into effect, October 7, by General Negley, assisted by General Palmer, resulting in the victory of Lavergne. It is worthy of note that the information of General Negley regarding the rebels at Lavergne was found correct in the minutest circumstances, and also that his plan and orders regarding the expedition were carried out and followed with a fidelity which reflects great credit upon the officers acting under him.

General Negley ordered General Palmer to move with his command, and instructed Colonel Miller to co-operate in the movement. The whole force moved promptly at nine o'clock on the night of Monday, the 6th of October, on the Murfreesborough road, while Miller took a direction to the left of the railroad. Palmer arrived at Lavergne at half-past three o'clock on Tuesday morning. Miller did not arrive in front of the enemy until the battle had begun, which was at daybreak. Before the encounter General Palmer captured some rebel pickets at Lavergne, and sent them to Nashville. The enemy, under General S. R. Anderson, opened upon Palmer, and attempted to flank him by throwing the 32d Alabama on his right. They also opened fire with one gun; but Houghtaling's battery, a short distance off, returned fire from two sections, and the second shot from our artillery went through the enemy's powder-magazine, causing its complete destruction.

When the Alabama regiment above referred to made its demonstration upon Palmer's flank, Miller's force had just arrived through a cornfield, and he threw his force across their front and on the Murfreesborough road on the right, while the 78th Pennsylvania Infantry formed in front of the retreating enemy when he attempted to pass his line to the left. Colonel Sirwell threw his regiment rapidly by the left flank, completely in front of the enemy in that direction. During this time the artillery was playing upon them with telling effect. The cavalry dashed against the line of the 78th, but was met by a succession of volleys of musketry. The 32d Alabama quickly threw down their arms, and the cavalry displayed a white flag, but the captain of our artillery, not seeing it, kept on firing. The cavalry then broke, and fled in great confusion to the woods. Meanwhile the 18th Ohio had arrived nearly at the place where the enemy's artillery made the first stand, and, by order of Colonel Miller, deployed as skirmishers to sweep the woods recently occupied by the Alabama regiment. The men swept the woods back to the rebel camps, and took numerous prisoners,—among them Colonel Maury. General Negley at an early hour on

Tuesday morning, deeming it expedient to risk no sacrifice of troops, sent out reinforcements from Nashville, when they were met by the victorious troops on their return.

The rebels had but one gun, which was captured. We also took from them four hundred small arms, a regimental stand of colors, fifty-six loads of flour, several hundred-weight of bacon, forty beeves, and a large number of horses. Our loss, as far as ascertained, was four killed and seven wounded. The rebel loss was thirty killed and eighty wounded, and three hundred prisoners, comprising two colonels, several captains and lieutenants, some ordnance officers, and a squad of sergeants and corporals.

On the 19th of October, General Negley also succeeded in routing Forrest's cavalry while crossing the Cumberland River. The following is his brief official report of the affair, which reflected much credit on all concerned :—

"HEAD-QUARTERS U.S. FORCES, NASHVILLE, TENNESSEE, October 20, 1862.

" Yesterday General Forrest commenced crossing a considerable force of cavalry over the Cumberland. The advance, about one thousand strong, encamped on the Gallatin pike seven miles from Nashville. I immediately sent a force under Colonel Miller, who attacked the enemy at daylight, speedily routing and driving them back over the river. In their consternation, they lost one of their cannon overboard from a flat-boat in recrossing, and strewed the pathway of their flight with arms (all new) and knapsacks. But few killed or wounded. A number of prisoners, including a colonel. The 78th Pennsylvania behaved handsomely. The result was very satisfactory,—especially as it is the third time we have completely routed the enemy's forces near Nashville.

"JAMES S. NEGLEY,
" *Brigadier-General commanding.*
"To COLONEL JAMES B. FRY, *Adj.-Gen. and Chief of Staff.*"

The rebel forces concentrated at Murfreesborough to operate

against Nashville were under the command of Major-General John C. Breckinridge. He had succeeded in accumulating about· five thousand infantry, an unknown force of cavalry, and a large amount of artillery, principally of a heavy character, and on November 5 made an attack on the city with his cavalry. At two o'clock on the morning of the 5th, Forrest, with three thousand men and four pieces of artillery, opened fire on our pickets on the Lebanon and Murfreesborough roads, driving them in,— they, in accordance with orders, making but feeble resistance, Negley indulging in the hope of drawing the enemy under the fire of the forts.

About the same hour a similar cavalry force under Morgan, two thousand five hundred strong, with one gun, attacked the works on the north side of the river, defending the approaches to the railroad and pontoon bridges, to destroy which was probably their purpose. The forces holding these defences quickly and gallantly repulsed the enemy; while about the same time the guns of Fort Negley opening on Forrest, his forces were dispersed and driven back. The enemy, however, soon rallied on the south, and took position with their cavalry and infantry a little beyond the original picket-line. Colonel Roberts, with two regiments of infantry and one section of artillery, advanced on the Murfreesborough road, while General Negley, with the 69th Ohio, 78th Pennsylvania, 14th Michigan, and a cavalry force, marched out on the Franklin road, quickly driving the enemy from their position there, who then fell back, closely pursued, seven miles from the city. At this point Colonel Stokes's Tennessee Cavalry was ordered to charge the rear of the retreating rebels; but their main body had succeeded in making a détour to the left, and, in the excitement of the charge, the cavalry and infantry pursued a small force in the direction of Franklin.

The enemy, with the view to cut off Negley from the city, soon appeared in his rear with the force making the détour, and planted a battery near the road. On learning of this movement, General Negley changed front, and advanced on the enemy in

their new position.   The artillery was soon got into action, and
the battery of the rebels was disabled,—shortly after which
they retired in confusion, with heavy loss.   It was soon after
ascertained that the enemy, greatly outnumbering our forces,
were about to make a charge with cavalry on Negley's flanks;
and he slowly retired towards the city and to more favorable
ground.   Stokes's cavalry were so disposed as to divert the
expected charge upon the rear; and the 14th Michigan was
stationed in such a manner that when the charge came the
enemy were received with so destructive a fire that they were
driven back in great disorder.

They then attempted to plant their artillery on the turnpike, but were driven from that position before the guns could
be discharged.   General Negley still continued to retire towards
the city, the enemy making but one more effort to get in his
rear.   In this attempt they were completely foiled by the reserve
force, which had been ordered forward.

Colonel Roberts, on the Murfreesborough road, met with
equal success, and drove the enemy back in confusion.   Their
loss here was four killed and seventeen wounded, and about
one hundred and fifty horses, which were captured running at
large in the woods.   The entire loss of the rebels was never
known, but was reported to be heavy.   Twenty-three prisoners,
including two captains from Morgan's command, were taken.
Our casualties were none killed, twenty-six wounded, and nineteen missing.

On the following day the advance of the Army of the Cumberland appeared at Nashville, and the famous siege was
raised.

General Negley next comes prominently into view at the
bloody battle of Stone River, in which he was a distinguished
actor.   On the evening before the great battle of December
31, his division had skirmished and fought into position, as
the centre division of the army, on a rolling ridge where
begins the slope to the west bank of Stone River.   The right
rested upon the Wilkerson Pike, hinging on to Sheridan's division,

while the line, diverging from the road, ran through a thicket
and rested upon the right division of General Crittenden's corps.
In the rear of the division was the since famous "Cedars,"—
that dark, gloomy, and almost impassable forest, which, ere the
day was over, witnessed one of the bloodiest contests of modern
days.   In his front, intrenched in an oak forest, were the divisions of Withers and Cheatham, holding the key to the commanding position which Bragg had deliberately chosen, resting
behind the *têtes-de-pont* erected to protect the bridges by which
he eventually retired.   From this position the rebels had a commanding view of our whole field.

Early upon the morning of the last day of 1862, the enemy in
force attacked the three divisions of McCook by a rapid advance
upon their lines, and simultaneously the artillery of Withers
opened furiously on Negley and Rousseau, receiving a rapid
and destructive fire in return; while on McCook's left General
Sheridan manfully withstood the impetuous assaults of Cheatham, and thrice repulsed him.   The rebels of McCowan and
Claiborne met with better success, as opposed to the divisions of Generals Johnson and Davis, who were driven before
the superior numbers of the advancing foe, leaving the as
yet successful Sheridan and Negley to be flanked and over-
powered by the enemy, now in their rear.   About eleven o'clock
Sheridan sent word to Negley that his ammunition was exhausted; and about the same time his division began to fall back
through the "Cedars."   Negley's artillery, having been hotly
engaged for four hours, was also short of ammunition.   The
rebels were in his rear, and already pouring a cross-fire into his
column.   Unflinchingly the division had withstood for four long
hours the destructive fire of the enemy, dying like brave men
in their ranks.   At last, our troops retiring from his right and
from his left to form on a new line which General Rousseau was
establishing in the rear of the "Cedars," and there being a heavy
column of rebel infantry in the forest, endeavoring to cut him
off, Negley was forced to withdraw.   He literally cut his
way through the enemy, succeeding, with the timely aid of the

brigade of United States Regulars which Rousseau sent to his assistance, in repulsing McCowan's division and reaching safely a second position. With maddened fury Withers attacked him as he retired, but was again gallantly repulsed. "Out of the 'Cedars' safely!" is an eulogium pronounced upon Negley and Sheridan whenever the phrase is uttered; for to say that they brought their men off safely from their perilous position is to declare them generals of superior ability, and to say of their men that each was a hero.

In the second position to which he was ordered, General Negley was permitted to rest for the remainder of the day. At noon on January 1, the division was sent to McCook's right, in anticipation of an attack upon the right wing; but none was made. On January 2, he was ordered to the left, to support Crittenden's corps, and took position in the rear of the line and on the west bank of Stone River.

On the events of the day following justly rests much of the reputation of General Negley. The troops of General Rosecrans were undeniably in rather low spirits. The repulse of our right wing when they had anticipated victory, the want of provisions, and various reports of rebel cavalry operations in our rear, tended to add to the prevailing despondency. Upon the afternoon of January 2, the second grand charge of the rebels was made. Their line had been naturally broken in their successful assault upon General Van Cleve's small division; and they were gathering themselves for a further advance and to cross the river, when General Negley, having obtained permission, ordered a charge of his whole division, now formed in échélon of brigades. His men sprang forward upon the double-quick, with fixed bayonets, and with cheers, evincing that the noble determination and enthusiasm of the corps were unbroken. The division crossed the river at a rapid rate, flanking the 2d and 4th Kentucky (rebel) Regiments—already at and nearly across the river—and forcing them to retreat, and immediately attacked Preston's brigade, capturing the 26th Tennessee Regiment and the battery it was supporting. At the same time the numerous batteries massed by General Rosecrans on the west bank of the river were playing furiously upon the rebels. The enemy recoiled before the terrible fire of these batteries and the intolerable fire and charge of Negley's division. Vainly attempting to rally his troops, Hanson fell, and the men fled in confusion. Breckinridge's staff officers were falling around him, Preston's brigade was scattered over the field, and the Washington (Ga.) Artillery, serving with Jackson's brigade, was in our hands; and now the enemy's entire right wing fled in general and utter confusion, pursued by Negley. Not once did they attempt to rally until behind the intrenchments from whence they had advanced.

The brief battle of the 2d was one of the bloodiest upon record. The rebels estimated their loss at the time at two thousand five hundred; but a month later a rebel newspaper declared, on the authority of Colonel Dana, of Breckinridge's staff, that their loss was two thousand eight hundred in the two hours' fight.

When night closed in, General Rosecrans ordered the division of General Negley to recross the river and resume its former position. On the morning of January 4, one of his brigades was ordered in pursuit of the retiring enemy; and on the 5th General Negley, with the rest of his command, went forward and continued the pursuit of the enemy, driving him rapidly and with considerable loss many miles south of Murfreesborough.

For his gallant conduct in the contest of Stone River, General Negley was specially commended by General Rosecrans and recommended for promotion to a major-generalship, which has since been bestowed upon him.

In person General Negley is a little above the medium height, stoutly built, with a healthy, florid complexion, and pleasing countenance. His manners are genial and courteous; he is easy of approach, being quite destitute of that official frigidity which repels acquaintance; and he is devoid of that ceremonious punctilio which measures friendship by rank and worth by position. Among his men he is very popular both because of his affability and his bravery. Mild and determined, generous and just, he is recognized throughout the army as a strict disciplinarian and a correct administrative officer. Treason and rebellion meet with no sympathy at his hands. In them he sees only crimes worthy of the severest punishment, and upon their advocates he draws a constantly tightening rein. His rule at Columbia—severe but just, once much condemned, because in advance of its time, in advance of public sentiment, yet attended with happiest results, —is an index of this phase of his character.

As a commander, he has the confidence of his superiors,—a confidence that has not been misplaced. Quick to see and prompt to act, he has proved himself a general in his skilful defence of Nashville and upon the bloody field of Stone River.

THE STAFF.

CAPTAIN JAMES A. LOWRIE, *Assistant Adjutant-General*, is the eldest son of Hon. W. H. Lowrie, Chief-Justice of Pennsylvania, and was born in the city of Pittsburg, January 23, 1833. In July, 1851, he graduated at Miami University, Oxford, Ohio, and in December, 1854, was admitted to the bar at Pittsburg. He practised his profession until April 17, 1861, when he enlisted for the three-months service, and served with General Negley, in Maryland and Virginia, until August 8, 1861. On the 7th of October, 1861, he was appointed assistant adjutant-general, with the rank of captain, and assigned to the staff of General Negley, with whom he has served constantly until the present time.

CAPTAIN CHARLES T. WING, *Quartermaster*, was born in Gambier, Knox county, Ohio, January 14, 1836, and graduated at Kenyon College in August, 1853. He removed to Columbus the same month, and was engaged in book-keeping for various mercantile houses and for the State Treasury Department until October 31, 1861, when he was appointed captain and assistant quartermaster of volunteers, and assigned to the post of Evans-ville, Indiana, in the Department of the Ohio. Here he remained until May 5, 1862, when he was relieved and ordered to Pitts-burg Landing, Tennessee, where he was placed on duty with the 7th Division, then in front of Corinth and under command of Brigadier-General T. W. Sherman. June 26 he was ordered to the posts of Eastport and Iuka, from which he was relieved July 27, and on the 7th of August stationed as post quarter-master at Dechard, Tennessee.

On the 7th of September he was assigned to duty with the 8th Division, then at Nashville and commanded by General Negley. In this capacity he served ably and faithfully until January 9, 1863, when he was temporarily relieved from duty and assigned as post quartermaster at Murfreesborough, Tennessee. His ability in this position, for four active, arduous months, is uni-versally conceded. May 1, 1863, he was relieved from duty as post quartermaster, and returned to his division, now the second of the 14th Army Corps.

CAPTAIN G. M. LAFAYETTE JOHNSON, *Division Inspector*, was born in Warren county, Ohio, November 4, 1837; but his early years were spent at Wilmington, Clinton county, Ohio. At the age of fourteen he removed to Cincinnati, Ohio, where he was engaged in mercantile pursuits up to the age of twenty-one. He then accepted a situation in a prominent mercantile house of New York, where he remained till the commencement of the rebellion, when he returned to Ohio and began recruiting for the artillery service. Being proffered a position, however, in a regiment already formed at Indianapolis, Indiana, he accepted it, and was commissioned October 5, 1861, as first lieutenant of Company D, 2d Indiana Cavalry, and was promoted to captain in the same regiment, March, 1862. He followed the varying fortunes of the regiment till the fight at Gallatin, Tennessee, August 21, 1862, against General John Morgan, when he received injuries from which he was detained for several weeks in hos-pital at Nashville. When sufficiently recovered, he reported for duty to the post commandant of Nashville,—General Negley, —who assigned him to duty as a member of his staff, where he is now acting as division inspector.

CAPTAIN JAMES R. HAYDEN, *Ordnance Officer*, was born in Oswego, New York, February 22, 1839, and removed to the city of Chicago in 1852, of which place he has since been a resident.

Captain Hayden's attention was directed towards military pursuits long before the breaking out of the present rebellion. As early as 1856 we find his name on the roll of the "Chicago National Guard Cadets," of which company the present colonel of the 19th Illinois Volunteers was at that time captain. After the disbanding of that corps, Captain Hayden became one of the most active assistants of the late Colonel Ellsworth in organizing the company which afterwards became so famous under the title of the "Chicago Zouave Cadets," of which he was elected second officer, and afterwards captain, *vice* Ellsworth, resigned, which position he held until the fall of Fort Sumter, when he was one of the first to respond to the call of his country, and raised the first company of volunteers for the war from Chicago, the date of its organization being April 16, 1861, and that of its departure from Chicago for the seat of war, April 19, 1861. At this time Captain Hayden had been elected major of Colonel Ellsworth's "Fire Zouaves;" but, receiving no notification of his election until he was on the way to Cairo with his new company, he did not accept the position. At the expiration of the three-months service the same company re-enlisted under Captain Hayden for three years, leaving Chicago again on the 12th day of August, 1861.

Captain Hayden has seen hard service since that time, in Missouri, Kentucky, Tennessee, and Alabama, and has proved himself a brave and efficient officer. On the 27th of August, 1862, while in charge of a train on the Nashville & Chattanooga Railroad, and having but seventy-five men under his command, he repulsed with severe loss a force of six hundred rebel cavalry who made an attack upon the train. Captain

8

Hayden is the senior captain of the State of Illinois, and during the fall of 1862 was in command of his own regiment for the period of three months. He was subsequently assigned to duty on the staff of Major-General Negley, as division ordnance officer, which position he has since occupied.

MAJOR FERDINAND H. GROSS, *Medical Director.* Though at present medical director of the 14th Army Corps, it is proper to represent Major Gross in connection with the staff of Major-General Negley, his services up to a late date having been almost entirely with that officer.

Surgeon Gross was born in Gutenberg, Germany, August 18, 1831. His father, Dr. Hermann Gross, emigrated with his family to America in 1833, and settled in Somerset county, Pennsylvania, but remained there only two years, when he established himself as a practising physician in the city of Pittsburg.

Young Gross there received his education, and at Washington College, a popular institution of learning in an adjoining county. On leaving this institution he entered upon the study of medicine, under the direction of his father, preparatory to attending lectures. Subsequently he attended the medical colleges of Cleveland, Ohio, the University of the City of New York, and the Jefferson Medical College at Philadelphia,—at the latter of which he graduated, March 10, 1855. Returning to Pittsburg, he joined with his father in the practice of medicine and surgery, continuing with but an intermission of a spring and summer which he spent on a visit to England and the continent of Europe. At the breaking out of the war, when General Negley raised his brigade in Pittsburg and the adjoining county, a number of medical gentlemen offered their services, and among them Dr. Gross, who was appointed by General Negley to the position of brigade-surgeon. It was subsequently discovered, however, that no provisions for brigade-surgeons had been made in the call of the President for troops. Dr. Gross, having enlisted as a private in the 13th Regiment Pennsylvania Volunteers, was immediately detached from the regiment and commissioned by

Governor Curtin as aide-de-camp, with the rank of captain. In this position he served during the three-months service on the staff of General Negley, and participated in Patterson's campaign in Maryland and Virginia.

At the close of the three-months service, being desirous of entering that branch of the service for which his professional acquirements best fitted him, Captain Gross appeared before the Medical Examining Board of Pennsylvania; and, being recommended by the Board, he was commissioned by Governor Curtin as surgeon. He acted as medical officer to the 100th Pennsylvania Regiment, then stationed near Washington, and commanded by Colonel D. Leasure. On the 17th of October, 1861, Surgeon Gross was appointed by the President to the position of brigade-surgeon, and he was so commissioned, and again ordered to join General Negley's command, then in the Army of the Ohio, operating in Kentucky.

Upon the 8th Division being organized on the 5th of September, we find Surgeon Gross announced as medical director of the division. During the defence of Nashville he remained with this command. On the advance of General Rosecrans's army to Murfreesborough, Surgeon Gross moved with the 8th Division, and participated in the bloody engagement of Stone River.

By unexpected changes in the line of battle, the hospital established by him on the 30th of December fell into the hands of the enemy on the morning of the 31st; but, partly through his efforts, nearly the entire ambulance train of the division was saved. Having been cut off from his hospital while with the staff, he remained engaged upon the field the entire day. After nightfall on December 31, he succeeded, by co-operating with General Rousseau's medical director, in re-establishing hospitals and obtaining shelter for the wounded on the Murfreesborough and Nashville road.

After the battle of Stone River, Surgeon Gross remained on the staff of General Negley until March 31, when, by order of General Rosecrans, he was promoted and assigned as medical director to the 14th Army Corps, and attached to the staff of Major-General Thomas, in which capacity he is now acting.

MAJOR ROSWELL G. BOGUE, *Medical Director*, was born at Louisville, St. Lawrence county, New York, May 3, 1832. At the time the rebellion broke out he was a practising physician in Chicago, Illinois, and on the 3d of August, 1861, was appointed surgeon of the 19th Illinois Infantry. This position he retained until March 31, 1863, when he was detached from his regiment and appointed medical director of General Negley's division.

LIEUTENANT NATHAN D. INGRAHAM, *Topographical Engineer*, was born at Granger, Medina county, Ohio, on the 18th day of May, 1835. He removed to Lockport, Will county, Illinois, in June, 1844, and was married at Gooding's Grove, Will county, to Miss Ruth Gooding, daughter of James Gooding, Esq., on the 27th of November, 1854. He went to the Rocky Mountains in July, 1860, and returned January, 1862. He enlisted as private in Company F, 100th Regiment Illinois Volunteer Infantry, July 25, 1862, and was commissioned first lieutenant of the same company August 30 following. He served with his company in General Buell's march through Kentucky, in pursuit of Bragg, in the fall of 1862, and, arriving at Nashville, Tennessee, November 26, 1862, reported to Captain J. C. St. Clair Morton (now Brigadier-General Morton) on the 27th as lieutenant in command of a detachment of pioneers, and was ordered to Gallatin, Tennessee, to work on fortifications, returning to Nashville December 13. On the 26th he was ordered by Captain Morton to report to General Negley as topographical engineer, which he did at Nolensville. At the battle of Stone River he was acting aide-de-camp to General Negley, as well as topographical engineer. By profession he is a surveyor and engineer.

LIEUTENANT CHARLES C. COOKE, *Aide-de-Camp*, was born at Pittsburg, Pennsylvania, February 27, 1837. At the commencement of the present rebellion he enlisted as a private in the ranks of the United States Zouave Cadets, a company then forming at Pittsburg, all of the members of which responded to the call for seventy-five thousand men by President Lincoln, April 12, 1861. In response to the call for six hundred thousand men, he enlisted and served as private in Company E, 77th Regiment Pennsylvania Infantry, said regiment composing a part of the Pennsylvania brigade, commanded by General James S. Negley, which landed at Louisville, Kentucky, October 22, 1861. October 31, 1861, he was elected by his comrades as second lieutenant of the company, in which position he remained one month, when he was assigned to duty as aide-de-camp on the staff of General Negley.

CAPTAIN W. H. H. TAYLOR was born at North Bend, Hamilton county, Ohio, on the 21st day of March, 1837. His father is now in command of the 5th Ohio Volunteer Cavalry. His mother was the youngest daughter of President Harrison. He entered the service as private in the first company that left Cincinnati, Ohio, for the defence of the city of Washington. He was appointed a first lieutenant in the 18th U.S. Infantry, May 14, 1861, and promoted captain August 11, 1862. His occupation before he entered the service was that of a farmer.

LIEUTENANT W. W. BARKER, *Commissary of Subsistence*, was born in Pittsburg, Pennsylvania, February 23, 1839, and at the commencement of the present rebellion was engaged in the produce and commission business in that city. Upon the call for seventy-five thousand three-months troops in April, 1861, he enlisted as a private in Company I, 12th Regiment Pennsylvania Volunteers, one of the regiments composing General Negley's 1st Brigade, but was detached from his command May, 1861, and stationed on the Northern Central Railroad, near Baltimore.

He afterwards enlisted as sergeant in Company B, 77th Pennsylvania Volunteers, September 13, 1861, and was detailed to the commissary department of General Negley's brigade at

Pittsburg, Pennsylvania, October 17, 1861, in which department he served until July 25, 1862, when he was appointed by Governor Andrew Johnson, lieutenant of Company B, 1st Regiment Tennessee Cavalry, and reported to General Negley at Columbia, Tennessee, for recruiting service. September 16, 1862, he was detailed as aide-de-camp to General Negley, then commanding the post of Nashville, and assigned to the command of his escort of cavalry. During the battle of Stone River, the escort was used as a courier line, and Lieutenant Barker acted as aide to the general. After the battle he was recommended to the President for promotion to commissary of subsistence, with the rank of captain. February 13, 1863, he was ordered on duty in the commissary department as acting commissary of the 2d Division, 14th Army Corps.

LIEUTENANT R. H. COCHRAN, *Provost-Marshal and Judge-Advocate*, was born in Belmont county, Ohio, May 25, 1836. His father was an honest, frugal farmer, grandson of Captain Thomas Cochran, who was slain by the Indians in West Virginia during the Revolutionary War. His mother is a daughter of Ellis Davis, deceased, who was a soldier in the War of 1812 and one of the early settlers of Ohio. In September, 1861, young Cochran entered the service as first lieutenant in the 15th Ohio Volunteer Infantry. At the battle of Lavergne, October 7, 1862, he was aide to Brigadier-General Palmer, where the enemy under the rebel General Anderson were signally defeated. At the request of General Negley, he was soon after appointed provost-marshal on the general's staff by special order of Major-General Rosecrans.

MAJ. GEN. PALMER

Eng⁴ by H.B.Hall.N.Y

AND

OFFICERS OF STAFF.

J.B. LIPPINCOTT & CO. PHILAD.ᴬ

Major-General John McAuley Palmer and Staff.

John McAuley Palmer was born on Eagle Creek, Scott county, Kentucky, September 13, 1817. His father, Louis D. Palmer (who is still living, at the advanced age of eighty-two), emigrated to Kentucky from Northumberland county, Virginia, in the year 1793, and was there married in 1813 to Miss Ann Tutt, a native of Culpepper county, Virginia. The ancestors of the family were from England, and among the earliest settlers of Virginia.

At the time of the birth of the subject of this sketch, what was then known as the Green River country was beginning to attract attention, and the elder Palmer, a soldier in the War of 1812, and fond of adventure, removed to Christian county, where he purchased a considerable quantity of the new cheap lands of that then almost wilderness, and engaged in farming. Here his son spent his childhood, attending the school taught in the neighborhood in winter, and rendering assistance upon the farm. This school was such as are common to early settlements. "To read and write and cipher" was the usual limit of the humble teacher's attainments; and in these branches young Palmer made satisfactory progress. But by other means his education was greatly enlarged. His father, who was an ardent Jackson man, was unusually fond of reading,—which led him to procure books and the newspapers of the time, particularly those of his own party, which were afterwards well thumbed by the children. His father was also an earnest opponent of human slavery, and thoroughly impressed his opinions upon his children, the family being at that time known as warm anti-slavery Democrats. In 1831, these opinions of the elder Palmer determined him to emigrate to the free States, and in that year he removed to Madison county, Illinois, and settled about ten miles from Alton.

The labor of improving a farm occupied the time until 1833, when the death of the mother broke up the family. About this time, the efforts which had for some time been making by the friends of education in Central Illinois to establish an institution of learning at Upper Alton were crowned with partial success, and "Alton College" was organized and opened upon the "manual labor system." In the spring of 1834, the subject of our sketch, and his elder brother Elihu, who has since become a minister of the gospel, and is noted for his learning and eccentricities, entered this school. They were almost without money, but in its place were possessed of most sanguine hopes. Several months were thus spent; and in the fall of 1835 he graduated, *for the want of money* to further prosecute his studies! From this time until the spring of 1839 he spent his time in a variety of ways. For a while he worked with a cooper; then he became a pedlar; and finally, in the fall of 1838, being then in Fulton county, Illinois, he was invited to take charge of a district school near Canton, which he taught "two quarters" to the apparent satisfaction of his patrons. During all this time he had been a constant reader of history, poetry, novels, sermons, and newspapers, and had amassed a respectable but most ill-arranged store of knowledge. In the summer of 1838 he first met with the late Senator Douglas, then a candidate for Congress and just entering upon his brilliant career. The district was large, and the vote close; but Douglas was young, eloquent, and a Democrat, and won at once the confidence of Palmer, who threw himself ardently into the contest and cast his first vote for the Democratic ticket.

This acquaintance with the rising statesman, by inflaming young Palmer's ambition and spurring him to effort, probably gave stability to his purposes and tended to shape his future course in life. During the winter of 1838 he obtained a copy of "Blackstone's Commentaries," and began a course of desultory reading with a view to the study of law, and in the spring of 1839 he entered the office of John L. Greathouse, then a lawyer of considerable standing at Carlinville, Macoupin county. On arriving at Carlinville, having walked thither from St. Louis, his entire stock of money was fourteen dollars, and his wardrobe consisted of an indifferent suit of clothes and an extra shirt. Here he found his brother Elihu, who was now married and preaching to a congregation in Carlinville. This brother—like himself, careless of money, but full of hope—advised him to remain in that place and pursue his studies, offering to board him, with a rather indefinite understanding as to payment in return; and accordingly, as we have stated, he entered the office of Mr. Greathouse.

In less than two months after this, at the request of the leading Democratic politicians of the county, he became a candidate for the office of county clerk. He engaged actively in the canvass, becoming involved in local politics to such an extent that he has never since been able to extricate himself,—but was defeated by a majority of one hundred and twenty-one votes. In December, 1839, after less than a year's study, having managed to buy the cloth for a suit of clothes, and having found a good-natured tailor who had faith enough in him to make them up on credit, he set out for Springfield, with five dollars in his pocket which he had borrowed from his preceptor to pay his expenses, and obtained from the Supreme Court a license to practise as an attorney and counsellor-at-law.

Mr. Douglas took much interest in the application, was appointed one of the examiners, and wrote the license, which is still carefully preserved, displaying throughout a kindness which was ever remembered with gratitude during the long and bitter contests of later years.

Our young attorney returned to Carlinville with the much-coveted license. His possessions consisted of a few books, the gift of Mr. David A. Smith, then, as now, an eminent Illinois lawyer, who, having supplied himself with new editions, kindly presented the old ones to the poor junior. He was not at once successful; and the only reason that he did not leave the village and seek a new home was that he could not procure money enough to pay his debts. Often since then he has said that this early poverty lies at the foundation of whatever success he afterwards attained.

In 1840 he participated in the canvass for the Presidency, earnestly supporting Mr. Van Buren and the Democratic nominees. In 1841 he devoted himself to his profession, his business having so increased that it afforded him a sufficient support. In 1842, being independent and self-minded, he made some personal enemies by refusing to support certain of the regular Democratic candidates. In December of that year he was married. In 1843 he was elected probate justice of the county, by over four hundred majority. The years 1844, 1845, and 1846 were spent in the practice of his profession, which had now become quite extensive. In 1847 he was elected to the Illinois State Constitutional Convention, and at the same election was defeated for probate justice by a combination formed against him. In 1848, his victorious competitor having resigned, he was again elected, by a large majority. In 1849 the new Constitution was adopted, and he was elected county judge, in which office he continued until 1851, when he was elected to the State Senate. In 1852, 1853, and 1854 he attended the sessions of that body. In the latter year he opposed the Nebraska bill. In 1855 he was re-elected to the Senate, and warmly supported many important measures, such as the free-school system, homestead law, &c. In 1856 he was a member and president of the first Illinois Republican State Convention, held at Bloomington. He was also a delegate to the National Republican Convention, and advocated the nomination of Judge McLean, though personally preferring Frémont. He entered actively into the canvass, exerting himself for Frémont, having first resigned his seat in the State Senate, upon the ground that, having changed his political connections after his election, self-respect and a proper regard for the true principles of a representative government demanded such a course. In 1857 and 1858 he was engaged in State politics, and in 1859 was nominated for Congress, but was defeated.

In 1860 he was a candidate for elector at large on the Republican ticket, was elected, and cast his vote for President Lincoln. In 1861 he was a delegate to the Peace Congress at Washington. In that body he advocated the call of a national convention for the settlement of our difficulties. That proposition having failed, and still eager to avoid civil war, or, if it could not be avoided, to secure unity of action in the Northern and border States, he favored the measures of compromise finally recommended by the conference.

When the second call for troops was made, he came forward as a common citizen and soldier, regardless of great home interests, and was unanimously elected colonel of the 14th Illinois Volunteers. For a time he was stationed at Jacksonville, Illinois, equipping, drilling, and perfecting his regiment. Affairs becoming threatening in Northern Missouri, the regiment was ordered thither, and during the month of July and the early part of August occupied various points on the Hannibal & St. Joseph and North Missouri Railroads. On the 10th of August the regiment arrived at Jefferson Barracks, and on the 12th, information having been received at St. Louis of the battle of Wilson's Creek and the death of General Lyon, it was ordered to Rolla, reaching that place on the 13th.

In September General Hunter assumed command at Rolla, and on the 23d of that month his command was ordered to Jefferson City, Missouri; and General Palmer's regiment marched with him from that place, by the way of Tipton, Warsaw, and Buffalo, to Springfield. On the 23d of October he was assigned to the command of a brigade by General Hunter, and returned with his brigade, after the removal of Frémont from the command of the department, to Tipton, going afterwards into winter-quarters at Otterville.

Colonel Palmer's brigade formed part of General Pope's expedition to Milford, which captured a large number of rebel prisoners. On the 20th of December he was commissioned brigadier-general, and placed in command of the post of Otterville. About the 1st of February, 1862, the forces at Otterville were ordered South, and General Palmer joined General Pope at Commerce, Missouri, for the expedition against New Madrid and Island No. 10. He commanded a division and took part in the operations before New Madrid, and on the 16th of March was ordered to occupy Riddle's Point with his division and some heavy guns. This was done, the men dragging the guns along the river-bank at night, wading a great part of the way. The course of the Mississippi River below Island No. 10, and the high stage of water, flooding the low-lands along its banks, made this a point of great importance in all operations against the enemy's works there. Island No. 10 is at the head of New Madrid. bend. The river, after following its course for twenty miles, returns within five miles of the island. The bottom along the banks for nearly this whole distance was overflowed; while at Tiptonville, Tennessee, within five miles of the island, the landing was good. Below Tiptonville the overflowed banks, and Rue Fort Lake to the south, cut off the rebel forces from the interior; and Commodore Foote had the river above. The landing at Tiptonville, then, was the only point of approach to the island which was open to the enemy. It was to command this landing that the expedition was sent to Riddle's Point, which is directly opposite.

On the morning of the 18th, at about sunrise, the rebels on the gunboats below discovered the work of the night, and were in motion at once. One boat came slowly steaming up the river, so steadily that it seemed to make scarcely a ripple upon the surface. When this boat had approached within about the distance of a half-mile, she fired a twenty-four-pound gun. The shot came dashing along, and struck the water in front of the earth-work. The response was prompt from our side. In a short time five other boats came up. A line was formed, and all opened upon Palmer's position. For two hours this unequal contest was maintained,—twenty pieces from the gunboats keeping up a constant roar, the shot plunging into the sand and burying the men in the pits, or tearing limbs from the trees. The steady but slow firing from our guns made each report appear like the last effort of exhausted men. Relying upon their superior fire, the boats approached the shore to land; but at the moment they got within one hundred yards of the shore the 47th Indiana Regiment, which occupied the rifle-pits, opened upon them with their rifles, and drove the men under cover.

Two of the boats were seriously damaged, and, after the repulse by the infantry, all withdrew.

After this the enemy made frequent efforts to reach the landing at Tiptonville, but were always repulsed. From this time until the reduction of the island, General Palmer's command was almost incessantly engaged with the rebel gunboats, six of which were engaged in constant efforts to introduce supplies to the island or to pass transports for the removal of the troops. They were unable to silence our guns by their fire, and all efforts to land were frustrated by our riflemen occupying rifle-pits along the shore; so that the relief and escape of the rebels became alike impossible.

After the capture of Island No. 10, General Pope's forces proceeded down the river to Fort Pillow, which was bombarded for some days; but before any definite result was attained they were ordered to join General Halleck before Corinth. On the 20th of April they landed at Hamburg, on the Tennessee River, and, General Pope then reorganizing his corps, General Palmer was assigned to the command of the 1st Brigade, 1st Division, of the Army of the Mississippi, composed of the 22d, 27th, 42d, and 51st Illinois Regiments and Hescock's Battery. As soon as all the regiments arrived, the army was put in motion, by short marches, for Corinth, with constant skirmishes along the front.

On the 3d of May, General Palmer's division was ordered to make a reconnoissance in front of the enemy's fortifications at Corinth. The second brigade, under General Morgan, attacked the rebel pickets at Seven-Mile Creek, driving them into the open field north of Farmington, and, passing out of the woods, formed on the north of the Farmington Road. General Palmer, with two regiments of his brigade and a battery, formed to the left, and moved forward under a brisk fire from the rebel skirmishers. After an advance of some three hundred yards, a rebel battery, posted near the point at which the road from Farmington to Purdy crosses the Corinth road, opened fire. After a few shots from our guns and a charge in line, the enemy fled. At night the division recrossed Seven-Mile Creek and encamped in the rear of the swamp through which that sluggish stream flows; and the next day it was joined by General Pope's forces.

On the 8th of May, Paine's division again crossed towards Corinth, advanced within a mile and a half of the fortifications, and, after skirmishing through the day, retired to camp. On the morning of the 9th, General Palmer was directed with his brigade to pass the swamp and camp near Farmington, which was then occupied by our pickets; and at nine o'clock the brigade, with its wagons and camp-equipage, was in motion. General Palmer, with a small escort, rode forward to select a suitable camping-ground. Between the crossing of the creek and the swamp (which was by a single road and narrow bridge, the ground on both sides of which is impassable) and Farmington there is a cluster of woods, of small extent, about a mile from the crossing, and nearly the same distance from the town, which conceals the entrance of the road into the swamp from the direction of Farmington and Corinth. After passing this clump of woods a short distance and reaching the open ground, the Federal pickets were met coming in, and considerable numbers of the enemy, infantry and cavalry, were in sight. About fifty of the cavalry, seeing the general in advance of his command upon the crest of the hill, made a dash to capture him. They came on at full speed, demanding a surrender; but, when they were within a hundred yards, two companies of infantry, which were concealed by the hill, opened fire upon them and emptied several saddles, whereupon the rest fled.

By this time heavy bodies of infantry had filed through Farmington and formed in a line extending east towards a point of woods in that direction. This movement was made with the double view of discovering the Federal forces behind the wood before spoken of, and of getting possession of the road across the swamp. As soon as this force was discovered, dispositions were made to repel it. Colonel Roberts, with part of the 51st Illinois and two or three companies from other regiments, was ordered to occupy a high piêce of ground which covered our left. Major Walworth was directed to seize a point of woods on our right, and the remaining troops, parts of the 22d, 27th, and 42d Illinois, formed in line, protected by some ravines and woods.

About the time these arrangements were completed, General Palmer received orders from General Pope to retire across the swamp to camp. At that moment the narrow road and bridge across the swamp were crowded with wagons and a brigade of Stanley's division which had occupied the ground in the rear of Palmer's brigade. To add to the embarrassment of the situation, three rebel batteries had opened fire from three different points, and heavy rebel forces had appeared upon the open ground in the direction of Corinth. Obedience to the order was, therefore, difficult. Wagons and baggage were ordered to the rear, however, and the determination formed to hold the enemy in check until the road could be cleared sufficiently to allow the troops to retire.

One section of Hescock's guns was by that gallant and skilful officer turned upon the battery upon the Federal right, and, after driving it off, was turned upon that to our left. The rebel infantry, in three divisions, came up in splendid style against our position. The 22d and 27th Illinois, protected as they were, received them with a galling fire, which at first checked them and then threw them into confusion, killing and wounding great numbers. Still, as the fact of the immense force of the enemy was developed, the danger of the little force opposed to them became painfully manifest. The enemy, not knowing at first but that Pope's whole army was concealed by the clump of woods, advanced slowly and cautiously, keeping up a tremendous cannonade from their eighteen guns. The Federal troops maintained their ground against this advance for two hours. About noon the rebels, having discovered, apparently, that Pope was not there, came on at a rapid pace, threatening to sweep every thing from the field, and were within twenty yards of our lines, when the troops were ordered to fall back. Walworth was withdrawn from the woods on the right, and had barely time to retire. The 22d and 27th Illinois retreated, closely pursued by the enemy, who burst through the woods within two hundred yards of Hescock and threatened to reach the entrance of the swamp before he could. Luckily, Hescock, with great sagacity and with a know-ledge of the full confidence reposed in him by General Palmer, had already sent his caissons and rifled guns to the rear, and now determined to give the enemy one more blow. He immediately double-shotted his howitzers with canister, and fired into the advancing columns, producing terrible slaughter, and then left the field. General Palmer, having remained at this point until he was assured of the safety of Hescock, rode to the rear to pre-pare to dispute the crossing of the swamp. Loomis's brigade had become engaged on the right, and, after a severe fight, were ordered to fall back. The 51st Illinois and 8th Wisconsin were formed behind the bridge, and the 42d and 47th Illinois were formed in the edge of the woods, on both sides of the road where it entered the swamp.

This arrangement was concealed from the enemy by the undulations of the ground; and their forces, disordered by the impression of a victory, now came on in a confused mass, whooping like Indians. General Palmer had sent his horse to the rear to assist in the concealment of the troops, and, standing behind his line, waited until the foremost of the rebels had approached within fifty yards, when he gave the order to fire. One volley covered the open ground to the front with killed and wounded, and the remainder broke and fled from the field.

This ended the struggle; and thus did this small force, aided by the favorable ground and the concealment afforded by the woods, after a closely-contested fight of several hours, escape from three rebel divisions. It ought to be stated, in addition, that the escape of Hescock was greatly aided by a charge upon the rebels on our right, made by the 2d Iowa Cavalry and ordered by General Paine, which checked the enemy for a moment. Our loss was twenty-two killed, one hundred and fifty-one wounded, and ten taken prisoners. The rebel loss was four hundred and eleven killed and wounded, among whom was Colonel Ingraham, of Van Dorn's staff.

After this affair our troops remained in camp until the 17th of May, when they advanced and took possession of Farmington. On the 18th, General Palmer, in command of the outposts, spent the day on the lines, and skirmished with the enemy, driving them back so as to gain possession of a ridge of hills which it was desirable to occupy. Towards sunset he succeeded in this, and returned to his quarters, but before midnight was attacked with pneumonia, and was confined to his bed until the morning of the 29th. On that day, under the impression that there would be a great battle, he went out upon the lines. While there, news came that Corinth was evacuated, and, still being very ill, he was ordered home by General Pope. He continued sick at home until about the 1st of August, when he took part in the efforts made to raise troops, and, under the authority of the Governor of Illinois, organized the 122d Illinois Regiment at Carlinville. On the 26th of August he left home, and on the 1st of September reached Tuscumbia, Alabama, when, General Paine being in ill health, he was assigned by General Rosecrans to the command of the 1st Division of the Army of the Mississippi, and ordered to join General Buell.

The 2d Brigade, being then at Tuscumbia, crossed the river near that place, and marched directly to Athens. The 1st Brigade was scattered along the railroad from Tuscumbia to Decatur. This force was concentrated at Decatur, and, under the command of General Palmer, crossed the river on the 5th, and reached Athens on the 6th of September.

There the first information was received of Buell's movements. A courier from him to General Paine, who was supposed to be in command of the column, was captured by some "peaceable citizens," who destroyed his despatches, and then exultingly

9

told the contents, which were orders to make forced marches to Nashville. A Union man gave information of this; and on the morning of the 7th the march was commenced. At this time the whole of Southern Tennessee north and east of the Tennessee River was abandoned by the Federal troops. The inhabitants, under the belief that the rebel authority was permanently established, were intensely malignant. Those who until that time had been faithful to our Government were disheartened; while the guerrillas were active in all directions. It being impossible, on account of the want of cavalry, to ascertain the movements of the large and active mounted force of the enemy, great vigilance was required to insure the safety of the long train which accompanied the march. The first appearance of the rebels was at Blowing Springs Gap. A party of bushwhackers here fell in behind our skirmishers, firing upon the column, and wounding three. The muskets of the 16th Illinois soon dispersed them. At night, from the camp at Buchanan's Creek, Colonel Roberts with two regiments was pushed forward to Pulaski, to surprise Biffles, who, with his cavalry, was in possession of the town. He heard of our movements in time to make his escape; but the party captured a mail, and, visiting his camp, secured the handsome donations sent in the morning by his friends in the shape of good cooked breakfasts.

On the morning of the 8th, in passing through Pulaski, a guard was detailed to protect the town, with orders to move up with the stragglers. When the rear of the column had passed out of the town, the *people ordered this guard to surrender as prisoners.* A few shots were exchanged, and the guard retired. At Reynolds's Station the train was attacked, and two unarmed, sick men, who had stepped aside to a spring, were murdered. The skirmish lasted for an hour, and ended in the repulse of the rebels. On the next day the train and rear-guard were again attacked. This skirmish lasted several hours, but upon reaching Columbia the rear-guard halted and drove the enemy off. On leaving the north bank of Duck River, at about five o'clock on the morning of the 10th, the rear-guard was again attacked; but a howitzer turned upon the enemy soon dispersed them with loss. At Rutherford Centre another attack was made. Here the Union force was greatly strengthened by a cavalry reinforcement, raised in a rather amusing way. As there was no cavalry force with the expedition, an order had been issued for all spare horses along the line to be mounted by active men, who were to act as scouts. By the time this order had reached the second regiment, it had assumed the form of a direction to the men to seize all the horses and mules to be found, for the purpose of mounting the infantry. On reaching Spring Hill, the general, much to his own surprise, found himself accompanied by a hundred mounted men, riding on all sorts of animals. Two were mounted on splendid jacks, which, to the great disgust of the riders, he ordered to be returned at once. At least fifty persons came into camp that night in search of horses and mules, all of which were returned,—"foolishly," as the general now says; for in a week afterwards they were in the hands of guerrillas. After the attack at Rutherford Centre the rebels made no further demonstration; and on the 11th of September General Palmer and his force arrived at Nashville.

During the so-called blockade of Nashville by the rebel forces of Wheeler, Morgan, and other commanders, for a period of several weeks, Generals Negley's and Palmer's forces were the occupants and defenders of that city. Several skirmishes occurred, and expeditions were undertaken, with generally favorable issues, as is fully narrated in the sketch of Major-General Negley given on preceding pages. The intercourse and co-operation of these two generals were at all times most friendly and hearty, with results beneficial to the cause and the country. The daily rebel threat of crushing the Union troops at Nashville was not fulfilled, and this strong key-point of Middle Tennessee was securely held. An onward movement and disaster to the rebellion followed in the last days of December, 1862, by which the rebels were destined to finally lose their hold upon the last—and to them the greatest and the best—of all the border States.

In the awful scenes of Stone River General Palmer acted a conspicuous part. His division at times occupied important and perilous positions. During the eventful 31st of December he held the advance for several hours after the falling back of portions of the right wing. At one period, when thus occupying an extreme point, the rebel musketry and artillery fire being directed upon his division from all sides, it seemed, we have heard him remark, as though his devoted command had become isolated and was forgotten. But he appreciated the importance of holding the position, and his batteries played with such vigor, and were supported by his infantry with such determination, that they receded not an inch from their position, but held the advancing hosts at bay whenever they approached along that line. Their gallantry was ere long recognized by General Rosecrans in person: he rode up to their position, with his escort, amidst the wildest of the storm, and spoke those words of approval and congratulation which are so cheering to the heart of every soldier. Thenceforward no rebel force could have driven in that battle-line; and, after several vain attempts, the design was abandoned, and the rebel advance on that portion of the bloody field was stayed.

For the gallantry and skill displayed by General Palmer upon this occasion, in connection with his previous career as a patriot and a soldier, he was nominated and confirmed as major-general of volunteers, his commission dating from the battles of Stone River,—a promotion which his troops, his many personal friends, and thousands of patriot hearts throughout the country, and particularly in the great States of the West, will endorse as well and nobly merited.

As a man, all who meet with General Palmer find in him an ardent, simple, pleasing friend, approachable, intelligent, and interesting. As a lawyer, he is one of the most remarkable, especially in a plea before a jury, to be found in Illinois or the West,—it being his forte to draw tears and smiles from beaming eyes and countenances and to wring verdicts from sympathetic jurors. As a statesman he has been honest and independent,—

his independence often leading him quite beyond the precincts of mere partyism, and his conscience restraining the wings of any sordid ambition, to take eventually higher and nobler flights. As a personal friend and a neighbor, the author, who has known him well for many years past, could write more of well-merited praise than perhaps ought to appear in a life-time biography. His thousand charities and kindnesses, his noble disregard of self-interest or aggrandizement, his almost reprehensible indifference to the acquisition of wealth, or even of a competence, his many ardent unrequited efforts for some friendless wretch or penniless suitor at the bar of justice, —all these, so well known to the people of Central Illinois, need not be related here.

Upon the opening of the rebellion, General Palmer was among the first to arm in defence of home and country. A civilian, solely, his tastes and habits in entire conformity with the sociali-ties of private life, and arrived at that age at which the ex-citable ardor of youth has merged into the fulness of manly reason, no other incentive than that of exalted patriotism could have led him to the tented field. He went there at great personal sacrifice, freely and cheerfully accepting the toil and the hazard,—went there without passion, without ambition, without revenge or resentment rankling in his breast. He saw an issue forced upon his country as if by the fiat of Heaven, and he calmly entered the arena as but one of the instruments by which perhaps that issue was to be determined.

During his military career in Missouri, General Palmer was particularly successful in his dealing with hundreds of half-de-cided followers of secessionism in that State. He was mode-rate and forbearing almost beyond measure, when that policy was deemed best by the Administration and the majority of the people of the country. As the rebellion progressed, and a more vigorous and determined policy was adopted, none was more justly severe than he in laying the hand of military power upon the neck of a rebellious race.

As a general, the subject of this sketch may be considered

neither wildly brilliant nor notably theoretic. He is plain, practical, industrious, sound. His men know him to be brave from principle, and to be determined and daring as a matter of correct judgment. As a general, he belongs to the class of which Rosecrans and Thomas are types,—not Napoleonic: this is not an age for Napoleons. Forces equal in military intelligence and determination and physical development now mingle in conflict. War, in the nineteenth century, consists in the marshalling of national resources of vast and varied extent and character, where the old-time personal prowess of leadership sinks in the comparative scale, and where power, well ordered, upon just and correct principles, will accomplish its certain and legitimate results.

THE STAFF.

CAPTAIN JACOB R. MUHLEMAN, *Assistant Adjutant-General*, was born at Thun, Canton of Berne, in Switzerland, November 24, 1824. His childhood was passed at the city schools, and in due time he received an education fitting him for the profession of a civil engineer. In this capacity he passed nearly three years in the employment of the government, superintending and assisting in the construction of public roads. At the beginning of his twentieth year, in accordance with the laws of the country, by which every able-bodied male citizen becomes a soldier in the national army, he was enrolled to serve eight years in the Elite, and entered the 6th Battalion Bernese Infantry as a private. In 1847 he was commissioned as second lieutenant in the Sappers, and participated in the "Sunderbunds Feldzug," or campaign against the Separate League.

In 1848, at the close of this campaign, he emigrated to Illinois, and settled, with a brother, upon a small farm near Alton. Subsequently he removed to Macoupin county, where he engaged in agriculture and other occupations. For nearly two years he was employed in the law-office of Palmer & Pittman, at Carlin-ville, the senior partner of which firm is now Major-General Palmer. At the beginning of the rebellion he enlisted, at Jack-sonville, in the 14th Illinois Infantry, of which General Palmer was then colonel, and was appointed sergeant-major of the regi-ment. In September following, he was appointed by General Frémont a second lieutenant of sappers and miners, and, until the change of commanders of the department, was on duty in St. Louis, superintending the erection of a portion of the fortifica-tions at that place. General Frémont being relieved, the engi-neer corps was dissolved, and Lieutenant Muhleman returned to his regiment, then stationed on the banks of the La Mine River, near Otterville, Missouri. Here he was tendered the position of regimental quartermaster, and, as such, accompanied the regi-ment during the year 1862 in its various wanderings through Tennessee, Alabama, and Mississippi. On the 23d of December, 1862, he was appointed assistant adjutant-general, with the rank of captain, and on the 31st of the same month was relieved of duty in the 14th Illinois, and reported to General Palmer.

CAPTAIN HENRY HOWLAND, *Assistant Quartermaster*, is a native of Conway, Massachusetts, where his parents now reside. In October, 1852, he removed to Chicago, Illinois, and for several years was extensively engaged in the lumber-trade in that city. He was commissioned as quartermaster of the 51st Illinois In-fantry, September 20, 1861, and left Chicago with his regiment on the 14th of February, 1862. On the 4th of March the regi-ment was ordered to join the Army of the Mississippi, then under the command of General Pope; and Quartermaster How-land was left at Cairo to attend to the transportation of the regiment. Rejoining it at New Madrid, Missouri, on the 13th of March, he was the same day detailed by General E. A. Paine, commanding the 1st Division, as quartermaster of the division. He acted as aide to General Paine in the battle of Farmington, May 8 and 9, 1862. On the 9th of June, 1862, he was appointed by the President assistant quartermaster, with the rank of captain, and remained with the old 1st Division of the Army of the Mississippi until December 10, 1862, when, by order of General Rosecrans, he was transferred to the old 4th Division of the Army of the Ohio, now the 2d Division of the 21st Army Corps.

CAPTAIN D. WOODMAN NORTON, *Division Inspector*, was born at Chelsea, Massachusetts, January 31, 1837, and lived principally in Boston until 1855, when, after graduating at the English High School in that city, he removed to the West, passing some time in Wisconsin, and finally taking up his residence in Chicago, where he was employed as a salesman when the war broke out. April 18, 1861, he enlisted as a private in the Chicago Zouave Regiment, and afterwards in the Douglas Brigade (now the 42d Illinois Infantry). Upon the organization of the latter regiment he was elected and commissioned as captain of Company E. He served with Generals Frémont and Hunter in their Missouri campaign against Price in the fall and winter of 1861, and was present at the occupation of Columbus, Kentucky, the bombardment of Island No. 10 and Fort Pillow, the siege and approach to Corinth, and the battle of Farmington. He also accompanied his regiment during the summer campaign in Mississippi and Alabama, and on the march from Alabama to Nashville.

In November, 1862, Captain Norton was selected by General Palmer as his division inspector, and as such participated with him in the battle of Stone River.

MAJOR S. G. MENZIES, *Medical Director*, was born in Woodford county, Kentucky, July 12, 1810, and in 1817 removed with his family to Fayette county, and thence, in the following year, to the adjoining county of Bourbon, where he began the study of medicine. In the spring of 1831 he graduated at the Transylvania Medical College, and for seventeen years practised medicine in Bourbon county. In 1848 he removed to Cincinnati, and remained there until the rebellion began, when he assisted in raising the 1st Kentucky Regiment of Volunteers, and entered the service as its surgeon on the 5th of May, 1861, continuing with it until January, 1862, when he was appointed brigade-surgeon of the 22d Brigade. August 18, 1862, he was appointed medical director of the 14th Army Corps,—the position which he now holds.

LIEUTENANT CHARLES C. PECK, *Commissary*, was born in the town of Barrington, Bristol county, Rhode Island, and prior to the rebellion was engaged in business as a jeweller. Upon the call of the President for troops, he volunteered as a private in the 6th Ohio Regiment, founded upon the Guthrie Grays of Cincinnati, and was afterwards promoted to quartermaster-sergeant. In December, 1861, he was appointed first lieutenant in Company K of his regiment, and in March, 1862, was detailed to act as commissary in the division commanded by General Nelson, in which position he served until August, 1862, when he was ordered to report to General Buell and act as post commissary at Murfreesborough, Tennessee. Upon General Buell's departure from the Army of the Ohio, Lieutenant Peck joined the staff of Brigadier-General William S. Smith as commissary for the 4th Division, and upon General Smith's being relieved by General Palmer he was retained in the same position upon the staff of the latter general. During the battle of Stone River he was very efficient in forwarding and supplying rations to his own division, besides issuing to other divisions one hundred and sixty thousand rations.

LIEUTENANT C. E. HAYES, *Topographical Engineer*, is a native of the city of Lancaster, Pennsylvania, and by profession a civil engineer. In May, 1861, he volunteered as a private in the 1st Pennsylvania Regiment Volunteer Infantry, and served through the three-months campaign. At the close of this campaign he entered the 79th Regiment Pennsylvania Volunteers, and on October 20, 1861, was mustered into the service as first lieutenant and acting quartermaster at Pittsburg, Pennsylvania. The regiment being in Brigadier-General Negley's brigade,

Lieutenant Hayes was second in command of Company K in their march to Pulaski, Tennessee, and Rogersville and Florence, Alabama, and back to Columbia, Tennessee, in the march under the same commander to Chattanooga and to Shelbyville.

At Bowling Green, Kentucky, he was detailed to act on the staff of Brigadier-General William S. Smith. Upon General Smith being relieved in December, 1862, by the present commander, General Palmer, the position of topographical engineer was proffered to Lieutenant Hayes and accepted.

LIEUTENANT BENJAMIN F. CROXTON, *Ordnance Officer*, was born in Stark county, Ohio, December 15, 1842. At the breaking out of the rebellion he was residing at Zanesville, Ohio, and on the 17th of April, 1861, enlisted as a private in the 15th Volunteer Ohio Infantry. Serving through the three-months campaign with this regiment, he re-enlisted for three years, October, 1861, as a private in the 51st Ohio Volunteers, under the command of Colonel Stanley Matthews. Soon after he was appointed a second lieutenant, and participated with his regiment in the campaign in Kentucky under General Nelson. He was afterwards stationed at Nashville, and served during the summer through Middle Tennessee. On the 17th of August, 1862, Lieutenant Croxton was appointed ordnance officer upon the staff of General Ammen. This position in the division he still retains, having acted in the same capacity upon the staff of General Smith, who succeeded General Ammen, and that of General Palmer, the present commander.

LIEUTENANT HARRY M. SCARRITT, *Aide-de-Camp*, was born in Alton, Illinois, December 29, 1842. At the age of fourteen he entered an academy at Cornwall, Connecticut, and remained there two years, when he entered Illinois College at Jacksonville, Illinois. Here he pursued his studies until April, 1861, when, the war breaking out, he enlisted as a private in the 2d company of the 1st battalion from his State (subsequently Company B of the 10th Illinois Infantry), and served through the three months of his enlistment. He then entered the service as first lieutenant of Company D, 10th Illinois Infantry, a new company partly raised by himself. In this capacity he followed the fortunes of the regiment through Southern Missouri to New Madrid, Island No. 10, and Fort Pillow, Pittsburg Landing, Farmington, and Corinth, and through the Northern Mississippi and Alabama campaign. In February, 1863, he was detailed as aide-de-camp upon the staff of General Palmer.

Major-General Philip Henry Sheridan and Staff.

PHILIP HENRY SHERIDAN, Major-General of Volunteers, and Captain and Brevet-Major 13th Infantry U.S.A, commanding 3d Division, 20th Army Corps, Department of the Cumberland, was born in Perry county, Ohio, in 1831. He was appointed a cadet at West Point from that county in 1848. Graduating in June, 1853, he was appointed brevet second lieutenant in the 1st United States Infantry in the following July, and joined his company at Fort Duncan, Texas, in the fall of the same year. From that time until the spring of 1855 he was engaged in active field duty against the Indians, when he was promoted to a second lieutenancy in the 4th Infantry and ordered to join his regiment in Oregon. During the months of May and June, 1855, he was in command of Fort Wood, in New York harbor, and in July of the same year embarked for San Francisco in charge of a body of recruits. Arriving there, Lieutenant Sheridan was detailed to the command of the escort of Lieutenant Williamson, for a survey of the route for a proposed branch of the Pacific Railroad from San Francisco to Columbia River, Oregon. This important expedition was accompanied by a large number of literary and scientific gentlemen, and resulted in eliciting much interesting and valuable information concerning the geography, topography, and natural history of the country, which has been spread before the people in the reports made by those in charge and published by Congress.

Detached from the escort of Lieutenant Williamson in September, 1855, at Vancouver, Washington Territory, Lieutenant Sheridan was ordered to accompany with a detachment of dragoons the expedition of Major Raine, of the 4th Infantry, to the Yakima country, against the Indian tribe of that name,

140

MAJ. GENERAL SHERIDAN

CAPT. GEORGE LEE

CAPT. A.F. STEVENSON

MAJ. GEN.
P. H. SHERIDAN.

AND

OFFICERS OF STAFF.

CAPT. H. HESCOCK

MAJ. D. J. GRIFFITH

Engᵈ by R.Thew

J.B. LIPPINCOTT & CO. PHILADA

and returned to the Dalles of the Columbia the same fall. He was specially mentioned in general orders for gallant conduct in an engagement with the Indians at the Cascades of the Columbia, April 28, 1856. In May following he was ordered to take command of the Indian Reservation in the Coast Range of mountains. In September, 1856, he was directed to select a post on this reservation in the Seletz Valley. In the spring of 1857 he was complimented by the general-in-chief for meritorious conduct in the settlement of the difficulty with the Coquillo Indians, on Yakima Bay. In the summer and fall of the same year he built the military post at Yamhill, on the Indian Reservation.

Promoted to a captaincy in the 13th Infantry, March 14, 1861, he was ordered to join his regiment at Jefferson Barracks, Missouri, in September of the same year. Soon afterwards Captain Sheridan was made president of the military commission to audit the claims arising from the operations of our army in Missouri during the summer of 1861. December 24, 1861, he was appointed chief quartermaster and commissary of the Army of the Southwest. In this position he organized the transportation, and supplied that army with the greater portion of its subsistence from the surrounding country, until after the battle of Pea Ridge. In March, 1862, he was ordered to St. Louis, and thence, in the latter part of April, to report at the head-quarters of General Halleck in front of Corinth, Mississippi. Upon his arrival at that place, he was appointed chief quartermaster and commissary on the staff of General Halleck, about the 10th of May, 1862.

His superior officers soon discovered, however, that his proper place was at the head of a regiment in the field; and on the 27th of May he was appointed colonel of the 2d Michigan Cavalry, and was ordered with his regiment to accompany the command of Colonel Elliott in his famous expedition to destroy the Mobile & Ohio Railroad at Booneville, Mississippi, about thirty miles south of Corinth. After making a circuit of about one hundred miles to the rear of the enemy, then concentrated at Corinth, the expedition burned the railroad-bridge at Booneville, captured and destroyed a large train and a great quantity of muskets and side-arms, and paroled two thousand prisoners. On the morning of May 30 he repulsed an attack of the enemy's cavalry under Colonel McNairy, scattering them in every direction.

Upon his return to Corinth, he was ordered to join the army near Booneville in its pursuit of the forces of Beauregard after their evacuation of Corinth. Accompanying the cavalry reconnoissance of Colonel Elliott to Blackland, he encountered the left wing of the enemy's forces at that place. Being in the advance with the 2d Michigan Cavalry, he repulsed an attack made by two regiments of infantry, two regiments of cavalry, and a battery of artillery, and, bringing off Powell's battery, fell back on our main force near Booneville. During a reconnoissance with his regiment on the 6th of June, he encountered a force of rebel cavalry under Forrest at Donelson's Cross-Roads, between Booneville and Baldwin, and signally defeated them. On the 8th of June, with the 2d Michigan and 2d Iowa Cavalry, he pursued the enemy, who were evacuating their position on Twenty-Mile Creek and falling back to Tupelo, captured the town of Baldwin, and drove the retreating rebels to Guntown, where they were forced to form in line of battle, with infantry, cavalry, and artillery. Thence he was ordered back to Booneville and with the army to Corinth.

On the 11th of June Colonel Sheridan assumed command of the 2d Brigade of the Cavalry Division of the Army of the Mississippi, composed of the 2d Iowa and 2d Michigan Cavalry Regiments, and on the 26th was ordered to take a position with his brigade at Booneville, twenty miles in advance of the main army, and cover the front. While at this place, he was attacked on the 1st of July by nine regiments of rebel cavalry, under General Chalmers, numbering between five thousand and six thousand men. After considerable skirmishing, he fell back towards his camp, which was situated on the edge of a swamp, —an advantageous position, in which he could hold the enemy at bay, in front, for some time. Finding that he was about to be surrounded, he selected ninety of his best men, armed with revolving carbines and sabres, and sent them around four miles to attack the enemy's rear at a given time, while he would make a simultaneous charge in front. This plan worked admirably. The ninety men appeared suddenly in the rear, not having been seen until near enough to fire their carbines, and, having emptied these, charged with drawn sabres upon the astonished rebels, who supposed them to be the advance-guard of a large force, not dreaming that so small a body would have the audacity to throw themselves upon an opposing body of six thousand, without the promise of speedy reinforcements. Before the enemy had recovered from the confusion caused by this attack in the rear, they were fiercely charged in front by Colonel Sheridan and his remaining handful of men, and, utterly routed, fled in wild disorder from the field. So panic-stricken were they, and so hasty was the flight, which ended only at Knight's Mills, some twenty miles south of Booneville, that the road over which they ran was literally strewn with arms, knapsacks, coats, and articles of every description. This battle, in which two small regiments of cavalry defeated nearly six thousand of the enemy, won for Colonel Sheridan his first star, —his commission as a brigadier-general dating from the day upon which it was so gallantly fought.

Twenty-Mile Creek was at this time the only place where water could be obtained by the rebels for their stock; and General Sheridan while stationed at Booneville frequently took advantage of this circumstance, making sudden expeditions in that direction and capturing at various times large quantities of stock. On one occasion, with the 2d Michigan, 2d Iowa, and 7th Kansas Cavalry Regiments, two companies of the 36th Illinois Infantry, and Hescock's Battery, he made a dash upon the enemy and succeeded in capturing and bringing away three hundred head of cattle. In August he was attacked by Colonel Faulkner's cavalry, near Rienzi, Mississippi, whom he defeated and followed to within a few miles of Ripley, dispersing the whole force and capturing a large number of prisoners and arms. He remained with his brigade in that vicinity until September 7, when he and his old regiment, the 2d Michigan Cavalry, were ordered to join the army in Kentucky, via the Mississippi and Ohio Rivers.

Arriving at Louisville, he was assigned to, and on the 20th of September assumed, the command of the 3d Division of the Army of the Ohio, consisting of ten regiments of infantry, one of cavalry, and two batteries of artillery. With this division he constructed, in the short period of a single night, the whole series of rifle-pits from the railroad-depot in Louisville around to the vicinity of Portland. On the 1st of October he took command of the 11th Division of the Army of the Ohio, and accompanied General Buell in his advance against Bragg. In front of Perryville, on the 8th of October, he was ordered to take position on the heights to the east of Doctor's Creek, for the purpose of securing the water for our men and animals. Gaining the heights (Chaplin Hills) early in the morning, with two regiments he repulsed an attack of a rebel brigade under General Leydell. At two o'clock the same day he was attacked by the enemy in strong force under command of General Hardee, who was handsomely repulsed. Soon afterwards he was again attacked, and a second time repulsed his assailants, driving them from the open ground on his front. The heights held by General Sheridan formed the key to the whole position: hence the desperate energy with which the enemy sought to drive him from them. After his second repulse of the rebels, some advantage having been gained by them upon our left, General Sheridan directed his artillery-fire upon them, and drove them from the open ground to which they had advanced. For a time the contest raged furiously at this point. The enemy came charging up with fixed bayonets, determined to take the position, but were driven back in disorder by the murderous fire which opened upon them, leaving the ground in front of the batteries covered with their dead and wounded. In this short but severe engagement the loss of General Sheridan's force was over four hundred in killed and wounded, and but for the sheltered position which he occupied it would have been much greater.

After the battle of Perryville, General Sheridan accompanied the army through Kentucky, until, early in November, he reached Nashville in command of a division of the Army of the Cumberland. Upon the advance to Murfreesborough on the morning of December 26, he had command of one of Major-General McCook's three divisions. Through the several days' skirmishing and fighting which terminated in the flight of Bragg and the evacuation of Murfreesborough, he was ever present and active, and by the skilful handling of his men contributed not a little to the successful issue of the battle of Stone River. For the part borne by himself and his division in that conflict, reference must be made to another chapter in this work, it being only necessary to say here that he was highly commended in the report of the general commanding, and recommended for promotion to a major-generalship. In the whole of that celebrated document, from the beginning down to "*non nobis*," no better compliment can be found than the following, paid to General Sheridan by one who, of all others, is the most competent judge :—

"Sheridan, after sustaining *four successive attacks*, gradually swung his right round southeasterly to a northwestern direction, *repulsing the enemy four times*, losing the gallant General Sill of his right and Colonel Roberts of his left brigade, when, having exhausted his ammunition, Negley's division being in the same predicament and heavily pressed, after desperate fighting they fell back from the position held at the commencement, through the cedar woods, in which Rousseau's division, with a portion of Negley's and Sheridan's, met the advancing enemy and checked his movements."

The major-generalship to which he was declared entitled by General Rosecrans by reason of his gallant and meritorious services was conferred on December 31, and he was confirmed in the position by the Senate at its extra session in March last.

To such a record, that of a man but thirty-one years of age, no word of commendation need be added by the author. Deeds speak with deeper meaning: by them let his life be judged,

10

upon them let his claim to popular favor be based. In person General Sheridan is rather under the medium size, with features strongly indicative of will and energy. Gentle and modest almost to a fault in ordinary intercourse, he is a very lion in daring when roused by the din of battle or momentarily swayed by the fierce passion called forth in imminent strife, and dashes into the fray with an ardor and impetuosity which usually attains its ends. As yet unmarried, his home is in the camp and field. His courage, kindness, and, above all, his soldierly abilities, have won for him the love of those whom it has been his fortune to command. He knows how to care for his men in the camp and how to handle them in the field,—qualities which a soldier never fails to appreciate. Very recently the officers of his division surprised him with an elegant and fitting testimonial of their regard, in the form of a magnificent sword, the blade exquisitely wrought, jewelled hilt, gold-plated scabbard, and the sword-belt woven with bullion. The present also comprised a set of silver service, a case of elegant, ivory-handled, silver-mounted Colt's pistols, and a general's saddle and bridle of the most gorgeous description. The cost of the sword alone was one thousand dollars, that of the whole present over two thousand dollars. Such a tribute from brave and gallant men to their commander is a sure index of the esteem in which they hold him.

THE STAFF.

CAPTAIN GEORGE LEE, *Assistant Adjutant-General*, was born in Yates county, New York, February 16, 1830, and was commissioned, by the Governor of Michigan, first lieutenant and adjutant of the 3d Battalion, 2d Michigan Cavalry, September 2, 1861. On the 10th of March, 1862, he was appointed acting regimental adjutant, at New Madrid, Missouri, by Colonel Gordon Granger (now major-general), then commanding the regiment. June 20, he was made acting assistant adjutant-general of the 2d Brigade of the cavalry division of the Army of the Mississippi, Colonel P. H. Sheridan commanding; and on the 11th of March, 1863, was appointed assistant adjutant-general, with the rank of captain, by the President, and assigned to duty with Major-General Sheridan. Captain Lee has been engaged in the following battles, expeditions, affairs, &c. :—New Madrid, Farmington, Booneville, Mississippi, May 29 and July 1, 1862, Chaplin Hills, and Stone River.

CAPTAIN A. F. STEVENSON, *Inspector-General*, was born in 1837, in the city of Hamburg, Germany, of Scotch-German parents. In 1854 he emigrated to America, and for several years cultivated a farm near Cambridge, Illinois. He then began the study of law with Judge Wilkinson, of Rock Island, and about a year thereafter was admitted to the bar. He continued in the practice of his profession until the beginning of the war, when he enlisted a company in Henry county, which, however, was not accepted by the Governor, a large surplus of volunteers having already offered. Under the second call for troops he enlisted a company for the 42d Illinois Regiment (Douglas Brigade), and served as first lieutenant in its Missouri campaign under Frémont and Hunter. He was afterwards appointed adjutant-general to Colonel Roberts, and remained with him in that position until the colonel was killed at the battle of Stone River. In the battles of Farmington and Stone River, and in the siege of Corinth and the pursuit of the rebels by General Pope after its evacuation, Captain Stevenson took an active part; and during the investment of the city of Nashville by the rebels, and its bombardment on the 5th of November, 1862, he was present with his command, participating in many of the skirmishes occurring in that vicinity. Soon after the battle of Stone River he was selected by General Sheridan as the inspector-general of his division.

CAPTAIN FRANCIS MOHRHART, *Topographical Engineer*, was born in Hesse-Darmstadt, Germany, October 23, 1823. In August, 1847, he came to the United States and settled in St. Louis, where he practised his profession as civil engineer until the war broke out. In April, 1861, he entered the service in the 2d Missouri Infantry, serving during the Frémont campaign in Missouri, and being present at the battle of Pea Ridge. With his regiment he joined the army of General Halleck before Corinth, and afterwards the Army of the Ohio under General Buell. Soon after the battle of Perryville, in which he was actively engaged, he was appointed Topographical Engineer on General Sheridan's staff, and in that capacity participated in the battle of Stone River.

SURGEON D. J. GRIFFITH, *Medical Director*, was born in Lampeter, South Wales, in 1830, and emigrated to the United States in 1841. Afterwards he began the study of medicine at Louisville, Kentucky, and graduated there in 1853. In October, 1861, he entered the army as assistant surgeon of the 2d Kentucky Cavalry. After serving some time in this capacity, he was promoted to be surgeon of the 2d Kentucky Infantry, and with that regiment was at Shiloh, where he, with a number of other surgeons, received special mention for efficient service from the general commanding. He was also at Corinth, and in Buell's campaign. Two days before the battle of Perryville he was appointed medical director to General Sheridan, and in that position was actively engaged in that contest, as he was also, later, at the battle of Stone River.

CAPTAIN HENRY HESCOCK, *Chief of Artillery*, is a native of Virginia, and about thirty-five years of age. He entered the United States service in 1846, served in the regular army as a sergeant during the Mexican War, was at Vera Cruz, Cerro Gordo, Huamantla, and Puebla, and afterwards in Texas and New Mexico. In January, 1861, he was stationed at Jefferson Barracks, and on the 17th of the same month was ordered, with a party of forty men of the 4th United States Artillery, to protect the United States Sub-Treasury and Post-Office at St. Louis, to prevent the seizure by rebel citizens of the funds deposited there. In the latter part of January he was stationed at the arsenal in St. Louis, and remained there until April 22, assisting General Lyon and Colonel Blair in the organization of the five regiments of volunteers enlisted in St. Louis. Having been appointed adjutant of the 1st Missouri Infantry, he participated in the actions of Booneville, Missouri, June 17, Dug Springs, Missouri, August 3, and Wilson's Creek, August 10, 1861, and returned to St. Louis in September with his regiment, which was then changed to a regiment of light artillery. Resigning as adjutant and joining Battery A, he marched from Jefferson Barracks, October 18, and participated in the battle of Frederickstown, Missouri, October 21. He was appointed assistant adjutant-general on the staff of Brigadier-General Schofield, November 21, in the Missouri State Militia, which position he held until February 25, 1862, when he was made captain of Battery G, 1st Missouri Light Artillery, and went with General Pope's army to New Madrid, sharing actively in the operations before that place until its evacuation, March 13. He was afterwards with General Palmer's brigade at Riddle's Point, in charge of a heavy battery, until the capture of Island No. 10. Accompanying General Pope to Hamburg Landing with his light battery, he took part in all the operations before Corinth, Mississippi, particularly the battle of Farmington, May 9.

July 4, 1862, the battery was attached to Colonel Sheridan's cavalry brigade. He left Mississippi, September 7, 1862, and arrived in Cincinnati, September 12, thence going to Louisville, whence he marched with General Sheridan's division, October 1, 1862, participating in the battle of Chaplin Hills, October 8. He afterwards went to Tennessee with General Rosecrans, and took part, with his battery, in the battle of Stone River. He was appointed chief of artillery on the staff of General Sheridan, September 30, 1862. Captain Hescock has seen at least as much of active and dangerous service as "any other man" now in the army.

LIEUTENANT ARAD J. DOUGLASS, *Ordnance Officer*, entered the service, July 6, 1846, in the Mounted Rifles United States Army, and served through the Mexican War as quartermaster sergeant. After his return to the United States at the close of the war he resided on his farm at Gambier, Knox county, Ohio, until September 19, 1862, when he was commissioned as a first lieutenant in the 71st Ohio Volunteers, and assigned for duty to General Sheridan as ordnance officer. Lieutenant Douglass has been in the following battles:—taking of Vera Cruz, Cerro Gordo, Contreras, Churubusco, Molino del Rey, Castle of Chapultepec, and the City of Mexico, and, in the present war, of Perryville and Stone River.

LIEUTENANT R. M. DENNING, *Aide-de-Camp*, was born in Princeton, Bureau county, Illinois, May 23, 1839. He entered the service at Morris, Illinois, August 1, 1861, as second lieutenant in the 36th Illinois Infantry, and served through Sigel's campaign in Southwestern Missouri. Previous to the battle of Pea Ridge, Arkansas, he was appointed aide-de-camp to Colonel Greaut, commanding a brigade in Sigel's 1st Division. His command at Covington, Kentucky, was attached to General Sheridan's division. Lieutenant Denning acted as adjutant-general of his brigade until October 8, the day of the battle of Perryville, when he was appointed aide-de-camp to General Sheridan. At Nashville, in November, 1862, he was promoted first lieutenant, and actively participated in the battle of Stone River.

LIEUTENANT FRANK H. ALLEN, *Aide-de-Camp*, was born in Craftsbury, Orleans county, Vermont, and went to Illinois in 1858. He enlisted in the 22d Illinois Infantry at Alton, and was mustered into service upon the formation of the regiment, May 11, 1861. He was promoted to the second lieutenancy of

Company B of the regiment on the 11th of February, 1862, and on the 13th of June following was made first lieutenant of the same company. In September, 1862, he was detailed as aide-de-camp to Colonel Geo. W. Roberts, commanding a brigade of the Army of the Mississippi, and was appointed aide to General Sheridan just before the battle of Stone River. Lieutenant Allen has borne a part in the following battles and sieges:— Belmont, New Madrid, Island No. 10, Tiptonville, Farmington, Corinth, and Stone River.

Brigadier-General Richard W. Johnson and Staff.

RICHARD W. JOHNSON, Brigadier-General of Volunteers, and Major of the 4th United States Cavalry, was born in Livingston county, Kentucky, February 7, 1827. He entered West Point Academy July 1, 1844, graduating July 1, 1849, and was appointed brevet second lieutenant in the 6th Infantry. On the 10th of June, 1850, he was promoted to a second lieutenancy in the 1st Infantry. On the 30th of October in the same year, he was married to Miss Rachel E. Steele, of Pennsylvania.

Soon afterwards he joined the 1st Infantry, in Texas, and served with it until March 3, 1855, and for the last two years was adjutant of the regiment. He was appointed by Jefferson Davis, then Secretary of War, first lieutenant in the 2d (now 5th) United States Cavalry, commanded by Colonel A. S. Johnston, —the rebel General Johnston who was killed at Shiloh. Colonel Johnston appointed him regimental quartermaster on his staff, in which position he continued until December 1, 1856, when he was promoted to a captaincy. Remaining with his regiment, he served during several Indian campaigns, and up to the time of the surrender of the United States forces by General Twiggs. After that surrender he left the country with a portion of his command, and arrived in New York shortly after the bombardment of Fort Sumter.

He now served as captain of cavalry under Generals Patterson and Banks, until September, 1861, when he was ordered to Kentucky as lieutenant-colonel of the 3d Kentucky Volunteer Cavalry. On the 11th of October he was appointed a brigadier-general, and from October 15, 1861, to March 29, 1862, commanded a brigade in General McCook's division. About this time he was taken ill and compelled to leave the field, thus being

152

BRIG. GEN. JOHNSON.

AND

OFFICERS OF STAFF.

J. B. LIPPINCOTT & CO. PHILADA

absent at the battle of Shiloh.   On the 13th of April he rejoined his command, and was present at the advance upon Corinth. On the 28th of May he was sent to the front with his brigade, and became engaged with a large force of the rebel infantry, which he routed, having killed fifty-three and wounded seventy-one of them.   After the evacuation of Corinth he marched with Buell's army through Northern Alabama to Battle Creek, Tennessee, where he was detached from his brigade and placed in command of eight hundred cavalry and sent in pursuit of the rebel General Morgan, who was making a raid upon the Louisville & Nashville Railroad and had succeeded in cutting off communication between Nashville and the North.   On the 22d of August General Johnson vigorously attacked him near Gallatin, Tennessee.   Morgan's forces were largely superior in numbers, and, Johnson being surrounded, and having lost about one hundred killed and wounded, about one-half of his command—himself among the number—were taken prisoners.   He made a desperate fight; and the enemy's loss is known to have been very severe.

General Johnson was paroled and subsequently exchanged. On the 10th of December, 1862, he was assigned to the command of the 2d Division of the right wing of the Army of the Cumberland, and served with it through the battle of Stone River.   In that engagement two of his brigades were on the extreme right, and one was guarding a train.   The enemy falling heavily upon our right, these brigades were forced back after a sharp contest, leaving Edgerton's and part of Goodspeed's batteries in the hands of the rebels.   The reserve brigade also, advancing from its bivouac near Wilkerson's Pike towards the right, made a gallant but ineffectual stand against the entire rebel left.   The heavy loss of the division and the punishment it inflicted upon the enemy prove that it did good service, though forced to give way before superior numbers.   No blame is attached to its leader for the reverse of that day.   His courage, gallantry, and skill are unquestioned, and the great loss of life in his ranks upon the battle-field of Stone River truly attests the bravery of his men.

General Johnson's division is now known as the 2d Division of the 20th Army Corps.

THE STAFF.

CAPTAIN TEMPLE CLARK, *Assistant Adjutant-General*, is a son of the late Major Satterlee Clark, United States Army, and was born in Utica, New York, October 23, 1826. When twelve years of age, he emigrated to Wisconsin, and resided at Fort Winnebago until 1843. Removing to St. Louis in the spring of 1846, he there joined the 2d Illinois Volunteers, under Colonel Bissell, and participated with the army of General Wool in the long march through Texas and Mexico and the severe battle of Buena Vista, returning to Wisconsin in 1847. On the breaking out of the rebellion, he was a lawyer, and had been in public life as a Democrat. He immediately raised a company in Manitowoc county, and in April, 1861, was assigned to the 5th Regiment of Wisconsin Volunteers as senior captain. He served on the Potomac in the army of General McClellan, was in the battle of Lewinsville and several skirmishes, and accompanied that army to the Peninsula. He left it early in April, 1862, to accept the position of assistant adjutant-general upon the staff of Brigadier-General Plummer, commanding a division under General Pope. Joining General Plummer at Tiptonville, he was with the Army of the Mississippi in the advance on Corinth, taking part in the engagements of Farmington, May 9, and of Corinth, May 28.

On the death of General Plummer, in August, 1862, Captain Clark was assigned by General Rosecrans to duty on his staff as assistant adjutant-general. As such he was actively engaged at the battles of Iuka and Corinth, and on the latter occasion received three wounds, one being a gunshot-wound through the lungs and reported as mortal. For meritorious conduct at Iuka and Corinth he was especially mentioned in general orders by the commanding general. January 3, 1863, he joined the Army of the Cumberland, and was temporarily assigned to duty with General Johnson as assistant adjutant-general.

CAPTAIN THEODORE C. BOWLES, *Quartermaster*, is a native of Ohio, and a lawyer by profession, but at the opening of the rebellion was engaged in commercial pursuits at the capital of his native State. He entered the service in August, 1861, as regimental quartermaster of the 15th Ohio Infantry, and in October following was, at the request of General Johnson, nominated by Colonel Thomas Swords, assistant quartermaster-general, as assistant quartermaster, with the rank of captain,— in which position he was confirmed by the Senate at its session in the spring of 1862. Since October, 1861, he has been on duty with General Johnson's command, and accompanied it in the noted Buell campaign through Kentucky, Tennessee, Northern Mississippi, and Alabama.

CAPTAIN WILLIAM E. MCLELAND, *Commissary of Subsistence*, was born in Clark county, Kentucky, September 21, 1814, but was raised in Jefferson county, Indiana, as a farmer. At the age of seventeen he entered a dry-goods store as clerk, and was engaged in mercantile pursuits until 1858, when he was elected sheriff of Jefferson county. This office he held until the 4th of July, 1861, when he entered the service. On the 26th of August following, he was appointed by Governor Morton first lieutenant and quartermaster of the 6th Regiment Indiana Volunteers, which office he filled until August 17, 1862, when he was detailed as acting commissary of subsistence in the 4th Brigade of the 2d Division of the Army of the Ohio, on the staff of Brigadier-General Sill.

On the 19th of February, 1863, he was appointed and commissioned by the President as captain and commissary of subsistence, and assigned to duty on the staff of General Johnson. Since the army first entered Kentucky, on the 20th of September, 1861, he has accompanied it in all its movements, participating in the battles of Shiloh and Stone River.

CAPTAIN J. R. BARTLETT, *Division Inspector*, was born in Seneca county, Ohio, July 16, 1830. In 1853 he was admitted to the bar, and continued the practice of the law at Frémont, Ohio, until July, 1861, when he organized a company for the 49th Ohio Regiment and was chosen its captain. He was in command of his company during the second day's battle at Shiloh, and was among the first to enter Corinth after its evacuation by the enemy. He also participated in the many marches and skirmishes in which his regiment was engaged through Northern Alabama, Tennessee, and Kentucky. On the 15th of November, 1862, he was appointed assistant inspector-general of the 2d Division, 20th Army Corps, and during the battle of Stone River acted as assistant adjutant-general upon the staff of General Johnson, commanding the division.

MAJOR LUTHER D. WATERMAN, *Medical Director*, was born at Wheeling, Virginia, November 21, 1830. He was educated at the High School in Zanesville, Ohio, and the Miami University at Oxford, Ohio. In 1853 he obtained his degree as a doctor of medicine from the Ohio Medical College, and for nearly three years practised his profession at Cincinnati. During the next two years he travelled in the West. He subsequently resided at Kokomo, Indiana, and on the 7th of September, 1861, was appointed by Governor Morton surgeon of the 59th Indiana Volunteers. He was present at the battle of Shiloh and the skirmishes at Rowlett's Station and Ridge Creek. For two months he was stationed at the general field hospital before Corinth, and was afterwards in charge of General Hospital No. 1, at Huntsville, Alabama. Dr. Waterman organized, and for six months had charge of, the Officers' Hospital at Nashville, and on the 16th of March, 1863, was assigned to duty on the staff of General Johnson as medical director of the 2d Division of the 20th Army Corps.

CAPTAIN ADOLPH G. METZNER, *Engineer Officer*, was born in Grand Baden, Germany, August 16, 1834, and arrived in New York December 7, 1856. August 24, 1861, he entered the service at Indianapolis as second lieutenant of Company A, 32d Indiana Volunteers, under the command of Colonel (now General) Willich. With his regiment he has served through the entire campaign, beginning with the skirmish at Munfordsville on the 17th of December, 1861, and ending with the battle of Stone River. On the 14th of February, 1863, he was promoted to the captaincy of Company K, and on the 17th of March was detailed as topographical engineer of the 2d Division of the 20th Army Corps.

LIEUTENANT JOHN J. KESSLER, *Aide-de-Camp and Provost-Marshal*, was born near Easton, Northampton county, Pennsylvania, in 1834. Entering the service at Frémont, Sandusky county, Ohio, as first sergeant of Company F, 49th Ohio Volunteers, he was promoted to the second lieutenancy, February 9, 1862, and on the 7th of April following to the first lieutenancy. At the battle of Stone River he was in command of his company, and on the 15th of March, 1863, was detailed as provost-marshal upon the staff of General Johnson.

Brigadier-General Jefferson C. Davis and Staff.

JEFFERSON C. DAVIS, Brigadier-General of Volunteers, and Captain in the 1st Regular Artillery, now commanding the 1st Division of the 20th Army Corps, was born in Clarke county, Indiana, March 2, 1828. His ancestors were notable men in early days in the West. His father was born and raised in Kentucky. His mother was born in Indiana, and is now sixty-two years of age, and is, probably, one of the oldest living natives of that State. His grandfather, William Davis, was an old Indian-fighter, who was an actor in numberless encounters and battles, among the more important of which was that of River Raisin. On his mother's side, his grandfather James Drummond was one of the earliest settlers of Kentucky, at the Falls of the Ohio. Several of his uncles were also active in the early settlement of that country, and participants in the battle of Tippecanoe and other Indian fights.

In 1841, young Davis, who was an apt scholar, entered the Clarke County Seminary, at that time one of the most prominent in the State. Here he remained four years, obtaining what was then esteemed in the West a liberal education, and was still attending school there in 1845, when the Mexican War broke out. The thrilling news from Palo Alto and Resaca de la Palma flushed thousands of hearts with excitement, and among them that of young Davis, now seventeen years of age. Love· of study was succeeded by a new and more absorbing passion, a thirst for the romance of camp and soldier life; and one morning he threw down his books, and in the afternoon was the first enrolled member of a volunteer company, called "the Clarke Guards," raised under the auspices of Captain T. W. Gibson, a West Pointer in earlier days, then a prominent lawyer of the

BRIG. GEN. DAVIS

CAPT. F. W. MORRISON.

CAPT. ASA D. BAKER.

BRIG. GEN.
EFF. C. DAVIS

CAPT. H. W. HALL.

LIEUT. F. E. REYNOLDS.

AND

OFFICERS OF STAFF.

Eng.d by S Thew

J. B. LIPPINCOTT & CO. PHILAD.A

county, and now one of the most notable attorneys in Louisville, Kentucky, or, indeed, in the West. The regiment of which it was a part was under the command of the now noted James H. Lane, of Kansas. The subject of our notice participated in the battle of Buena Vista, and in the entire Mexican campaign, without losing a day from sickness or other cause.

For gallant conduct in his regiment he was appointed second lieutenant in the 1st Regiment of Regular Artillery, to rank from June 17, 1848. Receiving his commission near the close of the war, Lieutenant Davis reported at Cincinnati for recruiting service, where he remained until October, obtaining in that time many recruits. Peace having been declared, he was ordered to join his company, which had just returned from Mexico and was then at Baltimore. Among his messmates and associates in the regiment were the present rebel generals Magruder, (Stonewall) Jackson, Hill, Winder, and Slaughter, and French, Brannan, Schofield, Baird, Vogdes, Anderson, Doubleday, and others now holding distinguished positions in the Union service. Of the officers of this regiment alone, twenty-one have become generals of mark and are now in active service. From Baltimore he was ordered to Fort Washington, on the Potomac, nine miles below Washington, where two years were spent on post duty and in professional study, his researches extending to every branch of military science. Much advantage was here derived by the young lieutenant from constant association with officers of skill and experience, whose theoretical knowledge had been tested and perfected by the trying scenes of the Mexican War. Young and full of life, he mingled much during these two years in Washington society, where he ever found a ready welcome. In the summer of 1850 his command constituted a portion of the escort at the funeral of President Taylor. In the fall of the same year it was ordered to New Orleans Barracks, then under the command of General Twiggs. In the fall of 1851 he was ordered to the Rio Grande to enforce the neutrality laws, and while there was engaged in several expeditions. That section of country was in a greatly disturbed

state, in consequence of the presence of a band of scheming filli-
busters, the survivors of the Cuban expeditions under the ill-
fated Lopez. Swarming upon the Rio Grande, many attempts
were made by them to revolutionize the adjoining country; and
in some parts of Texas they succeeded to a certain extent. The
danger becoming somewhat threatening, President Fillmore
issued a proclamation warning the participants to cease from
their illegal acts, and immediately entered upon prompt measures
to put an end to them. For this purpose troops were sent to
the Rio Grande, and among them, as we have seen, Lieutenant
Davis and his command. Lieutenant Davis himself captured
Colonel Wheat, the most noted of their leaders, and the band
was eventually defeated and broken up by the Mexicans at
Camargo, the battle being witnessed by Lieutenant Davis and
his men from the Texas side of the river.

February 29, 1852, he was promoted first lieutenant, *vice* T. J.
(Stonewall) Jackson, resigned. In the summer of the same
year he returned to New Orleans, and thence went to Pasca-
goula, where his ranks were fearfully decimated by the yellow
fever. In the succeeding autumn he was transferred to Florida,
and took a command on the Caloosahatchee River, on the
west coast, where he made several reconnoissances against
the Indians and was engaged in a number of skirmishes with
them. In June, 1853, after five years' continued service, Lieutenant Davis obtained his first furlough, and visited his home
in the West. Rejoining his command in the fall at Fortress
Monroe, he there spent two years at close study in the Artillery School of Practice. Old Point Comfort was at that time
a favorite summer resort of the wealthy and fashionable; and
the monotony of garrison-life was enlivened to our lieutenant
by many pleasant hours passed in this agreeable society. In
the fall of 1855 he was ordered to join French's Light Battery at Fort McHenry, Baltimore, and during his two years'
sojourn at this place became proficient in light-artillery practice,
being accounted one of the most skilful officers in that branch of
the service.

In the fall of 1857, having completed his detailed course of practice, as was then required, he was ordered to a station on Indian River, on the east coast of Florida, where he arrived in November. The winter and spring were occupied with Indian scouting expeditions, in which with his command he scoured that whole country from the Everglades to the northern boundary of the State,—a region some three hundred miles in extent. In May, 1858, in accordance with the provisions of the treaty then made, the Indians were removed to the West, and in June the troops were withdrawn from Florida and Lieutenant Davis and his command ordered to Charleston harbor. In August, 1858, he was placed in command of Fort Sumter with the first garrison that occupied it. Here he had charge of a large number of native Africans, the cargo of a slaver captured by the Dolphin, under command of Lieutenant Maffitt, now of the rebel navy. The people of Charleston, always ready to fan themselves into a blaze, were intensely excited, and threatened to take the negroes from his custody by force. The aid of the law was called in, and several writs of habeas corpus were served upon him. But Lieutenant Davis was firm in refusing to give them up; and in this position he was sustained by one of their most eminent judges, and by various editors in the State, who assumed the ground that negroes were not citizens, and consequently not entitled to the benefits of the habeas corpus act. While the controversy was pending, the yellow and ship fevers set in, raging with terrible fatality and carrying off large numbers of both garrison and negroes. The surviving blacks were sent to Liberia; and thus the difficulty was settled.

Lieutenant Davis remained nearly three years at Charleston, devoting himself to artillery practice, and finally passing a brilliant examination in that branch of the service. In December, 1860, when South Carolina seceded, by exerting his personal influence he contributed much to avert immediate collision between the citizens and the military. When Major Anderson cut down the flag-staff at Fort Moultrie, spiked the guns, burned the carriages, and retired to Fort Sumter, Lieutenant Davis was by his side.

11

During the four and a half months of the weary siege, he looked out from the walls of Sumter upon the line of batteries with which the rebels were encircling that devoted fortress. On the morning of April 12 he was on guard, and was upon the ramparts in the act of relieving the last sentry, when, at four o'clock, the first shell of the rebellion came over from Fort Johnson and exploded in the air forty feet above his head. It was still the gray of early dawn when this messenger of war was hurled against that small garrison, the sole representative there of that Government against which South Carolina had arisen in opposition. Unconnected with the saddening thoughts to which it gave rise, the general describes it to his friends as a magnificent sight. But there was little time then for melancholy reflection. The contest was upon them; and the little garrison of seventy-six were pitted against as many hundreds. All know the story of that memorable engagement,—how they fought long and well, but at length, wellnigh roasted by the flames of their burning quarters, were compelled to yield. During the bombardment, Lieutenant Davis commanded one of the batteries on the northwest face of the work, and directed his attention principally to the famous floating battery, silencing most of its guns and making it a complete wreck.

With Major Anderson and the garrison, Lieutenant Davis proceeded to New York after the surrender, when he received notification of his promotion to a captaincy, and found orders detailing him as mustering officer for the State of Indiana, with his head-quarters at Indianapolis. Here he remained several months, engaged in mustering volunteers and discharging quartermaster and commissary duties. His labors were severe and successful, the organization and equipment of many regiments having been furthered by him. The battle of Wilson's Creek and the death of Lyon now occurring, affairs in Missouri began to look dark, and the necessity for speedy reinforcements under competent commanders was proportionately increased. Captain Davis, being desirous of active service in the field, was commissioned colonel of a full regiment, the 22d Indiana, and ordered to

Missouri to assist in the defence of St. Louis. Three days after the receipt of the order, the regiment and its colonel were in St. Louis, and reported to General Frémont. Remaining there ten days, Colonel Davis was ordered to relieve General Grant of the command of all the forces between the Osage and Missouri Rivers. This territory constituted a district, with head-quarters at Jefferson City, and on the 28th of August Colonel Davis assumed command. At that time Price and McCulloch were at Springfield; and the new commander at once began to fortify the place and to dispose his forces—about fifteen thousand in number—with a view to its defence. He personally superintended the construction of the works, and so strengthened Jefferson City that the enemy deemed it unadvisable to make any attack upon what soon became known as one of the best-fortified posts in the West.

Leaving Jefferson City to the right, the rebels advanced upon Lexington and captured it. Colonel Davis repaired the Pacific Railroad, destroyed by the rebels, rebuilt the La Mine bridge, burned by Price, and pushed his forces to Georgetown, compelling Price to fall back from Lexington to Springfield, want of transportation on the part of our troops alone preventing his capture. During this period Colonel Davis's troops were actively engaged in scouring the country, and many small fights occurred, together with some severe ones, such as the desperate engagement at Booneville, which was successfully defended against largely superior numbers by Major Eppstein, and the fights at Lexington and at Arrow Rock.

Frémont now came up with his whole force, and took the field in person, appointing Colonel Davis an acting brigadier-general and assigning him to a brigade in General Pope's division. The army advanced to Springfield, and Price and McCulloch fell back before it to Arkansas. Frémont was at this juncture recalled; Hunter succeeded to the command, and the Federal forces fell back to the La Mine. General Pope was now assigned to the command of all the forces in Central Missouri, and Colonel Davis placed in charge of that district with about fifteen thousand men under his command, whom he was instructed to put into winter quarters. The month of November and a portion of December were spent in building quarters, instituting camps of instruction, &c. While thus engaged, Colonel Davis was ordered to join his captain's command at Washington; but through the influence of General Halleck, who wished him to remain, this order was countermanded.

On the 15th of December, Colonel Davis, in command of a brigade under General Pope, started upon the famous Blackwater expedition. The Union force—cavalry, infantry, and artillery— numbered about four thousand, and was divided into two brigades, the first under Colonel Davis and the second under Colonel (now Major-General) Steele, the whole commanded in person by General Pope. The object of the movement was to get between Price's army on the Osage and the recruits, escorts, and supplies on their way south from the Missouri River. On the first evening the force encamped fifteen miles west of Sedalia. That the enemy might be deceived as to the destination of the expedition, it was given out that Warsaw was the point aimed at, and the troops pursued the road towards that place several miles beyond Sedalia. On the 16th General Pope pushed forward by a forced march twenty-six miles, and at sunset, with his whole force, occupied a position between the direct road from Warrensburg and Clinton and the road by Chilhowee, the latter being the route usually taken by returning soldiers and recruits. Shortly after sunset the advance captured the enemy's pickets at Chilhowee, and learned that he was encamped in force (about two thousand two hundred) six miles north of that town. After resting a couple of hours, General Pope threw forward ten companies of cavalry and a section of artillery, under Lieutenant-Colonel Brown (now Brigadier-General), of the 7th Missouri Cavalry, in pursuit, and followed with his whole force, posting the main body between Warrensburg and Rose Hill, to support the pursuing column. Lieutenant-Colonel Brown continued the pursuit all night of the 16th and all day and part of the night of the 17th, his advance-guard occupying Johnstown in the course of the night. The enemy began to scatter as the pursuit grew close, disappearing in the bushes and by-paths, driving their wagons (common two-horse ones taken from farm-houses) into farm-yards distant from the road, and throwing out their loads. When the pursuing forces reached Johnstown, the enemy, reduced to about five hundred, scattered completely, one portion fleeing precipitately towards Butler, and the other towards Papinsville.

The main body of Pope's command now moved slowly towards Warrensburg, awaiting the return of Colonel Brown, who proceeded from Johnstown to scour the country south of Grand River to the neighborhood of Clinton. In these operations, sixteen wagons, loaded with tents and supplies, and one hundred and fifty prisoners, were captured, and the enemy's force thoroughly dispersed. On the morning of the 18th, Lieutenant-Colonel Brown rejoined the main body. Knowing that there must still be a considerable force to the north, General Pope on the 18th moved slowly forward towards Warrensburg, and when near that town the scouts sent out before leaving Sedalia reported that a large force was moving from Waverly and Arrow Rock, and would encamp that night at the mouth of Clear Creek, just south of Milford. General Pope thereupon posted the main body of his command between Warrensburg and Knob Noster, to close all outlet to the south from those two points, and despatched seven companies of cavalry, afterwards reinforced by a company of regular cavalry and a section of artillery, all under the command of Colonel Davis, to march on the town of Milford, so as to turn the enemy's left and rear and intercept his retreat to the northeast, at the same time directing Major Marshall, with Merrill's regiment of horse, to march from Warrensburg on Milford, turning the enemy's right and rear and forming a junction with Colonel Davis. The main body occupied a point four miles south, ready to advance at a moment's notice, or to intercept the enemy's retreat south.

Colonel Davis marched promptly and vigorously with the

forces under his command, and at a late hour in the afternoon came upon the enemy encamped in the wooded bottom-land on the west side of the Blackwater, opposite the mouth of Clear Creek. His pickets were immediately driven in across the stream, which was deep, miry, and impassable except by a long narrow bridge, occupied by the enemy in force under Colonel Magoffin. Colonel Davis brought forward his force and directed the bridge to be carried by assault. Two companies of regular cavalry, under Lieutenants Gordon and Amory, were designated for the service, and were supported by five companies of the 1st Iowa Cavalry. Lieutenant Gordon led the charge in person, carried the bridge in gallant style, immediately formed his company on the opposite side, and was promptly followed by other companies. The force of the enemy at the bridge retreated precipitately over a narrow open space into the woods, where his main body was posted. The two companies of the 4th Cavalry advanced, and were received with a volley of small arms. They continued to press onward, however; and the enemy, finding his retreat to the south and west cut off, and that he was in the presence of a large force and at best could only prolong the contest a short time, surrendered at discretion. The force thus captured consisted of parts of two regiments of infantry, and three companies of cavalry, numbering in all about nine hundred and fifty men, among whom were Colonels Robinson, Alexander, and Magoffin, Lieutenant-Colonel Robinson, Major Harris, a somewhat noted Missouri politician, and fifty-one commissioned company officers. About five hundred horses and mules, seventy-three wagons heavily loaded with powder, lead, tents, subsistence stores, and supplies of all kinds, and one thousand stand of arms, fell into Colonel Davis's hands. For his skilful management in this affair Colonel Davis was highly complimented by General Pope, and recommended to the special notice of General Halleck.

The prisoners and arms were at once sent to St. Louis, in charge of Colonel Davis, and arrived there the day before Christmas. Obtaining forty-eight hours' leave of absence, he made a flying trip to Indianapolis, was there married, returned with his wife upon a bridal tour to his camp, and rejoined his command at Otterville. Here he was ordered to join General Curtis's column moving from Rolla preparatory to an advance upon Springfield. The march overland to that place was a desperate undertaking,—indeed, was pronounced impossible by many military men; but General Halleck persisted in his order, saying that Colonel Davis's skill and energy would carry him safely through. Accordingly, it set out. Tents were left behind, and only such things carried as were indispensable. The Osage was very high, and was crossed on rafts in the midst of a heavy snow-storm. Three days and nights were occupied in the passage; and, as they ferried themselves over on the frail structures, many a soldier was probably reminded of the crossing of the Delaware by Washington,—more famous, but not more perilous.

In ten days from the time of starting he made a junction with Curtis at Lebanon, and his command became a part of the Army of the Southwest. As Curtis advanced, Price retreated, only stopping long enough to engage in a small skirmish with the Federal advance, commanded by Colonel Davis. At the Missouri line and at Cross Timbers, Arkansas, Price again made a stand, but was forced to continue his retreat. Colonel Davis now took command of all the cavalry, about eighteen hundred in number, and, on the exact line of thirty-six thirty, made a dashing charge on the enemy's rear brigade and a battery, driving them in confusion.

The army remained at Camp Halleck until Price, reinforced by McCulloch and Van Dorn, came back and gave battle at Pea Ridge. In that three-days engagement Colonel Davis's division fought, on the 7th of March, the battle of Leetown, one of the most sanguinary and decisive contests of the war. This division, numbering about three thousand, was opposed to McCulloch's command, reported at twelve thousand; and the latter were utterly routed, with the loss of Generals McCulloch and McIntosh killed and General Herbert taken prisoner. McCulloch was attacked in his own position; and the struggle was short and desperate, being decided in little more than thirty minutes. The next day Colonel Davis, with his whole division, stormed and carried the heights of Elkhorn, capturing five cannon and deciding the battle against the rebels.

After the battle of Pea Ridge, General Curtis began his memorable march through Arkansas, and Colonel Davis accompanied him as far as Sulphur Rock, where he received orders from General Halleck to take his command to Cape Girardeau and thence proceed by river to join the army in front of Corinth. Starting on the 10th of May, with two brigades, after an exhausting march of two hundred and forty miles through a rough and sparsely settled country, he reached Cape Girardeau on the 20th, thus averaging twenty-four miles of travel each day. Upon this march he received by a courier his commission as a brigadier-general, dating from the day of the Blackwater fight. Embarking on steamers, he reached Pittsburg Landing on the 24th, and marched at once to Corinth. There he was assigned to the left of Pope's command; and when the evacuation of Corinth took place he accompanied Generals Pope and Rosecrans in their pursuit of Beauregard. The pursuit over, the army fell back to Clear Creek, General Pope was ordered to Virginia, and General Rosecrans assumed command. By him General Davis was ordered to Jacinto, and remained there until about the 1st of July, when he was ordered to make a reconnoissance to Ripley, Mississippi. On this expedition he advanced to within a few miles of Holly Springs, when he was directed to return by forced marches to his original camp at Jacinto. This he did, remaining there until August, when ill health compelled him to retire from his command, and, with a twenty-days leave of absence, he visited his home in Indiana.

Soon afterwards Bragg advanced into Kentucky, and General Buell started in pursuit of him. The threatening state of affairs induced General Davis—still in ill health—to offer his services to General Wright to assist in the defence of Louisville. His division, which had been placed in charge of General Mitchel and attached to Buell's army, had arrived at Louisville, and he again assumed its command. While in the city, an unfortunate personal difficulty occurred between himself and Major-General Nelson, which resulted in the death of the latter and led to the arrest of General Davis. After a few days' arrest, he was released, much to the gratification of the public, and ordered to report at Cincinnati for duty, where he was assigned to the temporary command of the forces around Newport and Covington. After the subsidence of the fear of an attack on Cincinnati, he was ordered to take command of his old division, and did so at Edgefield, opposite Nashville. At the battle of Stone River this division was in the thickest of the fight, holding the centre of the right wing. After the attack upon General Johnson's division, the enemy fell upon it with crushing weight, and it too was forced back, but in comparatively good order. Its commander was faithful and brave as ever upon that memorable occasion; and that his efforts were appreciated is evident from the fact that in the official report the commanding general places him second on the list of those whom he recommends to be made major-generals, or, as he terms it, who "ought to be made major-generals in our service."

General Davis still commands his old division, which has marched more than five thousand miles and participated in ten battles and fights. *As a whole*, it has been engaged in five general battles—viz., Pea Ridge, Corinth, Perryville, Knob Gap, and Stone River—and in almost numberless expeditions and reconnoissances. It was the first organized division in the West, and still retains its original number and position. Its record and the histories of its commanding officers would fill a volume, and would constitute a history that would well compare in thrilling interest with any written upon the wars of continental Europe during the Middle Ages.

This old division, now the 1st of the 20th Army Corps, Army of the Cumberland, stands among the foremost in efficiency and popularity. Many of its gallant men sleep in heroes' graves, and its history is written in the blood of a wicked rebellion.

All honor to the loved and the lost from its ranks, and a country's gratitude to those who remain and are as determined as ever to maintain inviolate the integrity of the republic of the American fathers!

THE STAFF.

CAPTAIN T. W. MORRISON, *Assistant Adjutant-General*, was born in Bloomington and raised in Salem, Indiana, and is twenty-one years of age. His father, Hon. John J. Morrison, is a prominent citizen of Indiana, noted for his literary attainments, having for twenty-five years been Principal of the High School at Salem and the State University at Bloomington. In political life he is also known, having represented his county in both branches of the State Legislature.

The subject of this sketch enlisted, July 26, 1861, as second lieutenant in the 18th Regiment of Indiana Volunteers, and served during the campaign in Missouri, bearing a conspicuous part in the battle of Pea Ridge. On the 8th of February, 1862, he was appointed aide-de-camp by General Davis. Accompanying the general to Corinth, he acted in that capacity there and through the campaigns in Northern Mississippi, Kentucky, and Tennessee, ending with the battle of Stone River. For gallant conduct in this engagement, upon the recommendation of Generals Davis and McCook, expressed in the most favorable and complimentary terms, he was commissioned by the President as assistant adjutant-general, February 27, 1863, and assigned to the staff of General Davis, with whose command he has been intimately connected for nearly two years.

CAPTAIN ASA D. BAKER, *Commissary*, was born, January 18, 1828, in Waterloo, New York, where he received a business education. In 1859 he went to California, worked in the mines six months, and then engaged in mercantile business at Sacramento City. In 1851 he returned to his native home, where he remained until 1855, when he removed to Chicago, Illinois, and opened a railroad-furnishing goods and machinery depot. He was the first to introduce steam fire-engines into the city of Chicago, and sold the first five steamers used by that city. At the breaking out of the rebellion, he closed up his business and entered the service of the United States. He was one of the prime movers in the organization of the 37th Regiment Illinois Volunteers, and was with that regiment in its marches through Missouri under General Frémont.

In December, 1861, he was appointed by General Julius White (commanding the 2d Brigade of General Davis's division) acting assistant commissary of subsistence, and was with the brigade during their march across the Osage Mountains and into Arkansas. At the battle of Pea Ridge he acted as aide-de-camp to General White, and rendered gallant and important service. Having by his close attention to business qualified himself, he was recommended, immediately after the battle of Pea Ridge, by General Davis, General White, and others, for the appointment of commissary of subsistence, and was commissioned by the President November 18, 1862, and ordered to report to General Davis for duty, which he did on the 18th of January, 1863, at Murfreesborough, Tennessee.

CAPTAIN HAMILTON W. HALL, *Division Inspector*, was born July 17, 1837. At the age of sixteen he settled in the town of Urbana, Illinois, where, and at Mattoon, he spent several years in business pursuits. In April, 1861, he joined a company for military drill and discipline, and was made second lieutenant. During the summer of 1861, this company was offered to the Government through the Governor of Illinois, but, owing to the fact that a surplus had already been offered, was not accepted. About the 1st of August Lieutenant Hall and many others of the company determined to make another effort to get into the service; and, accordingly, he enlisted in a company raised by

Captain A. L. Taylor, in Charleston, Illinois, and upon its organization on the 14th of August was chosen second lieutenant. The company was mustered into the United States service at St. Louis Arsenal, 16th of August, as Company H, 9th Regiment Missouri Volunteers.

This regiment was composed entirely of Illinois companies who had been led to enter into an organization out of their State by the difficulty of acceptance at that time in Illinois regiments. Captain J. C. Kelton, assistant adjutant-general, became colonel, and with him the regiment entered the service at the time of Frémont's campaign, accompanying the division of General John Pope. Returning in November, the regiment spent the winter of 1861 and 1862 in tents or upon the march, at La Mine River, Syracuse, and Sedalia, Missouri, until January 25, when, under command of General J. C. Davis, the division marched to join General Curtis's expedition, well known in the history of the war as the "Campaign of the Southwest." Meantime the regiment had memorialized the President and secured a transfer to its own State, becoming the 59th Illinois.

After the battle of Pea Ridge, the expedition moved eastward, occupying the country south and east as far as Batesville, Arkansas. Up to that time (May, 1862) the regiment had marched over two thousand miles through a wilderness country, Lieutenant Hall having been with his company upon every foot of the march, in every bivouac, skirmish, or battle. Since then he has been assigned to duty as assistant regimental quartermaster, assistant adjutant, and assistant commissary sergeant of his brigade, occupying the latter position during the campaign of the Army of the Ohio in Kentucky, and until January 6, 1863, when he was appointed assistant commissary sergeant of 1st Division, 14th Army Corps. At the time of the advance from Nashville he volunteered to act as aide-de-camp to Colonel P. Sidney Post, commanding his brigade of General Davis's division. In this capacity he was employed during the engagement which resulted in the occupation of Nolensville on the 26th of December, and in the skirmishes of the advance upon the enemy's position on the 30th, and the engagement of the 31st at Stone River.

Upon the 16th of January, 1863, at the request of Company F, 59th Illinois, Lieutenant Hall was commissioned as their captain; and upon the same day he was assigned to duty as Inspector of the 1st Division, 20th Army Corps, on the staff of General Davis.

CAPTAIN THOMAS H. DAILY, *Aide-de-Camp*, was born in Charlestown, Clarke county, Indiana, December 4, 1842. He enlisted in the 22d Indiana Volunteers on the 6th of July, 1861, was promoted second lieutenant on the 12th of June, 1862, first lieutenant on the 21st of November, 1862, and captain on the 23d of February, 1863.

LIEUTENANT FRANCIS E. REYNOLDS, *Aide-de-Camp*, was born in Elmira, Chemung county, New York, May 12, 1836. His family removing to Aurora, Kane county, Illinois, May, 1844, he received his education at that place, and was engaged as clerk in the post-office for nearly five years previous to the outbreak of the rebellion. He enlisted as private, August 2, 1861, in Company A, cavalry, attached to the 36th Regiment Illinois Infantry, and was promoted, April 1, 1862, as first lieutenant of Company B, cavalry, attached to the same regiment, for meritorious conduct at the battle of Pea Ridge, Arkansas. For about four months he had command of the company, during which time it acted as escort for Generals Rosecrans, Gordon Granger, Jefferson C. Davis, and Robert B. Mitchell. On the 6th of January, 1863, he was appointed aide-de-camp on General Jefferson C. Davis's staff, for meritorious conduct during the battle of Stone River.

Brigadier-General Horatio P. Van Cleve and Staff.

HORATIO P. VAN CLEVE, Brigadier-General of Volunteers, was born in Princeton, New Jersey, November, 1809. In 1827 he entered the Military Academy at West Point, graduated in 1831, and served in the 5th United States Infantry till 1836, when he resigned his commission and retired to civil life. At the commencement of the rebellion he tendered his services to his country; and, being at that time a resident of Minnesota, the Governor of that State, on the 22d of July, 1861, gave him the command of the 2d Regiment of Minnesota Volunteers. He reported for duty with his regiment to General Sherman, at Louisville, and in December was assigned to the command of General Thomas, then at Lebanon, Kentucky. He commanded the 2d Minnesota at the battle of Mill Spring, on the 19th of January, 1862. After this battle he marched his regiment to Louisville, and accompanied General Thomas, by way of Nashville, to Pittsburg Landing. Having been promoted brigadier-general by the President on the 21st of March, 1862, on his arrival at Pittsburg Landing, General Buell gave him the command of a brigade in the division of General T. L. Crittenden, whom he accompanied in the campaign before Corinth, through Northern Alabama, at Battle Creek, and from Battle Creek, by way of Nashville, to Louisville. At Louisville, on the 1st of October, 1862, he took command of the entire division, General Crittenden having been assigned to the command of a corps. He joined in the pursuit of Bragg's army as far as Wild Cat, Kentucky, at which point he turned and marched his division, by way of Somerset and Columbia, Kentucky, to Nashville. In the latter part of December he marched with General Rosecrans's army to attack Bragg at Murfreesborough, and was engaged, with his division, at

BRIG.GEN.VAN CLEVE.

CAPT. E.A.OTIS

CAPT. LUCIUS H.DRURY

BRIG.GEN.

HORATIO P. VAN CLEVE.

CAPT. CHARLES A.SHEAFE

MAJOR SAMUEL D TANNEY

AND

OFFICERS OF STAFF.

Eng⁴ ᵇʸ W.G.Jackman

J.B.LIPPINCOTT & CO PHILADA

the battle of Stone River on the 31st. Having been disabled by a wound on this day, he was compelled to leave the field on the 1st of January, 1863. Upon his recovery he returned to the army and resumed the command of his division.

In the battles of Mill Spring and Stone River General Van Cleve rendered distinguished service, and won favorable mention from his commanding generals for his soldierly management. By his men he is beloved and esteemed for his gentle, kindly manners and the warm interest he manifests in their affairs. The oldest in years of any general in the Army of the Cumberland, he brings to the discharge of his duties, with his experience, the same ardor, energy, and patriotism that characterize his younger compeers. Courteous and affable in his manners, plain and simple in his life, and almost patriarchal in appearance, he presents a bright example of that patriotism which yields to the call of duty all that tends to make life comfortable and happy in its declining years.

THE STAFF.

CAPTAIN E. A. OTIS, *Assistant Adjutant-General*, was born in Calhoun county, Michigan, on the 2d of August, 1835. He commenced the study of law in the summer of 1856 at Kalamazoo, Michigan, graduated at the Poughkeepsie law-school in August, 1857, and immediately removed to St. Paul, Minnesota, where he commenced the practice of his profession in partnership with his brother, George L. Otis. He was commissioned as a lieutenant in the 2d Regiment of Minnesota Volunteers on the 19th of August, 1861, and since that time has been constantly in active service.

Upon the arrival of his regiment in Kentucky in the fall of 1861, he was appointed an aide-de-camp on the staff of Brigadier-General Johnson, then commanding a brigade in General McCook's division. He remained with General Johnson during the winter of 1861–62, marched with the command to Nashville and Pittsburg Landing, participated in the memorable battle of Shiloh, and was honorably mentioned by his superior officers for gallantry and good conduct. After the battle he was promoted to the position of assistant adjutant-general, with the rank of captain, on the staff of Brigadier-General Van Cleve. He shared in all the prominent movements of the army of the Ohio in the summer and fall of 1862, marched through Tennessee and Kentucky, and was with his command in the advance from Nashville in December. He was engaged in the battle of Stone River, where he again received honorable mention from his division-general for bravery and good conduct. Captain Otis is now assigned as assistant adjutant-general to the 3d Division, 21st Army Corps, commanded by Brigadier-General Van Cleve.

Captain Carter B. Harrison, *Division Inspector*, was born at North Bend, Ohio, September 26, 1840. At the outbreak of the war he was a student at Miami University. He entered the service of the United States on the 18th of April, 1861, as a private in a company of students raised at the university, and served with his company in Western Virginia until the expiration of the three-months enlistment. On the 12th of October, 1861, he was appointed adjutant of the 31st Regiment Ohio Volunteer Infantry, in which capacity he served until the 20th of November, 1862, when he was appointed brigade inspector on the staff of Colonel Stanley Matthews, commanding the 3d Brigade of the 3d Division of the 21st Army Corps. He was present at the battle of Stone River, after which he was promoted to a captaincy in his regiment. On the 1st of April, 1863, he was appointed acting assistant inspector-general on the staff of General Van Cleve, commanding the 3d Division of the 21st Army Corps.

Lieutenant Henry M. Williams, *Aide-de-Camp*, was born in Fort Wayne, Indiana, January 24, 1843. In January, 1862, he left the College of New Jersey, at Princeton, and entered the army as second lieutenant in the 11th Indiana Battery. October 7, 1862, he was appointed aide-de-camp to Brigadier-General Van Cleve, and served in that capacity during the battle of Stone River.

CAPTAIN LUCIUS H. DRURY, *Chief of Artillery*, was born at Highgate, Vermont, December 20, 1825. At the commencement of the rebellion he was a resident of Wisconsin, and on the 9th of September, 1861, received a commission as captain of the 3d Battery, Wisconsin Volunteer Artillery. Since October 1, 1862, he has acted as chief of artillery in General Van Cleve's division.

MAJOR SAMUEL D. TURNEY, *Medical Director*, was born in Columbus, Ohio, December 26, 1826, and entered the service, as surgeon of the 13th Ohio Infantry, May 2, 1861. March 21, 1863, he was appointed Surgeon of Volunteers, United States Army, and is now medical director upon the staff of General Van Cleve.

CAPTAIN CHARLES A. SHEAFE, *Provost-Marshal*, was born in Somerset county, Maine, September 7, 1832. At the beginning of the war he was engaged in the practice of law at Hillsborough, Ohio. Desiring to aid in the suppression of the rebellion, he was commissioned by the Governor of Ohio as a captain in the 59th Regiment of that State, and entered the service January 26, 1862. Following the fortunes of his regiment, he participated in the battles of Shiloh and Stone River, besides numerous skirmishes of lesser note.

LIEUTENANT EDWARD S. SINKS, *Acting Assistant Quartermaster*, was born in Bethel, Clermont county, Ohio, January 7, 1836. He entered the United States service in the 22d Regiment Ohio Volunteers, April 23, 1861. September 27, 1862, he was

12

appointed second lieutenant in the 59th Ohio Volunteers, and was promoted to first lieutenant and regimental quartermaster, August 1, 1862. In this position he continued until March 9, 1863, when he was detailed as acting assistant quartermaster upon the staff of General Van Cleve.

LIEUTENANT EDWARD KNOBLE, *Aide-de-Camp*, was born in Memphis, Tennessee, December 7, 1843. He entered the service of the United States, from Kentucky, September 20, 1861, as second lieutenant in the 21st Regiment Kentucky Volunteer Infantry. October 20, 1862, he was commissioned as first lieutenant by the Governor of Kentucky, and received the appointment of acting aide-de-camp on the staff of Colonel Stanley Matthews, and as such was present at the battle of Stone River. After this he was appointed acting assistant inspector-general of the 3d Brigade, and very soon afterwards received the appointment of aide-de-camp on the staff of General Van Cleve.

LIEUTENANT H. H. SHEETS, *Ordnance Officer*, was born at Indianapolis, Indiana, on the 9th of August, 1840. He enlisted in the service of the United States on the 8th of August, 1862, was commissioned as first lieutenant in the 79th Regiment Indiana Volunteers on the 21st of August, 1862, and was appointed aide-de-camp on Colonel Samuel Beatty's staff, 1st Brigade, 3d Division, 21st Army Corps, on the 22d of October, 1862, in which capacity he served up to and through the battle of Stone River, when he was appointed ordnance officer on General H. P. Van Cleve's staff.

LIEUTENANT T. FORREST MURDOCH, *Aide-de-Camp*, was born in Philadelphia, Pennsylvania, on the 2d of April, 1841. He enlisted as a private in the "Petite Zouave Guard" on the 18th of April, 1861. At the expiration of the three-months service he was commissioned by the Governor of Ohio as second lieutenant in the 13th Regiment Ohio Volunteer Infantry, and

served with his command through the campaigns in Western
Virginia, Kentucky, and Tennessee.   After the battle of Shiloh
he was promoted to a first lieutenancy, and on the 6th of
October, 1862, was detailed as aide-de-camp on the staff of
General Van Cleve, and in that capacity took part in the
battle of Stone River

Brigadier-General James St. Clair Morton and Staff, and the Pioneer Brigade.

OUR country is remarkable for the early development of her people; and this feature is well exemplified in the Army of the Cumberland. A large proportion of our generals, of our subordinates in command, of our men of responsible position, and of our gallant rank and file, are young men, the flower of the Great West. The North and the East have also given to us many of their valorous sons. A marked character among the latter is the subject of this sketch.

JAMES ST. CLAIR MORTON was born in the year 1829, in the city of Philadelphia. His father, Dr. Samuel George Morton, well known to science in Europe and in our own country as a naturalist and ethnologist, was the author of "Crania Americana," and other noted works upon that and kindred subjects. General Morton was educated at the United States Military Academy at West Point, and graduated, in 1851, second in a class numbering forty-two members. His first military duty was performed at Charleston, South Carolina, in 1851–52, as assistant engineer, in the completion of Fort Sumter and a variety of harbor improvements. He was next employed as engineer in the construction of Fort Delaware and of other river and harbor improvements in Delaware River and Bay. Subsequently he was made assistant professor of engineering at West Point, which position he filled for a period of two years, when he was appointed by the Treasury Department engineer and superintendent of the New York light-house district. Upon the completion of the necessary work of that district, he was selected by the Department of the Interior as chief engineer of the Potomac Water-Works,

BRIG. GENERAL

MORTON

CAPT. FRANCIS PEARSALL, ASST. ENGINEER.

LT. C.V. LAMBERSON, ASST. ADJT. GEN.

BRIG. GEN.

J. ST. CLAIR MORTON.

1ST LT. ABE PELHAM. A.Q.M.

LT. K.W. MANSFIELD, A.A.C.S.

AND

OFFICERS OF STAFF.

Engraved by Illman Bros.

J.B. LIPPINCOTT & CO. PHILAD^A

and charged with the duty of superintending the finished portion of the Washington Aqueduct.

In 1860, in pursuance of an act of Congress, General Morton was selected by the Navy Department to make an exploration of the Chiriqui country, Central America, to test the practicability of an inter-oceanic railroad-route across the Isthmus at a point midway between the present Panama and Nicaragua routes. With a party of eight white persons as assistants, and a squad of Indians hired as laborers, the expedition set out upon its romantic though perilous journey, in the midst of the rainy season. The country had never been explored by whites, and presented to the small band a continuity of matted jungle, dense forest, rapid rivers, and steep precipices. The journey was successfully accomplished, and an available railroad-route found. The expedition crossed mountains eight thousand feet in height, —the loftiest peaks of which commanded a view of either ocean, —and traversed swamps of vast extent, through one of which they were eight days in cutting their way. For days they subsisted solely upon cocoanuts; and monkeys, huge alligators, boa-constrictors, and the myriads of tropical insect and animal life, were their constant attendants and visitors. The sun poured its rays upon them vertically, and each person literally dwelt in his own shadow. The several months thus occupied by General Morton and his associates constitute an epoch in their lives never to be forgotten. A recital of those scenes now sounds more like romance than reality.

When General Morton returned to Washington, he was placed in charge of the entire work of the Washington Aqueduct. In March, 1861, he was sent to the Gulf of Mexico, for the purpose of putting the fortifications of the Dry Tortugas in a state of complete defence. These works are built upon a coral reef or island which rises about two feet above the surface of the Gulf of Mexico. The fort is planned to mount over four hundred guns, and is considered the strongest on the continent and the key to the Gulf.

Having been prostrated by a return of Chagres fever, General Morton was compelled to return North to recruit his health. Upon his recovery, in May, 1862, he reported for duty to Major-General Halleck, and was assigned as chief engineer to the Army of the Ohio, under General Buell. In that capacity he made the campaign of 1862, being busily engaged in superintending the building of bridges, stockades, and other defences upon railroads and pikes between Nashville and Huntsville.

Upon the march of General Buell's troops to Kentucky, Captain Morton was ordered to remain at Nashville and superintend the erection of fortifications in conjunction with Generals Negley and Palmer, it having been represented by him and others to General Buell that with proper fortifications the place could be successfully held. He pushed forward their construction most vigorously, employing the soldiery, and "pressing" the negroes of Nashville and vicinity, and teams of all kinds, without stint or scruple. The colored population of that city have probably not yet forgotten the suddenness with which his men gathered them in from barber-shops, kitchens, and even churches, and set them at work upon St. Cloud Hill, where was then a combination of rock and forest, but where now rise the frowning battlements of Fort Negley, commanding the entire city and surrounding country. The erection of this and other works unquestionably contributed greatly to the safety of the city, the rebel army not venturing an attack.

Upon assuming command of the Army of the Cumberland, General Rosecrans organized the Pioneer Brigade, as related elsewhere in this chapter, and placed General Morton in command. From that time until the present writing his labors have been constant and arduous,—at times dangerous. At the battle of Stone River he acted a conspicuous and gallant part, proving himself equally the brave soldier and the skilful engineer. The following special mention of the action of the Pioneers and their commander upon that occasion is copied from General Rosecrans's official report :—

"Among the lesser commands which deserve special mention for distinguished service in the battle is the Pioneer Corps, a body of seventeen hundred (1700) men, composed of details from the companies of each infantry regiment, organized and instructed by Captain James St. Clair Morton, Corps of Engineers, Chief Engineer of this army, which marched as an infantry brigade with the left wing, making bridges at Stewart's Creek, prepared and guarded the fort at Stone River on the nights of the 29th and 30th, supported Stokes's battery, and fought with valor and determination on the 31st, holding its position until relieved; on the morning of the 2d advancing with the greatest promptitude and gallantry to support Van Cleve's division against the attack on our left; on the evening of the same day, constructing a bridge and batteries between that time and Saturday evening. The efficiency and *esprit de corps* suddenly developed in this command, its gallant behavior in action, the eminent service it is continually rendering the army, entitle both officers and men to special public notice and thanks, while they reflect the highest credit on the distinguished ability and capacity of Captain Morton, who will do honor to his promotion to brigadier-general, which the President has promised him."

The promise of the President was faithfully redeemed, and Morton was nominated and confirmed brigadier-general, much to the satisfaction of his many friends and acquaintances. Since the battle of Stone River the Pioneers have been "the observed of all observers." General Morton planned the bridges and fortifications of Murfreesborough, which have been constructed with hardly a dollar of cost to the Government beyond the usual army expenses. The town is defended, as a base, and the work has given confidence to our army, and assured the secessionists of that region that we have gone there to stay, and intend to hold old Tennessee to the Union with triple hooks and bands of steel.

The principal characteristic of General Morton is his indomitable energy, coupled with extensive information and practical experience. He is out among his men early and late. If any special duty calls, he is always at hand. He does not say, "Go," but, "Come." This was recently exemplified at Stone River, where his new railroad-bridge was in danger of being swept away during a sudden freshet by the accumulation of drift-wood against the piers. Not satisfied with the progress of the work, he rushed into the water waist-deep, adjusted ropes to the logs and trees, and gave the command to "heave away." He is the author of several pamphlets treating of military subjects, most of which have been published by the War Department in its official reports, and also of a new theory respecting fortifications, which has occasioned considerable debate in military circles.

As we have already remarked, one of the most noticeable traits of the people of our country is their early development; and Brigadier-General Morton, with many other young generals and high officials in the Army of the Cumberland, may be cited as apt illustrations of the fact. The honors of such young men are true and lasting,—having been won through dangers, toils, and privations; and their grateful countrymen will freely acknowledge that they were well deserved.

THE STAFF.

LIEUTENANT CORNELIUS V. LAMBERSON, *Assistant Adjutant-General,* was born in New York City, and is now twenty-six years of age. Previous to the war he was in business at Chicago, Illinois, where his family still reside. He entered the service April 17, 1861, and was with the first company that occupied Cairo, as first lieutenant in the 19th Illinois Infantry. He was in the Missouri campaign, and in General O. M. Mitchel's campaign through Kentucky, Tennessee, and Alabama, also in the skirmishes of Tuscumbia and Leighton, Alabama, and Reynolds's Station, Tennessee, and participated in the battle of Stone River.

LIEUTENANT ABRAM PELHAM, *Quartermaster,* is a native of Delaware county, New York, and is now thirty years of age. His residence is Tecumseh, Michigan. He entered the service November 7, 1861. With his regiment he served under General

Buell in Kentucky and Tennessee, most of the time acting as quartermaster. He was with the army at Nashville when General Rosecrans assumed command, and was afterwards in the battle of Stone River. His rank and position is that of first lieutenant in the 13th Michigan Volunteers.

LIEUTENANT KILBERN W. MANSFIELD, *Commissary of Subsistence*, is a native of Stanbridge, Canada East, and is twenty-six years old. His residence is in Otsego, Michigan, where before the rebellion he was a law-student. October 24, 1861, he enlisted in the 13th Michigan Volunteers as a private. He served through Buell's campaigns, and was in the battles of Shiloh, Stevenson, Alabama, and Stone River.

LIEUTENANT THOMAS J. KIRKMAN, *Inspector*, was born in Jacksonville, Illinois, in 1837, and at the time of the outbreak of the rebellion was an attorney-at-law in his native town. May 7, 1861, he entered the service in the 21st Illinois Infantry, and served in Missouri and Arkansas under General Curtis, with General Rosecrans in Northern Mississippi, and with General Buell in the fall of 1862. He has been in the following skirmishes and battles :—Mount Washington, Fredericktown, Perryville, and Stone River.

LIEUTENANT JOHN B. REEVE, *Aide-de-Camp*, is a native of Rush county, Indiana, twenty-eight years of age, and enlisted in the 37th Indiana Regiment on the 10th of September, 1861. He served under General Mitchel in Kentucky, Tennessee, and Alabama, and was present at the cannonading of Chattanooga by General Negley in June, 1862. During the investment of Nashville by the rebels in October, 1862, he was on duty with the garrison, and in the battle of Stone River took an active and gallant part. He is a farmer by profession.

FRANCIS PEARSALL, *Assistant Engineer and Volunteer Aide-de-Camp*, is a native of Pennsylvania, and resides in Philadelphia.

His age is thirty-one; and he is a merchant and manufacturer as well as engineer. He served with General Morton in Central America and at Fort Jefferson, Key West. He joined the army at Nashville about the 20th of November, 1862, as assistant engineer, and in the battle of Stone River rendered valuable service.

THE PIONEER BRIGADE.

A NEW feature in the Army of the Cumberland is the Pioneer Brigade. The war for the suppression of the rebellion has peculiar difficulties and necessities. The armies are so large, and the territory traversed by them is so extended, that the construction and repair of roads, bridges, and railways have become matters of serious, often of vital, importance.

Early in the war, General Rosecrans saw the necessity of an arm of the service which should be organized specially for the performance of mechanical and pioneer duties, and upon taking the command of the Army of the Cumberland he organized the Pioneer Brigade from the ranks of the 14th Army Corps, by the following general order:—

"GENERAL ORDERS, No. 3.

"HEAD-QUARTERS 14TH ARMY CORPS, DEPARTMENT OF THE CUMBERLAND,
BOWLING GREEN, November 3, 1862.

"There will be detailed immediately, from each company of every regiment of infantry in this army, two men, who shall be organized as a pioneer or engineer corps attached to its regiment. The twenty men will be selected with great care, half laborers and half mechanics. The most intelligent and energetic lieutenant in the regiment, with the best knowledge of civil engineering, will be detailed to command, assisted by two non-commissioned officers. This officer shall be responsible for all equipage, and shall receipt accordingly.

"Under certain circumstances, it may be necessary to mass this force: when orders are given for such a movement, they must be promptly obeyed.

"The wagons attached to the corps shall carry all the tools, and the men's camp-equipage. The men shall carry their arms, ammunition, and clothing.

"Division quartermasters will immediately make requisitions on chief quartermasters for the equipment, and shall issue to regimental quartermasters on proper requisition.

"EQUIPMENT FOR TWENTY MEN—ESTIMATE FOR REGIMENT.

Six Felling-Axes.	Six Hammers.
Six Hatchets.	Two Half-Inch Augers.
Two Cross-Cut Saws.	Two Inch Augers.
Two Cross-Cut Files.	Two Two-Inch Augers.
Two Hand-Saws.	Twenty lbs. Nails, assorted.
Four Hand-Saw Files.	Forty lbs. Spikes, assorted.
Six Spades.	One coil Rope.
Two Shovels.	One Wagon, with four horses or
Three Picks.	mules.

"It is hoped that regimental commanders will see the obvious utility of this order, and do all in their power to render it as efficient as possible.

"By command of Major-General ROSECRANS.

"ARTHUR C. DUCAT,
"*Lieutenant-Colonel, and Acting Chief of Staff.*
"OFFICIAL:—
"——— *A. A. A. G.*"

The troops detailed in accordance with the above order numbered about three thousand men.

The duties assigned to them were the repair and construction of roads and bridges, the manœuvring of the pontoon-bridge equipage, the erection of fortifications, and, generally, the duties of sappers and miners. The distinction between their duties and those of the Michigan regiment of mechanics and engineers of the same army is that the Pioneers move with the advance of the army, all the work that is required there devolving upon them, while the latter is chiefly employed on the lines of communication.

The Pioneers, having been assembled in a camp of instruction at Nashville, were consolidated and organized as a brigade, the object being to enable the various descriptions of labor and workmanship demanded by the exigencies of a large army to be executed with more harmony and system, with less inconvenience, and with greater despatch than could be attained were it necessary to call upon each regiment in the army, whenever a bridge, a block-house, or a field-work had to be constructed, for its detail of mechanics suitable for the work, its share of the tools, materials, &c. A great difficulty would have been met with in endeavoring to concentrate the labor of the Pioneers, had they not been consolidated, in the details from each regiment not being able to rendezvous with their tents or cooking-utensils, seeing that each two men would belong to a separate mess in their regiment; nor could they have been organized, so as to draw their rations, to post guards, and to do military duty as it should be done,—viz. systematically and under the direction of the same officers. Many other sources of confusion and delay and bad work will present themselves to the commanding general; but enough has been mentioned to prove the soundness of his order consolidating the details of pioneers.

In that order it was required that the Pioneer details from the "centre" grand division of the army, now the 14th Army Corps, should constitute the first battalion, those from the "right," now the 20th Army Corps, the second, those from the "left," now the 21st Army Corps, the third. Each battalion was subdivided into ten or twelve companies of eighty or a hundred men, each of which was formed by aggregating the details furnished from the four or five regiments composing a single brigade. The field and company officers of the battalion were assigned according to rank,—the ranking lieutenant in each acting as lieutenant-colonel, and so on, the ranking lieutenant in each brigade detachment of eighty or a hundred men acting as captain of the pioneer company constituted by such detachment.

The campaign of Murfreesborough gave constant employment to the Pioneers; and the results of their labor show that the men and the organization are well adapted to the requirements of the service. Their constructions have been substantial and scientific, and are executed in a uniform style.

The system of administration for the safe-keeping and transportation of the immense store of implements and materials necessary on a campaign remote from supplies has proved judicious. As a unit, the brigade has on the battle-field proved itself as soldierly as any other troops in the army, and when separated into detached parts, working at distant points and on long lines of road, its discipline has always been observed.

There are at present in the ranks of the Pioneers sufficient proportions of the following-named trades and specialties,—viz.: military engineers, civil engineers, railroad engineers, surveyors, architects, sailors, draftsmen, printers, bridge-builders, carpenters, machinists, millwrights, wheelwrights, coopers, blacksmiths, saddlers, sawyers, woodmen; and there is no description of work that an army in the field can require, in all the multiplied occasions which arise in an enemy's country, that cannot be executed with despatch by the brigade, which is fully equipped with the proper tools for all purposes.

The Pioneer Brigade now comprises four battalions, numbering about three thousand eight hundred effective men. It has some fifty wagon-loads of tools, implements, and building and constructing apparatus of all descriptions. There is also attached to the brigade a pontoon-train of eighty boats, forty of which they can move at one time in line of march. A system of order and celerity has been adopted by which this brigade can plan and superintend work in two hours' time from the commencement, employing ten thousand men in its execution.

The labors already performed by this brigade are immense. It has fortified every railroad-bridge between Gallatin and Nash-

ville and between Nashville and Murfreesborough, and in such
a manner that the enemy have not as yet risked a single attack
upon them.   In and about Nashville it performed very important
work, especially in completing and perfecting the works of Fort
Negley, rendering it one of the strongest fortresses in the West.
As our army advanced upon the enemy from Nashville, the
brigade erected two bridges over Stewart's Creek, obtaining a
portion of the timbers by tearing down some large log houses in
the vicinity.   During one night it threw a temporary bridge,
some eighty feet in length, across Stone River, upon which troops
crossed and re-crossed.   Since the battle the brigade has built
two fine bridges over Stone River near Murfreesborough, at
points where the pike and railroad cross that stream.

Its last work has been, with the assistance of details of troops
of the line, the erection of the fortifications at Murfreesborough,
—said to be the largest and finest field-works upon this continent.
The several massive forts, the thousands of feet of high embank-
ments upon every hand, the long lines of warehouses for the
storing of army supplies, alongside of which railroad-tracks
have been laid, and the comfortable houses (frames) which have
been torn down elsewhere and re-erected within those works,
all speak volumes in praise of the efficiency of the Pioneers.
It must not, however, be inferred that the work upon the fortifications is performed by them alone.   The heavy earth-work—
the digging, the wheeling and ramming—is done by details of
soldiers and by hired refugees and contrabands.   During several
weeks some seven thousand workmen were thus at work upon
these fortifications, the Pioneers planning and superintending,
and executing the wood-work, &c. of the magazines and block-
houses.

Not only as composed of faithful workmen, but also of brave
soldiers, is the Pioneer Brigade known throughout the Army of
the Cumberland.   As will be seen elsewhere in this volume, it
occupied most responsible and important positions during the
battles of Stone River.   During the hottest of the battle of the
31st, when the fortunes of the day wavered between contending

hosts, the Pioneers were ordered by the general commanding to hold an important position with their battery (the Chicago Board of Trade Battery), which was successfully accomplished, the enemy being repulsed three times at that point with signal slaughter.

The members of this organization are proud of its success and its deserved popularity. The men are ever industrious and cheerful, and ready at a moment's call. So true is it that labor in camp, as well as at home, is the polishing process, to develop, preserve, and brighten the physical and mental forces. The Pioneer Brigade is a complete success,—fully realizing all that was expected of it by its practical, far-seeing originator, Major-General Rosecrans. No such body of skilful, energetic, intelligent men can be found in all rebeldom,—a little army of patriots who fight for their country equally well whether armed with the musket, the broad-axe, or the spade.

First Michigan Engineer Corps and its Officers.

THIS notable regiment was organized September 12, 1861, and left the State December 17, 1861. Crossing the Ohio River, it reported to General Buell, commanding the Army of the Ohio, and encamped near Louisville, December 18, 1861. Colonel Innes, with three companies, was ordered to report to General McCook; Lieutenant-Colonel Hunton, with three companies, to General Thomas; Major Hopkins, with two companies, to General Nelson; and Captain Yates, with two companies, to General Mitchel. Each of these generals commanded separate divisions of what was then the Army of the Ohio. The store-houses and forts at Green River were built by this command; and, in compliment to the colonel, one of the forts was named by General McCook Fort Innes. Miles of road were constructed by Lieutenant-Colonel Hunton's command, in order to enable General Thomas to reach Mill Spring. Had it not been for their energy, the ammunition and supplies could not have reached General Thomas's troops. Major Hopkins's command was with General Nelson, and for its excellent service was highly complimented by the general. Captain Yates's command built several bridges, and cleared the road from Green River to Bowling Green of all the obstructions placed there by the rebels. So rapidly was this work done that the march of the column was not interrupted. These two companies, supporting Loomis's Battery, were the first troops to enter Bowling Green. They rendered most efficient service in crossing the army over Barren River, the bridges being gone. When Buell's army arrived at Nashville, the regiment was ordered to duty under Colonel Innes; but so highly did General Mitchel value the detachment of Captain Yates that he persuaded General Buell to allow him

192

COLONEL INNES

LIEUT. COL. K. A. HUNTON.   MAJOR. ENOS HOPKINS.

COL. W. P. INNES

1ST MICH. ENGINEER

LIEUT. HENRY F. WILLIAMS Q.M.   ADJUTANT. CHARLES W. CALKINS.

AND

OFFICERS OF STAFF.

Eng⁴ by J. Rogers

J. B. LIPPINCOTT & CO. PHILADA

to retain them. The eight companies under Colonel Innes opened and repaired the Tennessee & Alabama Railroad as far as Columbia, Tennessee, thus greatly facilitating the shipment of supplies for Buell's army, then on the march to Shiloh. They also built several road-bridges; and the rapidity with which they performed their work enabled General Buell to reach the field of Shiloh in time to rescue the army of General Grant. In front of Corinth the Michigan Engineers were busily engaged in building roads, planting siege-guns, erecting hospitals, &c.

Captain Yates's command in the mean time was engaged with General Mitchel in Northern Alabama, who acknowledged that he was indebted to them for his supplies being always furnished and communication being kept open. Between Corinth and Decatur Colonel Innes's command repaired the railroad-track, and built two thousand seven hundred and fifty-eight feet of bridging, at an average height of forty feet, in thirty days. After the evacuation of Corinth, the engineers marched along the line of the Memphis & Charleston Railroad in advance of the whole army, and opened the road as far as Bear Creek. At this place they were attacked by a rebel force, which they quickly dispersed. They then opened the railroad as far as Decatur.

On the 3d day of July they arrived at Huntsville, and were joined by Captain Yates's detachment. The regiment then proceeded to open the Nashville & Chattanooga Railroad to Murfreesborough, building a large bridge at Cowen's Station, several smaller ones at different points on the road, and clearing out the tunnels. They opened the Tennessee & Alabama Railroad in an almost incredibly short space of time, building a bridge over Elk River six hundred and fifty feet long, three bridges over Richland Creek, each one hundred and forty feet long and thirty feet high, and rebuilding twelve hundred feet of trestle-work sixty feet high,—the most extensive piece of railroad trestle-work in the West. They also cleared out a tunnel three-quarters of a mile in length, which completed the opening of the road from Huntsville to Nashville.

At Stevenson, Alabama, the regiment built one hundred pontoon-boats in three days, which, however, were rendered useless by the falling back of Buell's army to Kentucky. Upon the evacuation of Stevenson Lieutenant-Colonel Hunton's three companies were the last troops to leave the post, and were highly complimented by the general commanding for the manner in which they discharged their duties, having destroyed every thing that could be of use to the enemy, and burned the railroad and other bridges as fast as crossed by the rear trains.

While at Stevenson, Colonel Innes, with five companies, was ordered to open the Louisville & Nashville Railroad, recently destroyed by the enemy; but while so engaged, having built three hundred feet of bridging and laid several miles of track, they were called off to take the advance of the entire army, which position they occupied throughout the campaign.

At Bowling Green the regiment was engaged in strengthening the fortifications at that place. Major Hopkins's three companies were in the hottest of the fight at Chaplin Hills (Perryville); while the rest of the regiment, with the commands of Major-General Crittenden and the late lamented General Sill, were not idle.

On taking leave of the Army of the Ohio, General Buell made personal mention of Colonel Innes, Lieutenant-Colonel Hunton, and Major Hopkins, complimenting them highly and giving the regiment great credit. They were the only field-officers of whom he made personal mention, and the regiment was the only one which he mentioned specifically.

The regiment arrived at Nashville November 7, 1862, when Colonel Innes was desired by General Rosecrans to open the Louisville & Nashville Railroad to Gallatin, and also to build the three bridges over Mill Creek on the Nashville & Chattanooga Railroad,—all of which was accomplished in the short space of two weeks.

On the 1st of January, 1863, while the battle of Stone River was raging, the Michigan Engineer Regiment was stationed at Lavergne for the purpose of protecting the supply-trains of the main army.

At one P.M. of that day they were attacked by General Wheeler's cavalry and a battery of artillery, the force numbering four or five thousand men.   Single-handed and alone, the regiment fought the rebels for four hours from behind breast-works of brush-heaps and rails, when the enemy sent in a flag of truce demanding an immediate and unconditional surrender. But the brave colonel told the officer bearing the flag to say to General Wheeler, "WE DON'T SURRENDER MUCH."   They again attacked, were repulsed, and left the field covered with their dead.   This was the first instance in the history of the war where a force attacked in this manner did not surrender.

By this gallant fight the entire rear of the army and nearly all its baggage-train were saved.   General Rosecrans in his official report gave the regiment credit for whipping ten times its number, and characterized the affair as one of the most brilliant of the war.

While at Lavergne, the regiment wielded the axe vigorously, and furnished sufficient ties to relay three miles of railroad-track. They were then ordered to Murfreesborough.   After remaining at Murfreesborough a · few days, the officers requested General Rosecrans to let the regiment open the Nashville & Chattanooga Railroad from Nashville to Murfreesborough, promising to do it in *ten* days.   On the *ninth* day the cars ran into Murfreesborough.   A citizen company had been for six weeks endeavoring to open the road, but had been almost daily driven off by guerrillas.

Colonel Innes next requested permission to open the Tennessee & Alabama Railroad to Franklin.   The work was done before the general commanding was aware it had been commenced.   The regiment has since constructed within the notable fortifications at Murfreesborough a large store-house capable of holding five million rations, a magazine one hundred and forty feet long, thirty-two feet wide, twelve feet high, and *bomb-proof*, and an ordnance-building one hundred feet long, thirty feet wide, and fourteen feet high,—all within thirty days' time. Its officers claim that there has not been an engagement of the army, from the battle of Mill Spring to the battle of Stone River, in which the regiment or some portion of it has not been engaged.   The Engineer Regiment is recognized as an independent corps, is not brigaded, and reports direct to the commanding general of the department.

Since the regiment has been in the service, they have laid over ten thousand lineal feet of railroad, built a number of highway bridges, erected store-houses, and made over twelve miles of corduroy road at Shiloh, Mill Spring, and elsewhere. But one man has ever been injured while at work; and he is now on duty.   The effective force of the regiment, May 1, 1863, is eight hundred men.

OFFICERS OF THE FIRST MICHIGAN ENGINEERS.

COLONEL WILLIAM P. INNES entered the service September 12, 1861. By profession a civil engineer, he was engaged for a number of years on railroads in the State of New York. In 1853 he went to Michigan, and became largely engaged in the railroad-operations of that State. At the time of his entering the service he was chief engineer and superintendent of the Amboy, Lansing & Traverse Bay Railroad. This is the largest "land-grant" railroad in the United States, except the Illinois Central. His residence is at Grand Rapids, Michigan.

LIEUTENANT-COLONEL KINSMA A. HUNTON entered the service September 12, 1861. Previous to that time he was engaged on various railroads in Massachusetts and New Hampshire. In 1853 he removed to Marshall, Michigan, as master-mechanic of the middle division of the Michigan Central Railroad, which position he left to enter the service. Residence, Marshall, Michigan.

MAJOR ENOS HOPKINS was formerly extensively engaged in manufacturing at the East. In 1854, business brought him to Michigan, where he has since resided. He became identified with this regiment on its first organization, leaving a large and lucrative business to devote his energies to the service of his country. Residence, Jackson, Michigan.

MAJOR JOHN B. YATES, a graduate of Union College, has been all his life actively engaged in civil engineering. He commenced his career in New York. He accompanied Colonel Innes to Michigan in 1853, and has been with him ever since. He entered the service as captain of Company A. He was promoted to be junior major, January 1, 1863, for gallant conduct at Lavergne. Residence, Ionia, Michigan.

SURGEON WILLIAM H. DE CAMP graduated at Geneva (New York) Medical College in 1847. After practising medicine in Western New York for eight years, he went to Michigan, and at the time of his joining the service he left a large and lucrative practice in the city of Grand Rapids, where he resides.

ASSISTANT SURGEON WILLOUGHBY O'DONOUGHUE graduated at Albany (New York) Medical College in 1850, and practised four years in the New York hospitals. In 1854 he moved to Michigan, where he has since resided. He entered the service September 12, 1861. Residence, Albion, Michigan.

JUNIOR ASSISTANT SURGEON WILLARD B. SMITH graduated at the Medical College, Ann Arbor, Michigan, in 1861. He was appointed by Governor Blair, December, 1862. Residence, Ann Arbor, Michigan.

FIRST LIEUTENANT HENRY F. WILLIAMS, *Regimental Quarter-master*, entered the service as a private in Company I, September 15, 1861. He was appointed sergeant-major September 18, 1861, commissioned as second lieutenant January 30, 1862, as first lieutenant July 30, 1862, and appointed regimental quarter-master December 1, 1862.   Residence, Grand Rapids, Michigan.

SECOND LIEUTENANT CHARLES W. CALKINS, *Adjutant*, entered the service, as a private in Company B, September 26, 1861. He was promoted to sergeant-major January 30, 1862, was commissioned as second lieutenant July 30, 1862, and appointed adjutant December 1, 1862.   Residence, Grand Rapids, Michigan.

MAJ. GEN. STANLEY

COL. R. H. G. MINTY.

COL. ELI LONG.

MAJ. GEN.

DAVID S. STANLEY.

COL. W. B. STOKES.

CAPT. ELMER OTIS.

AND

OFFICERS OF STAFF.

Eng^d by W. G. Jackman

J. B. LIPPINCOTT & CO. PHILAD^A

THE CAVALRY SERVICE AND ITS OFFICERS.

Major-General David S. Stanley.

DAVID S. STANLEY, Major-General of Volunteers, and Captain in the 4th Regular Cavalry, was born in Cedar Valley, Wayne county, Ohio, June 1, 1828. His father was a farmer. At the age of fourteen, upon the death of his mother, he became a member of the family of Dr. L. Fairstone, a physician of the county, with whom he remained until he was nearly nineteen. He then began in earnest the study of medicine; but, before he had completed or fairly begun his course, he was, in the spring of 1848, appointed a cadet at the Military Academy at West Point, by the member of Congress from that district, Hon. Samuel Lahm.

Entering the same summer, he graduated July 1, 1852, standing eighth in a class which numbered about one hundred and twenty at first, but graduated only forty-two. Among his classmates were Major-Generals McCook, Hartsuff, Slocum, and Sheridan, and Brigadier-Generals Hascall, Crooks, and Woods. Five members of the class were from Ohio, and all of them are now generals in the Federal service. After graduating, he was brevetted second lieutenant in the 2d Dragoons,—now the 2d Cavalry,—and for one year attended the school of instruction at Carlisle Barracks. In the spring of 1853 he was detailed as assistant to Lieutenant Whipple, in charge of the survey of a route for the Pacific Railroad along the 35th parallel, by way of Fort Smith and Albuquerque, New Mexico. Upon this service he remained nine months, crossing the continent to Santiago, California, by a then new and unexplored route, starting from an Indian village north of the Gila River, and going by way of the Mohave Valley to San Bernardino. Having in the mean while been promoted to a second lieutenancy, he returned to Washington at the close of his services in this expedition, in company with the present rebel General Hardee. Lieutenant Stanley's company was then stationed at Fort Chadbourne, Texas, whither he proceeded and remained one year on ordinary garrison duty.

In the spring of 1855, two regiments of infantry and two of cavalry were added to the army, in accordance with an act of Congress authorizing such increase. To command these new forces, officers were selected in equal proportions from civil life and from the army. Lieutenant Stanley now received a commission as first lieutenant in the 1st Cavalry, of which the late Major-General Sumner was colonel. The regiment rendezvoused at Fort Leavenworth, Kansas Territory, and Lieutenant Stanley was assigned to Company D, of which General George B. McClellan was then captain. Ill health, however, would not allow him to join his command; and he was transferred to duty at Newport Barracks, where he remained during the winter and spring. Thence he was ordered to take charge of the recruits at Governor's Island, New York harbor, and proceed with them up the Missouri River to join the force of General Harney, then commanding an expedition against the Sioux Indians. At the conclusion of this, he rejoined his regiment, then on duty in Kansas, engaged in preserving peace and order in the Territory, which was being ravaged by the two opposing parties, borderruffians and jayhawkers. In pursuit of one or the other of these, Lieutenant Stanley marched over the Territory, from one border to another. The lieutenant-colonel of the regiment was the present rebel General Joseph E. Johnston, who, to do him justice, took a bold, manly stand against the border-ruffians overrunning Kansas. A large force from Missouri, under command of Dave Atchison, threatening Lecompton and Lawrence, he interposed to save them, assuring the Missourians that they could only succeed in their attempt by walking over the force under his command. As this consisted of a full battery and a regiment or two, he thought they would find it a rather difficult thing to do. In this position Colonel Johnston was sustained by Lieutenant Stanley, with the other officers of his command, and the invading force, under these circumstances, deemed it advisable to retire. The fall and winter were spent in similar efforts to quiet the distracted Territory.

In the spring of 1857, Lieutenant Stanley was married to Miss Anna M. Wright, daughter of Surgeon Wright, U.S.A., of Carlisle Barracks, Pennsylvania. Soon afterwards he was engaged in an expedition against the Cheyenne Indians. The forces marched in two columns, which joined each other at Pike's Peak, on the spot where Denver City now stands. At that time, however, it was an unbroken wilderness, the presence of gold not being even suspected. From this point the expedition started on pack-mules, with twenty days' provisions, which were made to last two months. Supplying itself with buffalo-meat by the way, the expedition, after a most remarkable trip, came upon the Indians on Solomon's Fork, who were drawn up in line of battle about two hundred yards distant,—an unusual circumstance, and perhaps the first instance of the kind on record. Colonel Sumner at once ordered a sabre-charge, which put them to flight with the loss of several killed. This, with the destruction of their village, compelled them to sue for peace. Upon returning from this expedition, he was ordered to the Indian Territory west of Arkansas, and in the spring of 1858 was engaged in scouting, making several expeditions, in one of which he surprised a party of Comanches, killing several of them and scattering the remainder. For gallant conduct in these operations he was highly complimented by General Scott, in general orders. The next summer and winter he was stationed upon the frontiers of Northern Texas.

At the outbreak of the rebellion, having previously been promoted to a captaincy, he was stationed at Fort Smith, Arkansas. Here he rendered inestimable service to the Government by assisting in the successful abandonment of Forts Smith, Wachita,

Arbuckle, and Cobb. Notwithstanding the large rebel force in Arkansas and Texas, all the ammunition, clothing, and other property of the Government was safely brought away. With the garrisons of these forts he marched from Fort Cobb to Fort Leavenworth, Kansas, being one month on the road. Upon reaching the latter place, Captain Stanley found the rebellion under full headway and Missouri in a blaze of excitement. Many officers were joining the rebels, and many were uncertain what to do. The times were dark, the prospect gloomy; but he wavered not a moment. From the first he was uncompromisingly loyal; and now, with his whole heart in the work, he gave his influence and his aid to the support of the Government.

As a first step, he marched his command to Kansas City, Missouri, and took possession of that place. A considerable force of rebels had gathered at Independence, under the ostensible command of Colonel Hollaway, an old United States officer. The State of Missouri, though much excited, had not actually seceded from the Union, and there was really no war in the State, except that carried on by bushwhackers and guerrillas not as yet in any regular service. Under such circumstances, the gathering at Independence partook more of the character of a mob than of a military camp. Still, as it might prove the germ of something formidable, Captain Stanley determined to ascertain its real character and the intentions of those composing it. Accordingly, a few days after arriving at Kansas City, he proceeded with a flag of truce to Independence, and had an interview with Colonel Hollaway. While engaged in remonstrating with the latter upon his course, Captain Stanley observed that the rebels were closing in around him and his command. He directed Colonel Hollaway's attention to it, and asked him if his men did not mean to respect the flag of truce. Upon this Hollaway stepped up and waved the men back with his hand; but they were intoxicated and maddened with liquor, and either misunderstood the motion or purposely disobeyed it, and fired upon Captain Stanley and his company, killing Colonel Hollaway and one of the Federal soldiers. The interview had taken place in a narrow lane, and the rebels had ranged themselves upon each side of it. The day was hot, dry, and dusty, and Captain Stanley's men, in making their escape, raised such a cloud of dust that their exit was not noticed by the rebels, who continued a rapid firing across the lane, killing and wounding a considerable number of their own men. Discovering their mistake, they spent the night in a fierce quarrel among themselves, and the next day, disgusted with this experience, retreated southward to join Price. Colonel Hollaway was acting in good faith, and fell a victim to the drunken fury of the men whom he could not restrain.

Shortly after this, Captain Stanley crossed the river and captured a large squad of rebels on their way to Price's army. Marching southward with General Sturgis in pursuit of Price, he joined General Lyon at Clinton, Missouri, and participated in the affair at Dug Springs and the battle of Wilson's Creek. In this engagement he won due credit by his gallant conduct and by the skilful manner in which he handled his men. He also accompanied the expedition which captured Forsyth, Missouri, and there had a horse killed under him. After the battle of Wilson's Creek he returned with his command (the 4th Cavalry) to Rolla and St. Louis, and afterwards joined General Frémont in his march to Springfield. During the summer he received several offers of a colonelcy from Illinois regiments, and also one from an Iowa regiment, all of which he declined; and on the 28th of September, 1861, he was appointed a brigadier-general of volunteers. During a part of the following winter he was unable to take the field, because of a broken leg, caused by his horse falling with him. Upon his recovery he was assigned to General Pope, then on his expedition against New Madrid. At the latter place General Stanley's division was the first to occupy the trenches in front of the enemy's position, which compelled them to evacuate the town. It engaged in the operations at Island No. 10, and was the second to cross the Mississippi to the Tennessee shore at the time of the capture of that place.

After this he moved with the remainder of Pope's army down

the river to Fort Pillow, and, its capture being deemed impracticable, returned and ascended the Tennessee River, in pursuance of orders from General Halleck at Corinth. Here General Stanley had command of the 2d Division of the Army of the Mississippi, a part of which was engaged in the battle of Farmington. May 28, 1862, in a second engagement, he repulsed an attack of Cleborne's division upon our left wing. The fight was a desperate one, in which two of Stanley's batteries were captured by the enemy and were retaken in a few seconds thereafter. With his division he entered Corinth after the evacuation, and joined in pursuing the fleeing rebels as far as Booneville. Returning to Corinth, the division remained in camp until the latter part of August, when it occupied the railroad from Iuka to Decatur. After the battle of Iuka, in which it was engaged, it returned to Corinth and participated in the battle at that place. Here General Stanley commanded the left of the centre, supporting and occupying the ground about " Battery Robinette." It was the first time his troops had had occasion to use the bayonet; but the two regiments of his division which charged used it well. After the rebels retreated, General Stanley joined in the pursuit to Ripley, forty miles south, when the army was ordered to return to Corinth. Had the pursuit been continued, he is confident the entire rebel army would have been scattered or destroyed, and Vicksburg would have been occupied and held.

Upon General Rosecrans's assignment to the command of the Department of the Cumberland, he applied for the transfer of General Stanley to the command of the cavalry in that department, which request was granted, and he joined the army at Nashville in November, 1862. Since then he has been engaged in many raids, skirmishes, and heavier engagements,—a more detailed account of which will be found in the history of the operations of the Army of the Cumberland, as narrated in this volume. By his cavalry the enemy were first driven out of Franklin, where a considerable fight occurred. He next made pursuit of Forrest, then drove the rebels from Liberty and

Bradyville, and, lastly, was engaged in the battles of Stone River and Franklin. At the battle of Stone River he added largely to his already great reputation by the marked ability and skill which he displayed. Of his services there General Rosecrans thus speaks in his official report:—

"Brigadier-General Stanley, already distinguished for four successful battles,—Island No. 10, May 27, before Corinth, Iuka, and the battle of Corinth, —at this time in command of our ten regiments of cavalry, fought the enemy's forty regiments of cavalry, and held them at bay, and beat them wherever he could meet them. He ought to be made a major-general for his services, and also for the good of the service."

General Stanley is now in the prime of early manhood, and bids fair to give yet many days of gallant and honorable service to his country. In the annals of this war no brighter record than his can be found. Bold and dashing, his action is tempered and guided by skill and prudence, which make the successful commander.

Colonel Robert H. G. Minty.

COLONEL ROBERT H. G. MINTY, 4th Michigan Cavalry, commanding the 1st Cavalry Brigade, was born in the county of Mayo, Ireland, on the 4th of December, 1831. On the 9th of January, 1849, he was commissioned ensign in the 1st West India Regiment of the British Army, in which he served for five years in the West India Islands, British Honduras, and on the west coast of Africa. In September, 1853, he retired from the English service, in consequence of a severe attack of inflammation of the liver, contracted at Sierra Leone, and came to America. On the call being made for cavalry regiments, he joined the 2d Michigan Cavalry as major; but before that regiment left the State he was promoted to lieutenant-colonel of the 3d Michigan Cavalry, and on the 28th of November, 1861, took that regiment to Benton Barracks, at St. Louis. His command formed part of the Army of the Mississippi, which marched from Commerce. Missouri, on the 1st of March, 1862, under General Pope, and it took an active part in the capture of New Madrid on the 13th and of Island No. 10 on the 23d of March.

After the arrival of the Army of the Mississippi before Corinth, Colonel Minty was engaged in constant skirmishes with the enemy. He commanded the cavalry in the first battle of Farmington, and was favorably mentioned for his conduct on that occasion by Major-General Pope, in General Orders No. 104, of the 4th of May, 1862. On the 4th of July he was again favorably mentioned in General Orders No. 81, by Major-General Rosecrans, for having at Twenty-Mile Creek,—south of Blackland, Mississippi,—on the 16th of June, attacked and defeated four times his number of rebel cavalry,—his force consisting of one hundred and sixty-eight officers and men of his own regiment, the enemy's of Brewer's and Lay's regiments of mounted infantry, numbering eight hundred and seventy men. On the 4th of July, he commanded an expedition of one hundred and eighty-one men who marched from Rienzi to Salem, Mississippi, a distance of fifty-three miles into the enemy's country, returning after an absence of six days, with a loss of only two men.

On the 21st of July he was commissioned colonel of the 4th Michigan Cavalry, then about to be organized. He left the 3d at Tuscumbia, Alabama, on the 1st of August, 1862, having up to that time led the regiment in thirty-six battles and skirmishes, in every one of which it had been successful. He opened camp in Detroit, Michigan, on the 14th of August, and on the 28th mustered in eleven hundred and eighty-seven enlisted men, and the full quota of officers. Contracts were at once awarded for the purchase of horses, the last of which were received on the morning of the 26th of September; and at ten o'clock A.M. the entire regiment started for Kentucky, and arrived at Jeffersonville, Indiana, on the 28th, where there was considerable delay in procuring supplies; but on the 10th of October the regiment marched from Louisville for Perryville, leaving tents, wagons, and camp-equipage of every kind behind them. They joined

General Buell at Danville on the night of the 13th, and marched at one o'clock on the morning of the 14th, taking the advance in the attack on Stamford. Subsequently they followed Bragg as far as Crab Orchard, and were then sent in pursuit of John Morgan. At Munfordsville Colonel Minty was joined by the entire cavalry force under Colonel Kennett, and, after an unavailing chase of ten or twelve days, was, on the 7th of November, detached, and ordered to report to General Crittenden at Gallatin. He crossed the Cumberland the same afternoon, drove in the enemy's pickets, and sent one company to Nashville, where it arrived in safety, much to the surprise and gratification of General Rosecrans. At three o'clock next morning the infantry and artillery crossed, when Colonel Minty immediately mounted and advanced on Lebanon, driving the enemy's pickets for seven miles, and went into town at a gallop with five hundred and forty-three men, driving out Morgan with seven hundred and fifty men and two pieces of artillery, and capturing nine wagons, twenty-six mules, five thousand bushels of wheat, and large quantities of clothing and provisions of every kind. From that time until the 22d of November he scoured the country in every direction, having constant skirmishes with the rebels.

On the 22d of November, he was ordered to Nashville to report to General Stanley, chief of cavalry, and was assigned to the 1st Brigade, Colonel E. M. McCook commanding. Constant picket-duty and skirmishing, with two or three important and successful expeditions, occupied him while at Nashville. On the 23d of December, Colonel McCook obtained leave of absence, and Colonel Minty was assigned to the command of the brigade. On the 26th the army advanced from Nashville, the 1st Brigade in advance, on the Murfreesborough pike, met the enemy five miles out, and fought and drove them to Lavergne that night. Heavy skirmishing with the enemy's cavalry took place every day until the 29th, when the army arrived before Murfreesborough. The 1st Brigade, nine hundred and fifty strong, fought Wheeler, Wharton, and Buford, with two thousand five hundred men and two pieces of artillery, for three hours, on the 31st of December,—General Stanley leading one and Colonel Minty two charges,—and drove the rebels from the field with great loss.

From that time until the present the cavalry arm of the Army of the Cumberland has been continuously at work, constantly engaged and, almost without an exception, successful. Some of its most important expeditions and operations we will briefly mention.

On the 10th of January, the 1st Brigade, eight hundred strong, started in pursuit of Forrest, who had gone towards Harpeth Shoals with fifteen hundred men, and drove him across the Harpeth. The rising of that river rendering further pursuit impossible, they returned to camp after an absence of ten days, during which time seventeen men were badly frost-bitten.

On the 31st of January, the 1st Brigade, with the 4th U.S. Cavalry and part of the 3d Brigade, under Colonel Minty, marched with three days' rations. On the same day the 7th Pennsylvania made a sabre-charge, killing three and wounding forty-nine of the 8th Confederate Cavalry and taking a large number of prisoners, of whom ninety-four were sent the next morning to Murfreesborough. Forrest and Wheeler having gone to the attack on Fort Donelson, the cavalry followed them for the purpose of cutting off their retreat, but, learning near Charlotte that they had escaped through Centreville, returned to Murfreesborough, having been absent fourteen days, the only casualties being two men wounded, and having captured one hundred and forty-one prisoners, including two colonels, one major, and fourteen other commissioned officers.

On the 3d of March, the 1st and 2d Brigades, and two companies of the 4th U.S. Cavalry, under the command of Colonel Minty, moved out with four days' rations, and met the enemy, four hundred strong, at Rover. The 7th Pennsylvania, one hundred and seventy men, supported by the 4th Michigan and 4th Regulars (in all, four hundred and thirty-seven men), charged and drove them back on an encampment of six hundred more at Unionville, charged again, and drove them all at a gallop to within five miles of Shelbyville, where they ran into the infantry pickets and captured seven of them. The result of this dash was sixty-four prisoners, seventeen wagons, forty-four mules and harness, forty-three tents, and a large quantity of commissary stores. The command then marched to Franklin, and took the advance in the attack on Van Dorn at Thompson's Station, south of Franklin, where the squadron of 4th U.S. Cavalry and sixty men of the 7th Pennsylvania drove Armstrong's rebel brigade off the ground, killing five and taking thirteen prisoners. Crossing Rutherford's Creek in the face of Forrest's force, and driving him from the field with heavy loss, Colonel Minty followed Van Dorn to Duck River at Columbia, where the destruction of the bridge prevented further pursuit.

The 1st Brigade had the advance in the pursuit of the enemy to and attack on his position at Snow's Hill, east of Liberty, where the rebels met with a most signal defeat.

On the 20th of April, the 1st, 2d, and 3d Brigades, and the 4th U.S. Cavalry, under Colonel Minty, formed part of the expedition to McMinnville under General Reynolds. Colonel Long, with the 2d Brigade, destroyed the railroad about twelve miles west of McMinnville, and burned a train of cars and a large quantity of bacon. The 7th Pennsylvania took the advance in going into McMinnville, which place was entered at the gallop, completely surprising the rebels. Colonel Martin (rebel) was killed, and Major Dick McCann wounded and taken prisoner, in a charge made by Lieutenant Thompson, of the 7th Pennsylvania, with the advance-guard, twenty-five men. One hundred and thirty prisoners were taken, three railroad-bridges and large quantities of army stores were destroyed, in addition to what was burned by the mounted infantry under Colonel Wilder, and the expedition returned to camp, after an absence of six days, without the loss of a man.

14

Colonel Eli Long.

COLONEL ELI LONG, of the 4th Ohio Volunteer Cavalry, was born in Woodford county, Kentucky, June 27, 1836. His ancestors were from Wales on his father's side and from Germany on his mother's side, and his grandfather Long was among the early emigrants from Virginia to Kentucky. In January, 1852, he entered the Military Institute near Frankfort, Kentucky. Graduating at this institution in June, 1855, he went to Washington City, where he found employment in the Bureau of Construction under the Secretary of the Treasury and the immediate charge of Major A. H. Bowman, U.S. Engineer. He was assistant computer on the Treasury extension, and made the working drawings for the vault in the Treasury Building.

On the 27th of June, 1856, he was appointed second lieutenant in the 1st U.S. Cavalry, at the instance of Secretary Guthrie, and joined his company (H) at Lecompton, Kansas, in September, remaining nearly two months in that Territory. He was then detailed on recruiting service, and stationed at New Albany, Indiana, where he remained until April, 1857, when he rejoined his command at Fort Leavenworth, Kansas. In May he joined the column under General Sumner, then colonel of the 1st U.S. Cavalry, at a point very near Denver City, Colorado Territory. During this campaign he was distinguished by being the only white person in the command who killed an elk,—which he did after a long and desperate struggle, and great personal danger.

After the return of the Cheyenne expedition in the fall, Lieutenant Long was stationed at Fort Riley, Kansas, during the winters of 1857 and 1858, and was the first officer to escort the mail, in the month of December, 1858, to the crossing of the Arkansas River by the road to Santa Fe, New Mexico, a trip of nearly five hundred miles, for one hundred and fifty miles of which he was exceedingly ill, compelled to lie down in an ambulance provided for him. He succeeded, however, in getting his command safely back to Fort Riley, with the exception of six mules, most of which were frozen to death at night when tied up to the wagons. On one expedition his company was armed with Burnside's carbine, and he was ordered by the Ordnance Department at Washington to make a report upon them, which he did, receiving a letter of thanks for his "excellent and intelligent report" from the Chief of Ordnance at Washington. Changes and improvements were made in that arm in accordance with his suggestions; and those improvements appear on the Burnside's carbines issued by the Government at the present day.

In January, 1859, he made a march from Fort Riley of some two hundred and fifty miles through Kansas Territory, on which several teamsters and others—including himself—were frost-bitten, some of them severely. In the spring he marched, with a portion of his regiment, to the vicinity of the crossing of the Arkansas River by the Santa Fe road, where he formed a camp for the protection of the road, and remained there until the next fall, when the command, with the exception of Lieutenant Long and forty men, returned to Fort Riley. In the mean time war had broken out with the Kiowa Indians, and they had already killed some twelve of our people, including one lady and a mail-party, the most of whom were buried by Lieutenant Long, who was left behind with these forty men to escort two mails from Walnut Creek to the crossing of the Arkansas River, through the country of the Kiowas and the Comanches. This duty he performed, marching twenty-five miles per day for more than twenty days. Lieutenant Long was in command of his company upon an expedition to establish Fort Wise, Colorado Territory, and hauled the first load of timber to build that post, —a work which was complimented by European papers. This post was built with hardly any other implements or materials than those furnished by the woods and rock-beds. Here he remained until November, 1861, without any thing especial occurring except the capture by him in the summer of 1861, at a point some thirty miles southeast of Fort Wise, of a mounted and well-armed company of thirty-eight rebels *en route* from Denver City, Colorado Territory, to join Price in Missouri. They were taken completely by surprise, Lieutenant Long and forty-one of his men (dismounted) being within less than fifty feet of the party, with carbines cocked and at an aim, before they knew he had left the post. In this expedition he marched one hundred and twenty miles in thirty-two hours, with the loss of but one horse out of fifty-five, and captured fifty-two horses and mules. There were five or six murderers in the party, and a considerable number of horse-thieves, all of whom were safely lodged in jail at Denver City. When it is remembered that this party, had they not been apprehended, would probably have captured and destroyed two Government trains of un-guarded wagons, each loaded with ordnance and other stores, and worth from one hundred and fifty thousand to two hundred thousand dollars, *en route* to New Mexico, it will be acknow-ledged that it was a most important capture. In November, 1861, he went to Fort Leavenworth, Kansas, and remained there with his command until the 10th of February, 1862, when it was ordered to report to General Buell in Kentucky.

Arriving at Louisville about the 16th of February, Lieutenant Long served on Buell's escort until he was relieved by General Rosecrans. He was in the battle of Perryville until one o'clock in the day, when he was called in by General Buell. He was also with his regiment at the battle of Stone River, where he was wounded, while at the head of his company, in the left arm. On the 22d of February, 1863, Lieutenant Long was appointed colonel of the 4th Ohio Cavalry, on the re-commendations of Generals Stanley and Rosecrans. Some two weeks after he took charge of the regiment, about two hundred men under his command, and a smaller number of the 3d Ohio Cavalry, defeated a brigade of rebel cavalry at Bradyville, Tennessee, his regiment taking fifty prisoners. Again, at Snow Hill, near Liberty, Tennessee, with about one hundred dismounted men of his regiment, Colonel Long de-feated a part of three regiments of rebel cavalry, killing and wounding several, and driving them more than a mile through a thick wood and across a winding ridge.

In General Reynolds's late expedition to McMinnville, Colonel Long, in command of the 2d Cavalry Brigade, one hundred men of the 2d Kentucky Cavalry, and one company of the 1st Middle Tennessee,—in all about five hundred and fifty men,—burned a trestle-work on the Manchester & McMinnville Railroad, seven miles from Manchester, and three or four others between that and the large trestle-work at Morrison's Station, including the latter; also a locomotive, a train of cars, and the railroad depot, marching over forty-five miles in one day, and capturing many rebel soldiers on the road.

Colonel William B. Stokes.

WILLIAM B. STOKES, colonel commanding the 1st Middle Tennessee Cavalry, was born in North Carolina in 1814, and removed to Tennessee in 1818. He was raised a farmer, and has lived in the neighborhood of his present home—Liberty, De Kalb county—since his first settlement in the State. He has long been in public life, having twice represented his county in the Legislature, and De Kalb and Wilson counties in the State Senate for one term. He has ever been a Whig in politics, and at the time South Carolina seceded he represented the fourth district of Tennessee in the United States Congress. When the war broke out, he took a decided stand for the Government, and has been an unconditional Union man ever since. He worked and spoke earnestly against separation, and was the only ex-member of Congress in Middle Tennessee who made a regular list of appointments for public speaking and kept them until the very day of election.

The State having seceded and his Congressional term having expired, he remained in private life until July 22, 1862, when he was commissioned colonel, with authority to raise a cavalry regiment. He had scarcely enlisted a single company when he was put on duty by the Government, and has been almost constantly in active service up to this time. His regiment was recruited rapidly, almost entirely in Middle Tennessee, and has rendered important service, particularly by furnishing a large proportion of the guides and scouts necessary for the various expeditions that are continually sent into the adjacent country. Colonel Stokes has been in many skirmishes and smaller engagements, routing Colonel Bennett's guerrillas in October last, and participating in the battle of Lavergne, and in General Negley's fight on the Franklin pike, during the investment of Nashville. In the Stone River battles, from first to last, he was actively engaged, making a remarkable charge upon a largely superior force of rebel cavalry under Wheeler, on Wednesday evening, December 31, driving them for the distance of a mile, killing many and capturing a large number of horses. Upon the retreat of the rebels, with his regiment he followed them eight or ten miles on the Manchester road, constantly and sharply skirmishing with their rear.

On the 14th of March, 1863, ill health compelled him to resign his command, but, having again become able for duty, he was on the 16th of April, at the earnest request of his neighbors and friends and the men of his regiment, recommissioned, and again assumed command of his regiment. During the time, he was out of the service, he accompanied Colonel Wilder on his expedition to Snow Hill, camping one night within a mile of his own house. The next morning he proceeded thither with four or five men in the advance, and succeeded in capturing a number of rebel pickets who were breakfasting there. This was done by an ingenious device. One man was dressed in "butternut," and, advancing cautiously, beckoned to the rebel picket to come to him. Not suspecting any danger, he did it readily enough, and when he reached the place was quietly shown a number of concealed men and ordered to drop his gun. Resistance being useless, he had no alternative; and this operation was repeated until the whole were secured.

Colonel Stokes is but one of several thousand Tennesseeans in the Union service. Their patriotism is self-sacrificing, and allows nothing to stand in its way. For their country they have abandoned their home, family, friends, fortune,—every thing. Escaping from rebel despotism at the risk of their lives, they have shown their devotion to principle and their love of liberty by fighting for it. The services they have rendered, and are every day rendering, are invaluable. Their perfect knowledge of the country admirably fits them for guides and scouts; and as such they are constantly employed with manifest advantage to the service. In every contest they have acquitted themselves creditably; and many have sealed their devotion to the Union by their blood. When the history of this war is fully made up, no brighter page will be found than that on which is recorded the story of these loyal Tennesseeans, clinging to the Government and the faith of their fathers with a zeal and determination which cannot fail to excite the admiration of posterity.

Captain Elmer Otis.

CAPTAIN ELMER OTIS, of the 4th United States Cavalry, was born February 27, 1830, in Westfield, Massachusetts, and was left an orphan at an early age. His grandparents moved to Huntington, Lorain county, Ohio, when he was three years old, where he was raised by them to work on a farm. In the beginning of 1849 he procured, by his own exertions, an appointment at West Point, through the influence of Hon. Joseph M. Root, M.C. of that district. He graduated in 1853, in a class numbering fifty-two, and received a commission as brevet second lieutenant in the 1st United States Infantry. He served in Texas at different points until the middle of March, 1855, when he was promoted to a second lieutenancy in the 4th United States Infantry, and ordered to join his regiment, then serving in Oregon.

At this time four new regiments were being raised, two of cavalry and two of infantry. Having a partiality for cavalry service, he applied in person to President Pierce, and obtained the appointment of second lieutenant in the 1st United States Cavalry. He was promoted to a first lieutenancy on the 28th of February, 1856, and joined his company about the 1st of May the same year. Soon after he was detailed to take a company of recruits, belonging to the 1st Dragoons, to New Mexico, and marched them there, arriving with horses in good condition. He met their regiment about seventy miles from El Paso, turned over the recruits, and returned to Fort Leavenworth in October, and found himself detailed for recruiting service and ordered to proceed to Rock Island, Illinois, and open a rendezvous. He arrived there about the 1st of November, and remained until about the 1st of April, 1857, when he was ordered to return to his regiment at Fort Leavenworth, where it was preparing for a trip across the plains. The company to which he belonged formed a part of the force under Lieutenant-Colonel Joseph E. Johnston, for running the southern boundary of Kansas, as well as to co-operate with other troops against the Indians. This expedition returned to Fort Leavenworth the last day of October, and Lieutenant Otis remained in garrison during that winter, meanwhile making several small expeditions through Kansas with the object of preventing lawless bands from accomplishing their raids for plunder, &c. On the 18th of March, 1858, two companies of the 4th United States Cavalry were detailed upon the Utah expedition under the command of Lieutenant-Colonel Hoffmann. Lieutenant Otis's force was one of the companies detailed. He arrived at Fort Bridger, with supplies for the army, on the 9th of June. During this trip the command encountered several severe snow-storms, and on the morning of the 1st of May the snow was two feet four inches deep on a level. These two companies of Lieutenant Otis's regiment were the advance-guard of the army that marched into Salt Lake City. After making here several reconnoissances, the two companies started back on the 6th of August, and arrived at Fort Leavenworth on the 22d of October, having marched over three thousand miles in one year.

About the 1st of May, 1859, Lieutenant Otis with his force started, under command of Major John Sedgwick, on an expedition against the Kiowa Indians, and chased the Indians all summer, but came up with only a small party, all of the warriors of which were killed but two, and the squaws and children, together with about forty ponies and mules, were captured. During this summer, about the 1st of August, his command was ordered to establish and build Fort Wise (now Fort Lyon), on the Upper Arkansas. He arrived in the vicinity about the 28th of same month, established the post, and commenced laying stone for the quarters and stables on the 1st day of September. By the end of the month the horses of the four companies were in good stone stables; and the last of October found the men in comfortable stone houses.

Here Lieutenant Otis continued until the 1st of May, 1861, when he was promoted to a captaincy. About the same time he was left in command of the post, with six companies, and so remained until the 22d of November, when he received orders to take the two companies of the 4th United States Cavalry and proceed with them to Washington. He left Fort Wise on the 25th, and arrived at Fort Leavenworth the 18th of December. Here he reported to Major-General Hunter, and went into camp until further orders at Fort Leavenworth. On the 10th of February he received orders to report to General Buell at Louisville, and from thence was sent to West Point, at the mouth of Salt River.

About the middle of July, on his own application, General Buell assigned Captain Otis to duty, to report to Major Granger, at that time commanding the post of Louisville. He was then placed in command of Park Barracks. His regiment was subsequently the escort to General Buell, and accompanied him until he was relieved, in October last, by General Rosecrans. Captain Otis was during several months on General Buell's staff as chief of couriers. He immediately instituted a system of posts and relief stations connecting different points, somewhat upon the French courier system, and which he continued under the command of Major-General Rosecrans. In this way he has sent despatches thirty-two miles in two and a half hours.

Notwithstanding his position as chief of couriers, Captain Otis still retained command of his regiment. At Nashville he received authority to recruit from the volunteers to fill his thinned ranks. About the last of November, recruiting was commenced, and the regiment was filled up, and two more companies raised according to the new organization. He also obtained six hundred fresh horses, rearmed and equipped the whole regiment, and drilled his men very thoroughly.

This regiment was employed in running all the courier lines of different posts of the army, and, besides, formed the escort of General Rosecrans until he arrived in front of Murfreesborough. On the 4th of January, Captain Otis was ordered to report to General Stanley, chief of cavalry, and was relieved as chief of couriers upon his own application.

For gallant conduct and valuable services during the battle of Stone River, Captain Otis and his command were specially mentioned by the general commanding. Since then he has been constantly in the field except during a short period of illness; and his dashing, well-drilled cavalry, under General Stanley, have often made their mark upon the enemy. Captain Otis's record is an honorable one, showing years of active and zealous service in behalf of his country.

GENS AND COLS OF THE ARMY

BRIG. GEN. W. B. HAZEN.

COL. JOHN T. MILLER.

ANS C. HEC.

COL. W. Y. STOUGHTON.

W. BURKE.

BRIG. GEN. WILLIAM P. CARLIN.

Engraved by J.C. Buttre, New York.

OF THE CUMBERLAND.

J.B. LIPPINCOTT & CO. PHILADA

SKETCHES OF NOTABLE OFFICERS.

Brigadier-General Hazen.

WILLIAM B. HAZEN, Brigadier-General of Volunteers, was born in West Hartford, Windsor county, Vermont, in the year 1830. His father, Stillman Hazen, was a grandson of General Moses Hazen, a native of Connecticut, whose commission as brigadier-general bears the oldest date of any of that grade in the first Federal army of the Revolution. He was early associated with Generals Ethan Allen and Israel Putnam in their public services; and the friendship of the families was further strengthened by the marrying of the father of the present General Hazen to a direct descendant of "Old Put." When the colonies had achieved their independence, General Hazen and his two brothers, both of whom held commands in the army, emigrated to Vermont and located there the land granted for their valued services. The parents of General Hazen removed to Hiram, Portage county, Ohio, in 1833, and settled upon the farm which they now occupy. Here a family of three sons and three daughters have been reared. The sons and a grandson—all of the family capable of bearing arms—are now officers in the Union army. General Hazen was reared a farmer, receiving such an education as the limited means of his parents could command, until nearly twenty-one years of age, when, after much fruitless effort, he obtained the appointment of cadet at the national military school at West Point. At the time of entering this institution—in September, 1851—he was within two weeks of the limit which would have rejected him. In 1855 he graduated most creditably, and in July of the same year was appointed brevet second lieutenant 4th United States Infantry. Two months after this he was promoted second lieutenant in the 8th Infantry; but before informed of this promotion he had started to join his company in the 4th Infantry, then serving in California and Oregon. In October, the month of the commencement of the famous Indian wars of 1856, '57, he joined his company at Fort Inge, on the head-waters of the Sacramento, and on the following day was leading his men to Fort Lane, Rouge River, where the war had already become serious. Keeping the field during this campaign, he served creditably until April, 1857, when he joined his new company in the 8th Infantry at Fort Davis, Texas. Here he was soon actively engaged with the Comanches of Western Texas. He commanded successfully in five fights, until, in December, 1859, in a hand-to-hand contest with the Indians, he received a dangerous wound, the ball passing through the left hand, entering the right side, and passing into the muscles of the back, where it yet remains. Eight days afterwards, Lieutenant Hazen with his little force reached the settlement of Western Texas; but it was not until February, 1860, that, having submitted to repeated surgical operations, he was sufficiently recovered to set out for the Northern States. This closed the uniformly successful Indian service of the subject of this notice. Enterprise in the conception and energy and capacity in the execution of his plans were sufficiently apparent to attract the notice of the commander-in-chief of the army, and he was upon four occasions complimented in general orders. General J. E. Johnston, then assistant inspector-general of the army, in his report of the inspection of Lieutenant Hazen's post, commended that officer's "activity, perseverance, and courage" in his successful expeditions against the Indians; and the people of Texas, upon the occasion of his departure, after receiving his wound, held a public meeting at San Antonio, and adopted resolutions expressing their sense of the importance of his services to the State, and presenting him an elegant sword. The resolutions were as follow:—

" *Whereas*, Lieutenant W. B. Hazen, U.S.A., in his services for the protection and defence of our Western frontier from the ravages of hostile Indians, by his uniformly prompt, timely, and determined action in their pursuit, by his deeds of marked daring and bravery in their encounter,—of which he bears the unmistakable evidence in a dangerous wound received in his last Indian engagement, and which for a time threatened to prove fatal,—and by his repeated success in the recovery and restoration to our suffering frontier settlers of their stolen property, has deservedly won the confidence, high esteem, and admiration of the people of Texas, and especially of those upon the extreme frontier and of this community, and alike distinguished himself as a true and gallant officer, winning a high position in the army.

" *Resolved*, That the thanks of this community and the entire frontier are hereby tendered him.

" *Resolved*, That as an evidence of our appreciation of his distinguished services, and a token of our sympathy for his suffering and wounds, and as an acknowledgment of his noble gallantry, a sword be presented him.

" *Resolved*, That a copy of these proceedings be forwarded to the Secretary of War."

In consequence of the wound mentioned, twelve months' leave of absence was granted Lieutenant Hazen, with permission to travel in Europe. The expiration of that time found him with his arm still in a sling, but applying for duty; and in February, 1861, he was appointed Assistant Professor of Infantry Tactics at West Point Military Academy. In that capacity he served until his entrance upon the volunteer service in the present war. In June, 1860, he had been brevetted first lieutenant for meritorious services, and on the 1st of April, 1861, was promoted first lieutenant in the 8th Infantry. May 14, 1861, he was appointed captain of the 17th Infantry, but declined, having at the same time been promoted to a captaincy in his own regiment.

At the breaking out of the rebellion, Captain Hazen could not remain contentedly from the field of active service, and made strenuous efforts to obtain a release from duty at West Point. His ability was recognized in his own State, and, when the call for the first three hundred thousand men was made, many gentlemen of influence were anxious to have him in the army of volunteers which Ohio was then putting into the field. This influence availed, after the failure of his own efforts, and Captain Hazen was granted leave of absence to take command of the 41st Ohio Volunteer Infantry. This regiment was organized at Cleveland; and when Colonel Hazen joined it for duty, September 15, 1861, the enlistment of the men was not half accomplished. Taking it in this state, he conducted with a vigorous hand its recruiting, organization, and instruction,—assuming himself the entire schooling and drilling of the officers and sergeants until they were competent to instruct the men.

Being ordered to Gallipolis, on the Ohio River, then threatened by the rebels of Western Virginia, Colonel Hazen projected an important movement upon them at a point beyond the reach of the Union troops at that time in Virginia, but, although asking no force but his own regiment, failed to obtain permission of the department commander to march into his territory. In December, 1861, Colonel Hazen, with his command, joined the army then organizing at Louisville, Kentucky, under Major-General Buell. During these and subsequent marches and changes of station, the system of instruction of Colonel Hazen was carefully attended to; and when the regiment reached Nashville, in February, 1862, each company officer could drill the battalion, and had been instructed in every duty pertaining to his position.

On the 6th of January, 1862, General Hazen was placed by General Buell in command of the 19th Brigade of the Army of the Ohio, including his own regiment, and belonging to General Nelson's (4th) Division. The care and labor that had been bestowed upon his regiment was extended to the entire brigade now under his command.

At the battle of Shiloh, April 7, 1862, Colonel Hazen acted a conspicuous part. His brigade, arriving upon the field at the conclusion of the first day's fight, was immediately put in line, and, with the rest of Nelson's division, moved upon the enemy at daylight. General Hazen's skirmishers opened the second day's fighting on the left of the army; and for an hour his brigade was engaged under a sharp fire before the action became general. During this time, being in advance of the other troops, he was obliged to protect his position from flank attack, which he did successfully, and finally led his brigade in so fierce a charge that, although one-third of the officers and men were struck down before reaching the rebels, they forced back both of the enemy's lines, and captured a battery at the second line. During the subsequent operations of General Halleck at Corinth, and in the campaign of General Buell in Northern Mississippi and Alabama, Colonel Hazen served with his brigade. In the operations in Kentucky during the fall of 1862 his brigade performed many important services, driving the rebels sharply from Danville on the 12th of October. In the subsequent pursuit he was intrusted with the advance of General Crittenden's corps from Mount Vernon to London,—for eight days fighting with and driving Bragg's rear-guard through the passes of the mountains, until recalled from the pursuit.

The prominent part taken by General Hazen in the operations immediately preceding the battle of Stone River, and in that struggle, have been presented to the public in every complete published account of them. From the time of leaving Nashville until the battle, his brigade was twice engaged with the enemy; and in the great contest he maintained through the day the position taken in the morning. The official acknowledgment of the brilliant service there rendered is contained in the report of General Rosecrans. It was nothing less than the protection of the left of the army from being turned under simultaneous attacks by superior forces in front and flank, and this at the critical period of the fight, when, the right wing and centre having been driven back, General Rosecrans was exerting every power to form a new line. On the 2d of January he commanded a portion of the troops that drove Breckinridge's men from the field. When the army took position at Murfreesborough after the battle, Colonel Hazen's brigade was selected to hold the town of Readyville, twelve miles from the army, on the extreme left, and the most dangerous post in the line.

The subsistence for cavalry, artillery, and baggage-animals was drawn from the country in front; and, though this was constantly occupied by Morgan's and other cavalry forces, no loss was sustained. On the contrary, the enemy were constantly annoyed by expeditions against them, resulting in the capture of greater or less numbers of men and horses. On the 2d of April an expedition in command of General Hazen surprised a rebel camp at Woodbury, killing three and capturing about twenty-five men and horses, the entire baggage-train, with camp-equipage, &c., and dispersing the whole force.

From these operations and those during the pursuit of Bragg in Kentucky, "Hazen's Brigade" is probably better known among the rebels than any other in the army. It has never been attacked, though the enemy has often had four times its strength within a day's march. Finally, the general, always daring, has never attempted to lead his men against the enemy and failed: the rebels have never seen the backs of his men.

General Hazen received his commission as brigadier-general of United States Volunteers in April, 1863, after being three times nominated to the Senate by the President. He had for more than a year held a general's command, and had led it through two great battles and several minor operations. In treatment of subordinates, possessing in a remarkable degree the faculty of quickly and accurately judging the character and fitness of men, no one is kinder to those who make faithful effort to perform their duties, whether successful or not, but there are none more severe with those who wilfully neglect their obligations. Understanding thoroughly every detail of official duty, there is no portion of a soldier's life too trivial to receive his attention. With a vigilance that during three years of active service has never left him a moment unprepared or liable to surprise, a quickness to perceive and readiness to strike a weak point,—with a hearty love of the flag his fathers fought for, and, in the discharge of duty, an honesty not to be tampered with,—Brigadier-General William B. Hazen gives high promise that his future service will increase in value with the enlargement of the means intrusted to his control.

Brigadier-General William P. Carlin.

BRIGADIER-GENERAL WILLIAM P. CARLIN was born in Greene county, Illinois, November 24, 1829. In 1846, at the age of sixteen, he entered the United States Military Academy at West Point, where he graduated in 1850. He was assigned to the 6th Regiment U.S. Infantry as brevet second lieutenant, and joined his company at Fort Snelling, Minnesota Territory, in October, 1850. In 1851 he was promoted to the second lieutenancy of Company H, 6th Infantry, then stationed at Fort Ripley, Minnesota. Nearly four years were passed at the latter post and in the Indian country. In October, 1854, his regiment was ordered to Jefferson Barracks, Missouri, where it remained till March, 1855, when it scouted over the Western plains on the Sioux Expedition under General Harney. Having passed through that expedition, he was stationed at Fort Laramie, Nebraska Territory, as quartermaster and commissary of the post, and was occasionally in command of detachments and companies in expeditions against the Indians. In the summer of 1857 he commanded a company in the expedition of Colonel Sumner against the Cheyenne Indians, who were defeated and routed in a battle on Solomon's Fork, Kansas Territory, August 29, 1857. In September, 1857, he, with his company, was ordered into Kansas to protect the legal voters at the October election. In the spring of 1858, the 6th Infantry was ordered to join the Utah Expedition under General A. S. Johnston, then encamped at Fort Bridger, Utah Territory. Lieutenant Carlin acted as commissary of the regiment until its arrival near the North Platte River, near Bridger's Pass of the Rocky Mountains, when he, with forty men, was selected by the commanding officer to accompany the engineer company, under command of Lieutenant J. C. Duane, to open the road through that pass, to build bridges, ferries, &c. The regiment arrived at Fort Bridger about the 1st of August, 1858, when it was learned that the Mormon trouble

15

had been adjusted. The regiment then received orders to proceed to California. The journey was resumed, and the regiment arrived at Benicia, California, on the 15th of November, 1858, having marched two thousand two hundred and fifty miles during the season. Lieutenant Carlin's company, after a rest of three weeks, proceeded north to the head of Russian River, and was stationed in that region of Indian country for eighteen months. For nine months of the time, Lieutenant Carlin was in command of Fort Bragg, a military post on the Pacific coast and on the Mendocino Indian Reservation. From July, 1860, to September 1, Lieutenant Carlin—having been promoted to a captaincy on the 2d of March, 1860—was on recruiting service for the Regular Army. On the 15th of August, 1861, he was offered the colonelcy of the 38th Illinois Volunteers, which was accepted. He had previously been elected lieutenant-colonel of a New York regiment, and had been proffered the lieutenant-colonelcy of an Iowa regiment,—which were declined, as he had intended if he entered the volunteer service to go with men from his native State. Immediately after organizing his regiment it was ordered to Ironton, Missouri, where Colonel Carlin assumed command, being the senior officer present. The force consisted of the 21st, 33d, and 38th Regiments Illinois Infantry, and four companies of the 1st Indiana Cavalry. About the 14th of October, the rebel forces in Southeast Missouri made demonstrations of attack against Pilot Knob, and, as a preliminary, attacked the guard at the Big River bridge, on the Iron Mountain Railroad. A large portion of the force under Colonel Carlin being detailed to guard this railroad, his available force was not deemed sufficient to advance against the rebel forces, which had been concentrated, about the 15th of October, at Fredericktown, twenty-one miles southeast of Pilot Knob, and which were estimated at six thousand, under General Jefferson Thompson. General Frémont, commanding that department, being absent from St. Louis on his march for Springfield, Missouri, his adjutant-general, Captain McKeever, took the responsibility of ordering the 8th Wisconsin Volunteers, and part of the 24th Missouri Volunteers, with four pieces of artillery, to reinforce Colonel Carlin at Pilot Knob. The last of these forces arrived at the Knob on the 18th of October, and it was Colonel Carlin's wish to march against the enemy on the day following; but, the officer in command of the artillery having insisted that it was necessary to drill his horses, it was decided to delay one day. The forces marched on the 20th of October, and arrived at Fredericktown on the morning of the 21st. But the rebels had very hastily retreated, in consequence of having received information of the movement against them from Cape Girardeau, under Colonel J. B. Plummer. Plummer had sent a despatch to Colonel Carlin, calling for reinforcements, which despatch was intercepted by Thompson, who, not expecting an attack from Carlin, supposed that its possession would prevent the command of the latter from co-operating with Plummer. Thompson finally concluded to attack Plummer, and returned to the vicinity of Fredericktown and commenced the battle. The rebels were totally routed, the forces of Carlin and Plummer having formed a junction at Fredericktown about an hour before the fight began. This defeat of Thompson destroyed the rebel power in Southeast Missouri, except at the post of New Madrid, which they held until captured by General Pope in the spring of 1862.

Soon after General Halleck assumed command of the Department of the Missouri he appointed Colonel Carlin commander of the district of Southeast Missouri, which position he held till March, 1862, when he was relieved by General Steele. Colonel Carlin next commanded a brigade, under General Steele, in the expedition into Arkansas, and marched as far as Jacksonport, when he was ordered with the 21st and 38th Illinois Volunteers to Corinth, Mississippi, via Cape Girardeau, Missouri. He made forced marches to Cape Girardeau, and embarked immediately for Hamburg Landing, where he arrived on the 24th of May. Joining General Pope's army, he was at Farmington when the rebels evacuated Corinth, and participated in the pursuit of the enemy to Booneville, Mississippi. After returning from this pursuit, his command—a brigade of General Davis's division—formed part of an expedition towards Holly Springs, but was recalled before reaching that point, and till August was stationed in the vicinity of Jacinto, Mississippi. About the 10th of August, Colonel Carlin's brigade, with the remainder of the division, then under command of General R. B. Mitchell, was ordered to join Buell's army in Tennessee. Marching via Iuka, Eastport, Florence, Columbia, and Franklin, it arrived at Murfreesborough, Tennessee, about the 1st of September. After a rest of a day or two, the command proceeded to Nashville, and thence to Louisville, by forced marches. From Louisville Colonel Carlin marched with Buell's army to Perryville, Kentucky, where he was engaged in the battle of October 8, 1862. Colonel Carlin's brigade distinguished itself in that battle, as will be seen by reference to the official reports of General Mitchell, commanding his division, General Gilbert, commanding the corps, and General Buell, commanding the army. Colonel Carlin continued his march to Crab Orchard, Kentucky, and from thence to Bowling Green,—where General Rosecrans assumed supreme command,—and subsequently to Nashville, Tennessee. When the army of General Rosecrans moved towards Murfreesborough, on the 26th of December, Colonel Carlin commanded the 2d Brigade of General Davis's division, which had a sharp engagement with the rebel cavalry, under General Wharton, at Knob Gap, near Nolensville. Colonel Carlin's brigade here charged a strong position of the enemy, held by artillery and dismounted cavalry, and gallantly carried the position, capturing one gun and a few prisoners. On the 30th of December his brigade had a severe engagement with the enemy near Murfreesborough. On the 31st it passed through the terrific engagement of that day, and continued before the enemy till their retreat on the night of the 3d of January. Colonel Carlin's command suffered more severely during this series of engagements than any other in the army. The official reports of Brigadier-General Davis, commanding the division, and of General Rosecrans, commander-in-chief, afford sufficient evidence of the gallantry of that bri-

gade, consisting of the 21st and 38th Illinois, 101st Ohio and
15th Wisconsin, and the 2d Minnesota Battery. Colonel
Carlin was, subsequently to the battle of Stone River, promoted to the rank of brigadier-general, and still retains the
command of his old brigade.

The Scandinavian Regiment and its Colonel.

ONE regiment in the Army of the Cumberland—the 15th
Wisconsin Volunteers—is composed entirely of Scandinavians,
mostly Norwegians. With the exception of Company A, enlisted in Illinois, and Company K, from Minnesota and Iowa,
the regiment was raised in the State whose name it bears. Its
organization, which was effected about the 1st of October, 1861,
was mainly due to the efforts of its colonel, Hans C. Heg.

On the 2d of March, 1862, it left Camp Randall, at Madison,
Wisconsin, for the seat of war. Forming a part of the expedition against Island No. 10, it was the first regiment that landed
on the Tennessee shore on the 8th of April. On the 31st of
March, being yet quartered on transports, in company with the
27th Illinois, under the command of Colonel (now General) Buford, it started on an expedition against Union City, Tennessee,
where there was a rebel force about fifteen hundred strong.
The town and camp were completely surprised on the morning
of April 1, and the rebels driven in every direction. Nearly one
hundred horses and mules, several wagons, and all the camp-
equipage were captured, without the loss of a man by the
attacking party. On the 11th of June, eight companies of
the regiment left Island No. 10 for Union City, and thence
marched to Corinth and Jacinto, Mississippi, where they were
attached to Colonel Carlin's brigade, in which they remained
until recently.

Since the regiment joined Colonel Carlin's brigade, the histories of the two have been identical. It marched with General Mitchel's division from Iuka, Mississippi, by way of Florence, Alabama, and joined Buell's army at Murfreesborough on the 1st of September. Continuing with the Army of the Ohio, it endured all the hardships of the rapid march to Louisville. Leaving that city on the 1st of October, it participated in the battle of Chaplin Hills (or Perryville); and Company B of the regiment, deployed as skirmishers, were the first to enter the village of Perryville the morning after the engagement. Subsequently it took part in a skirmish near Lancaster, Kentucky, where a few of its men were slightly wounded. Reaching Nashville as a portion of General Rosecrans's army, it left that city on the 26th of December, as a part of General McCook's corps. On the same day, in company with the remainder of the brigade, it charged on a rebel battery at Knob Gap, and captured one gun and carriage, four horses, and three prisoners, Colonel Heg being the first man to reach the gun. In the battle of Stone River it played a conspicuous part, passing through that long and bloody contest with the cool courage and determined valor that have ever characterized its action, winning encomiums from the brigade commander, Colonel Carlin, and others, at the time.

On the 29th of April, by command of General Rosecrans, it was transferred from the 2d to the 3d Brigade of the 1st Division, on which occasion the following order was issued by Brigadier-General Carlin:—

"Special Order No. 2.

"Head-Quarters 2d Brigade, 1st Division, 20th Army Corps, April 29, 1863.

"The general commanding the brigade has to regret that the interests of the service have induced Major-General Rosecrans, commanding the department, to transfer the 15th Wisconsin Volunteers, Colonel Hans C. Heg, from this brigade.

"In parting with this regiment, the general commanding tenders to both officers and men his sincere thanks for the soldierly and honorable manner in which they have conducted themselves on all occasions. In camp they have been obedient and faithful to duty, and on the battle-field they have had no superiors in gallantry.   They may feel assured that they will carry with them the best wishes of the general commanding and the other regiments of this brigade.

> "By order of Brigadier-General W. P. CARLIN,
> "*Commanding 2d Brigade.*
> "SAMUEL P. VORIS,
> "*Captain and Acting Assistant Adjutant-General.*"

Though the Scandinavians in this country now number about one hundred thousand, scattered through the various States of the Union, but mostly in the Northwest, the 15th Wisconsin is the only regiment of its kind in the service of the United States; and it is as especially representing this vast, enterprising, and rapidly increasing portion of our population that it is worthy of notice.   But, though it be the only regiment representative of their distinct nationality in the field, thousands of Scandinavians have joined our armies, and may be found in every regiment organized in the Northwest.   They are among the best and bravest of our soldiers.   Descendants of the sturdy vikings of medieval times, they have in the long lapse of years lost none of that daring valor, power of endurance, and remarkable coolness in times of excitement, which characterized their ancestors.   Next to bravery, their most marked quality is calmness.   Always cool and collected, they act with the same deliberation and forethought in the trying hours of danger as in the transactions of every-day life.   Temperate and virtuous, obedient and well disciplined, they are in every respect model soldiers, and challenge the admiration and respect of all whose good fortune it is to mingle with them.   Long may they live to enjoy that freedom of speech and of thought for which they are so nobly contending !   And not less than America's own sons will they be honored in the days of returning peace,— when the sword shall once more be beaten into a ploughshare, and the spear into a pruning-hook.

HANS C. HEG, Colonel of the 15th Wisconsin Volunteers, commanding the 5th Brigade, 1st Division, 20th Army Corps, was born near the city of Drammen, in Norway, December 21, 1829.

In 1840 his father, Evan H. Heg, came to America and settled near Milwaukee, Wisconsin, being one of the first emigrants from Norway to this country. In 1849 the subject of this sketch, then twenty years of age, proceeded to California by the overland route, where he spent two years, returning in 1851. From that time until 1859 he resided near Milwaukee, engaging principally in farming and merchandising, and became one of the prominent business men of the State. In 1859 he was nominated by the Republican State Convention of Wisconsin for the office of State Prison Commissioner, and was elected by a large majority. This office he filled, with credit to himself and profit to the State, until he entered the service in 1861. That year Colonel Heg was nominated for the same office by both the Union and Republican conventions; but he preferred to serve his adopted country in a different sphere, and called upon his countrymen to rally around his standard for the defence of the Union and the Government. While yet in civil life, he was appointed by the Governor major of the 4th Regiment of Wisconsin State Militia, and in October, 1861, entered the service as colonel of the 15th Wisconsin Volunteers.

Since that time his history is identified with that of the regiment. With it he has served constantly and faithfully. Always at the head of his men,—the post of danger as well as of honor,—he has won their love and esteem by his cheerful participation in all their sufferings and privations. At the battle of Stone River he was with his regiment from first to last, never desponding for a moment, even when affairs seemed most discouraging. His services there and elsewhere have not escaped the notice of his superiors, and he has been highly complimented in the official reports of General Carlin. He is now in a position where his abilities as a military commander can be of even more service to the Government than heretofore, having on the 29th of April, 1863, been assigned to the command of the 5th Brigade, 1st Division, 20th Army Corps, to which his regiment was at the same time transferred.

Colonel Heg possesses the peculiar characteristics of his countrymen in a marked degree. His bravery, demonstrated in many engagements, is unquestioned. It is not, however, the reckless daring of an unskilled and careless man, but the cool and determined valor of a competent, thoughtful commander. He is prudent, but not timid; deliberate, but not slow in movement. In person he is of medium size, rather slender, and with features more than ordinarily prepossessing. With the courage he has the power of endurance so natural to the Scandinavian, and is as well calculated to share the hardships and privations of a march as he is to direct the movements of his command.

Colonel John T. Wilder.

JOHN T. WILDER, Colonel of the 17th Indiana Infantry, commanding the 1st Brigade of Mounted Rifles, was born in Ulster county, New York, in the year 1830. His is decidedly a fighting family. His great-grandfather, Seth Wilder, lost a leg at Bunker Hill; and his grandfather, Seth Wilder, Jr., then sixteen years old, served in his father's stead, and participated in the battles of Saratoga, Monmouth, and Stony Point, in the latter of which he was wounded by a bayonet-thrust. In the War of 1812 his father, Reuben Wilder, raised a company of light horse, and fought at Plattsburg and Sackets Harbor. He is still living, and, though lacking but a year of the allotted threescore and ten, his patriotism has not dimmed in the lapse of years, as is evidenced by the fact that he recently wrote from his home in Kingston, New York, to his son, asking permission to come to Murfreesborough and serve upon his staff.

The subject of our notice was educated as a civil and hydraulic engineer, and at the age of nineteen moved to Columbus, Ohio, where he remained three years. Removing in 1852 to Greensburg, Indiana, he engaged in the machine and foundry business, in conjunction with his more scientific professional pursuit of hydraulic engineering. In this he has been more extensively engaged than any other one man in the West,—in almost every principal town of which he has built mills, both steam and water. His labors extended beyond the State of his residence to Illinois, Wisconsin, Western Virginia, and even Tennessee, in which he has constructed several mills, and where he now owns several hundred acres of land. His nine years of work may be thus summed up. He has built over one hundred mills, has sent engines (all built by contract) to every part of the West, has constructed several large hydraulic works, and has been granted three patents on turbine water-wheels. When the war broke out, his business was in a flourishing condition. He had become a proficient in hydraulics, and was recognized as an authority in such matters to so great an extent that he was sent for as a witness and to act as umpire from all parts of the country. In politics he had been a Democrat; but when Mr. Lincoln was elected he fired a salute for him as his President, notwithstanding the objections of many of his brother Democrats. At the first sign of war he cast two steel six-pounder guns and donated them to the State. Artillery not being desired at that time, he interested himself, and was mainly instrumental, in raising the first three-years regiment from the State, of which he was appointed lieutenant-colonel.

Leaving his extensive shop and foundry, employing one hundred hands,—which, it may be remarked, is still in constant operation,—in charge of his foreman, he accompanied his regiment, then commanded by Colonel Haskell, to Western Virginia. Lieutenant-Colonel Wilder, however, was in command at Cheat Mountain and Greenbrier, and in all the severe skirmishes and fights under Generals Reynolds and Rosecrans. His regiment, the 17th Indiana, killed John A. Washington, was very prominent in the repulse of Lee, and at Greenbrier covered the retreat of General Reynolds, building, repairing, and maintaining the roads over which our forces moved. In December, 1861, Colonel Wilder marched with his regiment to Louisville, and accompanied Buell's army through all its varied fortunes.

Soon after the evacuation of Corinth he was taken ill with typhoid fever, and was compelled to absent himself from the field for nearly three months, the disease proving at one period nearly fatal. Soon after he recruited a company for his regiment, and also assisted in raising a regiment of thirty-days men, of whom six hundred and forty-one were enlisted during one day, to serve in Kentucky and repel the rebels at Henderson,—the same gang who had crossed into Indiana and had again recrossed the river. The men were raised, as stated, in less than twenty-four hours, and in forty-eight hours were armed, equipped, and in Kentucky, two hundred and sixty-five miles from Greensburg, Colonel Wilder accompanying them.

In September, 1862, in command of less than four thousand men,—of whom only twenty-two hundred were fit for duty,—he made his memorable defence of Munfordsville, repulsing a desperate attack of the rebels, nearly ten thousand strong, under General Chalmers, and maintained himself until he was surrounded by a force of twenty-five thousand, with forty-five cannon, under the personal command of General Bragg. By this brilliant and gallant defence Colonel Wilder gained due credit as a gallant and determined officer in whom confidence could be placed in time of need. For two months he was a prisoner, when he was paroled, and went to Washington, where he procured an immediate exchange, and at once rejoined his regiment.

When General Rosecrans assumed command of the Army of the Cumberland, Colonel Wilder was assigned to his present brigade, consisting of the 17th, 72d, and 75th Indiana, and the 98th Illinois. In December he was stationed at Gallatin, Tennessee, and on the 17th of that month joined in the pursuit of Morgan on his last raid, in company with General Reynolds's division. After the battle of Stone River he escorted a train of one hundred and twenty wagons from Cave City to Nashville. Since then he has been constantly engaged in raids and expeditions through the country, scarcely having a day of rest from active service.   Determining to mount his brigade and thus beat Morgan at his own game, Colonel Wilder began, with six horses, to capture others for his men.   On one expedition—the first—to Liberty and Lebanon he obtained some six hundred, on the second, about seven hundred, and on the third, five hundred and seventy-eight.   Gradually others have been procured, and three regiments are already finely mounted; and before this is seen by the reader the fourth will, without doubt, be similarly fortunate.   He has also procured an ample supply of fine mules for a battery of six rifled ten-pounder guns, also for one of four twelve-pounder mountain-howitzers; and this has been done without a dollar of expense to the Government. During the entire winter, and until the 1st of April, no corn or forage was drawn by this brigade for its animals,—they supplying themselves from the surrounding country.

Colonel Wilder's brigade is an independent command,—and in more senses than one.   It builds its own wagons,—ironing them from the wrecks of others scattered along the road,— shoes its own horses, and makes its own coal for its forges. Each man carries a hatchet with a handle two feet in length, —whence they have acquired the sobriquet of "The Hatchet Brigade."   Their hatchets are described as handy and effective both in bivouac and in fight.   Each company also makes for itself a fine mess-chest.   Every teamster, cook, and extra-duty man in the brigade is a negro, and every white is an effective soldier in the ranks.   The colonel is a firm believer in the friendship and good will of the negroes.   He relates numerous instances in which they have exhibited these qualities and rendered valuable service, among which is the following.

Upon one of his expeditions, during a dark, rainy night, he was visited in his camp by a very black negro woman, about twenty years of age, and married,—the property of one Hawkins, a large farmer living six miles from Lebanon, Tennessee.   She had walked the whole distance to his camp—six miles—in the mud and rain for the purpose of telling him where there were several barrels of salt hidden behind her master's garden-fence, as well as to reveal the locality of a certain cave where were concealed a number of horses and mules and some guns. "I could not help bringing her in with me," said the colonel; and he added, "The negroes are our best friends."

Colonel Wilder is emphatically what may be called a *live* man. He realizes the nature of the struggle in which we are engaged, and enters into the work with all his mind and strength. He believes in fighting, and plenty of it. Peace-upon-any-terms sticklers, and rebel sympathizers, meet with no sympathy from him. He was the first one to suggest the idea of having the soldiers appeal to their friends at home to unite in an earnest, hearty support of the administration in its efforts to crush the rebellion. To this end he used his influence among the Democrats in the army; and they co-operated with him,—with what result is known to the whole loyal North. Pure patriotism has impelled him in his course. His whole time and energies are devoted to the work. In addition to his salary, he has expended over seven thousand dollars for the cause,—having equipped from sixty to seventy men at his own expense. Still in the prime of life, understanding the nature of the enemy with whom he is contending, fertile in invention, and prompt in execution, Colonel Wilder and his mounted brigade cannot fail, in the days yet to come, to add largely to their already wide-spread reputation.

The brigade is composed as follows:—the 17th Indiana, Lieu-tenant-Colonel Jordan, 72d Indiana, Colonel Miller, 75th Indiana, Colonel Robinson, and the 98th Illinois, Colonel Funk-houser. It is called the First Mounted Rifles, and its services are in constant demand. Scarcely an expedition goes out of which it does not form a part; and wherever it goes it is sure to "make its mark." The rebels have learned to respect and fear it; and the name of its gallant leader has already become throughout the South a synonym for all that is bold and daring.

Colonel William L. Stoughton.

COLONEL WILLIAM L. STOUGHTON, 11th Michigan Volunteers, is a native of the State of New York, and was born March 2, 1827. Moving with his family to Ohio in 1839, he was educated at Madison Seminary. In 1849 he went to Michigan, and on the completion of his legal studies was admitted to the bar, and practised law till the fall of 1861. For four years he was prosecuting attorney of St. Joseph county, and had the reputation of being an able criminal lawyer. He was also a member, and one of the secretaries, of the National Republican Convention in 1860, which nominated President Lincoln, and took an active part in the subsequent canvass. In the spring of 1861 he was appointed United States District Attorney for the district of Michigan, and held the office till the fall of that year, when he resigned, and accepted the appointment of lieutenant-colonel in the 11th Michigan Infantry, and in April, 1862, was appointed colonel.

During the spring and summer of 1862 he was on duty in Tennessee and Kentucky. On the invasion of Kentucky by John Morgan in July, he was sent with the 11th Michigan to intercept him, if possible. He reached Cave City the next evening after Morgan's raid was known at Nashville, and made a forced march to Glasgow to attack him; but he had left five hours before the regiment arrived, and his command, being mounted on the best of stolen horses, escaped. From this point commenced the celebrated chase of Morgan through the State of Kentucky, in which our infantry constantly pressed the marauder, driving him from every point, but unable to make him fight. After this he was ordered to Nashville with his regiment, where he was assigned to General Negley's division, and was in Nashville during the blockade. In the course of the siege he was sent by General Negley, with three regiments and one section of artillery, sixteen miles down the Cumberland River, on a foraging expedition and reconnoissance. When near Fort Riley, the train was fired into by guerrillas, who were speedily put to flight. On reaching the road between the bluffs and the river, it was found to be cut away, leaving only a bridle-path, with trees felled across it to prevent the passage of wagons. With great labor the obstructions were removed, and the road bridged so as to allow the train to pass. On reaching the opposite side, the head of the train was again fired into by guerrillas; but they were repulsed and driven across the river, and an abundance of forage obtained. On the return of the train, the enemy made a spirited attack from a bend in the river opposite the bluffs, but were repulsed with the loss of sixteen killed and wounded. Colonel Stoughton was subsequently at the battle of Stone River,— where he acted a gallant and conspicuous part,—and was appointed provost-marshal of the post on the occupation of Murfreesborough. This position he has filled with notable success.

Colonel J. W. Burke,

OF the 10th Ohio Volunteer Infantry (Head-Quarters Guard), was born in Westport, county Mayo, Ireland, in the year 1836, and was educated for the English service, in which four of his elder brothers had reached high rank and distinction. Politically opposed to the Government and policy of Great Britain, and belonging to that class of young men whose genius and efforts in the cause of Irish nationality made the ill-timed Revolution of 1848 celebrated, he abandoned all idea of serving in "her Majesty's forces," and emigrated to the United States, where he devoted himself to the study of law, and practised his profession at the Cincinnati bar for three years before the breaking out of the war.

He commenced his military career as chief of staff to General William Lytle, commanding at Camp Harrison, and assisted that gallant officer in organizing some of the finest regiments Ohio sent into the field. Shortly after the call of the President for three-months troops, the Irish citizens of Cincinnati resolved to raise a regiment and send it to the field in defence of the Government. The Montgomery Regiment (10th Ohio) was thus organized,—composed mainly of this class of citizens,—counting among its officers some of the most promising and brilliant young men of the city. The regiment was commanded by Colonel (now General) William H. Lytle,—Colonel Burke entering as major. The regiment was among the first to leave for the war in Western Virginia, and served under General McClellan during his short campaign, until General Rosecrans took command.

Colonel Burke was put in command of an outpost,—a position requiring much tact and energy,—and soon gained the attention and confidence of his keen-sighted general. His regiment was the advance-guard of General Rosecrans's forces when the army marched to the Gauley River to engage the rebels under General Floyd, and distinguished itself highly at Carnifex Ferry, where it charged the works of the rebel general, mounting eight guns and defended by three thousand infantry. The brave Lytle was severely wounded within a few feet of the rebel redoubt, and the command of the regiment devolved upon Burke, who fought his men with the utmost courage and obstinacy until night put an end to the contest, when the rebel general retreated in confusion, leaving his works and large quantities of stores, ammunition, and arms.

The campaign in that region having been terminated by the expulsion of Floyd, Wise, and Lee, the regiment was ordered to Kentucky, and fell under the command of the lamented General Mitchel, serving with that officer in his brief but brilliant career in Northern Alabama. "The 10th" acquired the title of "the bloody 10th" at the battle of Carnifex Ferry; and the impression gained ground wherever they marched that it was composed of wild, lawless men: so that, it is said, citizens fled at the approach of the regiment, to return surprised that their horses and property were left unharmed. This impression prevailed particularly in Huntsville, Alabama; and great was the consternation among the citizens when Colonel Burke was announced as provost-marshal and his regiment as provost-guard. But the discipline and fine bearing of the regiment soon dispelled that impression.

When the Federal forces under Buell followed Bragg into Kentucky, the "10th Ohio" was assigned to the division of General Rousseau, of McCook's corps, and at the battle of Perryville was honored with the advance of the army. The gallant bearing of the regiment at that fight formed a theme for the admiration of the country. It went into action with five hundred and twenty-eight men, and lost two hundred and sixty-three killed and wounded. Surrounded at one time by masses of the enemy, their numbers diminishing at every step, the regiment cleared its way to the point where a great portion of the line had fallen back and taken up the final position of the day. Immediately on General Rosecrans assuming the command of Buell's army, he assigned to the regiment the highly honorable position of Head-Quarters and Provost Guard to the Army of the Cumberland,—a compliment well deserved by the gallant fellows who followed him with such devotion in his earlier campaigns.

At the battle of Stone River Colonel Burke and his command received the laborious and responsible task of keeping open the communications. Posted at Stewart's Creek, a short distance from the field, it protected large army-trains, rescued one from the rebel cavalry,—which it finally drove away,—kept open the line of communications, and returned to the army over two thousand stragglers who were found skulking to the rear. For these gallant services the general commanding publicly thanked Colonel Burke and his regiment,—an honor any officer might well covet. He also received the following despatch from head-quarters :—

"JANUARY 2, 1862, 8 o'clock A.M.
" LIEUTENANT-COLONEL BURKE :—

" The general commanding instructs me to say that your despatch is re ceived, and that your conduct is highly gratifying to him.

"Respectfully, yours, &c.

" FRANK S. BOND, *A.D.C.*

" By command of Major-General W. S. ROSECRANS."

In his official report General Rosecrans says :—

"The 10th Regiment of Ohio Volunteers, at Stewart's Creek, Lieutenant-Colonel J. W. Burke commanding, deserve especial praise for the ability and spirit with which they held their post, defended our trains, secured their cars, chased away Wheeler's rebel cavalry, saving a large wagon-train, and arrested and retained in service some two thousand stragglers from the battle-field."

The special correspondent of the "Cincinnati Gazette," speaking of the gallantry of the regiment, pays it the following high compliment :—

"To the heroic conduct of Colonel Burke at Stewart's Creek, where, with his unconquerable 10th Ohio, he so gallantly held his ground and repulsed the masses of Wheeler's rebel cavalry, is due the saving of an immense train of supplies, the loss of which, at a time when the army was reduced to horse-flesh and a scanty supply of hard crackers, might have been attended with the most disastrous consequences. Neither is it too much to say that his success, and that of Colonel Innes, of the Michigan Mechanics and Engineers, saved our army from an assault in the rear by the whole force of the enemy's cavalry."

In a short sketch like the present it is impossible to do justice to Colonel Burke and his brave men. The regiment, though decimated in number by its many fierce contests, has a well-earned reputation for discipline, dash, and fine appearance.

THE DEAD OF OUR ARMY.

WE have concluded our sketches of the living; and it is meet that we close this portion of the "Annals" with a tribute to the noble dead of the Army of the Cumberland. Fallen heroes!— sleeping upon the banks of the lonely river, upon adjacent cotton-fields, and among the cedars which skirt its meandering waters, they yet live in the memories of their surviving comrades. Unable to present their loved features in these pages, yet who of us who knew them so well can ever forget them? Perhaps *two thousand* of our gallant band have "slept the sleep" upon the battle-fields of Stone River, or have since languished and pined away unto death from wounds there received. Let the monument stand, an offering of the army and of the people, emblematic of their lineaments, their heroism, and their sacrifice.

The following sketches of prominent officers slain at the battle of Stone River, December 31, 1862, will be read with a deeper interest than any other chapter in this volume.

Brigadier-General Joshua Woodrow Sill.

(BY A LADY CONTRIBUTOR, CANANDAIGUA, NEW YORK.)

JOSHUA WOODROW SILL, the youngest brigadier-general in the army, and the only Union general slain at Murfreesborough, was the second son of the Hon. Joseph Sill and Elizabeth, daughter of Joshua Woodrow, of Hillsborough, Highland county, Ohio. He was born December 6, 1831, in the city of Chillicothe, where his father—a native of Northeastern New York—has resided since the year 1814.

Joshua's early education was watched over by his father, who spared from an active legal practice time necessary to give his son much instruction. As a child he was gentle, obedient, and studious; and before reaching the years of manhood he succeeded in mastering both rapidly and thoroughly some of the most abstruse sciences, particularly mathematics; while his proficiency in Latin and Greek, in standard English and French literature, gained for him the approbation and admiration of all. His father intended him for the legal profession; but this he declined, and, at his own request, was in 1849 appointed a United States Cadet from the Chillicothe Congressional District.

His life at West Point was remarkable only for the attention he bestowed on his studies and his strict performance of every required duty. He ranked among the first and best scholars, and graduated third in his class. Chosen for an ordnance appointment, he was in 1854 stationed at Watervliet Arsenal, West Troy. The following year he was recalled to West Point as one of the instructors. Two years passed, and he was ordered to Pittsburg Arsenal, where for a few months, awaiting further orders, he occupied himself with drafting for and testing ordnance. In May, 1858, he sailed for Vancouver, Washington Territory, to superintend the building of an arsenal there; but the Vancouver Island difficulty with the British Government prevented its construction. In September he returned, and was again stationed at Watervliet, but a few months afterwards was ordered to Fort Leavenworth. There his long-cherished intention of leaving the army took effect. Sill was willing to wield a sword when his country required it, but he could not endure the inactivity of army-life in times of peace.

Early in the spring of 1860 he gave notice of resignation; and in September of that year he accepted the Professorship of Mathematics and Civil Engineering in the Brooklyn Collegiate and Polytechnic Institute,—a position he filled with distinguished ability. For a few months he seemed happy in his congenial occupation and duties; but, as the time drew near when his resignation must be either perfected or withdrawn, the threatening aspect of affairs greatly disturbed and engrossed him. Many of our ablest statesmen believed the peril of civil war would be averted. Sill sought, and finally accepted, the advice of reliable military friends, and perfected his resignation. Still he was not content: a presentiment that the time would soon come when he must part from all the enjoyments of his new profession caused him anxious thought. The news of the bombardment of Sumter, flashing through the land, startling and firing the indignation of every patriot, found him calmly, quietly prepared. He resigned his professorship, and offered his services to the Governor of Ohio. In May, 1861, he was summoned to Columbus, and made assistant adjutant-general of the State, in which department he aided in the organization of the Ohio forces. In August, 1861, he was commissioned colonel of the 33d Ohio Volunteers. He accompanied General Nelson in his Eastern Kentucky expedition. After his return, his regiment being assigned to General Mitchel's division, Sill was placed in command of a brigade. He was promoted to the rank of brigadier-general, and confirmed by the United States Senate, July 29, 1862. After the promotion of General Alexander McD. McCook to the rank of major-general and to the command of an army corps, Sill was assigned to the command of a division. This division he led with consummate skill and energy; and, although engaged in constant skirmishing with the enemy, such was his vigilance and dexterity that he sustained but trifling losses. Upon the reorganization of the army under Major-General Rosecrans, he was assigned to the command of a brigade in General Sheridan's division. He fell at the head of this brigade, with which he had three times checked the furious onset of the rebels upon our right wing on the disastrous Wednesday of the battle of Stone River.

Gifted with more than ordinary abilities, he had by unwearied and successful culture trained them to a high degree of perfection. The unsullied purity of his life was rare and admirable.

He was gentle and sensitive to excess: yet in unswerving integrity, cool practical sagacity, chivalrous courage, and unyielding resolution, he verified his title to the noblest attributes of manhood.

It is an eloquent tribute that, when their brave leader fell, his men gave way to no shallow ebullition of sorrow. As the word passed down the line, there ensued no disorder, no confusion. Moved as one man by one fierce impulse of vengeance, they pressed forward and crushed the enemy who had slain him.

His loss, though keenly felt, should not be selfishly mourned. Through duteous self-sacrifice the brave, the gallant SILL has entered "the noble army of martyrs."

Colonel Julius P. Garesché.

COLONEL JULIUS P. GARESCHÉ (Chief of Major-General Rosecrans's Staff) was born in Cuba, of American parents. He entered West Point at the age of sixteen, and graduated in 1841, at twenty. He was married in 1849 to Miss De Laureal, of St. Louis. He served some years in Texas, and in Mexico during the war. During eight years previous to the rebellion he was on duty in Washington City as assistant adjutant-general. Upon the commencement of the war he became anxious for active service. He declined, however, a commission as brigadier-general,—not wishing to accept such an appointment until he had won it on the field. He was made chief of staff to General Rosecrans upon the latter's taking command of the Department of the Cumberland, and immediately proceeded to the West and entered upon his duties.

His life in the army has been one of work, and the services rendered by him to his fellow-officers and his country have been of the most important character. As chief of staff he was an invaluable aid to his commander, through his long experience and practical knowledge of martial affairs. Remarkably well versed in military law as regarded matters of rank and customs, precedents of courts-martial, &c., his decisions were universally respected; and his published orders are yet spoken of, among our army officers, as models of correctness, precision, and elegance of diction. As a man, modest, unobtrusive, kindly to all, and easy of access to both high and low,—to the humblest private as well as to the bearer of the sword and epaulette,—he was loved by all,—all mourn his loss.

A Washington correspondent of the "National Intelligencer" thus alludes to Colonel Garesché:—

"On one of the days of battle before Murfreesborough, during a critical moment of the conflict, Colonel Julius P. Garesché, chief of General Rose-crans's staff, was killed. There are things connected with the life and character of this gentleman, and with the years of his residence in this city, which make it fitting to allude to his death more at length than we have heretofore done, and, in a few words of special reverence to his memory, to call the attention of our citizens to the loss they have suffered in his fall.

"Of the high esteem in which he was held by the officers of the army nothing need be said. The grief expressed by his companions in the service sufficiently attests their appreciation of his stainless character and important services. His life in this city, to those who knew him best, seemed one continued act of charity. Prior to the war, when the duties of the Adjutant-General's office were not so pressing, his evening hours were almost invariably devoted to visiting the poor and sick. He sought for them in their homes, learned the history of their lives, consoled them in sorrow, and administered to them when in want. He denied himself many of the simplest comforts of life that he might be better enabled to alleviate the sufferings of the unfortunate. In the exercise of his charity he was at all times delicate as a true gentleman, generous as a perfect Christian. There are incidents in his life, familiar to a few, of such great heroism of virtue as would win for him, if widely known, the applause of all men. One of these we will relate. He learned of a family destitute of means and smitten with the small-pox. He visited them, finding the father beyond hope of recovery and one of the children dying. They were entirely deserted. Colonel Garesché visited them regularly, obtained for them the consolations of religion, stood by the bedside of the man when death closed his sufferings, and held the dying child in his arms while the priest administered baptism. Nor was this all. He went to three different undertakers, and each one refused to assist him to bury the dead. He applied to the city authorities, and was referred to one who conducts pauper funerals. He obtained this man's services, but defrayed the burial-expenses himself, lest the feelings of the widow should be hurt if her husband was buried as a pauper at the city expense. When one who had a right to remonstrate chided him for this exposure of himself and his family, this was his simple answer:—'I felt it to be my duty; I could not help it.'

"It was a splendid thing to die as he died,—suddenly, in the front of battle, in a deadly crisis of the day, fighting for a cause most pure and true; and it was proper that for such a man there should be reserved so grand a death. Yet in this there was nothing half so greatly heroic as the watching by the bedside and at the burial of that wretched victim of infection and the baptism of that smitten child.

" He was one of the founders of the Society of St. Vincent of Paul in this city, and was at the time of his departure the president of one of its conferences. He was a man of simple, unaffected piety, and untiring in charitable works. Those who knew him from youth never knew of him an evil deed or word. His wife and little ones, in their sudden bereavement, have the sincere sympathy of our citizens and of every officer, of whatever rank, in the army, and also the tears of many who in similar affliction found in him a consoler and a friend."

The manner of the death of Lieutenant-Colonel Garesche is well known. He was by the side of his general during the storm, advising, cheering, and executing orders. Calm yet courageous of heart, during that day he was observed, at an opportune moment, to retire to a private place, scan a page of his pocket-Bible, and to move his lips in prayer. He seemed, then, fearless of death: may we not say he was ready and willing to die for his country? Towards the middle of the day, while galloping over an open cotton-field upon a special mission, his head was blown away by a cannon-ball, a fragment of the lower jaw only remaining, his blood and brains being spattered over his attendants. Brigadier-General Hazen, one of the gallant spirits of that hour, and of the truly brave and pure of our army, thus writes:—

"IN CAMP, READYVILLE, TENNESSEE, June 4, 1863.

"AUTHOR OF ' THE ANNALS.'

" DEAR SIR:—At your request I pen you a few lines respecting poor Garesché. When killed, as you know, he was left just as he fell, there being no time then to give attention to the dead. About ten minutes after Colonel Goddard informed me of his death, I chanced to pass the spot where he lay. He was alone, no soldier—dead nor living—near him. I saw but a headless trunk: an eddy of crimson foam had issued where his head should be. I at once recognized his figure, it lay so naturally, his right hand across his breast. As I approached, dismounted, and bent over him, the contraction of a muscle extended the hand slowly and slightly towards me. Taking hold of it, I found it warm and lifelike. Upon one of the fingers was the class-ring, that (to me) beautiful talisman of our common school. This I removed; and, also taking from his pocket his Bible, I then parted with all that remained of one who in life was my dearest friend, and possessed of the highest virtues that grace the brave and honest man. There was no time for tears. I soon after sent an aide-de-camp, with men, who carried the body through the shower of iron that ceased not to rain upon that spot during most of that day, to a place where, whatever might be the fate of battle, it would be recovered. Yours, very truly,

"W. B. HAZEN."

The loss of Garesché was a shock to the army and to the country. Being killed within a few feet of General Rosecrans, the event thereby assumed a peculiar significance, and no battle-field death of this war has occasioned more thought and remark. His remains were buried in a little graveyard which chanced to be near where he fell, and after a few days were raised and taken to Cincinnati. His funeral honors are thus mentioned by the Cincinnati "Commercial" of January 14, 1863 :—

"HONORS TO COLONEL GARESCHÉ.

" The remains of this gallant officer reached our city early yesterday morning. The Young Men's Sodality received and escorted them to St. Xavier's Church, on Sycamore Street, where they were laid in state.

" A magnificent requiem mass was chanted over the body, the brother of the deceased, Father Garesché, S.T., being the celebrant. Rev. C. O'Driscoll, S.T., followed in a short panegyric.

"Guards were posted during the day, and a stream of visitors continued until the body was removed. About five P.M. the escort to accompany it to the depot was formed, in the following order :—

" Advance Guards.

Band.

Six companies of Infantry, in columns of platoons, with arms reversed.

Hearse.

Pall-bearers.

Band.

Young Men's Sodality.

Carriages.

" The procession was several squares in length, and, after a short détour, it proceeded to the Little Miami depot. The body will be forwarded immediately to the family of the departed hero, who reside in Washington City."

Colonel George W. Roberts.

COLONEL ROBERTS, 42d Illinois Volunteers, commanding 3d Brigade, 3d Division, 20th Army Corps, was born in Westchester county, Pennsylvania, October 2, 1833. After the necessary preparation, he entered the sophomore class at Yale College, and graduated in 1857. Adopting the law as his profession, he studied in his native county, where he was admitted to the bar, and continued to practise until the spring of 1859, when he removed to Chicago. There, while in the successful exercise of his profession, he determined to enter the army, and, in company with David Stuart, began recruiting for the 42d Regiment Illinois Volunteers. On the 22d of July he received his commission as major of the regiment, and on the 17th of September was elected lieutenant-colonel. Upon the death of Colonel Webb, December 24, 1861, he was chosen colonel. With his regiment Colonel Roberts took part in the well-known march of General Frémont to Springfield, after which the 42d went into quarters at Smithtown, Missouri. After the fall of Fort Donelson, the colonel proceeded with his regiment to Fort Holt, near Cairo, where he held command of the post, at that time garrisoned by the 42d Illinois, 8th Ohio, and a battery of the 2d Illinois Artillery. Thence he was ordered to Columbus, after its evacuation by the enemy, and next proceeded to Island No. 10, where he performed most valuable service during a night-expedition, in spiking a number of guns.

Here Colonel Roberts first made his mark, as one of the heroes of the army. Seeing that the boats could not pass the island unless the upper battery was silenced, the muzzles of the guns of which were but a few inches above the water, and which could have sunk any boat which might try to pass, he conceived the idea of spiking the guns. On the dark and stormy night of April 1, 1862, when almost a hurricane lashed the waters of the Mississippi, he embarked, with but forty men of his regiment in five small boats, upon that perilous expedition. Its success is history. The regiment was next ordered to Fort Pillow, and from there accompanied General Pope up the Tennessee and took part in the engagement at Farmington. He distinguished himself in that battle, where he with Company B, 42d Illinois, covered the retreat.

At the siege of Corinth he was in the advance, and was one of the first to enter the rebel fortification. In the pursuit of the rebels to Booneville and Baldwin he gained special praise from General Rosecrans for the rapidity with which he advanced.

He then served under Brigadier-General Palmer, and marched from Decatur to Nashville, in command of the 1st Brigade, 1st Division, of the Army of the Mississippi. Colonel Roberts distinguished himself in several skirmishes with the rebels while intrusted with this command, particularly during the siege of Nashville and its bombardment, November 5, 1862, in which he repelled the enemy from every point assigned to him to defend. Wearied with garrison-life, he soon after applied to General Rosecrans for more active duty, and was ordered to report with his brigade to General Sheridan. On the morning of December 30 he had the advance of the 20th Army Corps, and his skirmishers drove the rebels to their breastworks. On the 31st his brigade fought most bravely, engaging two rebel divisions at once,—one in front and one on the right flank; and not till a third division of the rebels came on his left flank and rear did his troops fall back. He then changed front along the Wilkerson pike, and, while gallantly inspiring his men with his words and deeds, a fatal ball struck him, wounding him mortally. One incident is worthy of mention. While a rebel division (Cleborne's) were driving some of our regiments before them, he asked permission from General Sheridan to charge upon the enemy, —which was granted. Galloping up before the 42d Illinois, he waved his cap and ordered them to fix bayonets. The men, filled with enthusiasm at this exhibition of bravery by their loved commander, rushed upon the rebel ranks with irresistible vehemence, and the enemy broke and fled in great confusion. The discomfiture of the rebel force at that moment was most opportune. It delayed their renewed attack upon our right wing for a considerable time, thus permitting the reforming of our broken columns, and, unquestionably, greatly contributed to stem the adverse tide of fortune, and to the achievement of the final victory.

Colonel Roberts needs no further eulogy. He yet lives in the memory and affections of our army.

Colonel Leander Stem.

(BY A CONTRIBUTOR, TIFFIN, OHIO.)

THE 101st Regiment Ohio Volunteer Infantry was organized under the call of the President for three hundred thousand additional volunteers, in July, 1862, rendezvoused at Camp Monroeville, and was mustered into the service of the United States on the 30th of August, with Leander Stem, of Tiffin, as colonel. It was ordered to active duty in Kentucky on the 5th of September, to assist in the defence of Cincinnati, then threatened by the rebel forces under command of General Kirby Smith.

It was subsequently ordered to Louisville, and accompanied the army of General Buell in the pursuit of Bragg through Kentucky. The regiment was present at the battle of Perryville, and, in connection with the 31st Brigade, to which it was attached, took part in the splendid action of the division commanded by General Mitchel. The coolness and courage exhibited by Colonel Stem on this occasion elicited high praise from his superior officers, and gained for him the admiration and confidence of the men of his command. This regiment also took a prominent part in the brilliant engagement at Knob Gap on the first day of the advance of General Rosecrans from Nashville upon Murfreesborough. Here again the perfect self-possession and indomitable courage of Colonel Stem was the subject of general remark among the officers who witnessed his conduct, and of enthusiastic praise among the men of his regiment.

The 101st was again hotly engaged at the battle of Stone River, where it suffered severely. Early in the morning of the 31st of December—that disastrous day of battle—Colonel Stem fell, mortally wounded. His gallantry, conspicuous on all previous occasions, here shone out with uncommon excellence. He fell while cheering on his men, close to the loved colors of his regiment, lamented by his superior officers and by the officers and men of his command, who felt for him the most devoted attachment and cherish his memory with the most affectionate tenderness.

The great epochs of history have always been marked by singular contrasts. While, on the one hand, the heart of the philanthropist has been sickened by the corruption of partisan leaders and the desolation of war, on the other it has been cheered and strengthened by the patriotism and heroic courage of those who have stepped nobly forward between their country and its peril. This truth has been eminently exemplified in the present rebellion. While some have labored energetically to destroy the most beneficent civil Government ever organized, others have displayed the most disinterested patriotism and self-sacrifice in its defence. The subject of this sketch is a signal illustration.

Colonel Leander Stem was born in Carroll county, Maryland, and was the third son of Jacob Stem deceased. When our country and Government were assailed by treason and rebellion, he manifested an intense interest, not as a mere party politician, but as a true friend of humanity. For years his hearty sympathy with human rights had led him to fear for free institutions while witnessing the plotting of their enemies. He felt it his duty to enlist in the military service of his country, and was appointed colonel of the 101st Regiment of Ohio Volunteer Infantry, and was with his regiment in the army, under the command of Major-General Rosecrans, at Nashville, Tennessee. He was wounded and captured at the battle of Stone River, on the 31st of December, 1862, and died at Murfreesborough, in a rebel hospital, January 6, 1863.

At the time he fell, his regiment was surrounded on three sides by the enemy, and was the last of the brigade to retire from the field. His last words on the field, while endeavoring to rally his men, were, "Stand by your colors, boys, for the honor of old Ohio!"

Colonel Stem was a man of most pleasing and urbane deportment, and interesting and improving in his social intercourse. As a legal advocate he was successful, and prosecuted his profession with acknowledged untiring industry. He will be missed and lamented the more for the gallant and heroic manner in which he offered himself up on the altar of his country. The following article from the Sandusky (Ohio) "Register," announcing his death, is a truthful tribute to his memory :—

"The death of Colonel Stem of the 101st Regiment, in the recent and terrible battle near Murfreesborough, is not one of the least important losses sustained in that bloody conflict. Though not a military man, unlearned in the art of war, he was a true man and a gentleman.

"Respected, esteemed, and trusted by all who knew him in all the business and social relations of private life, he had become alike respected and trusted by the men composing his regiment. The manliness of his nature, the good sense and sound judgment which he displayed in the performance of his military duties, and the interest which he felt in the men under his command, had made him what a colonel should be,—both the commander and the friend. The 101st Regiment, in the death of Colonel Stem has suffered an irreparable loss. Yet doubtless the influence of his example and his life will long be felt by them. But if his loss be irreparable to them, what is it to his family and friends? The hearts of the many who have suffered like bereavement only can estimate it.

"Colonel Stem is another of the victims of the accursed treason and rebellion which so many are now engaged in covering with a cloak of excuses and the drapery of palliation! How many more victims shall yet fall, God only can tell!"

THE DEPARTMENTS

OF THE

ARMY OF THE CUMBERLAND.

A DAY AT HEAD-QUARTERS.

THE Army of the Cumberland we will estimate, in round numbers, at fifty thousand men,—an extensive family, whose subsistence, discipline, and health are the daily care of its commander.

We are encamped at Murfreesborough,—have been located there for five full—but not solitary—months. Why so long a stay there? involves a combination of answers which the author does not feel called upon to give as "in duty bound." But the reasons are sound, as the result has shown. General Rosecrans moves when he is *ready;* and he knows the full meaning of that word. In all his military movements, without a single exception, he has made his "good ready," and by that sign has he conquered. In Western Virginia, at Iuka and Corinth, Mississippi, at Murfreesborough, and now upon his march into the vitals of central rebeldom, he *prepared* for victory, and so carefully and practically, that he has not yet failed in his advance, nor has he lost a foot of the ground, thus gained, by a forced retreat. When he moves on, it is to CONQUER and to POSSESS.

Say you, good reader, that here is a digression, and that we are no further on in our chapter than Murfreesborough? Not so. We do not propose to journey: we have aimed to "spend the day" at General Rosecrans's head-quarters with his bustling family. So sit you down, and, if it be your wont, fill up and light your pipe, ply your crochet, or unroll your knitting, and let us witness a day of in-door army life and appreciate this stated preparation for victory.

17   257

Let us first make ourselves masters of the position. Our army is drawn around Murfreesborough, in an elliptical circle, one and a half miles in diameter. Upon first entering the town, after the battle, this circle was much more extended,— say four miles in diameter, some of the division head-quarters being three miles from the court-house. This was needless; and the general commanding wisely reduced his lines, to avoid unnecessary travel, teaming, and picket-duty. So here we are, our divisions posted at every point of the compass from the court-house; and walk where we may, in any given direction, by day or by night, at the outer line of pickets (for we have town-pickets, street-patrol, &c. in addition) we are sure to bring up against a soldier, gun in hand, pacing his walk of fifty to two hundred feet, with a commanding "Halt!" And thus it is that if those "boys" on picket but do their duty, nor man, nor dog, nor rabbit, hardly, can steal into or out from this devoted town. We may add that far beyond the general picket-line, on every road, lane, and field susceptible of approach, we have posted cavalry pickets, singly, by groups, or in squads, as may be deemed prudent: so that surprise is impossible.

Thus surrounded by his great family, General Rosecrans has his head-quarters in the heart of the town. He has taken possession of the Keeble residence (if the author remembers the name correctly). It is a fine, two-story, country-town house, with a large, pretty garden attached. Its owner was a lawyer, county clerk, and secessionist, and now holds a position in the rebel army. He fled with Bragg after the Stone River defeat, during the memorable Saturday night, taking his wife and smallest children. The flight we know was sudden; it could not have been in the least anticipated by him, for on the next Monday, upon our entering, his house was found filled with family goods, as though he and his had simply turned the key and gone upon a stay-over-night visit. Of course this was all quite convenient, even to the kitchen-quarters, which shone with burnished stove-ware. Also gleamed there the ivories of a group of great and small Africans, mainly of the feminine gender. These were not quite so convenient, and were "sent to the rear." General Rosecrans and staff, who had been almost constantly in the rain and mud for ten days, now luxuriated upon white sheets and spring-mattresses, and "Philip," his steward, concocted dinners from army rations which were "fit to set before a king" in war-times. Truly, the "Yankee invaders" had arrived, and not only at this house, but at Colonel Ready's,—where General John H. Morgan had been married to his daughter, in the presence of Jefferson Davis, Bragg, Bishop Polk, and other rebel potentates, three weeks before,—and at the other best houses in the town.

True, these "Yankees" had only come to the possession and enjoyment of their "rights," after all. This house is but a concatenation of Yankeeism pure and (now) undefiled. Look about with us for a moment. It was planned by a "Yankee," or patterned after some pretty Northern double-story-porch-and-wing. It was built by educated "Yankee" labor, we are sure. It is painted with Northern oil and lead. Every carpet comes from the land of "white slavery," as also the tasty window-curtains, the bedspreads, and the snowy pillow-cases. See you those genuine "Yankee" mirrors and elegant picture-frames and mantel-ornaments? And, alas! we "see ourselves as others see us," by reflection from those highly polished black marble fire-fronts, wrought by miserable Vermont "mudsills" from quarries away up under the shadows of the old Green Mountains. Why, the elegant chair you sit in, friend, and the sofas and tables and stands and what-nots before you, were manufactured by low plebeians in the greasy town of Cincinnati; the clear white table-ware you notice spread out for dinner was sent here by some firm of sand-treading, clam-baking Jerseymen; while the knife and fork you may soon be invited to ply so industriously "grew," like Topsy, alongside of a counterfeit nutmeg, in some lowly vale of Connecticut. And open the carved doors of those showy library cases. Ah! what a concentration and intensity of Yankeeism! The brain of a Kent and of a Story finely preserved in Massachusetts calf for

Keeble; the glories of Irving and Bancroft and Willis, gorgeously clothed in "purple and fine linen" and tipped with gold by enterprising Northern publishers. Here, there, upon every shelf, are stored emanations of Northern art and genius, almost heaven-born, so beautiful and rare are they, by which are brought to view the lights and shadows of far-away foreign lands, the images of grand old mountains and the flashings of darksome ocean-caves, the fire-flash and the roaming buffalo of the prairie, the thunders of Niagara, Titus breaching the walls of fated Jerusalem, the landing of Christianity and democracy from the Mayflower upon the lonely rock, and Angelo's grand conception of the Resurrection. The possession of all this, the creation of Yankeeism, adorning hundreds of mansions in the "sunny South," and relieving the tedium of many a lazy hour, is the boast, while the creators are the sneer, of a race of uncreative aristocrats. Yes, here, there, everywhere, is the sign of the "Yankee,"—in every pane of glass and in every nail of this house "we live in;" and where, then, the impropriety of the Yankee coming to his own?

Surely here has been another digression. But what then? —we are getting slowly on, and to step aside and pluck a fragrant flower now and then relieves the tedium of a journey. The preliminaries settled, we are ready to spend our "day at head-quarters." We are there at nine o'clock in the morning, —no sooner; for the general arises at eight, and has just breakfasted. Ah! rather slow, say you? Well, no,—considered in the abstract. Great men have great ways, or, at any rate, various ways. Franklin arose at four to make ready to harness the lightning and drive sky-high. Humboldt arrived at four hours of constitutional sleep along about midnight. *Per contra*, the grandest brains of an age have incubated in bed after late breakfast-hours, and the finest poem of a century was written upon a stale pillow at hours as late as eleven o'clock in the forenoon. And there was Newton, who arrived at immortality just after an afternoon nap under an apple-tree. However, before

we conclude, we believe the "earliest bird" of a reader will not
be severe upon our general's breakfast-hour.

The day of our devotional general commences, we are sure,
with the morning prayer. This we have not seen, but, knowing
him, we know it to be true. After breakfast the first business
in order is the morning reports of any thing stirring "on the
front" during the past dark hours. Then reports from his
chiefs of staff of what large matter on hand for to-day. Then
comes the supervision and signing of important orders to corps
commanders, or to the commanders of posts at Franklin, Nashville, and elsewhere. And now begin to flock in the daily round
of visitors,—generals, colonels, and captains, upon this or that
errand, or for verbal instructions. A heavy army contractor
(perhaps *heavy* in a double sense) must confer with *him*,—is not
satisfied with the views or decision of an underling. An old,
rich planter is in trouble, and obsequiously squirms into the
general's presence, unless, more likely, he has sent his wife, a
sallow, plain, dejected-appearing woman. She was once, no
doubt, a pretty Southern belle; but Southern flowers fade as
early as they bloom. By this time there has assembled a crowd
of people,—officers upon errands, sutlers in trouble, and women
with children, and the distinct entity yclept "young ladies," all
after passes, or the restoration of property or other "rights;"
and all desire a full conference with the general upon their tiny
affairs, but are mainly attended to by his polite and excellent
aids.

Thus the busy work goes on, let us say, until two o'clock
P.M., when the general and his staff officers, with perhaps some
distinguished visitors from "abroad," will mount and take a
view of the camps, inspect the progress of the fortifications, or
call at the quarters of one of his sub-commanders. This is the
gala-hour at head-quarters. They have excellent horses; and
why not? They are dressed very neatly, as they should be,—
for then the general is "to be seen of men;" and we all know
the value of good example. As he rides along the lines, where
the troops are drilling by regiment or battalion, vociferous

cheering always greets him; and along the fortifications the same. For stretched all around him is a great army of men who love their commander as but few are loved, and he has shown a full return of affection for them, and that he is ever ready to do battle with them, and, if it is to be, to die by them.

The dinner-hour at head-quarters is four o'clock P.M. That might seem rather after the "St. Nicholas" and "Continental" style. But then it is the supper-hour also,—two meals per day; and thus the style is peculiar to our general. After dinner come a leisure hour and a siesta, a cigar and the daily papers. And as Sol marches flaming down the western slope, with his banner of light softly streaming in golden bars through the cedars and among the rocks of the yet torn and crumpled battle-field, and melts away beyond the forests which skirt the lonely river, the lamps are lighted; and now commences the second, and really the most important, half of the day.

From this time until long past midnight a continued stream of business pours into head-quarters. A hundred letters and notes are to be dictated, or to be perused, studied, and answered. Reports of many kinds; of courts-martial, as to "family jars;" of provost-marshal's matters of trade, passes, and concerning refugees and deserters; of sub-commanders respecting the enemy's movements along their fronts; to hear a written report of some spy just come in, and, if important, to see and question the man; to read and consider and answer telegrams from Nashville, Louisville, and Washington, often of vast importance; to confer, privately, with one or a group of his generals, and occasionally to hold a grand council of them; to have a kind, fatherly talk in private with some brave but erring officer; to call an old favorite—perhaps General Thomas, the "Nestor" of the camps —into "his corner," wheel around his chair against intrusion, and, in an under-tone, submit some important fact or uncertain point, and ask for an opinion which he knows well how to value, —all this goes on, and much more! Ah! here are decisions being made and plans laid affecting the lives of hundreds, and perhaps of thousands, of human beings,—which involve, possibly, the fortunes of an army, the fate of a government, or even those liberties which are the natural birthright of a great people.

While thus spending our day at head-quarters, good reader, you will be pleased to observe, we doubt not, the gentleness, almost quietness, which pervades the premises. The officers of staff, the visiting officers, and the secretaries, clerks, and order-lies in attendance, are neatly dressed, and are gentlemanly in their deportment. No shouting, nor loud talking, nor rude, boisterous laughter. An oath is rarely heard,—a loud one, never. The inordinate use of liquors is rarely noticeable,—is frowned upon. Due respect is paid to the Sabbath-day, the general attending his church-meeting invariably in the forenoon. We have not heard an angry word pass between members of this household during many months. Among the higher officers of our army, respect, confidence, and affection is the very general rule: the exception is rare. Especially has this been the case since the battle of Stone River. That great furnace of affliction seemed to purify and bring together in closer bonds the Army of the Cumberland. Men's hates and ambitions, passions and vices, assumed at least a much milder form, as though all were living in perpetual remembrance of those awful hours and of the dead. And the private soldier was thus equally affected with the officer. Truly, after that trial we had a better army of better men. As with our army, so it will be with the nation: —the gold is purified by the refiner's fire. Meriting this great trial as a people, we are being tried. And if we prove our-selves worthy of preservation, so will we be preserved, and will march on, higher and higher up the scale of national existence.

"Like master like man," is the trite saying of olden time; and it holds equally well in the new. The pleasing results just stated are easily traceable to their source. A cursing and carousing commander-in-chief gathers around him kindred spirits. The Christian and the gentleman, when invested with might and power, surrounds himself with the good and the true, "whose ways are pleasantness and their paths peace." Such has been our path, you will concede, kind reader, during our day's visit at head-quarters. Let us now retire, presuming it to be three o'clock in the morning,—an average hour of retiring for our general during the past eight months. And, while retiring, will you not join with him in what you may be assured is his earnest prayer to God, that peace and unity may soon be restored to our beloved and distracted country?

The Quartermaster's Department.

THE department of widest range in an army is that of the quartermaster. Upon its promptness and efficiency the success of all military operations in a great measure depends. The duties committed to its officers are most important, involving vast pecuniary responsibilities, and requiring for their faithful discharge the utmost energy and ability. The Quartermaster-General, in his late report, graphically and tersely sums up these duties as follows :—

" Upon the faithful and able performance of the duties of the quartermaster an army depends for its ability to move. The least neglect or want of capacity on his part may foil the best-concerted measures and make the best-planned campaign impracticable. The services of those employed in the great depots in which the clothing, transportation, horses, forage, and other supplies are provided, are no less essential to success and involve no less labor and responsibility than those of the officers who accompany the troops on their marches and are charged with the care and transportation of all the material essential to their health and efficiency. The quartermaster's department is charged with the duty of providing the means of transportation by land and water for all the troops and all the material of war. It furnishes the horses for artillery and cavalry, and for the trains; supplies tents, camp and garrison equipage, forage, lumber, and all materials for camps; builds barracks, hospitals, wagons, ambulances; provides harness, except for artillery horses; builds or charters ships and steamers, docks and wharves; constructs or repairs roads, bridges, and railroads; clothes the army; and is charged generally with the payment of all expenses attending military operations which are not ex-

pressly assigned by law or regulation to some other department."

The business of the department naturally divides itself into
three sub-departments, as follows:—

1. Clothing, camp and garrison equipage.

2. Transportation by land and water, with all its means and
supplies.

3. Regular and contingent supplies for the army and the
department.

The business which falls under the first head is immense; but
only general statistics can be given with safety and propriety.
Of tents, the regulations allow to each general in the field three;
to each staff officer above the rank of captain, two; to each captain or other staff officer, one; to every two subalterns of a company, one; and to every fifteen foot or thirteen mounted men,
one. The latter number are also entitled to two camp-kettles,
five mess-pans, two hatchets, two axes, two pickaxes, and two
spades.

Each soldier is allowed a uniform amount of clothing as stated
in the published table in the regulations, or, in lieu thereof,
articles of equal value. One sash is allowed to each company
for the first sergeant, and one knapsack, haversack, and canteen to each enlisted man. Commanders of companies draw
the clothing of their men, and the camp and garrison equipage
for the officers and men of their company. Other officers draw
their camp and garrison equipage upon their own receipts.
When clothing is needed for the men, the company commander
procures it from the quartermaster upon requisitions approved
by the commanding officers. Clothing is usually drawn twice
each year, but sometimes, in special cases, when necessary. The
price at which each article of clothing is furnished is ascertained
annually, and announced in orders from the War Department;
and when any soldier has drawn more than the authorized
allowance, the excess is charged upon his next muster-roll.
Officers furnish their own clothing, but may purchase from the
quartermaster, at the regulation prices, such articles as may be

necessary for their own personal use, upon certifying to such fact. No officer's servant, however, unless a soldier, is allowed to draw or wear the uniform clothing issued to the troops, except under-clothing and shoes, of which, when there is no other means of procuring them, a reasonable supply may be purchased of the quartermaster upon the officer's certificate to that effect.

Under the second division are included all the animals, wagons, ambulances, forage, steam and sail vessels, boats, railroads, and cars in use in the army. In the Army of the Cumberland there are about three thousand wagons, most of which are six-mule teams. One wagon is allowed to each regiment, ten to the brigade, and in the batteries one to each gun. In addition to these regular trains, there are also several extras. In the order of march, one hundred wagons extend over a mile of road; and if all the wagons in this department were formed in one line, they would extend thirty miles. The number of ambulances is about six hundred. The horses and mules number about fifty thousand head. These are purchased at an average cost of one hundred and ten dollars for horses and one hundred and five dollars for mules, and are also impressed from the surrounding country. Within the last three months a great number have been obtained in this way, many of which have been used in mounting Colonel Wilder's brigade. Three regiments have been furnished thus, and the work is still going on. Only about one-fourth of these are paid for,—disloyal citizens not being compensated therefor. Large as is the number taken by our forces, it has been greatly exceeded by the rebels, who from the beginning have supplied their armies by a system of most merciless impressment. The statistics of the losses of animals are not ascertainable. At the battle of Stone River it is estimated that over five hundred artillery horses were killed, and over one thousand belonging to the cavalry and wagon-trains.

Twelve pounds of hay and ten pounds of grain constitute the daily ration of each horse or mule. The amount necessary to supply such an army as that of the Cumberland is almost beyond belief, and must be seen to be realized. At present (April 20, 1863) the quartermaster has on hand some twenty-four thousand bales of hay and some two hundred thousand sacks of grain, stored away in houses and piled up out-of-doors. The hay costs at base of supplies about twenty-five dollars per ton, and corn one dollar and twenty-five cents per bushel. For three months the army was entirely supplied with forage from the country in which it was quartered. For every thing thus taken receipts are to be given, and upon proof of loyalty the party holding a receipt is entitled to a voucher for the amount. In many cases, however, receipts are not given at all, or it is done in an improper manner, or they are lost; and the proportion really paid for will not exceed one-fourth of the whole. The average cost of the feed for each animal is about thirty cents per day.

The railroad from Murfreesborough to Nashville is a military road, and is operated entirely by the Government superintendent and the quartermaster. All the freight for the army has been transported over it, and it has more than paid its way. Fifty car-loads—or three hundred tons—are daily brought to Murfreesborough from Nashville. Over the Louisville & Nashville road, which is taxed to its utmost capacity in transporting Government freight, the regular rates are paid. The road from Murfreesborough to Nashville has been in constant operation since the 1st of March; has been interrupted only once, when a train was captured and burned by the rebels. For passage and freight private persons pay regular rates.

All steamboats are bought or chartered by the quartermaster. This branch of the business is mostly transacted at Louisville; but a number were purchased at Nashville, by the chief quartermaster, to be transformed into gunboats for the Cumberland River service. For this item alone an immense amount of money is expended, a large part of the supplies for the army having been brought to Nashville by river.

The third division includes the regular and contingent supplies of the department,—hospitals, barracks, and quarters, fuel, stationery, secret service, and the numberless incidental expenses of the army.

Of fuel the consumption is enormous. Since the 1st of January one hundred and fifty thousand bushels of coal have been received at Nashville. It is estimated that six hundred thousand bushels will be used there before the river rises, next winter; and this amount was contracted for, to be delivered before the water becomes too low for transportation. In this estimate the quantity needed to supply the two hundred and fifty forges in the field is not included. Since the army arrived at Nashville—November 1, 1862—eighteen thousand cords of wood have also been consumed, and to this must be added the large forests that have been cut down and burned, of which no account is kept and for which no payment is made, and at least two hundred miles of fencing, mostly cedar rails. Board fences, and all lumber found in the country, are taken to make bunks, cots, and coffins. The coal costs at Nashville about fifteen cents per bushel, and the wood four dollars per cord.

The quartermaster also furnishes the stationery used in every department of the army, builds the warehouses at every post, repairs, refits, and furnishes all houses and offices for army use, provides all hardware and such building material as nails, glass, rope, &c., with all the machinery used, fits up hospitals for the sick, and furnishes coffins for the dead. He pays the mileage of officers, the expenses of courts-martial, the per diem of extra-duty men, postage on public service, the expenses incurred in pursuing and apprehending deserters, of the burials of officers and soldiers, of expresses, interpreters, veterinary surgeons, clerks, mechanics, laborers, and cooks.

The secret service alone requires about ten thousand dollars per month. The Quartermaster's Department at Nashville employs in the neighborhood of three thousand men as mechanics and laborers. These are engaged in shoeing horses, repairing wagons, making and repairing harness, and in divers other ways. Probably an equal number are similarly employed at Murfreesborough. The wages of white teamsters are from twenty-five to thirty dollars per month. Negroes, or "contrabands," are paid ten dollars per month. The latter are generally familiar with the management of mules, and are preferred by wagon-masters to careless white drivers. By their use in this service alone, nearly four thousand effective men have been added to the ranks of this army, and forty thousand dollars per month saved on their wages.

The policy in regard to the employment of negroes has been entirely changed. The principle now is, "keep all we get, and get all we can." Many of them are good mechanics and very shrewd. Negro women are worth five dollars per month to wash and work for the hospitals. In the performance of this labor their services are invaluable, and the Government can well afford to board and clothe them and their children. Cooks are allowed to each company; and for this purpose negroes are also employed as fast as competent ones can be found.

Still, the number of citizens necessarily employed in the differ-ent departments of an army is immense. Quartermasters, com-missaries, provost-marshals, provost-judges, and chiefs of police, if not themselves civilians, must have capable clerks who are, at wages varying from seventy-five to one hundred dollars per month. Then there are wagon-masters, agents, teamsters, scouts, and spies, all of whom come under the supervision and pay of the quartermaster. The money with which these pay-ments are made is sent to the chief quartermaster from the Treasury Department, in answer to his requisitions, which are sufficient in amount to meet the anticipated monthly expenses.

Full monthly reports are made to the chief quartermaster, by the corps quartermasters and each quartermaster in the service, of the expenditures of that month and the requirements for the next. The system is an admirable one, enabling the head of the department to know at a glance the amount of expenditures, the amount of stores on hand, and the amount, both of money and stores, necessary to be supplied. Still, with all the care and system possible, the labors of the chief quartermaster are in-cessant. He must maintain a constant watch over the river and railroad transportation, and anticipate every want of the army. With the commissary and the ordnance officers, he has to administer the affairs of, and provide for, a city, as it were; but upon him alone falls the duty of transporting the supplies and stores of the other two.

When General Rosecrans assumed command of the Army of the Cumberland, it was destitute of nearly every thing. Now it is abundantly supplied,—better, perhaps, than any other in the field. Nothing that could add to its health, comfort, or efficiency is wanting. Well clothed, fed, and paid, and well provided with camp equipage, it is in the best possible condition for effective service. This change, as gratifying as it is beneficial, is due mainly to the energy and perseverance of its chief quartermaster, seconded in all his efforts by the general commanding—by each of whom its value and importance are fully recognized.

THE CHIEF QUARTERMASTER.

LIEUTENANT-COLONEL JOHN W. TAYLOR, Chief Quartermaster of the Army of the Cumberland, was born in Saratoga county, New York, February 22, 1817. His father—John W. Taylor— was for twenty years a member of Congress from the Saratoga district, and was twice Speaker of the House. He is well known in the history of the country as one of the few who foresaw to what the country was tending through the continued agitation of the slavery question, and the disposition on the part of the South to make "the peculiar institution" supreme, and made the first speech in the House against the admission of Missouri as a State unless the question of slavery extension over free territory could thereby be permanently settled.

Colonel Taylor removed to Illinois in 1838, and has been a resident of the West since that time. At the time of entering the service, he resided in Dubuque, Iowa, where for several years he had been extensively engaged in business. In Northern Illinois and Iowa he is well and favorably known as an energetic, honorable business-man, and a gentleman of taste and refinement. June 22, 1861, he was appointed assistant quartermaster, with the rank of captain, being the second appointment to the quartermaster's department of the volunteer service. He was assigned to duty in the Western Department at Tipton, Missouri, then the principal interior depot of supplies for General Frémont's army. Thus Captain Taylor's first experience in the quartermaster's department was at this important post; and the business was so well conducted as to call forth the commendation of Major Allen, the chief quartermaster of the department, and to induce General Pope, then in command of the District of Central Missouri, to relieve him from that duty and order him to report to him as his chief quartermaster, in which capacity he remained with him during the whole of that general's Western campaign. The efficiency of the Army of the Mississippi bears testimony to his energy, prudence, and foresight.

When General Pope was ordered to Virginia and General Rosecrans was assigned to the command thus vacated, Captain Taylor was retained in his position. Upon General Rosecrans assuming command of the Army of the Cumberland, Captain Taylor, having gained the highest reputation for energy and efficiency in his department, was not permitted to leave Corinth until a peremptory order was issued from the War Department at Washington that he should be relieved and report to General Rosecrans. On the 13th of November, 1862, he was announced as Chief Quartermaster of the Department of the Cumberland, and on the next day promoted to a lieutenant-colonelcy. Since his entry into the service he has, without the loss of a day, been on constant and laborious duty at his post.

In the battles of Corinth and Stone River he was constantly at the side of General Rosecrans, and the highest commendation of his coolness and bravery during the latter engagement is found in the fact that the commanding general, in his official report, gives him the place of honorable mention next to the lamented Colonel Garesché. The fact that, notwithstanding its great distance from the base of supplies, the frequent interruption of railroad transportation,* and the long period during which the Cumberland River was unnavigable, the army has been so well supplied, reflects credit upon Colonel Taylor, its chief quartermaster.

THE ASSISTANT QUARTERMASTER'S CLERK.

H. A. HANSON, Esq., has been the chief clerk and cashier of this department during the entire administration of Colonel Taylor, and, as a faithful, energetic, and most accommodating official, merits brief mention in this connection. A native of Massachusetts, reared in the Western States, and now residing at Dubuque, Iowa, he has mingled amidst the scenes of camps and shared their ills, excitements, and alarms, and has faithfully played his part in the drama of civil war,—keeping his accounts and disbursing vast amounts of money, monthly, to the general satisfaction of the army and the people.

The Commissary Department.

THE Commissary Department is the great heart that sends the life-blood bounding through the veins of an army. Other departments are useful and necessary, but this is absolutely indispensable. To it the soldier looks for his daily food; without it no army could exist, no victories would be won. The wise commander will see that the haversack, not less than the cartridge-box, is well filled; for the hungry soldier, however abundantly supplied with powder and ball, is lacking in the one great essential to success,—physical strength and endurance. The immense importance of such a bureau, supplying the nerve and sinew of an army, caring for the lives and health of thousands of men, and involving such vast consequences as the fate of a battle or the result of a campaign, will be seen at a glance. Few of those inexperienced in military life, however, have any definite conception of its practical workings; and it is with the design of giving to the public an inside view of this department, as it exists in the Army of the Cumberland, that it is made the special subject of this chapter.

As remarked, the business of the Commissary Department is to supply the army with subsistence, or food. Of this subsistence the regulations provide that each man shall be entitled to a certain fixed amount daily, which amount is designated "a ration." Rations consist of beef,—salt and fresh,—pork, bacon, flour, pilot or hard bread, corn-meal, coffee, sugar, beans, peas, rice, hominy, molasses, vinegar, soap, candles, and desiccated vegetables. The latter are usually potatoes, cut, scalded, dried, and put up in barrels. When thus prepared they have very much the appearance of coarse corn-meal, and are used as a preventive of scurvy. Each day's ration—subsistence for one

274

man—in bulk averages three pounds in weight. A ration of whiskey—one gill daily—is allowed in cases of excessive fatigue and exposure, but is issued only on special o1 The negroes in camp also draw rations, principally made up of bacon, corn-meal, and molasses. All of these rations, forming the entire subsistence of the army, are under the charge of the Chief Commissary, by whom the corps commissaries are supplied; and these in turn supply the division commissaries. Brigade officers draw from the division commissaries, and regimental from brigade officers. The men draw their rations by companies; and they are then divided among the messes. The cost of each ration at Murfreesborough, including transportation, is about twenty cents.

All provisions are purchased by contract, proposals to furnish them having been invited by public advertisement. The salt meats and fresh beef for the Army of the Cumberland are brought from the north side of the Ohio River. About one hundred head of cattle are used per day; and they arrive in lots of some five hundred at a time. Those now at Murfreesborough came from Chicago, and nearly all that are used are from Illinois. The pilot-bread is chiefly made in Cincinnati, New Albany, St. Louis, and Chicago, and its average cost is about five cents per pound. The quartermaster provides transportation for all subsistence from the place of delivery by the contractors, to the army, and the buildings in which to store it. The special duty of the commissary is to keep watch of the amounts on hand, maintain a full supply, and notify the quartermaster to furnish transportation and storehouses when needed. The supply of corn-meal is constantly kept up. Large quantities of the kiln-dried article are brought from the North, and a mill is constantly in operation at Murfreesborough manufacturing it. When in camp, the entire army is supplied with fresh bread three days out of five. On the march the hard bread is used exclusively. Each brigade is, as a general thing, supplied with portable bake-ovens, with all the necessary appliances, such as kneading-troughs, baking-pans, &c. The yeast used is made of hops and, when they can be obtained, potatoes. Troops who have been some time in the service make mud ovens, wherever they are camped, similar to those found in primitive settlements. Their construction is easy and simple, and when completed they answer every purpose of a larger and more pretentious structure. A pile of wood is built up to fix the size and shape of the oven, and braces are put across the top to prevent the roof from falling in. The whole is then plastered over and covered thickly with mud, the wood burned out, and the result is a good oven, which lasts much longer than one would suppose. The heat cracks it sometimes, it is true, but the cracks are speedily stopped with mud, and the whole is as good as new again. The advantages of these ovens can hardly be estimated; for nothing contributes more to the health and strength of an army than good bread. In an emergency, troops can subsist upon it alone.

In camp each man consumes very nearly the whole of his rations. Whatever is saved by not drawing full rations is called the company savings, for which they are allowed a commutation in money. Each full company can save about fifteen dollars per month while in camp, and more when on the march, as but little over half the army ration is then consumed. The more active an army, the less the expense of transportation and subsistence; for the reason that men at leisure think more of their wants than they would if busily engaged. This is a matter of every-day experience with all classes of men. Any one who has ever travelled on a steamboat will acknowledge its truth at once. It is astonishing how little troops will sometimes subsist on when in active service. One of our generals recently re-marked, in speaking of the retreat from Huntsville last year, that he did not see how his men lived. They had scarcely any rations at all,—just enough to call them such,—and yet were in fine health and spirits. This explains why armies that march the most have the least sickness. They eat less and exercise more. The food of a soldier is strong and hearty, and is intended to produce stout and healthy men; but in camp too much is eaten and too little done to insure good health.

Of late, onions have been largely introduced as an article of food. These and potatoes are eagerly desired by the men,—so much so that if they could be constantly supplied with them they would be willing to forego one-fourth of their rations. Twenty thousand bushels of potatoes and ten thousand bushels of onions could be consumed in the Army of the Cumberland every month, with incalculable advantage to the men composing it. And yet, strange to say, they are so scarce that it is difficult, and at times impossible, to procure them in any thing like sufficient quantities. This, too, when the quarter of any county in the Ohio Valley—say, five thousand acres—will grow enough to feed the entire army for a whole year. Potatoes cost now (in the latter part of April, 1863) one dollar a bushel,—the contract price at the Ohio River,—and onions two dollars a bushel. At these prices the farmer can produce no more profitable crop. It is estimated that from eight hundred to one thousand bushels of onions can be grown on a single acre,—which, even at one-half the present prices, would prove most remunerative to the producer. Forty acres, thus planted, could be easily cultivated by a few contrabands, and, with half the labor expended on the more usual crops, be made doubly and trebly more profitable. These suggestions are thrown out in the hope that they may meet the eye of some one who will appreciate their importance, and induce him to take some steps towards remedying the scarcity which has called them forth. These vegetables are necessary to the health of the soldier. Without them and others, scurvy will inevitably make its appearance and the efficiency of the army be totally destroyed. But, if the war continues, the supply must be largely increased, or it will be absolutely impossible to furnish them, except in quantities too limited to be useful. Already prices have more than doubled, and are steadily increasing. The subject is worthy the attention of Northern farmers. The country is at war; and while the war continues, all the energies of the people should be directed to its prosecution. Such articles as are needed in the army should be produced to the exclusion of others,—especially when profit as well as patriotism prompts to such a course.

But potatoes and onions are not the only vegetables that are, or can be, used with similar beneficial results. Beans have become a staple article of food. Some two hundred and fifty bushels are used daily in this army; and so great is the demand that the price has risen from seventy and eighty cents to two dollars and eighty-eight cents a bushel. Sourkrout and pickles are also excellent anti-scorbutics, and are issued *pro rata* in lieu of other things, when procurable. But there is always a deficiency of these articles. The people should see that more of them are put up, and that less is allowed to waste and rot. They, too, command a good price, and with a little care an abundant supply for the whole army could be furnished. Another very excellent article, both common and cheap, is canned tomatoes. These can be used with great advantage at all times, and are especially desirable in hospitals. The necessarily coarse and substantial army fare, when long used and unvaried, wears upon the constitution and eventually breaks it down. These vegetables afford a variety, and prevent all injurious results, and thus save the lives of thousands of soldiers. The Government does every thing in its power to furnish a sufficient quantity; but upon the people at home the soldiers must mainly depend for them. The demand will always exceed the supply, and, unless more of them are grown, prices will necessarily rule too high to make them as abundant in the army as could be wished.

Other things being equal, the regiment that has the best cooks will be the healthiest and most effective. One good cook is worth ten doctors; as may easily be seen by an examination and comparison of the different messes in camp. One of our Pennsylvania regiments was especially noticed for the unusually healthy and contented appearance of the men. Inquiries revealed the fact that it was supplied with an excellent cook, whom the officers declared they would rather have than all the doctors in the army. This is a point which has been too much neglected, but is now coming to be better understood and appreciated. Many of the negroes who flock to the camps are fine cooks, and as such are very generally employed, to the manifest benefit of the men and an equal advantage to the service.

The Commissary Department of the Army of the Cumberland has been managed with signal ability. When General Rosecrans assumed command at Bowling Green, depots were at once established at that place. As it advanced towards Nashville, a depot was established at Mitchellsville, the then terminus of the railroad-route. When Nashville was reached, the supply of provisions was found to be scant, and immense quantities had to be transported by wagon-trains a distance of thirty-five miles. Even after the railroad was completed, this wagon-transportation was continued, and brought to the city large amounts of subsistence in addition to the many carloads that came daily by rail. By earnest and unremitting efforts during the delay at Nashville, thirty days' provisions were accumulated, and the army began its advance towards Murfreesborough, which it could not have done without this supply. The battle of Stone River and the period of rest necessarily following consumed nearly all of this stock, and new stores were gathered at Murfreesborough and Nashville. Taking advantage of the high water in the Cumberland, immense cargoes of every thing eatable were brought to Nashville and thence forwarded by rail to Murfreesborough. Many otherwise unoccupied houses in either city are filled from cellar to roof with commissary stores; and even then much of it is unhoused. The visitor at Murfreesborough is struck upon his arrival with the enormous piles of hard bread he sees near the depot. He has heard of a mountain of stuff, but never before so fully realized it. One mass is larger than a common two-story house, and around it are clustered other and smaller heaps, reminding him of the out-houses surrounding some stately mansion. Were all communication cut off with the North, the Army of the Cumberland, with the supply now on hand, together with what can be gathered from the surrounding country, could easily subsist itself for six months, and on short rations for a longer time. Such an accumulation inspires confidence in the masses of the soldiery. It tells of a foresight promising well for the future, and leaves no room for the disheartening influences which invariably attend an uncertain and irregularly-supplied commissary. They know that all which can be done for them will be done; and, with such assurance, they will put their hands boldly to the musket and look not backward until the end of their march shall have been reached.

THE CHIEF COMMISSARY.

LIEUTENANT-COLONEL SAMUEL SIMMONS, Chief Commissary of the Army of the Cumberland, is a native of Pennsylvania, born in 1826. His residence is St. Louis, Missouri, and he is by profession a lawyer. He entered the service May 1, 1861. He was appointed by General Nathaniel Lyon chief commissary on his staff, with the rank of captain. For several months, however, Claiborne F. Jackson, the Governor of the State, refused to issue any commission to him, the raising of the Missouri volunteers being in opposition to the Governor's wishes. During the organization of these troops he was stationed at the St. Louis Arsenal, and remained there until January, 1862. He was then ordered to St. Charles, where he acted as quartermaster and commissary for the post and the district of Northern Missouri, supplying the troops along the railroads with subsistence. Here he remained until after the fall of Fort Donelson, when he was ordered to the latter place, and became connected with the army of Tennessee under General Grant. Accompanying it to Pittsburg Landing, he was present at the battle of Shiloh, and until the evacuation of Corinth issued rations to three divisions of the army. Upon the assignment of General Rosecrans to the command vacated by General Pope, Captain Simmons was ordered to report to the former, and by him was assigned to duty as chief commissary of the Army of the Mississippi. In this position he remained through the campaign in Northern Mississippi, and was present at the battles of Iuka and Corinth and in the pursuit to Ripley. When General Rosecrans was ordered to the command of the Department of the Cumberland, Captain Simmons was retained on his staff as chief commissary, with the rank of lieutenant-colonel.

In his new department the duties devolving upon him were peculiarly onerous, owing to the disordered condition in which matters were found. The preceding account of the commissary department will show that its head sustains a responsibility hardly second to any in the army. At all times his services are very important, but in time of battle even more so,—if such a thing be possible. He must always be ready to issue when called upon, whether it be by day or night. He must also exercise a careful foresight with a view to meet contingencies of every kind. In short, it requires a peculiar talent, which every man does not possess, to become a practical, successful commissary. It is no small matter to cater for fifty thousand men and to so arrange that a full supply shall always be on hand. The efficiency and capability of the chief commissary of this army may well be inferred from the length of time he has held the position, and the universal satisfaction given by him, to which no word of comment need be added.

The Provost-Marshal General's Department.

THIS department of the Army of the Cumberland savors less of "villanous saltpetre" and the sword than others: yet without it an army would be grossly incomplete, and, but for the varied scenes of interest, of mirthfulness, and of sorrow there witnessed, camp-life would lose many of its rare concomitants, and the lesson of civil war would not be wholly learned. The provost-marshal is the social, internal regulator of the army. To him fifty thousand soldiers and the constantly changing crowd of citizens, strangers, and refugees throng for "passes" to go here and to go there. The entire trade of sutlers, merchants, cotton-dealers, and speculators of every name and kind comes beneath his notice and is subject to his "permit." Does a soldier commit an offence, or a trader sell liquor and other contraband goods? his case is also submitted to this official. Drunkenness upon the streets and highways is rolled into his presence, and thence is sent to be duly reduced and sobered off within the purlieus of the guard-house. Horse-thieves and house-breakers, swindlers and tricksters, street-loafers and the entire genus of camp-followers are brought to him for justice; and usually it is meted out to them to the full measure of their deserts.

And there, too, other and sadder scenes are of daily occurrence. A fond father or doting mother has come from the far West to find some trace of a loved and lost one who has fallen beneath the weight of wounds or disease, and whose body is resting somewhere in the red soil of Tennessee, and now they ask permission to undertake the sorrowful search, and crave assistance therein. A refugee family, a destitute wife and half-clad little ones, have just come in from rebel-cursed regions; and they are cared for, and the husband and father, who is probably

282

a soldier or laborer in the Union army, is to be found. A motley throng of men and women crowd his office-door, each awaiting an audience to tell the tale so common,—that a soldier has taken the last horse or cow or pig, or has invaded the peaceful sanctity of the chicken-roost. And here comes a procession of Union refugees, men and boys, who have fled for their lives; have lain hidden among the hills, rocks, and cedars of Eastern and Middle Tennessee to avoid the merciless conscription of the Southern leaders. They have reached our outer picket-posts in the darkness of night, and have been forwarded to the provost-marshal, by whom their names and statements are taken and themselves sent to the refugee-barracks to find food, shelter, and employment within our lines.

But all is not sadness. The ludicrous treads closely after the scenes of sorrow; and here we see still another procession entering the streets of Murfreesborough. These are contrabands, and truly a motley group; and they, too, are wending their way to the central dispensatory of army law and order. Negroes there are, big and little, old and young, in color black, blue-black, and yellowish tawny, or a mixture of all combined. They are on foot, and early travellers; for the dew has dampened the single coarse skirt of the negresses and their children, but not their ardor, and the dust of the road has adhered to the wet garment knee-high, giving a peculiarly expressive color to the fabric. The women invariably toil along with babies in their arms; the men and the larger boys and girls trudge past, laden with bundles of grotesque form and appearance; while the little picanninies mix in and patter on as would a flock of young quails in a wheat-field. Perhaps this scene is varied, the intelligent fugitives having *borrowed* " ole massa's" best horse, or mule, or yoke of cattle, and the large farm-wagon, in the night-time, and are coming in, bag and budget in hand, eyes shining and mouth agrin, and tattered duds flaunting in the breeze like banners on outer walls. These, likewise, are conducted by the guard in charge to that sanctuary of rest and fount of knowledge, the office of the provost-marshal.

Let us edge our way in at the door, and see what is to be seen within. Here is a special room, with clerks, and chairs, and desks, at one of which is seated the provost-marshal general, in the person of Major William M. Wiles. Perhaps—in fact, very probably—he is confronted by a number of elderly ladies and gentlemen who are *so* desirous of going beyond the lines to visit, to transact business, or to see sick children. They are peaceable, quiet folks, and have had nothing to do with this war. True, the ladies' husbands or sons are off in the rebel army; but how are they to blame for that? they query. Or may-be a bevy of prettyish young ladies, fair Eves of the South, are awaiting his answer to their application for a pass to lovers in Dixie or to dry-goods stores in Nashville or Louisville, and upon his refusal, most courteous and proper, a thousand daggers flash from beneath indignant eyebrows, and emotional skirts and furbelows grandly sweep from the hateful Yankee presence! Or perhaps—oh, rare chance, indeed!—the room may be empty of visitors; and then we will see the head of the department busily engaged in poring over the voluminous papers of some intricate case that has been referred to him for examination and report.

Passing into the next room, we see the rougher crowd of speculators, sutlers, visitors, and soldiers, each one elbowing his way to the first assistant provost-marshal general, Captain Cosper, for a pass or a permit, or for authority to do something, to get something, or to see about something. A sutler wishes permission to replenish his stock with a hundred boxes of wine, of which half will very probably be whiskey labelled "Heidseck" or "Sparkling Catawba." The captain glances up, characteristically strokes his beard, and intimates that a hundred boxes is rather a large supply,—enough to make a whole division drunk, much less a single regiment.

"Oh, no! It's a very harmless article, and very necessary. The officers must have it, they say. They are bilious, have fever and ague, are always dry, and want something for a tonic.

Here's their permit to sell it, and a recommendation for the shipment."

The captain meditates, and perhaps the sutler gets his permit, and perhaps he does not: more probably the bill is cut down a half or a quarter, and the limited quantity is allowed to come, to the delight of his customers and to his own profit. A seedy-looking individual of the butternut species prays for a pass, says he is a non-combatant, " don't take neither side,—this a'n't his war,—was agin it at the start, but when he found the Union was destroyed was bound to jine the South, as he lived thar, —would have no objection to the old Union as 'it was,'" and so on, *ad nauseam.* He is summarily passed out-of-doors with the complimentary ejaculation, "He's a fraud." Some better-dressed representative of a former uppertendom seeks a similar favor, and presents a letter in which he is described as the soul of honor and integrity, but never a word said of his loyalty,—of which he very probably has not a spark in his composition; and ten chances to one he follows in the footsteps of his more illiterate predecessor. A soldier wishes to visit a neighboring camp, an officer is going to Nashville or Louisville, a citizen would like to visit the hospital; and so, with one and another, the captain and his clerks are busy the livelong day, listening, questioning, and writing.

In still another apartment are other assistants and clerks, in charge of Second Assistant Provost-Marshal General Captain Goodwin. He is dealing with refugees and taking their names and statements, or questioning some disorderly soldier, or examining the case of some refractory or thieving negro, or wringing unwilling truth from some suspicious native who has drifted or leaked into our lines as a spy. The several clerks are busy copying statements, filing affidavits, examining papers, listening to complaints, or writing orders as dictated by their superiors. Every thing is life and activity, betokening the fact that here is neither time nor place for idle hands or minds.

Attached to this department is the office of provost-judge,—a position not recognized by the regulations, but created by General Rosecrans as a necessary auxiliary to the provost-marshal. The labors and duties of its incumbent somewhat resemble those of a police justice in our larger cities. Witnesses are sworn, papers examined and carefully preserved, and a regular docket is kept, in all cases involving the liberty or property of individuals, for future reference and mutual justice and protection. At first a single person was sufficient to dispose of all business brought before this branch of the department; but it steadily and constantly increased from day to day, necessitating the appointment of a number of assistant judges, all of whom now find ample employment.

All day long does the motley throng, which must be seen to be fully understood and appreciated, crowd the portals of the provost's office; nor do his labors cease upon the going down of the sun or when the Sabbath-day comes. The imperative calls of necessary business and the claims of suffering humanity alike render the duties of the provost-marshal general of our army, and those of his assistants, most varied, arduous, constant, and perplexing. The author has passed many hours there in witnessing scenes which he will ever remember,—scenes of the ludicrous and the saddening, of liveliest joy and deepest sorrow, of hope and of despair, the whole forming a moving mirror of all that attends battle-conflicts, deserted homes, and ruined families, and which, combined, present a grand, fearful panorama of that civil war now raging in the midst of and consuming a rebellious people.

WILLIAM M. WILES, Major and Provost-Marshal General of the Army of the Cumberland, was born in Columbus, Bartholomew county, Indiana, August 29, 1836, and has ever since resided there. In June, 1861, soon after the breaking out of the rebellion, he relinquished a profitable copartnership in the drug-business, and in connection with a fellow-townsman, Isham Keith, —a gallant young hero who was killed at the battle of Perryville, Kentucky, October 8, 1862,—enlisted a company, of which he was chosen first lieutenant. After serving several months in

the campaigns of Missouri and Arkansas, Keith was made major
to fill a vacancy, and First Lieutenant Wiles became captain of
his company.   He was detailed as aide-de-camp and provost-
marshal general upon the staff of Major-General Rosecrans at
Corinth, Mississippi, in May, 1862.   In this position his services
were so acceptable that he was retained in it upon the assignment of his general in-chief to the command of the Department
of the Cumberland.   He has passed through the heat of three
tremendous battles—Iuka, Corinth, and Stone River—unharmed,
but with imminent peril and several narrow escapes.   His coolness and courage have been fully tested, and his ready business
tact, coupled with an indomitable energy, admirably fit him for
the position he occupies.   Added to all is a fund of good humor
and genial kindness which never fails him, even when most
besieged by sleeve-pulling pertinacity or harassed by impor-
tunate audacity, which would be remarkable in a philoso-
pher of the oldest school, and is much more so in one whose
years still verge upon the spring-time rather than the summer
of life.

ELIAS COSPER, Captain in the 74th Illinois Volunteers, and First
Assistant Provost-Marshal General, is a native of Ohio, but
resides in Rockford, Illinois.   His age is thirty-nine.   His business was that of a banker, which he surrendered at the call of
duty, leaving a profitable position, an interesting family, and a
delightful home.   Failing health was about to compel him to
leave the service, when his many friends induced him to accept
his present position, to which he was detailed November 14,
1862.

ROBERT M. GOODWIN, Captain in the 37th Indiana Volunteers,
and Second Assistant Provost-Marshal General, was born in
Franklin county, Indiana, in 1836.   At the beginning of the war
he was engaged in a lucrative law-practice, which he resigned,
and enlisted as a private in a company forming in his county.
On the organization of the company he was elected first lieu-

tenant, and afterwards succeeded to the captaincy. With his regiment he participated in the campaign of Generals Buell and Mitchel in Kentucky, Tennessee, and Alabama, during the spring and summer of 1862. Upon Buell's retreat, his regiment was left at Nashville, and remained there during the investment. In the battle of Stone River he acted a gallant and conspicuous part. He was detailed to his present position February 22, 1863

Field Hospital, Murfreesborough, Tenn.

The Medical Department.

THIS chapter is appropriately introduced by the preceding illustration of the field-hospital at Murfreesborough, Tennessee. The cut is a faithful representation of the scene as taken from a distant stand-point: yet it fails to give—as would any single plate of its size and comprehensiveness—that vivid impression imparted to the visitor by a personal inspection, as he walks through the city of tents, with its broad streets, its alleys and walks, the streets neatly worked up and rounded at the centre, with gutters upon each side, and channels being also formed around each tent and house, and leading to main sluice-ways. Sidewalks of plank, cinders, gravel, &c. are laid along each street. The head-quarters' medical tents, the surgery, the house erected for hospital and sanitary stores, the post-office and news-depot, &c. occupy prominent positions in the centre of the village, from which the ground slopes away gently in every direction. Adjoining the hospital village on the west—for a village it is—is a garden comprising thirteen acres of rich bottom-land, which lies in a bend of Stone River, in which, as we write, may be seen a vast amount of " garden-truck," half perfected, and most luxuriant in growth. The river sweeps along the front of the village, and its " levée" presents an animated scene, at most hours of the day, of negro servants washing clothing and bedding, others "packing" water to the town, droves of horses and mules from distant camps being led to the stream upon the opposite side, to drink, and a multitude of invalid soldiers walking about, lounging upon the banks, angling, &c.

During the month of May, 1863, this hospital accommodated an average of eleven hundred patients; and it has proven a great success. As the season advanced, the ill-ventilated store-buildings of Murfreesborough became quite unsuitable for hospital purposes; and the benefit ensuing to the sick and wounded soldier from the cool and always fresh air of the clean, new tents was speedily apparent. This hospital was conceived and planned by the Medical Department of our army, and the grounds were thus scientifically laid out by the engineer corps of the Pioneer Brigade, all under the personal care and inspection of our humane and greatly interested commander-in-chief.

During the battle-week at Stone River, the Medical Department nobly sustained itself as an essential—in fact, vital—branch of the army. Regimental and brigade surgeons invariably followed their commands on to the sanguinary fields, and many were taken prisoners while operating amid groups of the fallen. The ambulance-trains were notably well handled, being drawn up in lines, and, upon the cessation of hostilities in any given direction, were rushed in, loaded with our wounded, and hurried away to the general hospitals in the rear. As an instance of celerity and efficiency, we may mention that within two hours after the battle of Friday evening, January 2, when Breckinridge's left wing was repulsed, our ambulance-trains had gathered the wounded, several hundred in number, by searching over upwards of a hundred acres of ground, after dark, and had them in hospital. And we might add, further, that by eleven o'clock of that night our dead were all decently buried.

The great American rebellion affords grand as well as terrible spectacles. The history of previous wars, of either ancient or modern times, presents no parallel to many features of the one now raging. We can especially instance one feature,—the humanity and tenderness of our nation for its wounded and enfeebled soldiers. Raising of armies was not an only thought. The surgical case accompanied the sword, and the cartridge was no more plenteous than lint and bandage. Medical men of professional reputation and high social character abandoned home and business, and accompanied the youth of their section to the battle-field; while the noble women of the land labored in their behalf with energy and success commensurate with the occasion. We need not dwell upon the fact—which has already become historic—that never was there a war in which such magnificent military hospital preparations were made, and so faithfully carried into effect, as the one now upon us.

The hall-hospitals at Nashville merit brief mention, as representative of that class which are located in buildings in cities and towns. The largest and best-ventilated store-buildings in the city were taken: if containing goods, they were at once vacated, and, where they were objectionable, partitions, shelving, &c. were removed. Walls were whitened, floors thoroughly scoured, and neat cot-bedsteads were made of suitable height and ranged in exact lines through the long rooms. Comfortable beds were prepared,—blankets spread upon ticks filled with fresh straw,—with a soft pillow in a clean white slip. Spittoons, &c. were at each bedside; and the author has heard more than one sharp reprimand fall upon some thoughtless or careless wight who had lodged saliva upon the floors. Several hospitals of this character exist in Nashville at the time of this writing, and, no doubt, in many of our large cities and towns. By such means and efforts hundreds of valuable lives have been saved,—to the praise of the people of this nation, as represented by their various sanitary commissions, volunteer nurses, and the Army Medical Department.

The surgeon who performs his duty faithfully and with skill occupies a laborious, difficult, and most responsible position. No less with him than with the commander upon the battle-field, the lives of the soldiers are intrusted to his care. Hospital scenes, daily to be witnessed within the lines of the Cumberland District, of faithful surgeons moving about at all hours of the day and night, examining, operating, dressing, prescribing, compounding, supplying delicacies, writing letters, breathing out to the afflicted spiritual consolation and hope, receiving last messages, and, finally, closing the eyes in death—and, oh! how many of such have been witnessed!—have won for the Medical Department of our army the lasting affection and gratitude of its members. Many names, thus eminent, could be cited in this connection; but to do so, and necessarily of only a part, would be invidious, and we forbear. Nor is it incumbent upon us to notice disreputable instances which may have occurred in this department, where fraud, intemperance, and professional murder can be charged to the wolves of the medical fraternity. They have been but few—very few—in the Army of the Cumberland; and we pass them by.

Those who witnessed surgical operations at the noted "Brick-house Hospital" during and after the battles of Stone River will never forget many of those scenes. There were the head-quarters for cases requiring amputation; and at times three tables were thus in requisition. Human limbs and pieces of flesh were cast outside of the house, through the windows, and, to use the words of a friend, "would fill a cart-load." The floors of the premises "ran rivers of blood," and the surgeons and attendants, in their dress and appearance, resembled butchers at work in the shambles. The long lines of graves, of both Union and rebel soldiers, now coursing down the sloping field in the rear of that "Brick-house Hospital," attest the many sad results of battle, in which these humane and skilful efforts to save were unavailing. The picture we have drawn is harrowing to the soul; but it needs be thus brought home that we may realize the deepest and most terrible ordeal of the army surgeon.

The Medical Department comprises 159 surgeons, 260 assistant surgeons, 84 contract physicians. There were 2500 attendants, as stewards, clerks, cooks, and nurses, on duty in our 35 general hospitals. The patients usually numbered 13,000, which was augmented to more than 20,000 by the battle of Murfreesborough. Our army has about 500 ambulances. Dr. Eben Swift, Surgeon U.S.A., until recently chief of the department, entered the army in 1847. He served during the Mexican War under General Scott, as aide to the surgeon-general, and established hospitals at Churubusco, Chapultepec, and at the city of Mexico. Since then he has been constantly on duty, and had charge of the Medical Department at the battle of Stone River.

The Artillery Service.

In the history of warfare no changes are more remarkable than those wrought by the improvements in artillery. From the first rude cannon used, to those employed at Stone River, is a long stride; and it would be interesting to trace the gradations through which this feature of warfare has passed. But the limits of this chapter forbid; and we can only give a brief description of the various kinds of artillery in use in the Army of the Cumberland, and a sketch of two or three of the more prominent officers connected with that department.

The importance of this arm of the service will be readily appreciated. Without it, in modern days, no battle worthy of the name has been or can be fought by an army. Upon its efficient management vast results depend; and yet outside of the army little is known concerning it. If the reader of this sketch shall obtain a clearer idea of the number and character of the guns used in one great battle, as well as of the kind, weight, and cost of the powder and projectiles expended, the object of the author will be fully attained. For prudential reasons, no reference will be made to the present condition of this department of the Army of the Cumberland; and the battle of Stone River has been selected as the basis of remarks under this head.

The artillery of the Department of the Cumberland, at the opening of the battle of Stone River, consisted of thirty-nine batteries,—heavy and field,—of which twenty-seven batteries of field-guns only were in the engagement.

It was divided as follows:—

RIGHT WING.

Chief of Artillery, Major CHARLES S. COTTER.

1st Division—Chief of Artillery, Captain O. F. PINNEY.

5th Wisconsin Battery......................Captain O. F. PINNEY.
2d Minnesota Battery......................Captain W. A. HOTCHKISS.
8th Wisconsin Battery.....................Captain T. J. CARPENTER.

2d Division—Chief of Artillery, Captain W. P. EDGARTON.

E Company, 1st Ohio Artillery............Captain W. P. EDGARTON.
5th Indiana Battery..........................Captain P. SIMONSON.
A Company, 1st Ohio Artillery...........1st Lieutenant E. B. BELDING.

3d Division—Chief of Artillery, Captain A. K. BUSH.

G Company, 1st Missouri Artillery......Captain H. HESCOCK.
4th Indiana Battery...........................Captain A. K. BUSH.
C Company, 1st Illinois Artillery.........Captain C. HOUGHTALING.

CENTRE.

Chief of Artillery, Captain O. H. MACK.

1st Division—Chief of Artillery, Colonel C. O. LOOMIS.

1st Kentucky Battery.......................Captain D. C. STONE.
1st Michigan Battery.......................Lieutenant G. W. VAN PELT.
H Company, 5th Artillery, U.S.A.........1st Lieutenant F. L. GUENTHER.

2d Division—Chief of Artillery, Captain F. SCHULTZ.

M Company, 1st Ohio Artillery...........Captain F. SCHULTZ.
G Company, 1st Ohio Artillery ....1st Lieut. ALEXANDER MARSHALL.
M Company, 1st Kentucky Artillery....1st Lieut. A. A. ELLSWORTH.

LEFT WING.

Chief of Artillery, Captain JOHN MENDENHALL, U.S.A.

1st Division—Chief of Artillery, Major T. RACE.

10th Indiana Battery........................Captain J. B. COX.
8th Indiana Battery..........................1st. Lieut. GEORGE ESTEP.
6th Ohio Battery..............................Captain C. BRADLEY.

2d Division—Chief of Artillery, Captain W. E. STANDART.

B Company, 1st Ohio Artillery.............Captain W. E. STANDART
M Company, 4th Artillery, U.S.A.........1st Lieut. C. C. PARSONS.
H Company, 4th Artillery, U.S.A.........1st Lieut. C. B. THROCKMORTON.
F Company, 1st Ohio Artillery............Captain D. T. COCKERILL.

3d Division—Chief of Artillery, Captain GEORGE R. SWALLOW.

7th Indiana Battery..........................Captain G. R. SWALLOW.

3d Wisconsin Battery.........................1st Lieut. C. LIVINGSTON.
26th Pennsylvania Battery.................1st Lieut. A. J. STEVENS.

PIONEER BRIGADE.

Chicago Board of Trade Battery..........Captain J. H. STOKES.

CAVALRY DIVISION.

D Company, 1st Ohio Artillery............2d Lieut. N. M. NEWELL.

The armament was as follows:—

RIGHT WING.

Eleven James rifled guns.
Seventeen six-pounders, smooth-bore.
Ten twelve-pounder howitzers.
Eight ten-pounder Parrott guns.
Four twelve-pounder light (Napoleon) guns.

CENTRE.

Four James rifled guns.
Three six-pounder smooth-bore guns.
Four twelve-pounder howitzers.
Twelve ten-pounder Parrott guns.
Four twelve-pounder light (Napoleon) guns.
Two six-pounder Wiard guns.
Two twelve-pounder Wiard guns.

LEFT WING.

Six James rifled guns.
Twelve six-pounder smooth-bore guns.
Ten twelve-pounder howitzers.
Sixteen ten-pounder Parrott guns.
Four three-inch Rodman guns.

PIONEER BRIGADE.

Two James rifled guns.
Four six-pounder smooth-bore guns.

CAVALRY.

Two three-inch Rodman guns.

It will be observed that seven different kinds of cannon were used in this battle, viz.:—

The twelve-pounder light gun.

The six-pounder smooth-bore.

" six-pounder James rifled gun.

" three-inch Rodman rifled gun.

" ten-pounder Parrott rifled gun.

" Wiard rifled gun.

" twelve-pounder field howitzer.

The twelve-pounder is a smooth-bore gun, made of bronze, called *light* twelve-pounder to distinguish it from the old heavy twelve-pounder, upon which it is an improvement. It was modelled from the French gun, and was introduced into our service in 1857. The improvements were suggested by the present Emperor, and the piece is generally known as the Napoleon gun. Its range is about fifteen hundred yards.

The six-pounder smooth-bore gun is the United States model of 1844, made of bronze, and previous to the present war was used in most of our field-batteries. Its range is about twelve hundred yards.

The James rifled gun is the United States smooth-bore, rifled by General James, of Rhode Island. The original name—six-pounder—is still preserved, although the elongated projectile weighs eleven pounds. James's invention refers more to the projectile than to the gun itself, his method of rifling presenting nothing that is new. The length of the projectile is twice its diameter, the front part conical, the rear portion made something like a *wheel-hub*, having a cylindrical cavity open towards the rear, and several cavities leading from this to the exterior, like the mortises of a hub which receive the spokes. A collar of lead encircles the exterior, and over this is a broad band of tin. The whole is covered by a wrapping of canvas steeped in oil. The projectile is made of such a size as to enter readily the bore of the piece. When the cartridge in the rear is ignited in firing, the expansive gases generated by the combustion of the powder enter the cylindrical cavity and the mortises of the projectile, and create a pressure against the wrapping, which yields, is forced into the grooves, and the projectile in its passage through the bore of the piece assumes the rifled motion.

The oiled canvas lubricates the grooves and prevents them from becoming "leaded." Its extreme range is about three thousand yards.

The three-inch Rodman rifled gun is made of wrought iron and named after the inventor, Captain T. J. Rodman, United States Ordnance Corps. The projectiles used in it are generally the Hotchkiss and Schenkl. They are both elongated, with conical points. The former has a collar of lead encircling it near the base. The base consists of a cup-shaped piece of metal, which is driven forward by the force of the powder in firing; and the rim, entering between the projectile and the leaden collar, forces the latter into the grooves and secures the rifled motion. The Schenkl projectile is terminated in rear by a conical spindle, around which fits a cylinder of *papier maché*, which when driven forward by the explosion of the powder is forced into the grooves, and the rifled motion is communicated to the projectile. The extreme range of this gun is about five thousand yards.

The ten-pounder Parrott rifled gun—named after the inventor, Captain R. P. Parrott, proprietor of the West Point Foundry, New York, and formerly an officer of the army—is made of cast iron, with a band of wrought iron shrunk on around the rear portion of the gun, to strengthen it. Its projectile—also the invention of Captain Parrott—is made of cast iron, with a cup-shaped piece of wrought iron attached to the base of the cavity towards the rear. This cup is expanded into the groove by the force of the powder, and the rifled motion thus secured. The range is the same as that of the three-inch Rodman gun.

The Wiard rifled gun—named also after the inventor—is made of steel. The same kind of projectiles are used as in the Rodman gun. The range of the six-pounder Wiard is very nearly the same as that of the ten-pounder Parrott.

The twelve-pounder howitzer is the United States model of 1841,—a short bronze piece for throwing shells, case-shot, and canister. Its range is about one thousand yards.

There were in all 20,307 projectiles thrown at the battle of

Stone River.   The average weight of metal in a projectile is ten pounds, and the average charge of powder one and a half pounds.   The entire weight of metal thrown was, therefore, 203,070 pounds, and the quantity of powder 30,360½ pounds. Assuming seven cents as the average price per pound for the different projectiles, the cost would be $14,214.90.   Twenty cents per pound for the powder would amount to $6,072,10. Total, $20,287.00.   This is taking the most economical view of the subject.

In the battle of the 31st of December, 1862, the following guns were taken by the enemy:—

        8 James rifled.

        6 twelve-pounder howitzers.

        9 six-pounder smooth-bores.

        2 ten-pounder Parrotts.

        1 six-pounder Wiard.

        2 twelve-pounder Wiard.

        1 James rifled (disabled).

Total, 29

The following were captured from the enemy:—

        1 Napoleon.

        2 ten-pounder Parrotts.

        2 twelve-pounder howitzers.

        1 six-pounder smooth-bore.

Total, 6

With the foregoing interesting and instructive statistics, furnished for this work by the Chief of Artillery, we take leave of the subject.

THE CHIEF OF ARTILLERY.

COLONEL JAMES BARNETT, of the 1st Ohio Artillery, Chief of Artillery of the Department of the Cumberland, is a native of the State of New York, and is forty-two years of age.   From boyhood he has resided in the city of Cleveland, Ohio. He was educated to the hardware-trade, and for many years has been a member of the hardware jobbing-house of George Worthington & Co., of that city.

At the beginning of the war he was in command of an independent artillery organization, and tendered its services to the State authorities. After the fall of Fort Sumter they were accepted, and on the 21st of April, 1861, the Governor of Ohio, by telegraph, ordered the command to report at Columbus. In accordance with this order, Captain Barnett, with a full company of men, and six guns, started the next morning, and, arriving at Columbus, proceeded, without halting, to Marietta, Ohio, where the guns were mounted, horses, &c. procured, and all fitted for service. Upon the occupation of Western Virginia by the Federal troops, one section of this battery moved with Colonel Steadman, of the 14th Ohio, by way of Parkersburg, and two sections by way of Benwood, to Grafton. During the three-months campaign these guns were constantly on duty, at Grafton, Philippi, Laurel Hill, Carrick's Ford, and other points. At the expiration of their term of enlistment the command returned to Columbus, and were honorably mustered out of service in the month of July.

In August it was decided to organize the 1st Regiment of Ohio Light Artillery, and Captain Barnett was commissioned as its colonel. This organization, consisting of twelve field-batteries of six guns and one hundred and fifty men each, was perfected, and the regiment was fully equipped and put into the field by January 1, 1862. The colonel reported to General Buell at Louisville, and upon the arrival of the army at Nashville, in March, he was placed in command of the artillery reserve of the Army of the Ohio, in which capacity he served until ordered to Ohio in July on recruiting service. Having obtained the requisite number of recruits for his regiment, he was assigned to duty in September upon the staff of General C. C. Gilbert, at that time commanding the centre corps of the Army of the Ohio. After the battle of Perryville the colonel was transferred to the staff of Major-General McCook as chief of artillery, which position he filled until November 24, 1862, when he was designated by General Rosecrans as chief of artillery for his department.

In the battle of Stone River, as well as in many previous ones, Colonel Barnett was constantly and actively engaged, and is mentioned with especial commendation by General Rosecrans in his official report.

THE ARTILLERY CHIEF OF THE 20TH CORPS.

MAJOR CHARLES S. COTTER, Chief of Artillery for the 20th Army Corps, is a native of Ohio, and was born September 20, 1827. Before the war he followed the silver-plating trade, and was doing a prosperous business. He was also captain of an independent artillery company, consisting of one gun and twenty-five men.

Hearing of the attack on Fort Sumter on Sunday, he closed his shop on Monday, and called a meeting of his company for the same evening. They voted to offer their services to the Government; and on Tuesday Captain Cotter reported to Governor Dennison. From that day to this he has not entered his place of business. His company was ordered immediately to Virginia, where he participated in the Kanawha Valley campaign under Brigadier-General Cox. At Scrag Creek the battery, consisting of two rifled pieces, was engaged, fired seventy-nine rounds, and dismounted three of the enemy's four guns. At Tyler Mountain a skirmish occurred, in which, with his battery, Captain Cotter burned the rebel steamboat Julia Moffatt.

In September, 1861, he enlisted a full six-gun battery at Ravenna and Cleveland, which was the first full one to go from Ohio. Passing through Kentucky and Tennessee, it reached Shiloh, but, being in the reserve, was not actively engaged. During the siege of Corinth he took part in a severe fight, in which four of his pieces fired two hundred and seventy-nine rounds, repulsing the advance of a brigade of the enemy and killing a number of them,—forty dead bodies having been found on the field. He then marched to Huntsville and Battle Creek. He was promoted major June 9, 1862. About the 1st of October he was assigned to Major-General McCook as chief of artillery. At the battle of Perryville, October 8, he had charge of twenty-six pieces, used them constantly, and lost none of them. Near dusk he rode to the rear for a supply of ammunition; and while he was thus absent from the front our forces fell back a few hundred yards. Not noticing this on his return,—it being too dark to distinguish more than the outline of men and animals,—he rode directly into the Confederate lines —they having advanced—and was taken prisoner by Major-General Polk in person. That night the enemy retreated, and he was carried with them to Harrodsburg, where he was detained as a prisoner for three days, and then paroled, when he regained our lines.

Returning to Ohio, he was ordered to Camp Chase, to take charge of the paroled artillery troops. Here he remained until he was exchanged, reporting to General McCook for duty February 15, 1863. He was at once appointed chief of artillery of the right wing of the Army of the Cumberland, or 20th Army Corps.

THE CHIEF OF ORDNANCE.

CAPTAIN HORACE PORTER (Ordnance Corps, U.S.A.), Chief of Ordnance, is a native of Pennsylvania, and was born in 1837. In June, 1855, he entered upon the five-years course at West Point, and in June, 1860, he graduated third in a class of forty-one. He was appointed brevet-lieutenant of ordnance July 1, 1860, second lieutenant April 22, 1861, first lieutenant June 7, 1861, and captain March 3, 1863.

At the opening of the war he was a bearer of despatches

from New York to Washington, and was subsequently on duty at Washington and at Watervliet Arsenal, New York. In October, 1861, he sailed with General T. W. Sherman's expedition to Port Royal, South Carolina, and at the bombardment of Fort Pulaski was chief of ordnance and artillery. At the attack on Secessionville, James Island, South Carolina, June 16, 1862, he was slightly wounded. In July, 1862, he joined the Army of the Potomac as chief of ordnance to General McClellan. In the following October he was assigned to the staff of General Wright, commanding the Department of the Ohio, as chief of ordnance, and in January, 1863, was appointed to a similar position on the staff of General Rosecrans, Department of the Cumberland.

The Army Signal and Telegraph Service.

THE Signal Corps of our Army is composed of officers and enlisted men, detailed from different regiments, with special reference to their fitness for the duties required of them. The officers are instructed in the use of the signals used before they go into the field, and are forbidden to carry with them any thing that would give the enemy information leading to the discovery of the system in case of capture. The object of the organization is to keep up constant communication between the different parts of the army and the different commanding generals, and to closely scan and discover the movements of the enemy. For this reason, the officers are furnished with powerful telescopes and marine glasses, and are usually located on the tops of high elevations, or other commanding positions.

When General Rosecrans assumed command of the Army of the Cumberland, he adopted the signal system and reorganized the corps. The officers and men were ordered to report to Captain Jesse Merrill, Chief Signal Officer of the Department, and were divided into parties, put in charge of competent directors, and assigned to the different army corps for duty. On the march from Nashville to Murfreesborough, officers were constantly on the alert, collecting and communicating intelligence. During the twenty-four hours previous to the battle of Stone River, communication was kept up from front to rear on the Murfreesborough pike, and on Tuesday, while our army was fighting its way to what was afterwards its line of battle, short lines of communication were maintained.

Soon after the occupation of Murfreesborough, two brigades were sent in the direction of McMinnville and Woodbury,— one as far as Readyville, twelve miles, and the other to Cripple

303

Creek, eight miles, from Murfreesborough. Between these two points, and a little north of the pike, is a high mountain, called Pilot Knob, and on its summit had been established a signal-station called " Fort Transit." This point commands the surrounding country in all directions for miles; and many items of inte· rest and importance were reported by the officers on that station They communicated with the central station in the cupola of the court-house at Murfreesborough; and daily and nightly, on these stations, flags and torches could be seen waving information and orders from one point to the other. As the lines of the army were extended, communication in the same way was opened between the different points. The station on the court-house at Murfreesborough communicates with one at Lavergne, fifteen miles distant, and one near Triune, seventeen miles distant. From the latter point a line of stations connects it with Franklin, and from the former communication can be had with Nashville whenever desired.

Major Albert J. Meyer, Signal Officer of the Army, has recently added greatly to the efficiency of his department by sending to Murfreesborough a signal telegraph train. This train consists of six substantially-built wagons, each containing a telegraph instrument, tool-chest, axes, reels, &c. Three of the wagons also contain five miles of wire each; the other three have fifteen empty reels, used in reeling up the wire after being laid out. The telegraph instruments are the most complete for field-purposes ever put in operation, and much superior, both in matter of economy and reliability, to others now in use. The dial-instrument is used and the electricity is generated at the time of operating, and without the use of acid. The instrument is contained in a box which can be carried by one man, and its mechanism is so simple that it is ready for use the instant the station in the field is selected. Three lines were put in operation at Murfreesborough, running to the corps commanders' head-quarters. The wire used is insulated by gutta-percha, and can be run out on the ground, hung on fences or trees, or put on poles. It is rolled upon reels, in one-mile sections, and, in running it or rolling it up, the horses are kept at a steady and rapid trot. This field telegraph is a recent invention, scarcely more than a year old; but it has been successfully used on the Potomac, and was of inestimable service at the attack on Fredericksburg in December last. The principal object aimed at in its use is to keep open a constant communication of the different commands of an army with each other and with head-quarters, and also to connect the army, or any portion of it, with the signal-station, which, from the necessity of its location on some high and commanding point, is almost invariably at some distance from the camp.

The full details of the system are, of course, known only to the initiated; for in its secrecy lies its success. A general idea of its character and management may be given, however, without injury to the service. In the first place, then, elevated positions are chosen, between which communications are made by means of a flag in the daytime and of a torch at night. The alphabet of the code consists of certain definite figures, different combinations of which represent the different letters of the ordinary English alphabet. Of these figures there are but few, a sufficient variety being obtained by different combinations of the same figures. Thus, 11, 14 may mean A, while 14, 11 may mean D; and so on. Each figure of the alphabet is represented by a definite number of dips or wavings of the flag or torch, thus enabling the experienced in the art to read messages at almost incredible distances with surprising rapidity.

To enable the reader more fully to understand the workings of the system, let him accompany the author to the signal-station in the cupola of the court-house at Murfreesborough. Here he will find two windows, one looking towards Fort Transit, nine and a half miles to the east, and the other towards Triune, seventeen miles to the west. By the side of each is a telescope, firmly fixed and bearing upon the station opposite. Outside of the opening is a platform, upon which the man waving the flag or torch stands. It being desired to open communication, the flag is waved to and fro until seen and answered by the other station,—which is generally but a moment or two, as somebody is always on the watch at the glass. The officer in charge seats himself at the glass, and, having observed the answer to his signal, calls to the man on the platform the figures which he wishes represented or waved. Thus, for example:

3—11; 21—5; 2—31—11; 1—43—5; 22—31; 14—22—23; 1—43—5; 11—1—42; 1—42—2; 23—11; 1—11; 5—55.

The substance of the above message is to inquire if a certain officer has arrived at a certain place, as expected. In what seems scarcely more than a single minute after the last word is sent, the answer comes from Fort Transit, and is read by the officer at the glass.

For the transmission of messages, different-colored flags are employed, as best suits the state of the atmosphere. There are now in use at Murfreesborough one black with a white centre, one white with a red centre, and one all red. Sometimes one can be plainly seen and recognized when another cannot be seen at all: hence the variety. As already said, there are two stations in the court-house at Murfreesborough, to which are assigned two officers and four men. The stations are kept open all the time, night and day, officers being constantly on the watch at the glass. When the station is " called" by one of the outlying stations, the officer in charge by whom the message is to be received and answered, if below in his office, is notified by the tapping of the court-house bell, two strokes calling him to one station, and three to the other. All messages sent and received are written out and copies of them preserved, which are often called for as evidence in courts-martial, &c. Messages received were formerly delivered at head-quarters by orderlies, but are now sent by the newly-arrived telegraph train.

The system now in use in all the Union armies was invented by Major Meyer, the Signal Officer of the army, since the beginning of the present war, the one previously in use having become valueless because of certain officers of the corps having gone with the South. The rebels, too, have a system, invented or perfected by one Alexander, formerly a lieutenant under Major

Meyer, but now understood to be a brigadier-general in the Confederate service. Our army system differs from that of the navy, in that the latter is worked by a series of preconcerted and set phrases, while by this any thing that can be written can be telegraphed with astonishing rapidity and certainty. A message of twenty words can be sent in five minutes, and answered in as many more. As an illustration of its workings, a single example will suffice. In the latter part of March, Major-General Palmer made an expedition to Woodbury, twenty-two miles from Murfreesborough, and in less than thirty minutes after he entered the town General Rosecrans was informed of the fact by means of the signal corps. The commanding general at once despatched to him certain orders; and in an hour from the time of sending them he was informed by General Palmer that they had been received and the troops disposed in accordance with them. The use of the field telegraph will materially add to the rapidity with which messages can be transmitted, by dispensing with the necessity of couriers between the headquarters of commanders and the signal-station.

The alphabet is not difficult to learn; but constant practice is required to enable the operator to send and receive messages without hesitation. The labor required of the corps is confining, but not severe. For days there may be little to do, and, again, both officers and men may be constantly employed during both the day and night. They sleep when they can, and are expected to be ready at a moment's warning. Messages, in very clear weather, can be read between Triune and Pilot Knob, twenty-seven miles, or between the Knob and Lavergne, twenty-five miles, without being repeated at Murfreesborough; and they have been sent direct from the Knob to Nashville, forty-five miles; but this distance is too great for the glasses now in use, and is not considered entirely reliable. In addition to the ordinary duty of transmitting messages, the officers and men of the corps act as scouts, keeping a constant watch upon the movements of the enemy, as they are able to do from their commanding location, and reporting the results of their observations to head-quarters without delay.

The Signal Corps of the Army of the Cumberland is under the direction of Captain Jesse Merrill, of the 7th Pennsylvania Reserve. He is a native of Pennsylvania, and an attorney by profession. He entered the service as second lieutenant, and served as such in the Army of the Potomac until January, 1862, when, having learned the code, he was detailed to the Army of the Cumberland to introduce it there and instruct the requisite number of officers and men in its mysteries. He is a thorough master of the system, and has rendered it highly effective, as the reader may judge from the foregoing account.

The Murfreesborough station is under the charge of Captain C. R. Case, of the 36th Indiana, and T. J. Kelly, of the 10th Ohio Infantry. The telegraphic train is under command of Lieutenant D. Wonderly, of Philadelphia, assisted by Lieutenants S. F. Reber and D. F. Jarvis. The corps of the department consists of about forty officers, and, inclusive of the telegraphic train, about one hundred and forty enlisted men, all of whom are detailed from their respective regiments for this service; and thus the signal service is rendered at but a trifling additional cost to the country.

The Army Mail.

Army Mail-Wagon escaping from Guerrillas at Lavergne.

A SOLDIER'S life is a life of privation. Like the migratory patriarchs of the olden time, he is only "a sojourner in the land;" but, unlike them, his wife, his children, and his household gods go not with him in his wanderings. Their homes were ever present with them; his can only be far away, in the forests of the free North or on the wide prairies of the West. "Home is where the heart is," sings the poet. "The heart is where home is," says the soldier; and not the daily stir of camp-life, not the march, with its ever-changing scenes, not even the

309

deadly shock of battle, can banish from his thoughts the dear ones whom he has left behind. Who, then, shall tell the heart-longings for home, for family, and for friends that crowd his hours of leisure and of rest? At dead of night, as the sentinel paces his lonely round, his mind is busy with fondest memories. Wrapped in his blanket, with only the stars above him, the soldier's weary body finds rest in sleep: yet he wanders from warlike scenes. No moonbeam brighter in its silvery flood than is his dream of that far-off home, where the good old father and mother sit by the chimney-corner and talk of their boy who has gone to the war,—where the loving wife presses the babe to her breast and gently whispers the story—alas! how true!—of its absent father,—where the maiden sleeps with dreams as pure and sweet as those in which he asks, "Are they of me?" and hers seem to answer, "Yes."

In the Army of the Cumberland there are fifty thousand men to whom this is no fancy sketch. They have been absent from their homes weeks, months, and even years. The interim has, perhaps, been fruitful of change in the dear home-circle. A mother, a wife, a child, has departed to the spirit-realm; the wedding-feast has been prepared in the household; or may-be another flower is blooming amid the family garland, unseen as yet by the war-worn father. With what eagerness, then, must not a visit to that home be desired! With what earnestness must not a furlough be sought! But we are in an enemy's country, a hostile army confronts us face to face, and furloughs must necessarily be denied. We may think and dream of home; but that is all. This privation, this heart-sickness, is the bane of a soldier's life.

Much, however, may be done to alleviate it. If we may not revisit those who nightly gather around the fireside, we may look upon their lineaments as painted by the sunbeam in its passage through the dark chambers of the camera. If we cannot whisper our thoughts and read the answer in loving eyes before the lips can give utterance, we can substitute pen for tongue, and, in return, gather from the thickly-covered page at least a part of what we would so dearly love to hear. As sight is the best of all God's gifts to man, and hearing the next, so the next best thing to a visit is a letter from home. Its influence on the soldier can hardly be overestimated. It is a messenger of love and hope, bringing words of comfort and cheer in those dark and trying hours which come alike, at times, to all. If it be in answer to tidings of victory, words of praise nerve him to still more daring deeds of valor. If of defeat, it bids him not despair, but, with faith in God and his own good sword, press persistently on to the inevitable triumph that awaits him. Uncertainty and suspense are ended, positive knowledge of home-affairs reigning in their stead. Discontent gives place to cheerfulness, and with firmer hope, higher aspiration, he re-enters upon his daily duty. A happier man and a better soldier, his country not less than himself is indebted for the change to the Army Mail.

At the outset it became evident that regular mails could not be supplied to our armies in the field through the usual agency of the Post-Office Department. Railroads were torn up; river-navigation was often interrupted, and became at all times dangerous; old mail-routes were suspended; mail-matter destined for the army accumulated at the distributing offices and at the termini of the regular routes, in hopelessly confused heaps, to be forwarded only at long intervals. Grave complaints unavoidably arose, and it became necessary to devise a military mail-system which, independent of, yet acting in concert with, the civil department, would supply the deficiency. Among the first to notice the evil and apply the remedy was Major-General Rosecrans. Himself a practical soldier and appreciating a soldier's minor wants, it is with him a settled policy to minister to the mind as well as to the body. In Western Virginia his efforts to secure regular mail-facilities to his men were attended with partial success; but it was not until called to the command of the Army of the Mississippi that he was enabled to inaugurate a thoroughly complete system of daily military mails.

Immediately on his arrival at Corinth, he appointed Colonel

William Truesdail his army mail agent. Messengers were at once placed upon the boats and railroads between that place and Cairo. An efficient general travelling agent—P. W. Currier, Esq.—was engaged; and it was one of his special duties to visit the various distributing offices at Louisville, Cincinnati, Chicago, St. Louis, and Cairo, and furnish them with accurate lists of the divisions, brigades, regiments, and smaller commands constituting that army, and to have forwarded from those offices bushels, and in some instances wagon-loads, of mail-matter found piled beneath tables and counters or stowed away in drawers, barrels, and back rooms.

Upon assuming command of the Army of the Cumberland, General Rosecrans found it in a worse condition even than had been the Army of the Mississippi in respect to mail-matter. Recently marched up from Alabama, through Kentucky and Tennessee, to the Ohio River, and now back again to Bowling Green, the troops had been almost everywhere in turn and nowhere long. Battles, skirmishes, and forced marches had followed each other in rapid succession; divisions and brigades were scattered here and there; and even regimental commands were divided between widely distant stations. No accessible record of their movements and localities had been preserved, and it had been found simply impossible to forward the long-looked-for mails. Thus thousands of soldiers and officers, as well as privates, had been weeks and months without tidings from home or friends, while tons of mail-matter lay mouldering in distant post-offices. To bring order out of this chaos was again the difficult duty of Colonel Truesdail, which was speedily accomplished, aided by his assistant, Mr. Currier, and other agents. Messengers were appointed and teams were arranged, and a system improvised ready for operation when the army should advance into the enemy's country. F. C. Herrick, Esq., an experienced employé of the civil department, was appointed army postmaster,—whose duty it was to move with the army and receive and distribute the mails, with instructions to operate in harmony with the United States mail authorities and have for his sole object the prompt delivery of the mails to the soldiers.

At this time, it will be remembered, Nashville was invested by the rebels, and for two months all communication with the North suspended. Not until our army reached that city was it relieved from the dearth of mail-matter. True, certain private parties had attempted to run the gauntlet with small letter-mails; but failure and loss of teams and mails had been the result. Now, however, daily mails were regularly received and sent, greatly to the joy of all. The Government then brought the mails only to Mitchellsville, Tennessee, distant from Nashville thirty-five miles. Between these places bridges had been burned and tunnels blown up by the rebels, rendering the railroad unavailing for several weeks. The mail-wagons were at once put on; and for two months a heavy mail passed each way through a wild guerrilla country, accompanied by a strong cavalry escort. Arrived at Nashville, it was at once distributed and sent to the various division, brigade, and regimental headquarters. Some idea of the business thus transacted may be gathered from the fact that not unfrequently twenty thousand letters were mailed at the Nashville office in a single day, besides two or three bushels of photographs, daguerreotypes, &c. From eight to twelve hundred dollars' worth of stamps were sold daily, and nearly all of them to the army.

When the advance towards Murfreesborough began, the army was again thrown beyond the reach of the Government mails; and again recourse was had to the army wagons and messengers, and daily trips were made, sometimes with, but oftener without, an escort. The route was through a dangerous country infested with roving bands of rebel cavalry : yet during many weeks the mails were thus carried safely and regularly, and in that time not a mail-bag, or, to the knowledge of the writer, a single letter, was lost. Early in March the railroad between Nashville and Murfreesborough was reopened; and since then daily mails have been received from and sent to Nashville by the army postmaster with great regularity, the Army of the

Cumberland receiving its mails more promptly and with less confusion, probably, than does any other army in the field. Upon an average, twenty-two thousand letters—amounting in bulk to fifteen bushels—leave the Murfreesborough military office daily, to be duly mailed in the United States distributing office at Nashville, from whence they are sent over the regular mail-routes to their respective destinations. The equally large mails received are sorted and distributed, by means of the mail-wagons, among the various camps and military offices with creditable energy and despatch.

In a correspondence of such magnitude it is idle to say that complaints do not arise. In spite of every care, letters will fail to reach their destination; but the wonder really is that so few are lost. In the Department of the Cumberland, embracing Western Kentucky and Middle and Eastern Tennessee, there are not less than twelve divisions, thirty-seven brigades, and more than two hundred regiments, besides independent organizations, such as pioneers, engineers, the signal corps, sharpshooters, batteries, scouts, hospitals, convalescent camps, &c. &c. Imagine the perplexity, then, of the army postmaster as he puzzles his brain over thousands of letters addressed, in the most unreadable hand, after this style:—"Mr. John Smith, Co. A, Rosecrans Army;" "Lt. Tom Jones, 3d Div.;" "Capt. Brown, 2d Brigade;" "Major Thompson, 21st Regt.;" and which he is expected to forward "in haste." The only possible disposition of such letters is to send them from regiment to regiment, until frequently they are literally worn out in their fruitless search for an owner.

Thus far the practical workings of the system have fully realized the most sanguine expectations of its originators. The cheerfulness imbued and the confidence inspired are well worth its entire expense; but, aside from these, the Government is abundantly remunerated for every outlay by the extra revenue derived from the thus largely-increased correspondence. With regular mails three letters are written where one would be without; and under the present system it only requires proper direction to insure prompt delivery. The simplest and plainest address is the best. The name, the title (if any there be), the company, the regiment, the State from which it comes, the arm of service to which it belongs, and the army or corps of which it is a part, comprise all that is absolutely indispensable to secure the safe and speedy delivery of army letters. The numbers of the brigade and division are not necessary; but it is better to add them if known. The same may also be said of the particular locality at which the command is stationed, and the route which the letter is to take. But such an address as this is sufficient:—" Robert Jasper, Co. H, 21st Regt. Illinois Infantry, Army of the Cumberland, via Louisville, Ky." "Cavalry" or "Artillery" may be substituted for "Infantry," as occasion requires. The distributing officers are furnished with lists of the regiments comprised in those armies whose letters they receive and forward, as well as their stations; and it is only necessary to know the particular army to which it is to go to insure the transmission of a letter thereto, and the company and regiment in that army, to secure its speedy delivery to the owner upon its arrival there.

A single incident will illustrate the occasional dangers of the military mail-service. During the week of battles at Stone River, the most important mail-matter was sent to and fro at considerable risk of capture from the rebel cavalry that had succeeded in getting between Nashville and the rear of our army and were burning wagon-trains on the road. On the evening of December 31, the day of the heaviest fighting, intelligence came that our shelterless men were wellnigh exhausted from continued exposure to storm and mud. Colonel Truesdail at once ordered a mail-wagon to be filled with choice refreshments for the general's head-quarters, which, with important mail-matter, he intrusted to the charge of S. A. Esterbrook, Esq., one of the oldest and boldest of the army mail-messengers. By ten o'clock, "Brooks," as he is called, was ready to start on his journey. Arrived at the outer pickets, he is told by the guards that the road is alive with rebel cavalry, that he will certainly be captured, and they flatly refuse to pass him beyond the lines. His protest is of no avail, and back he comes to the office. Colonel Truesdail, much disappointed, writes a peremptory order to pass the mail-wagon, assuming all risk himself. Again "Brooks" sets forth, and passes the pickets, but is scarcely out of sight or hearing when he meets a motley crowd of flying teamsters, pedlars, and camp-followers, each telling a more dreadful tale than the preceding of discomfiture to our arms, dangers along the road, raids of rebel horsemen, and flames of burning wagons. So strong the tide and so unanimous the story that "Brooks," concluding further advance fool-hardy, and, in this case, discretion certainly the better part of valor, again retraces his way, and at two o'clock in the morning is once more in Nashville.

The colonel had just retired, and was sleeping when "Brooks" came thundering into the office. Awakened by the noise, he is possibly a little vexed. Certes, he walks the room excitedly in rather scanty attire,—the shortness of army shirts being proverbial. Ere long, oaths fly about like feathers in a gale; and finally the intimation is heard that "Brooks is afraid." A still more wrathful explosion now occurs, "Brooks" declaring that wagon, mail, messenger, and driver will start again, and this time go without fail to Stone River or to——a much hotter place. "Yes," says the colonel, "go on: put 'em through; let the rebs get you if they can,—I want 'em to get you; but, if they do, lose your mails, destroy your despatches, and burst in your liquors, —— 'em !"

A third time our man starts, resolved to "do or die." It is almost dawn as his wagon rattles up the hill overlooking Lavergne, and a strange and fearful sight greets him at its summit. For a mile and a half the road is quite straight, descending a long slope into the valley in which Lavergne is built, and beyond the town again ascending a similar ridge. As far as eye can reach, the flames of burning wagons leap wildly up into the darkness, made tenfold darker by their lurid light. No living form is visible,—only the whitened surface of "the pike" and the sombre cedar thickets by its side. The authors of this havoc are lurking near by, or, more probably, are making good their escape with such plunder from our trains as can be carried on the backs of captured mules. Danger is ahead; but there is no escape: only the speed of his horses can save our driver now. Their mettle is of the best, and serve him well as he sweeps along like the wind, turning quickly out and in to avoid the burning wagons, listening all the while with bated breath for the whistling of bullets and the tramp of pursuing cavalry. The valley is reached, the town passed, the hill gained, and he is safe, and, the journey ended, he meets with a hearty welcome at head-quarters. His was a narrow escape, as, but half an hour previously that road was lined by a thousand rebel cavalry. An illustration of this scene precedes this chapter.

The Army Directory.

WHEN the Army of the Cumberland advanced southward from Bowling Green, the troops were gradually withdrawn from stations in Kentucky and elsewhere, and massed in the direction of Nashville, an aggregate of thousands, however, being unavoidably left behind on detached service, in hospitals, and absent on furloughs. Meanwhile an entire reorganization of the army was effected,—scarcely a regiment or battery remaining in its old brigade or division.

When Nashville was reached, and for weeks thereafter, not a day passed without the return of hundreds of these absentees to rejoin their commands, of whose whereabouts officers and privates were often alike ignorant. The military offices in the city were besieged with crowds of anxious inquirers, and for a time all was confusion. At length so great became this daily influx, and so considerable the time required to attend to it, that the general commanding committed the business to the care of the Chief of the Army Police; and to the usual crowd thronging the police office was now added this motley array of soldiery, too often weak and weary, and always without food or shelter.

Colonel Truesdail at once set about adjusting the difficulty in a speedy and practical manner. A tent was pitched on the vacant lot adjoining the police building, and an active and intelligent agent there duly installed as Army Director. The proper authorities were consulted, and an accurate schedule of the new army organization compiled. Messengers were despatched to ascertain the exact locality of each command, and lost soldiers were notified, by handbills posted through the city, to report themselves at this tent. The plan worked well, and

318

the military offices were soon rid of what had become an intolerable nuisance. The streets were cleared of stragglers, and the soldiers—many of them just discharged from hospitals, and sorely travel-worn—were promptly forwarded to their respective camps. When the army moved to Murfreesborough, the same difficulty was experienced; and an office was opened there, with a like good result. The department thus at first temporarily organized is yet continued, and is known as the Army Directory or Intelligence Office.

The cost to the Government of the office, which experience has proved to be a necessity in a large and ever-fluctuating army, is very slight, only a single clerk being needed. The benefits derived therefrom are incalculably great. Persons seeking for friends in the army have only to inquire at the directory to ascertain their whereabouts. Full and reliable burial-lists also may be found there, by means of which relatives in quest of the remains of deceased soldiers can at once be pointed to their resting-places. Not only lost soldiers are set right, but the hundreds of citizens, sanitary commissioners, nurses, traders, and others visiting the army are furnished with information indispensable to them in an army spread over two hundred miles of territory, and which is attainable in no other way. The good thus done, the suffering avoided, and the facilities afforded "the stranger within our gates" can be fully appreciated only by those who have mingled in the confusion of camp-life as witnessed during this rebellion.

The Army Chaplains.

No class of men connected with the army have been the subject of more hasty and ill-advised criticism than the chaplains. Their office and mission have been pronounced a failure by the depraved and thoughtless, and they have been classed as useless and an encumbrance, whose only aim and end was to draw their pay. Not unfrequently, discouraged at the results of their labors and doubtful of future success, some of our best chaplains have turned their backs upon the army and returned to their homes. At first blush, the assertion that but little good has been accomplished in this branch of the service in proportion to the numbers engaged and the means expended, would seem to be supported by observation and experience; but a candid examination of all the circumstances bearing upon the case will demonstrate its utter injustice. Were the army chaplains and their labors judged from a true stand-point, there would not be wanting words of gratitude and praise from every pen and tongue. But, their triumphs not being blazoned abroad on flaming banners, the influence they exert working secretly and without ostentation, the seed they sow not being followed for many years, perhaps, by the springing grain and the ripening harvest, they have been decried by men ignorant of the good they have accomplished.

The disadvantages and difficulties of the chaplain are almost innumerable. In every camp there will be found some bad men, whose influence goes far to neutralize that of the most faithful chaplain. Many officers are careless of the teachings of Christianity, and the soldier too often follows where his commander leads in the walks of every-day life as well as on the battle-field. In camp the restraints of home and society are removed, and wild passions hold a fiercer sway. Vice abounds on every hand, temptation to sin is everywhere present; and opposed to it all is oftentimes only the single voice of the chaplain. Under such circumstances, even favored with every assistance and encouragement, his task would be a herculean one, in which the chances of failure and success would be evenly balanced. But of assistance he has none, and of encouragement far too little. Congress provided for chaplains, and the people doubtless supposed that in so doing they had secured spiritual instruction and solace to our soldiers and the blessing of God upon our arms. But they made no provision for the accomplishment of this work. No system of duties is prescribed by the regulations, and thus they have no authoritative claim upon the time and attention of officer or private. Each chaplain is thrown upon his own resources, to do as best he can. By incessant labor he may accomplish much; but, with his opportunities circumscribed or totally restricted, according to the taste of those to whom he is subordinate, with the vile influences of camp-associations working against him, it is no matter of surprise that many a chaplain fails to accomplish all that may be expected or desired.

It is seldom, however, that the chaplain has to encounter the *direct* opposition of any of his superior officers. Many of the latter are Christians; and many more have so much regard for the gospel and its teachings that they take pains to render their chaplain every possible assistance. In such cases his success is proportionably greater, his influence more potent for good, and the results of his efforts more apparent. It is not of the outspoken opposition of either officers or men that the chaplains most complain. It is rather the bad influence of *their example* working upon that spirit of imitation which in army life becomes almost second nature. To combat this is their most serious task, requiring the exercise of the utmost patience, perseverance, and faith. Despite these difficulties and vexations, however, they labor on, and their labors are rarely wholly in vain. The good they do, the influence they exert

21

upon those around them, the suffering they alleviate, the wounds of body and spirit they bind up, may not now be fully known and appreciated; but there will come a day when in the light of perfect knowledge their labors will be recognized and rewarded.

That there are unworthy and incompetent chaplains in the army is not to be denied. Through base means and influence, some such have crept into the service, and some may have fallen away, even, as did Judas Iscariot from among the chosen twelve. Those who thus fail and fall attract special attention, and by them the remainder have too often been judged. The majority are earnest, industrious, God-fearing men, by whom every opportunity for good is faithfully improved. That they work for pay only is abundantly disproved by the fact that few of them save any thing from their salary. The numberless calls upon them by the sick, the wounded, and the destitute would consume an income vastly larger than that of a chaplain. Theirs is a labor of love and duty, for which they have left the comforts of home to endure the dangers and inconveniences of camp-life, and for which they can find their reward only in an approving conscience.

For various reasons, many chaplains have resigned and gone home. Some were unfortunate in manner and style. Not every clergyman can succeed in the camp. The soldier must be interested,—his attention withdrawn from all outside influences to the words of the preacher. A peculiar style of delivery is necessary. A monotonous "sing-song" tone will effectually ruin any camp-preaching. The eye, the hands, the posture, the tongue, the brain, and, above all, the Holy Spirit, are essential elements in all sermons, and especially those intended for the camp. Energy and industry, a buoyant spirit which no difficulties, no opposition, can daunt, and a faith that no temporary failures can cast down, are necessary qualities in every successful army chaplain. The motto inscribed upon his banner should be the divine injunction, "Whatsoever thy hand findeth to do, do it with thy *might*."

On account of the constant changes occurring in the positions of the troops in this department, it is impossible to preserve a complete register of the chaplains in the Army of the Cumberland. The following list comprises those who participated in the "Chaplains' Council," whose first session was held in Murfreesborough, Tennessee, beginning April 1, 1863.

Revs. Hiram Gilmore; E. A. Strong, 3d Ohio; T. R. Cressey, 2d Minnesota; W. H. McFarland, 97th Ohio; J. C. Thomas, 88th Illinois; John J. Height, 58th Indiana; William S. Cresap, 10th Indiana; Ed. Keller, 15th Missouri; J. M. Green, 81st Indiana; Hooper Crews, 100th Illinois; J. A. Frazier, 73d Indiana; B. R. Baker, 3d East Tennessee; L. H. Jamison, 79th Indiana; T. O. Spenser, 89th Illinois; J. M. Whitehead, 15th Indiana; O. P. Clinton, 21st Wisconsin; A. S. Lakin, 39th Indiana; J. Poucher, 38th Ohio; R. F. Delo, 30th Indiana; W. H. Rodgers, 69th Ohio; H. W. Shaw, 29th Indiana; Thomas M. Gunn, 21st Kentucky; W. M. Haight, 36th Illinois; G. S. Stuff, 42d Illinois; Lewis Raymond, 51st Illinois; Thomas B. Van Horne, 13th Ohio; W. S. Hearker, 86th Indiana; I. F. Roberts, 44th Indiana; James H. Bristow, 5th Kentucky; O. Kennedy, 101st Ohio; N. P. Charlot, 22d Indiana; E. D. Wilkin, 21st Illinois; H. A. Pattison, 11th Michigan; John W. Chapin, 59th Ohio; Jesse Hill, 72d Indiana; W. Price, 2d Kentucky; W. H. Black, 23d Kentucky; John H. Lozier, 37th Indiana, post chaplain at Murfreesborough.

In addition to the above, there are several others, who, for various reasons, could not be present at the council. Among these are remembered the names of Revs. Father Trecy, chaplain at head-quarters; Father O'Higgins, 10th Ohio; Father Cooney, 35th Indiana; S. Layton, 17th Indiana; N. M. Patterson, 42d Indiana; John Dillon, 18th Ohio; J. M. Morrow, 99th Ohio; Isaac Moufort, 68th Indiana; L. F. Drake, 121st Ohio; Wm. Cliff, 98th Illinois; Jacob Cooper, 3d Kentucky; Chaplain Matthews, 11th Kentucky; L. E. Carson, 38th Indiana; Chaplain Alington, 94th Ohio; J. W. Lane, 80th Indiana; and Levi Walker, 60th Illinois.

Of the above-named chaplains thirty-two are Methodists, six are Baptists, six are Presbyterians, three are Catholics, and one is a Campbellite. The religious denominations to which the remainder belong are unknown to the author.

The chaplains' council chose for its president Rev. E. A. Strong, of Ohio, and for secretary Rev. John J. Height, of Indiana. Before concluding an interesting session of three days, the council adopted the following resolutions, which were reported by a committee consisting of Chaplains Lozier, of Indiana, Pattison, of Michigan, and Black, of Kentucky, as an expression of the sentiments of the meeting.

"*Resolved*, That we, as chaplains of the United States army, in the Department of the Cumberland, at this our first meeting, express our unfeigned gratitude to Almighty God, through our Lord Jesus Christ, for the preservation of our lives and health in the midst of the ravages of war and disease, for all the good we have been enabled to accomplish in the cause of religion and humanity since we entered the service, and for the general health and indomitable courage of our officers and soldiers and their success in the field of battle.

"*Resolved*, That in the transfer of the Anglo-Saxon race to this Western world, in the enunciation of the political faith of our country, in the formation and adoption of our Federal Constitution, in our signal victories in the past on the field of battle and our present achievements, we recognize the hand of God, and we firmly trust that the heaven-inspired principles of American liberty shall not only be more firmly established in our own country, but shall become the settled political faith of the world; and that we regard the ultimate triumph of these principles of more value to us and our posterity than all the sacrifices involved in the present struggle.

"*Resolved*, That we heartily approve the sentiment of the late Senator Douglas, that there are but two parties in this country,—the friends and the enemies of the nation,—and that every man who does not sustain every measure necessary to uphold the Government is a traitor at heart, and that we have no sympathy with such persons, whether found in the North or South. He that is not for the Government is against it, according to the principles enunciated by our Lord Jesus Christ.

"*Resolved*, That the history of the past, the present aspect of things, and a brightening future, strengthen our determination to still labor and pray for the success of our President and military authorities in their efforts to save our country.

"*Resolved*, That we more than ever look on the work of chaplains in the army as of great necessity, utility, and responsibility, and that nothing shall discourage us in our work of faith and labor of love, but we will pursue our calling with the patience of hope, fully appreciating the approbation of

General Rosecrans at High Mass upon the Battle-field of Stone River.

our own respective officers and regarding their co-operation as a powerful auxiliary in the accomplishment of our work.

"*Resolved*, That we extend our sincere sympathies to all who have suffered or are suffering either from the wastings of disease, the terrible ravages of battle, or the crushing sorrow of the loss of friends, and in our prayers we will ever commend them to the God of all grace and consolation.

"*Resolved*, That we appeal to all who claim the exalted title of ministers of the gospel in this nation to use their influence wherever they go to sustain the principles and sentiments embodied in the foregoing resolutions, and to impress on all men the duty of rendering 'to Cæsar the things that are Cæsar's, and to God the things that are God's.'"

The renowned *fighting* as well as praying Methodist preacher, Colonel Granville Moody, of the 74th Ohio, occupied a seat in this council, and by his words of fervid eloquence more than once stirred the hearts of his younger brethren in the work.

Quite a number of the chaplains are detached from their regiments and placed on duty in the various hospitals. The chaplains thus detailed are under the general supervision of Rev. John Poucher, of the 38th Ohio, one of the most faithful and laborious of the fraternity. It is in the hospitals that the chaplains find their most promising field of operations. Here eager, willing ears are ever ready to listen to their words of hope and consolation. Many a spirit, not less sore than the wounded body, is soothed and calmed by their kind ministrations. In the future, long after the war is over, and when only its saddening memories remain, many a former soldier of the Army of the Cumberland will invoke a blessing upon the faithful chaplain who visited and cared for him when prostrated by sickness or wounds.

As an instance of valuable services rendered by the army chaplains, we may mention that during the battles of Stone River, Chaplain Lozier, of the 37th Indiana, was constantly on the ground, assisting in the removal of the wounded, exposing himself in the most fearless manner to the shower of shot and shell. His services upon that occasion were of inestimable value, as can be attested by many who but for him, helpless and

wounded as they were, might have met their death at the feet
of the trampling hosts rushing on to the fray.

It would be pleasant and just to extend this chapter and make
particular mention of other chaplains enumerated in the foregoing catalogue; but a volume would hardly suffice to do them
justice, and to discriminate would be unwise and unjust, where
all are worthy. That there are diversities of gifts among them
is beyond question, and that some are more abundant in labors
than others is equally true. To some are also accorded greater
opportunities than to others; and by these only should they be
judged. When they who read these lines have arrived at a
practical realization of the difficulties encountered by these
voluntary exiles from the refinements of home, and when they
shall know, in the full perfection of knowledge, all the good
resulting from their services in the field, the camp, and the
hospital, then may they pass their verdict upon them. But
until then let no one say that the army chaplaincy is a failure.

GENERAL ROSECRANS'S CHAPLAIN.

REV. FATHER TRECY, chaplain of the 19th Regulars and at
head-quarters, is so well known throughout the Army of the
Cumberland, and so generally respected and beloved, that we
need offer no apology for introducing a brief mention of him in
this work. He has been with this army from the beginning,
his cheering counsel and benign countenance imparting pleasure
and confidence wherever we meet him, whether in the camp,
or during the dusty march, or upon the battle-field. Among the
sick, the wounded, and the dying, be they Catholic or Protestant, saint or sinner, his labors are constant, and freely given,
" without money and without price."

He was born in Ireland in 1826, and with his parents and
family he emigrated to the United States in 1836, landing at

Philadelphia, and shortly afterwards removing to Lancaster, Pennsylvania. In 1844 he commenced study for the ministry, and was ordained at Dubuque, Iowa, in 1851. For a short time thereafter he had charge of the parish of Dubuque. In September of that year he was sent to the "Garry Owen" settlement, twenty miles back of Dubuque, where he labored during a period of four years, collected a congregation, and planned and accomplished the erection of a large stone church-edifice.

In 1854 Father Trecy was sent by Bishop Loras, of that diocese, to the country bordering upon the line between Iowa and Nebraska, where he collected several congregations or colonies. Thence he also made repeated visitations to the military posts of Fort Randall, Fort Pierre, Fort Kearney, and Fort Leavenworth, and to several of the Indian tribes of those regions. His travels during this period of five years extended over a vast region of country, and included a tour through most of the Southern States. During this time he also succeeded in collecting and establishing considerable congregations of his people at Council Bluff, Sioux City, St. Johns, and Omaha City.

In 1860, Father Trecy, at his own request, was sent to the South, his health having become affected by his labors and exposures in the Northwest. He arrived at New Orleans the evening previous to the day of the election of President Lincoln, and heard Mr. Yancey make his notable disunion speech at the base of the Henry Clay monument. Thence he proceeded to Mobile, and joined that diocese, and was sent out over the State of Alabama upon a missionary tour. At Huntsville, North Alabama, he found many of his people, who were scattered and neglected, and resolved to stay there for a time and aid them in building a church. His labors were successful, and he planned and commenced a building,—which had progressed to the windows of the main story, when the rebellion began and caused a suspension of the work. The edifice was designed to be of cut stone, and one of the finest in that section of country.

Father Trecy was always a Union man, firm and constant; and so were his entire congregation at Huntsville, excepting three families, who owned slaves, more or less. His ministerial course, however, was kind and conciliatory, his whole aim being the spiritual good of his people and to build the church. After the fall of Fort Donelson the general hospitals for the sick and wounded rebel soldiery were located at Huntsville. Hundreds of them were brought there and placed in negro pens and sheds; and their condition soon became shocking. Father Trecy was now constantly in attendance at these hospital-barracks. Alas that the same cannot be said of the rebel ministers and the secession ladies of that city! His complaints respecting the filthy condition of the hospitals met with no response, except that permission was given him to remedy the evil as best he might. He employed laborers, cleansed the premises thoroughly, provided bathing-tubs, and solicited donations to meet the expenses thus incurred. His widely diffused benevolence was duly appreciated by the hospital inmates and by most of the citizens of Huntsville; but, sad to state, there were narrow and illiberal souls in that region who charged these benevolent deeds to interested motives, declaring that Father Trecy was aiming to "Romanize the hospitals"!

Upon the approach of the Federal forces, under General O. M. Mitchel, these rebel hospitals were broken up, and the inmates were taken to Atlanta, Georgia, and Courtland, Alabama,—many of them dying from the effects of this sudden removal. Soon after, the battle of Shiloh occurred, and Father Trecy was solicited by the people of Huntsville to go to that place with medical and hospital supplies for the wounded of the rebel army. The forces of General Mitchel arrived at Huntsville soon after,—upon hearing which he started to return to that town, travelling about two-thirds of the distance on foot, and the remainder upon a mule. During the stay of the Federal army at Huntsville he was kind and courteous to all. Many well remember meeting him there often among our suffering soldiers in the hospitals, during the occupancy of Huntsville by the Union troops. To the eternal shame of the rebel Protestant ministers of that city be it here recorded that while Father Trecy was visiting the sick and attending the funerals of the dead, they were, for the public security, kept under close guard at the court-house, as the only means of restraining their rebellious tempers. The only ministerial courtesies then extended to any of our chaplains were from Father Trecy, the priest of Huntsville. When the army retreated northward, Dr. John R. Goodwin, of the 37th Indiana Volunteers, was left there in charge of the sick who could not be removed; and many were the deeds of kindness done to him and his patients by the same loyal-hearted priest. Such manifestations of Christian charity, however, did not suit the tastes of the chivalrous rebels, and Father Trecy soon had to flee for his life to the lines of General Rosecrans.

Shortly after the battle of Iuka, he returned to Huntsville to look after his personal effects. He was twice taken prisoner while on the way, and was each time in imminent danger of maltreatment. His journey was without profit, and he returned to Corinth; and from that time to the present writing he has remained with Major-General Rosecrans as his constant and faithful friend and spiritual adviser.

Father Trecy is no bigot: he meets all men with kindly spirit. His aid and charity are extended without question in barracks and hospitals. He was present upon the battle-fields of Iuka, Corinth, and Stone River, ministering to the dying. His gentle bearing and pure and simple mode of life is the exemplar of his religious teachings, and proves a constant yet pleasing rebuke to profanity, intemperance, and kindred vices, too common in army life; and his influence upon the young men, especially at the general's head-quarters, is very beneficial.

One of the most impressive scenes of the war was the celebration of high mass by Father Trecy in a rude log cabin upon the battle-field of Stone River, on Sunday morning, the 4th of January, 1863,—the day after the retreat of the rebels from Murfreesborough. It was a beautiful morning,—the first after a week of rain-storms. Dead soldiers and horses were still strewn

over the fields, and burial-parties were engaged at their solemn
task.   The general in command, his staff and guests, assembled
in and around that rude cabin, while the holy rites were celebrated, and a short address delivered by our chaplain from the
text,—

" In Ramah was there a voice heard, lamentation, and weeping, and great
mourning, Rachel weeping for her children, and would not be comforted,
because they are not."—MATTHEW ii. 18.

Every heart was touched, and the pent-up feelings of strong
men who had striven in these scenes of battle sought relief in
tears.

This memorable occasion is happily illustrated at the commencement of this sketch.

The Sanitary Commission.

WHEN the volunteer soldiers of the loyal States first took the field to aid in suppressing the present rebellion, the spontaneous inquiry arose in the hearts of those who remained at home, What can we do for the cause and for the soldiers of the Union? The appalling blunders of the English in the Crimean War, and the terrible mortality resulting therefrom, had called the attention of medical and military men to the necessity of better sanitary measures for preserving the health of armies than had before been adopted. The best medical men of the Union immediately took counsel, availed themselves of all the information which the system—or want of system—in other armies afforded, and, with the approval of the President, the Secretary of War, and the Surgeon-General, organized the United States Sanitary Commission.

The objects of its organization were primarily the preservation of the health of the soldiery while yet well, and their restoration to health when sick. For the first a system of general inspection was adopted, through which all information collected from reliable authorities and extended experience was distributed through the army; frequent inspections of camp and hospitals by competent medical men, suggestions as to camp police, care of the men, condition of every thing pertaining to the comfort and health of the men, their food and the manner of cooking it, &c. &c., made to the medical and other officers of each regiment, with the hope of securing a generous spirit of rivalry among the regiments, each striving to secure for itself the reputation of being the best policed and the most perfect in the army.

For the second purpose it established agencies throughout the army for the distribution to the sick and wounded of such articles of necessity and luxury as were contributed by the people or purchased by funds donated to the Commission,—it being one of the fundamental principles of the organization that in all its work it should be eminently national, making no distinction between different classes of soldiers, and should act in harmony with the regularly constituted military and medical authorities and be auxiliary to them,—that it should be, in fact, to the regular military and medical organization of the army what equity is to law : while the one is bound by necessary and rigid laws, adopted for the general good, but which bear with crushing hardship upon particular cases, the other should be flexible, ready to adapt itself to every emergency which may arise and leave no single case of suffering without a remedy.

At the same time, aid societies were established in the cities, villages, and townships of all the loyal States, and in almost every town and hamlet busy fingers were preparing articles of necessity, comfort, and luxury for the soldiers, which were forwarded by irregular and uncertain channels of communication, often injured or ruined before reaching their destination, often lost by the way, and often appropriated in a manner not in accordance with the wishes of the donors.

But, before the Department of the Cumberland was established, the United States Sanitary Commission had so perfected its agencies and systematized its mode of distribution of stores as to secure the confidence of the people; and to it the greater part of the local aid societies of the North had determined to intrust their contributions for general distribution,—the donors becoming convinced that they could best provide for the regiments in which they had an especial personal interest by uniting in a general effort to provide for all. The limits of this chapter will permit of only a brief notice of the work of the Sanitary Commission in this department of the army, through the agencies thus noted and the means thus supplied.

Medical inspectors, selected with care, and of established

reputation, have passed from regiment to regiment throughout the department, aiding the surgeons in charge in securing the adoption of all precautions and sanitary measures which experience has shown to be essential or conducive to the preservation of the health of the soldiery. By these inspectors careful and elaborate reports have been made of the sanitary condition of every regiment, the kind of camp-police maintained, and the extent to which all the regulations of the service looking towards the preservation of the health of the men and the care of the sick have been observed, and the apparent influences thereby exerted upon the health of the men and the efficiency of the army, which reports have been forwarded to Washington. A more frequent but similar inspection has been made of the general hospitals in the department, in which the inspectors have united with the surgeons in a joint effort to discover and remedy all defects in the general management of the hospital.

For the distribution of sanitary stores purchased by the Commission and intrusted to it by the managers of the patriotic "aid societies" of the North and West, depots have been established at important points in the department occupied by the Union forces, with competent and efficient storekeepers in charge. It has been the purpose so to locate these that every hospital and regiment could be supplied from them, and to secure to each its appropriate share. In distributing these stores, the agents of the Commission have acted upon the presumption that these stores were designed for the sick soldier, and primarily for the enlisted soldier, but that in places where the impossibility of furnishing delicacies has placed the officer and soldier in this respect on an equality, both should be treated alike and each receive a share. They have found by experience that these supplies—the articles of diet especially—must reach the sick, if they reach them at all, through the surgeons in charge, who are and must be held responsible for the diet as well as for the medicine administered to their sick, and who will not, and with safety to the patients cannot, allow outside volunteer agents to decide what they shall eat or drink, or to administer to them articles of diet without their approbation and direction. Compelled, thus, to act through the surgeons or abandon this part of their work, or, on the other hand, to distribute to the well man the articles designed for the sick, the agents have found, what they believed to be true in the beginning, that as a class the surgeons of the army are deserving of the confidence of the donors, are as honest, efficient, and competent a class of workers as can be found in the army, and for this very purpose as reliable agents as could be selected for so large a field of operations.

To enable the agents to account for all stores which have passed through their hands, and to fix where it justly belongs the responsibility of wastage and misappropriation should they occur, a full account is kept, showing where, when, to whom, and for what purpose, the goods have been distributed, and who has assumed the responsibility of their appropriation. Upon the establishment of a depot of stores, the surgeons in charge of hospitals and regiments are notified of the fact, and requested to send in an informal requisition, stating the number of their sick and naming the articles needed for their comfort. The quantities of each to be furnished are filled in by the storekeeper in accordance with the supply on hand and the number of sick to be supplied, and the surgeons requested to call again for further supplies when they are exhausted. Every evening the requisitions thus filled are charged in general account to the hospital or regiment receiving them, and the requisitions are filed. These accounts are at all times open to the inspection of any one interested, and, if charges of misappropriation are made, enable the agents to investigate them with a certainty of reaching a correct conclusion. Special cases of want are at once relieved by the agents of the Commission, wherever found; and on the same record an account of goods thus given out is kept, and the name and regiment of the recipient noted. By this means a steady and constant supply is afforded, which is distributed without confusion and without partiality, and an accumulation of stores in safe depots is secured for emergencies. In the rooms at Murfreesborough there is at present a large supply of hospital clothing, concentrated beef-tea, and other articles, not now especially needed, but indispensable in case of a battle, and which, from the facilities for transportation afforded by Government, to be furnished at a moment's notice should a battle occur, will be used to feed and clothe the wounded before the news of the engagement can reach the home of a single soldier.

With the present mode of distributing these stores in this department, it may be confidently asserted that ninety per cent. of those received for general distribution reaches the sick enlisted soldier. That some are misappropriated, and some are stolen, is unquestionably true. And when the people who contribute them remember that, with all their locks and bolts, their sheriffs and constables, their marshals and police at home, in every ward and township, they are compelled to try, every week or every month, some one among them for stealing, they ought not to be surprised that this vice is not entirely eradicated from the army,— unless, indeed, they regard it as a great moral reform association, with the power of working miracles in that direction,—which is not the general impression here of the character of army influences. On the whole, it is a matter of surprise and gratification to see how large a percentage of these stores does actually reach the sick; and it is believed that all that is now needed to satisfy their wants as completely as this can be done in the field is a more constant and liberal supply.

A single instance will illustrate the benefits derived by the army from this part of the work of the Commission. Early in April it became apparent that the army was seriously suffering from a long destitution of vegetable diet. Scurvy, or indications of it, appeared in almost every regiment, and the medical officers of the army became apprehensive of very serious results unless a remedy could be promptly applied. Some of them joined with the agents of the Commission in appropriate representations to the central office of the Western Department at Louisville, and to the branch associations in the principal cities of the West. Potatoes, onions, pickles, &c. were sent forward, in response, in such liberal quantities that the agents having their distribution in charge could say to all the surgeons of the army, " Let none of your men, whether in hospital or in quarters, suffer for the want of these vegetables. Give them to all, whether excused from duty or not, who show any symptoms of the approach of this disease. The supply will be kept up." It was kept up, thanks to the generous patriotism of the people; and the plague was stayed.

To relieve the anxiety of friends of the army at home, the hospital directory of the Commission has accomplished much. A statement of the working of the directory as it is, instead of a history of the labor of establishing it, must suffice for the limits of this article. Blanks for the morning reports of hospitals are furnished by the Commission to all the general hospitals in the West. The morning report shows all changes for the preceding day in the hospital, the name, rank, company, regiment, and disease of all who are admitted to the hospital, who die in it, or are transferred to other hospitals, or discharged to return to duty. The series, commencing with the establishment of the hospital, will furnish a hospital history of every soldier admitted to it. After being recorded at each post, these morning reports are forwarded from all the posts to the office at Louisville, where they are consolidated, recorded, and indexed: so that any one interested in the condition or fate of any soldier, by giving name, rank, company, regiment, in letter or telegraphic inquiry, can ascertain whether he has been admitted into any hospital, and, if so, his full hospital history. To make this directory a more perfect source of information, the list of casualties in different engagements, as they are made from time to time to the medical director of the department, are copied, and the copies forwarded to Louisville. If inquiries are made after soldiers whose names appear neither on the hospital records nor the records of casualties, or if more specific or general information is desired, the matter is written or telegraphed to the agent nearest the camp of that particular regiment, who promptly furnishes all desired information, if it can in any way be obtained. Many aching hearts are daily relieved by the prompt and reliable intelligence they obtain in this manner from distant friends; many sick in regimental hospitals are thus visited, and their condition communicated to inquiring friends; the last parting words and farewell messages of many are gathered up and forwarded to bereaved homes, to be garnered in life's most precious memories.

Another and not less important work of the Commission in this department has reference to the care of the discharged soldier. Too often in other armies the discharged soldier, worn out or broken down by hardships, and no longer fit for service, has been ruthlessly shuffled off as an excrescence, and been "turned out," like an old horse, to die. Munificently as our Government has provided for the soldiers, it has left much to be done by other agencies in this particular. Many of the discharged soldiers are crippled by wounds or prostrated by disease; and to such a ride in the ordinarily crowded railroad-car from Murfreesborough to Louisville, even when stimulated by the hope of meeting again the loved ones at home who have been long awaiting their return, has terrors more appalling than they ever experienced in the hardest fight. For such cases the Commission has fitted up hospital cars, both on the Louisville & Nashville and the Nashville & Chattanooga Railroads, which are run in connection with the regular trains, but in charge of an agent of the Commission. The cars on the Chattanooga road have recently been burned; but new ones are now building, with India-rubber springs, kitchen attached to the car, sleeping-berths, and every convenience that can be suggested for the comfortable carriage of the sick and wounded. These are the cars of honor, into which those alone are received who have been disabled or have worn themselves out in their country's service, and in which all their wants are carefully provided for. The soldier, taking one of these cars at Murfreesborough, on the arrival of the train at Nashville is received into the "Soldiers' Home," over the railroad depot, a hotel established

22

by the Commission for his special entertainment, where the exhibition of his discharge-papers or his crutch settles all bills, and where he receives all necessary aid in obtaining his pay, is directed on his route home, where to find similar places of entertainment at every necessary stopping-place on the way, where he can obtain food and lodging without charge, and, if entitled to a bounty or pension, or if he has any Government claim growing out of his military service, is directed to the proper parties, who will make out his papers without charge and forward them to the claim-agent of the Commission at Washington, who will secure as early attention to them as practicable, and, when allowed and paid, the soldier receives the whole amount, without any deduction for attorney or claim-agent's fees. If—as daily happens—on the presentation of his discharge and final statement at the paymaster's office in Nashville the soldier finds that he cannot obtain his pay, on account of some informality in these papers, so that, from some careless erasure or other cause, he would be deprived of a part of that which is justly due him, he returns to the Soldiers' Home, and his papers, with a memorandum of the defects to be remedied, are returned to Murfreesborough or to the office nearest to his regiment, and the agent writes immediately to the regiment, procures the necessary corrections and returns them by the next train to the soldier in the Soldiers' Home, who then receives his pay and goes on his way rejoicing. Visits to the regiments for this purpose and to answer the inquiries from the hospital directory or from friends at home, who write directly to the different offices, aid the agents in securing an impartial distribution and faithful application of the stores, as they thus learn the condition and wants of the regiments. Thus brought directly in contact with the men, in and out of the hospitals, they can accurately ascertain how far they are supplied by the stores furnished, and promptly investigate any alleged case of misapplication.

If the soldier finds his own way to the city, on arriving at Nashville he sees conspicuously posted through the streets a handbill, of which the following is a copy:—

"Discharged soldiers will find a resting-place and food without charge, also all needed assistance in regard to their papers and pay, at the Soldiers' Home of the United States Sanitary Commission, over the station-house of the Nashville & Chattanooga Railroad.

"L. CRANE,
"*Special Relief Agent U. S. Sanitary Commission.*
"March 11, 1863."

This guides him to the same asylum and place of relief, when the same helping hand is extended and the same kindness shown him as is here related. This bill, too, has attracted the notice of thousands of others, who else had been ignorant of the great work the Sanitary Commission is performing, and by them has been made the subject of favorable comment.

It is found that these different branches of the work can be carried on systematically and without confusion, each one aiding in the work of all the others, and each seeking, as far as possible, to relieve every discovered want of the soldier. The agents have received the cordial co-operation of all the military and medical authorities of the department, and have had promptly extended to them every facility needed for the successful prosecution of their work.

In the hospital cars, and under the care of the agents of the Commission, are also forwarded the sick and disabled soldiers who, under the recent order of Surgeon-General Hammond, are transferred to the general hospitals nearest their homes. All who have lived their allotted three months in hospital are placed within reach of their friends: from the hospitals of Nashville alone over one thousand have already been sent forward; and very many of them will owe their lives to the careful provision made for their comfortable transit by the Commission, and to the attentive care of its accomplished agent,—Dr. Barnum,—who has charge of this branch of the work.

The Commission also, without any extra expense or increase of its agencies, has provided for sending home the bodies of all soldiers who die in this department, if desired so to do by the friends of the deceased, when the undertaker's charges—

at rates less than the ordinary prices—are deposited to the credit of the Commission in Louisville, Chicago, Cincinnati, or Cleveland, and the name, rank, company, and regiment of the deceased soldier furnished. The agents of the Commission see that the work is promptly and properly done and the body forwarded. This saves to the friends the entire cost of a visit to the army, and enables them to secure the last remains of the soldier to be deposited with his kindred, at times when the exigencies of the service prohibit visits to the army for that purpose.

In part, also, the hospital gardens are the work of the Commission. It has furnished the seed to plant them, and the implements for their cultivation; and its agents have labored jointly with the medical director of the department, and with the surgeon in charge of the general field hospital near which the largest one is located, to secure thorough cultivation. One garden near Murfreesborough comprises about forty acres, most of which is already planted. A general variety of garden vegetables is cultivated by convalescent and contraband labor, under the direction of a competent gardener, detailed for the purpose from the 101st Ohio Volunteer Infantry. Already the fruits of this garden are beginning to come in. The health of the convalescents is improving from this cause, added to their light labor in the garden. In the long hot days of summer, when the North cannot furnish vegetables which will bear transportation to the army, the supply of potatoes, onions, beets, carrots, peas, beans, lettuce, radishes, turnips, tomatoes, cabbages, cucumbers, melons, squashes, corn, &c. &c., from the hospital gardens, will be of incalculable benefit to the sick, and will supply a want which at that time could be supplied in no other manner. The other garden is at Nashville, and will there prove of equal value.

The general commanding the department has given emphatic testimony to the value of the work thus accomplished, in the following letter of approval, which is accompanied by one from Colonel Moody, of the 74th O. V. I. These are given as a sample of many such, voluntarily sent to the agents of the Commission.

"TESTIMONIAL OF MAJOR-GENERAL ROSECRANS

"HEAD-QUARTERS DEPARTMENT OF THE CUMBERLAND,
"MURFREESBOROUGH, February 2.

"The general commanding presents his warmest acknowledgments to the friends of the soldiers of this army, whose generous sympathy with the suffering of the sick and wounded has induced them to send for their comfort numerous sanitary supplies, which are continually arriving, by the hands of individuals and charitable societies. While he highly appreciates and does not undervalue the charities which have been lavished on this army, experience has demonstrated the importance of system and impartiality, as well as judgment and economy, in the forwarding and distributing of these supplies.

"In all these respects the United States Sanitary Commission stands unrivalled. Its organization, experience, and large facilities for the work are such that the general does not hesitate to recommend, in the most urgent manner, all those who desire to send sanitary supplies, to confide them to the care of this Commission. They will thus insure the supplies reaching their destination without wastage or expense of agents or transportation, and their being distributed in a judicious manner, without disorder or interference with the regulations or usages of the service. This Commission acts in full concert with the medical department of the army, and enjoys its confidence. It is thus enabled with few agents to do a large amount of good at the proper time and in the proper way. Since the battle of Stone River it has distributed a surprisingly large amount of clothing, lint, bandages, and bedding, as well as milk, concentrated beef, fruit, and other sanitary stores essential to the recovery of the sick and wounded.

"W. S. ROSECRANS,
"*Major-General commanding Department.*"

" LETTER OF COLONEL MOODY.

"MURFREESBOROUGH, TENNESSEE, February 5.

"DR. A. N. READ, INSPECTOR UNITED STATES SANITARY COMMISSION:

"SIR:—I desire to express to you, and through you to the generous and patriotic donors sustaining the Sanitary Commission, my high appreciation of the works of love in which they are engaged. As I have visited the various hospitals in this place, and looked upon the pale faces of the sufferers, and marked the failing strength of many a manly form, I have rejoiced in spirit as I have seen your benevolence embodied in substantial forms of food, delicacies, and clothing, judiciously and systematically distributed by those who are officially connected with the army.

"If the donors could only know how much good their gifts have done, and could but hear the blessings invoked upon their unknown friends by the suffering ones, they would more fully realize the divine proverb, 'It is more blessed to give than to receive.'

"We would advise all who wish to extend the hand of their charity so as to reach the suffering officers and soldiers who have stood 'between their loved homes and foul war's desolation,' to commit their offerings to the custody of 'the United States Sanitary Commission,' an organization authorized by the Secretary of War and the Surgeon-General, having the confidence of the army, and affording a direct and expeditious medium of communication with the several divisions of the army, free of expense to the donors and entirely reliable in its character. It is also worthy of special note that the goods intrusted to the Commission are distributed to those who are actually sick or convalescent, and this is done under the security of the most responsible persons in its employ, and through regularly established official agencies in the army. If the patriotic donors of the several States would direct their contributions into this channel, it would save much expense of agencies, blend the sympathies of Union men of the several States, and prevent unpatriotic distinctions in the patients in the hospitals, who are from every regiment and from every State. Side by side they fought and were wounded, and side by side they suffer in the hospitals, and the Commission, through appropriate agencies, extends its aid alike to the sons of Virginia and Pennsylvania, Ohio and Kentucky, Indiana and Tennessee, Michigan and Missouri, thus giving prominence to our cherished national motto, 'We are many in one.' As an illustration, the other day an agent of a Wisconsin society came to a hospital with sanitary goods for Wisconsin soldiers, and went along the wards making careful discrimination in behalf of Wisconsin soldiers, but soon saw that it was an ungracious task, and handed over his goods to the United States Sanitary Commission. Learning this, one of the Wisconsin soldiers said, 'I am glad of that; for it made me feel so bad when my friends gave me those good things the other day, and passed by that Illinois boy on the next bed there, who needed them just as much as I did; but I made it square, for I divided what I got with him.' Brave, noble fellow! his was the true spirit of a soldier of the United States. We have a common country, language, religion, interest, and destiny; and we should closely weave the web of our unity, so that the genius of liberty may, like Him 'who went about doing good,' wear 'a seamless garment.' We believe in the constitutional rights of States, but most emphatically believe in our glorious nationality, which, like the sun amidst the stars, has a surpassing glory and is of infinitely greater importance, and should be cherished in every appropriate form of development.

"GRANVILLE MOODY,
"*Colonel commanding* 74th *Regiment O. V. I.*

If it be asked who has sustained the Commission in this work, furnished it means and money to carry it on, and contributed the clothing, dressings, articles of diet and luxury distributed, take the census of the people of all the loyal States, deduct therefrom the names of those who are sympathizers with the rebels in their effort to overthrow the Government, and the residue of the names will be those of the donors. Or if it be asked who among the ladies of the North—for in a great measure this is their work—are deserving of especial mention for their patriotic and zealous efforts, it may be truthfully answered, the record of their names would occupy too much space for the limits of this chapter or volume, and it would be invidious to give the names of a few to the exclusion of many others equally worthy.

Of the agents of the Commission who have been brought in contact with the officers and soldiers of this army, a few words may be appropriately added.

Among these, as entitled to the first place, as he is first in rank, stands the accomplished secretary of the Western Department of the Commission, Dr. J. S. Newberry, of Cleveland, Ohio, more recently of Washington. His superior scientific and general knowledge, his comprehensive mind, and his general acquaintance with the best men of the whole country, pointed him out upon the organization of the Commission. At the beginning he was placed in charge of the Western Department, comprising the whole of the army west of the Alleghanies, and has ever since had the superintendence of that large field. He has selected the agents, assigned them their duties, established posts, kept up the communication between the Commission and the people by public addresses, letters, and reports, exhibited the working and wants of the Commission, and at all times has discharged duties not less arduous and comprehensive, and hardly less important, than those of the military commander of a department. His energy and devotion to the work, his judgment, accurate in deciding, prompt in executing, have endeared him to the people and the army, and all agree that, for once at least, the right man has been assigned to the right place.

When the army of the Union first entered Kentucky, Dr. A.

N. Read, a physician of high standing and long experience, was summoned by telegraph to assume the duties of inspector for the Commission and follow the army in its progress South. He immediately gave up a lucrative practice, and has since labored incessantly and efficiently in the various departments of the West. When the Department of the Cumberland was established, the general superintendence of the work of the Commission in that department was intrusted to him. Under his management there has been no conflict or jealousy between the Commission and the authorities, mutual confidence has characterized their intercourse, and the whole work of the Commission has been so thoroughly systematized and perfected that it is difficult to say in what particular it can be improved. His head-quarters are for the present at Nashville,—although he makes frequent visits to all parts of the field, and when an engagement occurs is sure to be promptly at hand, aiding in the care of the wounded and directing his subordinates in the distribution of stores.

Mr. J. H. Robinson, of Cleveland, Ohio, is the storekeeper at Nashville. Mr. L. Crane, assisted by Mr. Merwin,—for a long time the storekeeper at Murfreesborough,—has charge of the Soldiers' Home at Nashville.

At Murfreesborough, M. C. Read, Esq., an attorney from Northern Ohio, has the general charge of the work, aided by Mr. Crasey, the attentive storekeeper.

The medical inspectors have no local head-quarters, but follow the army. Dr. Castleman and Dr. Bettleheim, thorough workers, and men of marked ability, are now with the army, acting in that capacity, and are just completing a renewed and systematic inspection of the whole army.

In closing this chapter, a few words may appropriately be added respecting female help in the hospitals. The Commission sends no ladies into the field as its agents, we are informed, but wherever it finds them doing a good work aids and encourages them. To the volunteer labors of many ladies the sick in the hospitals at Murfreesborough owe much,—many, their lives; all, very many comforts. Their labors here are especially mentioned because the writer has been stationed at this post and is not so familiar with their work elsewhere. They have not come here to control the hospitals, to assume authority over the surgeons and attendants; they have not come to gain a reputation or newspaper notoriety, but to do good as they should find opportunity. Assuming cheerfully such duties as the surgeon in charge assigned them, they have from day to day prepared the food of the low-diet patients, superintended the cooking and washing for all, aided much in securing neatness and cheerfulness throughout the hospitals, and, when the wards are put in order for the day, by their frequent visits and encouraging conversation with the sick and wounded have cheered their hearts, alleviated their loneliness, and have prompted many a poor soldier to thank God for the sunshine they have brought to his despairing heart.

The Army Police and its Chief.

THE police and scout service—one of the most interesting and important departments of the army—can have no better or more appropriate introduction than a sketch of the life of its originator and head.

WILLIAM TRUESDAIL, Chief of Police in the Army of the Cumberland, was born in Chautauqua county, New York, January 9, 1815, of American parents. At the age of eleven years he was bound to a merchant of Erie, Pennsylvania, at fifty dollars a year and three months' schooling,—but got no schooling. In the fall of 1835 he was elected deputy sheriff and police justice. While holding these positions, he devoted much attention to police-matters, and gained quite a local reputation for the skill displayed in investigating and developing numerous complicated and startling cases of fraud and crime. In a single instance nearly thirty thousand dollars was recovered by his agency. In the fall of 1836 he engaged in real-estate speculations, and in a short time cleared over fifty thousand dollars, having at one period between forty thousand and fifty thousand dollars cash in bank. In the general failure of 1837 this fortune was lost, with the exception of two or three thousand dollars. In 1838 he was appointed specie teller by the directors of the United States Branch Bank at Erie, and was confirmed as such by Nicholas Biddle, president of the parent institution. Six months afterwards he was made travelling agent for said bank, and continued in its service until its failure in 1841.

He then turned his attention to merchandizing at Erie, and remained in that business until 1847. By this time he had again accumulated a handsome competence, which was mostly lost in the crisis of the same year. We next hear of him as a

contractor on the Lake Shore Railroad, from Erie to the Pennsylvania State line, where he continued some two years, and until the road was nearly completed, finishing in that time four miles of heavy cut and realizing a handsome profit from his contract. In 1849 the Panama Railroad Company was organized; and in the fall of that year he made an arrangement with John L. Stephens, and others, of New York, to go out and superintend the building of the road across the Isthmus, at a salary of six thousand dollars a year and expenses paid. He left New York in November, 1849, taking with him two hundred and fifty men, having arranged for the forwarding of subsequent instalments of laborers in similar numbers. He remained on the Isthmus one year, in which time he completed the work across the Chagres swamp. Through all the terrible mortality which attended the construction of that work, and by which many thousands of lives are known to have been lost, his health was not materially affected by the climate. Of the fourteen hundred men, however, who were sent out to him, not more than three hundred returned alive. On his arrival at New York he was highly complimented by the Board of Directors, and was offered ten thousand dollars a year to return and superintend the completion of the enterprise. He accepted the proposition; but before the arrangements were fully effected the balance of the work was let to a private company.

In the fall of 1851 he proceeded to the West as the agent of H. C. Seymour & Co., and took charge of the western division of the Ohio & Mississippi Railroad, in conjunction with Professor O. M. Mitchel (late Major-General Mitchel, deceased), who was then chief engineer and bond commissioner of that great work. When the road was located and the money secured to build it, in company with others, he took large contracts in its construction, and built over sixty miles of the road between Sandoval and St. Louis. The same company, composed of three capitalists, subsequently built the St. Louis & Belleville Railroad, fifteen miles in length, the St. Louis & Alton Road, twenty miles in length, and the North Missouri Road for some sixty miles. These projects occupied some twelve years, and resulted largely to the profit of the contractors, although much of it was lost by the failure of the various companies to meet their payments. In these and many of his earlier operations the colonel lost heavily, indeed; but he never *failed*,—was never unable to meet promptly and fully all his obligations,—a fact alike remarkable and creditable in a business career of such great and varied extent.

In 1860, with two others, he embarked in the construction of the railroad from New Orleans to Houston, Texas, a distance of three hundred and twenty miles, and had completed and put it in operation from Houston to the Sabine River—one hundred and ten miles—at the outbreak of the rebellion. This great road, in which the colonel will have an immense fortune upon the return of peace and good times, is intended to be a national Southern route, connecting New Orleans with the Rio Grande, and thence across the country to the Gulf of California and the mouth of Yuba River. It crosses the Delta of the Mississippi and the high level plains of Texas, which latter were found so smooth and ready for the track that it was laid upon the grass for some sixty miles, the earth from the ditches at the side forming the filling between the ties.

Upon the fall of Fort Sumter the secession element in the State became too strong to be endured by Northern men, and early in May, soon after the violent deposition of Governor Houston, Colonel Truesdail left Texas and came to Missouri. Upon General Pope taking command of the army in Northwestern Missouri, he was appointed military superintendent of the North Missouri Railroad. Soon after, General Pope was recalled to St. Louis; and the colonel then contracted to supply General Grant's army with beef, and continued the business under General Jefferson C. Davis, and again under General Pope when he re-entered the field. With him he also had charge of the police and secret service, the scouts and couriers, and the forwarding of mails and despatches; and in these and other labors he performed valuable service in that wild, interior country. Throughout the New Madrid, Island No. 10, and Fort Pillow campaign, in the trip up the Tennessee, and during the operations in front of and beyond Corinth, he remained with General Pope, by whom the worth of his great services was freely and constantly acknowledged. When the latter general was ordered to Virginia, he invited Colonel Truesdail to go with him; but, preferring to remain in the West, where his family reside and his property is, and where he believed he would be more useful, he declined the invitation.

General Rosecrans, upon assuming command of the Army of the Mississippi, retained the colonel in his position. The completely unsettled condition of affairs in Mississippi at that time gave room for the display of his peculiar genius. The army mail and police service were irregular in their workings, and scarcely more than nominal in their existence. A new and complete organization of each was soon effected. Military mail-agents were placed on the boats and trains, and offices opened all along the route between Cairo and Corinth. A police system was put into operation that began at once to be felt throughout the army and all the country within our lines. The first arrest made under it was that of a high official in General Grant's employ, who was convicted of the fraudulent appropriation of several thousand dollars, and sentenced by that general to two years' imprisonment. Colonel Truesdail continued in this department until the assignment of General Rosecrans to the command of the Department of the Cumberland, when he was induced to accompany the general to his new field of operations,—although, personally, he was disinclined to longer service, having now been actively and constantly engaged since the beginning of the war, absent all the while from his home and family.

At Bowling Green the army mail system was organized, and policemen were put at work, not only there, but in the larger towns along the line of the Louisville & Nashville Railroad, and a surprising amount of knavery, smuggling, and guerrillaism was discovered. Upon reaching Nashville the police business at once assumed vast proportions. The city was full of violent and confessed rebels, most of whom were both smugglers and spies, as opportunity offered. The army had drawn thither its usual corrupt and festering element of camp-followers. The entire community was rotten, morally and socially. Murder, robbery, drunkenness, and all the nameless vices of rebeldom and war, were openly and shamelessly rampant. The Government was victimized at every turn. Horses and mules, stolen from neighboring farms and stables, were hawked about the streets for purchasers, at prices ranging from ten to fifty dollars per head. Arms were pilfered and sold for a trifle. Boots, shoes, uniforms, camp-equipage, ammunition, and supplies of every kind, serviceable to the rebel army, were daily sent beyond our lines in every possible way that the ingenuity of bad men and women could devise.

In our necessarily contracted space we cannot hope to give even an outline of the work accomplished by the army police. Suffice it to say that in a short time its influence was felt in every part of the city and army. His patrols were upon every road leading from the city, arresting and searching rebel emissaries, and at times confiscating considerable amounts of contraband goods. His detectives were in every hotel, and upon cars and steamers. Assuming the *rôle* of rebel sympathizers, they were introduced into the proudest and wealthiest secession families. Passing themselves off, in many cases, as spies of Wheeler, Bragg, and Morgan, they acquainted themselves with the secrets, the hopes, and the intentions of that entire people. Men were also busy among our own camps, detecting army vice and fraud. Their searching eyes were on the several army departments, hospitals, theatres, houses of ill-fame, and every centre of public interest. A minute report of all these investigations and their results would thrill the land; but better that it be not told to blanch the cheek and chill the heart of many a true wife and fond parent.

Many offenders thus detected were vigorously dealt with; and yet the police records of the department reveal instances of young men made wiser and better by the kindness shown and the advice given them.   Humane, benevolent, and far-seeing, yet prompt to visit with merited punishment the hardened offender, none more ready than our Chief of Police to temper justice with mercy.   The many instances of charity to the destitute, of forgiveness to youthful follies of the young men whom he has aided and counselled, of widows and orphans he assisted to fuel and bread during the hard winter at Nashville, of the young women found in male attire whom he and his assistants have decently clothed and sent to their homes, and of deserted children for whom he has found asylums, would of themselves fill many pages of this work.

In brief, the influence of the army police was felt in every ramification of army and city life throughout the Department of the Cumberland.   True, errors and wrongs may have been committed by its officials; many an arrest may have been made without good reason therefor, and many goods seized that ought to have been untouched; true, many bad men may have wormed themselves into its service; but, where such has been the case, none more ready to make restitution, none more severe in punishment of official treachery and knavery, than its justice-loving chief.   All in all, he has done well, and has exercised the utmost care in the selection of his subordinates.   For be it always remembered that there are but few men fitted for the business of a detective, and a still less number are found who will follow it.   In large cities, and with armies, the detective is a necessity; and yet it is a profession whose follower is and must be one continued counterfeit.   Bad men can make it detestable; but pure-minded, upright officers, operating secretly and in disguise though they may, CAN perform their duties with marvellous certainty in the detection of crime, with incalculable benefit to the public, and without injury to the innocent.

That the most worthy motives actuate the subject of this sketch in all his official dealings, the author has abundant reason to know.   Colonel Truesdail (he is called "colonel" by general consent, though a civilian and quite regardless of titles) is possessed of a handsome private fortune, which thus far has been diminished, rather than increased, by his army labors. Though a Southern man as regards the location of a great portion of his property and by reason of many years' residence in the slave States, he has been an original and uncompromising friend of the Union.

The results of the army police operations have been immense, both in gain to the Government and prevention of crime. Hundreds of horses and mules have been seized and turned over to the quartermaster's department. Scores of smugglers and spies have been detected and punished, thus largely curtailing this under-ground trade, alike beneficial to the rebels and detrimental to us. Large amounts of goods and medicines have been confiscated and sold, where the parties implicated were found *flagrante delicto ;* and thus this branch of the army has considerably more than repaid its entire cost to the Government. Connected with it, also, is the spy department, from which a line of communication has been constantly maintained throughout the rebel States, to the extreme limits of the Southern Confederacy. This interesting feature in its operations, systematic as it is under the watchful eye of the Chief of Police and under the personal direction of the general commanding, must, for obvious reasons, be imagined rather than described.

To illustrate the efficiency of the army police, a few of the very many cases of smuggling, spying, and treachery which it has developed are related elsewhere in this volume. They are compiled from the records; and, strange and improbable as some of them may seem, they are essentially truthful narratives of actual occurrence. Indeed, the facts are necessarily greatly abbreviated in a publication so comprehensive as this, the minutiæ—the smaller lines and threads which contribute to the beauty of the woof—being unavoidably omitted.

As may be readily supposed, such an extensive army organization ere long attained considerable notoriety. It marshalled its friends and its enemies in almost regimental numbers. Even in the army it has been violently assailed,—not only by the vicious in the ranks, but by officers whose evil deeds were *not* past finding out. If any direct charge was made, however, to General Rosecrans, it was at once and fully investigated; and in no one instance has the charge been maintained, as affecting the good character of its chief or of his principal aids. The breath of calumny has been even wafted to the Presidential ears, and the newspapers of last spring contained the announcement that a special commission had been appointed at Washington to investigate the operations of the police of the Army of the Cumberland. Many weeks elapsed, and this was not done. At the solicitation of its chief and his assistants, General Rosecrans then appointed a special inspector, Captain Temple Clark, formerly a member of his staff in Mississippi, and now chief upon the staff of Brigadier-General Johnson, to examine into the operations of his army police, and report. A portion of that report is herewith subjoined; and it constitutes an appropriate conclusion to our chapter:—

"NASHVILLE, TENN., June 2, 1863.

"MAJOR:—

"In compliance with your instructions, I have made a thorough examination of the books and papers connected with the Army Police Office and its operations in this department since its first organization, and I respectfully submit the following report as the result of my investigations.

"In arriving at facts and conclusions, I have taken advantage of every source of information at my disposal, except that of instituting a 'court of inquiry' and putting witnesses under oath.

"I find that the records of the operations of this institution, together with all important papers and vouchers connected therewith, have been kept with correctness and system, so that almost any official act of its employés can be easily traced from its inception to its result. This order and system greatly facilitated my investigation, and reflects credit upon the chief and his subordinates.

"The number of employés in this department, including scouts, spies, policemen, judges, clerks, mail-agents, &c., has at no *one time* exceeded fifty, although a much larger number appear to have been employed during the term of its existence,—most of them for short periods only. The expenses of the department from the middle of November, 1862, to June 1, 1863, are as follows:—

"For mail-service, six months and a half, $3,320; for salaries of clerks, scouts, and policemen in secret service, $66,564.55; making a total of expenses, including the military custom-house at Nashville, of $69,884.55;

23

of which amount the sum of $52,924.25 expenses up to May 1 have been paid, and the vouchers received and on file.

"The balance of $16,960 is for the expenses and disbursements for the month of May, not yet settled, though the amount is ascertained.

"Much of this last amount is for service rendered prior to the 1st of May last, and principally for secret service.

"The Army Police Department has seized and turned over to authorized agents of the Government, up to June 1, 1863, property to the value of $438,000.

"This property consisted of arms and ordnance stores, which have been turned over to ordnance officers; medical stores to a large amount which were found in the act of being smuggled through the lines to the enemy,—some of it stolen from our hospitals,—all being turned over to the medical director; and large quantities of goods and merchandise, which has been turned over to the custom-house officer and to the quartermaster.

"There has been placed in the hands of the United States District Attorney, with testimony for confiscation, the following property :—

"Stock of goods of Stewart & Co., Nashville, $25,000; stock of goods of Morgan & Co., Nashville, $35,000; stock of goods of Wilder & Co., Louisville, $80,000; gold from Mr. Lee, $109,000.

"For all the property thus disposed of, proper receipts and vouchers have been taken, and are now on file in the office, an abstract of which is hereunto annexed.

"Had the sphere of its usefulness ended here, the record of the army police would show well, and amply justify the wisdom of the commanding general in its establishment; but the great pecuniary profit arising to the Government from this institution is the least of its advantages; and the record of its services shows a long array of benefits to the army and the Government, only known to the members confidentially engaged in its service.

"The most important of these I propose to enumerate.

"1st. Through the agency of the secret police, especially selected for the service required, many rebel spies and smugglers have been arrested and brought to justice within this department, and information obtained and transmitted leading to the arrest of many more outside of the department.

"2d. The detection and prevention, to a great extent, of stealing in the army by officers and men; more particularly the stealing of horses and mules, at one time very extensively practised by both citizens and soldiers, now almost entirely suppressed through the successful vigilance of the army police. Over five hundred horses and mules stolen from the Government have been recovered by this organization and turned back to the proper channel.

· "3d. Discovering frauds on the soldiers, attempted to be perpetrated by Northern houses through the agency of swindling advertisements and the circulation of obscene prints and books. These last have been seized to a large extent, and destroyed, and a considerable amount of money which was being transmitted to these impostors has been returned by the police to the respective owners through army postmasters. A record has been kept, showing that each sum thus stopped and returned was duly received.

"4th. A perfect system of detection, reaching to the closets of traitors, and discovering who were the secret enemies of the Government within our lines, and guarding against their treasonable operations.

"5th. The employment of skilful scouts and spies to operate within and about the enemy's lines and furnish intelligence for the information of the commanding general. These men have been carefully selected for their peculiar duties. Most of them are well acquainted with the country and the inhabitants where they operate, and possess tact, self-possession, and nerve to a high degree.

"6th. A record of the character and political sympathies of nearly every adult inhabitant of the section of country through and in which the Army of the Cumberland has operated.

"7th. Knowledge and investigation of secret political societies, North and South, having for their object opposition to the Government and the prosecution of the war.

"8th. The detention and return of deserters,—of whom more than eight hundred have been arrested by the army police alone, and over two-thirds of whom would not have been reached through other sources.

"9th. Discovering and forwarding lost or stolen property belonging to officers and soldiers. The value of property so recovered and forwarded, or turned over to the authorized Government officers, exceeds $100,000.

"10th. Detection and exposure of fraud and irregularities in the military hospitals and other army departments, and the great improvement in the condition of our hospitals, which is chiefly due to the able medical officers more recently in charge of these institutions; yet a good share of credit is due to the detection, exposure, and punishment of grave abuses therein by the agents of the army police, who first occasioned the reforms by showing the necessity therefor.

"11th. The Army Directory, a record showing every regiment and detachment in the Department of the Cumberland,—in what brigade, division, and corps, and where stationed. This record is continued and every change noted. It contains also the name rank, company, and regiment of every officer and soldier who dies in the department, whether in camp or hospital; where he died, and where buried; the cause of death, and any circumstance necessary to be recorded as to the disposition of his effects, &c. The record has an alphabetical index attached.

"12th. The transmission of the mails done under the direction of its chief and by the employés of the army police. The mails have been delivered with surprising regularity and safety to every division and brigade in the army.

"That an institution like the army police, so vast and varied in its operations, assailing so many in their pecuniary, personal, and political interests, should have powerful and numerous enemies, is not to be wondered at; and that this enmity should develop itself in complaints and accusations is natural.

"Knowing this condition of public sentiment, I have inquired among all classes of people for the grounds of complaint against this institution. While I heard many *general* charges asserted and suspicions insinuated by persons who upon general principles or from personal motives believed that wrongs had been perpetrated and that the members of the army police were guilty of dishonest practices, I was only able to hear of one definite charge.

"This was a case where a valuable carriage—the property of a young lady—was said to have been seized and confiscated by the army police and then appropriated to the private use of members of the police force. The person making the statement to me merely gave it as a rumor, saying that he knew nothing of the facts, and had no positive reason for believing it, he making the statement only because I was asking for charges.

"An investigation showed that the carriage in question was the property of a secession family, the head of which had gone South: it was found secreted in separate parts and places, was taken by the police, and *immediately* turned over to the custom-house officer, who receipted for it and subsequently sold it at auction for five hundred dollars, and the proceeds were turned over to the Government.

    *   *   *   *   *   *   *   *

"I would therefore earnestly recommend that the army police be continued as a branch of your department. Professional villains can only be matched by professional detectives. The one turns every resource of his nature, mental and physical, to the successful perpetration of crime; and he can only be circumvented by one who concentrates all his powers to detection and prevention.

> "Very respectfully,
>> "Your obedient servant,
>>> "TEMPLE CLARK,
>>> "*Captain and Assistant Adjutant-General,*
>>>> "*Special Inspector.*"

HISTORY

OF THE

ORGANIZATION, THE EXPEDITIONS, AND THE BATTLES

OF THE

ARMY OF THE CUMBERLAND.

CONTENTS.

ORGANIZATION AND EARLY OPERATIONS OF THE ARMY.

A COMPREHENSIVE history of our army, however brief it may be, necessarily carries the reader back to the commencement of the rebellion,—from whence we follow it, from its inception, and through the campaign of General Buell, down to the present time. The few pages thus occupied will be as valuable as interesting.

The beginning of what is now the Army of the Cumberland, the nucleus around which our magnificent army has aggregated, was a small body of Kentucky volunteers, assembled, under Colonel—now Major-General—Rousseau, at Camp Joe Holt, near Louisville, Kentucky, in the spring and early summer of 1861. From this force was organized the Louisville Legion Infantry, the 2d Kentucky Cavalry, Stone's Battery of Artillery, and two companies of infantry which proved to be the beginning of the 6th Kentucky Infantry Regiment.

Prior to the assembling of this force, General Rousseau, in the Senate of Kentucky, was the fearless and eloquent advocate of loyalty to the Union. His words were confirmed by his deeds. He descended from his place in the Senate, and, raising the banner of his country, called upon all true Kentuckians to rally around it. In answer to his call there was soon assembled a force of nearly two thousand men. This was in the day when public opinion in Kentucky was unsettled; her Governor was a secessionist, and anxious to join the State to the "Confederacy;" her trusted commander of the organized Militia State Guard, now the rebel General Simon B. Buckner, was plotting treason, aiming to commit his force to a position in opposition to the Government. Many of her leading citizens were avowedly and actively disloyal, some of them, in the end, joining the rebel forces then assembling just beyond the southern border of the State, and all were using their whole influence to entice others to follow their wild example. The great body of citizens, however, did not openly favor the rebellion, nor the transfer of the State to the Confederacy: some were intimidated, probably, by the clamor, and hence declared themselves neutral; some adopted neutrality as a principle, others as an expedient: the first declared that Kentucky had nothing to do with the quarrel, which the belligerents might fight out at their leisure, and that they would repel by force of arms either party should they attempt to enter the State. This was tantamount to secession; for it assumed that the State was not a part of the nationality of the United States, but a nation of itself, with a right to stand aloof while other States, considered to be other nations, were contending around her. Those who resorted to this neutrality as an expedient hoped by that course to save the State from being prematurely committed to the rebellion during the first agitation, as had been done in Tennessee, North Carolina, and other States.

But beyond and above all these were the valiant few who patriotically proclaimed their brave and unconditional loyalty aloud, and flew to arms in answer to their country's call. The men under Rousseau, who assembled at Camp Joe Holt, were of this stamp. As early as June, 1861, there was a considerable force thus assembled; and they were speedily organized and accepted into the service of the United States. Such were also those raised, about the same time, by the late Major-General Nelson, at Camp Dick Robinson, in Garrard county, a more eastern part of the State. To these should also be added the two Kentucky regiments previously raised, who were at that time serving in Western Virginia.

In May, all Kentucky within a hundred miles south of the

Ohio River had been made a military department, and Briga-dier-General Robert Anderson had been assigned to its command. Early in September, he established his head-quarters at Louisville; and just about that time the rebel enemy on the Mississippi invaded the State, taking possession of Hickman and Columbus. They then intended to strike at once for Paducah, on the Ohio River; but Federal troops from Cairo, belonging to General Frémont's command, had anticipated them. But the day ever memorable in the annals of Kentucky and of the Army of the Cumberland is the 17th day of September, 1861. On that day war was fully inaugurated in the region of country lying between the Alleghanies and the Mississippi, and on that day General Rousseau's men from Camp Joe Holt, the initial element of the Army of the Cumberland, marched out to repel invasion. The rebel General Buckner, starting from Camp Boone, in Tennessee, just beyond the Kentucky line, attempted to reach the Ohio River at Louisville by the Nashville & Louisville Railroad. He meditated a surprise. There had been no intimation of his coming; but the train from Nashville due in Louisville early in the evening did nöt arrive, and the telegraph-wires had that day been cut. The managers of the road, suspecting no more than an ordinary accident, sent out a train to relieve the one expected. This did not return; and then a single engine was sent out. The trains had been seized by the enemy; but from the single engine a fireman escaped, and soon returned to Louisville with the news, having obtained a hand-car. General Anderson sent orders at once to Rousseau to move out with his men on the road, they, with the Home Guards of Louisville, being Anderson's only available force. The camp was on the opposite side of the river, and the order was brought in person by General W. T. Sherman, second in command to Anderson, at nine o'clock in the evening. By eleven o'clock they were all across the river, excepting a number of cavalrymen, who were not yet mounted, and were left behind with orders to come on the next day, bringing with them the tents, camp-equipage, and supplies. The men were in high

spirits and the best order. The rumbling of the artillery-
wheels and the regular tramp of the march of the men through
the streets of Louisville, like that of an army of veterans, were
the only sounds that broke the stillness of the night. There
was nothing like tumult, and no sign of disorder. Such of the
citizens as were wakeful remember the solemn sound; but few
were awakened from their slumbers. As soon as the cars could
be made ready, the troops were taken off, and accompanying
them a good force of the Home Guards of Louisville, who
turned out with infinite spirit, in unexpectedly large numbers.
General Sherman commanded the whole, General Anderson
remaining in Louisville to obtain reinforcements and forward
them as they might arrive. But this might not have foiled the
enemy in his purpose, perhaps, had it not been for the spirited
act of a loyal and intelligent young man of Bowling Green.
The trains with Buckner's army arrived and were detained for
a time at that place: he quietly set out, and, at a point a few
miles down the road, displaced a rail,—in consequence of which
the engine left the track and the rebel expedition was delayed.
This gave time to General Anderson, which he improved well,
as has been already stated. The enemy, nevertheless, got as
far as Elizabethtown, forty miles from Louisville; but there he
heard of the coming of the opposing force, and his heart failed
him. He had employed agents to destroy a high bridge over
the Rolling Fork of Salt River, by which the progress of our
forces was impeded,—but not long; for Rousseau, on foot, led his
men through the deep stream and onward. Buckner now
thought proper to retire, and subsequently intrenched himself at
Bowling Green, which place he held until the time of the fall of
Fort Donelson.

General Sherman established his camp on Muldraugh's Hill,
about three miles north of Elizabethtown, leaving guards at
each important point in his rear; and there he awaited the
gathering of such forces as could be obtained from contiguous
States. In a few days they began to come: among the first
were the 28th, 6th, and 39th Indiana Regiments, respectively

under Colonels Scribner, T. T. Crittenden, and Harrison; the 49th Ohio, under Colonel Gibson; the 24th Illinois, under Colonel Hecker; and two companies of the 15th United States Regulars, under Captain P. T. Swaine. These were in due time followed by other regiments; and this was the embryo of that army which, under the successive commands of Anderson, Sherman, Buell, and Rosecrans, has done such eminent service to the country, which by its gallant deeds has so glorified our country's history, and which on the battle-field has never met with a reverse.

When General Anderson, on the 28th of May, 1861, first took charge of this army, his command was called the " Department of Kentucky," and it comprehended so much of the State of Kentucky as lay within a hundred miles of the Ohio River. On the 11th of August it was extended over the whole State of Kentucky and the State of Tennessee, and was named the " Department of the Cumberland." In October, General W. T. Sherman took command, General Anderson's health failing. In November, Sherman was relieved by General Buell, and the limits and title of the department were again changed to the " Department of the Ohio," and now comprehended the States of Ohio, Indiana, and Michigan, all of Kentucky lying east of the Cumberland River, and the State of Tennessee. The Department of the Missouri, commanded by General Halleck, lay west of the Cumberland; and in the following March, General Halleck's command was extended eastward to a north-and-south line passing through Knoxville. This command was called the " Department of the Mississippi;" and in June this department was made to include the whole of Kentucky and Tennessee. The particular command of General Buell was called the " *District* of the Ohio," General Halleck having issued an order in April to the effect that the army of General Buell, as well as those of Generals Grant and Pope, would retain their original titles and organization. Until November 24, 1862, the title and limits of the District of the Ohio were retained. At that date there was a new arrangement of departments and of commanders. Tennessee east of the Tennessee River and Northern Alabama and Georgia were made a department, under the name, revived, of "Department of the Cumberland," into which Kentucky was again transferred. The Department of General Rosecrans is now essentially the same, though heavily reinforced, as that of the District of the Ohio which General Buell commanded.

As has been stated, our army, as formed under Generals Anderson and Sherman, was but a small beginning. Under General Buell it grew to formidable dimensions and an excellent organization, holding defensively such parts of Kentucky as the enemy had not gained possession of previous to its creation, and striking from time to time telling blows. Such blows were the battles of Piketon, Prestonburg, Middle Creek, Pound Gap, Rowlett's Station, and Mill Spring. The armies of Buell and Grant, and Commodore Foote's fleet of gunboats, made their simultaneous and masterly advance on the whole front of the enemy, extending from Columbus to Bowling Green,—of which the main features were the reduction of Forts Henry and Donelson in the centre, the capture of Nashville on the enemy's right, and the subsequent compulsory evacuation of Columbus on his left, which was speedily followed by the reduction of Island No. 10, in the Mississippi, by the gunboats and the co-operating army of General Pope.

On the 23d of February the army of General Buell entered Nashville; and there the general prepared for a continued advance southward to occupy Middle Tennessee and Northern Alabama and to co-operate with the forces of General Grant against Corinth. The forces of the latter were carried by transports up the Tennessee River to Savannah and Pittsburg Landing. Leaving a portion of his force under General O. M. Mitchel to advance directly south to Alabama,—which he subsequently did most gallantly,—General Buell led his main army towards the Tennessee River to join General Grant, and on the very hour of its arrival to plunge into the midst of the fight at Shiloh. How opportune his arrival it is needless now to tell. One day later, and who can tell how nearly fatal the disaster would have been? and one day earlier might have secured a victory with the most important consequences. The enemy, foiled and defeated, retired precipitately to his stronghold at Corinth. General Halleck now arrived and assumed command in the field, and the advance towards Corinth was continued, the army of General Pope, having reduced Island No. 10, being added as a reinforcement. Late in May, Corinth was evacuated; and the Army of the Ohio returned eastward in June, to rejoin the portion detached under General Mitchel in Northern Alabama. The line of communication with Louisville—a distance of three hundred miles by railroad—had been kept open meanwhile by a portion of the Army of the Ohio, on which the army depended for its supplies, excepting so far as the country furnished them. The Cumberland and Tennessee Rivers were of little value for navigation in their then low stage. So much of these roads as lay in Tennessee and Alabama were in a hostile country; and even Kentucky was subject to guerrilla raids of formidable character. In addition, garrisons were to be maintained at Nashville and other prominent places. The part of the army not thus employed encamped at Battle Creek and at other points in the vicinity of Chattanooga, threatening the rebel army of General Bragg at that place.

Such was the situation in July and part of August; and a great battle was expected daily. A battle was not, however, the purpose of the enemy unless attacked; for he was organizing an irresistible force with which to overrun Kentucky, to hold Louisville and the large towns on the Ohio River, and perhaps to capture Cincinnati. With this intent, the large army of Bragg began its march northward; and, to thwart his purpose, Buell had to release his hold on the country he had conquered, and to follow. He called in his forces from their several posts, and fell back on Nashville in a line parallel with the march of Bragg. At this city, where defensive works had been constructed within the month previous, he reorganized his forces with reference to the pending emergencies, left a small garrison there under General Negley, with orders to defend the place at every hazard, and pursued his rapid march towards Louisville, desiring to reach it in advance of his powerful enemy, who had three days the start. He effected this,—but at the cost of the sacrifice of the brave garrison at Munfordsville,—and secured his depots and protected his trains from the longing desires of the enemy. At Louisville he received heavy reinforcements, principally of new troops collected there, and again turned his face southward. On the 8th of October, near Perryville, a part of his army encountered the enemy and defeated him in the battle of Chaplin Hills. The army of Bragg, so magnificent in its preparation for the conquest of Kentucky, was defeated in its prime purpose, and now began its retreat from the State. There was dissatisfaction at this result, however. The nation was almost overjoyed that the invasion had been repelled; and yet nothing less than Bragg's annihilation would suffice. Three weeks after this battle, General Buell was relieved. General Rosecrans assumed command on the 30th of October, and the army continued its march southward under its new commander.

Thus plainly and briefly have we sketched the origin and early career of what is now the "Army of the Cumberland." The little force of Kentuckians that marched out under Rousseau to repel the invasion of Buckner was the germ that grew into the army which saved Kentucky and occupied and held for a season Middle Tennessee and Northern Alabama, which fought and won at Shiloh, and then returned and drove Bragg with a new rebel army from Kentucky. It has gathered strength by additions; but every regiment which has ever belonged to it is with it still, excepting such as have been retained in Kentucky, a part of the district to which until last November the army belonged. The generals who now command our three army corps,—Thomas, McCook, and Crittenden,—and hundreds of our best officers, all grew up with it while it was advancing to its present dimensions.

ADVANCE TO BOWLING GREEN AND NASHVILLE.

By General Orders No. 168, from the War Department, of date October 24, 1862, all of the State of Tennessee lying east of the Tennessee River, and such portions of Northern Alabama and Georgia as should thereafter be possessed by the United States forces, were erected into the Department of the Cumberland. Forts Henry and Donelson were subsequently added to this territory, inasmuch as they completely commanded the water-communications of the new department and had no necessarily intimate connection with the contiguous departments of Generals Grant and Wright. The troops now nearly a year under the command of Major-General Buell, and collectively known as the "Army of the Ohio," were by the same authority designated "The Fourteenth Army Corps." The command of this department and corps was assigned to Major-General Rosecrans, then at the head of the Army of the Mississippi, and just emerged from the smoke and carnage of the bloody and victorious fields of Iuka and Corinth.

In obedience to these orders, the new commander left Corinth on the 26th of October, and proceeded to his future field of labor. Passing two days with his family at Cincinnati, he reached Louisville on the 30th, and assumed command upon the same day. A short *résumé* of the circumstances under which this change was made, and a brief glance at the condition of the army thus consigned to the leadership of General Rosecrans, may not prove uninteresting, and will materially aid the reader in arriving at just conclusions as to the amount and value of the labor since performed within the lines of the department.

The successful escape of Bragg from Kentucky had greatly disappointed and somewhat disheartened the country. Marching his ragged regiments within sight of the Ohio River, he threatened both Cincinnati and Louisville, and yet, without sufficient force to capture either city, and, in all probability, abandoning all hope of doing so, he employed his time in feeding, clothing, and mounting his destitute men from the richly-stored granaries and well-stocked farms of the Green River country. General Buell, with a celerity for which he has not been given credit, had rapidly countermarched, and, throwing his troops into Louisville, was once more, with a largely increased army, in front of the enemy. On the 1st of October the Army of the Ohio was ready to move, and again, with high hopes of meeting and crushing the invading foe, set its face southward. Before this largely superior force Bragg retreated, eventually escaping into Tennessee in full possession of all his plunder. True, he had fought and lost the battle of Chaplin Hills; but it was a contest of his own seeking, in which, at the price of nominal defeat, he was entirely successful in the accomplishment of those ends to secure which he made the attack. To us it was a barren victory, dearly bought with the lives of hundreds of our best and bravest men. As a splendid illustration of heroic valor it will forever live in history; but it does not rank among the important and decisive battles of the rebellion.

It was now apparent that the ground gained by our arms in the South had been abandoned to the enemy; and, with the single exception of Nashville, garrisoned by the small divisions of Generals Negley and Palmer, but invested by a strong rebel force who were confident of its early capture, there was nothing to show as the result of nearly nine months' weary campaigning. Need it be wondered at that the spirit of complaint and discontent of the nation, which for months had with difficulty been repressed only by the hope that a crowning victory would speedily atone for the errors and follies of the past, again became rife, not only among the people at large, but even in the army? The Administration could not long withstand the complaints and refuse to grant the wishes of those upon whom it was dependent for support in its struggle to maintain unimpaired the integrity of the Union. Accordingly, while his columns, returning from their unsuccessful pursuit of

Bragg, were yet on the march towards Nashville, General Buell was relieved.

The Army of the Ohio was nominally large and effective. No labor nor expense had been spared in its creation and perfection. To it, while Bragg was yet in Kentucky, every available regiment and battery in the West had been drawn, as also the splendid legions which during the preceding spring had swept the rebel hordes out of Kentucky, planted the Stars and Stripes upon the dome of the Capitol at Nashville, turned defeat into victory at Shiloh, and overrun the whole of Northern Mississippi and Alabama. Surely it must constitute an army whose numbers and discipline would render it irresistible. So thought they who remembered only the men and material of which it had been composed, but were unmindful of the fearful manner in which its ranks had been thinned by disease, battles, and the nameless vicissitudes of war. In every respect it was largely overestimated. Nearly *seven thousand* of its numbers, disheartened and dispirited, had deserted. More than *twenty-six thousand* were absent by authority. The consolidated semi-monthly report for November 15, two weeks subsequent to the change of commanders, shows that a total of *thirty-two thousand nine hundred and sixty-six* officers and men—at least one-third of the whole army—were absent from their commands! Of these nearly ten thousand were sick in the hospitals of the West; the remainder were away on furlough or detached service, or had deserted. The army was composed in about equal proportions of veteran soldiers and raw recruits. The former were poorly clad and equipped, the latter inexperienced in drill or discipline, with officers often ignorant and sometimes incompetent. To add to the general incompleteness and inefficiency, there was a sad lack of cavalry; and even the small force of which the department could boast were so wanting in all the essentials of that branch of the service that they could be said to belong to it only because they wore its uniform and were mounted. To sum up all, briefly, the spirit of the army was broken, its confidence

24

destroyed, its discipline relaxed, its courage weakened, and its hopes shattered.

Such were some of the peculiar circumstances under which General Rosecrans assumed command. With a larger and more perfect army the task before him would have been difficult: it was rendered doubly so by the events to which allusion has been made. True, success had hitherto attended him in his military undertakings; but even this was a disadvantage, inasmuch as there was danger of its raising the hopes and expectations of the public to an unreasonable extent. He was profoundly conscious of all this; but any evidence of despondency or hesitation on his part will be sought in vain. He entered upon his duties with characteristic promptness and energy, and, tarrying but twenty-four hours in Louisville, he pressed on to Bowling Green, and there established his head-quarters on the 1st of November.

The divisions of the 14th Army Corps were concentrated at Bowling Green and Glasgow, with the exception of the two at Nashville, defending that city, as before stated. Bowling Green —seventy-two miles from Nashville—was the present terminus of the Louisville & Nashville Railroad, and the temporary depot of supplies. The Cumberland River was at a very low stage, and the subsistence and equipments of the army had to be brought by rail from Louisville over a road running through an unfriendly country. Our troops at Nashville were short of supplies, and before an advance could be made in that direction it was necessary that the railroad should be rebuilt; and then only by the greatest exertions could the army be supplied with provisions in sufficient quantities, so limited were the available means of transportation. Information touching the movements and designs of the enemy was difficult to obtain; but it was satisfactorily established that Bragg was yet in East Tennessee, marching towards Chattanooga with the purpose of ultimately concentrating his army at Murfreesborough, thirty-two miles southeast of Nashville, and that Breckinridge was already posted at the latter place with a strong division.

To become acquainted with, and gain the confidence of, his army,—to inspire it with all its former pride and zeal, to fill its thinned ranks, to perfect its organization and discipline, and to thoroughly clothe and equip it,—to extend his lines of railroad-communication, to procure and accumulate at convenient depots the requisite stores and supplies, to increase his knowledge of the country and the enemy, and, in short, to prepare for an active and vigorous campaign,—was the work to which General Rosecrans now addressed himself. In the words of one who is himself a gallant soldier, he "toiled terribly," night and day, scarcely taking for himself needed rest or allowing it to his subordinates.

Five millions of rations were sent forward from Louisville as fast as the limited capacity of the railroad would permit. Courier-lines were established between the different camps and garrisons of the department. Information concerning the topography of the country was collected, and military maps were made. Pioneer corps were organized in each command for the purpose of building bridges and repairing roads. Negroes were made useful as teamsters and laborers, as opportunity offered. Reviews of the divisions in the vicinity were held, and men and equipments examined with earnest scrutiny. The new troops were drilled incessantly. And, finally, authority was sought and obtained from the War Department to promptly muster out of or dismiss from the service "officers guilty of flagrant misdemeanors and crimes, such as pillaging, drunkenness, and misbehavior before the enemy or on guard-duty," as essential to the maintenance of discipline and good order.

Having thus inaugurated measures looking to the improvement of his infantry in discipline and efficiency, the general next vigorously applied himself to the reorganization and perfection of his cavalry. It was soon apparent that its feeble and unserviceable condition was owing in part to the want of capable officers to instruct and to lead them. Accordingly, he asked for the appointment of Brigadier-General David S. Stanley, with whom he had served in Mississippi, as his chief of cavalry; and that officer, in compliance with this request, was relieved from the command of a division of the Army of the Mississippi and transferred to the 14th Army Corps. A requisition was also made for five thousand revolving rifles: three thousand—all that the arsenals could supply—were obtained. Five thousand mules were ordered for pack-trains; but months elapsed before they were procured. An attempt was also made to perfect this arm of the service by combining with it light field-batteries for rapid movements; but the Government had not troops to man them, and it eventually became necessary to mount infantry and instruct them in this service.

General McCook's division was ordered to move, on the 4th, to Nashville, and, if possible, to reach that city by ten o'clock on the morning of the 7th. Upon receipt of information that the enemy were preparing to make an attack in force on the place they had so long invested, his columns were in motion by daylight on the 4th, and on the afternoon of the 6th had reached Edgefield Junction, twelve miles distant, when the thunder of heavy guns in the direction of Nashville hastened still more his rapid progress, and, pressing on, General Sill's division reached the Cumberland opposite the city at eight o'clock on the next morning,—two hours in advance of the designated time. The threatened attack had been made the day before, but had failed, as we have elsewhere fully narrated. This arrival relieved the city of all apprehension of further trouble, and established direct and regular communication with the head-quarters of the army.

By the 6th the railroad had been reopened to Mitchellsville, and supplies of all kinds were hurried forward with the utmost rapidity. Heavy supply-trains were put upon the road, and thus General McCook provisioned his own men, as well as the garrison of Nashville. The army was divided into the grand division, known as the Right, the Centre, and the Left, commanded respectively by Major-Generals McCook, Thomas, and Crittenden. The various columns were at once ordered forward; and in ten days from the time General Rosecrans assumed command, the whole army, with new life and energy instilled into every department of it, was moving with irresistible power towards the capital of Tennessee, in search of an enemy who had already twice escaped from its grasp. A vast amount of preparatory labor had been performed, plans for the ensuing campaign matured, communications established and suitably guarded, the army reorganized, and now its commander was ready to advance.

Accordingly, on the morning of the 10th of November, the head-quarters at Bowling Green were broken up, and the general and his staff proceeded by rail to Mitchellsville, whence, mounting their horses and escorted by a squadron of the 4th United States Cavalry, they rode to Nashville, reaching the city about nine o'clock the same evening. Head-quarters were immediately established in the Cunningham House, a large and elegant residence, whose owner was a quartermaster in the rebel army.

OCCUPANCY OF NASHVILLE.

THERE was work to be done. It was a rebel city, occupied as conquered territory, and swarming with traitors, smugglers, and spies. Of its male inhabitants a large number were in the rebel army, and its women, arrogant and defiant, were alike outspoken in their treason and indefatigable in their efforts to aid that cause for which their brothers, sons, and husbands were fighting. The city, in fact, was one vast "Southern Aid Society," whose sole aim was to plot secret treason and furnish information to the rebel leaders. To purify this tainted atmosphere, to establish order by the application of military law, and to impress this people with a sense of the strength and power of the Government, was the task to which General Rosecrans assiduously devoted himself while waiting for the accumulation of sufficient food, clothing, ammunition, and camp-equipage to make a further advance.

The police and secret-service department was organized and put into successful operation. The secret haunts of treason were penetrated, and its agents dragged forth to exposure and punishment. Smugglers and spies were pursued with a vigor so relentless that detection became the rule and escape the exception. Goods were seized and their owners sent to prison or expelled from the department, thus virtually putting an end to that contraband trade which had been of incalculable benefit to the rebels. All sutlers were ordered to their regiments, and it was announced that the Government would afford protection and trading privileges to all who would subscribe to an oath prepared for the occasion, and give bond with proper security for its faithful observance. Questions having arisen concerning the nature and binding force of this oath, they were definitively settled by an explanatory circular from head-quarters; and many embraced the opportunity thus afforded of procuring protection for themselves and property.

With all this care for the civil affairs of the department, the army was not neglected. No effort was spared to perfect it in drill, discipline, and equipment. An efficient signal corps was established. A new system of inspections was devised and adopted. A more careful attention to the proper performance of guard-duty was strictly enjoined. Sutlers were checked in their illegal and injurious practices. The authority obtained from the War Department to dismiss from the service incompetent and drunken officers was freely exercised. A cowardly trick of voluntarily surrendering to the enemy to be paroled, and thus escape the service, was summarily ended by the publication and subsequent enforcement of an order directing that all thus practically guilty of desertion should have their heads encased in white cotton night-caps, and, thus publicly branded as cowards, be marched through the streets and camps and sent North. The effect of this discipline was soon apparent; and in the six weeks spent at Nashville a long stride towards perfection was made by the army, thanks to the energy of its commander and the fidelity of its officers.

Meanwhile the enemy was sharply watched. His movements were for a time veiled by the strong cavalry force which he had thrown in front and which prevented our spies and scouts from obtaining ready entrance within his lines. The bridge across the Tennessee was known to be burned, and Bragg was said to be rebuilding it. The crowds of refugees thronging to our lines to escape the conscription, which the rebels were rigidly enforcing, reported that the road from the Tennessee to Murfreesborough was lined with camps. Still, it could not be definitely ascertained where the rebel general proposed to make a stand. Many believed that he would not attempt resistance to our advance on the north side of the Tennessee River, but would fall back from Murfreesborough to Chattanooga. But his movements and intentions were ere long developed by refugees, and the spies in the employ of Colonel Truesdail, Chief of the Army Police. In the latter part of November, Bragg was reported as having taken position in the rear of Stewart's Creek, nineteen miles from Nashville, with a force of sixty thousand effective men. His left rested on the Franklin pike, and his right on the Lebanon pike. His front was covered with strong cavalry vedettes, extending from the Lebanon pike to a point on the left of Nolensville, intersecting the Murfreesborough pike eleven miles from Nashville, and distant from our outposts scarcely two miles. Morgan, with a heavy force of cavalry and mounted infantry, covered his right, and Forrest his left, while Wheeler was posted at Lavergne and Wharton at Nolensville. His right wing was commanded by Kirby Smith, his left by Hardee, and the centre by Polk.

With his cavalry, in which he was immensely superior, the enemy constantly annoyed our outposts and forage-trains. The provision-trains between Nashville and Mitchellsville were constantly watched, and sometimes pounced upon, involving the loss, during the three weeks preceding the completion of the railroad, of a few men and wagons,—but were compensated for by equal captures on our side, however. Our cavalry was growing daily more efficient, and brisk skirmishes were of constant occurrence. Colonel John Kennett, acting chief of cavalry, captured large quantities of rebel stores, and eventually forced Morgan across the Cumberland. On the 27th of November he drove a large body of the enemy in confusion for some fifteen miles on the Franklin pike. The same day General Kirk, with a portion of his brigade, ran Wheeler out of Lavergne and destroyed a number of store-houses used by the enemy. Our loss was eleven wounded; that of the rebels was unknown, it being only ascertained that Forrest was among their wounded. The same evening Colonel Roberts, of the 42d Illinois, surprised a captain and squad of Morgan's men on the Charlotte pike, capturing the entire party, with their arms, equipments, and horses. About this time the enemy suddenly crossed the Cumberland near Hartsville, and captured a forage-train and the men accompanying, but were pursued by Major Hill, with a squadron of the 2d Indiana Cavalry, who succeeded, after a pursuit of eighteen miles, in recapturing the train, releasing the prisoners, and killing about twenty of the rebels.

On the 26th of November the railroad was completed from Mitchellsville to Nashville, and was immediately employed in hastening forward supplies. Up to this time it had been barely possible to subsist the army by running wagon-trains to that point, much less to attempt to accumulate supplies for the future. With railroad-communication re-established to Louisville, a vast improvement in this regard was expected. The supply soon began, but very slowly, to exceed the daily consumption, and in time, it was hoped, a sufficiency would be collected.

Thus far, in all the skirmishing, the rebels had gained no advantage. In fact, they had of late been badly worsted in their attacks upon our trains, &c. These successes—small, it is true, for the enemy avoided any contest of greater magnitude—inspired the army with hope and confidence. But now a reverse was in store that more than balanced all these minor advantages, and, in a measure, covered our arms with misfortune, if not disgrace, which stung our troops to the quick and filled them with a restless longing for action and revenge. This was

THE BATTLE OF HARTSVILLE.

THE main body of the centre division of our army did not advance to Nashville, but remained in the vicinity of Gallatin, to protect our line of communication to Louisville. General Dumont's division was stationed at Castilian Springs, in front of Gallatin, and he had thrown forward a brigade to Hartsville, for the purpose of guarding a ford and watching the road to Lebanon. This movement had been directed by General Thomas, and the brigade—the 39th—had taken position on elevated ground, where it was supposed they would be able to maintain themselves against a largely superior force. This post was first commanded by Colonel J. R. Scott, of the 19th Illinois, but on the 2d of December he was succeeded by Colonel A. B. Moore, of the 104th Illinois. According to Colonel Moore's official report, the brigade consisted of the 104th Illinois, the 106th and 108th Ohio, the 2d Indiana Cavalry, one company of the 11th Kentucky Cavalry, and a section of Knicklin's Indiana Battery, —in all, 1805 men. The troops were all new and untried, with the exception of the cavalry and artillery. Other authorities have placed the number at 1984; but the discrepancy is of no importance. The 2d and 40th Brigades were at Castilian Springs, about nine miles distant.

On Saturday, December 6, General John H. Morgan, of the Confederate Army, left Prairie Mills, eight miles south of Lebanon, Tennessee, and twenty-five from Hartsville, for the purpose of attacking the latter place. His force is stated by Colonel Moore at over five thousand, comprising six regiments of cavalry and two of mounted infantry (the 2d and 9th Kentucky,), and fourteen pieces of artillery, besides a considerable number of rebel citizens. Colonel Moore had not more than twelve hundred effective men, the balance being sick or on guard-duty with a provision-train. On Saturday night

Morgan encamped within five miles of Hartsville, and at early dawn the next morning moved to the attack. His advance-guard were clothed in Federal uniform, thereby completely deceiving Colonel Moore's vedettes, and capturing all of them without firing a gun. The enemy moved between Hartsville and Castilian Springs, and at sunrise were descried by one of the camp-guards, while approaching in the rear. A company of skirmishers threw itself forward and, by a sharp fire, checked the enemy, who approached cautiously, fearing stratagem. Time was thus given our troops to form in line of battle on the crest of a hill to the right of the camp. The enemy dis-mounted and, forming in compact line, moved forward, not-withstanding a heavy but scattering fire from Moore's line, and soon gained a protected position behind a fence at the foot of the hill on which our men were posted. The guns of Knicklin's battery were well handled, but the fire of the enemy was so destructive that the Ohio regiments were panic-stricken and gave way. The 104th Illinois stood its ground manfully for a time, but, being unsupported, was forced to yield to superior numbers. Strong cavalry detachments were harassing their flanks, and, after an hour and three-quarters' desultory and irregular fighting, the whole force was surrendered. The rebel cavalry had already dashed into the camps and made prisoners of the sick, straggling, and detached soldiers there found. Our loss in the affair was fifty-five killed and one hundred wounded. The enemy's loss was not far from the same. About thirteen hundred prisoners, two field-pieces, and a quantity of arms, ammunition, camp-equipage, and transportation, thus fell into the hands of the rebels. The defence was deemed unskilful, and the surrender premature. The fact that our troops had but just entered the service should be remembered in palliation, and their bravery has since been amply attested upon bloody battle-fields.

WHEELER DEFEATED BY MATTHEWS'S BRIGADE.

On the 9th of December another brigade was attacked by a strong force of rebel cavalry, mounted infantry, and artillery, all under the command of Brigadier-General Wheeler; but the result was vastly different. On that day Colonel Stanley Matthews, of the 51st Ohio, commanding the brigade, moved out upon the Murfreesborough pike with a large foraging-train guarded by the 51st Ohio, the 35th Indiana, the 8th and 21st Kentucky, and a section of Swallow's 7th Indiana Battery. Leaving the pike to his right, he crossed Mill Creek at Dobbins's Ferry, detailing a sergeant and ten men of the 21st Kentucky to guard the crossing. The train was filled, and just on the point of returning, when a sharp musketry-fire was heard in the direction of the crossing. Colonel Matthews immediately hastened on with the 51st Ohio and 35th Indiana, and, finding the enemy advancing through the woods in heavy force, at once opened fire, and, after a severe encounter, drove them a considerable distance, thus saving his picket-guard. Meanwhile the train and the remainder of the force had come up, and would have been a rich prize; but Colonel Matthews had no idea of allowing its capture by the rebel force, though apparently doubly superior to his own. Accordingly, with the Kentuckians protecting the rear and the Ohio and Indiana regiments in advance, he began a brisk march homeward. A short distance had been traversed, when the enemy was again discovered on the rear, moving forward rapidly and in strong force. No resistance was offered until they were within close range, when they were met by a fire from the Kentuckians so heavy and well directed that they recoiled. Soon reforming, they advanced and attacked again, but more cautiously than before, upon Matthews's flanks, and the fight became general. Their attempts to press his flanks, and a desperate effort to break his lines, were unsuccessful. The enemy was again driven back, and in a few moments fled from the field. Our loss in the engagement was five killed, thirty-five wounded, and four missing. The rebels subsequently confessed to a loss, on their part, of one hundred. The brigade marched safely to the city, and was warmly congratulated for the gallantry it had displayed.

General Stanley arrived and reported for duty about the middle of November. He at once organized the cavalry into two divisions, taking command of the first himself, and placing the second in charge of Colonel John Kennett. The revolving rifles had now arrived and been distributed, and the men were anxious to try them. To gratify them, General Stanley, with a considerable force, on the 11th of December, moved out on the Franklin pike, having in view a reconnoissance and the

CAPTURE OF FRANKLIN.

SOON after passing our outposts, skirmishing began with the enemy, and was continued all day, the latter's cavalry being chased and scattered in every direction. By night, Stanley and his men, tired and jaded, were beyond Triune, seven miles west of Murfreesborough, having destroyed two camps, dispersed numerous bands of the enemy, and captured a considerable number of rebel troopers and horses, with no loss to themselves. In front of them, at Nolensville, there was a large rebel force. Bragg, with his main army, was at Murfreesborough, and Buckner was in their rear, with his division. The attempt was hazardous, but General Stanley proceeded with his original design of making a dash at Franklin, and taking the garrison by surprise at night, if possible. The latter part of the plan was accidentally defeated. The enemy having been apprized of his presence, Stanley waited until daylight, when he advanced cautiously upon the town and drove in the rebel pickets. The 7th Pennsylvania formed line on the north bank of the Harpeth, a little to the right of where Fort Gilbert now stands, and opened fire on the enemy. Company I, of the 4th Michigan Cavalry, dismounting, took position near the bridge and opened fire on the mill; the remainder of the 4th Michigan dismounted under cover of the rising ground on which the 7th Pennsylvania were formed, advanced at the double-quick, passed the position of the 7th Pennsylvania, waded across the river, and drove the rebels from the town. Colonel Minty was the first man across the river, and, as he scrambled up the south bank, he took prisoner a rebel officer. The 4th Michigan had passed through the town and were following the enemy out on the Columbia and Carter's Creek pikes, *on foot*, before any of the mounted men had crossed the river. The enemy left one captain and four privates dead in the town, and ten severely wounded. Fifteen or twenty prisoners were also captured. General Stanley occupied the town an hour or two, destroyed a flouring-mill, captured a number of rebel horses, &c., and returned to his camp.

BATTLE OF STONE RIVER.

THE loyal people of the North were anxiously awaiting tidings of great events in the Department of the Cumberland. Far removed from the scene of action, they could not be expected to appreciate the vast amount of labor performed and the really wonderful progress made during the six weeks' stay at Nashville. To their minds, activity was indicated only by the shock of great battles, the thunder of artillery, the crash of musketry, and the groans of the dying. Nearly two months had elapsed since General Rosecrans assumed command, and no great results had as yet been realized by his grand army. From every side a pressure now began to bear upon the general commanding, urging a forward movement, especially after the re-establishment of railroad-communication with Louisville.

All such outside and—as our national experience has proven —improper influences, however, were firmly resisted by General Rosecrans. He declared that he would not move until the proper time,—that war was a business which not every one could understand,—and that he would not be driven by public clamor into a movement which his judgment could not approve. For many days after this impatience began to be manifested, the army was in no condition to move. It could not have moved more than three days without halting for supplies. On the 5th of December, nine days after the completion of the railroad, but five days' provisions had been accumulated; and with so scanty a store it would have been unwise and criminal to move the army from its base of supplies into the heart of the enemy's country. In his official report of the battle of Stone River, General Rosecrans alludes to the difficulties under which he labored, and explains satisfactorily the reasoning by which he was guided.

By Christmas thirty days' provisions had been collected and stored in Nashville; and now the general deemed it prudent to move. It had been satisfactorily ascertained, by means of spies and refugees, that the enemy had prepared his winter-quarters at Murfreesborough, and had sent one portion of his large cavalry force into West Tennessee to annoy General Grant, and another into Kentucky to destroy our railroad-communication. Polk's and Kirby Smith's forces were at Murfreesborough, and Hardee's corps was on the Shelbyville and Nolensville pike, between Triune and Eagleville. The enemy had been purposely deceived as to General Rosecrans's intentions, and supposed that he was going into winter quarters at Nashville, his force having been mainly collected in front of that city and extending over a strip of territory about ten miles in width. Under all these circumstances, it was adjudged that the time for an advance had arrived, and on the 24th of December orders were issued to the different columns to move at daybreak on the next day, Christmas. This announcement was received by the army with great satisfaction. For good reason, however, the orders were countermanded late that evening, after every preparation had been made for the morrow's advance.

On Christmas night a consultation was held at head-quarters,

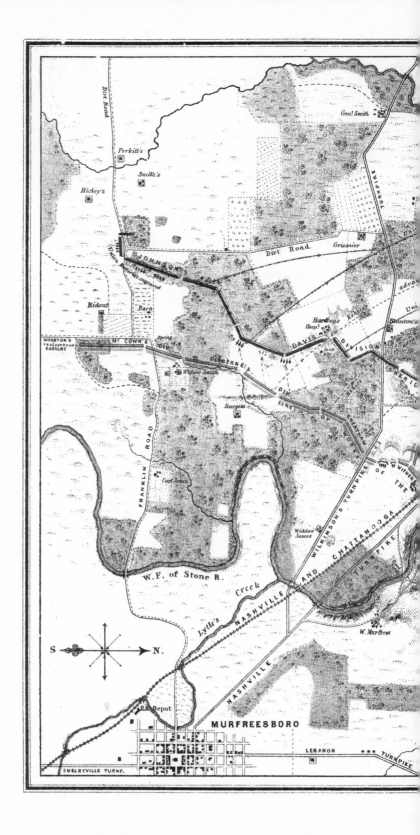

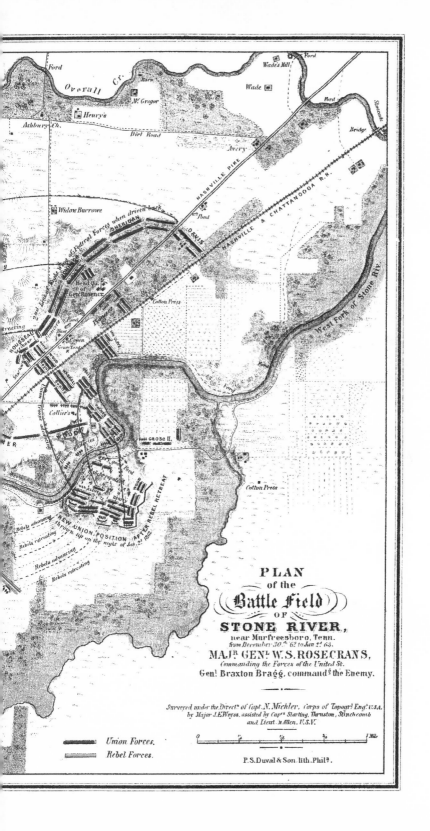

PLAN
of the
Battle Field
OF
STONE RIVER,
near Murfreesboro, Tenn.
from December 30.th 62 to Jan 2.d 63.
MAJ.R GEN.L W. S. ROSECRANS,
Commanding the Forces of the United St.
Gen.l Braxton Bragg, command.g the Enemy.

Surveyed under the Direct.n of Capt. N. Michler, Corps of Topogr.l Eng.rs U.S.A.
by Major J. E. Weyss, assisted by Capt.s Starling, Thruston, Stinchcomb
and Lieut. M. Allen, U.S.V.

Union Forces.
Rebel Forces.

0   ¼   ½   ¾   1 Mile

P. S. Duval & Son. lith. Phil.a.

at which the general announced that the army would move the next morning, and that the order and direction of the movement would be as follows :—

McCook, with three divisions, to advance by the Nolensville pike to Triune.

Thomas, with two divisions (Negley's and Rousseau's), to advance on his right, by the Franklin and Wilson pikes, threatening Hardee's right, and then to fall in by the cross-roads to Nolensville.

Crittenden, with Wood's, Palmer's, and Van Cleve's divisions, to advance by the Murfreesborough pike to Lavergne.

With Thomas's two divisions at Nolensville, McCook was to attack Hardee at Triune; and if the enemy reinforced Hardee, Thomas was to support McCook.

If McCook beat Hardee, or Hardee retreated, and the enemy met us at Stewart's Creek, five miles south of Lavergne, Crittenden was to attack him; Thomas was to come in on his left flank, and McCook, after detaching a division to pursue or observe Hardee, if retreating south, was to move with the remainder of his force on their rear.

General Stanley was to cover the movements with his cavalry. Dividing his force into three columns, he ordered Colonel Minty, with the first brigade, to move upon the Murfreesborough pike in advance of the left wing. The second brigade, in charge of Colonel Zahn, of the 3d Ohio Cavalry, was directed to move on the Franklin road parallel to the right wing, protecting its right flank. The reserve, consisting of new regiments, General Stanley himself would command, and precede General McCook's command on the Nolensville pike. Colonel John Kennett was assigned to the command of the cavalry on the left; and the 4th United States Cavalry, Captain Otis commanding, was reserved for courier and escort duty.

The morning of the 26th was dark, dreary, and rainy, but the camps were none the less scenes of active and busy preparation, and in due season the columns were in motion. McCook advanced on Nolensville, Johnson's and Sheridan's divisions moving upon the direct road, and Davis's division marching by way of the Edmonson pike to Prim's blacksmith-shop, whence it struck for Nolensville by a country cross-road. The advance of Davis's and Sheridan's commands encountered the enemy's columns about two miles beyond our picket-line; and from that point to Nolensville there was constant skirmishing. The enemy, occupying the town in considerable force, were driven out, and retired to a rocky range of hills about two miles beyond, through a defile in which (known as Knob Gap) the Nolensville and Triune pike passes. Here they made a stand, lining the slopes with skirmishers and placing a six-gun battery on a commanding position. A sharp fire was opened upon them by our batteries, and they were then gallantly attacked in front by Carlin's brigade and driven from their position with the loss of one gun and a number of prisoners. After taking possession of the defile and the hills, the right was encamped for the night, Johnson's division having arrived at Nolensville, without incident worthy of mention, at four o'clock. The loss of the right during the day was about seventy-five in killed and wounded.

The centre, consisting of Rousseau's and Negley's divisions and Walker's brigade of Fry's division, and numbering thirteen thousand three hundred and ninety-five effective men, was to encamp that night at Owen's Store, on the Wilson pike. Rousseau did so; but Negley, hearing heavy firing in the direction of Nolensville, left his train with a guard to follow him, and pushed on with his troops to the assistance of Davis, who was hotly engaged at Knob Gap. Walker's brigade camped at Brentwood, no enemy having been met during the day.

General Crittenden, in command of the left wing, thirteen thousand two hundred and eighty-eight effective men, moved along the Murfreesborough pike, Palmer's division in advance, followed by Wood's. Several miles north of Lavergne, a small town about equidistant from Nashville and Murfreesborough, portions of the enemy were encountered by our cavalry in the advance, and a running fight at once began. The country between Murfreesborough and Nashville was peculiarly favorable to the enemy in resisting and retarding our advance,—a small force being able to check the progress of a larger one. Large cultivated tracts occur at intervals on either side of the pike; but between these tracts are dense woods, often interspersed with almost impenetrable cedar thickets. The resistance the enemy was thus enabled to offer prevented our troops from gaining the commanding heights south of Lavergne on the first day, and so delayed their arrival at Lavergne that the necessary and customary reconnoissance could not be made. To guard against surprise, however, a regiment from each brigade was thrown well forward as a grand guard, and the front and flanks covered with a continuous line of skirmishers.

General Rosecrans, with his staff and escort, left Nashville at mid-day, in the midst of a drenching rain, and rode rapidly towards General McCook's head-quarters; but it was long after dark when the camp of the right wing was reached. McCook reported Hardee in his front, at Triune, seven miles distant, and said that he expected a stout resistance the next day. He was directed to move at daylight and push the enemy hard; and the general-in-chief took his leave, reaching his own camp at about one o'clock in the morning.

General McCook was ready to advance by dawn the next morning; but it had rained all the preceding day and night, and a dense fog, which prevented any thing being seen at a distance of one hundred and fifty yards, greatly retarded operations. The columns had moved about two miles when they encountered the enemy's cavalry, infantry, and artillery. The fog at this time was so thick that friend could not be distinguished from foe,—our cavalry being fired upon by our infantry skirmishers on the flanks. The enemy being conversant with the ground and our troops strangers to it, and having learned that Hardee's corps had been in line of battle all night, General McCook deemed it inadvisable to advance until the fog lifted.

He accordingly halted the column until one o'clock, when, the fog having disappeared, an advance was immediately ordered, and the enemy's cavalry were driven forward. On nearing

25

Triune, it was found that the main portion of the forces had retired, leaving a battery of six pieces, supported by cavalry, to contest the crossing of Wilson's Creek, a stream with steep and bluff banks, which could be crossed only with great difficulty, the enemy having destroyed the bridge. General Johnson, against a sharp resistance, finally gained a position overlooking Triune, and opened fire upon the rebels, who were formed in line, with their centre in the village. A few shots were sufficient to confuse them, and their battery, with the cavalry, fled down the Eagleville road. It being now nearly dark, and a severe and driving rain-storm having set in, they were pursued no farther. Johnson's division then crossed, and camped beyond Wilson's Creek, repairing the destroyed bridge. Sheridan's division also camped near the village, and Davis bivouacked at the junction of the Balle Jack road with the Nolensville pike.

On the centre, General Thomas moved Rousseau to Nolensville; but the heavy rains had so damaged the cross-roads that he did not reach that place until night. Negley remained at Nolensville until ten o'clock, when, having brought his train across from Wilson's pike, he moved to the east, over an exceedingly rough by-road, to the right of Crittenden, at Stewartsborough, on the Murfreesborough pike. Walker retraced his steps from Brentwood, and crossed over to the Nolensville pike.

The troops of the left were roused an hour and a half before dawn, and, getting their breakfast as speedily as possible, were formed in line and under arms before it was light. The enemy still occupied the opposite heights, and early in the morning began dropping an occasional shell into our lines,—thus proving the wisdom of the precautions taken. At eleven o'clock the left began its march to obtain possession of Lavergne, that being the first object. The enemy were strongly posted in the houses, and on the wooded heights in the rear, where they were enabled to oppose our advance by a direct and cross fire of musketry. Hascall's brigade advanced across an open field, and, quickly driving the rebels from their position, continued their forward movement, supported by Estep's 8th Indiana Battery. The enemy availed themselves of every opportunity to dispute their progress, but could not materially retard it. They continued to press forward through the densely-wooded country, in a drenching rain-storm, till the advance reached Stewart's Creek, distant some five miles from Lavergne,—a narrow, deep stream, flowing between high and precipitous banks, and spanned by a wooden bridge, of which it was a matter of cardinal importance to secure possession.

The enemy had lighted a fire upon it, but had been pressed so warmly that the flames had not yet communicated to the bridge. The skirmishers and the 3d Kentucky Volunteers—Colonel McKee—dashed bravely forward, under a steady fire from the opposing forces, threw the combustible materials into the stream, and saved the bridge. While this gallant feat was being performed, the left flank of the leading brigade was attacked by cavalry. The menaced regiments immediately changed front to left, repulsed the attack, and a company of the 100th Illinois succeeded in cutting off and capturing twenty-five prisoners with their arms, and twelve horses with their accoutrements. The result of the day's operations was twenty wounded in Hascall's brigade, and some twenty-five prisoners taken from the enemy. The enemy fell back in great disôrder from Stewart's Creek, leaving tents standing on the southern bank of the creek, and the ground strewn with arms.

This was Saturday night. On Sunday there was no movement, the troops resting, except Rousseau's division, which was ordered to move on to Stewartsborough, and Willich's brigade, which had pursued Hardee as far as Riggs's Cross-Roads, and, having determined the fact that Hardee had gone to Murfreesborough, returned to Triune. During the day General Rosecrans visited the front, and observed the enemy from the north bank of Stewart's Creek. A battery supported by a considerable force of mounted infantry was in plain sight, upon an elevated position in the road about a mile south of that stream, and the woods nearer its bank were swarming with rebels. The ground on the opposite side was admirably calculated for defence; and it was the general conclusion that the enemy would, in force, resist our crossing. Proper dispositions were made in view of the anticipated engagement, and, after a brief visit to General Crittenden's quarters, the general returned to his head-quarters, now at Lavergne.

Leaving the second brigade of Johnson's division at Triune, General McCook marched on the 29th by the Balle Jack road towards Murfreesborough, but, the road being very bad, the command did not reach Wilkerson's Cross-Roads (five miles from Murfreesborough) until late in the evening. His command was encamped in line of battle, Sheridan's on the left of Wilkerson's pike, Davis's division on the right of the same road, Woodruff's brigade guarding the bridge over Overall's Creek, and the two brigades of Johnson's division watching the *right. Believing that the enemy intended giving battle at or near Murfreesborough, he ordered the brigade left at Triune to join the main body, which it did the next day.

Negley's division crossed Stewart's Creek, two miles southwest and above the turnpike-bridge, and marched in support of the head and right flank of Crittenden's corps, which moved by the Murfreesborough pike, to a point within two miles of Murfreesborough. The enemy fell back before our advance, contesting the ground obstinately with their cavalry rear-guard. Rousseau remained in camp at Stewartsborough, detaching Starkweather's brigade, with a section of artillery, to the Jefferson pike crossing of Stone River, to observe the movements of the enemy in that direction. Walker reached Stewartsborough from the Nolensville pike about dark.

Crittenden's corps advanced, Palmer leading, on the Murfreesborough pike, followed by Negley, of Thomas's corps, to within three miles of Murfreesborough, having had several brisk skirmishes, driving the enemy rapidly and forcing him back to his intrenchments, saving two bridges on the route. About three P.M. a signal-message from General Palmer said that he was in sight of Murfreesborough and the enemy were said to be evacuating. An order was sent to General Crittenden to send a division to occupy Murfreesborough. Harker's brigade was directed by the latter to cross the river at a ford on his left, where he surprised a regiment of Breckinridge's division and drove it back on its main lines, not more than five hundred yards distant, in considerable confusion; thus he held this position until General Crittenden was advised that Breckinridge was in force on his front, when, it being dark, he ordered the brigade to recross the river,—a hazardous movement, but skilfully executed, with the loss of two killed and three wounded,—and reported the circumstances to the commanding general on his arrival, by whom his action was approved, the order to occupy Murfreesborough having been based on the information that the enemy were retreating from Murfreesborough. Crittenden's corps, with Negley's division, bivouacked in order of battle, about seven hundred yards from the enemy's intrenchments, our left extending down the river some five hundred yards. The Pioneer Brigade, bivouacking still lower down, prepared three fords, and covered one of them, Wood's division covering the other two.

At half-past three o'clock on the morning of the 30th, General McCook received orders to rest the left of his line on the right of Negley's division, and to throw his right forward until it became parallel, or nearly so, with Stone River, the extreme right to rest on or near the Franklin pike. At half-past nine the right wing began its march down the Wilkerson pike towards Murfreesborough. Soon after crossing Overall's Creek, the enemy's infantry pickets were encountered, and heavy skirmishing ensued. The line then moved forward slowly, as the enemy, under cover of heavy woods and cedar thickets, stubbornly contested every inch of ground. About noon, Sheridan's division joined Negley's right, the other divisions coming up on Sheridan's right, thus forming a continuous line, the left resting on Stone River, the right stretching in a westerly direction and resting on high wooded ground a short distance to the south of Wilkerson's Cross-Roads, and nearly parallel with the enemy's intrenchments thrown up on the sloping land bordering the northwest bank of Stone River.

Van Cleve's division being in the reserve, Rousseau's division, with the exception of Starkweather's brigade, was ordered up from Stewartsborough, reaching the position occupied by the army about four o'clock in the afternoon, and bivouacked on the Murfreesborough pike in the rear of the centre. During the morning, Negley's division was obliqued to the right, and took up a position on the right of Palmer's division of Critten- den's corps, and was then advanced through a dense cedar thicket, several hundred yards in width, to Wilkerson's Cross- Roads, driving the enemy's skirmishers steadily and with con- siderable loss.

The left was early in line of battle, Palmer's division on the right of the turnpike, his right resting on Negley's left, Wood occupying that part of our front on the left of the pike extend- ing down to the river, and Van Cleve in reserve to the rear and left. This position was maintained without material change during the day, though the skirmishing was sometimes heavy, particularly on the right, where McCook was approaching.

The entire cavalry force, except those detailed for escort and courier service, was engaged in guarding the flanks of the army. Some skirmishing occurred, but nothing of any importance. Just before midnight, General Stanley, with the 1st Tennessee and Anderson Cavalry, went back to Lavergne, for the purpose of protecting our communications. The commanding general remained with the left and centre, examining the ground, while General McCook moved forward from Wilkerson's Cross-Roads. At four o'clock in the afternoon, General McCook announced his arrival on the Wilkerson pike, joining Thomas, and the fact that Sheridan was in position there,—also that Hardee's corps, with two divisions of Polk's, was on his front, extending down towards the Salem pike.

Thus, on the night of the 30th of December the army of General Rosecrans, of forty-three thousand men, were drawn up in front of Murfreesborough, facing an enemy of considerably greater force. His line was continuous, about three miles in length, describing an irregular figure, with reserves in position, and whose extreme right bore away from the left towards the southwest at an angle of about thirty degrees. The left rested on Stone River, and the right on high wooded ground south of and near the Franklin pike. The extreme right brigade (Willich's) was formed at nearly right angles to the main line, making a bend towards the rear, to guard against a flank movement. The right wing occupied a wooded ridge with open ground in front, and was separated from the enemy by a narrow valley varying in width from two hundred to four hundred yards, which latter was covered by dense cedar thickets and oak forests. The centre was posted on a rolling slope in advance, joining Crittenden's right and McCook's left. The right brigade of the left wing rested upon a wood, the next stretched across an open cotton-field into a thin grove, and the left brigades were also partially covered by timber, with open ground in front. The enemy occupied a commanding crest in the open field, perhaps eight hundred yards distant from our line.

In rear of our line the country was undulating and rough, excepting on the left. Behind the right wing and centre there were alternate fallow fields, fences, and dense cedar thickets and ridges. Behind the left there was an undulating corn-field, rising into a crest which faced the enemy. On the right of the pike, going south, there was an irregular cotton-field, swelling to a crest and then falling off into thick-skirted swamps towards the north and into an open marsh towards the south, with its southern base fronting the centre of the enemy's right.

The railroad on high ground, to the left of the pike, the turnpike on low ground, intersected the left wing on Palmer's left, and crossed each other near the rebel line in a depression forming a sharp triangle, the base of which, a half-mile in the rear, was about five hundred yards wide. About half-way between the two lines were the walls of a brick dwelling, now famous as " Cowan's burnt house," occupying a knoll.

The enemy's right intersected Stone River nearly parallel

with our left front, and rested upon the heights east of the river, the extreme right obliquing to correspond with the course of the river towards our left. The left of their right and their centre were in position behind intrenchments on the crest of the cotton-field, sloping gradually towards our front and abruptly towards their rear. Their left was prolonged on a rocky ridge south of the Franklin road, and covered the roads going southward towards Shelbyville. The river was fordable at any place where it could be reached, so that, if necessary, the enemy could retire across it without trouble, and, with it in their front, could offer serious resistance to our forces should they attempt to advance across it.

The following diagram will enable the reader to understand at a glance the positions of the two armies as they came together, faced in line of battle, on the evening of the 30th and morning of the 31st.

DIAGRAM I.

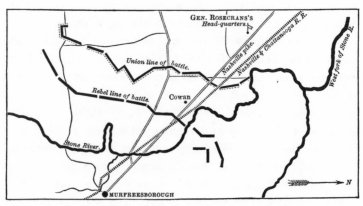

Positions of Contending Forces, December 31, 1862, 5 o'clock A.M.

At nine o'clock that night the corps commanders met at headquarters, and the following plan of battle was presented to them.

McCook was to occupy the most advantageous position, refusing his right as much as practicable and necessary to secure it,—to receive the attack of the enemy, or, if that did not come, to attack himself, and thus to hold all their force on his front.

Thomas and Palmer were to open with skirmishing, and gain the enemy's centre and left as far as the river.

Crittenden was to cross Van Cleve's division at the lower ford, covered and supported by the sappers and miners, and to advance on Breckinridge.

Wood's division was to follow by brigades, crossing at the upper ford, and, moving on Van Cleve's right, to carry every thing before them into Murfreesborough.

"This," said General Rosecrans in his official report, "would have given us two divisions against one, and as soon as Breckin. ridge had been dislodged from his position, the batteries of Wood's division, taking position on the heights east of Stone River, in advance, would see the enemy's works in reverse, would dislodge them, and enable Palmer's division to press them back and drive them westward across the river or through the woods, while Thomas, sustaining the movement on the centre, would advance on the right of Palmer, crushing their right, and Crittenden's corps, advancing, would take Murfreesborough, and then, moving westward on the Franklin road, get in their flank and rear, and drive them into the country, towards Salem, with the prospect of cutting off their retreat and probably destroying their army.

"It was explained to them that this combination, insuring us a vast superiority on our left, required for its success that General McCook should be able to hold his position for three hours; that, if necessary to recede at all, he should recede as he had advanced on the preceding day, slowly and steadily, refusing his right, thereby rendering our success certain."

The disposition of our forces on the morning of the 31st was as follows. To the left of the Nashville and Murfreesborough pike, one brigade of Wood's division formed the left of the Federal line; Palmer's division was deployed to the right of the pike, leaving two brigades of Wood's and the whole of Van Cleve's division as the reserve of the left wing; then the centre, with Negley's division deployed, and Rousseau's in reserve, but so located as to be available at the extreme left as well as the centre. The three divisions of the right wing were deployed, extending the line a considerable distance beyond the Nolensville pike. The cavalry—two brigades—were equally divided upon the flanks.

At daybreak the troops breakfasted and stood to their arms, awaiting the order to move. The movement was begun on the left by Van Cleve, who crossed at the lower fords, Wood preparing to sustain and follow him. But meanwhile the enemy had apparently, and as if by some wonderful fatality, anticipated General Rosecrans's plan, and during the night had massed his forces heavily in front of our right, advanced at early break of day, and with great vigor threw himself upon the extreme right of General McCook's line. Pressing rapidly forward in heavy columns, though losing largely at every step, he fell upon Willich's and Kirk's brigades of Johnson's division, who, after a desperate but unavailing contest, were driven back and crumbled to pieces, leaving Edgarton's and part of Goodspeed's batteries in the possession of the rebels. Edgarton had previously sent his horses to water, and they were still unhitched. He had barely time to put them in harness when they were shot; and, after firing a dozen rounds and having every horse killed, his guns and himself fell into the enemy's hands. Following up this advantage, the enemy fiercely attacked Davis's division, and, after desperate fighting, dislodged Post's, Carlin's, and Woodruff's brigades. Johnson's division, in retiring, inclined too far to the left, and also were too much scattered to make a combined resistance. The ground over which it passed, however, covered with the enemy's dead and those of our own men, showed that the field was warmly contested. Several times the lines were reformed and resistance was offered; but the columns of the enemy were too heavy for a single line, and the division in every case was compelled to fall back.

The right and centre divisions of the right wing having thus given back, the attack was made with redoubled fury upon McCook's left, Sheridan's division. Here the enemy met with a successful resistance for a time; but, the line on his right having given way, Sheridan was exposed in front, flank, and rear. Twice the heroic division changed front and hurled back the overwhelming mass of foes, and, when outflanked and nearly encircled, with every brigade commander killed or wounded, was retired in good order. Negley's division, hard pressed and out of ammunition, was also compelled to give way, and, with Sheridan, fell back through the cedar thickets.

Our right wing was now thoroughly broken, and its retiring divisions almost doubled backward upon the left. All had fought desperately, but all had been driven from their position. Eleven guns of Johnson's division and six of Sheridan's had been captured by the enemy. Hundreds of men had been killed and wounded, and nearly two thousand made prisoners. The enemy had gained sufficient ground in our rear to wheel his masses to the right and throw them upon the right flank of the centre, at the same moment attacking Negley and Palmer in front with a greatly superior force. The original plan of battle of our commander-in-chief was now utterly useless, the whole order of battle being changed; and so furious and persistent had been the assault and advance of the enemy that all this had occurred within scarcely two hours.

A forward movement of Palmer's division, to occupy a favorable crest preliminary to the grand assault by the left wing, was already in progress, when it was prevented by intelligence of the disaster to the right. While Negley's division was engaged, the reserve of the centre (lying behind the right brigade of the left wing) was ordered forward to his support. Rousseau's division moved into the cedars in Negley's rear and commenced its deployment. It was discovered at this critical moment that it was difficult, if not impossible, to move the artillery from the narrow roads which had been cut through the thicket into a position where it could be used to advantage. The deployment of the infantry was effected, but without engaging, save a battalion on the right, which was suddenly assailed in flank by the enemy and partially confused. The entire division was moved a considerable distance to the rear, and finally formed upon favorable ground directly in the rear of the right of Crittenden's wing. Negley, of course, could do nothing less than fall back then: his line had, in fact, already yielded for want of support. Sheridan's glorious resistance and the firmness of Negley's men had, however, covered the perambulations of the reserve, and that force was in readiness to receive the enemy.

At this stage it became necessary to readjust the line of battle to the new state of affairs. Rousseau and Van Cleve's advance having relieved Sheridan's division from the pressure, Negley's division, and Cruft's brigade from Palmer's division, withdrew from their original position in front of the cedars, and crossed the open field to the east of the Murfreesborough pike, about four hundred yards in rear of our front line, where Negley was ordered to replenish his ammunition and form his reserve in close column. The right and centre of our line now extended from Hazen to the Murfreesborough pike, in a north-westerly direction, Hascall supporting Hazen, Rousseau filling the interval to the Pioneer Brigade, Negley in reserve, Van Cleve west of the Pioneer Brigade, McCook's corps refused on his right and slightly to the rear on the Murfreesborough pike; the cavalry being still farther to the rear on the Murfreesborough pike and beyond Overall's Creek. Palmer's division, the right of Crittenden's line, was the only one still remaining in the original position.

The position of General Rosecrans was now in the form of a crotchet, the shorter line being Palmer's division. The left of this division, now the left of the army, was to the left of and at right angles with the Nashville pike, in a scanty grove of oaks, covering an inconsiderable crest between the pike and the railroad, which intersected at an acute angle, about four hundred yards in front. Stone River, crossing the pike some distance farther to the front, ran almost parallel and very near to it, within three hundred and fifty yards of Palmer's position, where it turned squarely to the left, and, continuing this course for several hundred yards, again turned and swept around towards the rear. The portion of the stream in front of Palmer's left was deep, with but one narrow ford, thus forming an excellent flank defence. Between Palmer's two brigades in the front line was an open field of three hun'dred yards (the left brigade had occupied this field; but its commander, seeing the impossibility of sustaining an attack in low, open ground, within musket-range of the enemy's cover, had moved to occupy the favorable crest mentioned), the right brigade lying in the skirt of cedar wood.

Palmer's division had sustained one attack successfully, and, while General Rosecrans was forming his new line, was assailed with extreme ferocity in front and upon the right flank, then exposed by the falling back of Negley. The right brigade was forced back in turn, exposing the left brigade to a flank attack and rendering the whole position critical. But Hazen, at the head of the left brigade, maintained his position with unflinching courage and good success, until the forces on his right were overwhelmed and driven back. When this occurred he was exposed to fire in flank and rear, and to the attempts of the enemy to charge in front. Its commander had but one regiment to protect this flank, but was furnished with two battalions from the division reserve. It required terrible fighting to beat back the enemy's double lines in front and flank; it cost a third of the brave brigade; but every moment the enemy was held back was worth a thousand men to the main line. General Rosecrans improved the time so well, in hurrying troops to the new position, that when the enemy assailed that line the fresh divisions of Van Cleve, Wood, and Rousseau, and the artillery massed on a commanding point, not only repulsed them, but they were charged while retiring by one of Crittenden's brigades. The enemy had also miscalculated the temper of Hazen's brigade, and Bragg was obliged to report, as he did in his first despatch, that he "had driven the whole Federal line, except his left, which stubbornly resisted."

The force that followed to engage the new line, when Negley fell back, was undoubtedly designed to operate in conjunction with the one now endeavoring to crush the short arm (Palmer's

division) of the crotchet line, and the two would then take the
main Federal line in front, flank, and rear, before its formation
was complete. The plan was well devised; for, with the division
protecting the left of his army removed, General Rosecrans's
prospects would have been hopeless. The persistence and desperate energy with which the enemy pressed this point indicated
that they were fully aware of the advantage success here would
give them.

A single brigade of thirteen hundred men, a mere handful in
comparison with the huge masses hurled against them, foiled
every effort of the enemy at this vital point. For this scarcely
less than miraculous result the country is indebted to the unflinching courage of the men and the ability of their commander,
who manœuvred them with wonderful skill. When the enemy
withdrew, the right of the brigade was swung to the rear,
bringing it behind an embankment of the railroad, which
formed a good breastwork and enabled it successfully to withstand subsequent flank attacks. In the temporary cessation of
fighting which ensued, General Rosecrans strengthened the
point with infantry and artillery.

But the battle was not yet ended. The enemy had been
repulsed with terrible loss; but it was hardly possible that he
would yield the signal advantage his success in the earlier part
of the day had given him, without at least one more desperate
struggle. Evidently unwilling to abide the test of a single
attack and repulse, he came forward again in solid columns; but
it was now too late. Rosecrans had been personally on the
field, and had newly formed his entire line of battle, having
discovered the enemy's object. McCook's troops and Negley's
division had been reformed in the new position. The enemy,
though inflicting severe losses, was unable to force the line
again, and was driven back with great slaughter. The right of
his line, when it came up to assault for the fourth and last time
Hazen's position on the left, was shattered and broken by a
single volley,—such a change had repeated repulses made in the

morale of troops that had fought with such frenzied desperation in the morning.

The day was now nearly spent. The confidence of the enemy was obviously shaken by the bitter experience of the last three hours. Still he exhibited a bold front and threatening aspect. Again his forces were heavily massed in front of the centre, as though the hazard of another assault would be attempted. But our artillery played upon them so effectively that only a small force could be urged up to the range of our musketry, and they were speedily driven back. An answering effort was made by their artillery, which opened upon our lines terrifically; but at sunset the roar of battle had ceased, and only the occasional booming of a single cannon or the more frequent but less heeded rattle of musketry disturbed the stillness of the night that was fast settling down upon that field drenched with the blood of thousands and thickly strewn with dead and dying.

"The day closed," said General Rosecrans, "leaving us masters of the original ground on our left, and our new line advantageously posted, with open ground in front, swept at all points by our artillery. We had lost heavily in killed and wounded, and a considerable number in stragglers and prisoners; also twenty-eight pieces of artillery, the horses having been slain, and our troops being unable to withdraw them by hand over the rough ground; but the enemy had been thoroughly handled and badly damaged at all points, having had no success where we had open ground and our troops were properly posted,—none which did not depend on the original crushing of our right and the superior masses which were in consequence brought to bear upon the narrow front of Sheridan's and Negley's divisions, and a part of Palmer's, coupled with the scarcity of ammunition, caused by the circuitous road which the train had taken and the inconvenience of getting it from a remote distance through the cedars."

Head-quarters were established that night in a log hut on the right of the road, within short artillery-range of the rebel front, and there a conference of the generals was held. Some of them were rather despondent; but not one advised retreat. All seemed to await the decision of the commander, with confidence in its wisdom. Indeed, there was much to sicken the heart,— much to depress the bravest and most sanguine of men. The day had begun in disaster, and it was not yet retrieved. More than seven thousand men were missing from our ranks. Many of the regiments had lost two-thirds of their officers; scarcely one had escaped without loss. Willich and Kirk, Johnson's ablest brigadiers, were not present: the first was a prisoner, the second desperately wounded. Sill, Schaeffer, and Roberts, Sheridan's brigade commanders, were dead. Wood and Van Cleve were disabled. Ten colonels, ten lieutenant-colonels, and six majors were missing,—dead, wounded, or prisoners. Of line officers the number gone was terrible. Sheridan alone had lost seventy-two officers. Out of fourteen hundred, the United States Regular Brigade had lost twenty-two officers and five hundred and eight men. The enemy held nearly two-thirds of the battle-field and one-fifth of our artillery. Communications were interrupted in our rear, and some of the subsistence-trains which had been ordered back to Nashville, to be out of our way and of danger, had been destroyed by rebel cavalry. Artillery ammunition was scant, and the rebel cavalry hovering in the rear made the obtaining of further supplies uncertain. The soldiers were weary and hungry, and now lay shivering in the cold December air, without fires. It was a gloomy night,— gloomy long before midnight, when the gathering clouds stretched across the heavens and poured upon the contending armies a deluge of rain, as if weeping over the slaughter.

The second position of the two armies, at the close of the battle of the 31st, is illustrated in the diagram on the opposite page.

The advantage was with the enemy thus far, and it was deemed probable that he would renew the attack in the morning: the question was how and where to meet him. The rebel leaders—as was subsequently ascertained—had no doubt that General Rosecrans would attempt to fall back on Nashville. But he had no such thought. Mounting his horse, he rode to the rear, examined the country, returned, and said to those about him, "Gentlemen, we conquer or die right here." If forced to fall back, he concluded that a successful stand could be made on the south bank of Overall's Creek; but he had no idea of taking

DIAGRAM II.

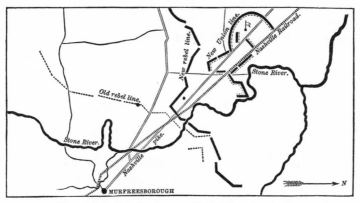

Lines of Contending Forces on the Night of December 31, 1862.

that position until driven to it. He found that he had ammunition enough for another battle, the only question being where it should be fought. By his personal exertions he had that day checked the tide of a terrible disaster, reformed his army in the face of the attacking enemy, rolled back their columns with appalling slaughter, and, if he had not achieved a great victory, had prevented a signal defeat. The same determination and hope which had inspired him in the darkest hours of that day's conflict were with him still, and, with unshaken reliance upon his trusty soldiers and implicit faith in a guiding Providence, he determined *to fight and to conquer*.

The consultation having resulted thus, arrangements were planned for the morrow. It was decided, in order to complete our present lines, that the left should retire two hundred and fifty yards to more advantageous ground, the extreme left resting on Stone River, above the lower ford, and extending to Stokes's battery. Starkweather's and Walker's brigades arriving near the close of the evening, the former bivouacked in close column,

26

in reserve, in the rear of McCook's left, and the latter was posted on the left of Sheridan, near the Murfreesborough pike, and next morning relieved Van Cleve, who returned to his position in the left wing.

It was also determined to await the enemy's attack in that position, to send for the provision-train, and order up fresh supplies of ammunition, on the arrival of which, should the enemy not attack, offensive operations were to be resumed.

At daybreak on Thursday (New-Year's day), General Rosecrans had his army in a position against which the enemy might have hurled his masses in vain. McCook's corps was disposed thus:—Davis on the right, Sheridan joining him on the left, and Johnson in reserve. Walker's brigade, relieving Van Cleve, was succeeded on Sheridan's left by Starkweather's brigade. Thomas's position was not changed. Crittenden had reunited his command, bringing them all together on the left of the turnpike, and took up a new line of battle about five hundred yards to the rear of the former line; Hascall's division rested its right on the position occupied by Stokes's battery, and its left on Palmer's right; Palmer rested his left on the ford, his right extending perpendicularly towards the railroad, thus bringing the line at right angles to the railroad and turnpike, and extending from Stokes's battery to the ford.

The enemy making no demonstration in the morning, Crittenden, in accordance with orders, sent Colonel Sam Beatty, with two brigades of Van Cleve's division, across Stone River, to hold a hill overlooking and commanding the upper ford, a mile below the railroad-bridge in front of Murfreesborough. During the day repeated attempts were made by the enemy to advance upon the centre; but they were kept back by a heavy artillery fire, and once were severely repulsed by Morton's Pioneer Brigade. About two o'clock in the afternoon, having previously shown signs of movement and massing on our right, the enemy appeared at the extremity of a field a mile and a half from the Murfreesborough pike; but the presence of Gibson's brigade, with a battery, occupying the woods near Overall's Creek, and

Negley's division and a portion of Rousseau's on the Murfrees-borough pike, opposite the field, put an end to this demonstration. The day closed with a similar demonstration on Walker's brigade, which ended in the same manner.

About eight o'clock on Friday morning, while the Pioneer Brigade were making crossings at the railroad, the enemy opened a sharp and rapid fire from four heavy batteries on the east side of Stone River, and at the same time made a strong demonstration of attack a little farther to the right; but a well-directed fire of artillery soon silenced his batteries, while the guns of Walker and Sheridan put an end to his effort there.

General Rosecrans still had faith in his proposed movement of throwing his left wing into Murfreesborough, and early in the afternoon rode towards the river to examine the position of Crittenden's left, across the stream,—the position being held by Van Cleve's division, supported by one of Palmer's brigades. At about three o'clock a double line of rebel skirmishers was seen to emerge from the woods in a southeasterly direction, advancing down the fields, and were soon followed by heavy columns of infantry, battalion front, with three batteries of artillery. The only battery on that side of the river was speedily placed in position, and at once opened upon the enemy. Their line, however, advanced steadily to within one hundred yards of Van Cleve's front, and began a furious attack. Their assault had all the vigor and rapidity that characterized the grand operation of Wednesday upon McCook. Van Cleve's division was driven from its position by overwhelming numbers, its fire scarcely lessening the speed of the advance, and retired in considerable confusion across the river, closely followed by the enemy. On came the entire right wing of the rebel army, in three heavy lines of battle, sweeping down the slope of a wide cotton-field, and to the very edge of the river.

Meanwhile, General Crittenden's chief of artillery had massed his batteries along the rising ground on the west side of the river, so as to sweep and enfilade the enemy, while our own left wing was well posted for their reception, and reserves were on their way. Fifty-eight cannon were soon pointing across the water and pouring forth their fiery streams of death. General Rosecrans had his army well in hand for a movement in any direction, and to quickly reinforce. A rapid counter-movement was made against the flank of the advancing enemy. The firing from both artillery and musketry was incessant, and the slaughter terrible. On came the rebel masses; and, as our artillery ploughed furrows through their columns, they were seen to close up, men rushing forward from the rear ranks to fill the gaps. So near was their approach that here, there, all along their front, their troops were seen to drop, incessantly, and occasionally by twos and threes, from the showering bullets of our musketry. Their front ranks were seen to waver,—the fire had become so murderous. Pushed and cheered on by their rear lines, they again advanced. A few yards farther down the glade, and again they wavered, and again they staggered on. A third time, and when almost at the river's brink, they stopped, some of them even stepping into the water. It was too much for human endurance: they gave way. As our troops now sprung upon them with the bayonet, fording the river, they began to fall back,—their retreat soon becoming a rout. They fled back over the ground upon which they had advanced, helter-skelter, throwing down their guns and all that would impede their flight. Our troops pushed after them upwards of half a mile, with cheers upon cheers, which were soon taken up and repeated along our entire line. The lost ground from which Van Cleve's forces had been driven was left far in the rear, and the rebels retreated beyond their original lines, having lost in forty minutes two thousand men. General Davis took one of his brigades and crossed at a ford below to attack the enemy on his left flank, and, by General McCook's order, the rest of his division followed; but when he arrived, two brigades of Negley's division, led by the glorious 19th Illinois, and Hazen's brigade of Palmer's division, had pursued the flying enemy across the field, capturing four pieces of artillery and a stand of colors. Darkness was now upon us, and put an end to the pursuit, or the enemy would have been followed into Murfreesborough. Crittenden's entire corps, however, passed over, and with Davis occupied the ground of our advance, which was formidably intrenched during the night.

This defeat of Breckinridge, so terrible in its mortality, imparted a new aspect to the situation. The Union army was exultant, and the more so because of its misfortunes on the 31st. The enemy had repeated his grand, sudden, and dashing attack upon the other wing of our army, and had been defeated. Long after dark, volleys of musketry were fired from the advance-pickets of the two armies,—so near were they stationed,—when rounds of cheers would go up from our lines, extending from one extremity to the other. What was the rebel plan of attack upon this occasion it is difficult to surmise. We have Bragg's version of it in his official report, in which he disingenuously attempts to lessen it in importance. His troops apparently aimed to cross the river with a rush and a storm, seize our batteries amid the confusion, as they did on our right, two days before, and drive back our left upon its centre, thus gaining the high ground we occupied on both sides of the river; from which position we constantly threatened their right, with nothing to prevent our swinging around and flanking or driving it, gaining their rear, and, over open and unobstructed fields, pushing in to Murfreesborough. The rebels were as greatly depressed by this result as the Federals were encouraged. Their first onset we had repelled after eight hours of unparalleled fighting, and had inflicted upon them even the greater loss; and their second had been nipped almost in the bud. The two armies had measured strength, and they were vanquished. The next day Bragg and his generals took council, and resolved to retreat,—and at night,—to avoid another battle. This decision was made in the forenoon. At three o'clock P.M. of that day, the rear rebel columns began their march from the battle-field, and through Murfreesborough towards the Tennessee River, leaving their front ranks in battle-line and keeping up brisk picket-firing at times, to cloak their retreat. Soon after dusk, their rear columns of exhausted and dispirited troops moved out from their intrenchments, and ere midnight of Saturday, January 3, 1863, amidst a wintry and tempestuous rain-storm, the grand army of Bragg, which had gone out to speedily annihilate Rosecrans or drive him back to Nashville and there besiege and capture him, had passed through Murfreesborough,—their rear columns a mob,—moving through mud and slush and darkness,—the confusion being worse confounded by the pelting storm and the bustle of hundreds of rebel townsmen and farmers, with vehicles of all descriptions, hastily laden with household stuff, who until a few hours before had been assured that all was going well,—that Bragg's army was victorious, and that Rosecrans was in full preparation for, if not in full tide of, retreat. The history of the retreat of Bragg's army, and the attendant fright and flight of the people of Murfreesborough and vicinity, afford a rare theme for pen and pencil. But to resume our narrative.

Soon after the battle just described, rain set in, and at daybreak next morning it was pouring down in torrents. The roads, camps, and fields were a wide expanse of mud; and military operations on any considerable scale were impossible. The ploughed ground over which the left was to have advanced was impassable for artillery, and the ammunition-trains did not arrive until ten o'clock. It was, therefore, determined to make no advance; but batteries were placed in position on the left, by which the ground could be swept, and even Murfreesborough reached, by the Parrott guns. The enemy kept up a constant picket-firing along the front, which at last became so annoying that General Rosecrans, in the afternoon, ordered the corps commanders " to clear their fronts,"—which was speedily effected. General Rousseau's front, however, was still harassed by the sharpshooters occupying the woods to the left of the Murfreesborough pike and " the Burnt House." A number of his men having been killed and wounded, General Thomas and himself obtained permission to dislodge them and their supports, they covering a ford. A sharp fire from four batteries was opened for ten or fifteen minutes, when Rousseau at dark sent two of his regiments, which, with Spear's Tennesseeans and the 85th Illinois Volunteers, who had come out with the wagon-train, charged upon the enemy, and, after a sharp contest, cleared the woods and drove him from his trenches, capturing from seventy to eighty prisoners.

The following diagram illustrates this advance of Breckinridge upon our left, his retreat, and the advance of our troops to a new position. The positions on our right were not changed by this battle; and thus both armies rested when the rebels evacuated Murfreesborough.

DIAGRAM III.

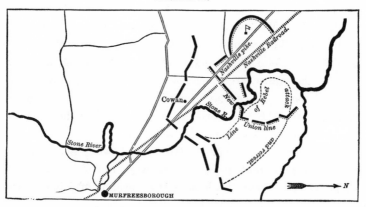

Lines of Contending Forces on January 2, 1863.

The next day being Sunday, it was probable that no offensive movements would take place on General Rosecrans's part. The night was no improvement on the previous one. It still rained incessantly. Every thing possible was done for the wounded, who had suffered greatly from the inclemency of the weather. About midnight, signs of a freshet appearing in Stone River, the left wing was withdrawn to the east side before daylight. Sunday dawned fair. Ere long news was brought that the enemy had fled; and the army rested, with the exception of the burial-parties and the cavalry, the latter following the enemy to reconnoitre.

Early Monday morning, General Thomas advanced into

Murfreesborough, driving the rear-guard of the rebel cavalry before him six or seven miles towards Manchester. McCook's and Crittenden's corps, following, took position in front of the town, occupying Murfreesborough. It was now ascertained that the enemy's infantry had reached Shelbyville by twelve M. on Sunday; but, owing to the impracticability of bringing up supplies, and the loss of five hundred and fifty-seven artillery horses, further pursuit was deemed inadvisable.

Of the results of the battle of Stone River we give the following general summary. We moved on the enemy with 41,421 infantry; 2223 artillery; 3296 cavalry: total, 46,940. We fought the battle with 37,977 infantry; 2223 artillery; 3200 cavalry: total, 43,400. We lost in killed, 92 officers; 1441 enlisted men: total, 1533. We lost in wounded, 384 officers; 6861 enlisted men: total, 7245. Total killed and wounded, 8778,—being 20.03 per cent. of the entire force in action. Our loss in prisoners was less than 3000. The enemy's force is estimated by General Rosecrans at over 62,000; and the reasoning by which he supports the estimate would seem to be conclusive.*

Thus ended the series of skirmishes and two grand battles at Stone River in front of Murfreesborough. The result of the enemy's retreat was the loss to the rebellion of Middle Tennessee and all hopes of an immediate lodgment upon the navigable waters of the Cumberland and Tennessee Rivers. Also it secured Kentucky from rebel advance in force, save by circuitous and hazardous marches through East Tennessee and the gaps of the Cumberland Mountains. Their retreat was truly a death-blow to the hopes of the rebel citizens of Nashville and throughout Tennessee and Kentucky. Up to that period the secessionists were confident that Bragg's great army would vanquish Rosecrans and drive him from their soil. Their surprise and bitter sorrow over his defeat were depicted on many a clouded brow, and were described by themselves in hundreds

---

* In the Appendix to this work we publish the official reports of Generals Rosecrans and Bragg, for future reference and candid criticism.

of intercepted letters. Above all, the result at Stone River destroyed the self-confidence of Bragg and his army. His troops were mainly from Tennessee, Kentucky, Alabama, and Mississippi,—confessedly the best fighting-men of the so-called Confederacy. And these men were here upon their own threshold, —battling, as their leaders would fain make them believe, for their homes, their altars, ana their firesides. The rebels had not yet fathomed the hollowness of their belief that each one of them was equal to three or even five of Rosecrans's men. How soon and how effectually this error was cut up by the roots, is attested by those awful battle-scenes and their clearly defined result. This point is thoroughly elaborated by Captain W. D. Bickham in his thrilling little volume entitled "Rosecrans's Campaign with the 14th Army Corps," from which work we copy as follows:—

"Bragg, confident in the superb discipline of his army, had misconceived the fighting qualities of our men. He assumed that at least half of Rosecrans's forces were raw, and therefore unreliable. He, therefore, not only concluded to give battle at Stone River, but it is asserted that he was preparing to fall suddenly upon the divisions at Gallatin, menacing Nashville with a sufficient force to prevent Rosecrans from sending succor to the forces at the former points.

"It is certain that he was sanguine of success, and his defeat, although compensated in some degree by his success of Wednesday, was a sore disappointment. Had he been satisfied to withdraw from Murfreesborough Wednesday night, the prestige of victory would have remained with him for a little while, though he would have been bitterly pursued and at all hazards. Bragg's mode of fighting was characteristic of the Southern people. It was all dash, and the admirable discipline of his troops told fearfully at every onset. They charged with splendid daring. But it was evident that they were best in onset. They did not at any time display the staunch stand-up fighting pluckiness which distinguished our troops. Where two lines were confronted in the field, man for man, the superiority of our troops was at once made manifest. Northern phlegm was too much for Southern fire. Their troops fought ferociously, ours with bitter determination. Now and then some of our regiments, galled to death by their marksmen, would rush infuriately forward and drive every thing before them. The rebels never attempted to resist a charge, though our troops resisted mad charges by them repeatedly. They overwhelmed the right wing and the 3d division of the left by avoirdupois,—not by fighting. Their grand tactics were conspicuous in this battle as they were at Gaines's Mills, where they defeated Fitz-John Porter, who, if he had possessed the skill of Rosecrans, would have utterly defeated the enemy, though vastly outnumbered by them. The rebel artillery practice was very fine. They had exact range all over our position. It was often remarked in the midst of battle that their gunners were very skilful. Nevertheless, the superiority of our artillery was established. Their sharpshooters were their most formidable arm. They swarmed in the forests, and during Wednesday there was not a point on the battle-field that was not within their range. Half of our officers who were wounded were struck by them. In McCook's front they had constructed platforms among the branches of the trees, from which to practise their devilish arts. Their mounted infantry were also signally serviceable to them. Without them their cavalry would not have been able to cut our communications so successfully. In fine, the rebels again illustrated in this battle the fact that they had thoroughly devoted themselves to war, —that they had rejected all theories; that they had adopted the wisest maxims of warfare, and had accepted the admonitions of experience. It was curious, however, that Bragg, whose reputation as an artillery officer stood highest in that branch of the service, should have been so thoroughly beaten with his favorite arm."

The contest at Stone River was one of the most memorable of the war up to that period. Nor has a battle since been fought attended with such mortality, such heroism, and such directly important results. As more recent events have shown, it destroyed the rebellion in Tennessee and struck a death-blow at the heart of the pretentious Southern Government. The loyal people of our country were paralyzed while the battles raged, and were correspondingly electrified at the result. The following telegraphic despatches transmitted to General Rosecrans breathed the heartfelt thanks of a grateful people to the heroes, dead and living, of Stone River :—

"WASHINGTON, January 5.

"To MAJOR-GENERAL ROSECRANS:—

"Your despatch, announcing the retreat of the enemy, has just reached here. God bless you and all with you! Please tender to all, and accept for yourself, the nation's gratitude for your and their skill, endurance, and dauntless courage.   A. LINCOLN."

"WASHINGTON, January 9, 1863.

"MAJOR-GENERAL ROSECRANS, *Commanding Army of the Cumberland :—*

"GENERAL :—Rebel telegrams fully confirm your telegrams from the battle-field. The victory was well earned, and one of the most brilliant of the war. You and your brave army have won the gratitude of your country and the admiration of the world. The field of Murfreesborough is made historical, and future generations will point out the place where so many heroes fell gloriously in defence of the Constitution and the Union. All honor to the Army of the Cumberland! Thanks to the living, and tears for the lamented dead.   H. W. HALLECK."

WHEELER'S REPULSE AT LAVERGNE.

WHILE the battle was raging before Murfreesborough, a most brilliant and decisive affair occurred at Lavergne,—which, the reader will remember, is a small village lying midway between Murfreesborough and Nashville, on the direct pike.

The 1st Michigan Engineers and Mechanics had been left at that place to protect communication, and had taken position on an elevated piece of ground in the rear of the village, surrounding themselves with a barricade of cedar brush, much in the nature of a common brush fence. The command numbered three hundred and ninety-one, officers and men. About two o'clock in the afternoon, the rebel General Wheeler, who had been busying himself in destroying trains upon the road, suddenly appeared before Colonel Innes's improvised fort with a force of about three thousand men and two pieces of artillery, demanding an immediate surrender. This was refused, and a charge made upon the garrison; but the rebels were spiritedly repulsed and driven into the neighboring thickets. Seven times the enemy attempted to carry the flimsy work, and seven times they were driven back with heavy loss. The scene was at times thrilling beyond description. The rebel horde, exasperated at the successful resistance of the little force, dashed their horses against the circular brush fence, which was only breast-high, with infuriate shouts and curses. But the Michigan troops were cool and determined: they loaded fast and aimed well, and, as the troopers rushed on upon all sides, they were met with staggering volleys almost at the muzzles of the muskets. Horses and riders recoiled again and again, until they despaired, and soon swept away through the dense forests, leaving over fifty of their dead upon the field, which were buried by our forces. The ground all around that small circle of cedar brush was strewn with dead horses of the rebel troopers, and with their clothing, guns, &c. Truly, this was one of the most gallant affairs of the campaign.

Meanwhile Colonel Innes had sent a messenger to Colonel Burke, at Stewart's Creek, five miles to the south, for assistance. The latter, with a portion of his regiment (the 10th Ohio), hastened rapidly to the scene of the conflict; but before he reached it the enemy had fled. For the gallantry displayed in this engagement, the Michigan Engineers Regiment was subsequently highly complimented by the commanding general.

OUR ARMY AT MURFREESBOROUGH.

HEAD-QUARTERS were established in Murfreesborough on Monday, the 5th of January, 1863. Taking up a position in front of the town, our exhausted army calmly settled down into the quiet of camp-life. The Pioneer Brigade and Michigan Engineers immediately began to rebuild the railroad and pike bridges across Stone River, and to repair the road beyond. The construction of a series of extensive earthworks, completely encircling the town, was entered upon, with a view of making it a base of future operations and an intermediate depot of supplies. Foraging-trains scoured the country in every direction, and collected grain and stock. A deserted mill was put into operation, and the troops supplied with meal. Preparations for advance movements were being made extensively; but the rainy season, now setting in, effectually put an end to present offensive operations. The constant and extraordinarily heavy rains, however, were not without beneficial results. The Cumberland River rose rapidly, and for months was navigable. Supplies were hurried forward and began to accumulate in large quantities at both Nashville and Murfreesborough. So passed the months of winter and spring, but not in idleness nor unmarked by important events.

On the 9th of January the army was divided into three *corps d'armée*,—the 14th, 20th, and 21st,—commanded by Major-Generals Thomas, McCook, and Crittenden, respectively.

The limits of a single chapter will not allow a detailed account of the most important expeditions and engagements which have occurred within the lines of the department; while many interesting minor events must be entirely ignored. All that can be attempted is an intelligible account of the considerable battles that have been fought, with allusions to some of the many expeditions which have been sent into the surrounding country in every direction.

FORAGING AND SCOUTING.

THE general and his officers were now occupied with the usual routine of business. The quiet of camp-life was enlivened, however, by the almost daily outgoing and incoming of foraging-trains, and occasionally the departure or return of a more formidable expedition,—usually cavalry, sometimes infantry, not unfrequently both. Of the former the experiences were as varied as their number. On other pages some of the incidents which befell those participating in them are related; and it is only necessary to say here that they were almost invariably attended with success, bringing in large amounts of wheat, corn, bacon, and stock. Of the larger expeditions a few of the more noted, with their results, are briefly narrated in the course of this chapter, and from them the character of the whole must be determined. The enemy was not idle. His cavalry, too, were out scouring the country, and occasionally our men and wagons were picked up by him. The grand object of his efforts was to cut off our communications and interrupt our supplies. To this end, the steamers upon the Cumberland were sharply watched, and more than one, in an unwary moment, was captured, robbed, and burned.

On the 31st of January, Brigadier-General Jefferson C. Davis with his division of infantry, and two brigades of cavalry, thirteen hundred and twenty-eight men, under command of Colonel Minty, left camp at Murfreesborough for an extended scout in the direction of Rover, Eagleville, and Franklin. Colonel Minty was ordered to proced to Versailles, where General Davis would form a junction with him. Sending two regiments, under Colonel Cook, to Middleton and Unionville, Colonel Minty proceeded to Versailles, and there learned that a body of four hundred rebel cavalry were at Rover. Proceeding to the latter place, he drove in the pickets, charged upon the main body, and routed them, driving them at a sharp gallop through the town, killing one, wounding forty-nine, and capturing forty-nine,—six of whom were officers. Among the prisoners were thirteen wounded, and all but one with the sabre. Not having heard from Colonel Cook, Colonel Minty proceeeded to Unionville, driving the enemy before him into and out of that town, and remained there about an hour. At this time a messenger arrived from Colonel Cook, stating that he had surprised a rebel force at Middleton and captured Colonel Douglas, a captain, a lieutenant, and forty-one men. The enemy had been reinforced and attacked him in turn, and he was in need of reinforcements. Ordering him to fall back to Eagleville, Colonel Minty joined him at that place, finding there also General Davis and division, who had met no enemy.

The next day Colonel Minty proceeded to Peytonville, intending to cross the Harpeth near that place and form a junction with General Davis near Boyce's Creek. Finding the bridges burned and no ford near by, he took the road to Poplar Grove, crossed at the ford west of the pike, and camped for the night beyond the junction with the Eagleville pike. The next day (February 2) he marched rapidly on Franklin, and found General Davis in possession of the place. Moving out on the Carter's Creek pike, he camped five and a half miles from Franklin, on the road leading to Hillsborough. On the 5th he passed through Hillsborough, on the 6th moved forward to Kinderhook, and, taking the road to Charlotte, camped after dark one mile south of the road leading from Nashville to Centreville. During the day Colonel Minty captured a colonel and major upon Forrest's staff, and two lieutenants and twenty-three men of Forrest's and Wharton's escort, one of them a courier with despatches for the latter. On the 7th the force returned to Franklin. On the 10th Colonel Minty camped on the north side of the Harpeth, and on the 12th marched through Triune to Eagleville. On the 13th General Davis returned to Murfreesborough; and Colonel Minty, with five hundred men, moved on Rover, drove the enemy out of that town, and arrived at Murfreesborough after dark. During the scout the cavalry captured one hundred and forty-one prisoners, including two colonels, one major, four captains, seven lieutenants, and one hundred and twenty-seven enlisted men. The only casualties upon our side were, one man severely and one dangerously wounded.

While this expedition was absent, events of greater magnitude were transpiring in another portion of the department. On Wednesday, the 3d of February; the rebel Generals Wheeler, Forrest, and Wharton, with a force of eleven regiments of cavalry and nine pieces of artillery, suffered a

REPULSE AT FORT DONELSON.

ON the 2d it was known that Forrest, with a command nine hundred strong, had taken position at Palmyra, for the purpose of interrupting the navigation of the Cumberland. Scouting-parties were sent out to watch his movements, and early on the morning of the 3d it was announced that the enemy was advancing upon the fort in force, both from above and below. The garrison of that fort consisted of nine companies of the 83d Illinois, a battalion of the 5th Iowa Cavalry, Flood's battery, and some wounded men,—in all less than eight hundred,—under the command of Colonel A. C. Harding, of the 83d Illinois. In addition to the battery, consisting of four rifled pieces, a single thirty-two-pounder siege-gun was mounted upon the northwest corner of the fort, near the old court-house. The cavalry was at once sent out on the different roads; one company of the 83d were deployed as skirmishers to the southward, near the outposts, and another on the ridge to the east, thus guarding the main approaches to the position. At about half-past one, the rebel commander sent in a flag of truce, demanding the surrender of the post and garrison, which was promptly refused; and Colonel Harding began vigorous preparations for defence.

One gun of the battery was placed upon a hill on the Fort Henry road, near the southwest corner of the fort, overlooking Colonel Harding's encampment and the surrounding country. Believing that the enemy would attempt to cut off communication with Fort Henry and thus make this the key to his position, Colonel Harding sent three companies of his regiment to support this gun. Another gun, supported by two companies, was ordered into position to the east of the rifle-pits, and a third was stationed behind the redoubts, at the southwest corner of the base. The siege-gun before mentioned as in position was a pivot-gun, and commanded every approach. The enemy now placed in position four guns, and opened a heavy fire upon the gun at the east end of the rifle-pits and the force upon the hill near the Fort Henry road. The companies of the 83d, not acting as supports to the guns in position, were deployed in a deep ravine on the west, where they were completely sheltered from the enemy's artillery. The latter now had nine guns in position, and were raining a constant stream of shot and shell upon Colonel Harding's small forces, occasionally changing their situation, in order to make their fire more effective. A heavy force was now menacing the position commanding the Fort Henry road, and the gun at the rifle-pits was sent to its defence. The enemy next attempted a charge from the low ground towards the river, but were driven back by the fire of the last gun of Flood's battery, placed in position for that purpose. All the guns were eventually concentrated on the hill, under the direction of Lieutenant-Colonel Smith, where they did good execution until their ammunition was exhausted, when they were retired with difficulty, as they had suffered severely in both men and horses. In the end one was lost, but the remaining three were brought safely off.

Forrest now led his large command of mounted men down the river to a point near the jail, and then by the flank up the street to the southward, forming them into successive lines of battle, which filled the whole open space in front of the fort. Rending the air with horrid yells, they advanced to the charge. In an instant the siege-gun was double-shotted with canister, turned upon them, and discharged into their ranks, blowing to atoms one of their number who was within ten feet of its muzzle, and making terrible havoc in the main body beyond. The infantry from the ravine now poured a galling musketry-fire upon the rebels at the crest of the ridge, and, with the aid

27

of the siege-gun, still belching forth its double charges of canister, checked their advance. While the column yet wavered, a bayonet-charge was ordered and the ground soon cleared, the enemy leaving forty prisoners in our hands. Again and again the charge was essayed, but each time was gallantly repulsed. In the last attempt, Colonel McNairy, of Nashville, was shot down while vainly endeavoring to rally his men, recoiling before the deadly fire from the fort.

Our artillery had now been withdrawn to the rear, and the force lying in the ravine near the siege-gun were ordered to the support of the right, where the rebels were advancing in large numbers. Advancing in line of battle, our forces drove the enemy before them until they came within range, when the line was halted and volley after volley delivered, till our ammunition was exhausted. The line moved towards a point known as "Mrs. Coble's House," where they were to some extent sheltered by the crest of the bluff. The enemy's firing had now ceased, and he was evidently preparing for another and final charge. Destitute of ammunition and far inferior in numbers, the situation of Colonel Harding's force was critical; but he was prepared for the emergency. A charge was ordered towards the rifle-pits and the ammunition. Advancing with wild shouts, the gallant Illinoisians drove the rebels before them in every direction and reached the position in safety. It was now too late for their artillery to inflict serious injury, and our men were disposed among the rifle-pits, where ammunition was distributed to them. The siege-gun, short of friction-primers, was imperfectly spiked and abandoned. Colonel Harding, placing his men to the best advantage, kept up a constant fire upon the enemy until about eight o'clock in the evening, when another flag of truce was sent in, Forrest again demanding a surrender, and saying that they had not yet brought into action half their number. The surrender was refused, as before, and the rebels, deeming further contest useless, retired in confusion.

In this gallant defence against immensely superior numbers, our loss was thirteen killed, fifty-one wounded, and twenty taken prisoners, not including a captain and twenty-six men of the command who were captured the same day while out on a scout. We also lost one gun without the caisson, and twenty-five mules and forty-two horses, killed, wounded, and captured. The enemy's loss, as far as could be ascertained, was two hundred and fifty killed, one hundred and fifty-five of whom were buried by our forces, six hundred wounded, and one hundred and five prisoners.

Thus far every thing had gone prosperously in the department. Constant success had attended our arms in the numerous skirmishes and scouts, and a large rebel force had been ignominiously defeated by a mere handful at Fort Donelson. The same success might reasonably be expected to crown our efforts in the future, and the army was hopeful and enthusiastic, confident in themselves and in their leaders. Foraging-trains still went out, expeditions of cavalry still roamed at will through the country, and all returned without disaster. The enemy was heard of and seen occasionally, but seldom made a stand; and in time it began to be questioned whether he would fight at all, after his experience at Stone River and since. So it continued for days and weeks, until suddenly the camps were startled by the news of the defeat and capture of a brigade at the

BATTLE OF SPRING HILL.

On the 4th of March, an expedition under the command of Colonel John Coburn, of the 33d Indiana, and consisting of parts of the 33d and 85th Indiana, 22d Wisconsin, and 19th Michigan, numbering in all fifteen hundred and eighty-nine, together with the 124th Ohio, and six hundred cavalry (detachments from the 2d Michigan, 9th Pennsylvania, and 4th Kentucky, under the command of Colonel Jordan, of the 9th Pennsylvania), and one battery of six small guns, was ordered to proceed from Franklin to Spring Hill, ten miles south on the Columbia pike and thirty miles from Nashville. About four miles out it met the enemy, and after a sharp skirmish drove them back, without loss on our side. Their loss was fifteen killed and wounded. Moving forward about two miles, the enemy were again encountered, but, owing to the lateness of the hour, the command went into camp.

On the morning of the 5th the force started early, the 124th Ohio being left in the rear of the wagon-train, which was large. After marching about two miles our cavalry met the enemy's pickets and outposts, and severe skirmishing was kept up until the expedition came in sight of Thompson's Station, the enemy falling back. About half a mile from the station the railroad approaches the pike on the west side and runs parallel with the pike, between two high hills, for six hundred yards, when it bears off to the west on a plain about half a mile wide,—hills rising again on the south side of the plain, the station being about half-way between the two ridges. When the point where the railroad joins the pike was reached, the enemy opened fire with a heavy battery.

Colonel Coburn at once formed his forces in line, ordered one section of the battery to take position on the hill on the left of the pike, and deployed the 19th Michigan and 22d Wisconsin to support it. The other three guns took position on the hill on the right, supported by the 33d and 85th Indiana. The enemy had two batteries on the range of hills three-quarters of a mile to the southward. The plain in front of our position was cultivated, and there were some six lines of rail-fence and one or two stone walls between us and the enemy, who showed no front. Colonel Coburn ordered the 33d and 85th Indiana to make a demonstration on the left of the enemy, to draw him out if in force, and if not to charge his battery. These two regiments marched out from the cover of the hills in columns of companies across the fields about six hundred yards, under a galling fire from the enemy's batteries, being all the while in plain view, having fences to tear down as they went, and wholly unable to return the fire by a single shot.

Upon reaching the station our skirmishers soon unmasked the enemy, and found at the foot of the hill, posted behind stone walls, fences, and brush, two whole brigades of dismounted cavalry. Seeing that it was impossible to advance farther, the two regiments lay down and were covered by the buildings and fences. No disposition to advance or attack, however, was shown by the enemy. The incessant firing of their sharp-shooters, to pick off our officers, seemed to content them. In a few moments the regiments were ordered to retire to the hill from which they had started, and Colonel Jordan was directed to send two companies of cavalry to their support; but the latter order, for some reason, was not obeyed. No sooner had they left their shelter than two regiments from Arkansas and Texas started in fierce pursuit, firing rapid volleys of musketry into the retiring ranks. The rebel batteries, meanwhile, were play-ing upon them, and both regiments lost several in killed and wounded. All this time they had been unable to fire a shot; but as soon as they reached the hill they turned and drove back the enemy faster than they had come, killing Colonel Earle, of Arkansas. The rebels again rallied and charged, but were again driven back. It soon became evident that Colonel Coburn had encountered the whole of Van Dorn's and Forrest's forces.

An advance was now made upon our left, where were sta-tioned the 19th Michigan and 22d Wisconsin. The latter at once opened fire upon the advancing enemy, and, the former coming to its support, the enemy was repulsed, and held in check for some twenty minutes. When the 22d Wisconsin was first attacked, that portion of the battery stationed on the left of the pike started rapidly up the road, and, notwithstanding the efforts of a staff-officer to induce it to stop and assist in checking the enemy, then charging upon the 22d, continued its retreat. Foiled in his advance here, Forrest at once made a circuit with his whole force, beyond the ground occupied by our force to the east, with the intention to turn our left flank.

Colonel Coburn now brought the 19th and 22d on the west side of the pike, and, leaving the 33d to protect the hill on its south face, the 10th and 85th were formed, facing the enemy, east, at right angles, with the 22d in the rear of the 85th, except three companies, which, with Lieutenant-Colonel Bloodgood, had without orders retired from the field when the 22d received the first charge, moving off by the left flank and joining the retreating cavalry and artillery.

The four regiments had hardly formed in line, lying down behind the crest of the hill, when Armstrong's brigade charged from the east and the Texans from the south. The fighting was now terrific. Our fire was reserved until the enemy were within thirty paces. Three times they gallantly charged up the hill from the east, and thrice were they forced back. In one of their charges the 19th Michigan captured the colors of the 4th Mississippi and four prisoners, and the contending parties were so near each other that one man was shot by the soldiers of the 85th from the window of a schoolhouse as he was trying to get in at the door. During this time one battery was throwing shells into our lines, and, having got possession of the hill on the east of the road, the enemy hurled grape and canister like hail. The battle raged furiously. Still, it was a hopeless struggle. Defeat was only a question of time. The ammunition was fast giving out, and Forrest, having got between them and Franklin, was closing in from the north. But officers and soldiers did their duty. A new line was formed with all four of the regiments, facing north, to meet the new foe, about three hundred yards farther to the west and about the same distance to the north.

Here Forrest was met and held in check until the last round of ammunition was fired. The brave little force then fixed bayonets, to charge and break the enemy's lines and try to escape. But, just as they were about to charge, it was discovered that Forrest had still *another line in reserve, and a battery* began to open and form a new position. Escape was hopeless; and, to avoid useless sacrifice of life, the command surrendered. Colonel Coburn, during the trying engagement, was calm and collected, displaying great energy and bravery. He made the best fight he could, and only yielded when further strife would have been madness.

Of officers and men thirteen hundred and six were made prisoners, and were sent south. The 85th Indiana had three hundred men in the fight, and two hundred and twenty-nine were taken. The cavalry were not engaged, and, with the artillery, escaped with little, if any, loss. The enemy were all cavalry and mounted infantry, but all fought on foot, every fourth man holding four horses; and the force consisted of six brigades, under Major-General Van Dorn, Brigadier-Generals French, Armstrong, Cosby, Martin, and Jackson. Infantry had no chance of escape after the fight once began. Somebody evidently blundered in the planning of the expedition, as Van Dorn's whole force had been at Spring Hill for three days before Colonel Coburn left Franklin, and, not knowing that the brigade had left Brentwood, were preparing to attack Franklin, and had started the day before for that purpose.

SUCCESSFUL EXPEDITION OF A DIVISION.

WHILE this battle was being fought, General Sheridan with his division, and Colonel Minty, with a force of eight hundred and sixty-three cavalry, were out on a ten-days scout. Colonel Minty drove the enemy out of Rover and Unionville, pursuing them to within five miles of Shelbyville, where the rebel infantry pickets were encountered. During this chase fifty-one prisoners, seventeen wagons, forty-two mules, thirty-one tents, and two wagonloads of bacon and meal were captured. Our only casualty was one man wounded. The colonel then fell back to Eagleville, taking the captured property with him, and was there joined by General Sheridan on the morning of the 5th. On the 6th he moved towards Triune, and on the 7th towards Unionville. Four miles beyond Eagleville he was ordered to return to Triune and proceed to Franklin. On the 8th he arrived at Franklin, and on the 9th marched out on the Carter's Creek pike to form a junction with General G. C. Smith near Thompson's Station. Six miles out, the enemy were met and driven to within a mile and a half of Thompson's Station, where a force of seven hundred cavalry were found drawn up in line. Declining fight, however, they fled, closely pressed by the 4th United States Cavalry and a portion of the 7th Pennsylvania. At Thompson's Station the rebels were reinforced by Starns's regiment (the 3d Tennessee); but, after a short and sharp skirmish, the whole brigade was driven from the field by two companies of the 4th Cavalry and about fifty men of the 7th Pennsylvania, with a loss of five killed and thirteen prisoners. Our loss was three killed and one wounded. Camping that night at Springfield, we advanced the next day, and found General Smith at Rutherford's Creek, the bridges over which had been burned. The next day the creek was forded higher up, Forrest and five hundred men disputing the passage but being driven to the woods with loss. The enemy had now dismounted, and advanced in line with their battle-flag flying; but, perceiving that they were likely to be surrounded, they rapidly remounted and fell back. Pursuing them five miles towards the Lewisburg pike, Colonel Minty then marched towards the Columbia pike. Upon reaching Duck River, it was found that Van Dorn's whole force had crossed during the day on a pontoon bridge and by the ferry-boat. Accordingly, on the next day, the 12th, the expedition began its return by way of Franklin and Triune, reaching Murfreesborough on the afternoon of the 14th, the whole loss during the ten days having been five killed and five wounded.

THE BATTLE OF MILTON.

ON the 18th of March an expedition, consisting of the 105th Ohio, 80th and 123d Illinois, and 101st Indiana, a section of the 19th Indiana Battery, and Company A of the 1st Middle Tennessee Cavalry,—the whole amounting to a little over fourteen hundred men,—under the command of Colonel A. S. Hall, of the 105th Ohio, left Murfreesborough in the direction of Liberty. The same night the command occupied Gainesville, capturing two prisoners. The next morning an advance was made towards Statesville, at which place a slight skirmish ensued. The enemy retired slowly down Smith's Fork on the pike, cautiously followed by Colonel Hall, until a regiment of cavalry, with those driven from Statesville, was found drawn up in line across the pike. Colonel Hall thereupon rested his forces for a couple of hours, which were occupied in reconnoissances. Becoming satisfied that the enemy greatly outnumbered him, he determined to draw them as near Murfreesborough as possible, and, accordingly, camping that night at Auburn, seven miles from Liberty, the next morning took up a position near Milton, which place is twelve miles northeast of Murfreesborough. Here he made a stand, fought the enemy, commanded by General John H. Morgan, and completely routed them, entailing upon that rebel general the first thorough defeat he had met with. This engagement was fought on the 20th of March, and has since become famous as the battle of Milton.

Colonel Hall had scarcely taken position when the enemy's advance made its appearance about fifteen hundred yards away. Flankers were at once thrown out, and the section of Harris's battery was ordered to open fire upon the rebels, who were approaching at a gallop. A few shells checked them; but the main body now came in sight, and, having dismounted, advanced on foot to the attack. Perceiving that the enemy outnumbered him almost two to one, Colonel Hall slowly fell back to the crest of the hill, where his men would have the advantage of an admirable position, and could avoid at the same time the possibility of being surrounded and compelled to surrender, he, meanwhile, sending a messenger to Murfreesborough for cavalry reinforcements.

The 80th Illinois was formed upon the right, the 123d Illinois in the centre, and the 101st Indiana on the left. The 105th Ohio was held in reserve as a support to the section of Harris's battery, which was ordered to fire upon each rebel line as it passed within range. The enemy now opened a fierce fire of shot and shell from their battery, and also advanced in strength on both our flanks. Morgan evidently hoped to be able to throw Colonel Harris's men into confusion while they were slowly retreating to the top of the hill, and made direct charges on his lines for that purpose. The nature of the ground over which he was compelled to pass was such, however, that he could not keep beyond the range of Harris's artillery; and his heavy columns passing to the left were two or three times cut in two by its terrible fire. The 80th Illinois also poured in a destructive volley, and so checked the enemy's ardor that all the regiments were enabled to reach the position on the crest of the hill without delay and in good order.

The enemy now advanced on the left in solid columns, making a vigorous onset upon the 101st Indiana and the left wing of the 123d Illinois, but were driven back in confusion. A second time they made a still more powerful attack. Some little confusion was at first manifested in the ranks of the 101st; but it was only for a moment, and the enemy were again driven back, with still heavier loss. Failing in his attempts on the left, he now moved in heavy force against the right, meanwhile opening a sharp fire upon the centre from four pieces of artillery. Here, too, he was driven back with terrible slaughter. The soldiers of the Illinois, Ohio, and Indiana regiments took deliberate aim, and at several places were forced to a hand-to-hand fight. They displayed the most invincible bravery. Our artillery was so handled as to do splendid execution. One of the enemy's field-pieces, a rifled six-pounder, was shivered to atoms while a shell killed the gunner belonging to another.

Failing to accomplish any thing on our flanks, the enemy next made an attack on the rear; but there also he was met and repulsed from the commanding position occupied by our forces, in such a tremendous storm of shot that the guerrilla gangs were literally mowed down. Again and again the rebels persevered, but each time without success, until at length (it being two o'clock, and the fight having lasted three and a half hours) Morgan withdrew his command.

He still continued his artillery-fire, however, and once, having received reinforcements, began a new and fierce attack, but ere long withdrew in confusion. At half-past four his artillery ceased firing, and the whole command left the field. He collected most of his wounded, except those within our rifle-range and those mortally injured, and carried them away with him. Four captains, two lieutenants, and fifty-seven men were, however, found upon the field, dead, or mortally wounded. Four surgeons were also left to care for the wounded, by whom Colonel Hall was informed that the wounded carried off the field amounted to about three hundred, including General Morgan, slightly wounded in the arm (his wound was afterwards found to be a more serious one), Colonel Grigsby, right arm broken, Lieutenant-Colonel Napier, thigh broken and amputated, Lieutenant-Colonel Martin, flesh-wound in the back, and many other officers of lower rank. Their total loss in killed and wounded could not have been less than four hundred. Ten prisoners, eight horses, and fifty-three stand of arms were captured and brought into camp. Colonel Hall's loss was six killed, forty-two wounded, and seven missing.

The courier whom Colonel Hall had sent for reinforcements magnified the danger, representing that he was surrounded and out of ammunition. Under these circumstances it was thought advisable to send Colonel Minty, with two brigades of cavalry, a brigade of infantry, and a battery, to the assistance of our beleaguered forces. Colonel Minty pushed on with all possible speed; but when he arrived at the scene of the fight, Morgan had left. It was already nearly dark; but Colonel Minty, thinking that perhaps the rebels had not gone far, advanced with his cavalry through the village and thoroughly reconnoitred the surrounding country. Not a rebel was in sight; and our cavalry returned to the hill and bivouacked for the night. The next morning Colonel Minty despatched reconnoitring parties to Gainesville, Statesville, and Liberty, all of whom returned without having seen the enemy.

The enemy's force was variously estimated at from three thousand five hundred to four thousand; but it was hardly so large. In his official report Colonel Minty estimates it at about two thousand two hundred and fifty, giving the number and names of the regiments composing it. There were four regiments of cavalry, averaging about three hundred each, and three of mounted infantry, averaging about three hundred and fifty each. The enemy also had one twelve-pounder rifled cannon, one howitzer (both brass pieces), and two small mountain-howitzers. Colonel Hall returned to Murfreesborough on the afternoon of the 21st, to receive the congratulations of the whole army for his gallant fight and his complete victory over the far-famed and not a little dreaded General Morgan.

EXPEDITION OF WILDER'S BRIGADE.

EXPEDITIONS were now more frequent, scarcely a day passing without the sending out or returning of one. The similarity of their movements and results renders separate mention useless. The most remarkable of them, however, have been made by Colonel John T. Wilder, of the 17th Indiana, commanding the 1st Brigade of Mounted Rifles. As a specimen of one out of many, the following account is subjoined.

On the evening of April 1, Colonel Wilder started with detachments of the following regiments, the 15th, 101st, and 123d

Illinois, on foot, commanded by Colonel Monroe, of the last-named regiment, and the 17th and 72d Indiana and the 98th Illinois, mounted, under Colonel Funkhouser. The brigade took with it four mountain-howitzers and four rifled Parrotts.

The entire force proceeded north to the east fork of Stone River, where it encamped for the night. The next day, after proceeding north for some distance in the direction of Lebanon, while the foot kept the direct road, the mounted regiments struck off to the right, scouring the country in all directions,— the whole force concentrating at Lebanon and spending the second night there. By different routes Colonel Wilder then marched his forces towards the northeast, sending scouts north to the Cumberland River on all the principal roads. While one part of the brigade marched on Rome, the other galloped into Carthage, taking possession of both these places at the same time.

After resting and scouting in this vicinity for some time, the command again turned towards the south, in the direction of Alexandria, up Caney Fork and Smith's Fork, marching over hills and mountains where the people had never before seen a Federal soldier. Even artillery went rattling over by-roads where scarcely ever a wagon had gone before. Hearing that a body of Wharton's cavalry had returned to Liberty and Snow Hill, whence General Stanley had driven a similar force but a few days before, Colonel Wilder laid his plans to capture them. His plan was perfect, and its execution would have succeeded even beyond his expectations, but for a mistake in a single road. Those ordered to take the rear wheeled to the right into the first cross-road, when they should have taken the second. This brought them into the main road of rebel retreat near the rear of their column, while the other would have placed them directly in Wharton's front. Still, several officers and a number of prisoners were captured. The position held by Wharton's battalion was well chosen, and so strong that a hundred resolute men ought to have held it against a thousand; but it was abandoned without any show of resistance.

Many Union families were found entirely destitute, and many rebels with abundance. The goods of the latter were distributed among the former, and many hearts made glad. To one a dollar's worth of captured cotton yarn would be thrown; to another a tired-out horse or mule would be given; and so the expedition marched through the country, stripping the rebels and supplying several families that had lost their all for the sake of the Union. Able-bodied negroes who chose to accompany the army were assured that they would find employment and protection in the Federal army, and large numbers accompanied it on its return.

The result of the expedition was as follows:—

Five hundred head of good horses and mules; eight thousand dollars' worth of tobacco and cigars, paid for by the Confederacy only two days before; four thousand dollars' worth of spun yarn; about eighty-six tons of hay and forage; four thousand bushels of corn; a large quantity of flour and meal; one hundred and four prisoners, including eight officers who were enforcing the rebel conscription; a rebel mail and mail-carrier, and one hundred and ninety-four able-bodied negroes. The expedition is recognized by all as one of the most brilliant and successful of the campaign, reflecting great credit upon the gallant officer in command.

An expedition, under command of General Palmer, to Woodbury, also proved very successful, resulting in the capture of sixty prisoners, one hundred horses and mules, a large quantity of hay and corn, and a considerable amount of cigars and tobacco.

VAN DORN'S ATTACK ON FRANKLIN.

EARLY in April, Major-General Gordon Granger, commanding a portion of our army at Franklin, learned that an attack would be made upon that place about the 9th or 10th of the month, by a rebel force estimated at from fifteen thousand to eighteen

thousand, and commanded by Major-General Van Dorn. General Granger's force consisted of Brigadier-Generals Baird's and
Gilbert's divisions of infantry, fifteen hundred and ninety-four
men and sixteen guns, and Brigadier-General Smith's Cavalry
Brigade, eleven hundred and twenty-eight men. To these were
added a cavalry force of sixteen hundred men and two guns,
under the command of Major-General Stanley.

The only artificial defence was the fort, not yet completed,
but which mounted two siege-guns and two three-inch rifled
guns from the 18th Ohio Battery. Rising about forty feet
above the general surface of the country around Franklin, it
commands most of the approaches to the place north of the
Harpeth, and all from the south save that part of the plateau
covered by a few blocks of houses in the southeast part of
the town.

General Granger's camps were on the north side of the river,
about two-thirds of a mile distant. The river is between thirty
and forty feet wide, and about three feet deep, with bluff banks
from six to ten feet high, and can easily be crossed at several
fords either above or below Franklin. Thus the town is easy
of approach from every direction.

As the enemy was mounted and in large force, it was anticipated that he would not attack directly in front, but would
seek to turn the flanks or gain the rear of General Granger's
forces. Accordingly, General Baird was directed to hold in
check any force attempting to cross the fords below the town.
General Gilbert was placed in position to meet any attack in
front or to reinforce either flank. General Stanley was stationed
four miles out on the Murfreesborough road, to guard the ford
at Hughes's Mill. General Granger's cavalry, under General
G. C. Smith, was held in reserve to reinforce General Stanley, if
necessary.

The day was propitious for the attack,—dark and smoky. The
wind, too, was high, and swept the dust from Franklin and the
dry roads into the faces of our men, so that at the distance of a
mile it was at times difficult to distinguish a line of horsemen

from a fence. The enemy advanced with great rapidity,—Van Dorn on the Columbia pike, and Cosby on the Lewisburg pike, while Starns and Forrest were sent around to gain Granger's rear by a road crossing the Harpeth three miles east of the town, known as the Nichol Mill Road. It was in anticipation of this movement that General Granger had placed General Stanley in the position he held. The first notice of Cosby's approach was the firing of our pickets, who were driven in about twelve o'clock, and fell back to the 40th Ohio, stationed on the south side of the town and there performing guard-duty.

By this force the progress of the enemy was stayed for an hour or more; but it was finally compelled to fall back for want of ammunition. The number of the enemy's dead and wounded, however, show that our men made a gallant fight against immensely superior numbers. In retiring they were followed into town by Major Jones's Mississippi cavalry, few of whom lived to return.

It was now about two o'clock, and a large force could be seen forming near the railroad on the Lewisburg pike, while another large force was collected between the Columbia pike and the railroad, about a mile and a quarter from the fort. Our guns at once opened upon the rebels stationed in the open field, and in a short time compelled them hastily to retreat. The enemy then posted two rifled guns in the edge of the woods, between the railroad and Columbia pike, directing their fire at the fort and General Granger's head-quarters, but without inflicting any damage. A messenger from Brentwood stating that the enemy had driven in General Morgan's pickets at that point, General Granger now thought it possible that Van Dorn's real intention might be to occupy his time and attention by a feint on Franklin, and thus prevent any attack upon him, while he attacked and captured the small force at Brentwood. To foil such a movement, he ordered all the cavalry under General Smith to reinforce General Morgan at Brentwood. After they had gone, however, it was ascertained that a gang of negroes had at a distance been mistaken for a rebel force, thus causing the alarm.

It was now evident that the real attack was to be upon his front; but it was too late to order the return of the cavalry force, which was to have supported General Stanley. To supply its place, two regiments of infantry, and two guns, from General Gilbert's division, were ordered forward.

Before they had moved, however, word was received from Stanley that he had crossed the river at Hughes's Ford, moved to the Lewisburg pike, and attacked the enemy in flank. It was here that Companies K and B of the 4th Cavalry distinguished themselves by one of the finest charges of the war, capturing a full battery of six pieces and between two hundred and three hundred prisoners, besides killing a large number, including a captain and a lieutenant. The enemy were routed at all points, with heavy loss in killed, wounded, and prisoners,— the latter numbering between four hundred and five hundred. Upon receipt of this information, General Granger at once ordered Stanley's reinforcements forward on the double-quick, so as to reach him before he was driven back. General Baird's division was also thrown across the river. These movements, however, were not quick enough. Van Dorn, discovering his precarious situation, abandoned his attack on Granger's front, and, concentrating his forces against General Stanley, forced him back, by the mere weight of overwhelming numbers, before his reinforcements had time to reach him. The battery could not be taken off, and was abandoned, four of the guns having been spiked. Most of the prisoners were also recovered by the enemy,—the cavalry only succeeding in bringing away thirty-four, among whom were a captain and a lieutenant.

Having thus extricated himself from a dangerous position, Van Dorn seems to have been satisfied with the day's work; for he immediately withdrew towards Spring Hill. His force was ascertained to have been nine thousand cavalry and mounted infantry, and two regiments of infantry. Their loss in killed, wounded, and prisoners was about three hundred, of whom about eighty belonged to the latter class. The loss of Generals Stanley and Granger was thirty-seven killed, wounded, and missing.

28

THE CAPTURE OF McMINNVILLE.

On the 20th of April, Major-General J. J. Reynolds, with his own division, Colonel Wilder's Mounted Brigade, and seventeen hundred and eight cavalry under the command of Colonel Minty, left Murfreesborough for McMinnville, to capture or disperse any rebel force that might be at that place. The cavalry camped that night between Readyville and Woodbury. At two o'clock the next morning, Colonel Long, with the 2d Cavalry Brigade, four hundred and eighteen men, was ordered to take the road leading through Jacksborough, strike the railroad at or near Morrison's as soon after half-past ten A.M. as possible, and to destroy the trestle-work at that place. The Manchester train, it was hoped, would be intercepted; but it escaped, though the work was well done, nevertheless. At three o'clock A.M., Colonel Minty, with the remainder of his command, marched for McMinnville, and was followed by Colonel Wilder with his brigade. About two miles from McMinnville, the 4th Michigan and one company of the 1st Middle Tennessee, with two of Colonel Wilder's mountain-howitzers, were detached and ordered to move on the Smithville road, the main body moving along the old McMinnville road. About half a mile farther on, the rebel pickets were encountered. Forming in line, they opened fire, but were charged and driven through the town. The entire force thus dispersed was about seven hundred,—six hundred cavalry, and the provost-guard, consisting of one hundred and fifteen men of the 2d Kentucky and 41st Alabama Infantry. These latter had left town with the wagon-train, by the Chattanooga road, about an hour before Colonel Minty's arrival; but, by pressing hard, a part of the 7th Pennsylvania succeeded in capturing three of the wagons and eight or nine of the men.

The cavalry scattered in every direction, part of them retreating at a gallop on every road leading from the town, and about fifty taking the railroad-train which started as our forces entered the place. In the charge made through the town by the advance-guard, consisting of Lieutenant Thompson and twenty-five men of the 7th Pennsylvania, Corporal Street mortally wounded Lieutenant-Colonel Martin, of Johnson's Kentucky Cavalry, laying open his skull by a sabre-stroke. General John H. Morgan was riding by the side of Colonel Martin, and barely escaped capture by the fleetness of his horse. The famous Major Dick McCann was also wounded and captured, but effected his escape the same night from a guard of the 4th United States Cavalry. Colonel Minty immediately sent the 3d Brigade and the 4th Michigan after the train which had just left, with orders to destroy it and also the new bridge over Hickory Creek. The 4th Regulars were sent to the support of the 7th Pennsylvania, on the Sparta and Chattanooga road. Colonel Minty then encamped for the night on the hill west of McMinnville, and early the next morning was rejoined by the 2d and 3d Brigades and the 4th Michigan.

On the 22d he camped at Snow Hill, and on the 23d passed through Liberty and Alexandria, Wheeler's, Wharton's, Harrison's, and Duke's brigades retreating before him. Camping three miles west of Alexandria, he remained there until the morning of the 25th, when he began his return, and, camping that night near Cainsville, reached Murfreesborough the next afternoon. The expedition resulted in the capture of one hundred and thirty prisoners (all but seven of whom were taken by the cavalry), the destruction of the trestle-work below Morrison's, the burning of the railroad-buildings, one locomotive, and two cars at that place, the burning of the railroad-bridge across Hickory Creek and the capture there of a large amount of bacon and other commissary-stores, the recapture of fifteen of the 2d East and 1st Middle Tennessee Cavalry, and also the capture of thirty horses, twelve mules, and three wagons. A large amount of property and stores—including a cotton-factory and other Government-buildings—was destroyed at McMinnville by Colonel Wilder,—who also brought in a large number of horses and mules. All this was effected without a single casualty.

On the 27th of April, General Granger's escort—detachments of the 7th Kentucky Cavalry, Major Vemouth, 6th Kentucky, Colonel Wickliff Cooper, and 6th Kentucky, Lieutenant-Colonel Roper,—in all, about five hundred men, commanded by Colonel Watkins, of the 6th Kentucky—made a brilliant dash upon a camp of rebels upon the Carter's Creek pike, eight miles from Franklin. Moving at two o'clock in the morning, they completely surprised the rebels at daybreak, killing two, wounding ten, capturing one hundred and thirty-two privates and six officers,—three of them captains, and all of the 1st Texas Legion. About one hundred and fifty horses, one hundred mules, eight wagons, and an ambulance, were also among the trophies.

A large camp, covering several acres, was completely broken up, and all the camp-equipage that could not be conveniently transported· was destroyed. Only a mile distant was another and much larger camp, before which Colonel Watkins drew up his men as though preparing to attack it. Under cover of this demonstration, he withdrew with his captures, reaching Franklin in safety.

EXPEDITION TO NORTHERN GEORGIA.

WHILE the expedition to McMinnville was being consummated, still another was in progress, in another direction, with a view to stir up the rebel enemy at their homes and to destroy their army-supplies and lines of communication. Colonel A. D. Streight, of the 51st Indiana Volunteers, was placed in command of the 80th Illinois and portions of two Ohio regiments, which, with his own regiment, numbered about eighteen hundred men, with instructions to proceed to Northern Georgia and harass the enemy's rear in every possible manner. The expedition was successful in accomplishing a part of its projected work, but was closely followed by superior rebel forces, and, after five days of constant fighting, was compelled to surrender, its ammunition being exhausted and further resistance useless.   Inasmuch as Colonel Streight and the commissioned officers of his command have been refused an exchange and are now confined in Southern prisons as common felons, we subjoin the instructions given to Colonel S., upon which the expedition was based.

"HEAD-QUARTÉRS DEPARTMENT OF THE CUMBERLAND,
"MURFREESBOROUGH, April 8, 1863.

COLONEL A. D. STREIGHT, 51st Indiana Volunteers.

"By special field orders No. 94, Paragraph VIII., you have been assigned to the command of an independent provisional brigade for temporary purposes. After fitting out your command with equipments and supplies, as you have already been directed in the verbal instructions of the general commanding this department, you will proceed, by a route of which you will be advised by telegraph, to some good steamboat-landing on the Tennessee River, not far above Fort Henry, where you will embark your command and proceed up the river.   At Hamburg you will communicate with Brigadier-General Dodge, who will probably have a messenger there awaiting your arrival.   If it should then appear unsafe to move farther up the river, you will debark at Hamburg, and without delay join the force of General Dodge, which will then be en route for Iuka, Mississippi.   If, however, it should be deemed safe, you will land at Eastport and form a junction with General Dodge. From that point you will then march in conjunction with him to menace Tuscumbia ; but you will not wait to join in the attack unless it should be necessary for the safety of General Dodge's command or your own, or unless some considerable advantage can be gained over the enemy without interfering with the general object of your expedition.   After having marched long enough with General Dodge to create a general impression that you are a part of his expedition, you will push to the southward and reach Russelville or Moulton.   From there your route will be governed by circumstances ; but you will with all reasonable despatch push on to Western Georgia and cut the railroads which supply the rebel army by way of Chattanooga.   To accomplish this is the chief object of your expedition ; and you must not allow collateral or incidental schemes, even though promising great results, to delay you so as to endanger your return.   Your quartermaster has been furnished with funds sufficient for the necessary expenses of your command.   You will draw your supplies and keep your command well mounted from the country through which you pass.   For all property taken for the legitimate use of your command, you will make cash payments in full to men of undoubted loyalty ; give the usual conditional receipts to men whose loyalty is doubtful ; but to rebels nothing.   You are particularly commanded to restrain your command from pillage and marauding.   You will destroy all depots of supplies for the rebel army, all manufactories of guns, ammunition, equipments, and clothing for their use, which you can without delaying you so as to endanger your return.   That you may not be trammelled with minute instructions, nothing further will be ordered than this general outline of policy and operation. In intrusting this highly important and somewhat perilous expedition to your charge, the general commanding places great reliance upon your prudence, energy, and valor and the well-attested bravery and endurance of the officers and men in your command. Whenever it is possible and reasonably safe, send us word of your progress. You may return by way of Northern Alabama or Northern Georgia. Should you be surrounded by rebel forces and your retreat cut off, defend yourself as long as possible, and make the surrender of your command cost the enemy as many times your number as possible. A copy of the general order from the War Department in regard to paroling prisoners, together with the necessary blanks, are herewith furnished you. You are authorized to enlist all able-bodied men who desire to join the 'army of the Union.' You must return as soon as the main objects of your expedition are accomplished.

" Very respectfully, your obedient servant,

"J. A. GARFIELD,
" *Brigadier-General and Chief of Staff.*"

"ADDITIONAL BY TELEGRAPH.

"April 9, 1863.

"THE written instructions you have received are designed to cover the cases you allude to. It is not necessary that a manufactory be directly in the employ of the rebels to come under the rule there laid down. If it produces any considerable quantity of supplies which are likely to reach the rebel army, it is to be destroyed. Of course small mills, that can only supply the necessaries of life to the inhabitants, should not be injured. Any considerable amount of supplies likely to reach the rebel army are to be destroyed. If you dress your soldiers in the costume of the enemy, they will be liable to be treated as spies: you should not do this without the consent of the men, after they have been fully advised of the possible consequences.

" (Signed) J. A. GARFIELD,
" *Brigadier-General and Chief of Staff.*"

Thus instructed, Colonel Streight moved with his command to near Fort Donelson, on the Cumberland River, by steamers from Nashville, and thence marched across the neck of country to a point on the Tennessee River near Fort Henry, while the steamboats went down to the Ohio and came up the Tennessee River to meet him. While thus crossing, his men scouted through all that region for horses and mules, and soon the entire force of the expedition was mounted. Proceeding by steamers to Eastport, the force disembarked and marched up the country, effecting a junction with General Dodge's force, advancing upon Tuscumbia and defeating the rebel troops stationed there, with considerable loss to the latter. Colonel Streight now pushed on to Northern Georgia, hoping to reach Rome and Atlanta, and there destroy the rebel stores, machine-shops, and magazines, render useless their railroads, and in every way to commit irreparable damage to the rebellion, if possible. The forces under General Dodge, meanwhile, turned off southward to make a sweeping raid into rebel territory in North Alabama and return to their head-quarters at Corinth.

Colonel Streight was hardly under way when information of his movements reached Forrest's and Roddy's cavalry, which were then within striking-distance, as it happened. They moved on rapidly and, by pushing across the country, came in upon the rear of the Federals; and then commenced a running fight of four days' continuance, during which there occurred two severe battles and several spirited skirmishes, resulting in considerable loss of life,—mainly on the part of the rebels, who rushed into well-laid ambushes and were several times signally repulsed. Upon one such occasion they lost two cannon, which our forces took along with them and used with effect until the ammunition was expended, when they were spiked and left behind. Thus, for a distance of over one hundred miles, our gallant troops marched towards the heart of the rebellion, doing immense damage as they progressed, by destroying bridges, large supplies of corn that had been collected for rebel army-use, burning a large foundry where cannon and shot were being cast for the Southerners, and stripping the country of whatever animals were needed for the expedition. Aside from this, strict discipline was maintained, private property was respected, and the people along the route were not needlessly harassed. At length the rebel force in the rear became augmented to overwhelming numbers, and, his ammunition being expended and his men thoroughly exhausted, Colonel Streight surrendered his command, at a point fifteen miles from Rome, Georgia. His men, about thirteen hundred in number, were paroled and sent

to Virginia, where they were exchanged some two months after
their capture. He and his officers were retained and closely
imprisoned, upon the demand of the Governor of the State
of Georgia, who claimed them as prisoners of state (felons),
alleging that they had incurred the penalty fixed by a statute
of that State for inciting slaves to rebellion. The charge was
made that, at the time of the surrender, negroes were found
with Streight's command, uniformed and bearing arms. Our
returned privates, however, deny the charge,—stating that but
very few—not more than five or six—negroes were with the
command, that those persons started with them from Nashville
as servants, &c., that they refused to permit negroes to accompany or follow them during the march, and that at the time of
the surrender only one of these negroes could be said to be
armed, and he was carrying his master's (or employer's) sword,
as a servant.

So stands this matter at the present time of writing. For
this unjust detention and imprisonment our Government has
retaliated by refusing to parole or exchange rebel officers, and
hundreds of the latter have since accumulated and are now pining
in Northern prisons. In consequence of his detention, no official
report of Colonel Streight's expedition has been made; and the
author has gleaned the foregoing account from various sources,
and in the detail it may not be strictly accurate. The following
letter from Colonel Streight, addressed to Brigadier-General
Garfield, Chief of Staff, from his cell in the Libby Prison, Richmond, Virginia, is all the official light as yet afforded us respecting this expedition:—

"RICHMOND, VA., May 24, 1863.

"GENERAL:—I hope this may reach you; but whether the bearer of it
(Captain Brown, formerly of the gunboat Indianola) will be able to get it
through, I am unable to say.

"Though painful in the extreme, I am under the necessity of announcing
to you that after four days and nights of almost incessant fighting,—the
enemy being fully four thousand strong, commanded by General Forrest,—
we were compelled to surrender for want of ammunition. Our loss in the
several engagements, in killed and wounded, does not amount to more than
one hundred. I regret to say that Colonel Hathaway is among the killed.

he fell, mortally wounded, on the evening of the third day, and expired in a few moments. The loss of the enemy in killed and wounded—according to actual count on some of the principal battle-grounds, together with the most positive information obtained through one of my surgeons, who was left in charge of our wounded—will amount to not less than five hundred in killed and wounded; among the latter is Captain Forrest (brother of General Forrest), mortally. I am proud to say that the whole command—both officers and men—acted nobly and gallantly,—drove the enemy from the field in each and every engagement. I will be glad to give you all the particulars when I have more confidence that they will reach you. We (the officers of my command) are now confined in the celebrated Libby Prison, and hope you will exercise your influence and judgment in getting us released as soon as possible, as our condition is any thing but pleasant. I had forgotten to say to you that we captured in the first engagement two pieces of artillery, which we used to good advantage until the ammunition was expended, when they were spiked, the carriages destroyed and abandoned. I had also forgotten to mention that a portion of our ammunition had become damaged, which rendered our further resistance impossible at an unexpected time.

" Truly, your friend,

" A. D. STREIGHT.

" To Brig.-Gen. J. A. GARFIELD."

ADVANCE UPON TULLAHOMA.*

UPON the 23d of June, General Rosecrans issued orders for an advance in force upon the enemy the following morning at day-break. His plan of operations was to create the impression of a main advance upon the enemy's left and centre by feint move-ments and demonstrations on our right with the lesser part of the army, in the direction of Shelbyville, while the decisive blow of the campaign was to be struck by rapidly marching with the principal body upon the enemy's right, turning or pushing it out of the way, and thence moving quickly, via Manchester,

---

* From this point the operations of the army are given by the author as gathered from verbal and unofficial reports, and may not be entirely accurate. Also, portions of our forces may not be mentioned as they merit. The author hopes for indulgence from the army, should this prove to be the case. The "Annals" were nearly ready for publication, and to wait for the official reports would have occasioned material delay.

upon Tullahoma, seizing the enemy's base at and lines of retreat and communication from that point, and thus forcing them to fight on our own terms, or surrender or scatter. To General McCook's corps the part of making the first advance from our right was assigned.

The three divisions of the 20th Corps were under arms before sunrise on the 24th. Owing to the delay in receiving marching-orders, General Sheridan's, which was to have the advance, did not get under way on the Shelbyville road until about seven A.M. It marched over that road, preceded by five companies of the 39th Indiana Mounted Infantry, under Lieutenant-Colonel Jones, until it came in sight of the enemy's outposts, when it halted and bivouacked, according to orders, in the woods on each side of the road, paying no attention to the desultory musketry and artillery fire the rebels opened upon it at intervals. Johnson's and Davis's divisions turned to the left when six miles out, as ordered, and took the road to Liberty Gap.

Up to the morning of the 24th, there had been a long term of fine, cool, clear weather. The roads were dry without being dusty; but the very hour the troops marched out of their cantonments rain commenced falling, as was the case also in December last, when the army moved out from Nashville upon Murfreesborough.

Before daybreak on the 24th, Colonel Wilder's mounted infantry struck tents, and were soon in motion along the pike leading to Manchester. General Reynolds, with the remainder of his division, followed. Later in the day, Generals Negley and Rousseau left camp in the same direction. Colonel Wilder was directed to move forward to within a few miles of Hoover's Gap, rest until the infantry should come up, and then to carry the works. Nine miles from Murfreesborough the advance-guard came upon the enemy's pickets. Two companies were deployed as skirmishers, and the column moved forward, driving the enemy before it. From the citizens and prisoners Colonel Wilder learned that the works commanding the gap, and carefully constructed under the supervision of Bushrod Johnson, were not occupied at present; and he determined to move forward and take possession before the knowledge of our movement could reach the enemy and enable him to move into the fortifications, which he successfully accomplished, driving back the rebel outposts and skirmishers and taking several prisoners.

This gap afforded strong defensive points at its entrance; but so sudden was our appearance that the enemy made but little resistance. Learning that the farther extremity of the gap offered opportunity for serious resistance to our advance, Colonel Wilder resolved to hurry forward and take position on the hill that commanded the road and the enemy's camp. The vanguard dashed forward and captured a train of nine wagons on the way to the rebel camp, a drove of fine beef-cattle, and twelve or fifteen prisoners. The long roll was heard in the enemy's camp soon after his arrival, and he immediately disposed his troops for battle. Captain Lilley, with his 18th Indiana Battery, hurried forward and took position on a cleared eminence used for pasturing-purposes, while the 123d Illinois, Colonel Monroe, moved up to its support. A howitzer was planted on a less commanding eminence near the creek, and the 72d Indiana formed in line of battle near it. Colonel Jordan, with the 17th Indiana, took position, while Colonel Funkhouser, with the 98th Illinois, formed some distance to the right, but on the same ridge. Soon after, the thunders of the artillery announced the opening of the battle, and the replies of the rebel gunners indicated a readiness to engage. Five regiments of rebel infantry rose from the low ground near the stream, and, cheering like men confident of easy victory and disposed to inspire terror in their antagonists, came charging across the rolling but open field towards the 17th. The enemy approached within range, and received a volley from the 17th, that checked but did not stay them. Supposing our guns exhausted, a cheer followed the report, and they moved on. Again Wilder's exhaustless weapons—the Spencer Rifles (twelve-shooters)—pour in their rain of bullets, and still the enemy press on. The rebels were nearing the line in largely superior force, and the colonel looked anxiously for assistance. The bayonet might prolong the struggle, but ultimate capture seemed inevitable. Not a man left the line. Comrades were falling rapidly; but threatening disaster only nerved the men to greater exertion, and they still bravely poured in their fire. Just as hope was giving way, successive volleys on the right announced the arrival of reinforcements. The enemy faltered, staggered back, and, as if hurried to a decision by a united fire of the 98th and 17th, turned their backs and fled, leaving a large portion of their dead and wounded on the field. The right of their line charged our batteries; but the 123d Illinois, rising from its cover, charged over the crest, poured in a few well-directed volleys, and the day was won. The importance of this victory was evinced by the remark of the general commanding. He is reported to have said, after examining the formidable position, "Wilder has saved us thousands of men." The loss of the command, in the two hours' fighting, was sixty-three killed and wounded. Deserters from the enemy and prisoners captured gave their loss at over five hundred killed and wounded; and among the former was Major Claybrook, of one of the Tennessee regiments engaged. The rebel forces engaged were Liddell's, Wharton's, and Bates's brigades, numbering fifteen regiments.

During this time brilliant work was being done at Liberty Gap, through which the command of Major-General McCook was to pass in advancing upon Cleborne's division of the rebel army. Since the battle of Stone River, General McCook's troops had longed for another trial of valor with the enemy. At Liberty Gap it came to them at last, and most handsomely did they improve it. Colonel Harrison, in the advance, with one battalion of the 39th Indiana Mounted Infantry, discovered a force of about eight hundred rebel infantry, about one o'clock P.M., when within a short distance of the entrance of the gap. After dismounting part of his men and deploying them as skirmishers, he reported the fact to General Johnson, who directed General Willich, whose brigade led the column, to drive the enemy. General Willich at once halted his brigade and made the necessary dispositions. He then ordered the entire line forward. It pushed on, under a heavy fire, through the open fields, with loud cheers, and, with its flanks outreaching and turning those of the enemy, had soon gained the hills and driven the rebels into precipitate flight, capturing their tents, baggage, and supplies.

General Johnson now ordered General Willich to rally and rest his brigade, and Colonel Baldwin's to take the lead and clear the upper end of the gap from the enemy. Advancing as rapidly as the narrow valley permitted, Colonel Baldwin soon found the enemy in force, afterwards ascertained from prisoners to have consisted of an entire brigade of infantry and a battery of artillery, in a strong position on each side of the road. Placing the Louisville Legion (5th Kentucky) on the right and the 6th Indiana on the left of the road, with skirmishers in front and the 1st and 93d Ohio as reserves, and directing a section of the 5th Ohio Battery, under Lieutenant Ellison, to engage the rebel artillery, he moved to the attack under a severe fire, and, after a short but sharp combat, drove the enemy in gallant style from and occupied their position.

On the following day General Johnson, in obedience to instructions, kept up the delusion of the enemy as to our real intentions, by holding the position his command had won the night before. In the forenoon Willich's brigade was ordered to picket the front. Its pickets kept up a brisk exchange of shots with those of the enemy. Towards noon they commenced feeling us by repeatedly advancing within range with skirmishers, supported by cavalry. They were driven back as often as they advanced. At two P.M. they repeated their attempt with a reinforced front of skirmishers, but again failed. Between three and four o'clock they came to a formal attack in line of battle. Simultaneously they posted a section of artillery in front of our left, and another bearing upon our centre, but still did not succeed in forcing back our picket-lines, which, after being strengthened by the support-companies, counter-charged, and drove the enemy several miles. At about three o'clock the ammunition of the 32d Indiana and 89th Illinois giving out, General Willich ordered the 15th Ohio to advance in support into the front line. The men of the 15th divided their ammunition with those of the 32d and the 89th, and the three regiments thus kept the enemy in check.

Soon after, General Willich ordered the 49th Ohio behind the centre of the line, and placed Goodspeed's battery upon a hill, somewhat in the rear, where it opened a vigorous and effective fire upon the enemy's artillery, and some houses sheltering rebel infantry, on the opposite heights. At about the same time General Willich sent word to General Johnson that the fight was becoming serious.

Between five and six P.M., the ammunition of the 15th Ohio, 32d Indiana, and 89th Illinois being about exhausted, General Willich ordered the 49th Ohio to charge. Upon returning from captivity, General Willich had introduced into his brigade a new form of attack by skirmishers. This the 49th now executed for the first time in action. Upon the order to move forward, the regiment advanced in steady line, cheered by the remainder of the brigade and joined by the men of the other regiments still provided with a few cartridges, through the open woods, towards the cornfields forming the valley across which the enemy had been operating. Having arrived within close range, Colonel Gibson gave the order, "Advance, firing." The regiment formed in four ranks. The first rank delivered a volley, next the fourth advanced to the front and fired, and then the second and third, in succession. At the second volley the advancing enemy wavered; at the third and fourth they broke and ran.

General Johnson, in the absence of General Davis in consequence of illness, had ordered General Carlin's brigade of the 1st Division, which had gone up the gap during the engagement, to the support of the 2d Brigade. Advancing across the valley with a dash, it came up on the right of the latter, after losing from twenty-five to thirty men. General Davis, having left his sick-bed upon the first sound of battle, arrived in front just in time to see the first charge of his men. Shortly after the appearance of Carlin's brigade, the enemy abandoned the contest. The orders of our generals being only to check but not to attack them, the fight ceased. In the earlier days of the war these two affairs at Liberty Gap would have commanded the public attention to a full extent. But, amidst the contemporaneous struggles of mightier numbers for more important issues in other parts of the country, they will pass as of minor importance. We sum up the result of these movements as follows :—

Wilder's mounted infantry defeated a superior infantry force at Hoover's Gap on the 24th, and on the same day Willich's brigade of McCook's corps drove two regiments from a strong position at Liberty Gap. The next day Willich's, Wilder's, and Carter's brigades completely routed a rebel division under General Cleborne, who is said to have fallen in the action. The Union loss was forty killed and one hundred wounded.

These gaps were the key of the position, and their loss to the enemy at once determined him to retreat; for as soon as General Rosecrans advanced, through them, to Manchester and Winchester, he flanked Bragg, at Tullahoma; and the latter, with Vicksburg and Port Hudson fresh in his memory, hastily evacuated. Upon ascertaining this fact, on the 1st day of July General Rosecrans threw forward his force in rapid pursuit, Thomas moving on the Manchester road from Manchester, and McCook on the one from Tullahoma. Thomas moved rapidly in hopes of striking the enemy, moving nearly due east, to get on the military road built by Bragg, parallel with and five miles east of the railroad. This General Thomas failed to do until the enemy was well beyond the angle and when he was crossing Elk River. The division of General Negley encountered the rear of Hardee at a point about four miles north of Elk River, and skirmished with it all day, losing four or five men killed and wounded. The enemy's rear-guard, under Wheeler, made a stubborn resistance, delaying Negley so that the rebel trains got beyond the river. During the night, by great exertions, Bragg escaped with his reserve of artillery—twenty-six pieces —across Elk River, at Estelle Springs, and reached Tin Mountains. The enemy, on both roads, burned the bridges, and the rear-guard took up positions in hastily-built works on the opposite side of the river. It was readily understood that this was to delay our crossing as long as possible, in order to enable the infantry and trains to get into the mountains. To aid them in this, heavy rains came up, and the river rose very high.

General Crittenden, with a full corps, was sent by a rapid march to take possession of the road leading from Dechard, via Tracy City, to Chattanooga. This was successful, and forced the enemy to take roads across the mountains.

On the morning of the 2d, General McCook crossed at the mouth of Rock Creek, below the enemy's position in front of our right, and thus flanked the road to Winchester and the mountains. At the upper bridge, where Negley was, a similar manœuvre was made, with still better success. Rousseau and Brannan were sent to the upper crossing to come down on the rear of the enemy, whom Negley was to detain,—not to drive. It was thought that Rousseau could cross by ten o'clock; but the swollen state of the river prevented, and only a few troops got across in time. In the mean time a cavalry brigade came in upon the right flank of the enemy. Their firing was mistaken for that of Rousseau, and Negley opened with two batteries on the rebel position, one thousand yards distant. The first fire dismounted one gun and killed several of the rebel gunners. They were taken completely by surprise, and made but few replies, retreating precipitately to the mountains. General Turchin had engaged the rebel right, and after a fight of two hours drove it and the entire rebel force from the field, killing thirty-five of them. The fight only commenced at two P.M., and the troops were unable to cross until the morning of the 3d. They moved only a short distance, Negley encamping on the battle-field, and Rousseau and Brannan on the bank of the river. McCook in the mean time advanced, and occupied Winchester, Dechard, and Cowan. On the morning of July 4, our whole force advanced to the foot of the mountains at Cowan, to find the enemy gone, in full retreat upon Chattanooga and the Georgia border.

Meanwhile Generals Stanley and Granger marched on and took possession of Shelbyville, meeting with but little opposition from retiring rebel skirmishers, and are reported as having captured several pieces of cannon and some three hundred prisoners,—among them a colonel and a lieutenant-colonel. The Union citizens of Shelbyville greeted our troops with waving of flags and expressions of delight. From thence General Stanley has penetrated to Huntsville, Alabama; and we now hold that entire section of country.

Bragg's retreat from Tennessee has demoralized his army, and discouraged the rebel people of that section. When the order was given to his troops to relinquish the fortifications and retreat in the direction of the Tennessee River, the disaffection that had existed among the Tennesseeans broke out in open denunciation and unreserved expressions of determination to abandon the cause and return to their homes. General Cheatham's division of Tennessee troops is said to have dissolved, and the flying fragments are making their way through the mountains to the Federal lines. Sixty deserters came into Tullahoma in one day and took the oath of allegiance. A colonel of a Tennessee regiment, on announcing the order to retreat, boldly avowed his intention of quitting the rebel service, and advised his men to escape to the mountains and make their way home.

We here close our record of the operations of the Army of the Cumberland. It has saved Kentucky and recovered Tennessee—two of the most valuable of the Southern States—to the Union fold. Its operations have been uniformly successful, and it has fought one of the greatest battles of modern times. As we close, the note of busy preparation is heard upon every hand for an advance beyond the Tennessee River, to free the crushed Union men and to overwhelm the rebel traitors of the Gulf States.

TULLAHOMA, TENNESSEE, August 1, 1863.

29

ADDITION TO FOURTH EDITION.

A BRIEF REVIEW OF THE LAST ADVANCE.

THE fourth edition of this volume being required by the public demand, the author makes some material additions, which, he believes, will render the work still more valuable to the Army of the Cumberland and to the friends of Major-General Rosecrans. Since the issuing of our previous editions, a vast army movement has been undertaken and concluded, and a terrific battle has been fought, resulting in the displacement of the enemy and the occupancy, by the Union forces, of another of the strongholds of the rebellion.

With this there has also been a change of commanders of our army; and hence we deem it especially appropriate to add to this record a brief account of the moving of General Rosecrans's forces across the Tennessee River, the flank movement upon Bragg, the battle of Chickamauga, the successful occupancy of Chattanooga (the grand object for which the battle was fought), and the construction of the defences of that place, with a few remarks on the relieving of the commander of the Army of the Cumberland and on the general situation. This addition, it is hoped, will render the "Annals" still more acceptable, as a complete history of the operations of the Army of the Cumberland under Major-General William S. Rosecrans.

Before proceeding with our narrative of the direct advance of the army upon Chattanooga, it will be well to take a retrospective glance. The advance of the army from Murfreesborough was planned by General Rosecrans with one grand purpose in view,—THE POSSESSION OF CHATTANOOGA. The rebel army was

then entrenched at Tullahoma and Shelbyville, and there a
momentary delay was anticipated; but the nook in the bend of
the Tennessee River, walled up by grand old mountains upon
every hand, was the object aimed at. The accomplishment of
this purpose, however, was a matter of extraordinary difficulty.
The rebels held the line of railroad, and, if compelled to retreat,
would unquestionably destroy it as much as possible to prevent
pursuit. The wagon-roads leading in that direction were rude
and rough in the extreme, over continuous hill, valley, and
mountain, passing through the entire Cumberland range, and
preparations must be made at Murfreesborough to move the
army through the wilderness, across mountains, and over rivers,
by the ordinary modes of land-conveyance. The utmost that
could be hoped from the railroad was that if repaired in time it
would serve to bring on supplies in the rear of the army. The
preparation for such a movement involved the collection of a
vast number of horses, mules, wagons, compact army stores, the
thorough equipment and clothing of the men, and the thousand
minor arrangements always to be made ere marching a great
army upon an interior summer campaign. Here was one cause
of the long stay of our army at Murfreesborough,—our friends
at home becoming in the interim most restive at the delay.

A second reason was, the great lack of cavalry. This defect
was fully demonstrated at the battle of Stone River, where the
largely superior numbers of the rebel-cavalry enabled them to
come upon our rear and make the complete circuit of our army,
destroying our supply-trains with impunity. General Rosecrans
at once set about remedying this want; and the efforts he made
to secure animals, by purchase, by inland expeditions of impressment, and even by the wholesale "pressing" of horses at
Nashville and vicinity, are described elsewhere in this volume.
By such tedious means the four regiments constituting Welder's
brigade of infantry were mounted. While this supply of horses
were being procured, a goodly share of them, purchased for our
army at Louisville, were necessarily taken at that city to
mount General Burnside's forces in their expedition to the

Cumberland Gap, and also to go in pursuit of the rebel General John Morgan, who was then passing through Kentucky and Indiana on his last and most notable raid. The want of cavalry was finally remedied, to a limited extent, after much procrastination and difficulty, that arm of the service being brought up to about six thousand effectively mounted men,—a force which was deemed sufficient to protect the immense trains of the army and to do scouting and pioneer service upon the march South.

Another, and a very potent, reason, weighed in the minds of the general and corps commanders of our army. The siege of Vicksburg was progressing, and to advance was not deemed politic,—since if Bragg were driven from the valley of the Tennessee, the probability was that he would retire to Chattanooga, and, leaving a small force there behind intrenchments, would send the bulk of his army to operate with Johnston against the forces of General Grant. This view was taken by all the officers of the army, and was at length adopted by the people of the country. The result proved—many idle reports at that time to the contrary—that Bragg's army lay quiet at Shelbyville and Tullahoma, and thereabout, intact; only Breckinridge, and, a small portion of the uneasy element of the rebel army, leaving it in that direction. The defensive works at both of these places were of the most formidable character. The rebels had been industrious, and, aided by the labor of some three thousand slaves sent up mainly from Georgia and Alabama, intrenchments were thrown up, earth forts, &c., quite surpassing the famed rebel works at Corinth, Miss., which for several weeks held at bay a Union army of one hundred and twenty thousand men. At Shelbyville these rebel works extended over a circuit of five miles.

It must also be remembered that the co-operation of the forces of General Burnside was expected in the advance movement, he penetrating into East Tennessee,—which was eventually and successfully done. But further delay inevitably arose from this source, although commendable despatch was exhibited on the part of that auxiliary command.

At length, when the above-mentioned preparations had been made, and when General Rosecrans was fully satisfied that the investment of Vicksburg was complete and must result successfully, he ordered the advance from Murfreesborough, as stated in a preceding page, on the 24th of June. Even then the means for a forward movement were not such as could have been desired, and many doubts troubled the minds of the old campaigners of the army, the most of whom had participated in the advance to the Tennessee River, under Buell, the year before. They well knew the rugged character of the country, and the long and unprotected rear line through a destitute and hostile region. It is a fact worthy of mention, that the corps and division generals of our army were by no means enthusiastic as to the position on their front. When requested by General Rosecrans to advise with him upon this matter of an immediate advance, the unanimous opinion, in writing, of those seventeen generals, was that an advance at that time was inexpedient. General Rosecrans, however, deemed it best to advance, and the army was soon put in motion. Some time before this, the War Department had issued to the commander-in-chief strenuous appeals and orders to advance. General Rosecrans asked in return if such orders were peremptory, stating that if so, he would tender his resignation rather than encounter the fearful consequences. The orders were decided to be merely advisory; and the general assured the War Department that preparation was going on in all possible haste, and that the fall of Vicksburg he hoped was nearly a certainty.

The author advances the opinion, for which he is alone responsible, that short and ill-tempered orders from the War Department, over the telegraphic wires, upon this matter, developed a feeling of contentious opposition, if not of unjust action, on the part of the Secretary of War and his advisers at Washington, continually manifest since that time, and which has recently cropped out in a remarkable manner. That Rosecrans and Thomas, and the entire corps of generals of the army, were correct in their views, has been conclusively proven by results.

The cavalry, that hitherto lame-leg of the army, was now able to cope with the rebel horsemen, especially since the loss to the latter of John Morgan's command. Teams and supplies were selected and compacted which carried our army over two hundred miles of difficult land-travel, and enabled it to wage a two days' battle, and to successfully enter and retain Chattanooga. Bragg's army was prevented from marching to the relief of Vicksburg,—although the country was assured by divers alarming reports that it had been divided, and even decimated, for that purpose, leaving a mere shell of *Quaker* camp-equipage and cannon to oppose to the Army of the Cumberland. That bubble was speedily pricked. Let it be borne in mind that the generals who thus confronted the mandates of the War Department are now in command of the Army of the Cumberland, and most deservedly enjoy the confidence of the army and of the nation.

The advance of our army upon Tullahoma by flank movement, —the rushing into mountain-gaps, driving back, by gallant charges and sharp hand-to-hand encounters, the rebel forces stationed there,—the astonishment of Bragg at finding our forces marching past him and threatening his rear and railroad,—his sudden flight, abandoning all his works, forts, and vaunted military resources of surrounding produce and forage, —his hasty retreat to the Tennessee River, followed so closely by our forces that he must needs fight the while, and had no time to injure the railroad, further than to destroy nearly every bridge upon it,—the swoop of our gallant troops across the Cumberland Mountains in pursuit, treading upon the enemy so closely that he failed in completely destroying the great bridge over the Tennessee, several of the extensive spans midway being saved,—all this is history, and is in great part narrated in the preceding pages. The series of marches from Murfreesborough to the Tennessee River, and the attending brilliant successes, have no parallel in the history of this war. An army of at least forty thousand men were forced from their fortified works by flank approaches, through mountain-passes which the rebels deemed they had sufficiently guarded, after most vigorous and galling charges! But this great victory, achieved by strategy, rapidly and gallantly executed, excited little comment,—and very naturally. Vicksburg had recently fallen, and the nation was aglow. The smaller success was enveloped by, or rather was incorporated into, the greater. Had the Army of the Cumberland stormed the ramparts of Tullahoma, spiked its seventy pieces of cannon, and driven back its rebel defenders at the cost of ten thousand men, the victory would have been chronicled in story and in song. But to win victory at the least cost has ever been the study of General Rosecrans.

Although successful in this movement upon the enemy at Tullahoma, a keen sense of disappointment was experienced in this regard. Our generals had planned the movement with a view not only to drive out Bragg, but to reach his rear, and, forcing him to a battle at a serious disadvantage, to overwhelm him and destroy his army. The weather had been most favorable, and the country roads were in good order. It was midsummer, when continued rains are unusual. But upon the morning of the advance the rain commenced, and continued as if the very windows of heaven had been opened. For seventeen consecutive days the rain fell in remarkable quantity. No such stormy period had visited that country for twenty-six years past. The army moved on through the storm; but the roads were soon cut up, and the rear squadrons and columns, with the supply and ammunition trains, were for several days completely "stalled" in the mud. This of course delayed our advance, and permitted Bragg to retreat upon his railroad with all his material.

CROSSING THE TENNESSEE RIVER.

THERE was some delay in the advance of the army as it approached the foot of the Cumberland Mountains. This was caused by the period of incessant rain, the mud of the country roads impeding army locomotion, and the teams becoming exhausted and requiring rest. Meantime, vigorous railroad repairs were being effected; bridges were erected, the railroad-tunnel below Cowan was cleared out, and, by the time the army had reached the river, the shrill shriek of the locomotive again pierced the valleys, and the roar of hundreds of bread-and-forage-laden cars echoed back from the mountains of Northern Alabama.

The crossing of the Tennessee River by our army was a remarkable feat. After the completion of the means of crossing, four days were consumed in the passage of the army at the various places. The constant measured tread of infantry; the tramp of thousands of cavalry; the rattle and shout, and the crack of the whip, as those four thousand heavily-laden wagons, in trains miles in length, bounced from the banks on to the narrow pontoon causeways; the heavier jar and crash, as the huge artillery vehicles rumbled over the planks,—all must be heard to be duly appreciated. The quick passage of our army over that wide, swift-running river, without the loss of a single man or animal, is a feature in army experience worthy of note. To effect this crossing of the larger part of the army, General Rosecrans ordered one pontoon bridge to be laid down at Caperton's Ferry, three miles from Stevenson, twelve hundred and fifty feet in length, and another pontoon bridge at Bridgeport, twelve miles up the river, of twenty-seven hundred feet. Not having pontoons enough to complete the latter, his engineers finished out the bridge by setting down trestles and planking them over.

CHATTANOOGA TAKEN BY STRATEGY.

WE should state here that, previous to this time, General Crittenden's corps had crossed to the Sequatchie Valley, midway towards Chattanooga, to operate against Bragg on his front, from the north and opposite side of the river, while the com-

mands of Generals McCook and Thomas were crossing the river
below. The Union commander had resolved upon capturing
Chattanooga by strategic movements. In fact, he could not
hope to enter it by a direct forward movement from the north.
Bragg was there, in the nook; his front a broad river, over
two thousand feet wide, whose banks on his side were lined
with cannon, ready to sweep off men from pontoon bridges as
fast as they stepped upon them, or to destroy boats, rafts, or
bridges entire. Therefore a plan was adopted to this effect:
Crittenden's corps was to go up on the north side of the river
as far as Chattanooga, and there feign the intention of crossing
and making the attack in front,—*à la* Fredericksburg, Va. His
men made a toilsome march across and among the Cumberlands,
dragging their cannon over precipices by hand, and accomplishing their task in about four days' time. Thus temporarily
located in the Sequatchie Valley, he despatched four brigades—
two of cavalry, Colonel Minty's and Wilder's mounted infantry,
and Generals Hazen's and Waggoner's brigades of infantry—to
proceed to points on the river opposite Chattanooga and immediately above and below that town, and make the feigned attack.
This was done. Some of Wilder's troops above the town let
ends of logs and rails and bits of lumber float down past Bragg's
front, as if they were preparing a bridge; other troops slapped
boards together, to make a lumbering noise; while Wilder un-
limbered his artillery and shelled the town. Some of his balls
raised a dusty sensation over the way, one of them, it was said,
having struck a church during the services of a Sabbath morning.

While Bragg's attention was thus being occupied, the two
pontoon bridges below were thrown over and fords were worked,
as already stated, and the main army of the Cumberland, under
Generals Thomas and McCook, crossed the river. Our cavalry,
meanwhile, went mostly by another and more western route, by
way of Athens, passing through the town of Huntsville,—thus
going around (flanking, in military parlance) the most abrupt,
of the Cumberland Mountains. The plan devised for gaining
Chattanooga we will now more fully elucidate. While Critten-

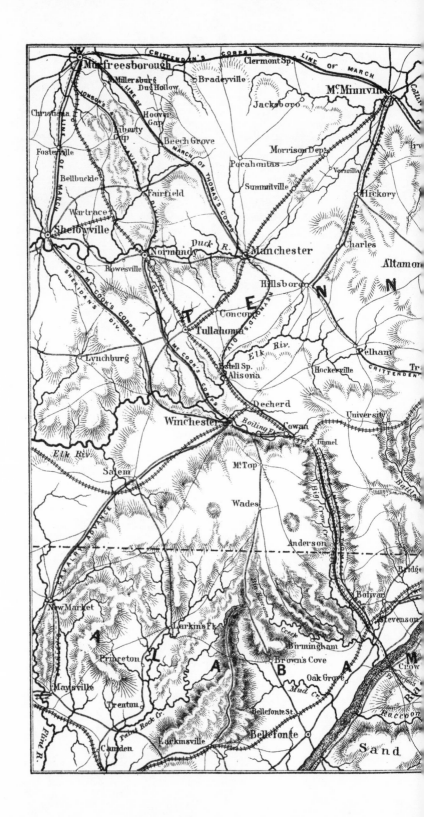

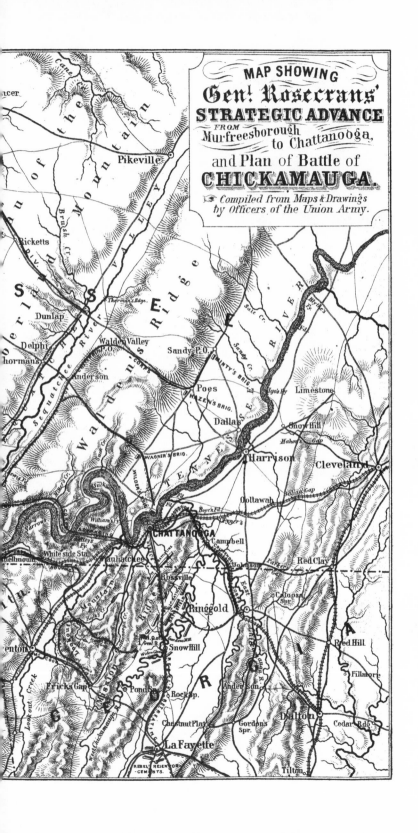

MAP SHOWING
Gen! Rosecrans'
STRATEGIC ADVANCE
FROM
Murfreesborough
to Chattanooga,
and Plan of Battle of
CHICKAMAUGA.
Compiled from Maps & Drawings
by Officers of the Union Army.

den was thus to threaten with his four brigades on the opposite side, below and in front of that place, to mislead Bragg, the main body of the army was to march down into Georgia to two gaps piercing Lookout Mountain, and, passing through them, to come in on Bragg's rear. Lookout Mountain is a high range, or spur, running back from the river, just below Chattanooga, into the heart of Georgia,—a "hog-back" ridge, so to speak, terminating at the river in a steep bluff. It is of great height, and its descent upon either side very abrupt and rugged. The railroad creeps along upon a shelf cut into the solid rock under this knob, near the water's edge, where the mountain appears to have been separated from its kindred links across the river by the floods of the Tennessee, which for countless ages have rolled down upon and past this barrier in resistless might. The river west of Chattanooga, in its general direction, runs southwest. Skirting it is the Raccoon range, of which the Sand Mountain, where the army passed over, is part. After marching over a plateau twelve or fifteen miles in width, the Sand Mountain is descended, and the Lookout Valley is gained, some two miles wide, running southwest, and bounded on the east by the Lookout Mountains, running parallel with the Raccoon range.

With this explanation (which we will soon demonstrate to the reader by tracing the campaign with him upon our map), we proceed with our account of the movement. Lookout Valley, coursing down along the west side of Lookout Mountain, ends against an angle, or another spur of that mountain, and this place is called Valley Head. Here there is a break in the direct line, where the rugged mountain melts away into a wild scattering of considerable hills, near which the road is abruptly turned through winding valleys,—not forgetting, however, a jagged and stubborn spur which rears its head at this point. This, like some other mountain-ranges in North Georgia, is quite wide on its top, and, in many places, susceptible of cultivation: so that the traveller will occasionally meet with a small patch of a farm, with usually wretched improvements. Says one of the correspondents of the Cincinnati "Commercial," writing of the pass at Valley Head:—

"After reaching the top, another plateau, some dozen miles wide, is encountered, so level and gently rolling, that one laughs at his preconceived ideas of the tops of mountains,—if, indeed, he does not forget that he has left a valley. No peaks from which to unfurl a flag, if any one should be geographically poetic; no sugar-loaves where one can clamber, and feel like a giddy explorer standing on a heavenward land's-end. There are groves and fields, and smooth-flowing streams, where the imagination pictures verdant crags and cascades."

Thus General McCook's corps safely and speedily climbed the abrupt Raccoon Mountain, which faces Bridgeport and Stevenson, and thence directed their course across, over Sand Mountain, through Valley Head, over Lookout Mountain, at Winston's Gap, until they reached the next valley, called Broomtown Valley, directly threatening the rebel rear. This was a memorable march, over a distance of forty-nine miles. From this newly acquired point General McCook sent a reconnoitring force to Alpine, three miles farther south, to threaten Bragg's rear. Still farther down, our own mounted forces were upon the move to mystify the rebel general, a detachment of Colonel Brownlow's Tennessee cavalry going within five miles of Rome.

Leaving McCook thus located in Bragg's rear, we will explain the movement of the corps under General Thomas. He marched south from Bridgeport, over spurs of mountains and through deep wooded gulches, to the Lookout Valley, followed that narrow and meandering channel to another depression, crossed through at Cooper's and Stevens's Gaps, after toilsome marches over the roughest of mountain roads, and took position at the mouths of those gaps, in Bragg's rear. This division thus marched fifty-one miles from Bridgeport, and was now twenty-six miles south of Chattanooga by the nearest practicable wagon road. McCook's division was seventeen miles farther south, being a total of forty-three miles below Chattanooga, and his outpost at Alpine, over sixty miles.

The rebel commander now became fully aware of Rosecrans's intention, but too late, if he had even had the force, to prevent its execution. By taking possession of the gaps on his side of Lookout Mountain, he might have fortified them and prevented the passage of our troops. This had not been done; and the Federals were now in his rear many miles below, threatening his railroad and subsistence, and preventing the arrival of reinforcements. On the 8th of September, General Thomas had full occupancy of those gaps, and on the 9th of that month, General Bragg's army evacuated Chattanooga, going south, mainly by the Rome road. In passing down the valley, in front of Thomas, Bragg endeavored to cut off some advanced regiments; but Thomas cautiously drew them up to him, within the jaws of the gaps, and the rebel hosts marched southward rapidly, but in regular order.

Meanwhile General Crittenden was moving. He proceeded to cross the main body of his troops over the Tennessee River at and above Bridgeport, following Thomas, and then took up his line of march for Chattanooga over the very brow of Lookout Mountain. Arriving upon the mountain, he found that Bragg had fled, leaving the town quite deserted. He entered the place at once, and was soon after joined by his four brigades from the opposite side of the river. This accomplished, General Crittenden moved his corps out to Ringgold, on the railroad, to reconnoitre the enemy. His advance speedily ascertained that Bragg had fallen back only to Lafayette, and had taken position. He at once moved with all possible haste across to Lookout Mountain, to be within reach of Thomas, for it was now apparent that the enemy were becoming more bold and belligerent. The reader will find no difficulty in understanding that the sole aim of all this strategy and hard marching was *to force Bragg out of Chattanooga and to get in there ourselves.* Not a plan was laid, hardly a thought was indulged in, which did not refer to that purpose. Chattanooga was the object of that campaign.

We had taken that place,—or, rather, our smallest corps of

troops had passed into and through it. But our army was mainly down among the mountain-ranges of Georgia, and its occupancy of Chattanooga was yet to be. General Rosecrans and staff had also marched into Chattanooga, and he there fixed his general head-quarters. As for himself, however, and his other officers, with the exception of clerks and office-men, his head-quarters were in the field, miles below, solely intent upon consolidating and bringing his columns north. There were newspaper reporters also in Chattanooga upon the entry of Crittenden, and they represented to the world that the town was gained and securely held, and that the great Army of the Cumberland were now marching in pursuit of Bragg, and might possibly pursue him even to Dalton and to Atlanta. And there were shouts of a joyful people at the North at this great success, as announced in the daily newspapers. But this news and this joy were premature. Not so felt the several Union commanders. Rosecrans, and Thomas, and Palmer, and their *confrères*, were then aware of what was soon fully developed,—*the reinforcement of Bragg*, and his turning upon our army.

The strategic movements of Rosecrans at once alarmed the Southern Confederacy. He was moving on them; but how, was the mystery. But they rallied their troops from every section. A large portion of Stonewall Jackson's division of Virginia veterans were sent down from Lee's army, with Longstreet, Lee's best general, in command. Brigades were hurried up from Charleston and Mobile. Buckner's army of ten thousand came down from East Tennessee, and a large force was received from Johnston's Mississippi army, which had failed in succoring Pemberton at Vicksburg. It is ascertained, also, that a considerable number of rebel troops captured and paroled at Vicksburg had joined Bragg's army, as well as some eight thousand of Georgia State militia hastily collected for the emergency. Thus Bragg's army was swelled, *in one week's time*, from about forty thousand to upwards of eighty thousand men. We shall prove this conclusively farther on. Bragg marched to a short distance below, and, at a point opposite the gaps where our forces

lay, halted and took position. Here he met his first heavy reinforcements; and others began to pour in. He left Chattanooga on
the 9th of September; on the 16th of the same month he
addressed a notice to his army, to the effect that, having been
heavily reinforced, they were now to assume the offensive and
drive the invaders from the soil of Georgia.

Of this Rosecrans was early made aware, and to concentrate
his army and get to Chattanooga, or, at least, to be able to select
his position and prepare for the grand battle that was threatening, was his great object. McCook was ordered to come to
Thomas, and Crittenden to remain within close supporting distance of the latter general. We have stated that the gap where
McCook's corps had crossed, and in which it now lay, was seventeen miles below the force of General Thomas. McCook was
instructed to use all possible haste, and, fully advised of Bragg's
strength and preparations for attack, he moved with great
celerity. He was informed of a road on the mountain-top that
would lead him north in an almost direct course to the upper
gaps; but, relying upon the assertion of scouts and refugees
that no such practicable route existed, he retraced his march
through the gap, across the mountain, to Valley Head, thence
up Lookout Valley, to the gaps where Thomas had passed, and
marched over the same route, joining Thomas at the mouth of
the gaps,—whereupon Thomas moved away from the gap a short
distance, towards Chattanooga and Crittenden. Thus McCook
marched four days and a half over a distance of forty-six miles,
when he could have come by the cross-road on the mountain,
seventeen miles, in a day and a half. He acted, however, on
what he supposed to be his best information, and the error was a
very natural one. His corps made extraordinary marches during
those memorable four and a half days, and he and his gallant
men are entitled to the thanks of the nation.

But in this delay there was fearful danger and loss of advantage. The rebel hosts were marshalling and advancing upon our
army. Had they moved only a day or two sooner, and driven
Thomas back within his gaps, holding him there with a portion

of their forces while they advanced upon Crittenden with their main army and forced him back to Chattanooga, and into the river, or among the mountains, how completely foiled would have been the Union army! The campaign would have been lost, and we would have been left with our forces divided far down among the inhospitable mountains. These few days were days of deep anxiety to the general commanding and to his staff and advisers! But Bragg, it was subsequently ascertained, was not ready to attack: his forces were not well in hand, and when he moved upon us it was too late to prevent the concentration. The delay occasioned by the roundabout march of McCook's corps was mainly unfortunate in this: it prevented the Union commander from choosing his battle-field.

How imperfectly was all this strategy understood, except by the generals in command and their confidants! The soldiers and the reporters were equally in the dark as to the object of the movements. The retreat of McCook through the mountains, to join Thomas, was described by a writer to a prominent paper in the Northwest, after the battle and so-called "failure," or "defeat," as a hasty and mistaken march farther south, to try to get in Bragg's rear and cut off his retreat; and the editor of this Northwestern paper was fain to believe, with due sorrow and mortification, that Rosecrans had been completely outwitted, and thereby badly defeated. Other army correspondents sent to the world joyful accounts of the utter demoralization of Bragg's army, of his weakness and retreat, as they followed down with Crittenden's corps in his march to the support of Thomas! In their mistaken zeal, they already pictured Rosecrans at Dalton and Atlanta. They could not perceive the gathering of the rebel clans among those mountain-valleys not more than ten miles beyond. Had our commander-in-chief called into his tent these gentlemen of the press, and explained his plans and revealed the tidings brought him by his spies and scouts, they would not have fallen into such errors and have so grossly misled the public. But such revelations cannot be made. Better that the newsmen err than that Bragg be informed, through the Louisville, Cincinnati, and New York papers, of the scheme that has been so carefully and skilfully elaborated, by which he is walked out of his fortified places and great natural defences without the firing of a gun. To hide his forces here and there among the valleys,—to move in such a way as to baffle the intelligence of the enemy,—to have the main army forty miles in the enemy's rear, when he fancies it on his front and just below him,—such was the strategy of General Rosecrans; and to publish it before its accomplishment, would be far more disadvantageous than to permit the people of the Union to be so grossly deceived by the eager and well-intentioned news-gatherers of the public press.

CHICKAMAUGA.

WE have shown that Bragg evacuated Chattanooga on the 9th of September. He marched down past the valley of Chickamauga Creek, some thirty miles, to Lafayette. McCook's corps was at once set in motion to rejoin Thomas, which feat was accomplished on the 18th. Bragg began to march back on the 17th, to attack our corps in detail, before their junction was effected. In this he failed: McCook had come in from the south, and Crittenden from the north, in support. The reader will remember that Bragg attributes this failure to two of his subordinate generals, Polk and Hindman, and after the battle relieved them from their commands. Bragg now strikes for the main Rome road, leading into Chattanooga, hoping thus to get between our army and the river. General Rosecrans foresees this, and orders an advance in force to secure this road. General Thomas breaks camp at sunset, Friday, the 18th, and makes his memorable night march, over hill and through forest and valley, and by sunrise next morning reaches it and takes position. Within two hours there after, the rebel advance reaches this road, a short distance below our forces, and remains quiet. General Thomas sent out a strong reconnoitring force to feel the enemy, about ten o'clock on Saturday morning, the 19th. They found the rebels in force and advancing, and brisk skirmishing soon merged into severe fighting. The rebels were apparently surprised to find the road occupied in their advance, and gave battle with their accustomed impetuosity, following back our reconnoitring column to the Union lines, when the battle became general along the entire front. Thomas, by his night march, filing to the left past Crittenden, became the left wing, leaving the latter the centre, and McCook, retaining his first position, on the right.

We shall not attempt to give the movements of the two days' battle in detail: the official report of the commander-in-chief describes them fully and correctly. Our present aim is merely to give a general outline of the battle, in connection with the strategic plans of the campaign of Chattanooga.

The battle of Saturday resulted in our general success. The contest raged along hillsides and amid forests and ravines. The army lines extended over nearly three miles of ground; and only by the smoke that rose above the heights, and the dust that ascended above the forest-trees in the valley, or as the cannon's roar and the rattling discharges of musketry were heard upon surrounding hills, could the observer note the ebb and flow of the tide of battle.

When the rebels advanced upon Thomas in heavy line of battle, he informed General Rosecrans of the fact; and the latter, who was at the right, personally inspecting the lines, arranging batteries, &c., instructed Thomas to hold his position on the main road by all possible means, and that, if necessary, he should be amply reinforced. The battle raged all day, darkness alone ending the conflict. The fighting was constant, and occasionally furious. Brigade after brigade of the Union forces was moved into the conflict, until every brigade in the army had participated. At one period two of our divisions were badly driven by immensely superior rebel forces; but the lost ground was soon after fully recovered. No signal advantage had enured to either side when the day's conflict closed, each having taken prisoners. But this day of battle had fully demonstrated the fact that the Army of the Cumberland was contending against fearfully superior numbers of determined and exasperated veterans. It was reported that some of the rebel Virginia soldiers cried out, as they charged upon the walled lines of Thomas, "You are not fighting with conscripts now!" to which the answer would be shouted back by the Western boys, "You are not fighting with Eastern store-clerks!" On the evening of this day there was a consultation of commanders at General Rosecrans's head-quarters, at the "Widow Glen" house, where it had been during the day, within musket-range of the line of battle. Each reported that every brigade had been in the day's fight, and that our troops had acted finely; but all agreed that in every severe attack made upon us we had been invariably outnumbered. It was plain that the next day's contest must be for the preservation of the army and the holding of Chattanooga.

After due consultation with his corps commanders, the following plan for the second day's battle was decided upon, and was announced at one o'clock that morning. General Thomas, with Johnson's division from McCook's corps, and Palmer's division from Crittenden's corps, was to maintain his present position. McCook was to post the remainder of his corps on the right of Thomas; while Crittenden was to place the remainder of his corps in reserve, near the point of junction of the other two corps, and to support either, as circumstances might require. These positions were assumed by daylight. It soon becoming apparent that the enemy would wage strongest battle on Thomas's left, with a design to turn him and reach the main road, Negley's division was ordered from McCook's line to take position at the left of Thomas, and McCook was instructed to close up the gap thus made in his line.

The rebels commenced the battle early; and it raged with tremendous fierceness, at times, along the entire lines. General Thomas reported that the pressure upon him was most severe; and he was instructed, in return, to hold his point without fail, with the assurance that, if necessary, he should be reinforced by the entire army. The rebels invariably attacked, and were as invariably repulsed, their object appearing to be to find some point where our lines might be penetrated. It was in consequence of this manner of fighting, the rebels moving while the Federals were in position, the latter often lying down and thus loading their muskets, only rising to fire and to repel a charge, that the rebel killed and wounded greatly exceeded our own. A multitude of important orders were given during this time, and many movements were made, their results conforming to this general outline. All went favorably, the enemy being held firmly in check and undergoing terrible slaughter, until about one o'clock in the afternoon, when, by the misconception of an order, one of our divisions was moved in the wrong direction, and a gap was left open in our battle-front at the point of junction between Thomas and McCook. This the enemy quickly perceived. They advanced rapidly and heavily, and poured their columns in at the gap, taking both McCook and Thomas on the flank, crushing Crittenden, and completely changing the order of the battle at that point. General Davis's gallant old division charged in to stay the rushing tide, but in vain. General Rosecrans was speedily present, and ordered forward Sheridan with two light brigades; but they were also swept back before the rush of the now exultant foe. In fact, the right wing of the army was partially cut off, and Crittenden's reserve was forced back in confusion. Thus it was that seven brigades were isolated from Thomas and the main body of the army. Sheridan retreated in tolerable order, and by a quick movement eventually succeeded in getting to the support of Thomas. On both sides of this gap the fighting was irregular and against us, we there losing most of the prisoners and guns taken by the enemy. The rebels now charged down the valley, and among hills and forests, surrounding, crushing, and capturing, until they were recalled by their leaders to assist in the necessary driving of Thomas from the main road.

General Thomas was still in strong position with his corps,

reinforced by Palmer's, Wood's, and Johnson's divisions, and one brigade of Van Cleve's division. The rebels now bent all their energies to the dislodging of our main army. They attacked, and were repulsed, again and again. Our troops fought well: they were nobly led. Thomas, Palmer, Johnson, and other Union generals, won imperishable honor by their coolness and bravery. From two o'clock until sunset the battle thus raged in front of our lines. The rebels, in despair, hurled their entire army upon the devoted Union forces, who were now outnumbered by more than two to one and were greatly exhausted. General Granger's command, however, of three fresh brigades, arrived, soon after the breaking of our line of battle, from towards Rossville, and at this critical juncture they bore the brunt of the shock. General Stedman, the Ohio fighter, marched to a gap which was being attacked by Longstreet's men, with two of the fresh brigades, and for forty minutes the most furious contest of the battle took place. He repulsed the advancing horde three times, with frightful slaughter, himself losing nearly one thousand men from his command. The rebels now gave up the contest and withdrew.

Thus ended the battles of Chickamauga. The enemy were too severely cut up to again offer battle. Their desperate charges were led by their officers in person: hence their loss in generals, twelve of whom were said to be discomfited,—four of them being killed, four mortally and four slightly wounded. Their loss in colonels and subordinate officers was proportionately severe. The cannon of Thomas, at times, mowed down their advancing troops as the grass falls before the reaper. During the night of this last day of battle, General Thomas, not knowing what the enemy might attempt the next day, fell back three miles, unmolested, and took up a much stronger position near Rossville. Here the Union forces formed in line of battle, and remained during the next day,—Monday; and, the enemy not appearing, on that evening the army took up the march for Chattanooga, a distance of five miles, and entered it in order, with all their material.

General Rosecrans, when our line was pierced, and after vainly attempting to stem the rebel tide with the troops at hand of Davies's and Sheridan's divisions, started with his attendants to reach General Thomas. The enemy being between them and that officer, and the country being of the roughest character imaginable, without roads or even horse-paths, the party also being strangers to the locality, they determined to debouch to the rear and gain the main road at Rossville, a distance of four miles, and then repair to the main army. At or near Rossville was a reserve force under General Granger; and the intention of General Rosecrans was to order this reserve forward to the support of Thomas forthwith.

Arriving at Rossville, it was ascertained that Thomas was holding his own, with prospects of keeping the enemy at bay until night; also, that Granger's reserve had already started to his support. Thus, all was as yet well in that quarter. But General Rosecrans's attention was now drawn to Chattanooga. The wildest confusion reigned there and along the roads. The seven brigades of McCook and Crittenden, numbering perhaps ten thousand men, were much demoralized. In general terms, and to give a clear understanding of the matter to the reader, without pretending to accuracy in figures, we will say that perhaps one-half of these broken troops were halted, reformed, and gradually moved back to the rear of Thomas during the afternoon, while the remainder, numbering perhaps five thousand men, together with teamsters and the usual array of camp-followers and attendants, were directing their way through the forests and by every footpath towards Chattanooga.

General Rosecrans was as yet uncertain of the general result. It was now about three o'clock in the afternoon, and appearances were much against him on his right. He consulted with his attendants, and soon decided—as would any prudent commander whose army was in fearful jeopardy—to aim at two points first, to hold the enemy at bay, if possible, until night, and then to retreat into Chattanooga; secondly, to have that place put in due state of defence. Having thus determined, and deeming it most important that he should look after his rear, he despatched his chief of staff, General Garfield, to the front, to convey intelligence and orders to General Thomas. General Rosecrans proceeded to the town, arriving there about four o'clock in the afternoon, and set about preparations for defence. The thousands of teams that filled the main streets in rows four and five deep, were ordered across the river. The stragglers were put to work, and many of them were reformed and sent back to the army. Breast-works were planned and commenced in the rear of the place, ready for a new and last line of battle, should such a struggle come. Our troops had been out twenty-one days, and their supply of rations and ammunition was nearly exhausted. The long lines of our supply trains were near Chattanooga, in the valley, ten miles distant from the main battle-field; and General Rosecrans well knew that, were those trains cut off and destroyed by the rebel advance, our forces would be starved out of Chattanooga as well as fought out of it. The safety of those trains, and the security of the several fords and of his pontoon-bridges, were not forgotten by our general in that hour of critical danger. Although Thomas was holding the greatly superior enemy in check, the latter might succeed in a flank movement, causing our forces to fall back to the town, perhaps in haste and disorder. The commander-in-chief had been constantly upon the battle-fields. He was most fearful of the failure of our right, weakened as it had been by reinforcements sent elsewhere. Throughout he was busy in receiving reports, despatching orders, posting troops, and personally overseeing the placing of batteries. Cool, clear, and calm as an autumn day, and, though most anxious, yet hopeful, his manner, as upon the open fields at Stone River, was cheering, and his words encouraging. But the country was so broken that his two miles of army lines were in a great measure hidden from his view. He was not able to judge of events upon the instant, nor was the ground susceptible of such action on his part as was exhibited upon the cotton-fields of Murfreesborough. The reader will remember that the line of the Chickamauga was an accidental battle-field to both contending armies. It afforded few opportunities for the ordinary field display of generalship. In such a contest, success lay mainly with the bravest and the greater numbers, accident, etc.

General Garfield, chief of staff, proceeded to General Thomas and explained the condition of affairs, informing him that, if he deemed it advisable, he could retire the army to Rossville after night and there take a stronger position, or that, if necessary, he could come in to Chattanooga. This was Sunday night; and the town was, as above stated, filled with "demoralized" soldiers, teamsters, sutlers, and camp-followers, including, perhaps, we ought to add, sundry newspaper reporters. Each person had his own version of the scenes of the battles and of our "awful defeat." Those who flee invariably magnify the cause of their flight. While the main bulk of the glorious Army of the Cumberland was in good order, and successfully repelling the attacks of the enemy, our "Bohemian" corps—as represented by at least two or three of its prominent members—were busily engaged in shedding their befogged ideas upon paper, assuring the country that our army had been fighting the entire Southern Confederacy and had been terribly defeated.

To show conclusively that the battle of Chickamauga was a necessity, that it was forced upon our army, let us advert to the dates of the various movements. General Thomas accomplished his march through Lookout Mountain in Bragg's rear on the 12th of September. General McCook passed through Winston's Gap, and took position on the 10th. General Bragg evacuated Chattanooga on the 8th and 9th, and passed southward, in front of Thomas, on the 12th. McCook was ordered to retire and join Thomas on the 12th, which task he mainly accomplished by the 18th. Crittenden moved to the support of Thomas on the 18th. Bragg issued his order to his troops, assuring them of reinforcements and their ability to drive "the invaders," &c. on the 16th, and he commenced his advance movement upon our army and Chattanooga on the 17th. On the 18th his pickets and cavalry had constant skirmishing with our forces, and on the

19th and 20th were fought the great battles. It will thus be perceived that General Rosecrans lost no time in marching upon
Chattanooga and in concentrating his army, when the rebels
assumed the offensive.

We should here state—in justice to our subject and to individuals—that so apparently necessary and expedient was this
action upon the part of General Rosecrans, that not until soon
after his removal, which took place some four weeks after the
battle, was a breath of reproach heard respecting it. One circumstance, probably, tended to call attention to the fact that he left
the battle-field before the close of the conflict,—viz.: the entry of
Major-Generals McCook and Crittenden into Chattanooga without their commands. It is due to those gallant officers, than
whom we know none more brave and determined upon the field
of battle, and to the officers upon their staffs, and to the soldiers
of the Army of the Cumberland who were under their command,
that the following facts should be made known.

We have stated that the commands of McCook and Crittenden
were depleted, to reinforce Thomas, at the main point of the
battle. We have shown that their line of battle was pierced by
the enemy at the point where their forces joined on to Thomas,
partly through an error in the movement of a division, which
caused a gap in the lines, and partly on account of the overwhelming numbers of the rebel army, which then centred at that point,
after having been repeatedly foiled in their attacks elsewhere.
The reader has seen that Davis and Sheridan gallantly plunged
into the breach with their divisions, and were quickly thrust aside
by the advancing tide. The crumbling in pieces of those seven
brigades amidst those forest-clad hills and valleys, in midsummer, where the foliage and unevenness of the locality precluded
to a great extent any comprehensive view of the situation, has
been duly commented upon. Generals McCook and Crittenden
labored with all possible zeal and ardor to repair the disaster
of the hour. They rode hither and thither, in various directions, endeavoring to collect their scattered forces. They found
their men wherever they rode, completely disorganized, some-

times in squads and groups, but more often singly and by twos and threes, all urging their way back through the thickets towards Chattanooga. To reform the men, under such circumstances, was a sheer impossibility. That they attempted it, and made all possible exertions to retrieve the fortunes of the day, will, we are assured, be fully established by their official reports. Under the circumstances,—it being then after three o'clock in the afternoon,—they deemed it advisable to repair to Chattanooga. We speak of them in connection for the sake of brevity only. They came in separately, neither knowing of the whereabouts of the other. Not until they reached the town could they ascertain the situation of affairs with General Thomas. They reported to General Rosecrans; and he bade them wait until intelligence came in from General Garfield. Upon its arrival, with the assurance that our army held its position firmly, they returned to the front, and assisted in the falling back, during the night, to the new line of defence near Rossville, and, finally, came into Chattanooga with the army.

No complaint was uttered against these two officers by General Rosecrans. The Secretary of War, however, found reason for ordering their immediate suspension from their positions, and commanded them to appear at Indianapolis, Indiana, there to undergo trial as military felons. We have fully and candidly stated the facts: from them let the people of our land render judgment. The army was surprised and shocked at this sudden action, attended as it was by the instant consolidation of the 20th and 21st Army Corps. It was considered an imputation on the bravery of hundreds of officers and thousands of men in the Army of the Cumberland, too monstrous to be entertained.

MAP OF THE STRATEGIC MOVEMENT.

To afford valuable instruction is one of the main objects of this volume. We have fully portrayed with our pen the march of the Army of the Cumberland upon Chattanooga. Still further to aid the reader, we have prepared a map with much care, upon which the entire movement can be traced. Let the reader turn to it, and accompany us in its examination.

Our army is starting from Murfreesborough. The several blue lines indicate the marching of the several commands. General McCook's corps take to the right, and Thomas and Crittenden to the left; and thus they flank Bragg at Tullahoma, and he retreats. Our army soon pushes on, reaching Stevenson, Bridgeport, and Jasper. The Tennessee River is now crossed by McCook and Thomas, and their lines of march are readily traced down among the valleys and ridges and through Lookout Mountain to the rear of Bragg. The rebels evacuate; and Crittenden, who has meanwhile crossed the Tennessee and marched up towards Chattanooga, now enters that town, and then sets out for Ringgold. It will be perceived that Bragg is now heavily reinforced, and turns upon Thomas and McCook. The march of the latter back to form a junction with the former is shown by the dotted blue lines. Bragg now marches for the main road to Chattanooga, and to get in front of our army, as is seen by the course of the red lines. Thomas also makes for the same road; and the battle ensues.

The reader will be amply repaid, in the study of these army movements, by the acquisition of knowledge respecting military strategy accomplished upon American soil and attended by one of the greatest battles of modern times.

GENERAL SUMMARY AND CONCLUSION.

THE occupation of Chattanooga was accomplished. For seven months past, since the taking of Murfreesborough, this had been the task for our army to perform. The entire object has been gained; and we are quite unable to perceive wherein lies "the defeat," "the disaster to Rosecrans," &c. &c., that the patriotic people of the North and West have been solicited to believe. That such a wrong impression respecting a great battle could arise, appears almost incredible: yet, under the peculiar circumstances, it may be explained. The partial occupancy of Chattanooga by Crittenden's corps would lead the world to believe that the army of the Cumberland was there. The regretful thought would then arise, our army having got so snugly into Chattanooga, why race down among the mountains fifty miles to get up a fight with rebels, reinforced as they unquestionably would be? Some reporters stated that McCook and Thomas were going on to Dalton, and Atlanta, and Savannah, and Charleston, leaving Bragg penned up in Chattanooga with our army at his door! When once understood, as we here endeavor to explain it, the American people will appreciate the fact that the strategic campaign of Rosecrans on Chattanooga was one of the most extensive, the grandest, and the most successful of the war.

To show how completely deceived were very many able men as to our having gained Chattanooga, we copy the following editorial from the New York "Tribune" of September last, which assumes that the Army of the Cumberland was then in that place safe and snug:—

"CHATTANOOGA.—The occupation of Chattanooga by General Rosecrans is a more brilliant success than if achieved by help of a victory. 'Battles are the last resort of a good general,' said one of the greatest. We are a little slow to believe it; but General Rosecrans is so thorough a teacher that the dullest of us shall yet prove apt scholars under his instruction. The popular imagination delights to conceive him in the storm of bullets, amid which his courage and capacity turned defeat to victory at Murfreesborough. Magnificently done it was; but Chattanooga is a still higher talent. Needless to remind ourselves that it was a famous rebel stronghold. Its impregnability has been vaunted in every rebel journal for a twelvemonth past. Nature had done her utmost to secure it from assault, and engineering science had trebled its natural strength.

"General Rosecrans might have buried half his army on its craggy slopes before he had fought his way into its recesses; but he turns its terrors into triumph by skilful strategy, and a simple flank movement discloses the weakness of this formidable fastness. It is simple, however, only in the same sense in which nearly all grand manœuvres are simple. They are the exact application of simple general principles in difficult circumstances, the natural obstacles being in this case the greatest to overcome. Rivers, mountains, impracticable roads, a country barren of supplies,—these are what test a commander's capacity, and what General Rosecrans has just proved himself master of."

Even by the officers and privates of our army the strategy of their commander was very imperfectly understood at the outset, and it was by them grossly, though innocently, misrepresented. But by the time the result was attained, the whole army fully appreciated it, and they now consider this achievement as the grandest and most important of all. It is said that while riding along the lines after the final occupancy of the town, General Rosecrans thus addressed his troops in return for their cheers:—

"Fellow-soldiers:—We struck for Chattanooga,—we fought for Chattanooga,—and here we are!"

An appreciative officer of our army (unknown to the author) writes as follows to friends in Wisconsin:—

"IN THE TRENCHES AT CHATTANOOGA,
September 25, 1863.

"MY DEAR UNCLE:—

*   *   *   *   *   *   *   *   *

"The campaign I regard as one of the most brilliant and successful of the war. We have occupied the most important stronghold in the hands of the enemy against a vastly superior force. When Bragg evacuated this place, he expected, with the aid of large reinforcements, to take advantage of the weakness of our line, McCook's corps (right wing) being nearly forty miles distant from Chattanooga, where our left rested. This extension of our right was necessary in order to execute the flanking movement. Nothing seemed easier than for Bragg to cut us in two, and annihilate our comparatively small army by whipping us in detail. It was a skilfully laid and evidently long-matured plan of Bragg, and was foiled only by the consummate strategy of Rosecrans and the determined pluck of his troops.

"The right wing marched all night, fought and marched all day, thereby shifting itself to the centre before the enemy had time to strike; the left wing, aided by Granger's Reserve Corps, at the same time successfully prevented the efforts of the enemy to turn our left flank and get between Rosecrans and Chattanooga. For three days we contended against the overwhelming numbers of the enemy in this disadvantageous position, when Rosecrans finally succeeded in concentrating his army, saving his trains, and in occupying Chattanooga—the coveted position—in such force as to insure its permanent possession.

"The object of the campaign has been fully accomplished, and we have had to contend with much greater difficulties than ever we anticipated. The enemy has been baffled and outwitted; he has gained no compensating advantage for the loss of Chattanooga in any way; and I believe that his loss in killed, wounded, and prisoners is even heavier than ours. We in the army can appreciate better than you at home the genius of our commander in extricating us from our perilous position."

That officer could not have stated the case more clearly had he had his general's maps and notes in hand.

General Rosecrans's official report admits a loss (displacement) of sixteen thousand men, and General Bragg officially confesses to a loss of seventeen thousand. The Union commander announces in the same report that the enemy took four thousand nine hundred of our men prisoners, including the wounded on the battle-field; while we took two thousand rebel prisoners, none of them wounded.

As regards the extent of the rebel forces at the battles of Chickamauga, General Rosecrans assumes that they had at least seventy thousand men, upon this basis. We took prisoners from one hundred and fifty-three rebel consolidated regiments. They will average four hundred men to each regiment,—sixty-two thousand. Add to this at least eight thousand men for artillery. The rebel prisoners generally concurred in that estimate.

The Marietta (formerly Chattanooga) "Rebel," soon after the battle, stated that Brag was "surrounded by a galaxy of higher military talent and backed by a larger army than he ever before commanded during his whole military career."

When the rebel newspapers gave the names of their generals who were killed, it was easy to see to what extent reinforcements had been sent to Bragg. Hood's, McLaws's, and Gregg's divisions—the two former of Longstreet's and the latter of Ewell's corps—are represented in their list of officers killed and wounded. The two divisions out of three of Longstreet's corps show forty-two regiments and about fifteen thousand men. Gregg's division, which is the third of Ewell's corps, numbers about ten thousand men. Thus Lee sent to Bragg from twenty-five thousand to thirty-one thousand men. When we add to this Bragg's original army, swelled by conscripts to at least thirty-five thousand men, ten thousand men under Buckner, together with material reinforcements from Johnston and Pemberton's old armies, the latter having been declared released from their paroles given at Vicksburg, the magnitude of Bragg's army is well established. B. F. Taylor, Esq., who is now with the Army of the Cumberland as the war-correspondent of the Chicago "Journal," writes to that paper under recent date (October) as follows:—

"The business before us is formidable,—how formidable I fear the country does not quite appreciate. No such enemy ever sat down before a Federal hold, no such host ever before looked us face to face. No such stake has been ever before to be played for. One hundred thousand seasoned men will not exhaust the rebel roll. We here shall see the most terrible battle ever fought on this continent."

The value of the results of the campaign for Chattanooga is now universally recognized. The following, from the Knoxville "Register," at present published at Atlanta, Georgia, shows how important the rebels feel it to be to recapture East Tennessee:—

"If any one doubts the necessity which would impel President Davis to sacrifice Richmond, Charleston, and Mobile, all to reacquire East Tennessee, he need only ask the Commissary-General by what agencies and from what source the armies of the South have been sustained during the first year of the war. East Tennessee furnished the Confederate States with twenty-five millions of pounds of bacon. Last year the State of Tennessee fed the army."

And says the Richmond "Examiner" of October 31:—

"For a long time the importance of East Tennessee to the Confederacy seemed to be unappreciated. Not until that country fell into the possession of the enemy was its incalculable value realized. Except what was furtively obtained from Kentucky, the whole army supply of pork came from East Tennessee and the contiguous counties of the adjoining States. The product of corn in that region was very heavy, and no portion of the Confederacy, equal in extent, afforded as large a supply of forage and winter pasturage. The occupation of East Tennessee by our own armies was not only important in itself, but it was important also in respect to the contiguous country which it protected. A great line of railway was secured, continental in its dimensions and in its value. The saline and lead mines of Virginia, which produce all the salt and lead used in the Confederacy, were protected so long as East Tennessee was ours.

"But the evacuation of that region, and its surrender without a single battle to the enemy, has lost us all these advantages. The railway is broken up, and there can be no communication between General Jones at Bristol and General Bragg at Chickamauga, who are less than one hundred and fifty miles apart, except by a circuit of twelve hundred miles through Petersburg, the Carolinas, and Augusta. The hogs of East Tennessee, affording twenty-five millions of pounds of pork, are now being slaughtered for the Yankee armies. The vast corn-crops and forage-supplies of that department, sufficient to winter all the live stock of the Confederate armies, are being fed to the fifty thousand horses and mules belonging to the forces of Grant. The salt and lead works of the Confederacy, and the numberless caves of Southwestern Virginia, from which immense supplies of saltpetre are obtained for the Ordnance Department, are now imminently threatened by the close presence of hostile armies, requiring the presence of heavy forces of our own for their protection."

After gaining Chattanooga, General Rosecrans vigorously pushed forward his earth-works in the rear. As at Corinth, at Nashville, and at Murfreesborough, he at once prepared *to stay*, and to make the place an extensive military depot. During four weeks he labored incessantly and effectively.

Notwithstanding the false impressions already mentioned, as to our "defeat," "disaster," and to our being "out-generalled," &c., the Union patriots of our land honored our army and its commander as greatly as ever, for the last display of their labor, their fortitude, and their bravery. It was not, therefore, on account of any public dissatisfaction that General Rosecrans was relieved from his command. The order came to him, unannounced, at four o'clock P.M. on the 19th day of October. At nine o'clock that evening he turned over his army to his old and tried friend and confidant, General Thomas. Desiring to have no commotion in the army, he prepared the following order to be issued after his departure, and at eight o'clock the next morning, October 20, just one year to a day from the time of his leaving his army at Corinth, Mississippi, to take this command, he bade farewell to the Army of the Cumberland:—

"GENERAL ORDERS, No. 242.

"HEAD-QUARTERS DEPARTMENT OF THE CUMBERLAND,⎱
"CHATTANOOGA, TENN., October 19, 1863.　⎰

"The general commanding announces to the officers and soldiers of the Army of the Cumberland that he leaves them, under orders from the President.

"Major-General George H. Thomas, in compliance with orders, will assume the command of this army and department.

"The chiefs of all the staff departments will report to him.

"In taking leave of you, his brothers in arms,—officers and soldiers,—he congratulates you that your new commander comes not to you, as he did, a stranger. General Thomas has been identified with this army from its first organization. He has led you often in battle. To his known prudence, dauntless courage, and true patriotism, you may look with confidence that under God he will lead you to victory.

"The general commanding doubts not you will be as true to yourselves and your country in the future as you have been in the past.

"To the division and brigade commanders he tenders his cordial thanks for their valuable and hearty co-operation in all that he has undertaken.

"To the chiefs of the staff departments and their subordinates whom he leaves behind he owes a debt of gratitude for their fidelity and untiring devotion to duty.

"Companions in arms,—officers and soldiers,—farewell; and may God bless you!

"W. S. ROSECRANS, *Major-General.*"

The causes of this action on the part of the Government have not been made public; but it is the duty of all patriots to presume that they are ample. Injurious and defamatory reports against General Rosecrans have arisen in this connection to die almost as soon as born. The author passes them by unnoticed farther than to leave them to be refuted by the enemy.

From the Richmond "Examiner," October 26.

"Meantime, Lincoln is helping us. He has removed from command the most dangerous man in his army. A variety of mean and damaging pretexts for Rosecrans's removal have been published by the Yankee press. But the true reason is the fact that he failed at Chickamauga.

*　　*　　*　　*　　*　　*　　*　　*

"Rosecrans thus retired is unquestionably the greatest captain the Yankee nation has yet produced. His performances in the field are too fresh in the memory of every reader to necessitate recapitulation. We may, however, mention, in proof of his intellectual ability, that he graduated fifth at West Point in a class of fifty-six, in which General G. W. Smith graduated eighth and Longstreet fifty-fourth."

The gigantic efforts now being made by the rebels to recover Chattanooga and its concomitant, East Tennessee, and the determination of the Federal Government to retain it, best attest the value of General Rosecrans's last campaign. As we have remarked of his strategic and bloodless victory at Tullahoma, so we may claim of Chattanooga, that, had he attacked and stormed it in front at a cost of five thousand of his soldiers, the world would hail it as a glorious and substantial victory. The result of the campaign is the same,—Chickamauga was the inevitable price of Chattanooga.

Thus we close our history of the Army of the Cumberland. To its future, under its wise and beloved leader, General Thomas, are committed, to a great extent, the hopes of the patriots of our land. May those hopes be gloriously and speedily fulfilled!

The theatre of war is now apparently changed; and upon the Georgia frontier are to be witnessed the culminating scenes of the rebellion. The Union armies are there assembling under the direction of Major-General Grant, the successful hero of Fort Donelson and Vicksburg. The next campaign of this grand army of the Union, thus commanded, will constitute an epoch in the history of our nation and of the world.

POLICE RECORD

OF OPERATIONS OF

SPIES, SMUGGLERS, TRAITORS, ETC.

OCCURRING WITHIN THE LINES

OF THE

ARMY OF THE CUMBERLAND.

CONTENTS.

ARMY POLICE RECORD.

A Rebel Minus One Hundred and Nine Thousand Dollars!

ONE of the most important and interesting cases upon the records of the Police of the Army of the Cumberland occurred at Louisville, Kentucky, about the time when Major-General Rosecrans was assuming its command in October last. The Chief of his Army Police, and some of his assistants, had hardly arrived in that city before they got upon the track of the case, and fully developed the facts, which are as follow.

On the last day of October, 1862, as the mail-boat from Cincinnati to Louisville was ploughing its way down the Ohio River, well thronged with passengers, a party of three persons were to be seen in the saloon, seated before a table, enjoying themselves over a friendly glass and whiling away the hours with a game of euchre. The three were, comparatively speaking, strangers,—had not met with each other previously. Either by accident, by mutual attraction, or by *spiritual* affinity in the double sense (and whether these small, yet great, events in life come by chance, or are foreordained, we leave to casuists and philosophers to determine), it so happened that these three persons took to cards and cocktails from nine o'clock at night until two in the morning. One of these parties was Mr. John W. Lee, a well-dressed, smooth-faced, courteous, middle-aged gentleman, bearing the appearance of a prosperous and well-regulated country merchant. The second person was a resident of Cynthiana, Kentucky : his name or business is of no importance, as the only figure he cuts in this story is—like that of the deuce-spot in the game—to count. The third party at the table was a detective; and that is enough to know, gentle reader, to appreciate fully the story.

The game of euchre proved the entering wedge for another kind of game. The influence of cocktails and brandy-straight opened wide the door of friendship and confidence, and Mr. Lee intrusted to the keeping of his new-found acquaintance the weighty secret that he had in his charge a large amount of gold and greenbacks *in transitu* to its owners in Dixie. Mr. Lee further intimated that he would like to purchase some twenty thousand dollars' worth of goods to take to Kentucky to sell, and if he could get passes and permits of the military authorities at Louisville to get his money and goods through, he would be all right. Much conversation ensued that night and during the following morning, the result of which was that Mr. Lee and

485

his friend were to go into partnership in the merchandise, and the friend was to be instrumental in getting the passes, or, if necessary, in running the blockade. Franklin, Kentucky, was the point fixed upon as a good locality for selling the goods, and, of course, the nearest and best point to rebeldom in Tennessee for smuggling purposes.

Arrived at Louisville, Mr. Lee and his friend proceeded to the express-office in that city,—the latter by invitation of the former. Passing along the streets, Mr. Lee more fully explained that he had about one hundred and sixty thousand dollars in gold and treasury notes; that he had taken English sterling bonds for his friends in Knoxville, Tennessee, to New York and there cashed them; that he had sold the bonds for thirty-two per cent. premium; that he had bought some gold at about the same rate of premium; that the money was to come to Louisville by express, and was there now, very probably. Upon inquiry at the office Mr. Lee found this to be the case. He asked the agent if *five* bags of gold were there for John W. Lee. The agent replied, "No," and said, "Have you not made a mistake in the number of bags?" Mr. Lee looked at his receipt, and said, "Yes; there are *seven* bags." This was correct, and the agent expressed his readiness to deliver it upon Mr. Lee procuring the usual identification. The twain were rather nonplussed: however, Mr. Lee remembered that M. B. Whiteside, Esq., of that city, knew him, and would vouch for him; and they left the express-office. The detective volunteered to find Mr. White-side. He did so; and that gentleman remarked that he merely knew Mr. Lee, but of his loyalty he knew nothing, and declined to vouch for or identify him. The new friend, however, did not despair; he saw Mr. Lee, reported progress, or, rather, no progress, and said *he* had friends in the city whom he would introduce, and who could not only identify, but also procure the requisite passes. All now was well. Mr. Lee and friend *smiled* most pleasantly in that very luxurious but rather one-sided apartment, the saloon of the Galt House. But—alas for the evanescent bliss of the happiest of mortals! —at this juncture a policeman tapped our tapsters on the shoulder, and they followed him to the shades. Mr. Lee was informed that he was under arrest; that his money had been seized where it lay in the express-office; that he would not be confined, however, but liberated on his parole not to leave the city. The new friend was hustled off to prison summarily, as an old offender; *i.e.* he was marched away from Mr. Lee under arrest; and then, most probably, set off to work up some other case of rascality, possibly a little sad at the loss of his prospective partnership in the country store at Franklin, or, *more* possibly, smiling at the trick that Mr. Lee was playing upon him, in holding out to him such an inducement to aid the smuggler on his way.

There was now a shadow upon the countenance of John W. Lee aforesaid. He paced to and fro through the public halls of the Galt House, as if tormented by a perturbed spirit. The close observer might have noted as much at a glance; and one person there was, lingering around that hotel, in and about, who was thus taking notes. He was a gentleman familiar with the purlieus of the Galt House, and, probably, of many other houses in the city of Louisville. Some trivial pretext for conversation soon occurred, and this gentleman introduced himself to Mr. Lee as a paroled Confederate surgeon and a Mississippian, who enjoyed the privilege of the city through the interposition of influential friends. Our quondam surgeon had also come heavily to grief, and at once proceeded to unbosom himself to the interested Mr. Lee. He told him that, because of his prominence and influence as a Southern Rights man, his name was not placed upon the regular cartel for exchange, recently made out by Major-General Buell, that he was about to proceed to Bowling Green, then the head-quarters of Major-General Rosecrans, to have his name thus properly placed, and that he would then proceed home speedily, and without taking the oath of allegiance to the Federal Government.

This tale was pleasant to John W. Lee. It was told with such earnestness and unction, and was so well concocted, that it threw him completely off his guard. Here was trouble with which he could heartily sympathize. By this time the twain were cosily seated in the gentlemen's parlor of the Galt House, and Mr. Lee seemed to crave for friendly sympathy in return. To insure its extension, he gave this account of his affairs and their present condition.

During the last autumn two persons from Kentucky passed through the North and proceeded to the city of Augusta, Georgia. There they purchased of Thomas Metcalf English sterling exchange to the amount of nearly two hundred thousand dollars, paying for it entirely in Confederate scrip, all of which proved to be counterfeit. Upon ascertaining this fact, Metcalf at once sent to Knoxville for Lee, asking him to come to Augusta: he did so, and it was agreed that he (Lee) should have thirty-three and one-third per cent. of all the amount he could recover. This was a bright idea with our Southern brother Metcalf; for Lee was known at home as a good Union man, and could travel about among the Yankees and hunt up the money at will.

Mr. Lee was faithful and energetic in his search for the lost treasure. Aladdin never rubbed his lamp with more ardor than did this gentleman seek for sterling bonds or their proceeds. He found his way back to Morganfield, Union county, Kentucky, on the 16th day of October, 1862. He crossed the Southern lines upon passes furnished him by Metcalf; and, of course, he could pass through the United States upon the strength of his Unionism pure and undefiled. He obtains an introduction to Mr. George R. Ellis, of that town,—the latter being an officer, a constable or deputy sheriff, we believe, —and hires his assistance to find two persons, by name, Frank Payne and Martin Hancock, telling him that these persons had passed counterfeit Confederate money on the firm of Metcalf & Co., of Augusta, Georgia, to the amount of one hundred and sixty thousand dollars, or thereabouts; that they lived somewhere in that vicinity, and that he wished to find them.

Lee and Ellis, after a vigorous search, found Hancock in Henderson county, and ascertained that Payne was either dead or had left the country.

They invite Hancock into a room, and Lee produces a letter from Metcalf &
Co. (And here, by the way, we should remark that the latter gives two or
three different names of parties in Georgia who owned the sterling bonds.
In stating the case to the supposed Confederate surgeon, at the Galt House,
Louisville, he gave the owner's name as Thomas Metcalf, of Augusta,
Georgia; and in stating it to Mr. Ellis—as we see by Ellis's affidavit—he
gave the owners' names as Whiteman & Co., of Augusta, Georgia.) This
letter Lee read to Hancock; it charged him (Hancock) and Payne with
passing off the counterfeit money. Hancock at once admitted the fact, and
then and there agreed to refund the whole amount involved to Lee, as agent
for the owners, informing him that the money was in New York City, and
that he would go on with him and make it all right. Lee then employed
Ellis to accompany them to watch Hancock and make all sure, agreeing to
pay him five hundred dollars for the service. The three soon started for
the East; and at Cincinnati Hon. Judge Trigg joined the party as counsel,
procured by the far-sighted Lee. To be brief, they reached New York City,
and there recovered one hundred and forty-five thousand dollars in money,
and Hancock gave his note to Lee for fifteen thousand dollars, payable
three months thereafter at Nashville, Tennessee.

The party returned to Cincinnati, bringing the money in two large trunks,
which were so heavy that Lee feared they would excite suspicion, and there
telegraphed back to New York respecting the exchange of the gold for
Southern scrip, or something that would answer the purposes of the owner.
Mr. Ellis and Judge Trigg parted from Lee at Cincinnati, and the latter
came on to Louisville with the money, as related in the beginning of this
chapter.

So much for the story of John W. Lee, told to our confidence-man, the
Confederate surgeon. The latter heartily sympathized with his friend, and
with the Southern owner, who, he hoped, would yet get his money from
the Federal clutches. The surgeon remarked,—

"I have a heartfelt interest in your case. I am a native of Georgia.
I know Thomas L. Metcalf, of Augusta, well, and he is a true, uncompromising friend of the South. He is very wealthy,—a heavy cotton-dealer
and ship-owner, &c. When the war broke out, Mr. Metcalf raised and
equipped a company called the Metcalf Guards, which company fought at
the first battle of Bull Run, and was, sad to say, almost annihilated."

"I am pleased to hear this," replied Lee, "and that Mr. Metcalf has
another friend here. But one thing let me caution you about: don't
breathe a word here about his Southern Rights course, as you respect
him and love the cause. Be very careful; for I shall now insist that he is a
good Union man, and think that I can thus get his money back and save my
portion of it."

The surgeon of the Confederacy promised faithfully to be silent on that
point. It was also further arranged that he would at once go to Bowling
Green, see Major-General Rosecrans, get his exchange papers adjusted,
and return to Louisville, when Lee would have letters ready for Mr. Met-

calf explaining the ills that had happened to their plan, which letters were to be taken to the sunny South by the surgeon.

The story is told. Mr. Lee saw the surgeon no more ; nor did his old steamboat friend again turn up. His money is now in possession of the United States Government, and the trial of the case is pending, we believe, in the United States District Court at Louisville. When we last heard from John W. Lee, the good Union man, he had feed a lawyer for ten thousand dollars to win the case, at Washington, where he expected to get back his bargained share, thirty-three per cent. of the sum total. This statement is compiled from the evidence of the two witnesses,—the surgeon and Mr. Ellis of Kentucky,—and, if the facts are as thus stated, Mr. Lee will have a happy time of it in recovering his percentage.

A Nest of Nashville Smugglers.

For many weary months after its occupation by the Federal army, Nashville was the great centre to which thronged all the hordes of smugglers, spies, and secret plotters of treason, whom a love of treachery or of gain had drawn to the rebel cause. The aid and encouragement received from the wealthy Secessionists of the city enabled them securely and successfully to carry out their designs, which, added to its proximity to the heart of the Confederacy, made it a peculiarly advantageous base of operation. Through them, lines of communication were kept open to every part of the South, and the rebel army supplied with valuable goods and still more valuable information. Their shrewdness and secrecy seemed to defy every attempt at detection. The regular pickets, do what they would, found it impossible to prevent the transportation of contraband goods beyond the lines ; and it was only when mounted policemen were stationed on every road leading from the city that a noticeable decrease in the operations of these aiders and abettors of the rebellion became apparent. As an illustration of the beneficial effects of the new arrangement, and to show to what great results a trifling circumstance will sometimes lead, the case of the three Friedenbergs and the developments to which it gave rise are here narrated.

On Sunday, the 28th of December, 1862, as two of these policemen were patrolling the Murfreesborough pike, they saw coming towards the city a buggy in which were seated three men. At first glance there was nothing to distinguish them from ordinary travellers ; but when they had drawn near enough to see the policemen, the youngest and smallest of the three jumped from the buggy and made for the woods with desperate speed. This, of course, excited suspicion, and he was at once pursued, but unavailingly. His two companions, however, were halted and sent under guard to the police-office. An examination of themselves and vehicle revealed the presence of nothing contraband ; the only thing found upon them being several hundred dollars in Southern money. Their names, they said, were Besthoff and Friedenberg. They had been engaged in merchandizing at Atlanta, Georgia, before the war, and had remained there until recently. Finding they could no longer keep out of the rebel army, they determined to escape; had closed out their stock at what it would bring, and with the proceeds were now on their way North. Of the young man with them when first seen, they either could or would say nothing more than that he was a stranger whom they had found at Murfreesborough, and who had begged a passage in their buggy to Nashville. Such was the substance of a very pitiable story of hardships, suffering, and heavy losses, related with much volubility and feeling, and, there being no evidence contradictory of it, or warranting their further detention,—whatever private reasons there may have been to suspect its truth,—they were released.

Attention was again directed to the young man—or boy, rather—who had escaped. His hasty flight indicated something wrong, and detectives were put upon his track. For several days nothing was heard of him; but one morning he was seen gliding stealthily through an alley in the city, and, chase being made, was this time soon caught. He was found to be a German Jew, not yet sixteen years old, but bright and quick-witted far beyond what is usual at such an age. An examination at the police-office disclosed upon his person about six hundred dollars, which was taken from him. On being questioned, he said that his name was James Wilson; that he formerly lived in Cleveland, East Tennessee, but had been peddling in Atlanta, Georgia. His story was much the same as that of Friedenberg and Besthoff; he had sold his goods, was anxious to get away and go to Germany, was tired of the business, had lost heavily, &c. As in the case of the others, this was reasonable enough in itself, and he was about to be released, when a gentleman sitting in the office—formerly a resident in the South, but now in the army police service—called Colonel Truesdail to one side, and said to him,—

"That boy is lying to you,—is telling you a series of lies right along. I know him, and know who and what he is. I saw him at Murfreesborough peddling contraband goods, where he was generally known to be a smuggler, and I recognized him at once while he was talking to you."

"Take him into another room, then," said the colonel, "and work upon him. Talk sharp to him; tell him that you know all about him, and how you know it. Convince him that you have seen him in the South and know what he was doing there, and then tell him that if he will own up, tell all he knows about these smuggling operations, and disclose the names of those engaged in it, we will return him his money and let him off without punishment; but, if he won't do that, we'll keep his money and send him to the penitentiary."

This was done; but the boy still persisted for some time in his original story. Finding, however, that he really was known, and that it was likely to fare hard with him, he finally yielded and made a new statement, which was in substance as follows.

His name, he still said, was James Wilson,—this was afterward found to be untrue,—and he had been living in Cleveland, as he first stated, for two years. He was a native of Germany, and his parents still resided there. About two months since he came to Nashville,—purchased goods, succeeded in smuggling them through the Federal lines, and took them to Atlanta, Georgia, where he sold them. The goods were purchased of Staddler & Brother, No. 2 Public Square, and Kleinman & Co., on Market Street, and consisted entirely of fine combs, for which he paid one dollar and twenty-five cents per dozen. These he packed in two satchels, and, wishing to get them out of the city, was introduced to one F. W. Keller, residing about one and a half miles out on the Zollicoffer Road, who took him and his goods out to his house the same evening, with his children, as he carried them home from school. Keller also took out with him at the same time a box of goods which he said he had bought of the Friedenbergs. For helping him out, Wilson paid Keller fifty dollars, and received from him the next morning a note to one Avis Brown, in which it was stated that the bearer was a smuggler who wished to get away as soon as possible, and requesting Brown to assist him in doing so. From Keller's Wilson made his way, partly on foot and partly on a horse which he purchased on the road, to Brown's, who received him kindly and showed him the way. Thence he went to Franklin and Murfreesborough, where he sold his horse and took the cars for Atlanta. Here he sold the combs for one dollar each, and then returned by rail to Murfreesborough, where he met Friedenberg and Besthoff, with whom he came to Nashville, arriving there—or rather in sight of the policemen—on Sunday, the 28th of December. This trip occupied about twelve days, and proved very profitable to him; and it was now his intention to go home to Germany.

Respecting others engaged in smuggling goods through the lines, he said that he knew a Mr. Wolff, living in Atlanta, who had recently purchased an assortment of buttons, needles, pins, gold lace, &c., which he had carried out in a two-horse wagon that had a false bottom to the bed, and taken to Chattanooga, where the witness had assisted in unloading them. One A. Haas had a two-horse carryall with a false bottom, and had the previous month taken in it a load of goods from Nashville to Atlanta, where he also resided. The false bottom, he said, was put into the carryall in Nashville. Leo Cohen also had a false-bottomed wagon, which he had made in Nashville, and with which he had smuggled a load of contraband articles to Atlanta. About three months ago, a man living at Selma, Alabama, had come to Nashville and purchased two wagon-loads of goods, which he took through the lines with him to Chattanooga, whence he made his way to Selma. He knew, he said, further, that Schwab & Co., a heavy firm in Nashville, had been engaged in smuggling, but not to what extent. As to the Friedenbergs, &c., he did not know, of his own knowledge, that they had been running goods through the Federal lines, but he did know that Abraham Friedenberg had on several occasions taken goods to the South from Nashville, and had seen him in Murfreesborough and Chattanooga with them, and he knew that they were the goods which he had seen loaded into a two-horse wagon, furnished with a false bottom, at the store of B. F. Shields & Co., in Nashville, and he was afterwards told by Friedenberg that they had been sold by him in Chattanooga and Atlanta. These were the only persons engaged in contraband trade of whom he had any knowledge.

Having thus fully revealed these matters, the boy was released, his money returned to him, and himself sent North. The information given by him was at once improved by the arrest of Keller, at whose house was found and seized a large amount of dry goods and clothing. Keller, upon his examination, stated that about five weeks previously he had come to the city to sell some butter, and while at the market was approached by two Jews named Friedenberg, who inquired where he lived. On being informed, they asked him if he could not take out to his house some goods for them, for which service they would pay him well. After some conversation, and on being assured that there was no danger in it, he agreed to take them out, and came the next day, as requested, with his wagon for them. The Friedenbergs loaded the wagon with a large quantity of hoop-skirts and several small boxes and bundles of unknown goods. These he carried to his house, and the same evening another Jew, named Besthoff, came out with a new wagon, drawn by two mules. Stopping there a few minutes, he went down the road, and, returning the next morning, informed Keller that he had taken down a load of goods in that wagon, concealed by a false bottom. He then requested the Jew to take the goods from his house, or he would throw them out into the yard. Besthoff said he would come back and get them on his return from the city in an hour or so,—which he did,—loading them into the same wagon which he had with him on the day previous, and giving him at the same time an order on Friedenberg, written in Hebrew, for his pay. This order was presented the next day, and the amount—five hundred dollars— promptly paid by Friedenberg, who remarked that they would make fifteen thousand dollars on that load. There were three Friedenbergs, all of whom were in the habit of going out on the same pass which Besthoff had used, and which was in one of the Friedenbergs' name. Whoever used it would leave it at Keller's house, and he would take it back to town for the others.

At one of his visits to these Friedenbergs they induced him to take three boxes of gray caps out and go with them to Murfreesborough, saying that he could sell them there for five or six dollars each, and that they would divide the profits with him. About ten days before Christmas he went with the caps to Murfreesborough, where he found great difficulty in disposing of them at all, but finally closed them out for one dollar each, in Confederate scrip, which realized about seventy cents to the dollar. Here he met Besthoff and Friedenberg, the latter of whom informed him that he was then going to Atlanta, but that he would soon return, and would then want more goods brought through the lines. Returning on Christmas day, Keller went immediately to see the other Friedenbergs, who told him that they would furnish him some goods to take out and sell, which would pay a great profit. The arrangement proposed was that he should pay them the cost-price of the goods when he took them to his house, and that they would pay him his money back, and fifty per cent. in addition, when the goods should be delivered to their partner, the other Friedenberg, on his return from the South. To these terms he agreed, and took out the goods which were found at his house and seized there, and for which he had advanced over nine hundred dollars. Abraham Friedenberg returned to Nashville, but, instead of coming for the goods, as promised, went to Louisville, and the other Friedenbergs then said that they would send somebody else to get them; but before they could do so their arrangements were broken in upon by his arrest and the seizure of the goods. The Friedenbergs and Besthoff were all partners,—they had told him so, many times; also that they were smugglers, and did nothing else. The goods which he carried out were sometimes taken under a quilt or blanket in his market-wagon; or sometimes he would put the boxes under bundles of oats; and when they were large he would throw manure over them. He made five trips to bring out the goods, for which they paid him the five hundred dollars. At the time he was about to start for Murfreesborough with the caps he did not keep it a secret, and about that time he met one Salzkotter, who requested him to say to his partner Schwab, if he met him, not to come back, for if he did the Yankees would catch him. Besthoff had told him that this same Schwab had made twenty thousand dollars on hats which he had smuggled through the Federal lines in feather beds, and that he and his firm—Schwab & Co.—had been engaged in the same kind of business ever since the war began.

Keller also related the history of his acquaintance with the boy Wilson, whose real name, as he had been informed by Friedenberg, was Solomon Guthman. This did not differ much from the boy's own statement, but contained the additional information that Wilson was connected with the Friedenbergs, always procured his goods from them, and seemed to be one of them. He had made five thousand dollars, he boasted to Keller, by smuggling goods through the lines, and he was now going on to Philadelphia to buy another stock, on which he would make five thousand dollars more. Keller stated, in conclusion, that he was a vegetable gardener, and had been doing well before the rebellion, but had found it impossible to make a living since. He had been driven into this business through sheer poverty and ignorance: he had no wish or design to injure the Government,—was not in favor of the rebellion. By the seizure of the goods he had lost every thing he had; and, as they did not really belong to him, but to the Friedenbergs, by whom he had been inveigled into carrying them to his house, he hoped that the military authorities would force them to refund him his money, or a portion of it, at least.

In consideration of all the circumstances, and believing that Keller did not engage in the business for the purpose of aiding the rebellion, but rather through actual fear of coming to want, and that he might be made of some service to the Government, it was proposed to him that he should turn around and assist in developing the case against the Friedenbergs and Besthoff, so as to secure their punishment and the confiscation of their goods. If he would do this, and work faithfully, he was promised that he should not be a loser by it, but should be remunerated for the money he had advanced to the Friedenbergs. Keller gladly accepted the offer, and went to work at once, following the matter up diligently and faithfully, and since then has been almost constantly employed in the secret service. Through his instrumentality Isaac and Mike Friedenberg were arrested, and some nine hundred dollars in money, besides personal property, as watches, &c. were found upon their persons and seized. Diligent search was made for Abraham Friedenberg and Besthoff; but they had gone to Louisville to purchase goods, and, by some means hearing of the affair, made good their escape. At the same time a large stock of goods, valued at between four and five thousand dollars, stored in the auction and commission house of B. F. Shields & Co., was seized as the property of the Friedenbergs. Isaac Friedenberg, when arrested, had little to say, further than to admit that he had sold the goods to Keller, but claiming that he did not know that the latter intended to smuggle them through the lines, though he did know that Keller had previously taken goods to Murfreesborough to sell. Mike Friedenberg, however, made quite a lengthy statement, which resulted in the arrest of still other parties, and was in brief somewhat thus:—

In March, 1857, he went to Columbus, Georgia, and remained there, engaged in merchandizing with his brother Isaac, until March, 1862, when he came to Nashville. The reason of his leaving Columbus was that he did not wish to enter the rebel army, and could not longer remain there without doing so. He had not been back since leaving there, and his business there was still in an unsettled condition. His brother Isaac was at that time in Richmond, whither he had gone when the Federal army occupied Nashville, and had written to him as he was about leaving Columbus to stop at Nashville and take charge of the balance of a stock of goods which he had left there. This he did, moving them first into the store of a Mr. Stein, and. on the latter's leaving for New York, to the store of Shields & Co., where he began selling them out. On the 16th of June, 1862, he was taken sick, and for two months was unable to attend to any business. Just before this, however, Isaac had returned from Richmond, and proceeded immediately to New York to buy more goods. He returned, however, without any, and Mike, on recovering, went himself to New York, and remained there two months, when he again came to Nashville, reaching there on the 28th of November, 1862. In the mean time his brother Isaac had bought of two parties in Nashville a considerable stock of boots, shoes, hats, caps, and gentlemen's furnishing goods, which he then had in Shields's store, and which he said belonged to himself, Mike, and their nephew, Abraham Friedenberg. After his return from New York, Mike himself purchased from A. Laob & Co. a lot of hats, which were still in the store of Shields & Co. when seized by the police. Abraham Friedenberg was in partnership with himself—Isaac— some five or six weeks, and then left them and went with Besthoff; but what they did he did not know. One day Abraham Friedenberg came to him and wished him to buy him a wagon and two mules, which he did, paying for them four hundred and seventy dollars. The next day Besthoff came and requested him to get Mr. Smith, a carpenter, to make a false bottom to the wagon. He said Mr. Smith knew all about making it, and that when it was finished he—Besthoff—would call for it. Smith agreed to make, and did make, the false bottom, as he desired, and Friedenberg afterwards saw it in the wagon. Keller's arrangement for carrying goods out to his house was entirely with Besthoff and Abraham Friedenberg. He carried out five or six loads for them, and Abraham Friedenberg furnished the five hundred dollars to pay him. Besthoff and A. Friedenberg loaded their own wagon— the one with the false bottom—twice, and went with it into the country, where they remained until December 28, when they returned, and in two or three days afterwards went North. Through them he became acquainted with Keller, and sold him seventy-four dozen fine combs, which cost one dollar and fifty cents per dozen, for two and a half or three dollars a dozen, eighteen pounds of flax thread, and some other goods.

This testimony of Mike Friedenberg led to the arrest of John L. Smith, who made the false bottoms, and who stated, on examination, that he was a carpenter, and had a shop on the corner of Lime and High Streets. In the latter part of February or about the 1st of March, 1862, a Mr. Salzkotter, of the firm of Schwab & Co., merchants of Nashville, called at the shop and requested him to make a false bottom in a light spring-wagon, and afterwards sent the wagon to the shop, where the bottom was made and put in. The way in which it was made was this. Side-pieces were put on each side of the bed inside, and one through the centre, the whole length, and on these pieces planed boards were secured, leaving between the two floors a vacant space of from two and a half to three inches. When finished, Salzkotter himself came after the wagon and took it away, but neither at this nor at any other time did he say for what purpose he intended to use it. Since then he had made five or six similar ones for other parties, all of whom had been introduced by this same firm of Schwab & Co. He objected to making them at first, but finally was induced to do so, though he knew it to be wrong. Salzkotter paid him five dollars for the job; Haas, the only one of the other parties whose name he could remember, paid him ten, and the remainder fifteen dollars. After the wagon for Salzkotter was finished, and before he took it away, he sent to the shop a dray loaded with boxes, the contents of which he said he wished to pack into his wagon. Smith gave him the key of the shop; and during the night they were unloaded and packed,—as the wagon was gone in the morning, and the boxes were there empty. Mr. Smith did not know what was in these boxes; but Mahlon Jones, one of his workmen, testified that he helped remove them from the dray, and, in so doing, one of them fell upon the ground and was broken open, exposing the contents, which were quinine and other medicines.

It was now Salzkotter's turn to receive the attention of the police, as a smuggler and dealer in false-bottomed wagon-beds; and some three or four thousand dollars' worth of liquors and domestics were seized as belonging to him. He was immensely indignant, of course, and unblushingly endeavored to lie out of the scrape in which he found himself. When questioned, he stated most positively that he had been keeping books for Schwab & Co. in

Nashville for three years, until some three months previous, when the store was closed. He had never been in partnership with Schwab. The firm—composed of Schwab and his brother-in-law, H. Dreyfoos—owed him some four thousand to five thousand dollars, for which he held their notes. Schwab and his partner had both left the city, and he believed them to be in Knoxville, where they had ·a branch house. They had left him about one thousand dollars' worth of liquors to sell for them, and he had sold all but about two hundred dollars' worth. He also had some two hundred dollars' worth of liquors of his own, which they had given him in settlement. He had never had made, for himself or anybody else, a wagon, carriage, or vehicle of any description, with a false bottom, and he did not know anybody who had. He had never bought any wagon for himself or other person, nor had he been, directly or indirectly, connected with anybody in running goods through the lines to the enemy or to any disloyal persons. Schwab & Co. had had considerable trade with the South, but it was all before the war. Their books and papers were left with him to settle up, and he was to pay himself out of the proceeds. He never knew of Schwab having had a wagon or carriage made for carrying goods through the lines. He knew Mr. Smith, the carpenter, but had never visited his shop for the purpose of having a false bottom made to a wagon or other vehicle. Of the other parties who had testified concerning them he knew nothing. When asked by Colonel Truesdail if he would make oath to this statement, he rose from his chair and said he would. The colonel, however, would not allow him thus to perjure himself, but immediately called up the witnesses Smith and Jones, who reiterated in his presence their former statements, and identified him as the man whom they called Salzkotter and who had several times been to the shop for the purpose of having the false bottoms made.

Mike Friedenberg was then called in, and, in the presence of Salzkotter, stated that his nephew, Abraham Friedenberg, told him to go to Mr. Salzkotter's store and inquire of him who could be hired to make a false bottom to a wagon. Accordingly, he went to Salzkotter one Saturday, some five or six weeks before, and made the inquiry, to which the latter replied that he would introduce him to a Mr. Smith who would make it, but that Smith would not make it if he went to him alone. After supper he called on Salzkotter by invitation, and together they went to Smith's, to whom he was introduced, and with whom, in Salzkotter's presence, he made an arrangement for the making of the false bottom. This testimony being rather damaging, Salzkotter endeavored to weaken it by a cross-examination ; but Friedenberg still persisted in his statement, and further said that the wagons were made for the express purpose of smuggling.

The complicity of Salzkotter in the wagon-bed transaction was now fully established ; and witnesses were next examined to prove that both he and the house of Schwab & Co. had been extensively engaged in smuggling goods through to the rebels. Edward Speckel testified that he lived in Nashville, knew Salzkotter well, and that the latter had told him some five months previously that he had been smuggling goods from Louisville to

Nashville. They were principally quinine and other medicines; and he had made eighteen hundred dollars on one trip. The goods were taken by a carriage to a way-station some distance from Louisville, and thence shipped by rail to Nashville. Near Louisville he just escaped detection by saying that the trunks contained only the clothing belonging to a family who were to join him at the station. Salzkotter said that his father-in-law, Schwab, had taken the goods South from Nashville and sold them, he being a partner in the transaction. He further said that he had been South himself before this occurred, and that he had cleared eighteen hundred dollars by the trip,—of which he had one half and Schwab the other. He had often remarked, laughingly, that they could make more money than the Union men, and seemed to make no secret of his sending goods to the South.

David Kuhn, who had lived in Knoxville eight years, testified that he knew the firm of Schwab & Co. Salzkotter was connected with them in some way, but he did not know whether he had an interest in the store or not. In Knoxville they sold liquors, cigars, and notions, but they had closed their store some eight months before. It was the general belief, and he knew, that the house was engaged in smuggling goods through the Federal lines. He knew that they had brought goods from Nashville, but did not know that they had brought them in wagons with false bottoms. Both Schwab and Dreyfoos had told him they had smuggled goods through since they closed their store, and in October, 1862, Salzkotter came to Knoxville in a light spring-wagon, with goods, as was believed. His reputation was that of a smuggler.

William Müller, who was formerly a clerk for Schwab & Co., corroborated Kuhn's testimony, and added that it was common report that Schwab & Co. and Salzkotter were in the habit of running goods through the lines by means of wagons having a false bottom. While clerking with them, he had heard the firm say that they were smuggling medicines and other goods through the lines; and he knew of pistols and knives having been sent to the Knoxville house of Schwab & Co. early in 1862. Salzkotter went to Knoxville in the summer of 1862; and it was the general report that he had taken goods with him. It was his impression that Salzkotter was a silent partner in the house, on account of having failed in business at Knoxville.

Salzkotter's case was now hopeless; and he seems at last to have given it up himself, as he made no further efforts to avert punishment by holding out against evidence so strong and positive. His liquors were turned over to the United States Marshal for libel and confiscation in the United States District Court, his domestic goods were put to immediate use in the hospitals, and he was sent to the Alton Military Prison, but has since been released, and is now again in Nashville. His money—of which he had some twenty-three thousand dollars—was not found, though long and thorough search was instituted for it. He admitted, however, afterwards, that the officers came within an inch or two of the place where it was secreted. In the case of the Friedenbergs, Isaac was imprisoned in irons for some time; but finally he and Mike were paroled not to come south of the Ohio River again during the war. Their goods seized in the act of smuggling were confiscated at once, and those in store at Shields & Co.'s were turned over to the United States Marshal for libel and confiscation in the District Court. Their watches and money, after deducting enough to repay Keller, were returned to them. Smith, the carpenter, was released without punishment.

Thus ended this remarkable case, or rather series of cases, all resulting from the trifling incident of a boy jumping from a buggy in which he was riding, and escaping to the woods. It disclosed a vast network of fraud and villainy, and resulted in the punishment of three persons, the pardon and subsequent good behavior of numbers of others, and the confiscation of some ten thousand dollars' worth of goods. But, more and better than all this, it demonstrated the sleepless vigilance of the Government in the discovery of guilt, however secret and well planned, and the heavy hand of justice not yet too weak to visit upon the violators of its laws the full penalty so deservedly prescribed. It taught a lesson which could not but be heeded, and disclosed a power which must be respected and feared, if not loved.

The Hollow-Heeled Boot.

IN the earlier days of the rebellion there lived in Southeastern Missouri one Ogilvie Byron Young. He was a wild, graceless scamp, rich in the blood of his ancestors, but poor in purse. To the pride of Lucifer he added the courage of Falstaff and the honor of Iago. A scion of Virginia's aristocracy, he deemed himself a statesman from birth and an orator by nature. Showy in manner and superficial in attainments, he could act the accomplished gentleman or the bullying braggart as best suited the occasion. Vain, reckless, and boastful, he was scorned as a visionary enthusiast by some, feared as a bold, bad man by others, but admired as a genuine Southern cavalier of the old school by those who knew him least. Wildly imaginative, but immensely unpractical, he plunged madly into the first waves of rebellion, and, while Sterling Price was yet a Union general and Claiborne F. Jackson a loyal Governor, dared to avow and advocate opinions of the most ultra-Southern character. Fine-drawn theoretical arguments on the right and duty of secession were spread before the people of the State, in column after column of letters published in newspapers and to which was attached the full signature, "Ogilvie Byron Young." The rough backwoodsmen of his county were momentarily swayed by his presumptuous clamor, and he was sent to the first Missouri State Convention. Here he was the only member that took strong ground in favor of secession *per se*, gaining thereby not a little notoriety. The State did not secede; but Ogilvie Byron Young *did*, and for some months he was not so much as heard from.

In the fall of 1861 he was arrested at the Spencer House, Cincinnati, as a spy. In due time an indictment and trial followed; but, though there was

abundant evidence of guilt, he escaped conviction by means of some tech-
nical informality in the proceedings. He was ordered to leave the city,
however, and did so. In the following spring he was found in Covington,
Kentucky, under an assumed name, aiding and abetting the rebels by furnishing information, and was again arrested. He had been cautioned by
some one, it would seem; for there was found nothing upon him in the way
of papers or letters to warrant his detention, and he was again released, to
again disappear from sight for some months.

In November, 1862, he is again met with, in Nashville, where he had been
for some weeks as a paroled prisoner, but acting all the while in his old
capacity of smuggler and spy. In this business he seems to have had
remarkable success, until his career was fortunately arrested by a combination of circumstances and the watchful shrewdness of the army police.
About the last of that month Young was introduced to a gentleman
who represented himself as a hostage for the return of certain loyal Mississippians captured at Iuka and treated by Price as traitors, contrary to the
terms of the cartel between the Federal and Confederate Governments. At
first he was shy and suspicious, but was finally convinced that his new
acquaintance was really what he purported to be, and heartily entered into
all his plans for the advancement of the Confederate cause. As his confidence grew stronger, he remarked that he had been of more benefit to the
South, as a spy, than any brigade of rebel soldiers. He had encouraged de-
sertions in the Federal camps, and made out paroles in the names of Morgan
and Kirby Smith. The business was getting a little dangerous now, however, and he should get beyond the lines as soon as possible. He would
have gone long ago, only that he had expected to be saved the trouble and
expense of the trip by the fall of Nashville.

Our Iuka hostage then informed him that Mrs. Major Ranney—wife of
Major Ranney of the 6th Texas Regiment—was in the city, under his
charge, and just returned from Europe, whither she had been on diplomatic
business for the Confederate Government. She had in her possession very
important despatches, and was anxious to get safely through the lines with
them. Young said, in reply, that he would bring his influence to bear upon
the army officials in her favor, but in case she should be searched it would
be well to provide for such a contingency. There was, he said, in the city
a man by the name of Thompson, ostensibly a citizen, but really a rebel
lieutenant in Bragg's army, and now acting as a spy. He had made the trip
through the lines ten or twelve times, and could do it again. He was now
engaged in drawing a map of the fortifications around Nashville and procuring information as to the numbers of the troops, &c., which should be
forthcoming in due season. These secret despatches of Mrs. Ranney's,
together with this map and other papers, could be hidden in the heel of a
boot, which would be made for them by a bootmaker of the city in the
employ of the Confederate Government. His name was C. J. Zeutzschell,
and his shop was on Union Street.

This plan was agreed to, and Young was to assist in the execution of it;

in return for which, he was to be placed in a high position at Richmond. Young's reputation, however, was not of the best, and the bootmaker would do nothing for him, when called upon, without first making inquiries among his friends and consulting with our hostage, for whom the boots were wanted.

Accordingly, Zeutzschell came to his room one evening and said that Young had been to his house and wished him to make a pair of boots and to secrete important documents in them so as to defy detection. He had no confidence in Young's honor, and did not wish to do it for *him*. He knew him as identified with the Confederates, indeed, but he was a bad man, low in his habits and associates, never had any money, &c. He (Zeutzschell) had been inquiring of the *friends* of the South—undoubted secessionists—concerning him (our Iuka hostage), and was convinced that he was a gentleman and a true Southerner. He would do any thing to promote the cause,—money was no object,—he would lay down his life for it. If Young could be thrown off the track, he would make the boots and secrete in them a map of the fortifications about Nashville. His brother-in-law, Harris, would go out and see if any new ones had been erected. If not, he had a perfect plan of them in his head, to prove which he immediately sat down and drafted one. He remarked that he had recently sent several such to General Morgan. He had made the boots for all the spies in the same way, and not one had ever been detected. He had sent valuable information in a common pipe.

"Can you get a pass for your man?" asked our hostage. "Certainly," was the reply; "as many as you like. There is a German at head-quarters who steals blank passes for me, and I fill them up myself. I give him whiskey for them."

He would like to go South, too, he said, in conclusion. He could describe the fortifications so much better than in a map.

Both parties being satisfied, an agreement for the boots was made. Zeutzschell was to get the exact distances of the defences, the number and disposition of the troops, &c., and secrete them, together with Mrs. Ranney's despatches, in the heel of one of the boots. This he did, according to promise: the boots were made and delivered on the evening appointed. Instead of reaching Generals Bragg and Morgan, as intended, however, the maps, papers, boots, owner, maker, and spy, suddenly found themselves in the hands of the army police, much to the astonishment and chagrin of all parties concerned. Zeutzschell and Young were sent to the military prison at Alton.

The Pseudo "Sanders."

PROMINENT among those thronging the head-quarters of Brigadier-General Boyle, in the city of Louisville, one morning in November, 1862, might have been noticed a bright, handsome woman, who seemed exceedingly anxious for the success of some suit in which she was engaged. Her dress and manner indicated that she belonged to the higher walks of life, but otherwise there was nothing in her conduct or appearance by which a careless observer would distinguish her from the hundreds of others who daily gather at the office of a commanding general, seeking favors as numerous and diverse as the applicants themselves. The practised eye, however, could easily discern certain suspicious circumstances attaching to her and suggestive of the idea that beneath all this pleasant exterior there might be an under-current of deceit and treachery. But her story was plausible, her manners winning, her conversation sprightly and interesting. The impression made by her upon all with whom she came in contact was in the highest degree favorable, and it seemed both ungallant and unjust to harbor the shadow of a suspicion that she was otherwise than a high-minded, honorable woman, who would scorn any of the petty meannesses of such frequent occurrence within our lines.

It subsequently transpired that her name was Ford, that her husband was a Baptist clergyman,—a man of ability and reputation, formerly editor of a religious paper in that city, and now representative in the Confederate Congress from that district of Kentucky. She herself belonged to one of the first families of the city, and moved in the highest circles of an aristocratic society. To a naturally brilliant mind, strengthened and polished by a thorough education, were added the ease and grace of an accomplished Southern woman. In the palmy days of peace she had been the centre of a bright galaxy of wit and beauty, dispensing to her admirers a bounteous hospitality, as genial as it was welcome. Now all was changed. These social gatherings had long been discontinued, the family circle was broken and scattered, her husband was a fugitive from his home, and she was seeking from the Federal authorities permission to pass southward beyond their lines and join him in his exile.

Lounging about the same head-quarters, on the same morning, with seemingly no particular business or present occupation save to watch the movements of others, was a quiet-looking man, who now and then cast sharp, quick, and stealthy glances at this Mrs. Ford, apparently regarding her with much interest. Presently, seeing her somewhat apart from the crowd, he approached, and, in a respectful, diffident manner, engaged her in conversation, which continued for some time, and, from the animated character it gradually assumed, was evidently upon some subject in which both parties were deeply interested. That it was of a confidential and private nature was easily inferred from the caution maintained during its continuance. It seems that, after some commonplace talk, the stranger informed her that he was not what he then seemed, but in reality Captain Denver, of the Confederate army, visiting Louisville as a spy upon the movements of the Federal army in that portion of Kentucky. Highly gratified at this intelligence, the lady became very friendly, and at once invited the captain to visit her house. The invitation so warmly given could not be declined without apparent rudeness, and so was accepted, but with, as the lady thought, a rather unnecessary and suspicious hesitation.

Whatever unwillingness the captain may have outwardly exhibited in accepting the proffered invitation, he was not slow in availing himself of its present privileges and prospective pleasures. Calling soon afterwards at the residence indicated, he was cordially received by the family, whom he found strong in their sympathy with the South. Conversation naturally turned upon the war, and by a warm espousal of the Confederate cause he soon succeeded in ingratiating himself into their confidence, and, by way of showing *his* confidence in them, revealed his intention of presently escaping through the Federal lines to the nearest Confederate command, taking with him as large an amount of quinine, morphine, and other medicines as he could safely carry. Confidence thus implicitly reposed in the acquaintance of but a few hours could not be otherwise than pleasing to the fair hostess; and surely a reciprocal confidence would be little enough expression of gratitude in return. It was not safe; it was not wise; but "there can be no harm in trusting so true and firm a Southerner as Captain Denver," thought Mrs. Ford.

It was her purpose too, she said, to smuggle through the lines large quantities of medicine, and at the same time carry to the Confederate authorities valuable information of Federal movements and plans. Her husband was in the South, and she apprehended no difficulty in procuring a pass allowing her to go to him, so soon as the circumstances of her case could be brought to the personal notice of General Boyle. The enterprise in which both were about to engage now became the exclusive topic of a lengthy conversation, in the course of which the captain remarked that he had not sufficient money to make as extensive purchases as he wished, and was desirous of assistance from the friends of the cause in Louisville. Mrs. Ford thought this need not trouble him. She could arrange it to his satisfaction, and appointed an interview for the next morning, at which she hoped to report the complete success of her efforts. The evening passed rapidly, and the captain took his departure, leaving his entertainers highly pleased with him as a valuable acquaintance and colaborer in the cause of the South.

The same evening the captain chanced to meet in the office of the Galt House an old friend, Dr. Rogers, surgeon on the staff of General Sterling Price, a paroled prisoner, and now, by order of General Rosecrans, on his way to Cairo to report to General Tuttle for transportation by the first boat to Vicksburg. According to the terms of the cartel agreed upon by the Federal and Confederate authorities, surgeons were held as non-combatants and not subject to exchange; but the doctors, with others, found in the hospital at Iuka, had been detained by General Rosecrans, in retaliation for the arrest and imprisonment by General Price of certain Union soldiers in Mississippi, and as hostages for their return. Their release had been followed by his; and he was now, as stated, *en route* for Cairo. At their meeting the next morning, Captain Denver mentioned the doctor to Mrs. Ford as his friend and an intelligent and accomplished gentleman, with whom she would no doubt be highly pleased, at the same time remarking that he was on his way South, and it would be greatly to their advantage to go thither under his protection. To this she readily assented, and desired the captain to procure her an interview with the doctor. This not very difficult task was speedily accomplished, and the doctor called upon her that evening. Some time having passed in conversational pleasantry, the doctor adverted to the carrying of contraband goods, and spoke discouragingly of its policy, saying that any thing of the kind would be a violation of his parole and might lead to his arrest and imprisonment. With apparent sincerity, Mrs. Ford promptly replied that though an enemy of the Federal Government she was an honorable enemy, and would engage in no enterprise to which the military authorities would refuse their sanction.

The doctor seemed satisfied, and did not revert to the subject, but, instead, imparted to her, in strict confidence, a secret of the utmost importance. It will be remembered that some months previous to this, George N. Sanders had successfully escaped from the rebel States and made his way to England for the purpose of negotiating a Confederate loan. High hopes of success, on his part, were entertained, and his return was anxiously looked for by the rebels. Mrs. Ford, with her whole heart and soul in the cause, was more sanguine even than her most sanguine friends; and imagination can scarcely conceive the bright colors with which she painted the future of the embryo Confederacy. Who, then, shall describe her surprise and joy when told by the doctor that their friend Captain Denver was no other than this same George N. Sanders, who had eluded the guard at the Suspension Bridge and was now on his return to the Confederate capital? She was also informed that his mission had been completely successful,—that the loan had been taken by the Rothschilds, and that Sanders had in possession the evidence and documents connected therewith, all written in cipher. She was cautioned against hinting a word of it to anybody, or even intimating to Sanders that she knew him in any other character than as Captain Denver. He would accompany them to Vicksburg in his present disguise, and, until that point was reached, safety required that it should be penetrated by no one, however friendly to the South. The interests at stake were too vast to be hazarded by exposure to a mischance, which a single careless word might bring upon them. In case, however, he should be suspected, it would be their business to assist him in the secretion of his papers.

The arrangements for the journey were discussed, and the suggestion of the doctor warmly espoused by Mrs. Ford. Her eyes sparkled with delight as she asked a thousand questions about Sanders: how he had managed to escape the vigilance of the Federals; by what means he had accomplished his mission; what was the state of feeling in Europe, the prospects of recognition, and so on. The doctor answered as best he could, and at length took his leave to make final preparations to start the next evening. Passes were obtained, tickets bought, trunks checked, berths secured in the sleeping-car. Every thing bade fair for the successful termination of the enterprise. The night was passed comfortably in sleep, from which they were wakened, on arriving at Cairo, to find themselves under arrest. Denver and Rogers were indignant, but Mrs. Ford trembled like an aspen-leaf, and had the earth opened under her feet, revealing a bottomless chasm in which she must inevitably be buried alive, she could not have been more astonished and horrified. She could find neither tongue nor heart to utter a word in defence, and was led away in silence. A personal examination brought to light a number of letters and a large quantity of quinine concealed about her clothes. The trunks were found to contain similar contraband goods and much information of value to the rebels. Grieving will not restore lost opportunities, nor bring to the surface sunken treasures: else had not the hopes of Mrs. Ford been thus ruthlessly dashed to the ground, her letters and goods fallen into the hands of her enemies, and the riches of the Confederate loan taken to themselves wings and flown away.

After a protracted investigation, Mrs. Ford was sent South,—since which time she has engaged in the business of publishing a book giving an account of her experience and treatment under Federal rule. Captain Denver, *alias* George N. Sanders, *alias* Conklin, it is needless to say, was simply a member of the detective police of the Army of the Cumberland, and Dr. Rogers, of Price's staff, also a member of the same corps.

Dr. Hudson the Smuggler, etc.

THE stroller about Nashville and its vicinity, in some of his more extended walks, may have noticed, on the summit of a considerable elevation about three hundred yards north of the Penitentiary, a large white house, half hidden in a beautiful grove of sugar-maples. The broad grounds in front, with their well-filled flower-beds, winding walks, and neatly trimmed shrubbery, tell of wealth and taste combined. Apart from the business portion of the town, with its constant hum, the air is redolent of perfume. Even the winds, seemingly, pause to dally in luxurious idleness with the cedar-boughs, and from the birds in the heavy-leaved magnolias are heard the notes of gladness. Surely here, if anywhere, under the shade and in the quiet of these magnificent trees, one could spend a life of happy content, alike ignorant and careless of the noisy world beyond.

In character with the house and its surroundings was the family that dwelt within, a few short months ago. Its head—Dr. J. R. Hudson—was a large, stalwart man, whose whitened hair and beard would have indicated that fifty-odd years of life had weighed none too lightly upon him, had not the signs of present comfort been visible in every feature of his cheerful face. And, indeed, he had but few of the world's troubles to breast. The possessor of an elegant residence, and the proprietor of extensive iron-works near Harpeth Shoals, with three thousand acres of land attached thereto, and the owner of slaves and other property, he could now well afford to sit beneath his own vine and fig-tree, secure in the full possession of his ample fortune, and look out almost unconcernedly upon the wild waves of rebellion's stormy sea. His wife—a comely and interesting lady—was much younger and smaller than himself, but not less the embodiment of an untroubled and self-satisfied mind. A bright, keen eye told of acuteness and penetration, to which even her liege lord, physically great as he was, must bend the knee of inferiority. Three daughters, and a son, the youngest of all, constituted the family then at home. Two of the daughters were young ladies grown, and the third was just on the verge of womanhood: they were attractive in feature and manner, and possessed of many of those graceful accomplishments which mark the perfect woman.

To such a family, dwelling amid such scenes of beauty, and in the enjoyment of all that earthly riches could give, it would seem that the future could not well be otherwise than an unruffled sea of happiness. But life, like an ocean-voyage, is full of uncertainties. And so with this household. At the very moment in which we have looked in upon them, they were treading upon the threshold of a great disaster. But we will not anticipate, further than to say that the story about to be told is a striking illustration of that wild spirit which will peril all the blessings and comforts of life to gratify a reckless malice and hate.

One afternoon in the first week of January, 1863, the doctor was visited by a young lady, a Miss Roberta Samuels, a rebel sympathizer of Nashville, in company with a young man whom she introduced as one of Ashby's cavalrymen and a Confederate spy. In the most gracious manner the doctor expressed his gratification at having such a guest under his roof. The call being one of mere introduction, the visitor took his leave after about an hour's conversation, in which his host somewhat guardedly expressed sympathy for the Southern cause, and invited him to call again and often. In three or four days the spy called again,—this time in the morning, remaining until after dinner. The doctor, for some reason, was more communicative than on the previous visit, and, by way of showing his hearty good will towards the Confederacy, related the story of his assisting some fourteen rebel prisoners to escape from the penitentiary at Nashville through the Federal lines. On a very dark night, he said, they came to his house, where he secreted them until the way was clear, when he took them into the fields, pointed out the Federal picket-fires, and showed them where they could slip by in the darkness without being seen. By one of them—Samuel Y. Brown—he had also sent out a fine revolving rifle and pistol and various other articles. He turned to his visitor, and asked,—

"Of what does your command stand in most need?"

"Pistols and ammunition," was the reply. "And it is the principal part of my business here to-day to make arrangements with you to get a supply and have them run through the lines. You can help me, can't you?"

"I am just the man to do it," said he, earnestly, clapping his hand on the knee of his companion. "How many can you manage to carry out? I can get you as many as you want."

"I can get through with fifty, I think."

"Well, I'll look around and see about them. The next time you come I'll let you know, and I doubt not it will be all right."

The second day after, the doctor was again visited by this friend, who brought with him a Mr. Walker, whom he introduced as a paroled Confederate prisoner. They were gladly welcomed, and presented to the family in the sitting-room. The doctor remarked that he had been too busy since the last call to do any thing about the pistols, but he hoped "to get to work at it soon." He interested himself also in Mr. Walker's case, and asked him if he did not wish to get away from Nashville by running through the lines, without waiting to be exchanged.

"If you do," said he, confidently, "I can get you through any time you want to go. I can pass you out as one of the hands employed in my iron-works down on the Cumberland River, or I can send you out as a carriage-driver or wood-chopper. I have passed out several in these ways; and sometimes I give a man an axe to go out to chop wood, and he quite forgets to come back."

At this witticism all had a hearty laugh; and a still more lengthy and confidential conversation ensued, developing, however, nothing materially different from the points already touched upon. Highly pleased, the party at length broke up, with the promise on the part of the two Confederates to call again in a week or ten days and make further arrangements about the pistols, &c.

This appointment was kept according to agreement,—the two friends walking out to the residence one cold, rainy evening. They found that the doctor had a visitor before them,—one Captain Redman, a Federal quartermaster. This, of course, precluded the further transaction of the business on which they came, and might have embarrassed a less politic man than Dr. Hudson. He met the difficulty boldly, introduced them to the captain as workmen from his iron-works, questioned them as to affairs there, asked them if they had passes to go back, talked to them as Union men, and took every occasion to mock and jeer at the rebels and their cause, slyly winking, however, the while, at the two Confederates. Accompanying them to the door, the doctor was told by the spy that he had just returned from the steamboat-burning expedition near Harpeth Shoals, and that the Confederates were greatly in need of pistols; they wanted fifty at once.

"You shall have them," he exclaimed, shaking his hand energetically. "I have some Federal Government vouchers, to the amount of several hundred dollars; I am expecting to get the money on them every day;

and with it I'll buy the pistols. When shall I meet you to go and see about them?"

"I can't go at all. It will not do for me to be seen on the streets of Nashville," was the reply.

"Sure enough! But there's Mr. Walker,—he'll do just as well. I'll meet him to-morrow, at eleven o'clock, at McNairy's store in Nashville, for the purpose."

This was agreed to, and the parties separated for the night. The next morning Hudson and Walker met, as proposed, and went directly to a gunsmith's shop on Deadrick Street, kept by one William Rear. Rear was in the front part of the shop when they entered, but, without a word being said, all three walked through to the back room. Here the doctor, without introducing Walker, said,—

"I want fifty pistols for a friend of mine who is going to run the lines."

"I have but two," replied Rear, producing them.

"What is the price of them?"

"Twenty-five dollars apiece."

"Well, I'll take them; and I want you to get some more right away."

Then, turning to Walker, he added, "I'll go out now and see if I can't get some from Captain Redman's clerk; and I will leave a line here to-morrow morning, letting you know what I have done."

The two then left the shop, leaving the pistols until more could be procured. The doctor did not come to town the next day, as promised, nor the day after; and Walker began to fear that something had happened to him. To set his mind at rest, he sent him a note, which was answered by the doctor in person the next morning, at Rear's shop. In reply to Walker's queries he said,—

"I couldn't get any pistols, as the teamsters and soldiers from whom I expected to buy them were all gone. But I have something here that's pretty good, I think," exhibiting a bullet-mould made to run twelve at a time.

"You had better have some balls run with it," remarked Walker, as he examined it carefully.

"I'll have a peck of them run at once; and if you can't get them out, I will. I can put them under sacks of bran, or I will keep them at the house to load the pockets of prisoners when they run the lines. I can find ways enough to get rid of them; for Confederate spies and escaping prisoners always stop at my house. In fact, they make it their head-quarters," he said, laughingly, as he bade Walker "good-morning."

The doctor saw no more of Walker after this,—which he accounted for by the supposition that he had made good his escape from Federal restraint. Other parties and other business soon claiming his attention, he thought but little about it, indeed. On the last Monday of January he was surprised and pleased by a visit from his old friend the Ashby cavalryman and spy, of whom he had lost sight for some time. The sitting-room being occupied by a Federal soldier,—there as a guard to protect his property,—the doctor and his guest retired to the parlor, where they had a long conversation touching the matter in which both were so deeply interested. The former was exceedingly communicative, and did most of the talking. He had recently secured, he said, through a Dr. Ford, a pair of fine revolving pistols and a revolving rifle, which his wife had taken out on the Charlotte pike to Mr. Charles Nichols, residing fifteen miles from Nashville, and there left them for a friend, who had doubtless got them by that time. He declared that his whole time and attention were devoted to assisting the Confederate cause, and that his principal object in taking the contract to furnish the Federal hospitals with milk was that he might pass the lines at will with men and materials to aid the South. He dwelt particularly upon the fact, and boasted of it as a shrewd trick, that he was kind to the Federal sick and wounded in order to pass as a good Union man and thus accomplish more for the cause he was engaged in; and it had been of great service to him; for he had been enabled to get many rebel prisoners and friends through the lines on his own pass and in other ways. At one time he had on his back porch eight Confederate soldiers just escaped from the penitentiary, while he was entertaining four Federal officers in the house. His particular aim was to keep arms passing into the guerrilla region on the Cumberland, to harass steamboats and the rear of General Rosecrans's army, and thus keep alive the spirits of the rebels. Towards the close of this conversation he said to his visitor,—

"My friend Dr. Ford is afraid of being arrested by the Nashville army police. Can you get him through the lines?"

"Yes, I can; but it will be in a risky way. He will have to run his chances, and may get shot," was the answer.

"Never mind, then: I can easily do it myself."

The spy now rising to take his leave, and intimating that he might not see him again, the doctor accompanied him to the porch, where he stood in his stocking-feet to say many parting words. When cautioned against it, he merely replied,—

"I would be glad to walk to the State-House on my bare feet ten times, if I could advance the Southern Rights cause by so doing."

Four days afterwards, on the morning of the 30th, a Mr. Newcomer called at the doctor's house and presented him a letter of introduction from J. Prior Smith, living twelve miles from Nashville, on the Hillsborough pike. His business, as stated in the letter, was to obtain assistance in procuring negroes, especially negro children, and running them through the lines to Smith, to be sold at the South. The enterprise, if successfully managed, would prove exceedingly profitable; and the doctor entered heartily into the arrangement. Having unbounded confidence in Smith, he was not at all reserved in his expressions, but repeated much of what he had told to Walker and the Confederate spy, ending by making an appointment to meet Newcomer at Rear's shop, there to aid him in the purchase of pistols to carry South. Here they found five pistols,—the same which had been procured for Walker, but which were finally sold to Newcomer. The doctor also purchased on his own account several pounds of Minie balls to send to the rebels. His wife, he said, was now beyond the lines for the purpose of taking out a fine horse which he had bought from a soldier for a trifle. Newcomer advanced Rear money for the purchase of other pistols, Hudson promising to see that they were forthcoming at the proper time, and, just before leaving, made an arrangement with the latter to procure for Smith the requisite number of negroes and run them through the lines. He was to procure a pass for his driver and servants to go out into the country for milk for the hospitals; and in that way they could get the negroes out and such other articles as Newcomer wished to carry with him,—the latter acting as driver. (We should have stated, ere this, that Dr. Hudson had quite a herd of cows, and supplied milk to the Nashville hospitals, to a considerable amount, daily.) The doctor assured him that he could be relied on in every emergency, and that he would not hesitate to do any thing to assist the cause of the South.

The next day Newcomer called again, and paid the doctor two hundred dollars, taking from him the following receipt:—

"$200.

"Received two hundred dollars of Mr. Newcomer, to be appropriated as distinctly understood, or accounted for on sight, or sooner.

"J. R. HUDSON.

"January 31, 1863."

The understanding referred to was that he should purchase pistols and ammunition to be carried South by Newcomer. The next day the doctor showed Newcomer the pistols, a double-barrel shot-gun, and a place which he called his arsenal, prepared by him for the express purpose of secreting arms whenever he should deem it necessary, and which, he said, would hold a thousand stand.

The doctor was now engaged heart and soul in the pistol and negro business, and for the next two weeks held almost daily consultation with his friend Newcomer as to the best means of procuring and getting them to their destination. In a week or so they had obtained six likely boys, who, Smith was informed, would be delivered at any place he should name outside of the lines, and the doctor had procured the promise of four more. So far every thing was progressing favorably; but the operations were more limited than suited the tastes of either, and each was constantly on the watch for some opportunity of materially enlarging them. Meanwhile the doctor was visited by numbers of persons representing themselves as paroled prisoners, spies, &c., to all of whom he extended a welcoming hand. With one in particular— introduced by Newcomer as a spy of General Wheeler—he became very intimate, and revealed to him his real·sympathies and feelings quite at length. To him he said, on his first visit,—

"I am a strong Southern Rights man; and not a day passes over my head that I do not do something to assist the Southern cause. I am watched by the detectives, I know, and have been frequently reported, but have not yet been imprisoned, because I play my cards right. I have in my house frequently, and am friendly with, many Federal officers, and, when reported, I prove by them that the charge is false. I have aided in the escape of many prisoners, but they have always thought me innocent."

Mrs. Hudson, however, did not seem as confident and easy as the doctor. She repeatedly cautioned their new friend to be very careful, as they were watched on all sides, and she had reason to suspect that certain suspicious-looking men who had been there a few days since were nothing else than spies sent there by some of the officers. She was assured by him that he was sharp enough to evade any detectives that could be sent to watch him or them,—at which she seemed satisfied and more at rest and confidential than before. Some of their friends, she said, with great glee, had recently escaped from the penitentiary, and intimated that she and a neighbor lady had assisted them to do so, without, however, saying it in so many words. The doctor made an appointment to meet him in town that day,—which he did, and pointed out to him on the street a number of friends whom it would do to talk to, gave him the names of others living in the country who would be of great assistance, and invited him to visit him at his house often, and to call upon him for any thing in his power to give.

At this time large numbers of negroes were employed upon the fortifications at Nashville ; and it was here that the doctor hoped to procure all that he wished to run South. Accordingly, he called upon Dr. or Lieutenant D. J. Deardurff, Acting Assistant Adjutant-General of the Engineer Camp, and inquired if he could be spared some negroes long enough to build up and repair his fence,—saying that he would be very much obliged if he could be thus accommodated. The lieutenant replied that he might have them as soon as they could be spared, calculating, however, that this would not be until the works were finished, and not intending to let him have them until then. Soon afterward he was instructed by higher authority to confer with Dr. Hudson and consent to arrangements with him to furnish negroes, and was informed that the doctor would call on him soon,—which he did in four or five days. Being treated with some courtesy, he proposed the trapping of boys from ten to fifteen years old, and said to the lieutenant that if he would engage with him in the business and turn them over to him, he could get at least one thousand dollars for every boy large enough to plough, and for able-bodied men from fifteen hundred to two thousand dollars, and that they would divide the proceeds equally. He further said that he could get any kind of a pass he wished, as he had a farm outside the pickets, and would have no difficulty in getting through and disposing of them as fast as they could be furnished. Deardurff assented to the proposition, and told him he could have as many as he wanted ; whereupon the doctor took his leave, promising to call for them on the following Monday.

The next thing now was to see Newcomer, report his success, and make arrangements for the future ; and for this he was not compelled to wait long, as the latter called upon him that very evening. The doctor reported that he had sounded Lieutenant Deardurff, with whom he had just taken dinner, in regard to the negro-smuggling business, and that the lieutenant had agreed to go into partnership with him. He said, further, that he was going to-morrow to see Dr. Seamore and try to get three or four little negroes from him to take South, and also would go to Lieutenant Osgood and ask for a pass for himself and servants through the lines, upon which, if he obtained it, he would take out all the negroes he was to get from Deardurff and Seamore. Newcomer was highly pleased, and congratulated the doctor upon his excellent management. He had just returned from outside the lines, he said, and had taken with him six negroes, whom he had sent South.

" And while there," he continued, " I found a letter addressed to me from General Frank Cheatham, enclosing five hundred dollars, with which he requested me to purchase quinine for the use of his hospitals. I suppose I can procure it from Drs. Cliff and Ermy, of this city, can't I?"

" I am well acquainted with Ermy," replied the doctor; "and I don't doubt I can get all we want from him."

" But how will we manage to get it through the lines?"

" I think we can get Dr. Ford to carry it. At any rate, Ford, you, and I will meet at Rear's to-morrow and arrange it all."

Newcomer was at the place appointed in due season, but found neither of the others there. Somewhat disappointed, he sent a note to Hudson, asking the reason of it, and received word that there had been a misunderstanding about the place of meeting, with a request that he would call at his house, as he was anxious to see him. Going at once, he was told by the doctor that he had seen and talked with Dr. Ermy about the quinine, and that they could have one hundred ounces for four hundred and seventy-five dollars. Hudson had offered four hundred and fifty dollars, and Ermy said *he* would not object, "as it was for *suffering humanity*," but his partner, Dr. Cliff, would have four hundred and seventy-five dollars, which he had finally agreed to give, thus closing the bargain. Newcomer expressed himself fully satisfied, and was about to leave the house, when he was approached by Mrs. Hudson, who said that there was in the penitentiary a Confederate officer by the name of Russell, the son of an old friend of her husband, whom she was very anxious to get out and run through the lines.

" Yes," said the doctor; "I would gladly crawl on my elbows from here to the prison, the stormiest night that ever blew, if by doing so I could release him."

" If you can get him out, I give you my word that I will take *good care of him*," was Newcomer's reply.

" I will see him, then, to-morrow," remarked Mrs. Hudson, "and tell him that one of General Wheeler's spies is in the city, who will take charge of him and see him safely through the lines if he can only get out of prison."

It was now the Monday on which the doctor had promised to call again upon Lieutenant Deardurff, and he was prompt to fulfil his appointment. The interview was a pleasant one; and the doctor stated that he had made all the necessary arrangements, and was ready for business at any time, asking, finally,—

" Do you see any chance of being caught in it?"

" No," returned the lieutenant; "I can manage my part of it without any trouble. So far as I am concerned, I have no fear at all, and am satisfied that if the thing is properly managed there is no danger in it. Besides, didn't you tell me you could get a pass of any kind at any time you wanted it?"

"Yes," he answered, at the same time taking out and showing a pass. "I have one here. You see, it says, for myself *and servants.* I told them I had a farm beyond the pickets, and, as I was just commencing work on it, might want to take out more hands some days than others. They had better make it 'servants,' I said, and then it would pass out any number,—which they did; and all I will have to do now will be to say that they are my servants. The pickets are changed every day; so they'll not suspect any thing: and I think it's perfectly safe. At any rate, I'll risk it. If there's nothing risked there'll be nothing won, you know. We can make a very good thing out of it, and nobody will be the worse for it; because they are runaway slaves, anyhow, whom their masters will never get again, and so will lose nothing by our operations."

Other features of the plan were discussed for nearly three hours, when the doctor asked Deardurff to order his horse and go with him to select the best route to get them away, and also to call at his house and talk with his wife about it. He did so, and found Mrs. Hudson considerably more shrewd than her husband, but eventually gained her confidence, and was invited to dinner the next day. He accepted the invitation, and was generously entertained by the doctor and his family. During the meal, the former inquired if he could let him have any number of negroes, from four to twelve, that evening or night or the next morning, at any place that would suit.

"Do you know what you can do with them?" queried the lieutenant.

"I'll take them out on the farm, and then see what can be done with them and how many can be disposed of."

"If I were in your place I would go and see Prior Smith and two or three others of your friends, and see what they say about it," continued Deardurff, anxious to implicate as many as possible and at the same time convince Hudson that he was very much in earnest about the matter.

"That's a good idea. I'll go to-morrow morning, and report to you immediately on my return."

With this they parted, the one to go to his camp, the other to make ready for his journey. Whether this was ever performed it is not necessary to state; but certainly it was not the next day, for the doctor had more important business with Newcomer, which he must have forgotten when making this arrangement with Deardurff. The next morning Newcomer came early with the money to buy the quinine which had been engaged of Dr. Ermy. When told what he had come for, Hudson at once ordered his buggy, and was just ready to start for the medicine, when his wife returned from the city, bringing word from Dr. Ford to have nothing to do with it, as he had reason to know that something was wrong. Mrs. Hudson also said that Dr. Chalmers, of Hospital No. 15, had told her that she and the doctor were watched at head-quarters, and that passes were only given them for the purpose of catching both of them,—that he had known it some time, and would have told her sooner, only he had been cautioned not to say any thing about it; but, notwithstanding, that he would warn them of their danger. He was surprised they were not already arrested; and they must keep a good lookout, or they soon would be.

"I don't believe a word of it," said Newcomer. "At any rate, I'll find out before night whether any thing of the kind is in the wind, from one of General Mitchel's clerks, who is in my employment."

At this both were much pleased, and said they felt perfectly safe so long as they had such a shrewd friend to watch over them.

Newcomer called again that evening, and found the doctor as ready as ever to assist in getting the quinine through; but Mrs. Hudson was still much alarmed. Promising to come again in the morning, he left without making any arrangements about the matter. The next day he was informed by the doctor that Deardurff had dined with him a day or two before, and that all arrangements about the negroes had been satisfactorily agreed on between them. Newcomer now said that he had seen the clerk he had spoken of, and that he had told him there was nothing on file at head-quarters against him or his wife, and that all Dr. Chalmers had said was false. This made matters right again in a moment; and Newcomer handed to Hudson the five hundred dollars, taking for it this receipt:—

"$500.
"Received five hundred dollars, to be appropriated as directed and understood.
                                             "J. R. HUDSON.
   "March 6, 1863."

The doctor said he would get A. W. Hendershot, a druggist of the city, to take the five hundred dollars and buy the quinine from Ermy, and he would send his servant to bring it to the house. From thence he would get his wife and daughter—Mrs. Ward, who lived five miles out on the Charlotte pike—to take it beyond the lines to the house of the latter, and there leave it for Newcomer. They would, he said, tie twine around the necks of the bottles, and adjust them around their waists, under their clothes, and thus carry them out of their lines safely. He then introduced Newcomer to Mrs. Read,—wife of General Read of the Confederate army,—and gave him several letters which Mrs. Ford wished sent South. The ladies were very agreeable, showing him marked respect, inviting him to call often, and assuring him that he would always be treated "as a friend indeed." Hudson started at once to make arrangements about the quinine, and Newcomer soon followed him.

The next day, Hudson said that he had bought the quinine, and that fifty ounces were then hidden in his house, and that to-morrow he would have the remainder there. Newcomer thanked him for his promptness, and engaged in conversation upon other matters. There was a Federal commissary store burned in town last night, he said, and he believed it had been done by some friend of the South.

"I have no doubt of it," said the doctor.

"If I knew who did it I would make him a present of one thousand dollars."

"If that is all you want, I can find you as many men who will do that kind of work as you wish. I will go and see about it to-morrow and let you know."

"All right. I will pay well for it if it is well done."

"Well, I don't think it is any worse than to capture a train of wagons loaded with the same kind of goods. I'd make the match to set the buildings on fire myself. It is easy enough to do, too. All that is necessary is to take a piece of punk and wrap around it cotton soaked in turpentine; then set fire to the punk, and it will not blaze for hours after it is put in the building; so that a man will have ample time to get away before the fire breaks out."

This ended the conversation and the acquaintance of the doctor and Newcomer, who will at once be recognized as the scout and detective. And here, too, it may be stated—as has probably been already surmised—that Walker, the Ashby cavalryman, and Wheeler's spy, the doctor's three friends, were simply members of the army police. Before the doctor had time to put into operation any of his plans for smuggling negroes or medicines through the lines, he was arrested, together with his wife and the gunsmith Rear. An examination of his house revealed a large amount and variety of contraband goods,—among which were nine revolvers, three shot-guns, two muskets, one rifle, three bags of bullets and buckshot, a large quantity of domestic and woollen goods, three bottles of morphine, and *ninety-nine* ounces of quinine. This latter, it seems, his daughter had refused to assist in carrying beyond the lines, and therefore it was found just where he had secreted it. Hudson and his wife were imprisoned—the former in the penitentiary, and the latter at her house—while their case was pending. The decision finally arrived at was to send them South beyond the lines, whither they had aided to send so many others. Rear was released on parole and bond, and is, we believe, still at large.

Thus was the home-circle broken up; and where was once only happiness is now misery. Though the guilt of the parents is not that of the children, they feel its weight, and in sorrow must mourn it for many days. "The way of the transgressor is hard," was said of him who violated the laws of God's kingdom; and it is not less true of those who rebel and plot against a Government at once so beneficent and *so powerful* as ours. If at any time, now or in the future, the fate of Dr. Hudson, his wife, and the children upon whom his crimes have entailed sorrow, shall convey aught of warning to others, the labor spent in compiling this chapter will not have been in vain.

In this case there were two ruling passions developed in the aged and wealthy rebel,—one to aid the rebellion, and the other to make money for himself. For the one, the plea of a mistaken, fanatical principle **might** be offered as an apology, but for the other none can entertain the **least** respect. The reader may exclaim against the seeming *temptation* resorted to in this case; but there was really no temptation. The detectives were strictly enjoined in this, as in all other cases, simply to afford facilities to the secret evil-doers of Nashville in this hour of general rebellion and peril to the Government; and the above record is evidence that they kept within the line of their instructions. The schemes of Dr. Hudson were his own, or arose incidentally from his surroundings. Had plans and schemes been deliberately made up for him, one can hardly conjecture to what extent his principles and feelings would have carried him.

Newcomer the Scout.

HARRY NEWCOMER was born in Lancaster county, Pennsylvania, in March, 1829. Born and raised in a hotel, he was employed as a bar-tender until he reached the age of about fourteen, when his mother died and his father broke up housekeeping. Thus thrown out of present employment, he soon afterwards went to Ohio, where he was apprenticed to learn the milling business. Serving out his time, he continued at this some years, until his brother-in-law, a Mr. ——— Gates,—now County Auditor of Ashland county, Ohio,—was elected sheriff, when he was appointed one of his deputies. In 1857 he went to Cleveland, and was employed by Jabez Fitch, United States Marshal for the Northern District of Ohio, as a detective officer. This situation he retained some three years, during which time he was quite successful in developing several noted cases of crime and bringing to punishment men who had grown gray in villany. One of these cases is so remarkable in its history and character, and was productive of such startling results, that the author thinks it worthy of a detailed narration, as an example of the skill displayed by our detective, and an illustration of the practical truth of the saying that "murder will out."

Information had been obtained by the authorities that a large business was transacted in the manufacture and sale of counterfeit money in Geauga county, Ohio. Though it was certain that the information was correct, it had thus far been found impossible to obtain any positive evidence by which to fix the guilt upon the suspected parties. By his previous operations Newcomer had acquired the reputation of being an ingenious and successful detective, and it was determined to send him down to try his hand at the case. He was instructed to make the acquaintance of an old blacksmith named Jesse Bowen, who lived near a place called Burton Square in that county. This Bowen, in addition to his trade, cultivated a small farm, and had long been known as a lawless character, engaged in every manner of fraud and crime, but had, nevertheless, managed to escape detection and punishment. He was now some seventy-eight years old, and lived a friendless, unsocial life, his house being shunned by all who had any care for their reputation and standing. To this man Newcomer introduced himself as William H. Hall, an extensive manufacturer of and dealer in counterfeit money. To substantiate this representation of himself, he exhibited large quantities of counterfeit bills on various banks,—with an abundance of which he had been furnished before leaving Cleveland. Two or three interviews were had, in which he succeeded in so completely gaining confidence that the old man gave him the names of all the parties in that vicinity dealing in counterfeit money. He was then working a small patch of corn, and as soon as he could finish hoeing that and cut and get in his hay, he said, he would take him around and introduce him to them, when he could easily dispose of all his money. Newcomer now went to work with the old man, and assisted him about his corn and hay, that he might get through as soon as possible. During this time he stayed with Bowen, sleeping up-stairs, while the old man and his wife remained below. Scarcely a night would pass that some one of the gang of thieves, robbers, and counterfeiters who made this their head-quarters would not come and knock on the side of the house. The old man would thrust out his head and ask, "Who's there?" If the password was correctly given, the door would open at once. By lying awake at nights when he was thought to be asleep, sometimes getting out of bed and listening at the window or peeping through the cracks in the floor, Newcomer soon ascertained that this password was "Washington," heard much of their conversation, learned their plans, and often saw them buying counterfeit coin of Bowen.

Day by day the old man's confidence in him became stronger, until at last he imparted to him all his secrets, took him to his shop, dug up from one corner his tools, moulds, and other apparatus for coining money, and explained to him the whole business. Newcomer now assisted him in the manufacture of bogus coin, and soon they had a considerable stock on hand. One day the old man called him out into a small orchard near his house, and, sitting down under an apple-tree, told him to take a seat beside him, as he wished to talk with him.

"I have," began he, "something to tell you,—something I never told to anybody before, not even to my wife. It seems strange, perhaps, that I should tell it to you *now*, a comparative stranger, whom I have known but a few days; but I feel something within me that prompts me to it. Forty years ago, when I lived in Vermont, my brother and myself murdered our brother-in-law in the woods one day. He was a simple, shallow-witted fellow, and was in the habit of wandering off by himself and remaining for some time away in the woods. On one of these occasions we waylaid and killed him. For a time nobody knew what had become of him; but by-and-by some portion of the body was found and identified, and we were arrested as the murderers. Nobody had seen the murder done; but there were certain things tending to fasten the guilt on us, and the possession of the considerable property he left was supposed to be motive enough for the deed. The evidence was entirely circumstantial; but it convinced the jury: we were convicted and sentenced to be hanged. The case was desperate, and it seemed impossible to escape. The day of the execution was drawing nigh, and we had about given up all hope,—when relief and release came very unexpectedly. Some of our friends accidentally fell in with a man in New Jersey who was the very image of the murdered man. His most intimate friends could not have told them apart. I myself, when I first saw him, was ready to sink through the floor with fear, thinking that our brother-in-law had returned to accuse us. This man was brought into court, and swore that he was the identical man whom we had been accused and convicted of murdering. Nobody could gainsay it, and we were released. He remained there just long enough for this, and then disappeared as mysteriously as he came, never having been seen or heard of since. My brother remained in Vermont, and died there. What little property I had was entirely used up in the expenses of the trial, lawyer's fee, &c., and I came here to Ohio, where I have been ever since. I was poor, and this counterfeiting business suited my taste, and I have been engaged in it, more or less, during all the time I have lived here. Our case has been often published and cited as a striking instance of the utter unreliability of the strongest circumstantial evidence, and as a narrow escape from death of two innocent men; but nobody knew that we actually did kill him, and that his return was all a made-up scheme to effect our release, based upon the extraordinary likeness of the man to our murdered brother-in-law."

To say that Newcomer was not astonished and horrified at this strange revelation of long-concealed crime would be to say that he was not human in his sympathies and feelings; but, whatever he may have thought and felt, he artfully avoided any expression of it, and as speedily as possible changed the conversation to other subjects. The old man's work was now done, and the promised trip around the county was made. Some fifteen or twenty dealers were visited and traded with. Newcomer bought, sold, and exchanged counterfeit money with them, and thus gained their confidence as fully as he had gained Bowen's. Many of them afterwards came to see him at the house of the latter, where they had long conferences and together laid out plans for future operations. The circle of Newcomer's acquaintance rapidly increased, and soon numbered the more considerable counterfeiters, burglars, horse-thieves, &c. of that whole region. Several weeks passed in this way, when urgent business called him away, and he returned to Cleveland to report progress to Marshal Fitch. Officers were immediately despatched to the place, and five of the gang arrested,—among whom was Bowen. Large quantities of bogus coin, together with the moulds and metal used in its manufacture, were found in his shop. They were brought to Cleveland and confined in jail, where Bowen was visited by many citizens, to whom he confessed that the facts as here stated were substantially correct. They were all tried, convicted, and sentenced to the penitentiary,—Bowen for six years, and the others for terms ranging from one to five.

During his stay in Cleveland, Newcomer was engaged in many other cases, some of them of scarcely less importance than the one just mentioned; but they cannot even be alluded to in this brief sketch. Suffice it to say that he obtained a wonderful local reputation for skill and sagacity in the development of difficult and complicated cases, and that his services were in demand in various parts of the country. In 1860 he went to Pittsburg, where he made the acquaintance of Robert Hague, Chief of Police in that city, and was by him introduced to Biddle Roberts,—then United States District Attorney, now a colonel in the Federal army,—who at once employed him as a detective. At this time ——— Campbell, an able and energetic officer, as well as an accomplished and courteous gentleman, was Marshal of the Western District of Pennsylvania. The wilds of Western Pennsylvania had long been notorious as the hiding-place of innumerable thieves, counterfeiters, and murderers. Many efforts had been made to break up their gangs and rid society of so disgraceful an element, but, for some reason, they had all ended in failure. The United States authorities were now determined to make another attempt to discover the whereabouts and arrest the leaders and members of this wide-spread association of criminals. It was a task in which only the utmost ingenuity and enterprise could hope to succeed; and the subject of our sketch was selected as the proper person to whom to commit it.

For half a century, a place in Butler county—known as the Stone House— had been designated as the head-quarters of much of this villany. It was in a wild, dreary region, at a crossing of public roads where stages were in the habit of stopping for meals and a change of horses. About a mile from this tavern, in a dense forest near the iron-mountains, lived the leader and head of the gang, Charles Coventry by name, but known among his confederates as "the Old North Pole." He was a desperate, daring man, fearing nothing, and feared by all. Tall and heavy-built,—weighing at least two hundred pounds,—dark-skinned as a negro, with a strong black beard and a thick bushy head of hair, he was the very beau-idéal of a reckless, law-defying bandit. To the lair of this "wild man of the woods" Newcomer was sent, with instructions to ascertain as nearly as possible his whereabouts, habits, and associations, and to obtain such other information concerning him as could be gathered up about the neighborhood. Having no recommendation to him, he could not at this time hope to do more than this, as Coventry was too shrewd and practised a rogue to be easily caught. His instructions were fully carried out, and he returned in a few days to Pittsburg, reporting progress to the authorities. He had not seen Coventry, but had reconnoitred the neighborhood and prepared the way for future operations in the same direction.

While at Pittsburg two events transpired that gave him a foundation to work upon in his second and more elaborate attempt. In themselves they were trivial circumstances, and seemed to afford little promise of results; but give our detective the smallest fissure wherein to insert his entering wedge, and he will speedily drive it to the head. The facts which Newcomer now eagerly seized were, first the arrest and imprisonment in Philadelphia of an intimate friend and former partner of Coventry's, on a charge of counterfeiting, and, secondly, the opportune return to Pittsburg of an old acquaintance and colaborer of his own,—Dr. Joshua Webb. The doctor was acquainted with Coventry, and, in some way, had managed to ingratiate himself into his confidence and esteem. It was arranged between Webb and Newcomer that the former should at once go down to Coventry's house on a visit and remain there for a time. In a week or so the latter would follow, and introduce himself to Coventry as an acquaintance of Coventry's imprisoned friend and the bearer of a message from him to Coventry,—his own character and standing being vouched for by Webb, should occasion require. This programme was carried out,—Webb going down, and Newcomer following in a week after. On the way from the Stone House to Coventry's nobody was seen but a little girl, who was coming from the house and passed on down the hill to a buckwheat-patch, where a number of men were at work cutting the grain. Newcomer went to the house, climbed a high fence by which it was surrounded, and knocked at the door. No answer being given, he shook it, tried the latch, attempting to open it, but found it fastened. Concluding nobody was at home, he turned to retrace his steps, and had just gotten over the fence again, when his attention was attracted by a short, quick coughing, or rather hemming, of somebody inside. The house was a story-and-a-half log cabin, of which only the lower part was "chinked and daubed,"—as it is called,—the crevices between the logs of the upper portion being left open. It was through these that the voice evidently proceeded; and soon a nose and mouth made their appearance at one of them. In a loud, hoarse whisper, the mouth said,—

"They're all down in the buckwheat. Don't look this way, but turn around and look towards the woods, as if you were watching for somebody, while I talk to you. It's rather dark up here, and you can't see me very well; but you know me, don't you?"

"Yes, Doc: it's you, isn't it?"

"Yes. We've got the press up, and I am cutting out two-dollar-and-a-half pieces. The old man is out cutting his buckwheat, and I am helping him make coin. We'll soon have lots on hand."

"Well, Doc," replied Newcomer, gazing intently into the woods, "I'll go back to the Stone House and come again when he's at home. You can say that somebody came to the house, but you didn't know who it was, lest he should accidentally have seen me and suspect something."

So saying, he walked slowly back to the tavern, and loitered about there until evening, when he again went to Coventry's, and at some distance from the house saw him sitting under a shed, talking with one of his *confrères*, but was not seen by them. Near the house, meeting the girl whom he had seen in the morning, he stopped and said to her,—

"Does Mr. Coventry live here?"

"Yes," was the reply.

"Are you his daughter?"

"Yes, sir."

"Well, my little girl, won't you run back and tell your pa that there is a gentleman here who wishes to speak with him for a moment?"

The girl did as requested, and Coventry came out at once, holding out his hand in a very friendly way. Newcomer introduced himself as H. C. Myers, and informed him of the situation of his Philadelphia friend. He had seen him recently in prison, he said, and had been requested by him to call on Coventry and tell him that he was in trouble, and was very anxious to have him come and see him, if possible.

Coventry was surprised, and evidently uneasy. "He was one of the best and keenest men in the business," said he; "and it is very strange that he should be jugged. I am very sorry about it,—would almost as soon be in prison myself, and, if necessary, will spend every dollar I have to get him out. But come; let me introduce you to a friend of mine here."

Newcomer went with him to the shed where he had been sitting, and was introduced to the man whom he had seen talking with Coventry a few moments previous. The latter accompanied the ceremony with the remark, "He's all right, I know; or my friend wouldn't have sent him to me." The three talked together for some time, Newcomer all the while, with inimitable tact, drawing him out and working upon his sympathies, until he gained his confidence as completely as he had that of many others before. Wishing to see and perhaps buy some of his wares, the old man went into the house and brought out specimens of bogus coin and a pair of fine steel dies for stamping it, which Newcomer agreed to take at another time. Coventry gave him the names of several other parties engaged in the same business, and recommended him to them. Our detective now took his leave, first making a bargain, however, to come again in ten days and purchase a large amount of counterfeit coin.

At the time appointed, in company with Robert Hague and five policemen, he started on his promised return. At Somerset they arrested a merchant, one of the parties recommended by Coventry, and then proceeded on their way. About three o'clock in the morning they had arrived within a mile of his house, and there left the wagon, with two of the officers in charge. Newcomer, with Hague and the other three, started towards the house. Knowing the desperate character of the man, and that he always kept two or three double-barrelled guns loaded ready for use, they did not seem to relish the idea of marching boldly up to the house; and, to avoid danger, Newcomer proposed to go and decoy him out of his stronghold. The night being too dark to distinguish persons, it was arranged that when they were heard coming back along the path the officers should spring out and arrest the foremost one. He went to the house and called Coventry out. The latter was in bed, but soon came down, without stopping to put on his coat. He seemed much pleased to see Newcomer, and asked him to come into the house.

"No," was the reply; "I can't, just now. I brought down a large lot of ones and twos on the State Bank of Ohio, but I didn't know who I might meet here, and concluded it wasn't quite safe to bring them to the house first thing. So I left my satchels out in the woods; and, if you'll get your coin, a candle, and some matches, we'll go right out and make our exchange there."

Coventry assented, went into the house, and in a few minutes returned with the coin and the steel dies, which he put in his pocket. They felt their way along until they reached the place where the officers were concealed, Newcomer dropping to the rear, and at this time being a considerable distance behind Coventry, who was in his shirt-sleeves still, and the more readily distinguishable. Just as he was fairly opposite them, all four of the ambushed officers jumped upon him, whereupon ensued a desperate struggle; and it was fully half an hour before they succeeded in getting the handcuffs upon him. During all this time he kept constantly shouting, "I'm trapped! I'm arrested!" &c., in order to alarm Webb, who was yet in the house, and give him a chance to escape. He succeeded also in throwing away the dies, and, though search was made for them the next day, they were never found. Secured at last, he was placed in the wagon, and the whole party drove up to his house, where an immense amount of counterfeit money, moulds, dies, and a heavy iron press used for striking off bills, were found. Coventry was subsequently tried, convicted, and sent to the penitentiary for five years.

Newcomer remained at Pittsburg through the administration of Marshal Campbell, and for some time with his successor, Marshal Murdoch. On one occasion he went to Johnstown, Pennsylvania, and arrested nine counterfeiters, with all their dies and instruments and a large amount of coin. Many other smaller but interesting cases were developed by him, some sixty-eight in number, and embracing every kind of vice and crime. Some jealousy having arisen on the part of the city police, caused by his extraordinary success, he deemed it inadvisable to remain there longer, and about two years ago came to Chicago, where he had several interviews with C. P. Bradley, Chief of Police; but, finding nothing important on hand or in prospect, he concluded to return to Ohio. In Logan county, Indiana, he met with an officer recruiting for the Eleventh Indiana Battery, who induced him to enlist in the same as a non-commissioned officer. At Louisville he joined the battery, and came with it to Nashville. Thence he accompanied Buell in his severe march over almost impassable roads and through swollen streams to Pittsburg Landing and Shiloh,—not arriving, however, in time to participate in the battle. Thence he went to Corinth, remaining there until its evacuation by the rebels, and thence to Huntsville and Stevenson, Alabama. Here, the monotony of camp and stockade life becoming irksome, he began to vary it by scouting on his own account. Frequently at night, after tattoo, he would mount his horse, slip past the pickets, scour the neighboring country in quest of information and adventure, and return again before reveille, his absence seldom being noticed by any one. On one occasion something of more than ordinary importance having come to his notice, he reported it to Colonel Harker, of the 65th Ohio Volunteers, then commanding the brigade stationed at that post, stating the means by which he had obtained the information, and giving some account of his previous midnight scouts. The colonel, highly pleased, at once gave him passes, and instructed him to continue the business as he had time and opportunity.

Frequently he would go down to the Tennessee River in sight of the rebel pickets; and one night he concluded to cross the river and get a nearer view of them. Striking the stream at a point three miles from Stevenson, he built a raft of rails and paddled himself across. Crawling up the bank through the bush, he came close upon the pickets, seven in number, without being observed. After watching their movements a while and finding nothing of particular interest, he returned safely as he went. Soon afterwards a negro told him of an island in the Tennessee River, some ten miles below Stevenson, on which a company of guerrilla cavalry were in the habit of rendezvousing every night. This opened a large field of operations for our scout, and he determined to visit the island forthwith. One afternoon, borrowing a suit of butternut from a negro at Stevenson, he set forth in that direction. The butternut clothes were carried under his saddle until he was fairly outside of our lines, when he exchanged his own for them and went on in the character of a genuine native. Reaching the river opposite the island after dark, he again constructed a raft of rails, fastening them together this time with grape-vines, and shoved across the narrow channel to the island, landing in a dense canebrake. Carefully feeling his way through this, he came soon to a corn-crib, around which twenty-five or thirty horses were feeding. It was now ten o'clock, and quite dark, but clear and starlight. Examining the crib, the entrance was discovered about half-way up, and our adventurer at once clambered up and put his head and shoulders through. Careful listening revealed the presence of sleepers within. Putting his hand down to see how far it was to them, it came in contact with the body of a man. Wishing to know in what direction he was lying, he felt along carefully and came upon a pistol in his belt. Working at this, he soon drew it out, and, finding it a good Colt's revolver, put it into his pocket and got down again. Exploring around, he came to a corn-patch and a cabin near by, in which there seemed, from the noise within, to be a family or two of negroes. Crossing to the south or rebel side of the island, he found that the stream was much narrower there than on the other side, and that close to the shore a number of boats and scows, in which the band crossed and recrossed, were tied. It was now time to think about getting home, and he circled around the crib and cabin to reach the place where he had left his raft. When he came in sight of it, there was also to be seen a human form standing by the water's edge and apparently regarding the raft with no little astonishment. In the uncertain light, it was impossible to tell whether it was man or woman, white or black; and there was nothing to do but wait until it disappeared. Crouching down amid the canes, he soon saw it turn and begin to climb the bank directly towards him, and as a precautionary measure took out the pistol and cocked it, though he could not see or feel whether it was loaded or not. The person proved to be a negro, and passed by, unconscious of the presence of any one so near, soliloquizing to himself thus:—"Mighty quare boat dat ar; 'spec's some of Masser John's work." This danger having passed, our self-appointed spy descended and re-embarked on his raft. Lest any one should see him, he lay flat upon it, paddling with extended arms, the whole presenting very much the appearance of a floating mass of driftwood. By the time he reached the opposite shore his butternut suit was pretty thoroughly soaked, but, without stopping to dry it, he mounted his horse, which he found straying about the woods, rode on to Stevenson, and reported to Colonel Harker. An expedition for the capture of this band—afterwards ascertained to be Captain Rountree's company—was just about starting, when orders were received to evacuate the place and fall back to Nashville with the remainder of Buell's army.

The battery went no farther backward than Nashville, remaining there during the famous investment of the city and until the Army of the Cumberland again reached it. Meanwhile, Newcomer was occasionally employed by General Negley as a detective; but most of the time was spent with his command. Early in December the police and scout system was fully organized and in successful operation. Our former scout, thinking that he could serve the Government to better advantage in the business with which he was so familiar, made application to Colonel Truesdail for employment as a scout and spy. The colonel, pleased with his appearance and conversation, at once made an engagement with him, and procured his detail for that special service. Having previously made the acquaintance of one Cale Harrison, a livery-stable-keeper, he now called on him, and, exhibiting a forged certificate of discharge, told him that he was on his way to the rebel army. Harrison, of course, was highly pleased to hear it, and gave him some valuable hints and information for his guidance in the matter. There was, he said, a man living on the Charlotte pike, by the name of Spence, whose son was an aide-de-camp on the staff of General Polk, and who would undoubtedly assist him in getting South and give him a letter of introduction to his son. In this event the road would be clear, and no difficulty need be apprehended in making the trip.

Thus directed, he set forth from Nashville on a scout South, with saddlebags well filled with fine-tooth combs, needles, pins, thread, &c., and carrying two fine navy revolvers. Going directly to Spence's, he introduced himself, said he had called by recommendation of Harrison, made known his business, and asked for a letter to his son, on General Polk's staff. Spence received him cordially, but would not furnish him with the desired letter. He referred him, however, to J. Wesley Ratcliffe, living about one mile from Franklin, on the Lewisburg pike, as a person likely to render him very material assistance. This Ratcliffe was a rebel agent for the purchase of stock and commissary stores, and was well known throughout the whole country. Pushing on, he accordingly called at Ratcliffe's, and made his acquaintance. When informed of his plans and purposes and shown the goods, Ratcliffe was much pleased, and soon became very friendly, advising him to go to Shelbyville, where such articles were greatly needed and could easily be disposed of. Newcomer accordingly started for Shelbyville, and for some time met with no incidents on the way. Between Caney Springs and Rover, however, he fell in with a band of rebel cavalry belonging to General Buford's command, who, on being made acquainted with his business, advised him not to go to Shelbyville, as considerable trouble might be experienced there. Their bushy shocks of hair suggesting that they were combless, he offered his stock for sale, chatting meanwhile with them about matters and things in general and in that vicinity in particular. Combs which cost two dollars per dozen he sold for two dollars each, and other articles in proportion, and, by the time his trading was finished, had ascertained that General Buford was stationed at Rover to guard a large mill full of flour and meal,—the size of his command, the number and calibre of his guns, and other items of importance, and also what generals and troops were at Shelbyville. The cavalrymen now wished him to go back to Nashville and bring them some pistols on his return. This he agreed to do, and, having obtained all the information he cared for at this time, turned his horse about and once more set his face towards Nashville. The two pistols which he had carried with him he had not shown, and still had them in his possession, —which circumstance was the cause of a slight adventure on the way home. He had proceeded but a little way when he met with a small squad of cavalry, who halted him, as usual, and demanded his name, business, and where he was going. These questions satisfactorily answered, he was next asked if he had any pistols about him. He replied that he had two, and was forthwith ordered by a rough-looking Texan to produce them, which was hardly done before they were coolly appropriated by his interrogator. Remonstrance was followed by abuse and threats of violence; and it was only by the intervention of the other parties that the matter was compromised by the sale of the pistols at fifty dollars each, and our traveller allowed to go on his way rejoicing. Without interruption head-quarters were reached, and a report of operations duly made.

Remaining two days at Nashville, he started again, with three pistols and the balance of the old stock of goods. The first night was spent at Ratcliffe's, and the next day both went to Murfreesborough in a buggy. Ratcliffe had business to transact with the provost-marshal and a number of the generals and inferior officers to see, and Newcomer was taken round and introduced to all as a colaborer in the cause of the South. During his four days' stay he was all over the town, through several of the camps, in many of the houses, drank whiskey with General Frank Cheatham, went to a grand party at the court-house, and made love to a dozen or more young ladies of Secession proclivities,—aided in all this by a perfect self-possession, an easy, graceful manner, and a winning face. In addition to pleasure-seeking and love-making, he also drove a thriving business in the sale of pistols and other contraband goods, and, with pockets filled with money and head stored with information, returned with Ratcliffe to his house, and thence to Nashville,—having first made an arrangement with the former to accompany him to Shelbyville the next day. Arriving at Nashville after dark, he remained there until morning, and then made preparations and started for a third trip.

With a pair or two of cotton-cards, a lot of pistol-caps, and some smaller knick-knacks, as passports to favor, he set forth once more to join Ratcliffe;

but, having been unavoidably delayed in starting, he found him already gone. Nothing was now to be done but to push boldly ahead in the hope of over-taking him on the road or meeting him at Shelbyville. With the exception of Ratcliffe, not a soul there knew him. Trusting to good fortune, he travelled on, and reached Shelbyville in due season without trouble. The usual questions were asked him by guards and pickets, to all of which he replied that he lived in Davidson county, was going to visit some friends in the 44th Tennessee Regiment, and had, moreover, a small stock of contraband goods for sale. These answers proving satisfactory, he was passed through, and reached the town early in the forenoon. Most of the day he spent in riding about, looking into quartermasters' and commissary depots, inquiring the names of officers, the number of troops, commanders, &c., until he had ascertained all that he wished. By this time night was drawing near, and it was high time to think about getting out of town; for should he remain after dark he was certain to be arrested. Ratcliffe was nowhere to be seen; and on inquiry he was told that he had gone to Atlanta, Georgia, on the train, and that nobody knew when he would be back. Here was a desperate state of affairs. Get out of town he must, and to get out he must have a pass. It was easy enough to come in, but very difficult to get out. Nobody knew him ; and, in fact, for once in his life, he was at a loss what to do. While thus troubled, he met some citizens of Davidson county who had been over the river to the camps of Cheatham and McCown's division and were now on their way to the provost-marshal to procure return passes. Misery loves company, and, with long face, he told them his trouble,—dressing it up with a considerable amount of fiction to suit the occasion. By way of adding earnestness to his entreaty and to open a sure path to their sympathies, he bought a bottle of whiskey and invited them all to drink with him. The liquor warmed their hearts as well as stomachs ; and while hobnobbing together he asked them if they wouldn't vouch for him to the provost-marshal and thus enable him to procure a pass. Being now in a condition to love the world and everybody in it, they promised to do so, and in due season all went for passes. His seven newly-made friends found no difficulty in their suit, their names being all written on a single pass ; but our scout was left unnoticed. The attention of the provost-marshal was called to him, when that functionary asked if any of them was personally acquainted with him. Though rebels, they would not lie,—possibly they thought it was not necessary,—and answered, "No," but they would vouch for him. But that would not do. His situation now was worse than ever. He not only had no pass, but had not the slightest chance of getting one. The whiskey investment had proved a losing speculation ; and he knew not where to turn for relief. The loungers about the office began to eye him suspiciously, and even the dogs seemed disposed to growl and snap at him as having no business there. The place was getting too hot for safety ; and his only hope of escape was to hurry out and lose himself in the crowd.

His new friends were still outside, waiting for him ; and with them a long consultation was held as to what had better be done about getting away, as every moment added to his already serious danger. Finally, one of the party suggested that he should go with them anyhow,—that the pickets would not be likely to notice that his name was not in the pass, there being so many already on it. In default of any thing better, this proposition was agreed to, and all set out together. Newcomer, however, was still far from easy about the matter, and was fearful that the plan would not work. As they were journeying along, he proposed to the one who had the pass that he should be allowed to write his own name on the pass with a pencil, and if any objection should be made to it they might say that he belonged to the party but did not come in until the pass was made out, and that the provost-marshal, to save writing a new one, had inserted the name in pencil-mark. This was assented to and done. The amended pass carried them safely through, and the last cloud of anxiety was lifted from his troubled mind.

Some twelve or fifteen miles having been passed over pleasantly, Newcomer purposely lagged behind and allowed the others to get far ahead, when he turned off and struck across to the Lewisburg and Franklin pike. Travelling on this about ten miles, he stopped for the night, with five of Wheeler's cavalry, at the house of a man who had a son in Forrest's command. Starting the next morning betimes, he reached Ratcliffe's the same evening, but found he had not yet reached home. Stopping a few moments, he passed on through Franklin towards Nashville. He had gone some seven miles, and was near Brentwood, when he saw four cavalrymen riding furiously down a lane just ahead of him. They and our hero reached its entrance at the same moment. The leader of the squad—who proved to be Captain Harris, a scout of John Morgan's, and who, as well as his three men, was very drunk—roughly halted him, and, riding up, pistol in hand, shouted,—

"Who are you? and where do you live?"

"My name is Newcomer, and I live six miles from Nashville, near Brent Spence's," was the ready, respectful reply.

Spence was well known to all, and no further trouble was apprehended; but the drunken captain was not so easily satisfied. He soon asked,—

"Where have you been? and what in the —— are you doing here?"

"I have been to Shelbyville to see Spence's son, and I took along some contraband goods to sell."

"You can go back to Franklin with me, sir!"

Protestation was unavailing; and without more ado he turned about and all started towards Franklin. On the way Harris asked if he had any arms with him, and, on being told that he had two fine revolvers and some cartridges, ordered him to give them up, which was done. With a savage leer he then said,—

"I know all about you. You're a —— Yankee spy. You have been going backwards and forwards here so much that the citizens of Franklin have suspected you for a long time, and have reported you. I am satisfied that you are a Yankee spy; and I am going to hang you, —— you. Bragg has ordered me never to bring in spies, but to shoot or hang them like dogs, on the spot; and I am going to make a beginning with you, now, this very night."

"If you do that," was the reply, "you'll take the life of a good and true man. I can show by J. W. Ratcliffe that I am a true Southerner, that I have done much good for the cause,—very likely much more than you have,—and that I am doing good every day I live."

"Captain," said one of the men, "it may be that he *is* an important man to our cause; and you had better see Ratcliffe and inquire into his case."

Harris studied a moment, and finally concluded to go with the prisoner to Ratcliffe's and confer about the matter,—at the same time assuring him that it was of no use, for he should certainly hang him anyhow. At Franklin all stopped to drink, and Harris and his men became beastly drunk. Reeling into their saddles, they were once more on their way to Ratcliffe's, but had gone only a short distance, when Harris wheeled his horse and hiccoughed out,—

"Boys, there's no use in fooling. I am satisfied this fellow's a —— Yankee spy; and here's just as good a place as we can find to hang him. Take the halter off that horse's neck and bring it here."

It was indeed a fitting place in which to do foul murder. Not a house was to be seen; and the road wound through one of those cedar thickets so dense that even in mid-day it is almost dark within them. It was now night, and the sombre shade even more gloomy than ever, as Harris jumped from his horse, and, taking the halter, made a noose of it, and, fitting it around the neck of the unlucky scout, drew it up uncomfortably tight, until, in fact, it was just about strangling him.

Now or never was the time to expostulate and entreat. In a moment it might be too late; and then farewell home, friends, and all the joys of life! It is not hard to die in peace, surrounded by weeping friends, or even to meet the dread king in the shock and excitement of battle; but to hang like a dog!—the idea is sickening, appalling; and it is no sign of cowardice to shrink from it. One more effort, then, for life, even if it be to supplicate for mercy from a drunken rebel.

"Captain," said he, with great feeling, "it is wrong to take a man's life on so slight a suspicion. It is a vast responsibility to take upon one's self; and you may do something for which you will be sorry by-and-by, in your calmer moments, and for which you may be even punished when it comes to the knowledge of General Bragg."

To which came the rough and heartless answer, "I know my business; and I don't want any advice from a —— Yankee spy. When I do, I'll let you know. Come along," shouted he, seizing the rope and dragging his victim towards a tree. "I know my duty, and am going to do it, too. Come on, men, and let's swing up this —— rascally spy."

They refused to come to his assistance, however, saying that they were as ready as he to do their duty, but they wanted to be a little better satisfied about the matter. It was only half a mile to Ratcliffe's, and it would be a very easy thing to go and see what he said about it. Harris would not listen a moment, and again ordered them to come and help him, which they dared not longer refuse.

The case now appeared hopeless. Death stared him in the face, and life, with all its memories and pleasures, seemed passing dreamily away. Looking into the cedars hanging heavy with darkness, they seemed the entrance to the valley of the shadow of death, beyond which lay the infinite and mysterious future. On the verge of the grave life was yet sweet,—yet worth striving for; and, as a last effort, the unfortunate man went up to Harris, placed his hand on his shoulder, and asked him if he would promise, on the word and honor of a gentleman, that he would go to General Bragg and give him a true statement of the affair, narrating every circumstance as it actually occurred. Then, turning to the men, he asked them if they would do it, provided the captain did not. Less hardened than the captain, they feelingly answered that they would; and the earnestness with which they replied was proof enough that they would make good their words. This set the captain to thinking. He evidently didn't like the idea of Bragg's hearing about it, and, after some moments' reflection, concluded to go to Ratcliffe's and see what he would say. The rope was removed, and they resumed their journey,—the captain still swearing it would do no good, as nothing could save him, for he was bound to hang him that very night.

Life still hung on a thread, however. In the afternoon, when Newcomer had been there, Ratcliffe had not returned, and if he were not now at home nothing would prevent Harris from carrying out his threat, which he seemed determined to execute. That half-mile was the longest ride Newcomer ever took. No lights were to be seen; but it was near midnight, and it might be that all were abed. Harris left the prisoner at the gate, in charge of the other three, and went up to the house. He knocked on the window, and Newcomer thought it was the thumping of his own heart. Fortunately Ratcliffe was at home, and came hurriedly to the door, without stopping to dress. The two conversed in a low tone for some time, when Ratcliffe was heard to exclaim, " I'll be —— if you do !" and instantly started down towards the gate. Coming up to the prisoner, and throwing one arm around his neck, while he took his hand in his, he said to him,—

" Great God! Harry, how fortunate that I am at home !"

After they had talked a while together, Harris came up again, and called Ratcliffe to one side, where they had another protracted conversation in a low, whispering tone. While they were thus engaged, a large owl on a tree near by began hooting, and was speedily answered by another some distance up the road. The three men mounted their horses at once and galloped to the road, shouting, at the top of their voices,—

" Captain, we're surrounded! This is a trap. Don't you hear the signals?"

The captain stepped to the road, listened a moment, and then, with a volley of oaths, ordered them back for " a pack of —— fools to be scared at an owl." Still quaking with fear, which did not entirely leave them until they were fairly away from the place, they resumed their places, the owls hooting lustily all the while.

Harris and Ratcliffe continued their conversation for a few minutes, when the former came towards Newcomer with a pistol and some papers in each hand, saying, as he gave them to him,—

"I release you, and restore your property, on the word of Quartermaster Ratcliffe. He assures me that you are one of the most important men in the South, and a secret agent of the Confederacy. I am very sorry that this thing has occurred, and will make any amends in my power. If you desire, I will go with you to the Charlotte pike as an escort, or will do you any favor you may ask."

"No," said Ratcliffe: "he must come in and stay all night with me. I can't let him go on to-night."

While standing at the gate, during this conversation, our released prisoner sold his pistols to the cavalrymen for Tennessee money. Just at this moment, too, a squad of cavalry belonging to Starns's command came by. One of them—to whom Newcomer had sold a pistol some weeks before—recognized him at once, and shook hands with him very cordially. He corroborated Ratcliffe's statement, saying that Newcomer was on very important business for the South, which was rendered still more so by the fight having begun at Stewart's Creek. A short time was passed in general conversation, when all left except Newcomer, who hitched his horse to the porch and went in with Ratcliffe. When sufficient time had elapsed for them to be well out of the way, Newcomer said his business was of too much importance to brook delay, and he must be off at once. Ratcliffe said if he must go he could not urge him to stay. "I will go with you to your horse," said he. "Meanwhile, take this to keep you from further trouble. If anybody stops you again, just show them this, and you will be passed at once."

So saying, he took from his pocket a large Government envelope,—of which he had an abundance,—and wrote on it,—

"*All right.*

"J. W. RATCLIFFE."

Armed with this, he started again, and reached the pickets of the 5th Kentucky Cavalry, who brought him into the city. It was nearly three o'clock in the morning when he arrived at the police-office: but the colonel was still up, and immediately telegraphed his report to head-quarters.

The next day, nothing daunted, he set out again, and went, as usual, first to Ratcliffe's, where he remained all night,—thence the next morning travelled, by way of Hart's Cross-Roads and Caney Springs, to Murfreesborough, reaching that place on the Saturday evening closing the week of battles at Stone River. Riding about the town, he observed that nearly every house in it was a hospital. Every thing was confusion and excitement. Immense crowds of straggling soldiers and citizens were gathered about the court-house and depot. Commissary and quartermaster stores, artillery, ammunition, and camp equipage, were being loaded on the cars, and trains were starting as fast as loaded. An evacuation was evidently on hand, and that right speedily; and he determined to leave as soon as possible. The only trouble was how to get out. After wandering around some time, seeking an opportunity, he came across a train of small wagons, with which the neighboring farmers had come to take home their wounded sons and brothers. Quick to embrace opportunities, he saw that now was his chance to escape. Dismounting from his horse, he led him by the bridle, and walked demurely behind one of these wagons, as though it was in his charge. Clad in butternut, and in every outward appearance resembling the others accompanying it, the deceit was not discovered, and he safely passed all the pickets. It was now nearly two o'clock in the morning, and he rode rapidly on, in a cold, driving rain, until fairly benumbed. Some nine miles out, he came to a deserted school-house, which he unceremoniously entered, leading his horse in after him. Within, a large fireplace and an abundance of desks suggested the idea of a fire, and a huge blaze roaring and crackling on the hearth soon demonstrated its practicability. The next step was to wring the water out of his well-soaked garments and partially dry them. Both horse and man enjoyed themselves here until near daybreak, when he mounted again and rode on to Ratcliffe's, reaching there about three o'clock Sunday afternoon. Here he remained a while to converse with his friend, refresh the inner man, and care for his horse,—neither having eaten a mouthful since the morning before. Ratcliffe was rejoiced to see him, and wished him to remain longer; but he pushed ahead, and reached Nashville late that evening, wellnigh worn out with hunger, fatigue, and want of sleep. His report was immediately telegraphed to General Rosecrans; but he had been so long in making his way back that the general did not receive it until he had himself entered Murfreesborough.

Late the next night he started again, with a single pistol and a small stock of needles, pins, and thread. On Monday evening he reached Ratcliffe's, and, staying but two hours, rode on two miles farther to the house of one M. H. Perryear, with whom he remained all night. Thence he travelled, by way of Hart's Cross-Roads, towards Caney Springs, but before reaching the latter place fell in with some of Wheeler's cavalry, with whom he rode along friendly and companionly enough. Some of them were old acquaintances and very confidential. They were, they said, just on their way to burn a lot of Federal wagons at Lavergne and Triune, and, deeming him a good fellow well met, invited him to go with them. Thinking that there might be some chance to save the wagons, he declined the invitation, urging the pressing nature and importance of his mission as an excuse. It was soon found, however, that every avenue of escape northward was guarded, and the whole country filled with the cavalry, of whom there were, in all, about three thousand. There was nothing to do, then, but to leave the wagons to their fate and push on, which he did, and, arriving at Caney Springs, remained there over-night. The next morning the cavalry began to loiter back from their marauding expedition in squads of from fifteen to a hundred or more, and from them he learned the complete success of the enterprise. Making the acquaintance of a lieutenant, he was told that they were going at once to Harpeth Shoals, to burn a fleet of boats which was then on its way to Nashville. This determined him to abandon the idea of going to Shelbyville, and he accompanied a detachment back as far as Hart's Cross-Roads, where they went on picket-duty at a meeting-house by the road. Bidding them good-day, he started on alone towards Ratcliffe's. Stopping at Perryear's, he was told that Forrest was in Franklin, that the roads were all guarded, and that there was a picket just at Ratcliffe's gate. Perryear then gave him an open letter of introduction, recommending him to all officers and soldiers of the Confederate army as a true and loyal Southern man, engaged in business of the highest importance to the Government. With this he again set out, and, as he had been told, found a picket at Ratcliffe's gate. Requesting to be admitted, he was asked if he was a soldier, and, on answering negatively, was passed in without hesitation. Ratcliffe corroborated Perryear's statement, saying, furthermore, that Forrest was very strict, and that it would be much better for him to remain there until they had all gone down the river.

"But," added he, "if you must go, I'll go with you as far as Franklin and help you through."

The town was found to be full of cavalry, who were conscripting every man whom they could lay hands on. Ratcliffe introduced his companion to Will Forrest,—a brother of the general, and captain of his body-guard. The captain was profuse of oaths and compliments, and, withal, so very friendly that Newcomer at once told him his story and business, all of which was endorsed by Ratcliffe. More oaths and compliments followed. The captain was glad to know so important a man, and, by way of business, asked him if he had any pistols to sell.

"No," was the reply; "I have nothing but a single navy revolver, which I carry for my own defence, and which I wouldn't like to part with. But I am just going to Nashville for more goods, and, fearing trouble in getting away, I thought I would come and see about it."

"Oh, I guess there will be none," said the captain. "The general wants to know something about Nashville, and will be very apt to send you there to get the information for him. Come; let's go and see about it."

The two set forth, and found the general, surrounded by the usual crowd, at his hotel. Calling him to one side, the captain pointed out his new friend, and, explaining who and what he was, concluded by remarking that he wished to go to Nashville for goods, and would bring him any information he desired. The general, not just then in the best of humor, swore very roundly that he knew as much about Nashville as he wanted to,—it was men he wanted,—and concluded by ordering the captain to conscript his friend into either his own or some other company. Turning on his heel, he walked briskly away, leaving his brother to his anger and our would-be rebel spy to his disappointment. The captain fumed with great, sulphurous oaths, and consoled Newcomer thus wise :—

"He's a —— fool, if he is my brother. You are the last man I'll ever bring to him to be insulted. But you sha'n't be conscripted. Come with me, and I'll help you through. You can go with my company, but not as a soldier, and I will send you to Nashville myself. My company always has the advance, and there'll be plenty of chances."

Making a virtue of necessity, this proposition was gladly accepted, and all started on the march. By this time Wheeler had come up and taken the lead, Forrest following in the centre, and Starns bringing up the rear. About eight miles from Franklin the whole command encamped for the night, and our hero slept under the same blanket with Captain Forrest and his lieutenant,—a Texan ranger named Scott, whose chief amusement seemed to consist in lassooing dogs while on the march, and listening to their yelping as they were pitilessly dragged along behind him. Towards midnight, one of their spies—a Northern man, named Sharp, and formerly in the plough business at Nashville—came in from the Cumberland River. Captain Forrest introduced Newcomer to him as a man after his own heart,— "true as steel, and as sharp as they make 'em." The two spies became intimate at once, and Sharp belied his name by making a confidant of his new acquaintance. He had formerly been in Memphis, and acted as a spy for the cotton-burners. More recently he had been employed with Forrest; and now he had just come from Harpeth Shoals, where he had learned all about the fleet coming up the river, and to-morrow he was to guide the expedition down to a place where they could easily be captured and burned. Early next morning the march was resumed, and at the crossing of the Hardin pike General Forrest and staff were found waiting for them. Upon coming up, the captain was ordered to take his company down the Hardin pike, go on picket there, and remain until eleven o'clock; when, if nothing was to be seen, he was to rejoin the expedition. These instructions were promptly carried out,—a good position being taken on a hill some eight miles from Nashville, from which could be had a view of the whole country for many miles in every direction. About ten o'clock the captain came to Newcomer and said he was going to send him to Nashville himself; at the same time giving him a list of such articles as he wished, consisting principally of gray cloth, staff-buttons, &c.

As may be imagined, no time was lost in starting, and still less in getting into Nashville, where he arrived in due season to save the fleet. A force was at once sent out on the Hillsborough pike to cut off the retreat of the rebels, and another on the Charlotte pike to attack them directly. The latter force succeeded in striking their rear-guard, and threw them into confusion, when they hastily fled across the Harpeth River, which was at the time very high. Our forces, being principally infantry, could not cross in pursuit, but the troops on the Hillsborough pike succeeded in killing, wounding, and capturing considerable numbers of them. They were thoroughly scattered, however, and the fleet was saved,—which was the main object of the expedition.

General Rosecrans had now been in Murfreesborough several days, and

Colonel Truesdail immediately on his arrival sent the scout to that place. Here he made a full report, and, having received instructions for another trip, returned to Nashville the next day to make ready for it. The only item of interest on this trip was that at Eagleville he met Wheeler's command, by many of whom, and by the general himself, he was well and favorably known. Here Wheeler employed him as a secret agent, and gave him a permanent pass, which he still retains. Borrowing from one of his officers one hundred dollars in Tennessee money, the general gave it to him, and instructed him to buy with it certain articles which he mentioned,—among which were gray cloth and staff-buttons, always in demand for uniforms. Stopping at Ratcliffe's on his return, he showed him the pass, and related the circumstances of getting it, at which the former was highly gratified,—" as," said he, " you'll have no more trouble now, Harry."

At Nashville Wheeler's bill was filled, such not very reliable information as Colonel Truesdail and General Mitchel saw fit to give was obtained, and another trip began. Wheeler was now at Franklin, quartered in the court-house. The goods and information were delivered, much to the gratification of the general, who forthwith instructed him to return to Nashville for more information and late Northern papers. So well known and highly esteemed was our man now, that the cashier of the Franklin Branch of the Planters' Bank of Tennessee, on this trip, intrusted to him to carry to the parent bank the accounts and valuable papers of the branch, which he did, delivering them at Nashville. On the way back he stopped at the house of one Prior Smith, whom he knew as an ardent rebel and extensive negro-dealer. Smith, naturally enough, inquired who his visitor was, and was told the usual tale. He then inquired if a good business might not be done in running off negro boys from Nashville, buying them cheap there or kidnapping them, and if he wouldn't like to engage in it. Newcomer said that it would doubtless be a splendid thing, but he did not dare to venture into it: it was too public, and might endanger his other operations, more important than any private speculations. Smith still insisted, and said he would give ten dollars a pound for likely children, and would furnish him with a letter of introduction to his "right bower" in Nashville. The right bower proved to be Dr. Hudson, who was afterwards called on by Newcomer and various other detectives in the secret service, as is narrated in a preceding sketch.

Obtaining the papers desired by Wheeler, and various items of information, Newcomer now set out on his sixth and last scout. At Franklin he found that Wheeler had gone on to Shelbyville, leaving only a squad of cavalry behind. That evening Ratcliffe and himself sat down and wrote out the information, sealed it up with the papers in large Government envelopes, and gave them to the lieutenant in charge of the company, who sent them by a courier to Wheeler. Remaining all night with Ratcliffe, he returned the next day to Nashville, where his services were needed in the development of the Hudson and other important cases, full details of which are given in other pages of this work. Since then he has been constantly employed as a detective, with equal credit to himself and benefit to the Government.

In all the annals of police and spy life it will be difficult to find a career marked by such uniform and brilliant success as has attended Harry Newcomer in his adventurous enterprises. He has never undertaken a case whose mystery he did not solve. Friendly and companionable with his own sex, he is equally a favorite with the ladies. With many a high-born rebel lady he has held converse by the hour, she little dreaming, meanwhile, that her strangely pleasant guest was a "Yankee hireling." With a perfect self-control and self-confidence, a quick perception, and a faculty of adapting himself to circumstances on a moment's notice, he has proved one of the most useful men in the secret service of the Army of the Cumberland.

General John H. Morgan's Female Spy.

ON the 16th of December, 1862, while the rebel army was at Murfreesborough and the Army of the Cumberland at Nashville, a lady of middle age and fine personal appearance was walking along the road leading from the former to the latter place. Between Lavergne and Nashville, not far from the Federal pickets, she was overtaken by a gentleman named Blythe, —a Union man and a paroled prisoner,—who had that day procured a pass from General Bragg to go to Nashville in his buggy. Seeing that she was weary with long walking, he invited her to ride, and they proceeded in company about three-fourths of a mile, when they came upon a party of Federal and rebel officers, consulting about some matter under a flag of truce. Blythe, because of his parole, was allowed to pass within the lines, but the lady was detained outside until her case could be submitted to headquarters and permission obtained for her entry. While thus delayed, Blythe overheard Lieutenant Hawkins, in charge of a rebel flag, saying to her, in a cautiously modulated voice, "If they won't let you in you can go across the country—about four miles—to my father's, and there they will run you through the lines anyhow." This aroused his suspicions, and determined him to report her case at the Police Office, with his ideas of her character, and the suggestion that a strict watch be maintained upon her movements.

The next afternoon she was brought in, and immediately sent to headquarters. Here she gave her name as Mrs. Clara Judd, the widow of an Episcopal clergyman who had died the year previous, leaving herself and seven children, without property and in debt. She was on her return from Atlanta, Georgia, whither she had been on a visit to her son, a boy, who was living there and learning the printing-business. She wished to go to Minnesota, where the remainder of her children were, and where she then claimed to reside. Her story was told in so simple, artless a manner, and with such an air of sincerity, that the sympathies of all present were at once enlisted in her favor,—it not being in the heart of man to doubt, for a moment, the truth of all she said. The examination ended, a pass was given her to Louisville, and she was allowed to depart in peace. From the Police Office she made her way to the Commercial Hotel, where she expected to meet an old friend, but, finding that he was out of the city, and that the hotel was too full to obtain lodgings, she went to a sutler of her acquaintance, named Becker. He also was absent; but she remained over-night with his partner and wife,—Mr. and Mrs. Beaden. Knowing that Blythe was at the Commercial Hotel, she wrote him a note, requesting him to call and see her on important private business.

Early in the evening Blythe called at the police department, inquiring if Mrs. Judd had come in, and was told that she had just gone, a pass having been issued to her. He seemed disappointed, and remarked that they had been fooled,—that in his opinion her story was essentially false, and she a bad woman, whom it would be well to watch. His reasons for so thinking were freely given, and, though they did not entirely destroy the confidence she had inspired, they served to weaken it materially, and to excite doubts as to the truth of her statements and the honesty of her intentions. Returning to his hotel, the note from Mrs. Judd there awaiting him fully confirmed his previously-formed opinions. So strong were they now, and so solicitous was he to fathom and disclose the mischief which he felt to be brewing, that he again went to the Police Office that evening, taking the note with him and exhibiting it to the authorities there. He was advised to call as requested, and endeavor to ascertain her true character and designs. He did so, and found her at Mr. Beaden's, as stated. After some unimportant conversation, she said to him, "Are you loyal?" His decidedly affirmative answer she construed to mean that he was a friend to the South and favorable to its cause. It may here be explained that, though Blythe at his first meeting did not recognize her, she at once remembered having seen him in Murfreesborough, where he had been detained some eight or nine weeks before he was allowed to proceed to Nashville. As he seemed while there to be under no restraint whatever, she knew nothing of his being a paroled prisoner and a Northern man. The fact of his having a pass from General Bragg, taken in connection with certain remarks casually made by him, was to her proof positive that he was a Southerner and a rebel. To this very natural mistake she was indebted for all the misfortune that eventually befell her.

Completely self-deceived, she immediately took him into her confidence, and entered upon an explanation of her business and plans. She was going, she said, to Louisville, for the purpose of purchasing quinine and other medicines for the Southern Confederacy, together with a considerable amount of dry-goods and groceries for herself and others. But this was only a portion of her business, and of no importance in comparison with the remainder. John Morgan was about to make a raid upon the Louisville & Nashville Railroad, and was only waiting for information as to the strength of the garrisons and the disposition of troops along its track, necessary to determine the most available point of attack. This information she had engaged to obtain and furnish to him on her return to Gallatin, where certain of his men were to meet her, by appointment, on a fixed day. This day was now at hand; and accordingly she was anxious to start for Louisville the next morning, so that she might have ample time to purchase her goods and be back to Gallatin on the day appointed. Unfortunately, however, her pass did not allow her to leave Nashville until the morning after, and she wished he would try and exchange it for one allowing her to go on the morrow. Blythe obligingly consented, and further said that, as it would save her a good deal of trouble in Louisville, he would get her a pass to go and return as far as Gallatin. With the old pass he immediately went a third time to the office, stated his wish, and related the conversation that had passed between himself and Mrs. Judd. Colonel Truesdail gave him the desired pass, and insisted upon his accompanying her to Louisville, at the same time instructing him to afford her every facility for the perfection of her plans, but to neither encourage nor restrain her.

Blythe returned with the new pass according to promise. In the conversation that ensued, he warned her of the danger of the business she was about to embark in, cautioning her as to the watchfulness of the Federal authorities, and endeavored to dissuade her therefrom. His advice, however, though well meant and kindly enough received, was of no avail. It was her duty, she said, to do all that she could for the South; and, as they were God's chosen people, she was not afraid of any harm befalling her. Seeing that she was determined in her purpose, Blythe affected a deep solicitude in her welfare, and finally told her he would postpone his business for the present and go with her to Louisville then, instead of waiting a few days as he had intended. It would be a great accommodation, as well as pleasure, to him, he remarked, laughingly, for then he could sit with her in the ladies' car,—no small matter on a train literally jammed with passengers, as that one usually was. Madam was highly pleased at this exhibition of kindness, and with many thanks endeavored to show her gratitude therefor. Thenceforward she placed implicit confidence in Blythe, and unreservedly told him all her plans, together with much of her past history and experience. This was her second trip, she said. The previous one had been quite profitable to her, and had enabled her to furnish a large amount of valuable information to the rebels.

Throughout the entire journey to Louisville she was ever on the alert for the smallest scrap of information. At every station, out of the window would go her head, and the bystanders be plied with guarded questions concerning the strength of the place, means of defence, number of troops and names of regiments there, &c. Blythe was evidently annoyed, and time and again pulled her dress, begging her "for God's sake to sit down and keep quiet," or she would attract attention and ruin both herself and him. She replied that it was a part—and a very important part—of her business to observe, make inquiries, and take notes; she must do it.

At Louisville Blythe paid her every attention, assisted her in her purchases, introduced her to one of the best dry-goods houses in the city, and went with her to New Albany, where she bought several hundred dollars' worth of drugs and medicines. Here she was well acquainted,—a fact which she explained by saying that she had made purchases there before. These drugs she intended to pack in a trunk with a false bottom, but was told by Blythe that it would not be necessary, as he would see that her trunk was passed without examination. Occasionally he would absent himself for several hours, accounting for this by representing that he was engaged in buying a large stock of goods, with which he designed returning immediately to Murfreesborough. One day he was taken quite ill, and was attended and nursed by her in the kindest manner. In addition to her confidence, he seemed now to have gained her affections. She devoted herself to him as only women do to those whom they love,—anticipating his slightest wishes, and providing for his every want in the most warm-hearted and loving manner. Blythe's pretended sickness was soon over, but it left him weak; and he wished her to remain at Louisville another day. No; she could not stay. Morgan's men had made a positive engagement to meet her that night at Gallatin, and she would not disappoint them for the world. She was to tell them, then and there, all that she had seen and heard down the road, and to advise them where to tap it. In return, they were to assist her in getting her trunks through the lines, which could easily be done by putting them in the bottom of the wagon-bed and covering them with fodder. Seeing that she could not be induced to remain, Blythe determined to return with her. Flattered by this mark of attention and appreciation, she was highly delighted, and more affectionate than ever. Arrangements were at once made for the journey, Blythe in the mean while visiting General Boyle, explaining the whole matter to him, and procuring an order dispensing with the usual examination of baggage in their case, and also telegraphing to Colonel Truesdail, at Nashville, to have them arrested at Mitchellsville, just before reaching Gallatin.

On the way back she was in the best of spirits, and could hardly refrain from frequent exhibitions of her elation at the success of their schemes. Blythe begged her to be careful, or she would expose herself and him to ruin. "You know," said he, "if any thing should happen to you it will get me into trouble, and that would make you feel bad; wouldn't it?" He asked her if she was not afraid of being watched,—if she did not think she was already suspected,—seeking by this means to prepare her mind for the arrest which was soon to occur, and at the same time to allay any suspicions she might otherwise entertain of his complicity therein. She replied that she was, and that there was then in that very car a person whom she believed to be watching her. She betrayed considerable anxiety, and seemed quite uneasy about the matter for some time, but finally fell into her usual careless mood. At Mitchellsville she took on board two large trunks of goods and clothing, left there on her former trip because of her having had too many to get safely away at that time without exciting suspicion. Just after leaving

Mitchellsville, Blythe said to her, "Now, this is a dangerous business you are in; and you may not get through. At Gallatin I shall leave you, but will go straight through to Murfreesborough; and if you have any word to send I will take it with pleasure to anybody you may name." In reply, she wished he would see Lieutenant Hawkins and tell him that she had arrived safely at Gallatin with her goods, but that there was a larger force there than she had expected to find, and she might be troubled in getting out; or, if Lieutenant Hawkins was not then at Murfreesborough, he might tell any of Morgan's men, and their general would be sure to get the news and devise some means for her assistance. At this time, as well as on previous occasions, she seemed to be on very intimate terms with Morgan and to rely implicitly upon him and his followers. She further informed Blythe that her home was in Winchester, Tennessee, but that she was on her way to Atlanta, Georgia, where her son had a situation in the Ordnance department, and that the knitting-machine purchased by her was intended as a pattern for the manufacture of others, there being nothing of the kind in the South.

This conversation was scarcely concluded when both were arrested, and Blythe—according to previous arrangement—roughly handled. Mrs. Judd turned very pale, and was strangely excited; though she seemed more affected by Blythe's situation and danger than her own. Blythe, however, seemed to take it coolly enough, and as a matter of course,—which but the more increased the sorrow of Mrs. Judd, it being for her only that he had thus ventured and lost. But regrets were useless now, and both were brought on to Nashville at once. Mrs. Judd was put under guard at a hotel, and assured that Blythe would be hung the next morning. At this intelligence she became quite distracted, begged and implored to be heard in his favor, asserting with broken voice and tearful eyes that he was an innocent man and that the guilt and blame of the whole transaction were hers alone. Making no impression upon those about her, she went so far as to write and send to head-quarters a petition that he might be spared from a punishment he did not deserve. Blythe, of course, was released at once; but she did not know it, and to this day remains ignorant of his real fate and location. Her baggage was examined and found to contain many hundred dollars' worth of contraband goods,—unquestionable evidences of her guilt. Among its contents was a Bible, with Blythe's name written in it by herself, which she had purchased in Louisville, intending to present it to him when they should meet again in Murfreesborough.

The circumstances, when known, created not a little excitement in army circles, and the case was personally examined by the general commanding and his staff. The crime was the highest known to military law; the importance of the consequences involved in the success or defeat of the scheme, almost incalculable. In short, it was one of those little pivots on which the fortunes of a campaign or the fate of an army might turn. For such an offence the only adequate punishment was death; but the person implicated was a woman; and that reverence for the sex which brave men ever feel would not allow the application of so extreme a penalty. To pass her lightly by, however, could not be reconciled with a sense of duty; and it was deemed necessary to make an example of her, by confining her in the military prison at Alton, Illinois, during the war, where she is at this present writing.

Norris the Kidnapper.

ONE of the most marked results of the war has been the escape from rebel masters of large numbers of slaves. Flocking to our camps, where they are universally known as "contrabands," they have been made useful in a multitude of ways by the Army of the Cumberland. As cooks, as waiters, as teamsters, as laborers, in the hospitals, in warehouses, in stables, on the fortifications, on steamers and railways, they have been constantly employed with advantage to themselves and the Government. By as much as they have been a gain to us they have been a loss to the rebels, who rely upon them not only for their army labor but for the cultivation of their plantations and the production of the supplies necessary for the support of their troops in the field. At first no particular caution seemed to be exercised to prevent their escape, or any considerable efforts put forth for their recovery. Their whilom masters were apparently content to let them go or stay as they pleased, congratulating themselves that it was simply so much pork and corn-bread saved when they abandoned the lean larder of a Southern plantation for the ample store of a Yankee camp. Those left behind were enough for all their present needs, and too many to be decently fed and clothed from the scanty crops and scantier stocks of the Southern Confederacy.

With the last New Year, however, another policy seems to have been inaugurated, either by the civil authorities at Richmond or by the military leaders in camp. Whether it was that the number of fugitives had become alarmingly large, or that the influence of the emancipation policy was feared, whether it was the dread of an armed insurrection or a general stampede to the Federal lines, or whether it was all of these combined, that caused this change of policy, is not easy, and not necessary, to determine here. Suffice it to say that measures were at this time taken to remove into the interior and southward these slaves in Tennessee and other border States that could be reached, and to recover from the Federal lines as many as possible of those who had escaped thither. The spies and scouts of the secret service soon scented this new game, and were on the alert. It was found that considerable rewards had been offered in Murfreesborough and other places in the Southern Confederacy for the delivery of negroes within the rebel army lines. Emissaries were found in Nashville, engaged in trapping and carrying away by force such likely negroes as they could lay their hands upon,—at the same time acting as spies and furnishing the rebels with important information.

Measures were at once taken for the detection and punishment of those engaged in this nefarious traffic. A suitable person was despatched to Franklin, Tennessee, where resided several men formerly well known as extensive negro-dealers, for the purpose of obtaining reliable information of the parties in the business and the means by which it was carried on. With one of these men—J. Prior Smith, who had one million dollars of Southern money for investment in negroes—this agent became very intimate, and finally engaged to purchase for him men, women, and children. For likely children from one to eight and ten years of age he was to be paid *ten dollars per pound;* and for every man and woman that he would get out of Nashville and vicinity he was to be liberally rewarded. Smith also gave him letters of introduction to two prominent citizens of Nashville, both of whom entered cheerfully into the scheme and suggested various means of carrying on the business. One of them—Dr. J. R. Hudson—was particularly interested, and for months busied himself in kidnapping young boys and running them South. He tampered with the officers of the engineer corps in charge of the fortifications then being constructed, offering them half the profits, or five hundred dollars each, for every man they would permit him to steal out of their squad of laborers. He would procure passes for himself and servants to go out to his farm, and the servants would never come back. He would send them out with his wood-wagons, and when once beyond the lines they would be passed on to their destination and sold. His speculations, however, were interfered with materially by the Army Police; but he was indefatigable in the business, and only ceased trapping negroes when trapped himself.

It was found, too, in addition to this organized scheme of theft in which these unprincipled speculators were embarked, that some of the night police of Nashville, employed by the city government, had engaged in a similar business. Scarcely a night passed but some fugitive slave was arrested and jailed by them, on the demand of pretended owners or their agents. For such services they were paid from five dollars to one hundred for each arrest. James A. Steele testified that he had caught, within three weeks, six negroes, for which he had received about one hundred dollars in all. J. F. Ingalls testified that he had assisted in the arrest of six negroes for Dr. Oden, and received for the same ten dollars. James Hinton paid him forty dollars for arresting ten negroes belonging to a relative. He had also been approached by other parties, and been offered from fifty to two hundred dollars each for the arrest of other negroes, many of whom were in Government employ. William Mayo was paid sixty-six dollars for arresting a man, a woman, and two children for Watt Owens. Mr. Gillock was to pay him from fifty to seventy-five dollars for arresting his negro woman. Mr. Everett paid him twenty-five dollars for a like service, Mr. Hatch ten dollars, and Mrs. Cunningham had offered him twenty-five dollars to get back a woman for whose arrest she had already paid fifty dollars, and who had again

NORRIS THE KIDNAPPER.   541

escaped. Similar revelations were made by other policemen and officers of Nashville.

The records of the Army Police Office abound with cases of reported abductions,—one of which may serve as a sample of the remainder. In the pleasant little village—or "city," as it is styled—of Edgefield, just across the Cumberland River from Nashville, resided, before and in the early days of the war, a certain Rev. Dr. McFerran, or, as he was commonly called, Preacher McFerran. The fortunate possessor of a score or more of negroes, he was also otherwise blessed with an abundance of this world's goods. Waxing wealthy and fat, he fared sumptuously every day, until the approach of the Union army, when, having preached the gospel according to Jeff Davis, he found it advisable to travel southward. His departure was considerably hurried,—too much so to allow of his taking with him the larger and more valuable portion of his movable property,—the negroes above mentioned. Left to shift for themselves, they did much as they pleased,—some running away and others remaining. About a year afterward McFerran turned up at Connerville, Alabama, and began to think it would be a good idea to have his negroes there too; they certainly would be worth considerably more than where they were. He accordingly cast about for some means of getting them out of Yankee hands and into his own.

He puts himself in communication with one Silas Norris,—a carpenter by trade, living in Edgefield, and who for some years had been acting as constable. Norris being a man that will do any thing for pay, however dirty the job, an arrangement is made between them by which McFerran is to get his negroes,—all that are left of them, seven in number,—and Norris eight hundred dollars. Norris at once begins preparations, and, as a first step, buys a wagon, for which he pays thirty-five dollars. He engages two men—William Bradlove and James Stuart—to go with him, and promises the former one hundred and the latter two hundred dollars for their services. The next thing, and the most difficult, is to catch the negroes and load them into the wagon. They lived in a cabin about two miles from Nashville, outside of the picket-lines. The most feasible plan seemed to be to go in force and capture them at night. Accordingly, he takes with him five men, —some of them armed,—and in the middle of the night makes a descent upon their cabin, and has them in his hands before they fairly know what is the matter. Four of the men he chains by locking their legs together with trace-chains, and fastens them together by twos. In an adjoining cabin are four other negroes, belonging to James Anderson, son-in-law of McFerran, in three of whom Norris claims to have some interest. While his hand is in, he concludes he may as well take them along too, and they are surprised and secured in the same way. Resistance is vain: yet they struggle as best they can, howling, begging, and imploring not to be taken "down Souf." They might as well appeal to a stone. He knows no mercy, and shows none. Once in the wagon, they are driven off as rapidly as his four horses can draw them. By twisting and turning from one road to

Norris kidnapping Negroes

another, he evades the Federal forces, and in about eight days reaches his destination, Huntsville, Alabama, when the negroes are turned over to their ministerial master and Norris receives his reward.

This was during the last weeks of December, 1862. On his return the next month, Norris was arrested, and, after a careful examination, convicted of kidnapping and sent to the military prison at Alton, where he yet remains. His well-merited punishment had a good effect,—largely diminishing the number of similar transactions, previously of such common occurrence; and the subsequent energetic movements of the Army Police have wellnigh ended the business within the bounds of their operations.

Phillips, the Bogus Kentucky Unionist.

THE arrest of the parties mentioned in the sketch headed "The Pseudo Sanders," which will be found on preceding pages, was for a time the town talk. Gossips discussed it in every conceivable aspect, and Rumor found employment for her hundred tongues. The hotels, the steamers, the railways, the bar-rooms, and even the streets of Cairo, Illinois, were full of it. It penetrated the sanctity of private residences, and sat down with their inmates around the family hearth. The doctor and captain were soon recognized, pointed out, and everywhere made the cynosure of wondering eyes. Speculation was busy with their probable fate, and expressions of sympathy or scowling looks of contemptuous indifference greeted them, according to the character and feelings of those whom they saw and met. Mrs. Ford, too, was not forgotten in all this. Pitied and despised in turn, she was thought and spoken of by many; but, not being visible to the rabble, she was hardly the object of so much interest as her two companions.

On the evening following the arrest, while the doctor was comfortably ensconced within an arm-chair in the sitting-room of the St. Charles, he was accosted by a fine-looking, elderly gentleman, who introduced himself as Mr. Phillips, of Louisville, Kentucky. For the liberty thus taken he apologized by saying that he had heard him spoken of as a Confederate surgeon under arrest and in trouble, and that if he could be of any assistance to him he would most cheerfully render it. He lived, he said, three miles from Louisville, just outside of the Federal lines, and was there known as a Union man of the straitest sect,—so much so that General Boyle had given him a pass to come into the city and go out at will. He had taken oaths of allegiance—bitter and detestable as they were—out of policy, and for appearance's sake. His heart, however, was with the South, in whose service part of his family now were. His son-in-law, Dr. Keller, was chief surgeon on Hindman's staff, and his own son held a position in the rebel army. He owned a plantation in Mississippi, which had formerly been well stocked with negroes. He had heard, however, while at home, that the Yankees had overrun the plantation and run off the negroes, and that most of them had been brought up the river to Cairo. He had at once procured from General Boyle a pass to Cairo and a letter of introduction to General Tuttle, in which he was endorsed as a sound, thorough-going Union man, in whom all confidence could be placed, and stating also that he was now in search of certain negroes supposed to be in Cairo, and that any assistance rendered him in their recovery would be considered a particular favor by the writer, who regarded it as no more than an act of justice to a loyal man. On the strength of these representations he had recovered the negroes, and was now only waiting for a boat to take them home with him. In the mean while, if he could be of any service, he had only to mention it. He had some money left, and if it was money the doctor wanted, it was at his command. If there was not enough of it, he would procure more for him. He would sign a bond, would endorse any statement, would make any sort of representations to General Tuttle in his behalf, and, with the character given him by his letters of recommendation, he thought he could arrange the matter with the general and procure his release.

The doctor thanked him warmly, but said that it would be of no use, as it was beyond the power of General Tuttle to do any thing in the premises. He had been implicated in smuggling contraband goods through the lines, and had been ordered to be sent back to General Rosecrans, to be dealt with for the violation of his parole. His own case was bad enough, to be sure; but it was not for himself he cared. His life was worth nothing, and he would die any time to serve the Confederacy: it did not matter whether he ever returned to the land of his love. It was not for his own sake he wished it, but to relieve the sufferings and save the lives of his companions-in-arms. There was a great scarcity of all kinds of medicines in the South, and hundreds were dying for the want of them. He had hoped, in his poor way, to do something for them, but he had been betrayed by a pretended friend. But even this failure, involving the consequences it did, was a small matter compared with the detention of his fellow-traveller. That was a public calamity which it was of the utmost importance to remedy at once; for, to speak confidentially, Captain Denver was not Captain Denver at all, but George N. Sanders, just returning from England with the acceptance of the Confederate loan, by the Rothschilds, in his pocket. This he had managed to save from the general confiscation; and if any way could now be devised to get him away and through the lines immediately, all would yet be well, and the Confederacy financially be recognized as an independent nation. As for himself, he had no particular desire to go again to Nashville if it could be avoided, but Sanders must be helped through at all hazards, without reference to himself or anybody else. Some time previously, it will be remembered, the noted George N. Sanders escaped to England through Canada; and this tale was concocted to correspond with that event and seem plausible.

During this narration Phillips was deeply interested, and at its close so much excited that he could hardly speak. After gazing abstractedly for a few moments, he invited the doctor to his room, where they could talk more privately and with less danger. There he repeated that, though professedly Union, he was heart and hand with the South, and always had been. He had aided it at every opportunity,—had smuggled through clothing, medicines, arms, and ammunition, had acted as a spy, and when Bragg was threatening Louisville had sent his negroes to him, time and again, with valuable information, and on one very important occasion had gone himself. His earnest professions of loyalty had completely deceived the Federal authorities, and he was trusted by General Boyle as a friend, and the standing thus acquired had made him of considerable service to his Southern friends, and he had expected to continue in his assumed character somewhile longer; but now he thought he could do more good by throwing off the mask.

"Come straight back to Louisville with me," he said. "I will put you and Sanders both through, and go myself in the bargain. I am tired of Yankee rule; don't care a —— for them, and ask no odds. I've got money enough, every thing I want, and can get along without them. It will be easy enough to get away. Nobody will suspect me, and I can get a pass from Boyle to go anywhere. I've got some of the best horses in the country, —can't be beat for speed and bottom; and we will fix up a light wagon, fill it with medicines most needed, and be away beyond reach before anybody'll think of such a thing as pursuit."

The doctor assenting, an immediate return to Louisville was agreed upon, where the three were to meet again and make all necessary arrangements for the trip. On reaching that city, the doctor went at once to see General Boyle, when the following colloquy ensued:—

"General, do you know a man by the name of Phillips, living some three miles out of town?"

"Oh, yes, very well. He's a particular friend of mine."

"Do you know his wife and his daughter Mrs. Dr. Keller?"

"Yes,—know the whole family."

"What is their position, general, on the war question?"

"Oh, they are loyal. He's one of the very best Union men we have in Kentucky."

"Ah? But, general, what would you think if I should say I had made an arrangement with him to poison you?"

"That you were mad as a March hare."

"Well, I don't mean to say that I have exactly any thing of that kind against him; but I do say that he is not a Union man at all, but, on the contrary, a rebel and a spy."

"How do you know that?"

"Oh, simply enough. He told me so himself; that's all. I met him in Cairo a day or two since, and we had a long talk." (Here the doctor narrated the circumstances, and gave the conversation as it occurred.) "I'll fix it upon him in any way you wish. He shall give money to anybody you name, to buy contraband goods and medicines with. He shall leave his house on any night you say, in any kind of a wagon you say. You shall examine that wagon, and in it you shall find contraband goods. You shall arrest him at any point you please, and you will find our man Conklin [Denver] in the wagon, blacked and disguised as a negro. You shall find upon him letters to Southern rebels; or you may secrete yourself behind a screen and hear him tell his own story, how he has deceived you, how he smuggled goods through to the rebels times without number, how he kept Bragg informed of what was going on last summer, and how he is now preparing to go South with an amount of medicines, important despatches, &c."

"Good God! Is it possible that he is such a man? I would have staked my life on his loyalty and good faith. But can't you stay and work the case up for me?"

"I will stay to-morrow and do what I can; but the next day I must be in

33

Nashville. I will arrange matters so that your own men can fix the whole thing upon him, but I am expected back day after to-morrow, and dare not stay longer."

"I don't like to trust them: it's too important a case. I'll telegraph to the Chief of Police, and, if your business isn't a matter of too much importance, get permission for you to stay a few days. How will that do?"

"Very well."

The doctor then took his leave, and the next morning was shown a despatch authorizing him to remain in Louisville so long as General Boyle should require his assistance.

That day Phillips came to see the doctor at the Galt House. The project was discussed more at length, and a plan of operations partially agreed upon. At length Phillips said to the doctor,—

"Do you know my son-in-law, Dr. Keller?"

"Very well; have seen him a hundred times."

"Do you know his wife?"

"Yes: I met her frequently in Memphis. She was connected with some aid society there, and I saw her often about the hospitals."

"Did you? She's at my house now, and will be crazy to see you."

The doctor saw that he was getting himself into a scrape. Known to Mrs. Keller by another name and in another character, how should he meet her now, in new garb and guise, without revealing the deception and frightening away his game? The only escape from the dilemma was to put a bold face on the matter, and by sheer audacity overcome any difficulties or obstacles that might be thrown in his way by reason of old acquaintance. He would be very happy to meet the lady, he said, but could not call on her. He did not think it wise to leave the hotel, and especially to go beyond the lines. It was only a matter of courtesy that he was allowed the liberty he enjoyed. Charged with breaking his parole, strict military usage would demand close confinement under guard, and he was anxious to do nothing to which the least exception could now be taken. Any further mishap to him would endanger the success of their new enterprise, and it was vitally important that Sanders should get through this time without fail. If his daughter could be induced to call upon him at the Galt House, it would confer a personal favor upon him, and would relieve him from the necessity or temptation of doing any thing incompatible with the terms of his parole and the strictest sense of honor. Phillips acknowledged the justness of this view of the case, and promised that Mrs. Keller should visit him the next day.

Sure enough, the next morning in came Mrs. Keller. Hardly had she alighted from her carriage when the doctor welcomed her in his most graceful manner.

"How do you do, Mrs. Keller? I am delighted to see you. How well you are looking! How are the children? When did you leave Memphis? How long have you been in Louisville? When did you hear from Dr. Keller? How did you leave all the friends in Memphis?"

And so for full five minutes the doctor launched at her question after question, with the utmost rapidity of his rapid utterance, scarcely giving her time to hear, much less answer, the first before her attention was called to a second, a third, and so on, until she was so hopelessly confused and perplexed that she could say just nòthing at all. By the time she had recovered, the doctor, with diplomatic skill, had diverted the conversation into new channels, still giving her no time to advert to their acquaintance in Memphis and the spirit of change which had since come over him. At length, by shrewd management, she edged in this simple question:—

"When did you see Dr. Keller last?"

The road now being clear, the doctor answered more at leisure, but not less elaborately:—

"It has been a good while,—some five or six months. I have been a prisoner three months or more, and General Hindman had gone to Arkansas some time before I was captured, and I have not seen the doctor since he left with the general."

"I had no idea you had been so long a prisoner. How did you happen to be taken? and how did you escape?"

"We were taken in the Confederate hospital at Iuka. Ordinarily, surgeons are not treated as prisoners, but are considered non-combatants. We, however, were retained as hostages for the return of certain Federals imprisoned by General Price in violation, as the Yankee commander alleged, of the rules of war and the cartel agreed upon by the contending par-. ties. A very intimate friend of mine,—Dr. Scott,—also of the Confederate army, and captured with me, married a cousin of the Federal General Stanley; and through the influence which this relationship gave him we were released on parole, the remainder being still in captivity."

The doctor then proceeded with a relation of the occurrences of the past two or three days, dwelling particularly upon the unfortunate detention of Sanders. Mrs. Keller's sympathy was at once excited. She entered warmly into their plans and purposes, and freely offered every assistance that it was in her power to render. She would go herself, but circumstances over which she had no control would not permit it. She had a younger, unmarried sister, however, who was very anxious to accompany them, and she would dress her in boy's clothes to avoid suspicion and trouble.

Just then Phillips himself came in, flushed with excitement, and eager to be off at once. His whole mind was bent on the enterprise, and he could not be easy until they were fairly started. His arrangements were all perfected, and he knew just where he could buy every thing he wanted; he would take the articles out to his house a few at a time, and nobody would imagine any thing out of the way. He could easily make two trips a day; and it wouldn't take long at that rate to load the wagon. He wanted every thing ready, so that they could be off at a moment's notice.

"Certainly," said the doctor, thoughtfully; "it will be well to have every thing ready. But since I saw you last I've been thinking about this thing of carrying contraband goods with us, and I've about concluded it won't do.

It is true that the medicines would do an immense amount of good,—possibly save many lives; but there's Denver: he must be got through, anyhow. It won't do to risk any thing. We must have a sure thing of it this time. Then, again, I don't want to act in bad faith by violating my parole. Our people want such things badly enough, but they must get them in some other way. It will be glory enough for us to get Denver through: 'twill be better than winning a battle; whole generations will rise up and call us blessed. Don't let us attempt too much and spoil it all. Better avoid all needless risk, and stick to one thing. We are made men if we succeed in that."

But Phillips was not convinced. He didn't believe there was any risk at all, and wasn't going with an empty wagon,—not he. It should be packed as full as it could hold with drugs and other needed goods. He had money, and was going to use it; and if he, the doctor, was afraid to go with him, he might find some other means of getting there.

To this, the doctor only replied that he still thought it unwise, but he was not the man to back out of any enterprise. Still, he would not violate his parole,—would not knowingly engage in any contraband trade. But Denver was under no such restraint, and, said the doctor,—

"You had better talk with him. He knows just what is wanted. He's a mild, quiet fellow, however, and never intrudes himself upon anybody's notice. He wouldn't think of suggesting such a thing; but if you furnish him money he'll buy just what can be used to the best advantage. He can buy and you can load the goods; but I don't want to know any thing about them. You can be ready to start on such a day, and I will meet you at some station on the railroad and take passage with you there."

Phillips was satisfied with this, and at once sought out Denver and gave him one hundred and fifty-five dollars,—all the money he had with him,—directed him to a particular store where he could get all the quinine, &c. that he wanted, told him to buy as much as he thought best and pay this money down as an earnest of good faith in making the purchase. In the mean while he would draw from the bank as much more as would be needed, and with it he could settle the bill the next day. Denver went as directed, but found that the merchant would sell him nothing without a special permit from General Boyle. This was reported to the doctor, who promised to have that obstacle removed without delay

While Phillips and Denver are arranging other matters, the doctor goes to General Boyle, reports progress, and asks him to issue a permit for the sale of the quinine. The general hesitates, doesn't exactly like to do it, and finally asks if they can't mark some boxes "quinine," nail them up, load them into his wagon, and have them found there when arrested. "But no," he continues: "that won't do at all. He'd beat us in that game. We couldn't show that he had any thing contraband in his wagon. Of course he'd deny it, and it would be necessary for us to prove it. Can't we borrow enough to answer our purposes?"

"Possibly; but it would be better for the Government to buy it, if you won't let him do it.   It would be worth more than five or six hundred dollars to get rid of such an arrant old traitor and spy."

"I guess we can get along by borrowing."

The borrowing project very nearly defeated the whole matter, by the delay incurred; but the quinine was finally obtained, given to Denver, and safely packed in Phillips's wagon.   Every thing was now ready for a start.   The doctor took the cars for the place of meeting, and Phillips set out in his wagon, Denver, disguised as a negro, driving.   The doctor arrived safely at the appointed rendezvous ; but not so Phillips.   He was scarcely well started when he was arrested and brought back to Louisville.   Too proud and haughty to betray the least emotion, there was no "scene" at any time during his arrest or examination, and he vouchsafed not a word in his own behalf.   Defence there could be none.   His guilt was too patent for doubt. Conviction followed as a matter of course ; and, instead of finding a home on his Mississippi plantation, he became an involuntary recipient of the widely-dispensed hospitalities of Camp Chase.

Moore and Blue, the Scouts.

ROMANCE in real life is not less abundant than in novels.   The history of many a man unknown to fame, if written and published, would prove infinitely more fascinating to the reader than thousands of the pages of fiction so eagerly devoured.   In times of peace these heroes of unwritten adventure are seldom withdrawn from the quiet into which they have settled, and the story of their lives—told only to a few friends—passes at their death, with all its wonder and romance, into the great storehouse of unremembered things.   Not so in these days of war.   The active, the bold, and the daring have opened to them an unlimited field for the exercise of their peculiar characteristics.   They are brought into contact with thousands to whom they would otherwise never have been known, their history is told and heard, and ultimately finds its way to the public in the columns of the newspaper or the pages of the book.   Thus has it been with the two whose names head this chapter.   Theirs has been a strange, varied, and sometimes lawless life. Together they have wandered over many wild and unknown regions, passed through many scenes of interest and danger, and, by the experience and sagacity thus acquired, made themselves of no little service to their country during the present war.   Firm and constant friends in all their adventures and trials, their story is not less remarkable for its intrinsic interest than as that of a modern Damon and Pythias.

In 1856 two young men—Frank M. Blue, formerly of Michigan, but now from Illinois, and Henry W. Moore, of Brooklyn, New York—met in Leavenworth City, Kansas, whither they had come for the purpose of pre-empting land in that Territory.   Taking a fancy to each other, they set out for the interior in company. At Ossawatamie they met John Brown, joined him in scouting after border-ruffians, and participated in the fight at Hickory Point, where Brown, his son, and twenty-seven men routed forty of them strongly posted in a blacksmith's shop, by backing up against it a load of hay and burning them out. Leaving Brown, they next went to Jennison's camp at Mound City, which was made in such a shape as to resemble a group of hay-stacks. While here, they, in company with eight others, crossed the Missouri River, surprised the town of Rushville, captured thirty border-ruffians and a number of the citizens, broke their guns, and carried away their horses, money, watches, &c. Afterwards they joined the Utah Expedition under General A. S. Johnston, and with it went through to Salt Lake City. Leaving there on their own responsibility, the fame of the Mexican silver-mines attracted them to Puebla, where they remained four months in company with a mixed crowd of miners, Indians, and Mexican peons. Having accumulated a considerable amount of silver, the spirit of adventure led them to Santa Fe, where, some of the party getting themselves into a difficulty, a hasty flight northward became necessary. Procuring a Mexican boro (jackass), and loading him with a few crackers and their personal effects, they set out for Fort Union, one hundred miles distant. Here they procured a mule and crossed over to Bent's Fort, where they joined the Kiowa Expedition under Major Sedgwick. Returning from this, they proceeded to Camp Floyd, and thence across Kiowa Pass to Pike's Peak, where they "jumped" a claim and went to mining. Here they spent the summer, and in the fall hired to Joe Doyle, a Mexican trader and ranchero, to go down the Waifoma River and oversee his peons and take charge of his herds. Remaining all winter on his ranch, they went again next spring to Leavenworth, and hired as riders to the California Overland Express Company, in which business they remained until the outbreak of the rebellion.

With the prospect of active service, they could not stand idly by and see others engaged, and accordingly recruited ten men, with whom they joined Captain William Cleaveland's independent company for the defence of the Kansas border. Their first exploit was a dash into De Kalb, Missouri, where they captured twelve or fourteen prisoners and forty horses and mules. A large party, however, pursued them, overtook and captured them at Atkinson's Ferry, carried them to St. Joseph, and lodged them in jail. The good people of St. Joseph were very anxious to have them tried and sent to the penitentiary at once; but there was no court in session, and the only recourse was to lock them up in the jail, where they did not remain long. The guard was made drunk with drugged whiskey, the negro cook was bribed with a twenty-dollar gold piece to steal the keys from the jailer, the door was unlocked at midnight, and the whole party walked out just ten days after they had been incarcerated. One John Seelover, a friend, had a skiff near at hand to cross them over the river, and a conveyance on the other side to take them to Atchison the same night. The next night, nothing daunted by their recent jail-experience, the same party crossed in a flat-boat to

Missouri, captured from the rebel farmers horses enough to mount themselves, and returned again, after giving the people thereabouts a good scare. The evening following, a negro came to their head-quarters at Pardee, eight miles from Atchison, and said that his rebel master, John Wells by name, and living twelve miles south of St. Joseph, was to leave the next morning for Price's army with two wagon-loads of goods and a coffin full of arms. The company started over immediately, the negro acting as guide. The rebel was found, and so were the goods, consisting of bacon, flour, sugar, coffee, tobacco, whiskey, powder and lead, but no arms. Demand was made for the latter, but the prisoner denied having any. A lariat was then thrown over his neck and drawn tight for a few minutes, when he disclosed their place of concealment,—a newly-made grave, with head and foot board,—in which were found twenty stand of arms of all kinds, and a box of pistols, all of which were taken to Fort Leavenworth and turned over to the United States Government.

Many other expeditions were made, until Cleaveland and his band were known and feared all over that country. On one of these it was ascertained that Major Hart, of Price's army, was at his home, fifteen miles from Weston, with ten men. The company immediately set forth to capture them, a woman—Mrs. Chandler—acting as guide. The major, his men, and the stock on his farm, were taken and carried to Geary City, Kansas, where the stock was just put away and twelve men left as a guard over the prisoners, when forty Missourians rode up and demanded their surrender. Chandler, who stood in the porch, said they would never surrender,—when he was shot dead, eleven bullets being found in his body. His wife and the remainder fired from the house, and picked them off so fast that they were compelled to retire to Fort Leavenworth, eight miles distant, whence they brought up a company of the 1st Missouri Cavalry, under Captain Fuller, to their assistance, and finally succeeded in capturing the little garrison. They were taken to the fort, and, no one appearing against them, were speedily released by Major Prince, of the U. S. Regulars, commanding the post. Not long after this, Moore, Blue, William Tuff of Baltimore, and Cleaveland, dashed into Kansas City and levied a contribution of some thirty-three hundred dollars in coin upon two secession bankers who had rebel flags flying at their windows. They were pursued, but made their escape, divided the money equally, and all four went to Chicago to spend it, which they did most liberally, and in June, 1861, returned to Leavenworth.

Here Moore and Blue, who had become fast friends, separated, the latter going into Missouri on several jayhawking expeditions, and the former acting as guide to General Sturgis and participating in the battles of Dug Spring and Wilson Creek. Moore relates many interesting adventures which befell him while thus engaged, of which one is here given as an illustration of his shrewdness and foresight. Having been sent by General Lyon to ascertain about certain guerrillas that were lurking about the country, he dressed himself in butternut uniform and set out. Thinking, however, that he might be captured on the trip, he determined to avail himself of a trick he had somewhere read of, which was to take a large minie ball, cut the top off, hollow it out, and then take the other part and make of it a screw to fit on again, thus forming a kind of little box. He then took a piece of parchment paper, and, writing on it in a peculiar hand a commission in the secret service of the Confederate army, and signing to it the name of General Price, enclosed it in the bullet, screwed it up, and started on again. He had gone but a little way when, sure enough, he fell into the hands of Sy Gordon's guerrilla band, who proposed hanging him at once. Gordon told him he had orders to hang all such suspicious characters as he was, and that he should do it. Moore replied that he had very little to say, but he wished he would do him the favor to take that bullet to General Price after he had hung him. Gordon seemed much amused at so trifling a request, and said to his prisoner that he must be either crazy or a fool. When informed that there was more about the bullet than he had any idea of, he insisted that he should be shown what it was; but Moore refused, saying that he was sworn to say nothing about it. Gordon was non-plussed for a while, but, examining the bullet very closely, soon saw the trick, unscrewed the top, and took out and read the contents. Turning to Moore, he told him he was "all right," and furnished him with a better horse than he then had, on which he at once started back. On arriving at camp, he related his adventure, whereupon a body of cavalry was sent out in pursuit, and the next day succeeded in capturing a number of the band.

Late in the fall Moore and Blue again met in Leavenworth, and both went towards Springfield as guides and spies for Lane and Sturgis's commands. On Christmas-day both were sent by General Steele into Price's camp, whither they went, and returned on January 3, 1862. Four miles from Warsaw they found Christmas was being celebrated by a ball, at which many rebel officers were present. In company with some rebel teamsters, they devised a plan to scare these officers off, and secure to themselves the field and the girls, by rushing up to the house and shouting, at the top of their voices, "The Feds are coming! the Feds are coming!" The plan worked admirably: the officers rushed away in hot haste,—one even falling into the well,—and our plotters were left in full possession of the premises. Coming back to Sedalia, they were engaged by Colonel Weir as guides. Going ahead one day to select a camping-ground, they came to a house where was a man very hospitably inclined, asking them to stop, put up their horses and feed them with corn, of which he had plenty. Representing that they had been pressed into the service, but were in heart with the rebels, their entertainer grew confidential, and told them something about himself,—that he acted as a spy, carried despatches wrapped in a cigar; &c. The information thus obtained from him contributed to the capture, by General Pope, at Blackwater, of thirteen hundred rebels with all their equipments. They accompanied General Pope on his expedition to Warrensburg, where he captured Colonel Parke's rebel force, and then returned to Kansas, where they jayhawked for a month or two. Going again to Missouri, they learned that Quantrill's guerrilla band was in the vicinity of Independence. With eleven comrades, they went there, captured the town, quartered themselves in the court-house, and badly frightened the people, who thought, of course, that they were only the advance-guard of a larger body behind. Quantrill soon came into the place with forty-five men, and demanded their surrender. This was refused, and a skirmish commenced, the occupants of the court-house firing out of the doors and windows, and finally succeeding in dispersing the besiegers, who went off for reinforcements. The thirteen now thought it best to retire, which they did, skirmishing for one and a half miles to a stone fence, when the guerrillas mounted. The jayhawkers now ensconced themselves behind the fence. Holding their position until dusk, they then scattered, having killed five and wounded seven of the guerrillas. Pursuit was made by the latter; but the darkness enabled them to escape, and they soon put an effectual end to it by cutting the telegraph-wire and stretching it across the road from fence to fence.

The twain now joined Generals Curtis and Sigel as couriers, and made several dangerous trips between the army and Rolla, carrying despatches each way, on one of which Blue was taken prisoner and held as such for six weeks. Both accompanied General Curtis in his terrible march through Arkansas to Helena, and met with many stirring adventures by the way. One day while they were riding in company with Newton Blue, a brother of Frank and also a scout, they came suddenly upon five rebels in a lane, with whom they stopped and talked for some time, representing themselves as Southern men. The rebels soon heard a bugle behind them, however, and, suspecting that all was not right, made a charge upon our scouts, who killed three of them and captured their horses, the remaining two falling into the hands of the Federal advance. At Helena they engaged in buying cotton for the speculators, and in one of their excursions were captured by the guerrillas. Pretending to be rebels, they joined a portion of Jeff Thompson's gang, and, remaining with them eleven days, obtained much information concerning him. Having had enough of guerrilla life, they planned an escape, in this wise. An old negro, of whom they knew, was just going into Helena with a load of cotton for sale. By him they sent word to General Steele of an arrangement which had been made to rob him on his return of the proceeds of the cotton. The message was carried and delivered faithfully, and on his way back the negro was robbed, as proposed, of his eleven hundred dollars in greenbacks, which were found hidden away in his boots; but just as the thirty-one guerrillas were dividing the spoils, the second battalion of the 1st Missouri Cavalry came up and captured the whole party, all of whom were subsequently sent to St. Louis as prisoners.

From Helena Moore and Blue next went to Columbia, and then to Corinth, where they detected and arrested two counterfeiters, making a great haul of counterfeit St. Louis city treasury warrants and gold dollars, both of which were well executed. Accompanying Colonel Truesdail's police force to Louisville, they there played the rebel, and hunted out Palmer and Estes, who burned the ammunition-steamers at Columbus and were afterwards sent to Camp Chase. With our army they came on to Nashville, and afterwards ran as mail-messengers,—a very dangerous service. Getting on the track of a band of guerrillas between Bowling Green and Nashville, they piloted a cavalry force to the neighborhood, and captured a considerable number, who were brought to Nashville and were properly dealt with. They next made a successful spy-trip to Murfreesborough, going by way of Lavergne and crossing at Sanders's Ferry. Dr. Goodwin, of the rebel army, whom they had fallen in with on the way, vouched for them, and they passed the pickets into the town readily enough. Once in, they made the circuit of the town and camps, obtaining all the information they could, and then began to think of getting back. It was arranged that Moore should go to Chattanooga for further observation, while Blue would return to Nashville and report what they had already seen and heard. With this understanding, both went at once to the provost-marshal's office for passes. At that time Captain William Brenton was provost-marshal, whom they found somewhat crabbed and chary of words. Making known their wants, they were saluted in this manner:—

"Want a pass to Chattanooga, do you? Lots of people in that fix. What d'ye want to go there for?"

"We want to join Jack Jones's cavalry company," replied Moore, at a venture, who had heard of such a company.

"If that's all you want, you needn't go to Chattanooga for it. Jones and his company are here now."

This was a new and not pleasing phase of affairs; and, to add to their difficulty, Captain Brenton called Jones in at once, and told him here were two men who wished to join his company, and he'd better have them sworn in right away. Fairly caught in their own trap, there was no escape, and, trusting the future to good luck, they yielded to their fate, and were sworn in. Three days afterwards, they with three others were detailed to duty on the second picket-line, and determined to take advantage of this opportunity and make their escape. Some distance from their station was a house where whiskey could be obtained at exorbitant prices; and Moore and Blue proposed to their companions that if they would go and get the whiskey they would pay for it, and guard the post during their absence. This was agreed to; and the whiskey-seekers were hardly out of sight when our two scouts rode off in hot haste to the outer pickets, two guards being on duty in the road, the remainder of the pickets being near by at their fire, and their horses tied close at hand. They were accosted by the guard with the usual—

"Halt! who comes there?"

"Friends, with the countersign!" was the answer.

"Dismount; advance, one, and give the countersign," was now the order.

Our scouts had foreseen this, and planned accordingly. Hence they rode up briskly to the pickets; and while they pulled and tugged upon the bridle-reins to hold in their fiery steeds, the spurs upon their heels were doing equally good service in urging the animals forward, and they could not be stopped until abreast of the pickets and nearly touching their opposing muskets. Moore then leaned forward, without dismounting, as if to give the password, and suddenly jerked to one side the bayonet and loaded gun of the nearest guard, while with his other hand he shot him dead with his pistol, suddenly drawn from his holster. The ball penetrated the forehead, the guard falling over backward, his mouth wide opened. Blue at the same time drew a pistol and shot the other guard dead in his tracks, and away they flew down the road, and were speedily lost in the darkness and distance. The rest of the rebel pickets did not pursue them, but our scouts could hear them shout after them long and loudly, "Oh, you —— infernal Yankees!" &c. &c. The scouts soon took to the woods, travelling all night in the direction of Nashville, and meeting with no further adventure until soon after sunrise, when one of them espied a moving object in their front, at a considerable distance. A second glance revealed it to be a "butternut," with gun in hand, who at that instant glided behind a tree and took deliberate aim at them. Our scouts, who were also in butternut, were not taken aback. Keeping on at an easy horse-walk, and apparently noticing no one, one of them begins to sing, in a brisk, cheery voice, a verse of the "Dixie" song, ending,—

> "In a Southern land I'll take my stand,
> And live and die in Dixie," &c.

As they neared the butternut, he was observed to lower his gun and emerge from behind the tree. When abreast, he accosted the twain:—

"Halloo, boys! which way?"

"All right!—taking a little scout this morning," was the answer.

The "butternut," who was a rebel scout or guerrilla, was now near them, unsuspecting, and inclined to be inquisitive and sociable, his gun over his shoulder. But our men were in haste, and had a vivid remembrance of that previous moment when he had drawn a bead on them, in such a cold-blooded manner, from behind the tree. One of them draws his revolver as quick as thought and shoots him dead; and again they ride forward briskly for a while, and eventually reach the Federal lines near Nashville in safety, but through dangers to be feared upon every hand, from behind each tree, or rock, or bush,—as they were traversing debatable land, between two great contending armies, and known to be swarming with scouts, spies, and troops, and especially rebel guerrillas or "partisan rangers."

Acting as secret policemen and detectives, they now assisted in developing several important cases, a full mention of which would fill many pages of this work. Occasionally they varied their daily routine by acting as guides to cavalry expeditions, in which they rendered efficient service. One of their adventures in Nashville is worth relating.

After the battle of Stone River large numbers of rebel prisoners were sent to the city and allowed their parole, whereupon the wealthy secessionists of the place seized every opportunity to feed, clothe, and encourage them. One day, as Moore and Blue were walking down High Street in the dress of Confederate prisoners, they were invited into an elegant residence and were kindly entertained by Miss Hamilton, one of the reigning belles of Nashville. Conversation naturally ensued concerning the relative merits and demerits of the North and South, in the course of which Miss Hamilton said she had done every thing in her power to aid the Southern cause. She had sent letters of encouragement, she said, and also a Southern flag, through the lines. She told them of an old Irishwoman who was in the habit of carrying out goods in a market-wagon which had a false bottom. She said, too, that Governor Andy Johnson once had her brought before him and gave her a severe lecturing, but she soon talked him over, and persuaded him into giving her a pass to go two miles out of the city to see her aunt, and that when once beyond the lines she went to the rebel army at Murfreesborough. She further said that a Mrs. Montgomery, who lived two miles out on the Franklin pike, had taken out more goods than anybody else in Nashville. When she went to Murfreesborough she took out with her letters, and had given to Southern soldiers coming into Nashville large quantities of clothing, and finally demonstrated her good will by presenting Moore with a fine pair of pants and other clothing and a pair of new boots. In return for these acts of kindness, Colonel Truesdail sent her the following letter of thanks:—

"OFFICE CHIEF ARMY POLICE, January 10, 1863.

"MISS HAMILTON, HIGH STREET:—

"DEAR MISS:—Please accept my grateful acknowledgment for your kindness—during the arrival of a large number of Confederate prisoners in the city from the battle of Stone River, and their stay here—in calling into your beautiful residence one of my secret police, and for the kind and benevolent treatment you extended to him. Also for the new suit of clothes and the cavalry boots given him, the valuable information of your labors in the Confederate cause furnished to him, and the knowledge afforded me of your persevering energy as a spy and smuggler. I shall endeavor to profit by it, and may have occasion to send another officer to you.

"Respectfully,

"WILLIAM TRUESDAIL,

"Chief Army Police."

After this they accompanied a cavalry police expedition for the purpose of capturing Captains Young and Scruggs,—the leaders of a band of guerrillas on White's Creek, who were a terror to the whole country. They were at the house of an old man named McNeill, which was surrounded and a demand made for Young and Scruggs. There being some sixty troops to back the demand, the old man did not dare to deny their presence, and, without deigning any reply, turned at once, went into the house, and bolted the door. This slight barrier was speedily broken down, and the crowd rushed in. Search was made everywhere,—down stairs and up, under beds, in chimneys, and under the floor; but neither Young nor Scruggs was found. As a last resort, they went to the girls' bedroom; and there—in bed, between two full-grown young women—the valiant Young was found snugly hidden away. He was unceremoniously dragged out, and Scruggs in the mean while having been found in a hay-loft, both were taken to Nashville, and are now in the penitentiary at that place, awaiting their trial.

For the last five months Moore and Blue have been constantly engaged in the investigation and development of many minor cases; and both look forward to yet many days of adventure for themselves and of usefulness to the Government.

Trainor, the Traitor Wagon-Master.

In the early part of February, 1863, there was boarding at the City Hotel, in Nashville, a lady of ordinary appearance and apparently about forty-five years of age. Her husband and three sons were in the rebel Morgan's command, and she was known by the proprietors of the house and by Mrs. Winburn—the wife of one of them—as entertaining strong sympathy for the Confederate cause. In reality, however, she was a Union woman, and in the employ of Colonel Truesdail, Chief of the Army Police. From the position of her relatives, and her former place of residence, aided by her expression of Southern sentiments, she was considered a genuine secessionist, and had completely won the favor of Mrs. Winburn, by whom she was made a friend and confidante. Mrs. W. told her on several occasions how much aid she and others of her lady friends had rendered to the Confederates, and how much more they intended to do for them. When visitors arrived at the City Hotel and made known their Southern sympathies, she was introduced to them as entertaining the same sentiments, and at once admitted to their confidence and councils. In this way she learned the existence there of a club, or rather association of persons, of rebel tendencies, the members of which made use of a certain password, without which none could gain admittance to their meetings, and this password was "Truth and Fidelity."

About the middle of February there arrived at the hotel from Louisville a certain Mrs. Trainor, who was there joined by her husband, John Trainor, —the latter understood to have formerly been master of transportation in the Ordnance Department of Major-General Buell's army. Mrs. Trainor was introduced by Mrs. Winburn to her confidential friend our detective as one who had at heart the welfare of the Southern Confederacy, and Mrs. Trainor presented her to Trainor, her husband, saying that he too was a friend of the South and ardently desired its success in the struggle for independence. This interview proved the precursor of many others, in which Trainor and his wife made many interesting statements concerning themselves and the assistance which they had rendered to the rebel army.

From Trainor she thus gained the following remarkable information. In the fall of 1861, he said, he had run the Federal blockade and brought from Louisville to Nashville, for the use of the Confederate army, several wagonloads of arms, ammunition, drugs, and medicines. These he had purchased in Louisville,—the arms and ammunition from a Mr. Bull, and the drugs and medicines from Dr. Pile. While in Nashville on this business, he made the acquaintance of General Zollicoffer, who advised him to abandon the neutral position he then occupied in regard to the war and engage in the service of the Confederates. This he agreed to do; and, the better to accomplish his ends, he was to obtain the position of Master of Transportation in the Ordnance Department of the Federal army. On his return to Louisville he had applied for the situation, which was given to him. Since then he had improved the advantages it offered, by following the Federal army down into Alabama with wagon-loads of contraband goods, which, according to previous arrangement, he disposed of at different places. During the whole Buell campaign the rebels knew, at all times, the strength of the escort which accompanied him, and if they did not capture his train it was not his fault. In the different skirmishes between the two armies he so managed that his train was never in its right place, and frequently the rebels would capture a portion of it, but would not take him prisoner, as it would be against their own interests to do so.

He regretted very much that the Confederates had not captured a train of one hundred and sixteen wagons, once under his charge, while General Buell was on his march to Kentucky in September last. He had requested Mrs. Winburn to inform Generals Morgan and Forrest where they could find the train and how many men the escort numbered. This she did; and he was so sure they would capture the train that he took Mrs. Winburn and his wife along for some distance from Nashville to see the fun of the capture. He had with him a young man—formerly in the Confederate army, but at that time in his employ—who was so disappointed because the train was not captured that he blew up and destroyed twenty-five of the wagons as they were passing over a certain bridge, and this, he said, was done with his own knowledge and consent, and partially at his suggestion.

After General Rosecrans assumed command of the Army of the Cumberland, Trainor said he began to purchase from Federal officers and soldiers, and from others who would sell them, pistols for General Wheeler, Dick McCann, and the guerrilla bands in the country. Some of them he carried to the rebels himself, and the balance he sent by a man named Nevins, who lived in Kentucky and had a contract to furnish cattle to the Federal army. This Nevins usually had with him some of Morgan's men, through whom he kept the Confederates continually informed of the number and movements of Federal troops along the line of the Louisville & Nashville Railroad, and he had acted as guide for Kirby Smith when the latter invaded Kentucky last fall. Trainor further said that he (Trainor) now had charge of the army transportation at Nashville, and that about the time of the battles at Stone River he was in the rebel camp and gave information. At this the lady remarked,—

"That accounts for the success of the Confederates in capturing so many of the Federal wagons."

"You may come to what conclusion on that subject you please," answered Trainor.

The young man, he continued, who was with him at the time of Buell's retreat and blew up the twenty-five wagons, was still in his employ; and one night not long since, by his management, five hundred mules belonging to the United States had stampeded and mysteriously disappeared from their corral. Many other interesting things which the young man had done for the benefit of the Confederate Government Trainor related with relish, and seemed desirous to impress upon the mind of his hearer that he himself was at all times anxious to serve the rebels and injure the Federal Government in every possible way. Seeing this disposition on his part, she suggested that he could now do more good by purchasing arms, quinine and other medicines for the use of the Confederate army than in any other way, and adding that she had a friend in Louisville who was a secret agent for that very purpose, and who would assist him in getting them South.

Trainor replied that he had then on hand one and a half pounds of quinine and two or three splendid pistols, which he would like to send South, and that he could procure any quantity of pistols if the money was furnished to purchase them.

The lady then proposed to buy his pistols and quinine, if he would deliver them to her friend in Louisville, who would send them through the lines.

Trainor assented, and sold her the quinine and four pistols, for which he received from her two hundred dollars. He also proposed to, and did, write to Mr. Bull and Dr. Pile, of Louisville, requesting them to furnish the secret agent above mentioned such quantity of quinine, pistols, and knives as he might wish for the Confederate service. He further said that he had a friend by the name of Kellogg, in whom he had confidence, and for whom he had obtained a pass and transportation to Louisville, and that he would send the quinine and pistols by him, instead of by his wife, as had been previously arranged. Implicit faith could be reposed in Kellogg, as he had recently engaged in running horses to the Confederacy, and was now trying to assist a rebel prisoner to escape from the penitentiary. His friend Mr. Bull, continued Trainor, had a brother who was chief clerk in the Quartermaster's Department of the Union army, and as good a secessionist as his brother, and who had a much better chance to serve the South than he had. He thought the Federals would have a good time whipping the Confederates, when many of the important offices of the different army departments were filled by friends of the latter.

The reason assigned for sending the quinine and pistols to the South by the way of Louisville was that it afforded less chance of detection than to send directly from Nashville, as the Federal army had a vigilant police, and it was almost impossible to get them through the lines in that direction. Accordingly, as agreed, Trainor, about the middle of March, did send to Louisville, by his friend Kellogg, the quinine and pistols that had been purchased of him, and which, on their arrival, were delivered to the supposed secret agent of the Confederacy, as will hereafter be related.

About the same time there arrived at the City Hotel a gentleman representing himself as Dr. Dubois, an agent of the Confederate States Army, and just from Bragg's command. As he had with him a genuine pass, signed by General Bragg and countersigned by General Breckinridge, his statement was readily accepted as true by the proprietors of the hotel and its *habitués.* For nearly a week after his arrival he was confined to his room by a severe sickness, during which he was carefully nursed by Mrs. Winburn. As soon as recovered, he was introduced by Mrs. W. to Trainor, as a friend of hers who had just come to Nashville from Bragg's army to purchase medicines and goods to be sent South through the Federal lines. Dubois at once expressed his desire of purchasing pistols and medicines, and requested Trainor to assist him.

Trainor eagerly assented, and said, "I will furnish you nine."

"But I want and must have more."

"Well, I will get them for you, and will leave them at Mrs. Davidson's, six miles out on the Charlotte pike. Some of my army-wagons are going out that way after wood, and I can easily carry them with me."

Mrs. Winburn had previously sold Dubois three pistols, for which she had been promised twenty-five dollars each, two of which Trainor took with him to his camp to add to those he had there, and to take them all out together as soon as possible. Dubois said that he would conceal in the muzzle of the third pistol important information, written in cipher, and a letter to General Cheatham, telling him that a lot of pistols had been procured through the influence of Captain Trainor, and were now on their way South, to which was added a request that he would set Trainor right with the Confederates when they got possession of Nashville. This pistol Trainor called for and carried away the next evening, but on the day following returned and said that he was totally unable to carry them out to Mrs. Davidson's, as he had expected to. Dubois then told him he had a friend who would take them out, and he might bring them back to the hotel,—which he agreed to do the next evening.

He came as he had promised, bringing with him eight revolvers on his person, some of them in his waist-belt and some in his boot-legs. As he handed them over, and while Dubois was putting them under the blanket on the bed, he remarked that he had on several occasions taken out on his person as many pistols as he had just brought in. Mrs. Winburn, who was present, boasted that she had taken out four blankets on her person, and that a lady friend had carried out beneath her skirts, in the same way, a cavalry saddle. While this conversation was still progressing, all parties, including Mrs. Winburn, Trainor, and Dubois, were arrested, the latter being ironed and sent out,—ostensibly to prison, but more probably to some other field of operations, where his skill in detecting rebel smugglers and spies might be made equally useful.

Mrs. Trainor had already returned to Louisville, and had been there some days. The medicines which had been forwarded by Kellogg were in her possession, and she was anxiously awaiting a visit from the secret agent of the Confederacy, to whom she could deliver them and make with him arrangements for the purchase of more. She had been telegraphed by her Nashville friends that he would call on her in a few days; and, as some time had elapsed since the receipt of the despatch, she began to wonder why he did not come. One day, as she was returning in a carriage to her house, in what is known as California Suburb, on Fifteenth Street beyond Kentucky Street, she espied coming from it a well-dressed, handsome-appearing young man, who wore conspicuously a large red-white-and-red cravat. As he came opposite to the carriage, he hailed the driver, and asked,—

"How far are you going?"

"Just to yonder house," replied the coachman,—pointing to Mrs. Trainor's, the house he had just come from.

"Very well: I will wait here for you, then, and go back with you."

During the time occupied in this colloquy, and as long as she could see him from the carriage-window, Mrs. Trainor eyed him earnestly, as though she suspected he was the person she was so anxious to see. Nothing was said, however, and on reaching home she went in and found on the table a note for her from one H. C. Davis, stating that he was the secret agent of the Confederacy, that he had just called to see about the medicines, and was sorry to find her out. The signature to the note was "Truth and Fidelity,"—a sure guarantee that there was no deception in the matter. Meanwhile the coach had returned to where the prospective passenger was left standing, when that gentleman took his seat inside and directed the driver to turn around and go again to the house he had just left. Mrs. Trainor met Davis at the door and welcomed him most cordially. Holding out her hand, she said,—

"I thought as much. I was sure it was you when I first put my eye on you."

"Why, madam, what could have made you think so?"

"Oh, that cravat! Nobody else would wear it. But you must be careful about it. It isn't safe. You'll be suspected."

"Oh, I guess there's no danger. I have friends enough in Louisville to take care of me."

The two then entered the house and engaged in earnest conversation. Davis said that he was just about shipping some goods to the South, and he would like to send what medicine she could furnish along with them. He made it a practice to make as few shipments as possible, in order to avoid suspicion.

It was all ready, she said, and he might have it as soon as he wished.

Davis made arrangements to have them delivered at an appointed time, and proposed the purchase of a large quantity in addition to that she had brought from Nashville. She entered eagerly into the business, and said she would ascertain at what prices she could obtain quinine, morphine, and pulverized opium. The next day she reported that she could get them from a man named Tafel, who kept a small prescription-store,—the quinine for six dollars an ounce, the morphine at eight dollars an ounce, and the pulverized opium at fourteen dollars a pound. Davis thought this rather high, but said he would take them at that price. He wanted a thousand ounces of quinine and smaller quantities of the others. After making arrangements for the purchase of the medicines and a supply of pistols,—which was

34

to be furnished by Mr. Bull at thirty dollars each,—Davis went to the city to prepare for their shipment South.

The next evening he called again to invite Mrs. Trainor to the theatre, and was told that there was a difficulty about the medicines. Tafel was fearful that he could not make so large a purchase on his individual credit, and that he wished the money advanced to buy them with. Davis replied that he never did business in that way. He would pay cash on delivery, and if Tafel could not furnish them on those terms they must look elsewhere. Mrs. Trainor thought there would be no difficulty about it. Tafel was to procure them of a wholesale druggist named Wilder, and the matter could doubtless be arranged to the satisfaction of all concerned. In fact, she could safely promise that it should be ready by the next afternoon. At his next visit, Davis was told that the medicines had been purchased, and were ready for delivery, when and where he pleased.

He wished them delivered at her house, he said, early the next morning. He was all ready to ship, and was only waiting for them. Mrs. Trainor engaged that they should be there without fail, and Davis returned to the city, having first arranged with a Federal soldier whom he found at her house—a deserter from the Anderson Cavalry—to go South and act as a scout for General Breckinridge in his expected movement into Kentucky. The next morning, instead of himself coming to receive the goods as he had promised, he sent out a force of policemen, who reached there just as the wagon containing the medicines drove up to the door. Mrs. Trainor, the driver, and the deserter were taken into custody, and the former was sent immediately to Nashville. The wagon was found to contain drugs—mostly quinine and opium—to the value of about five thousand five hundred dollars according to the wholesaler's bill, and eight thousand eight hundred dollars at Tafel's prices. The pistols did not come, Bull having failed to procure them. Wilder and Bull were also arrested, and the store of the former seized, with its contents, valued at from fifty thousand to seventy-five thousand dollars. Tafel's prescription-shop was converted by General Boyle into a medical dispensary for the hospitals of Louisville, and is now used as such. Since her arrest, Mrs. Trainor has been heard to say that she was fearful that secret agent of the Confederacy was only "one of Truesdail's spies," in which supposition she was more than usually correct, he being no other than our old friend Newcomer, who played so important a part in many of the cases here and elsewhere recorded.

The following statement of the army policeman who was sent from Nashville to Louisville to arrest Mrs. Trainor and her cotemporaries and abettors in crime sheds additional light upon this remarkable and important case:—

" As per instructions of Chief of Army Police, at Nashville, I proceeded to the house of Mr. John Trainor, in Louisville, Kentucky, where I arrested Mrs. Trainor, Mr. Tafel, a deserter, and one other gentleman. They were put under arrest and placed in the guard-house. Mrs. Trainor was put under guard at her own residence. Next morning they—Mrs. T. and the three gentlemen—were brought to Nashville, under guard. The house at

Louisville was searched, where was found a military saddle, which was taken; also between eight thousand and nine thousand dollars' worth of quinine and opium was taken,—as per bill found with them,—which said articles were ready to be sent to 'Dixie.' During that night I had various conversations with Mrs. Trainor, in all of which she stated her object to be to make money, for which she undertook the risk. On my return on the train from Louisville to Nashville I brought eight persons as witnesses in the Trainor case and connected with Wilder, the smuggling firm. At various previous interviews had with Mrs. Trainor, she declared that her husband was not implicated in the smuggling, &c. with herself. But she afterwards confessed he was,—stating she had bought quinine, arms, equipments, &c., and shipped to him at Nashville, to be sent through the lines. After having made her final statements,—during which time she was kept in confinement some two or three weeks under guard, with strict orders allowing no person to converse with her,—she was notified that she could see her husband. Upon being admitted to the room, she embraced him, and then fainted, and was in that condition for several minutes. She was accompanied by her two small children,—a girl and a boy, aged five and seven years. The manacles were taken off from Trainor prior to Mrs. T. and the children's entrance. The proper restoratives were administered to her by myself,—the husband being greatly alarmed, saying, 'Do you think she will recover?' 'Is it not a very long time to remain in this condition?' 'I am afraid she will die,' &c. When the restorative took effect, his countenance lighted up with joy. After she was fully restored, a friend who was present, and myself, retired and left them to each other's society. They were together during the whole day, and at night were separated,—he being sent to jail and Mrs. T. to her quarters, there to await the final decision of Major-General Rosecrans."

The evidence against Trainor as a smuggler is conclusive. As regards his confessions to the female detective at the City Hotel, Nashville, of the crime of treason while in the employ of the United States Government under General Buell last year, no further proof has been as yet discovered. When arrested, the bearing of Trainor was defiant to the last degree: he laughed scornfully at the officers and men who stood near or around him, and retained the same bold manner during his several days' imprisonment at the police office.

At the time of this writing (May, 1863) the decision in the case of Trainor has not been made public, if arrived at. He may have concocted all that story of his betrayals under Buell to tickle the ears of silly people; but probably not. The Chief of Police was shocked at the revelation, and desired cumulative evidence of its truth beyond the confidential confession of the wretched party to his detective. So far as possible, this was obtained, and "Dr. Dubois" was put upon the track, resulting in confirming the statement of the first detective in every respect, so far as it extended.

In this connection comes up the case of Wilder, the wholesale and retail drug-dealer of Louisville. His immense concern has been closed, and his goods will probably be confiscated. His greed and his rebel sympathies have proved his ruin. As one item against him, it is certainly true that he had coats manufactured and on hand stuffed and quilted with quinine, which he sold to spies and travellers and traders to be taken South. The property thus confiscated in this case alone will defray the expenses of the Army Police for several months.

A Spy on Morgan and Wife and his Nashville Kin.

ONE of the most interesting cases of spying that has occurred in our army, though perhaps not so important as some others, was that in which a shrewd young Union soldier, whom we will name Johnson, was the actor, and by whom the notable General John H. Morgan and family were completely duped, as the following pages will reveal.

"NASHVILLE, February 8, 1863.

"STATEMENT OF A. B. JOHNSON IN RELATION TO GENERAL MORGAN, ETC.

"I am a personal acquaintance of General John H. Morgan; he is acquainted with my family in ——, Kentucky. I saw him at Lexington. I met him with about one hundred men about three miles from Stewart's Ferry, on the Wilson pike, on Tuesday, one week ago. He was pleased to see me, and, after due conversation, I agreed to scout for him. I came down with him to Stewart's Ferry, where he captured five Federal soldiers in the following manner. General Morgan and his men had on United States uniforms; on reaching the ferry-boat, he saw the Federals on the opposite side of the river. He was hailed by the Federals, Captain Powell saying, 'What command are you?' He answered, '9th Kentucky.' Then Morgan asked him, 'What command are you?' They answered, 'Scouts from Nashville.' When Morgan asked him, 'What news?' 'Nothing of importance.' Then Morgan ordered eleven men aboard the ferry-boat, and sent them across and captured five men, *and shot one who tried to escape.* We left, and went to near Lebanon that night, next day to Liberty, and the next day (Thursday) to McMinnville, where I stayed four days, when I came to Liberty on Tuesday, where I was arrested by some of Morgan's men, and taken to Woodbury, where I was released by Colonel Clark, and then went to Ready-ville. From there I went to General Crittenden's head-quarters, and thence to General Rosecrans's head-quarters; and there I was ordered to report to Colonel Truesdail, at Nashville.

"My instruction from General Morgan was to go to Nashville, deliver letters to his (Morgan's) friends in Nashville, and then to learn whether there were any commissary stores at the Chattanooga & Nashville depot; to see Mrs. Hagy if she knows of such commissary stores, and also ascertain where the commissary stores in Nashville are, particularly, and how all the steamers lie in the river, how many gun-boats, and how they lie in the river. For this information, promptly delivered, he would give me five hundred dollars in greenbacks. He very pointedly charged me to beware of Truesdail's detective police, &c. I saw Mrs. Hagy to-night, after advising with Mrs. Cheatham, who advised me to put on United States uniform, which I got of Colonel Truesdail, and went and saw Mrs. Hagy and others, and to visit all parts of the city to obtain the information the general directed. A shoemaker—first house on the left-hand side of Church Street after you leave the penitentiary—is making boots for me with false bottoms for carrying despatches. I have not his name: it begins with ' H.'

(Signed)   "A. B. JOHNSON."

"NOTE FROM CHIEF OF POLICE TO GENERAL ROSECRANS.

" GENERAL :—I have sent Johnson back with information not very inviting to General Morgan: yet I am of the opinion the latter will make a raid upon some point in your command within ten days. He has a chain of scouts this morning extending from Stone River, perhaps into the city, all the way through to Lebanon, Greenville, Smithville, and McMinnville, his general head-quarters. One hundred of his men were at Stone River last night, I am informed.

"Yours, &c.,   WILLIAM TRUESDAIL,
                                     "Chief of Army Police."

The spy Johnson was sent back to Morgan with proper instructions, made his trip successfully, returned, and reported as follows:—

"I left Nashville February 9th, and stayed at Stewart's Ferry that night; next morning went four miles beyond Beard's Mill; next day went five miles beyond Liberty. On the 12th went to McMinnville to General Morgan's head-quarters. When I went into his office, the general was not there, but his brother—Charlton Morgan—was in. He said to me, 'Is it possible that you have got through?' He then called one of the boys, and sent word to the general that a man wanted to see him on important business. The general came over, and, as he came in, said to me, 'Mr. ——, I am very glad to see you.' He then turned to his brother, and said, 'I told you he would go through, Charlton. I am hardly ever deceived in a man.' I told him that I had some things for his wife from Mrs. Dr. Cheatham. He then invited me over to Dr. Armstrong's, where he was boarding. We went in, and he introduced me to his lady, saying, 'Here, my dear, is the gentleman I told you of; he is just from Nashville.' She invited me to be seated ; and the general then asked me for information about Nashville. I told him that they were receiving heavy reinforcements there,—that there were fifty-seven transports lying at the levée, loaded with troops and provisions. He asked me if they had not been burned yet. I told him they had not. He says, ' Well, they will be.' He asked when I would be ready to go to Nashville again;

and I told him I was ready at any time. He asked me if I did not want some money ; I told him I did; and he gave me one hundred dollars,—part in Confederate and part in greenbacks and Tennessee money. He then said he wanted me to leave on Sunday or Monday for Nashville. On Monday I started from McMinnville. He told me to find out how many troops there were here, where they were going to, and how many transports there were here, and their location. Also how many gun-boats there were here, and whether they lay above or below the railroad-bridge. He said for me to get all the information I could of the movements, location, and number of the army. Monday night I stayed at Mr. Bradford's, five miles the other side of Liberty ; next night stayed at Widow Buchan's, five miles beyond Lebanon ; next, stayed two miles this side of Green Hill ; next day (Thursday) came to Nashville. While I was in the general's office at McMinnville, Colonel Clarke, commanding Duke's brigade, came in and asked the general if the troops could not be paid off before going to Kentucky. Morgan said they could be paid. He asked the colonel if he wanted any money. The colonel said, ' Yes ;' that he wanted commutation for fifty days. In marching they do not issue rations. Heard Major Steel say that the command would be at Sparta in the morning. Learned from officers at McMinnville that there were near twenty-five thousand troops at Tullahoma, that they were fortifying there and at Manchester and Shelbyville, and that Breckinridge was at Manchester. While at McMinnville I saw the telegraph-operator, who invited me to his office. He was just sending to Bragg the news I had brought. While in his office, he received a despatch from either Richmond or Charleston, saying that France had interfered, and that commissioners were to meet in Central Mexico.

(Signed)   "A. B. JOHNSON."

When Johnson started on this trip, he carried a letter from Mrs. Dr. Cheatham, of Nashville, to her sister,—Mrs. General Morgan,—Mrs. Cheatham supposing our man to be one of them and all right. He brought back an answer, which we copy, as follows :—

"MRS. JOHN MORGAN TO MRS. DR. CHEATHAM.

" MY DEAREST SIS :—I was made very happy last Thursday by the reception of your sweet letter, and felt almost as if you were with me : each little article had been purchased by yourself, and put up by your own hands. My best of husbands came hurrying over from his office with the *detective*, knowing how happy he could make me. We read the letters and feasted over them ; and as I untied each bundle he sat and watched my delight with eyes full of pleasure. Oh, I do wish you knew him well ! you could but love him; and I often tell him the same thing of you. It will be a happy day when we can return home again and not see all the dear ones left there compelled to submit to the despotism of Yankee rule. My life is all a joyous dream now, from which I fear to awaken; and awake I must, when my husband is called to leave me again. But he says that shall not be soon ; he keeps his command constantly at work, but will not take more rest himself. Did you know he was within five miles of you a week or two ago? You would have had a visit from him in your own home, but for one little circumstance,—of which I will tell you when I do many other things which in these uncertain times cannot be written. Allie is not now with us. Horace took her to Knoxville, where she had been intending to go for some time previous. My husband is with the army: and with this portion of the army we may have to move at any moment. My husband says he wants me to remain with him, and of course I much prefer it. They say we are a love-sick couple: at any rate, I know my liege lord is devoted to me, and each day I am forced to love him more. His disposition is perfect. I know you will say, sis, that every topic I commence runs into praise of my husband; but the truth is, I cannot help it, and one of these days you will not be surprised at it. I never knew whether you received my letters written from home or not. I sent you several; and in one my husband added a post-script and directed it. If you have ever received it, you could not have mistaken the handwriting on the *little slip of paper*. The man who took it was very much amused at you, and told us every thing you said; he also saw mamma and papa, but did not make himself known. I wish very much I had the things you sent to mamma for me: I really need them: for a bride, my wardrobe is very scant. You could not have sent me any thing, sis, more acceptable than the things you did send; and I am sure I can say the same for Allie. I miss her very much: she is not married yet, although it has been published recently in the Mobile papers. I will send her one of the skirts, perhaps, and other things you sent, immediately. The general is delighted with his fur collar; he says you are a great sis. He has really been in love with you since the first time he saw you. He has searched his trunk through to find some trophy for darling little Mattie S. He is at it now, but I think he cannot find any thing: I sent his trunk of trophies to Knoxville for safe-keeping. He sends a great deal of love to you, and says, 'Tell sis to kiss her sweet children for me a thousand times.' I can correspond with you almost regularly now, sis; and it is such a comfort to me to be able to hear from you all. I will send letters to you for mamma, and get you to send them to her. There is another charm of my darling husband: he leaves nothing undone to contribute to my happiness, and he knows nothing will please me more than to hear from you. The bearer of this goes principally on my account. We are very comfortable here: my new brothers have all been with me, and I love them very much; Mrs. D. is coming this week. Write me something, please, of Uncle Sam's family; he writes to me about twice a week, and I should like to give him some news of his family in my next letter. Give a great deal of love and a kiss to brother Will for me, and to aunt and cousin Myra. Sis, do you realize that I am married? What would I not give to see you, and for you to know my dear husband and see our happiness! I have been writing most of the time, sis, with the room full of men talking to the general on all sorts of business, and I have all the time had one ear open: so I think you will have a crazy letter to read.

What about the gowns, sis, I wrote for ? This man can bring out any thing, sis, you desire to send ; and I should be so much obliged to you if you will send me two pair of slippers, Nos. 4 and 4½, and some pins, large and small. I could write all evening, but the man must start to-night. I will write soon again. If you cannot get the green dress the general sent for, get a lilac one : I prefer it, at any rate. I knew nothing of his sending before : he did it as a surprise for me. I have a gay riding-habit, sis, and can get nothing to trim it with. It is cloth, very handsome, and I should like blue velvet to trim it with. The man is sitting waiting, and asks me to tell you he is not a 'detective.' He is as true as steel, and would do any thing for the general. I must close now. I have some things I would like for you and brother Will to have, but I am afraid to send them. Please write me a good, long letter ; we enjoy them so much. Perhaps Cousin Myra would write too : I wish she would. Kiss the darlings for me a thousand times, and their uncle. You and dear brother Will must kiss each other for me. How I wish I could see you ! Good-bye. God bless you !

" Your devoted sister,

"_____ _____.

" P.S.—Allie is not married, and does not expect to be, that I know of. In Dixie paper, as every thing else, is getting scarce."

(POSTSCRIPT, BY GENERAL MORGAN, TO HIS WIFE'S LETTER.)

"MY DEAR SISTER :—You cannot imagine how very anxious I am to see you again. Have you forgotten our first meeting? Had hoped to have seen you some days since, but accident alone prevented. The bearer can explain the cause of my failure. Mattie talks of you all the time, and is so anxious to see you. Kiss your sweet little girl for her new uncle, and tell her I love her a good deal. Regards to the servants. It would be folly for me to tell you how very happy I am, knowing Mattie as you do.

"Your affectionate brother,

"_____ _____."

(POSTSCRIPT NO. 2.)

"I came very near forgetting, sis, a very important thing which I want to tell you of. It is this : I have made me an elegant evening dress, cut it out by a low waist that I happened to have with me, and it fits me so nicely, and is so stylish, that the general is so proud of it he will not consent to let my letter go without this postscript. He brought the dress from Kentucky for me. Is his own taste. It is a beautiful *rose deschaum* color. I wore it to the ball given in honor of us last Friday night, with a black lace flounce round the bottom, headed with black and pink velvet, a black lace vest and sleeves, and a fall of black lace around the waist. It was magnificent, and very much admired. The ball was an elegant affair,—beautiful decorations and delicious supper, two magnificent bands of music from Tullahoma, and scores of gay, handsome officers. I wished for some of the pretty girls of

Nashville to enjoy it with us. I had a splendid time, and, of course, was something of a belle,—as the ball was in honor of the bandit and his bride. I think now I can rival Mrs. McK—— in evening dresses, but would prefer not being under the necessity. Alice has made her a handsome riding-habit. The Confederacy teaches us industry, does it not? I think the general would try to preserve the wonderful dress in *alcohol*, if he thought the color could be retained. I have the dress you sent to me: it is made becomingly and handsomely. I don't care to undertake another: my *reputation is established on one.* You will see your friend, who carries this, often; and I wonder if you will enjoy it as much as I will. I ride every evening on horseback with the general, and enjoy it *so much.* I have written quite a postscript. Brother Will, don't laugh at it. I have so much to say I cannot bear to close. Will, I will see you some day, I hope; and then what a time we will have talking! This is full of love. Good-bye again.

"Your devoted sister,

"——— ———.

"P.S.—Please send me some large hooks and eyes, and a corset,—if possible, No. 21. Sis, please send me some black stick pomatum: I want it for my husband."

This letter, after being duly read, discussed, and copied in the office of the Chief of Police, at Nashville, was delivered by the "brave fellow" in person, at the house of Cheatham, in the small hours of the night. That he was hugely welcomed who will doubt? The parlor *tête-à-tête*, the wine, &c., is imaginable. He promises them to return to General Morgan in a day or two. They agree to have letters ready, some little articles for Mrs. General Morgan, &c.; also they will apprize their friends, who will send many letters by him. At the appointed time "our man" gets at their house a large packet of letters, and the following articles for Mrs. Morgan. It will be seen, by the way, that the articles are all base "notions" of "Yankee" make:—

100 Envelopes (white and nice).
6 quires Letter and Note Paper.
Half-dozen Black Stick Pomatum.
1 gross Hooks and Eyes.
2 packs Pins.
2 pairs Slippers.
1 copy Godey's Lady's Book for March, 1863.

The letters were mainly harmless epistles of family matters and gossip. The following letter and postscript, from Mrs. Cheatham to Mrs. General Morgan, will repay a leisurely reader's perusal:—

(TO MRS. GENERAL MORGAN.)

"NASHVILLE, Feb. 20, 1863.

"MY DARLING MATTIE:—At half-past two last night the door-bell rang, and

who should it be but 'our man'? He looked so bright, and with a triumphant air handed me a letter from Mrs. M. 'You know that handwriting,
madam?' 'Oh, yes!' said I. 'Sit here on the sofa by me, and tell me
every thing.' I looked at the letter and talked to him at the same time.
Bless your dear heart! I can see your bright, happy face before me now,
but *I can't write.* I shall never get over not seeing you a bride; and when
I attempt to write, it is so unsatisfactory I am inclined to throw my pen
aside and *cry,* instead of writing. I have so much time for reflection, dear
Mattie; and sometimes I am very sad, but would not for worlds cast a
shadow upon your bright horizon. You are very happy, and ought to be,
for you have every thing to make you so. Don't you remember, though, I
fell in love with your dear, good husband first? You didn't see him on the
turnpike, with the blouse and coon-skin cap on. That day I was so excited
about old Mrs. Flowers and her flag. He looked so amused. The fiery
ordeal I have passed through since that day! All my spirit is gone. I am
as submissive as a whipped child (except sometimes). Oh, if this man
should be caught, and hung as a spy, it would kill me. For Heaven's sake,
Brother J., don't come to Nashville! It would frighten me to death. I
cannot bear to think of your running such risks. Why, if they were to take
you they would put you in an iron cage and carry you all over the country.
I was so thankful you did not come. My dear husband is at Louisville,
and that road is to be destroyed. If they would only wait until he gets
home! I came very near going with him. I wish I had; then we would
have been taken prisoners together, and been carried to 'Dixie.' I should
have said to them, '*Please take me prisoner.*' I hope Dr. C. will send
Penny on to you. She is coming with him. She entreated to be sent for;
and, without consulting papa, Dr. C. went. Eliza and Caroline are in Cincinnati. I hear from mamma very often. She writes cheerfully. Ell is
still with her. I sent for Cous. Nina this morning, and we have had a good
time together. She is writing to you. I wish you could have passed on us
this morning. We had a good laugh about the silk dress from Kentucky.
Do you know the 'Feds' say he took fifteen hundred dollars' worth of fine
silks from Elizabethtown? Mrs. Fogg says she wants one: so you must not
make them all up. I regret very much not having a dress ready-made to
send you, but will have the next time I have any letter ready for you.
Now, since I know I can send them, I shall always be thinking of getting
ready. If they don't catch that poor man! I am miserable about him
now. We don't see the bright side here, Mattie. It is nothing but gloom.
When our prisoners come in we are sad, and go to work to clothe and feed
them. These horrid prisons would make your heart sick. Hospitals on
every street; and our poor wounded Confederates, how they did suffer!
Many of them froze to death at Camp Douglas. Even the Journal spoke
of their sufferings, but blamed the Confederate authorities. They were
sent from here on boats that severe weather. Many of them were in a
dying condition when they started. Dr. —— has resigned in disgust. I
believe he is a good man. He took me to Murfreesborough after the battle,

when old Mitchell would not even allow mothers to go to look after their wounded sons. Poor Mrs. McNairy has Frank's body in the house yet. It was embalmed. She is afraid to bury it. Johnny Kirkman was buried by his mother's side. What do your army people think of that Fort Donelson affair? From our point of view it seems to have been a miserable '*faux pas.*' I can't understand Wheeler's being major-general of all the cavalry in Tennessee. Won't you explain? You must take time, dear Mattie, and write me a long, satisfactory letter. Write me more of Alice and Horace. Tell me of General Hardee. Mamma is very fond of him. Has Hor. good clothing? I cannot forgive myself for not sending him; but it never occurred to my mind once that Bragg would retreat from Murfreesborough. I expected to see Rosecrans's army flying through Nashville, and *ours* enter in triumph. The disappointment was terrible and miserable. Poor old Rutherford county! Such devastation! The people have been robbed of every thing. Speaking of robbing, my horses have been taken. I never expect to have another pair, for when the war is over all the horses will be dead. I prized my horses very highly, and tried so hard to keep them! How does Margaret behave, Mattie? I hope she makes herself useful to you. If she is *good*, give her a kind remembrance from me. My servants are the wonder of all my acquaintance. They are just as good as they have always been. I did not finish my letters to-day, and was constantly interrupted whilst writing. It is now almost the hour for 'our man' to come. Dr. C. did not come to-night. I am some troubled for fear the road will be torn up to-morrow and he will be detained. I send you, dear Mattie, the few little articles you sent for. There are very few really nice things in Nashville. Our old merchants have nothing. I send you some paper, and shall expect many good, long, sweet letters. Write me all about yourself and your dear husband. What would I not give to see you! Cous. Nina sends much love, and will write the next time. I send you some letters to mail for our friends. Read this one for Charleston. Mrs. W. will write you all about '*Uncle Sam's Family.*' Try and send me some Southern papers, Mattie; they would be so acceptable. I cannot write more now. Good-bye.

"Your devoted

"SIS.

(POSTSCRIPT TO GENERAL MORGAN.)

"DEAR BROTHER:—Another little word for you. I am *very anxious* to see you, but you *must not come* whilst the *foe* is *near.*

"I need not say, take good care of Mattie. I know you will send me a letter whenever you can. If you could only witness the eagerness with which I receive them, you would feel fully repaid. We have so little to cheer us. Good-bye. Kiss Mattie for me.

"Affectionately,

"SIS.

"P.S.—Nashville affords no English pins. I send Yankee ones. I must see you wear that ball-dress you made yourself. Take good care of it. I send you Godey, hoping it will prove acceptable in Dixie.

(ADDITIONAL TO MRS. GENERAL MORGAN.)

"SUNDAY, Feb. 22, 1863.

"MY DARLING M.:—'Our man' did not get off yesterday, as he expected: so I cannot refrain from sending you a postscript, which I expect will quite equal yours in length. How I long to be with you! I do *not* realize that you are married, although your husband has taken a deep hold upon my affections. You know the reason—because Mattie is so devoted to him; and then he tells me he is so happy. Dear M., you think the honeymoon will never pass, don't you? I feel a little inclined to tease you, but I won't. There is that plaguey door-bell! I never sit down to write but some one comes. Oh, 'tis some music good neighbor Fogg has left for Mattie. There is the bell again! I have to go down. Now it is a man from Louisville, with messages from Brother Will. Poor Brother Will! he has had an annoying time. If he does not come to-night, I shall give up looking for him. He sent the children a box of candy, and they send some to aunty. Matty S. says there is a bonnet for you and a hat for Uncle M. The dear little creature wonders how mamma will send it. I told Rich a Federal officer would send it out with a flag of truce. He believes it. M. S. looks wise, and guesses better. I started with M. yesterday to have their photographs taken for you, but it commenced raining. I will have them taken, and send you. I must have a *good* likeness of General M. in return. The one I have is not good: it is something like the one you had with whiskers. He only wears moustache now. Do you want that black pomatum to black it? I send you six sticks. Is that enough? I could get no blue velvet, Mattie, for your riding-habit. How would blue cloth answer? Your gowns are not finished. You shall have them next time, but must not wear them. They are too thin for winter. I fear you will not like the corset; but it is the best I could get. Do you want gloves? Make a memorandum, and I will fill it if I can. What has become of Kate and Mary R.? Their mother is very anxious to hear from them. I send you some letters that I hope you can send. Mrs. W. is *crazy*, I think. [Puss!] She says she is going South. You need not be surprised to see her at *your head*-quarters very soon. I do *not* make a *confidant* of her. I feel very uneasy about 'our man.' I gave him a note to papa. He lost yours. It frightens me for any one to run such risks. I am very glad 'accident prevented' that visit from your husband. He must not wear Federal uniform again. He will think, I am sure, it is well I am not a soldier's wife. I send you Rosecrans's order. I am afraid of him and his 'detectives.' Times are not as they used to be when Negley was commandant.*

"*Sunday Night.*—Brother Will has come at last. Penny *declined* coming

---

* No army police then.—AUTHOR.

with him. The deceitful creature! I hope mamma will be fully satisfied now that there is no hope of getting her. [A slave.] Will went to gratify mamma. I have been writing this letter all day, Mattie. Have had a visit from a Fed. officer since I commenced, and now Cous. Bob and Will C. are sitting with us, all smoking pipes. I am almost suffocated. Will has told me of Brother John's visit to Springfield last summer or fall. There is a report here that Dave Yandell is dead. I hope it is not true. Do you think you can answer all my questions, dear M.? Mrs. Fogg expresses great interest in you. Don't forget to send her a kind message in your next letter. Nina was much gratified at your kind mention of her. Poor Will will never be himself again. He walks very badly. Aunt Em is very miserable. Brother Will sends bushels of love, dear M., and wishes he could be with you. 'Tis now very late, and the man has not come. May-be he is a prisoner, and will never see this. Mattie, do you always pray for peace? It is my most earnest prayer. God bless you, and protect you and your noble husband!

"Your devoted

" SIS.

"I will try and get you some paper like this. 'The man' says you want some. I used to write to Brother Charlie on this paper. My liege-lord says I must stop writing to-night. I *must* obey. Good-night."

———

Not only were the ladies thus wickedly deceived by "our man," but General John Morgan was so completely sold by this—his own—spy, that we may reasonably suppose he has had his ears measured repeatedly of late, to ascertain their increased length. The following facts will show how Morgan's brother lost his liberty and "our man" came within view of a halter.

Coming into Nashville on his second trip, he brought a letter from Captain Clarence Morgan (the general's brother), addressed to their mother, in Kentucky, to be mailed at Nashville. This letter advised the mother that its writer would be at Lexington, Kentucky, upon a certain day, and desired her to meet him there. This letter also contained the following note,—from the devoted Charlton Morgan to his lady-love, as it would seem:—

"McMinnville, Feb. 14, 1863.

"Dear Mollie:—Meet me at Lexington. I will be there in four or five days.   Charlton."

Directed to
"Miss Mollie Williams,
Care of Mrs. Mary Atkinson,
Russellville, Kentucky."

Of course, this letter came to the hands of the inevitable Colonel Truesdail, and he forthwith advises General Boyle, commandant at Louisville. The latter sends a force and arrests Captain Morgan, and he was sent to Camp Chase as a prisoner of war or a spy,—we are not positive which.

Returning on his third trip to Morgan's head-quarters at McMinnville, "our man" found himself in trouble at once, and under arrest, as a traitor to the South. General John Morgan had received the day before a copy of the Nashville "Union," containing an account of the arrest and imprisonment of his brother in Ohio. He well remembered that Johnson had that letter in charge, and he could not imagine any other cause for the calamity than Johnson's betrayal of the trust. But "our man" was equal to the emergency. He swore by all that was blue above that he had faithfully carried the letter and placed it in the Nashville Post-Office,—which was true enough.

"You know full well, general," said he, "that old Truesdail and his gang have the complete run of affairs at Nashville; and if Captain Morgan was captured because of that letter, they must have read it while in that office. That the letter went to your mother is plain; for it seems she got it, and met your brother; and it was by watching her that they caught him."

What could Morgan say? Johnson was discharged from arrest. But matters were not easy, as before. Morgan was cloudy and ill at ease. Finally, Johnson was sent to Tullahoma and court-martialed, was tried, and discharged for want of convicting evidence. "Our man" was now satisfied that his *rôle* was about ended, however. Suspicion once attaching to a spy, his work is done and his neck is spanned by the halter. It is only the blind, generous confidence that suspects nothing that serves the ends of the successful scout. Johnson returned to Nashville speedily and secretly. While at Tullahoma, however, he made the acquaintance of the rebel General Forrest, who wished to employ him as a scout, with apparently full confidence in his loyalty to the South. But one trial by court-martial was enough for Johnson.

Arrived at Nashville, he reported at midnight to the Chief of Police. The next day he was publicly arrested on the streets, as a spy of John Morgan, and thrown into the penitentiary, where had just been confined a large number of Nashville rebels, preparatory to being sent to the North and to the South. He obtained their confidence and sympathies, and "dug up" some items of much interest to the Union cause.

Racy Rebel Letters.

THE history of the Army of the Cumberland, and of the rebellion, would be incomplete, and the future historian would be robbed of one of his spiciest subjects, should we fail in preserving a sample of the letters of the bitter, shrewd, wild, reckless women of the South. That they are discovered so plentifully by our secret police and through ordinary military capture, &c., is no reason why their existence should be ignored. The action of the secession females of the South has already become history in outline and in notoriety: let us devote a page or two of the "Annals" to the minutiæ of the subject.

It is no wonder that the separated Southrons should write to and fro through our lines. .Divided husbands and wives, parents and children far apart, sentimental bathers in moonlight, and revellers in absent lovers' dreams, most naturally take to pen and paper. Fully sympathizing with hundreds of aching hearts, the Chief of the Army Police devised many plans, and afforded convenient facilities, for the carrying of these soothing epistles. The Nashville Post-Office, and other adjacent post-offices, were open to their reception; and old Uncle Samuel took them along, as usual, in his capacious mail-pouches, over hill and dale. But ah! the many midnight hours spent by prying clerks and secretaries in dampening the gum of those envelopes, opening and reading the outpourings of Southern traitors' hearts, and airing the amorous sighs and tears of lovelorn maids and swains! Not only this, but Colonel Truesdail established a special "grape-vine" mail for Nashville and vicinity rebeldom,—so accommodating, indeed, that he actually employed daring Southron spies to evade the Yankee pickets, run the lines, and bring to the secesh doors at dark hours of night, or through back alleys and cellar-ways at mid-day, the dear missives from the South. Thus has he sent messengers from his office directly into their very parlors and inner chambers, where wines, gold, and rich gifts were lavished upon them with unsparing hand.

The following letter, discovered while passing through the Nashville Post-Office, was written by a rebel officer. We entitle it

A GOSSIPING LETTER.

APRIL 5th, 1863.

"MRS. McW———.

*　　　*　　　*　　　*　　　*　　　*　　　*　　　*

"Mrs. General Bragg has been dangerously ill at Winchester, Tenn. The general wrote Sweazy a few days since that the crisis was past, and she was now believed to be out of danger. The 'soldier' and S., you perceive, are, as ever, on favorable terms, and friendly. Mrs. General Morgan has been spending most of her time recently with her husband, at McMinnville, Tenn., where she visits the hospitals daily, in company with the general, to the gratification of all the boys. Miss Alice thinks so much of General Hardee that she actually kisses him whenever they meet.

"Miss Lady Ewing, daughter of Hon. Andrew Ewing, told me a few days ago that the gentleman at whose house Miss Alice is stopping in Winchester says that he saw Miss Ready embrace and kiss General Hardee. The gentleman in question supposed the stranger, from his appearance, to be Miss Ready's father: so he advanced, and said,—

"'How do you do, Col. Ready?'

" 'Col. Ready, indeed !' exclaimed Miss Alice. 'Allow me, sir, to introduce to your acquaintance my friend, Gen. Hardee.'

"Astonishing as you may deem this, it can hardly be questioned, as Miss Lady herself said the gentleman *himself* told *her* what is herein related, and says the scene transpired at *his own house.*

"Hardee is eminently a devotee of society,—emphatically a lady's man. Last week he visited Huntsville, it is said, to see Mrs. Williamson, your classmate at the Nashville Academy. However, the general is quite general in his attentions to the ladies generally, and it is difficult to locate him.

"Mrs. M., of Clark, has returned to Kentucky. She expects to be back in Dixie soon. She promised to write you from her old home. She passed here in company with Mrs. Gen. Helme. Is a young lady in years and appearance, of medium size, pleasant manner, and frank, cordial address,— not petite, yet handsome, and withal a woman of attractive social qualities. She is stopping in Athens, East Tennessee. So is Mrs. Gov. Foote. Mrs. E. M. Bruce, wife of an M. C. from Kentucky, in Confederate Congress. resides here. She dresses splendidly, and appears on public occasions glittering in diamonds. She attended a soirée given Gen. Johnston some time since at this place, and it was remarked by all that she wore on that occasion more jewels than any lady had ever been known to wear in the South before. Her husband you may remember as a large Government contractor and pork-packer at Nashville during the early stages of the existing Revolution. He is very wealthy. Mrs. General Breckinridge is at Winchester. She is of a quiet, retiring disposition, and few have ever seen her there. Col. Wm. Breckinridge's wife is at Lexington. Sweazy has been contriving letters to her by the under-ground mail line. She was Miss Desha. His first wife was a Miss Clay, daughter of Charles Clay, and grand-daughter of great Harry of the West. You know the Breckinridges. always marry into the oldest and most intellectual families.*

"Mrs. Gen. Joe Johnston is at Jackson, Mississippi, but the general is at Tullahoma. Mrs. Gen. Buckner is with her husband at Mobile. Mrs. Gen. Wm. Bate is at her father's, in Huntsville. Mrs. Gen. Withers is at Shelbyville. So is Mrs. Gen. Geo. Massey. Mrs. Maj. Stevenson, Mrs. Maj. Cunningham, and Mrs. Maj. Schon are with their husbands, at Atlanta, Georgia. Maj. Gen. McCown, of Tenn., is under arrest for sending off one of his staff without Gen. Bragg's permission: so the newspapers state. Col. Burch Cook has resigned his commission in the C. S. Army: cause, bad health. Col. John Savage has resigned, because Lt. Col. Maurice J. Wright, his junior, was promoted over him. Public opinion justifies Savage's course. He is said to be very bitter in abuse of Gov. Harris and others. Though not popular personally, yet all admit that a better colonel than Savage was cannot be found in either army, while all equally agree that few, if any, would surpass him.

"As Brigadier-General Bob Foster and his brother William make this place

---

* Mrs. Bruce, above spoken of, has her chapter in this work.—AUTHOR.

head-quarters, Mrs. Bolling, of Nashville, is here. It is said she is treated with so much kindness (!) by Federals and others at Nashville, that she contemplates an early return to the capital. At all events, such is the street-gossip, and is credited here. Henry Watterson, editor of 'Chattanooga Rebel,' is said to be very much in love with Miss Fogg, sister to the A.Q.M. Col. Reece, formerly paymaster in the Army of Tennessee; ditto Miss Rutledge. Lt. Cooper, of Georgia, it is said, is the fortunate suitor for the hand of Mollie Bang. Capt. Frank Green will be married to Miss Pattie so soon as the war ends. The Misses Ewing, of Nashville, are here, and receive much attention, of course. Yours, respectfully, visits them when he can, but not often. We hear funny—yes, very facetious—reports concerning a Miss B———, of Edgefield. We have it in Dixie that she has been enlisting soldiers in our ranks. Is it so? We hear—— But no matter! We defer interrogations for those who write to us. The Southern prisoners, when out from Nashville, all have something to tell about Nashville girls. One tells us he heard Miss Bellie curse a Yankee soldier.

"Dave Jackson passed here recently, en route to Richmond. When he returns, will hand him his mother's letter. Joe Pickett is in Charleston. Tom Cook left here on the 30th of March for La. He was well,—well pleased with his visit to all. J. Jr. is sick. He has been confined to his room for two weeks. He has some kind of fever—nothing serious. Should he become seriously ill, will advise his father's family. Dr. Smith is at Winchester. He has letters from Edgefield dated 23d March. Shelby Williams is here, and wishes his wife to know he is well. Neil Brown, Jr., is travelling as special messenger for Major Bransford, Chief of Transportation at this place. Tom and Tully are with Capt. Cheney at Tullahoma. All quite well. Mr. McWhisten, at Kingston, and his father-in-law at Talladega, both well. John Green has gone to Atlanta to live. Rawworth and Morgan remain. Ike, Dan, Gabe, and Allen are here—all well. Moss Goodbar is in distress. He has not received his ——, and his —— has been broken up. The wagon gentleman is thought to be doing well. He is at Gainesborough. His sister's letter was forwarded to him. He sends us many newspapers. Mr. Darrah, of Breckinridge's staff, is in Lagrange, Georgia, making love to Miss Lucy Seifer. Maggie S. and Fanny C. are both well, and both wish to return. Bob B. has been advised to tell them to stay where they are—the former, at least—until ——. Tom Cook's ambrotype and Dave Jackson's photographs are here in our keeping for their friends and relations at home."

The foregoing letter was addressed to Mrs. Dr. A. G. McWhorter, residing at Edgefield, opposite Nashville, a noted admirer of Southern "rights," and an uncompromising rebel, whose husband we have heard mentioned as a surgeon in the Confederate army.

The following are extracts from letters written by rebel citizens of Nashville, to be sent through our lines, and which were intercepted and passed upon or pigeon-holed by the Chief of the Army Police, as was deemed advisable.

35

(A Lady in Connecticut to her mother, MRS. B. PRINGLE, at Charleston, S.C. Sent by MRS. CHEATHAM to MRS. MORGAN, to be mailed.)

[*Extract.*]—"Recent events show so plainly that, if man proposes, God disposes. You can imagine how I shuddered when I heard Federal officers tell their friends how easily my dear old home is to be captured; their plan being to run their iron MONSTERS *so close under Sumter* that her guns *cannot* be depressed, while they fire their Satanic balls of 450 pounds each at her walls, and crumble them as they wish. You know these iron boats fire *two* guns from one side, making a discharge of 900 pounds, they say, upon Sumter. God grant that your noble B. [Beauregard] knows more about this than the 'Feds' imagine!"

We have not space to spare for the insertion of the above letter, entire, as it merits. Its author, to judge her by her letter, is one of the wildest rebel women yet put upon our record,—albeit she is enjoying all the rights, privileges, and comforts of a Connecticut home. The Chief of Police very greatly regrets that he was unable to ascertain her name and publish it in this connection. There was no signature attached to the letter.

(From "GERTRUDE," at Nashville, to FRANK S. SCOTT, February 19, 1863.)

[*Extract.*]—"When will redemption from these despots come to us? When—how long—ere with shouts of joy we shall make the welkin ring at the entrance of *our South's noble boys?* Come! We crouch to the foe, and await but your coming to spring up and help you to strike for liberty!"

(From GERTRUDE to "ROB," February 19, 1863.)

[*Extract.*]—"To say you were in the battle of Murfreesborough, that admits you into the confidence and hearts of all Southern friends. Bravely, boldly, gloriously, knights of imperial valor, you withstood the overwhelming numbers of the Huns, who indeed have proved the 'scourge' of God. From atrocities committed, they place themselves in history with the Flemish banditti under William de la Mark; and our defenders climb to the summit of chivalry and nobility's heights, and o'ershadow the Scottish Archers' Body-Guard, who existed and fought at the same date in history. Perhaps ere this reaches you another Golgotha will sadden the land, already draped in 'trappings of war.' Once more our sacred soil will receive to its keeping those caskets rifled of the pearl which makes them so beautiful, so dear to friends and associates. Not many sweet smiles and kindly words are wasted on the *would-be* elegant officers of the *grand Federal Army.* Arrests are still being made, Donigan & Calhoun being the last victims I have heard of. 'Tis said they are to be held as hostages for two Yankee pedlars taken by General J. H. Morgan. The penitentiary received them as inmates. Forty-six escaped a night or two since, one being a spy for the general just mentioned. Frank McNairy and Johnnie Kirkman's remains have been brought up and buried. The former had *not been treated* as we heard."

(From "NANNIE," Balcony Place, Nashville, February 20, 1862, to
DR. L. T. PAYNE, *per* DR. WILLIAMS, S.C.A.)

"You have doubtless heard of that unfortunate affair at Fort Donelson, which resulted in a defeat, with the loss of some gallant officers, among whom were my brother-in-law's youngest brother and nephew,—the *choicest flower of our land.* So young, too! But the hardest of all is, after treating the corpse with every *indignity possible*, they [the Federals] refused even a Christian burial: not a *prayer at the grave*, nor any demonstration whatever!"

(From MRS. WILLIAMS [Nashville], Home, February 20, to her husband,
ROBERT A. WILLIAMS.)

"Poor Colonel Frank's [meaning Frank McNairy] remains are still at his mother's. She is almost a maniac, and cannot decide what to do, as he has been denied the right of a Christian burial. Is it not sad?"

[N.B.—General Rosecrans refused any other than a respectful private burial.]

(From —— ——, Nashville, February 20, 1863, to her sister, MRS. H. J. JONES.)

"Can it be that the South regards with suspicion all who are in Nashville? If so, I do not know who they may regard as true: certainly not those who have fled from Nashville, leaving it to be no less than a Union town. There is more good accomplished by remaining here and bearing the brunt of this terrible time—of holding up the hands of those who fall— than to take a musket into the ranks. This town now is settled alarmingly with Northern people; and although the old residents may stand firm, of course they will ever (if voting should be allowed) be outnumbered. Frank McNairy has not been buried yet. They are afraid to do so, for fear of some violence from the base Tennessee [Union] troops. You know that foolish and unfortunate advertisement for bloodhounds has exasperated Governor Johnston, and unjust vengeance is muttered."

(From Mrs. Dr. Hall to her brother in the Confederate Army.)

[*Extract.*]—"The detective police system here exceeds any thing you ever saw. Not wishing to fall into their hands, I have not even asked for a pass these three months."

The foregoing letters and extracts may well be preserved, as evidence of the course of Southern women.

A Cincinnati Spy.

For several months past the Army of the Cumberland has known a jovial, smiling, wide-awake personage (a native of the "Green Isle," but who is remarkably well cut-and-dried and seasoned, nevertheless), by the, name of M. E. Joyce. He corresponds for different Northern papers, visits around among the camps, is always in with his laugh and his story, and is as fond of accompanying an expedition, sharing danger, and having a rough time, as "any other man."

Who of our army officers does not remember little Joyce,—or "Jice," as we term him? That he is useful as well as ornamental, and that his brains were put in pretty nearly the right place, let the following facts be ample proof.

In November last, while plodding in the vicinity of Nashville, crossing over from one camp to another, our hero was picked up, or, rather, pulled down, from his horse by some rebel guerrillas or patrols. He was rather taken aback; but for an instant only. He was soon entirely "aisy" with them,— telling them all sorts of a story, and, as he states it, "letting on secesh like the d——l," as a butternut citizen. Satisfied that he was "a good enough Morgan" for them, he was not retained long; and he hastily scrambled back to the city, highly elated with his adventure.

"Hark'ee, now, Joyce; you are just my man," said Colonel Truesdail. "You can go to Murfreesborough without any trouble,—can get me the information we desire. I will get you a good horse and outfit, and pay you three hundred dollars for the trip, if you are quick and smart."

The newspaper-man's chuckle rounded into an attentive period, as he pondered over the idea, and heard all about the "how to do it" from the Chief of Police. He was to ride boldly up to the rebel lines and claim to be the regular correspondent of the Cincinnati "Enquirer,"—a man of conservative sentiments, who was friendly to the South, was opposed to the war, was in the Union army as regular correspondent, had written something to offend General Rosecrans, and the latter had imprisoned and abused him; and he was now determined to injure Rosecrans and his crowd all he could. Joyce liked the idea. It was novel and feasible,—would take him into tall company, and would pay well. Joyce, therefore, prepared;

and about the 25th of November last he sallied forth as boldly as would the knight of La Mancha, and as happy as Sancho, his squire, when at his best estate, as "governor of an island."

The joke and Joyce succeeded admirably. He was taken to Murfreesborough, and into the august presence of Bragg. He told his tale with an air of injured innocence, and swore great oaths of vengeance against the "stupid Dutchman," the leader of the Yankee fanatics and cowards at Nashville, &c. His assertions were partially borne out by one of General Bragg's principal officers, who stated that he had recently seen an account in a Nashville or Louisville paper of a difficulty with some writer of the Cincinnati "Enquirer," whom the Union commander had imprisoned and then banished from his army lines.

Bragg was not a little pleased at the incident. A tyrant in his own "bailiwick," he was gratified to hear of the malignant fanaticism and injustice of the opposing commander.

"I am glad to see you, sir," he said, addressing the humble representative of Cincinnati, "for I respect your occupation and admire the men who employ you. The Cincinnati 'Enquirer' is the only paper in the West that does the cause of the South even common justice. I will protect you within my lines, and render your stay as comfortable as possible."

Mr. Joyce was thankful and at ease: he always is. He was again slightly severe on the "Dutchman" in command at Nashville, and on the "Abolition fanatics" of the North, and, now that he was in the proper position, it should not be his fault if he did not write home to the Cincinnati "Enquirer" some homely truths, *pro bono publico*. His only fear was that he would not be able to send his productions to the "Enquirer."

"Never fear about that," replied General Bragg: "I will see to that. My man John Morgan is superintendent of the railroad-system in the Southwest, and will get your letters through by first trains."

Pleased with the conceit, Bragg and Joyce both smiled over a nip of quite new and sharp Robertson county whiskey. Supper being announced, Joyce was invited to the table, and, with the usual modesty and timidity of his ancestry in the ascendant, he sat down to his rations of beans, coffee, and corn bread. Bragg and his staff were there assembled, and the tale of Joyce was again unfolded to admiring auditors. After supper Joyce retired to a vacant corner, and with pen and paper he toiled for an hour, writing up one of the most scathing and glowing diatribes upon low-lived "Dutchmen" and high-toned gentlemen, the horrors of war, the blessings of peace, and the ignorance and folly of Northern Abolitionists and fanatics. The epistle was properly enveloped, addressed in style (for Joyce is an elegant and rapid penman) to the editor of the Cincinnati "Enquirer," and handed to an aide of General Bragg's to be forwarded by the Morgan line; and thus ended the task of our quondam correspondent. He strolled over the town in company with an under-officer or two, and a fair cigar. To his companions he expatiated largely upon Nashville army affairs and Northern sentiments and sympathies; and it need not be specially set down, for aught we know, that he told any more of "whoppers" than the time and occasion would warrant.

Next day the man of the "Enquirer," after breakfasting with some officers at Bragg's head-quarters, set out to view the town, as per assurance of the officers that he was quite at liberty to do. The railroad-depot, the store-houses, the outer works, &c., were visited, in the most indifferent and uncon-cerned manner. Ere long, however, some military officer, dressed up in a little "brief authority," accosted our explorer after items and demanded that he give an account of himself.

"To the divil with ye! An' is it the likes of you that is afther stoppin' me and axin' me name an' business? Go to Major-General Bragg, an' he'll tell ye who I am!"

The officer was not to be thus put aside: he collared Joyce forthwith, and led him to the provost-marshal's office, near by, supposing him to be a shirk-ing soldier or skulking conscript. The provost-marshal was of the same opinion.

"I'll send you to your regiment. What is it?" asked the marshal.

"You'll not do the likes at all, now," said Joyce; "for I don't belong to any."

"Oh, ho! you don't? Then you're just the man I want; for I know of a regiment that has just room for you," replied the marshal.

Matters began to look serious for Joyce. The town was all astir, for this was but a few days before the battle of Stone River. He told his story to the marshal, and it was agreed that if he should go back at once to Bragg's head-quarters and get a pass, or endorsement, it would be all right. Joyce did so; and an actual pass was granted to him, over Bragg's sign manual, giving him the run of the town,—which pass Joyce showed to the marshal with considerable glee and, withal, a slight taste of impudent defiance.

After looking about the town, our correspondent took the cars for a trip down towards Bridgeport,—was away two or three days, going as far as Atlanta, Ga., ascertained the general condition of the rebel rear, and returned to Murfreesborough. Again he basked at times in the presence of General Bragg and his officials, and wrote lively and caustic philippics for the able "Enquirer," and sat at Bragg's table and discussed the war and his mut-tons. And, to cap the very climax of absurdity and impudence, our man mounted his "Rosinante"—the horse he sallied forth with from the police stable at Nashville—and rode out to one or more of the grand division reviews with President Jefferson Davis, Bragg, and his escort,—Davis being then on his Southern tour.

It was now time for Joyce to be off, while his budget was full of news and the signs were favorable. Some officers invited him on the night of the review to go out with them to see some fair maids and have a good time. The girls were at an out-of-the-way place; and the less said about their chastity the better,—so reports Joyce. Arrived there, the party dismount, hitch their horses, and make themselves agreeable within-doors. Joyce watches his opportunity, slips out for a moment, unties the horses and turns them loose in the darkness to prevent possible pursuit, stealthily mounts his own horse— or, more probably, the best one of the lot—and makes off for dear life. He was fortunate enough to elude the pickets, the night being very dark; and ere morning he made his way across to the Cumberland River, and thence to the Federal lines.

His information was received with the liveliest satisfaction, and the joke thus perpetrated upon both Bragg and the Cincinnati "Enquirer" was the talk of the day. Its importance can be estimated when we state that the Union army advanced towards Murfreesborough a short time after his return. His statements were corroborated by two other spies just in from Murfrees-borough, and two days after his return there came into our lines a most respectable citizen, previously and now a merchant of Murfreesborough, who also confirmed Joyce's story, not only as to his army information, but as to the *rôle* he had played and the manner in which it was done.

There is something more than a joke left in the mind of the thoughtful, patriotic reader. There is a future, when the actions, the motives, and the errors of men will be truly judged by posterity. That time will soon come throughout the United States, if it is not already here. The editors of the Cincinnati "Enquirer" will be arraigned before that bar of enlightened, patri-otic public opinion, and the question will be asked, Where was *their* influ-ence during the darkest hours of the slaveholders' rebellion against liberty and human rights as guaranteed to their descendants by the Revolutionary fathers?

Two Rebel "Congressmen's" Wives.

ON the evening of the 26th of December last, a carriage containing two ladies and three children, and trunks and packages betokening the party to be travellers, came to the picket-line of the Army of the Cumberland, some four miles out from Nashville, on the road leading from Murfreesborough. Being utter strangers, and having no pass or permission to enter our lines, they were sent in to head-quarters under guard, as is the invariable rule.

Arrived in Nashville, the carriage was driven to the office of the Chief of Army Police, and the case was investigated by the provost-judge, in con-junction with the Chief of Police. The facts elicited were as follows, and were freely and candidly stated by the ladies.

Their names, Mrs. L. B. Bruce and Mrs. E. B. Burnett,—late residents of Kentucky. Their husbands, they said, now resided within the lines of the Southern Confederacy,—were at that time in or about Richmond, Virginia, in attendance upon the so-called Confederate Congress, of which body they claimed to be members, representing two Congressional districts of the State of Kentucky. These men had been members of the United States Congress for those districts at the breaking out of the rebellion. They seceded and joined the Confederate Congress, declaring at the same time that Kentucky had also seceded. For thirteen months past these ladies had lived within the lines of the new Government, they stated, their husbands being thus "in Congress" a portion of the time: the balance of the year they had dwelt in East Tennessee, as near to "the old Kentucky home" as they could well get.

In reply to queries of the provost-judge, the ladies stated that they had come to our lines in order to pass through to their homes in Kentucky. When informed that he feared this might not be permitted, they were apparently astonished.

"What! stop women and children from passing to their homes?" they exclaimed.

Even so. But they were assured that their cases should be stated to the general commanding, whose decision would be final. The ladies were much distressed at the thought of being prevented from "going home." Mrs. Burnett said she had two little sons in Kentucky, and all her relatives and friends, whom she had not seen for thirteen months, nor heard from for many weeks. Mrs. Bruce said she was the daughter of ex-Governor Helm, who resided at Elizabethtown, Ky. She *must* go home to her parents, for a cause that was plainly apparent,—her approaching confinement.

The day had been raw and cold, for it was mid-winter, and the ladies and children were chilled, tired, and dismal in feeling indeed. They were made as comfortable as possible before a cheerful fire. Some remnants of Christmas confectionery, stowed away in the pigeon-holes of the judge's desk, were distributed to the little ones, who devoured them as only children can. Remarking their glee, one of the mothers observed,—

"Ah, sir! that is the first candy they have had for a long time. There is none to be had where they have just come from."

The ladies further stated that they presumed they would remain permanently in Kentucky. When told that this would involve entire separation from their husbands, they looked blank astonishment; and they knew not what to answer when informed that if allowed to pass on to Kentucky they probably would not be permitted to return. They appeared to realize very feebly, if at all, the actual condition of their section of the country,—and had been of the opinion that, as ladies and non-combatants, they could pass about as freely as in times past.

They stated, also, that they had taken this latter step of their own accord,— their husbands neither advising nor restraining them. Mrs. Bruce said her husband had expressed to her his fears, or doubts, when they parted, that perhaps the Federals would not receive them within their lines.

The pseudo-Congressmen had come with their wives and babes to Murfreesborough, and there left them and returned to East Tennessee and Richmond,—to their warm and congenial nests in that mansion of political bliss, the Confederate Congress, composed of Virginia and Carolina negro-driving aristocrats.

Without detaining the ladies and their little ones longer, they were driven to the St. Cloud Hotel, and the best in the house was speedily at their disposal. The Chief of Police made up his report of the facts, and sent it forthwith to the general commanding. The report, ere midnight had elapsed, elicited the following response. For the sake of brevity we omit the formalities and signatures of the documents :—

"SIR:—In your report of this evening you state that two ladies, their children and baggage, with vehicle and driver, came to our lines without permit to enter; that they were apprehended and reported to your office. Their statements made in writing are to the effect that they are the wives of men prominent in aiding and abetting the rebellion, who now seek protection from a great and good Government which their husbands are aiming to destroy.

"The Provost-Marshal General will provide conveyance for these ladies and their children beyond these lines in the direction of Murfreesborough, from whence they say they came; or they may be carried quite to Murfreesborough, upon the pledge of the ladies, for themselves and for their husbands and friends, guaranteeing the safe and speedy return of the driver and carriage.
"By command of," &c. &c.

Early the next morning the following order was handed in to the ladies' rooms, at their hotel :—

"The ladies herein referred to—Mrs. Bruce and Mrs. Burnett—are respectfully informed that, in accordance with the foregoing order of the general commanding, a conveyance will be in attendance upon you at eight o'clock to-morrow (Saturday) morning, to convey you as indicated.
"Respectfully, yours," &c.

So far had the case progressed, when an unseen difficulty sprung up. This day the Federal army was under orders to march on to Murfreesborough, and the awful scenes of the tragedy of Stone River were about to commence. No hack-driver nor team could be hired in Nashville to take the party back to Murfreesborough, for fear of trouble—conscription, confiscation, etc.—upon the road, lined as it was with rebel guerrillas and thousands of rebel troops. At length the Chief of Police procured one of his own employés, and pressed the horses and carriage of a colored hackman, upon the ladies' giving the following document to satisfy the unwilling driver:—

"NASHVILLE, TENN., December 27, 1862.

"MR. GEORGE F. MOORE.—SIR:—This is to assure you that you, in undertaking to drive us to Murfreesborough, will not be molested by the forces or pickets of the Confederate Army; and we guarantee your safe and speedy return to Nashville upon the day following our arrival at Murfreesborough, or at safe quarters for us within the Confederate lines.

"MRS. L. B. BRUCE.
"MRS. E. S. BURNETT.

While giving this assurance to their driver, the ladies cried as if their hearts would break at their disappointment and unlucky predicament. They complained of the destitution and discomfort of life at the South, and of their long absence from children, parents, &c.; and there was much sympathy expressed for them by the officers at head-quarters, who, nevertheless, acknowledged the justice and necessity of the action of their general. The Chief of Police having made all needful arrangements, the carriage was ordered up, when a heavy rain-storm set in, continuing until after dinner, and their departure was postponed until the next day. Perceiving the scantiness of the children's clothing, &c., he gave the ladies permission to purchase such articles of personal comfort as they might desire,—a privilege eagerly accepted. They shopped for two or three hours during that afternoon, each purchasing some twenty dollars' worth of small articles, for which they gave orders on their relatives in Kentucky to the obliging storekeepers, the ladies being quite without money, it seemed.

The next morning the rain was falling briskly,—a continuous drizzle. The carriage was at hand, and the party was ensconced therein, they receiving due attention from several officers about head-quarters. New blankets were purchased, to wrap around the children and to stop up the cracks of the carriage-doors. It was a miserable day; the army was in motion, too, and there was fighting going on out on the Murfreesborough pike, cannonading being heard at intervals. A circuitous route of over forty-five miles must be travelled to avoid the armies. The carriage drove away upon its tedious, dreary journey, and at nine o'clock that night entered the town of Murfreesborough. There all was on the *qui vive*. The rebel army was preparing to meet General Rosecrans on Stone River, a mile or two north of the town, and the people feared that the place might be destroyed ere the contest was decided. After inquiring all over the town, shelter was at last found for the exhausted party. But times were stirring. People were fleeing. Our Congressmen's wives and little ones were among the early birds next day, leaving Murfreesborough before daylight for their husbands in Richmond, Virginia, or in East Tennessee, by the five o'clock train. One of them remembered her pledge, and spoke to an officer about her driver. The officer may have promised; but that was all. The next day our man was allowed the run of the town; but as for a pass through the lines to Nashville, nobody had any ears for his case. The battles of Stone River commenced a day or two afterwards, and the driver and his team were pressed to haul in wounded soldiers from the battle-field to the town hospitals. When the rebel army evacuated in the night, they carried off his horses and vehicle, and would have taken him, he thinks, had he not hidden himself in an old outbuilding or house and escaped the notice of their press-gangs, which swept over the place, taking the active negroes and able-bodied white men with their army.

Upon the Union troops entering Murfreesborough, the most joyful man of the hour was this carriage-driver. As for the team, it was gone, none knew whither, and must be paid for. The non-return of our driver also frustrated a very nice little arrangement our police had planned,—to make a good spy of the driver on the rebel movements at Murfreesborough!

Some weeks now elapsed, and the matter had quite passed from mind (except an occasional dun from the poor darkey at Nashville, whose carriage and horses were gone, and for which he was promised payment), when the Chief of Police learned that these ladies—or at least one of them—had arrived in Kentucky; and, without any desire to harass rebel women, but simply to recover the value of the lost property, to pay it over to its owner, he resolved to investigate the matter still further.

The discovery was accidental; and we relate it as an apt illustration of the importance of apparent trifles, all through life. John Morgan's gang had made their raid into Kentucky, destroying the Louisville & Nashville Railroad, some two weeks before, and stages were now running between the break, where two very high trestle-work bridges were destroyed, at Muldraugh's Hill. One morning, at Elizabethtown, before daylight, the stage-agent overheard two negro hostlers conversing about affairs at "Mass'r Helm's," while currying their horses. Says one of them,—a bright, likely slave, owned by ex-Governor Helm, of that town,—

"I say, Joe, somefin gwine on at mass'r's house. Did yer know dat?"

"What is it, Bill? Didn't know of nuffin."

"Well, ole mass'r's daughter, Mrs. Bruce, has jest slipped in from de Souf; and quite a time dar last night, shore."

The stage-man was from Nashville, and conversant with the facts above related. He questioned the negro, and learned that Mrs. Bruce had got home secretly, *via* the Cumberland Gap route. As the train went down to Nashville next day, he saw the provost-judge of the department on the train, by mere chance: he also happened to remember, as a simple incident, the conversation of the negroes; and he asked, for information, whether the general had revoked his decision respecting the traitors' wives. Proper steps were now taken; and thus, ere the lapse of many days, the vigilant Chief of Police was officially apprized that one of these ladies—Mrs. Bruce—had arrived at Elizabethtown, Kentucky, and was then at her father's house. He reported the case to head-quarters, with the following order as the result:—

"SIR:—Your report respecting the return of one, and probably of two, ladies,—Mrs. L. B. Bruce and Mrs. E. S. Burnett,—wives of two notable rebels, formerly of Kentucky, and now assuming to be members of Congress in the so-called Congress of the rebels at Richmond, Virginia, claiming to represent the loyal State of Kentucky therein, has been submitted to the general in command.

"You state in said report that one of the ladies in question, after having been refused entrance within these lines at Nashville, and having been sent back to the rebel army at Murfreesborough in December last, has since then passed into Kentucky through the Cumberlands without permission of the United States Government or military authorities, and is now in our midst, in the enjoyment of rights and privileges due only to loyal citizens, the husband of this lady meanwhile being still at his nefarious work of violence against the nation and fraud upon the people of Kentucky.

"As appears from documents in the office, copies of which are hereto annexed, the ladies in question were furnished with a carriage and two horses and a driver, to convey them from our lines back to Murfreesborough, they guaranteeing safe and speedy return to head-quarters of the same. You report that said property was never returned, but was taken South by the rebels when they evacuated Murfreesborough several days thereafter. Also you report the special guarantee to the driver of the carriage (a copy of which is also hereto annexed) was not in the least observed by the ladies in the premises nor by the rebel authorities, and that said driver was held as a prisoner, and hid himself in a building when the rebels evacuated Murfreesborough, to prevent their forcing him away as a prisoner or conscript.

"This exceeding bad faith on the part of the ladies above named, coupled with their act of stealing within our lines against the express order in their case, has received the serious consideration of the general commanding.

"You are herewith ordered to send a competent officer to where they may chance to be, if within this department, and there demand and receive speedy and full payment for the value of the said horses and carriage, and also proper compensation to the driver for his wrongful detention, the amount being left to your judgment, or others who knew the property and its value; and, in case of refusal of said persons so to do, you will have them arrested at once and sent to these head-quarters.

"If not in this department, you will confer with proper authorities where they are. You will, further, prepare a full statement of the case, together with a copy of this order, and transmit the same to Brigadier-General Boyle, presenting the case to him as to whether he deems such persons, under such peculiar circumstances, entitled to residence within his lines.

"You will report especially to these head-quarters your action in these premises.

"By order of," &c. &c.

In accordance with the above order, an officer was sent to Kentucky, who found one of the "Congressmen's" wives at the house of her father, ex-Governor Helm, in the full enjoyment of all the blessings—peace, comfort, and *dry-goods*—vouchsafed to her people by the good old Union. The lady prayed that she might be allowed to stay. Her father begged and implored. He paid nine hundred dollars cash for the lost horses and carriage; and the lady was permitted to remain, as a matter of humanity. Thus ended a chain of events which at the time created no little remark in official army circles; and, although of no remarkable importance as respects war results, these cases may well be preserved as matter of minor history for future reading, which will "point a moral or adorn a tale."

As will be seen by reference to "A Gossiping Letter," in this volume, written by a rebel officer to a secesh lady of Nashville, our friend Mrs. Bruce soon returned to the land of Dixie, where she has since cut a very superior figure, through the aid of silks, jewelry, &c., that she was able to purchase at Louisville and eastward, probably from the pay of the bogus Congressman her husband, and from his army contracts with the Southern clique of masters.

Morford, the Daring Spy.

"JOHN MORFORD"—so let us call him, good reader—was born near Augusta, Georgia, of Scotch parents, in the year 1832. A blacksmith by trade, he early engaged in railroading, and at the opening of the rebellion was master-mechanic upon a prominent Southern road. Being a strong Union man, and making no secret of it, he was discharged from his situation and not allowed employment upon any other railroad. A company of cavalry was also sent to his farm, and stripped it. Aggrieved at this whole-sale robbery, Morford went to John H. Morgan,—then a captain,—and in-quired if he would not pay him for the property thus taken. Morgan replied that he should have his pay if he would only prove his loyalty to the South. Morford acknowledged this to be impossible, and was thereupon very liberally cursed and vilified by Morgan, who accused him of harboring negroes and traitors, and threatened to have him shot. Finally, however, he was content with simply arresting him and sending him, charged with disloyalty, to one Major Peyton.

The major seems to have been a somewhat talkative and argumentative man; for upon Morford's arrival he endeavored to reason him out of his adherence to the Union, asking him, in the course of a lengthy conversation, many questions about the war, demonstrating, to his own satisfaction at least, the necessity and justice of the position assumed by the seceded States, and finishing, by way of clenching the argument, with the inquiry, "How *can* you, a Southern man by birth and education, be opposed to the South?" Morford replied that he saw no reason for the rebellion, that the Union was good enough for him, that he should cling to it, and, if he could obtain a pass, would abandon the Confederacy and cast his lot with the North. The major then argued still more at length, and, as a last resort, endeavored to frighten him with a vivid description of the horrors of "negro equality,"—to all of which his hearer simply replied that he was not afraid; whereupon, as unskilful advocates of a bad cause are prone to do, he became very wrathy, vented his anger in a torrent of oaths and vile epithets, and told Morford that he ought to be hung, and should be in two weeks. The candidate for hempen honors, apparently not at all alarmed, coolly replied that he was sorry for that, as he wished to live a little longer, but, if it must be so, he couldn't help it. Peyton, meanwhile, cooled down, and told him that if he would give a bond of one thousand dollars and take the oath of allegiance to the Southern Confederacy he would release him and protect his property. After some hesitation,—no other plan of escape occurring to him,—Morford assented, and took the required oath, upon the back of which Peyton wrote, " If you violate this, I will hang you."

With this safeguard, Morford returned to his farm and lived a quiet life. Buying a span of horses, he devoted himself to the cultivation of his land, seeing as few persons as he could, and talking with none. His house had previously been the head-quarters of the Union men, but was now deserted by them; and its owner endeavored to live up to the letter of the obligation he had taken. For a short time all went well enough; but one day a squad of cavalry came with a special written order from Major Peyton to take his two horses, which they did. This was too much for human nature; and Morford, perceiving that no faith could be placed in the assurances of those in command, determined to be revenged upon them and their cause. His house again became a secret rendezvous for Unionists; and by trusty agents he managed to send regular and valuable information to General Buell,— then in command in Tennessee. At length, however, in May, 1862, he was betrayed by one in whom he had placed confidence, and arrested upon the charge of sending information to General Crittenden, at Battle Creek. He indignantly denied the charge, and declared that he could easily prove himself innocent if released for that purpose. After three days' confinement, this was assented to; and Morford, knowing full well that he could not do what he had promised, made a hasty retreat and fled to the mountains, whence, some days afterwards, he emerged, and went to McMinnville, at which place General Nelson was then in command.

Here he remained until the rebel force left that vicinity, when he again went home, and lived undisturbed upon his farm until Bragg returned with his army. The presence in the neighborhood of so many officers cognizant of his former arrest and escape rendered flight a second time necessary. He now went to the camp of General Donelson, with whom he had some acquaintance, and soon became very friendly there,—acting the while in the double capacity of beef-contractor for the rebel army and spy for General Crittenden. Leaving General Donelson after some months' stay, although earnestly requested to remain longer, Morford next found his way to Nashville, where he made numerous expeditions as a spy for .General Negley. Buell was at Louisville, and Nashville was then the Federal outpost. Morford travelled about very readily upon passes given him by General Donelson, making several trips to Murfreesborough and one to Cumberland Gap.

Upon his return from the latter, he was arrested near Lebanon, Tennessee, about one o'clock at night, by a party of four soldiers upon picket-duty at that point. Halting him, the following conversation occurred:—

" Where do you live?"

" Near Stewart's Ferry, between here and Nashville."

" Where have you been, and what for?"

" Up to see my brother, to get from him some jeans cloth and socks for another brother in the Confederate army."

"How does it happen you are not in the army yourself? That looks rather suspicious."

"Oh, I live too near the Federal lines to be conscripted."

"Well, we'll have to send you to Murfreesborough. I reckon you're all right; but those are our orders, and we can't go behind them."

To this Morford readily consented, saying he had no objection; and the party sat down by the fire and talked in a friendly manner for some time. Morford soon remembered that he had a bottle of brandy with him, and generously treated the crowd. Further conversation was followed by a second drink, and soon by a third. One of the party now proposed to exchange his Rosinantish mare for a fine horse which Morford rode. The latter was not inclined to trade; but objection was useless, and he finally yielded, receiving seventy-five dollars in Confederate money and the mare. The trade pleased the soldier, and a present of a pair of socks still further enhanced his pleasure. His companions were also similarly favored, and testified their appreciation of the gift by endeavoring to purchase the balance of Morford's stock. He would not sell, however, as he wished to send them to his brother at Richmond, by a person who had given public notice that he was soon going there. A fourth drink made all supremely happy; at which juncture their prisoner asked permission to go to a friend's house, only a quarter of a mile off, and stay until morning, when he would go with them to Murfreesborough. His friend of the horse-trade, now very mellow, thought he need not go to Murfreesborough at all, and said he would see what the others said about it. Finally, it was concluded that he was "right," and might; whereupon he mounted the skeleton mare and rode rejoicingly into Nashville.

On his next trip southward he was arrested by Colonel John T. Morgan, just as he came out of the Federal lines, and, as his only resort, joined Forrest's command, and was furnished with a horse and gun. The next day Forrest made a speech to his men, and told them that they were now going to capture Nashville. The column immediately began its march, and Morford, by some means, managed to have himself placed in the advance. Two miles below Lavergne a halt for the night was made; but Morford's horse was unruly, and could not be stopped, carrying its rider ahead and out of sight. It is needless to say that this obstinacy was not overcome until Nashville was reached, nor that when Forrest came, the next day, General Negley was amply prepared for him.

At this time Nashville was invested. Buell was known to be advancing towards the city, but no scouts had been able to go to or come from him. A handsome reward was offered to any one who would carry a despatch safely through to Bowling Green, and Morford undertook to do it. Putting the document under the lining of his boot, he started for Gallatin, where he arrived safely.

For some hours he sauntered around the place, lounged in and out of bar-rooms, made friends with the rebel soldiers, and, towards evening, purchased a small bag of corn-meal, a bottle of whiskey, a pound or two of salt, and some smaller articles, which he threw across his shoulder and started up the Louisville road, with hat on one side, hair in admirable disorder, and, apparently, gloriously drunk. The pickets jested at and made sport of him, but permitted him to pass. The meal, &c. was carried six miles, when he suddenly became sober, dropped it, and hastened on to Bowling Green, and there met General Rosecrans, who had just arrived. His information was very valuable. Here he remained until the army came up and passed on, and then set out on his return on foot, as he had come. He supposed that our forces had gone by way of Gallatin, but when near that place learned that it was still in possession of the rebels, and so stopped for the night in a shanty between Morgan's pickets, on the north side, and Woolford's (Union), on the south side. During the night the two had a fight, which finally centred around the shanty, and resulted in driving Morford to the woods. In two or three hours he came back for his clothes, and found that the contending parties had disappeared, and that the railroad-tunnels had been filled with wood and fired. Hastily gathering his effects together, he made his way to Tyree Springs, and thence to Nashville.

For a short time he acted as a detective of the Army Police at Nashville, assuming the character of a rebel soldier, and living in the families of prominent secessionists. In this work he was very successful; but it had too little of danger and adventure, and he returned again to scouting, making several trips southward, sometimes without trouble, but once or twice being arrested and escaping as best he could. In these expeditions he visited McMinnville, Murfreesborough, Altamont, on the Cumberland Mountains, Bridgeport, Chattanooga, and other places of smaller note. He travelled usually in the guise of a smuggler, actually obtaining orders for goods from prominent rebels, and sometimes the money in advance, filling them in Nashville and delivering the articles upon his next trip. Just before the battle of Stone River he received a large order to be filled for the rebel hospitals, went to Nashville, procured the medicine, and returned to McMinnville, when he delivered some of it. Thence he travelled to Bradyville, and thence to Murfreesborough, arriving there just as the battle began. Presenting some of the surgeons with a supply of morphine, he assisted them in attending the wounded for a day or two, and then went to a hospital tent in the woods near the railroad, where he also remained one day and part of another. The fight was now getting hot, and, fearful that somebody would recognize him, he left Murfreesborough on Friday, and went to McMinnville. He had been there but little more than an hour, having barely time to put up his horse and step into a house near by to see some wounded men, when two soldiers arrived in search of him. Their description of him was perfect; but he escaped by being out of sight,—the friend with whom he was supposed to be declaring, though closely questioned, that he had not seen and knew nothing of him. In a few minutes pickets were thrown out around the town, and it was two days before he could get away. Obtaining a pass to Chattanooga at last, only through the influence of a lady acquaintance, with it he passed the guards, but, when once out of sight, turned off from the Chattanooga road and made his way safely to Nashville.

General Rosecrans was now in possession of Murfreesborough, and thither Morford proceeded with some smuggler's goods, with a view to another trip. The necessary permission was readily obtained, and he set out for Woodbury. Leaving his wagon outside the rebel lines, he proceeded on foot to McMinnville, arriving there on the 19th of January last, and finding General John H. Morgan, to whom he represented himself as a former resident in the vicinity of Woodbury; his family, however, had moved away, and he would like permission to take his wagon and bring away the household goods. This was granted, and the wagon brought to McMinnville, whence Morford went to Chattanooga, representing himself along the road as a fugitive from the Yankees. Near Chattanooga he began selling his goods to Unionists and rebels alike, at enormous prices, and soon closed them out at a profit of from four hundred to five hundred dollars. At Chattanooga he remained a few days, obtained all the information he could, and returned to Murfreesborough without trouble.

His next and last trip is the most interesting and daring of all his adventures. Making a few days' stay in Murfreesborough, he went to McMinnville, and remained there several days, during which time he burned Hickory Creek Bridge, and sent a report of it to General Rosecrans. This he managed with so much secrecy and skill as to escape all suspicion of complicity in the work, mingling freely with the citizens and talking the matter over in all its phases. From McMinnville Morford proceeded to Chattanooga, and remained there nearly a week, when he learned that three of our scouts were imprisoned in the Hamilton county jail, at Harrison, Tennessee, and were to be shot on the first Friday in May. Determined to attempt their rescue, he sent a Union man to the town to ascertain who was jailer, what the number of the guards, how they were placed, and inquire into the condition of things in general about the jail. Upon receipt of his report, Morford gathered about him nine Union men, on the night of Tuesday, April 21, and started for Harrison. Before reaching the place, however, they heard rumors that the guard had been greatly strengthened; and, fearful that it would prove too powerful for them, the party retreated to the mountains on the north side of the Tennessee River, where they remained concealed until Thursday night. On Wednesday night the same man who had previously gone to the town was again sent to reconnoitre the position. Thursday morning he returned and said that the story of a strong guard was all false: there were but two in addition to the jailer.

Morford's party was now reduced to six, including himself; but he resolved to make the attempt that night. Late in the afternoon all went down to the river and loitered around until dark, when they procured boats and crossed to the opposite bank. Taking the Chattanooga and Harrison road, they entered the town, looked around at leisure, saw no soldiers nor any thing unusual, and proceeded towards the jail. Approaching quite near, they threw themselves upon the ground and surveyed the premises carefully. The jail was surrounded by a high board fence, in which were two gates. Morford's plan of operations was quickly arranged. Making a prisoner of one of his own men, he entered the enclosure, posting a sentinel at each gate. Once inside, a light was visible in the jail, and Morford marched confidently up to the door and rapped. The jailer thrust his head out of a window and asked what was wanted. He was told, "Here is a prisoner to put in the jail." Apparently satisfied, the jailer soon opened the door and admitted the twain into the entry. In a moment, however, he became alarmed, and, hastily exclaiming, "Hold on!" stepped out.

For ten minutes Morford waited patiently for his return, supposing, of course, that he could not escape from the yard, both gates being guarded. Not making his appearance, it was found that the pickets had allowed him to pass them. This rather alarming fact made haste necessary, and Morford, returning to the jail, said he must put his prisoner in immediately, and demanded the keys forthwith. The women declared in positive terms that they hadn't them, and did not know where they were. One of the guards was discovered in bed and told to get the keys. Proving rather noisy and saucy, he was reminded that he might get his head taken off if he were not quiet,—which intimation effectually silenced him. Morford again demanded the keys, and the women, somewhat frightened, gave him the key to the outside door. Unlocking it, and lighting up the place with candles, he found himself in a room around the sides of which was ranged a line of wrought-iron cages. In one of these were five persons, four white and one negro. Carrying out the character he had assumed of a rebel soldier in charge of a prisoner, Morford talked harshly enough to the caged men, and threatened to hang them at once, at which they were very naturally alarmed, and began to beg for mercy. For a third time the keys to the inner room, in which the scouts were, were demanded, and a third time the women denied having them. An axe was then ordered to be brought, but there was none about the place: so said they. Morford saw that they were trifling with him, and determined to stop it. Snatching one of the jailer's boys standing near by the collar, and drawing his sabre, he told him he would cut his head off if he did not bring him an axe in two minutes. This had the desired effect, and the axe was forthcoming.

Morford now began cutting away at the lock, when he was startled by hearing the word "halt!" at the gate. Of his five men two were at the gates, two were inside as a guard, and one was holding the light. Ready for a fight, he went out to see what was the matter. The sentinel reporting that he had halted an armed man outside, Morford walked out to him and demanded,—

"What are you doing here with that gun?"

"Miss Laura said you were breaking down the jail, and I want to see McAllister, the jailer. Where is he?" was the reply.

"Well, suppose I am breaking down the jail: what are you going to do about it?"

"I am going to stop it if I can."

"What's your name?"

"Lowry Johnson."

By this time Morford had grasped the muzzle of the gun, and told him to let go. Instead of complying, Johnson tried to pull it away; but a blow upon the neck from Morford's sabre soon made him drop it. Morford now began to search him for other weapons, but before he had concluded the operation Johnson broke away, leaving a part of his clothing in Morford's hands. The latter drew his revolver and pursued, firing five shots at him, sometimes at a distance of only six or eight paces. A cry, as of pain, showed that he was struck, but he managed to reach the hotel (kept by his brother), and, bursting in the door, which was fastened, escaped into the house. Morford followed, but too late. Johnson's brother now came out and rang the bell in front, which gathered a crowd about the door; but Morford, not at all daunted, told them that if they wanted to guard the jail they had better be about it quick, as he was going to burn it and the town in the bargain. This so frightened them that no further demonstration was made, and Morford returned to the jail unmolested. There he and his men made so much shouting and hurrahing as to frighten the people of the town beyond measure; and many lights from upper-story windows were extinguished, and the streets were deserted.

A half-hour's work was necessary to break off the outside lock,—a splendid burglar-proof one. Morford now discovered that the door was double, and that the inner one was made still more secure by being barred with three heavy log-chains. These were cut in two with the axe; but the strong lock of the door still remained. He again demanded the key, and told the women if it was not produced he would murder the whole of them. The rebel guard, Lew. Luttrell by name, was still in bed. Rising up, he said that the key was not there. Morford now ordered Luttrell to get out of bed, in a tone so authoritative that that individual deemed it advisable to comply. Scarcely was he out, however, before Morford struck at him with his sabre; but he was too far off, and the blow fell upon one of the children, drawing some blood. This frightened the women, and, concluding that he was about to put his threat in execution and would murder them surely enough, they produced the key without further words. No time was lost in unlocking the door and releasing the inmates of the room. Procuring their clothes for them and arming one with Johnson's gun, the whole party left the jail and hurried towards the river. Among the released prisoners was a rebel with a wooden leg, the original having been shot off at Manassas. He persisted in accompanying the others, and was only induced to go back by the intimation that "dead men tell no tales."

Crossing the river in the boats, they were moved to another place at some distance, to preclude the possibility of being tracked and followed. All now hid themselves among the mountains, and the same Union man was again sent to Harrison, this time to see how severely Johnson was wounded. He returned in a day or two, and reported that he had a severe sabre-cut on the shoulder, a bullet through the muscle of his right arm, and two slight wounds in one of his hands. Morford and his men remained in the mountains until all search for the prisoners was over, then went to the Cumberland Mountains, where they remained one day and a portion of another, and then proceeded in the direction of McMinnville. Hiding themselves in the woods near this place during the day, seeing but not seen, they travelled that night to within eleven miles of Woodbury, when they struck across the road from McMinnville to Woodbury. Near Logan's Plains they were fired on by a body of rebel cavalry, but, though some forty shots were fired, no one of the ten was harmed, Morford having one bullet-hole in his coat. The cavalry, however, pursued them across the barrens, surrounded them, and supposed themselves sure of their game; but Morford and his companions scattered and hid away, not one being captured or found. Night coming on, the cavalry gave up the chase, and went on to Woodbury, where they threw out pickets, not doubting that they would pick up the objects of their search during the night. Morford, however, was informed of this fact by a citizen, and, in consequence, lay concealed all the next day, making his way safely to Murfreesborough, with all of his company, the day after.

Fraudulent Transfer of Rebel Goods.

On the 10th of December, 1862, the Chief of Police of the Army of the Cumberland seized the large wholesale store and stock of goods of Morgan & Co., a noted dry-goods house at Nashville, Tennessee, previous to the breaking out of the rebellion. When war convulsed that section of country, the store was closed, and upon the occupancy of Nashville by the Union troops, after the fall of Fort Donelson, Samuel D. Morgan went South with the rebel army, with which he was identified as a contractor, as a manufacturer of percussion-caps, and as a very wealthy, ardent, Southern secessionist. After the store had been closed several months, it suddenly was made known that this stock of goods, $26,000 in value, had been sold to Messrs. Moore & Kyle, who were formerly clerk and book-keeper, respectively, in the same store,— who were notoriously young men of no capital, and were not known as Union men in that community. The facts we glean from the papers in the case to be as follows:—

This stock of goods was the property of Samuel D. Morgan and Charles J. Cheney, partners, doing business under the style of Morgan & Co. At the breaking-out of the rebellion, and before the State of Tennessee seceded, Samuel D. Morgan, a zealous rebel sympathizer, started a factory for the manufacture of percussion-caps. He was chairman of an ordnance bureau. He applied to Andrew Anderson, a foundryman and machinist in Nashville, to make machines for making the caps, and on his refusal called him a Union man, and threatened to have his property seized by the authorities if he refused to make them. Upon this Anderson made the machines, and Morgan took from him his foreman, Horatio North, to superintend the manufacture of the percussion-caps. He manufactured about one million caps per week, and shipped them to Richmond, Mobile, New Orleans, &c. On the fall of Fort Donelson, Morgan fled with the Southern army. On the secession of the State, Morgan turned the factory over to the Confederate authorities, and he has never returned since.

This stock of goods remained in store until the summer of 1862, when said Cheney, who is Morgan's son-in-law, executed a sale of it to John F. Moore and James Kyle. It is not pretended that either of these persons had any means. Moore had been a clerk in the house of Morgan & Co. and Kyle had also been a clerk. Moore is shown to have been a secession sympathizer; nothing is stated as to Kyle's political views. To these persons the stock was sold for the sum of $26,000 (it is stated that the stock is of far greater value), on a credit, their notes being taken for $2000 each, payable to Morgan & Co. every three months, making a time-sale running through thirty-nine months. It is stated that the firm of Morgan & Co., owed a heavy debt in New York and other Eastern cities of from $25,000 to $30,000, and that it was their intention to pay this indebtedness, and that it was the desire of Mr. Cheney to apply the amounts of these notes in liquidation of this debt.

Mr. Cheney states the indebtedness due the firm of Morgan & Co. at $300,000; that the notes of Moore & Kyle, together with all the notes due the firm, were sent by him to Mr. Morgan, then in Middle Alabama, in September last.

It appears from the statement of Mr. Moore that the amount of the first note has been fully paid in supplying the families of Morgan and Cheney, still in the city of Nashville, with necessaries.

It is stated by Mr. Cheney, and by other testimony, that the stock of goods was four-fifths Morgan's and one-fifth his; that the store was closed from the time of the taking of Fort Donelson, February, 1862, until the sale in the same summer, because licenses were required. It appears that the requirement for a license was the oath of allegiance; but no effort appears to have been made by Mr. Cheney to obtain a license, although, as he states, the goods were damaging. It further appears that on the sale to Moore & Kyle they obtained license by taking the oath of allegiance.

Moore & Kyle state that if the seizure of these goods be preparatory to the confiscation thereof as the property of Morgan, it is inflicting a severe and disastrous blow upon them; that they owe the notes, but, if the goods are taken, have no means of payment; that if the object were to reach the property of Morgan, they suggest that the notes should have been seized; that the transfer to them was a *bona fide* transaction; that, at any rate, it is a proper case for civil, not military, proceeding, and that they suggest the propriety of seizing, by process in the nature of attachment or injunction, their indebtedness to Morgan & Co.; and that they have acted in perfect good faith in this transaction throughout.

The foregoing is the substance of the evidence in this case, though it is hoped that the evidence of Mr. Joseph Clark, of Liberty, De Kalb county, Tennessee, can be obtained.

The facts show,—

1st. That this stock was owned by parties hostile to the Union and sympathizing with rebellion; one of the parties being in active hostility, not as an individual merely, but with a wide-spread influence as a man, and rendering assistance to the rebellion of the utmost importance as a manufacturer.

2d. That Morgan, whose only two sons are, or were, in the rebel army, fled with the Southern army as a rebel, and engaged in rebellion, leaving his property and goods; and that Mr. Cheney, from his own statements, though not an active participator, was and is a rebel sympathizer to such an extent that he either did not dare to take steps to procure license for the sale of the stock, or did not choose to.

3d. That from these facts alone it would appear that, so far as Morgan was concerned, he fled, leaving these goods because he had not time to make a proper disposition of them; that they remained as lawful prize to the army of the United States; that, by the very nature of the transaction, the title became vested in the United States as a military capture,—not as goods subject to confiscation.

4th. The sale to Moore & Kyle seems to have been only a sham. Morgan has with him in the South, sent there in September last by Mr. Cheney, the substance of the concern,—$300,000 of evidences of debt due the house, and the notes of Moore & Kyle. It is not presumable that men engaged as he and Cheney should be willing, upon the policy of the South, to pay Northern debts; to the contrary of the assertion of Mr. Cheney to that effect, the proceeds of the sale of these goods have so far been applied to the support of the families of Morgan and Cheney.

In case this stock of goods is not to be looked upon as a military capture, it was respectfully recommended by the provost judge that they be turned over to the United States Marshal for libel and confiscation.

This latter recommendation was approved by the general commanding, and the case is now before the United States District Court, to be heard at its next sitting at Nashville. Of course good Union lawyers will be feed to prevent the confiscation of these goods if possible. But the case is a plain one, from the above showing. At all events, this chapter is worthy of perusal, as representative of the multitude of cases of confiscation that will flood upon the country upon the close of the war.

Mrs. Y——'s Boots and Dry-Goods.

ABOUT the 15th of December, 1862, while the Army of the Cumberland
was occupying the city of Nashville, Tennessee, the rebel army being but
thirty-two miles south, at Murfreesborough, and smuggling and spying at
full tide, the following important and amusing case occurred.

A Mrs. Y —— entered the house of a neighbor in that city at the time
above mentioned, both being Southern sympathizers, and spoke of her intention to go South soon to her husband; also, she desired to take with her
a quantity of clothing for him and other friends in the Southern army
especially some boots, coats, &c.; and, furthermore, she had a large lot of
store goods, which would pay well, and also greatly aid the cause, if she
could run them through safely. She said she had recently made a trip to
the rebel army, cheating the Yankee authorities badly; that she took with
her quite a lot of goods, letters, &c., but that she had no conveyance, and
was compelled to walk several miles at one time: she now desired to get a
team to go with, &c.

There was present at this conversation a man whom the ladies thought to
be all right; and so he really had been. They freely consulted with him
he having been at one time in the Southern army. A change, however, had

come over this man, and he had silently come to the conclusion that the rebellion was wrong and would prove a failure. As soon as Mrs. Y—— departed he also left the house, and ere long the whole matter was known to the Chief of the Army Police.

The man was instructed to aid Mrs. Y—— in all her movements, but was particularly cautioned not to encourage or advise her to do unlawful acts. He returned to that house, and soon was assisting her in that spirit and intent. She wanted a team: he assisted her in purchasing two mules and a double-spring wagon. He procured boxes and bales at her request, and helped her to stow away her things in a friendly manner. It seemed that her husband or friends had formerly kept a store in Nashville until the war set in, when it was closed, and the goods taken to her dwelling and there hidden away in back-room, garret, or cellar.

At length she was ready; and so was the Chief of Police. Several days were required to perfect all her arrangements, down to the final one of getting her pass to move South with her household goods; for this was her pretence, and at that time the general commanding permitted Southern sympathizing families to go South. Of course a pass was granted to her. The informer often cautioned her as to the risk of detection, and the sure confiscation that would follow; but she was fearless and reckless and determined.

Mrs. Y—— and party left Nashville one morning in style, as follows:— two mules drawing spring wagon, with a black man as driver, and herself and her black female servant mounted high upon the load of beds, bales, and bundles of what seemed to be common household "plunder." Arriving at the outer lines, the wagon was halted and the pass demanded and exhibited. "All right; pass on," were the cheering words of the picket-guard; and Mrs. Y—— must have breathed much easier as the team started on cheerily for the land of Dixie. Her exultation was short-lived. Some Federal patrols (policemen), whom Colonel Truesdail has constantly on that road, were on the alert. The wagon was again halted, the pass exhibited, and then the lady, her driver, and the woman-servant were invited to dismount, that the goods might be examined. Mrs. Y—— protested, expostulated, and stormed; but it was of no avail; alight they must. She did so, followed by the driver. Her black woman then essayed to get down; for she was fat, old, and clumsy, and had on hoops, and negro-finery of latest pattern. When almost down, she gave a jump, and brought up on the ground "all standing." Alas for that jump! A string broke from about her waist, and down tumbled to the ground from beneath her well-developed hoops *two pairs of long-legged cavalry boots.* The surprise and mortification of the lady, the horror of the darkies, and the smiles of the officers and men may well be imagined. Our artist has presented the scene on the foregoing page.

This evidence was sufficient to warrant the detention and return to Nashville of the party. The policemen, however, knew their business, and a moment's examination of the beds, &c. satisfied them of other mysteries packed away in the wagon. The party were at once returned to the city police office,—the lady in a state of mind more easily imagined than described.

Then occurred another scene, to be witnessed but once in a lifetime. The wagon-load of bedding was taken into the police office and examined. In the midst of feather beds, &c. were found new shoes, boots, balls of ribbon, articles of clothing, hoop-skirts, packages of gloves and stockings, bunches and spools of thread, whole pieces of lace and edging, dress-patterns of various hue and texture, entire pieces of domestic and muslins,—in short, the remnant of a considerable stock from a city dry-goods store, which would have been worth to Mrs. Y——, once safely in rebeldom, five hundred per cent. more than the original cost, and which she counted good to her for eighteen thousand dollars.

As the negro servants and orderlies worked away in uncovering and disembowelling the goods, the large parlor of the noted Zollicoffer mansion, where the army police office has been located for several months, presented a singular appearance. A pile of goods was made in the middle of the floor like a pyramid, reaching above the centre-table. The atmosphere was thick with downy feathers which came out with the goods. Around the room were standing crowds of officers from head-quarters, who had heard of the event and come over to witness the developments. At one time the general commanding was an interested witness. The facts were noised about the neighborhood, and for some time afterwards the police office was a "curiosity-shop" of the highest pretension.

Upon the person of Mrs. Y—— were also found some eight hundred dollars in money, a gold watch, &c., which were retained for the time, and she was permitted to go to her home. The case was reported to head-quarters; and orders were thereupon issued that her store-goods and team, and five hundred dollars of her money, be turned over to the United States Government as subject to confiscation, and that she be sent south of our lines, with her household goods proper, clothing, &c., with strict command that she return to the North no more during the war.

The following letter was found upon Mrs. Y——'s driver, and contains some interesting items:—

"NASHVILLE, December 17, 1862.

"IRA P. JONES, ESQ., CHATTANOOGA, TENNESSEE.

"DEAR SIR:—It is now nine o'clock at night, and, feeling quite lonely, my mind runs back to pleasant hours that I have spent with you, your dear wife, and sweet little darlings, and, thinking a word from me would be exceptable to you, I will write a line informing you of our good health. I say our,—and mean sister, the black ones, and I; for these compose my family. Since you left here we have all had fine health; and well that it is so, for we have had but little else to cheer us; but I have as little to complain of as any one, for as yet not one tree, bush, or shrub has been destroyed inside of my home place. I hope it may continue so. Your home is in like condition. Soon after you left, I got a man to go in the house, and he is still there. I have claimed the property; and so far all is well taken care of. We have a hard way of getting on now: every thing is high and scarce; and I suppose it will be so while the war continues. Do you see any thing bright or hopeful in the future? Oh, I wish it was stopped! but God only knows when it will cease. I think it very doubtful whether you get this note or not: if you do, please write to me, for I would be glad to hear from you and any of the children. Mr. Armstrong and family are all well. My servants are all with me yet, but I am looking for an outbreak with them. The men have been working on fortifications nearly all the summer. They are quite free; but still they are home. The servants are ruining! our country is ruining! all, all are ruining! Please write if you can.

"I am, as ever, yours,

"I—— P——."

The Case of Mrs. Molly Hyde.

In April last, Mrs. Hyde, of Nashville, a young, ardent, handsome, and smart rebel lady, mother of two children, and whose husband was in the rebel army, was arrested within our lines as a spy and a dangerous political character. Also her sister, Mrs. Payne, likewise a resident of Nashville, was subsequently arrested as connected with, aiding, and abetting her.

A detective policeman, whose *rôle* was to get into the confidence of notable secessionists, had become acquainted with the lady and all her ways. He reported to Colonel Truesdail, and at the proper time the arrest was made. We will call the detective by the name of Randolph, and let him tell the story. We only publish two statements made after her arrest, as they give a fair insight into the case,—one of them made by her to her *confidential* friend, as she supposed, and the other an open, defiant confession, made to the police-officer who had her in charge. Says Randolph,—

"Mrs. Molly Hyde has told me that when she was last at General Morgan's head-quarters she gave Harry Morgan a fine horse; that she paid eight hundred dollars for him; that Harry Morgan was a cousin of John Morgan; that she was glad that she did it, for the Yankees would have got him if she had delayed it any longer, and that she would rather see the horse shot than to see them get him; that he was in good hands now; and that if she ever needed a horse she could get as many as she wanted of Morgan.

"She told me that she wanted to be sent South. She did not care if she did have to go by the way of Vicksburg; she would be at Morgan's head-quarters as soon as she could get there, and that would be in two weeks after her arrival at that point; that she regretted nothing that she had done for the Confederacy, for her whole heart was with the South, and she would remain as true as steel.

"The only thing that she was sorry for was that she had taken the oath of allegiance to the United States Government. She wished she could have an opportunity to scratch her name from that paper: she regretted it more than any act of her life; but, said she,

"'If ever I get my liberty, *the oath won't stop me. No, sir!* Not until every one of old Truesdail's devils is caught and hung. I would rather Morgan would catch him than any other man in the world. He has had a man on my track ever since I took the oath. If he had not known that I went to the Southern army, he would not have stopped my letters at the Nashville post-office. I wish he was hung for that! I have sent word to every one of my friends that I could, not to write to me through the post-office any more, for if they did I would not get them.

"'I think that old Church Hooper has told something on me that makes Truesdail or some of the Yankees watch me so,—and Clay Drake too. He offered me five hundred dollars to get him released from the conscript that was on him. I would not get him released for one thousand dollars: they will shoot him if they ever get him,' &c. &c.

"She then repeated,—

"'I wish they would send me South; but I will not let them know that I want to go there, for if I do they will be sure to send me North. I am going to tell them that I am not at all particular where I go, they may do just as they please with me. But I tell *you*, Mr. ——, if I do go to the Alton or Camp Chase prison, I want you to come and see me and help me out.'

"'That will be a very difficult task to undertake,' I remarked.

"'I know that,' she replied, 'but where there is a will there is a way; and if you want money to do it with, my friends will furnish all your wants, and you can do it easy enough. These Yankee officers are easy enough bribed: you know that *yourself*, for you was one *yourself* once, or *thought you were as good as any* of them, and *now* see *how you feel* towards the *whole Lincoln tribe*. I am glad that you are now going to do something for people that can appreciate your services and not treat you like a dog.'

"Mrs. Molly Hyde stated to me yesterday—my last interview with her—that Captain Dick Gladden, who was discharged from the 1st Middle Tennessee Infantry,—Union,—was now an officer in the Confederate army; that he went from here to Columbia, Tennessee, with a man from Edgefield by the name of Madison Stratton, who was held in hostage for D. D. Dickey, when the Confederates had him; that Gladden had recognized several men from Nashville from Yankee regiments, who were supposed to be spies, five of whom were hung. She saw the execution take place, and expressed much regret that there had not been twice as many. She saw Gladden at Tullahoma, about eight days before her arrest. Mrs. Hyde said she carried very important papers and information to Generals Wheeler and Van Dorn, which officers made a great ado over her upon her arrival. She said she bribed the Federal pickets on her return home with apples, cakes, and candy, which she obtained of her aunt, who lives near Columbia. I did not learn the name of her aunt and uncle."

The foregoing is the substance of Mrs. Hyde's revelations to the detective. She prevailed upon Randolph to go and see a Federal officer and get assistance from that quarter. He did so,—with the following result, says Randolph:—

"During an interview with Captain ——, of the Ohio cavalry, he stated to me all of the friendly relations that existed between himself and Mrs. Hyde and Mrs. Payne. He said he had known them for some time, and that they had been very kind to him in several instances. When he was sick they visited him, and brought all sorts of delicacies to him, and nursed him as kindly as his own mother could have done. 'And now, Randolph,' said he, 'I cannot forget such kindness. I do not want to do any thing that will *criminate me*. I am in the Government service; but I will exert myself to any honorable extent to relieve them from their present confinement.' We talked of every plan by which their release could be effected. The captain's opinion was that the best thing they could do would be to go before the military authorities and acknowledge they had done wrong, and that they had been influenced to do as they had by those who had pretended to be their friends, but in whom they had lost all confidence, and that they were now willing to abide by the laws of the Federal Government while they occupied this country. If this policy did not gain them their liberty, it would have a very good influence upon the general commanding the post, also with General Rosecrans, &c. &c."

Thus the reader will perceive the craft and deceit of these secession females, in paying ladylike attentions to Federal officers, to gain favors and protection, while in their hearts are only hatred and curses. In this case we are pleased to see that the officer properly remembered their kindness to him in sickness, but was true to his flag. Finding all hopes of release vain, Mrs. Hyde puts on a bold air of defiance, and reveals her doings to the police-officer at the hotel who has her in charge. We will also let him tell his part of the story:—

"Mrs. Hyde told me, in a conversation I had with her alone at the City Hotel, in Nashville, on May 1, 1863, that she had been doing an immense deal of service for the rebel Government for the last twenty months,—had been all through Southern Kentucky, in fact, all over the State. Near Lexington, Kentucky, she bought the fine blooded mare that John H. Morgan now rides. She presented it to said Morgan; and it is the same one which he rode when he made his escape from the Federals at McMinnville about one week ago. She further said she was in McMinnville last winter; she was then employed by said John H. Morgan in obtaining information for him of all that would be of any advantage to him, of the movements of the enemy, or of their whereabouts, &c.

"In presenting the mare to Morgan, she told him the mare had done her good service: 'Take her, and do all the good you can with her for our cause.' She further told me she made a trip for Bragg into East Tennessee last winter to gather all the information she could in regard to who were in sympathy with the Lincoln Government, and to ferret out the bridge-burners in that region. She also said she was in Middleton last winter when Major Mint Douglas and his men were captured by the Federals,—said she saw the whole of it. She then came to Murfreesborough, and stopped at the house of Mrs. Davis.

"On the same night Mrs. Story, of Shelbyville, came and stayed at the said Mrs. Davis's. Said she slept with a lady at Mrs. Davis's, but did not tell me her name. Her object in coming to Murfreesborough was to get all the information of the movement of the Federal troops and of their strength,—in fact, she said, all that would be of any value to the Confederate forces. Said she had for the last twenty months out-generalled the Yankees, but they had at last beat her, and she was resigned to her fate, be it what it might. Said she had done nothing she was sorry for, and would do the same again if she could get the chance; said it was not the amount of money she was to receive for her labor, but it was done for the good of the rebel cause. Said her sister knew nothing of her secrets. She did most of her travelling by night. Said she had furnished rebel generals with important information, and a large amount of it.

"The circumstances under which I obtained this information from Mrs. Hyde were as follows:—I was in charge of Mrs. Hyde and Mrs. Payne at the City Hotel, to see that they were well provided for; and, after she thought that the Federals knew all she had done, she told me that it would not make her case any worse, and she gave me this history of her own accord. I did not seek it: she told me of her own free will. I carefully avoided asking her any questions, but treated her with due deference and kindness."

It appears from the evidence that Mrs. Molly Hyde was the travelling member of the firm of spies, while her sister, Mrs. Payne, collected the news and letters, and superintended generally the Nashville terminus of their grape-vine line of communication. We have given enough of the evidence, from the great mass before us, to properly illustrate the case, and will bid adieu to the ladies in question, one of whom was ordered to be sent North, to remain until after the war. Mrs. Hyde is now an occupant of the Alton (Illinois) military prison.

The Adventures of Two Union Spies.

THE following statement of two young members of the army police is strictly reliable, and will amply repay a perusal.

"On the 15th of April, 1863, we were sent from Nashville by Colonel Truesdail, Chief of the Police and Scout service, to gather knowledge of parties engaged in smuggling goods through the lines, and to gain all information possible as to the strength and position of the enemy's forces. Assuming the character of deserters from the Federal army, we started out, and arrived at the house of one Thomas Hooper, below Sam's Creek, twenty miles from Nashville, on the 17th instant, at evening. We remained at his house one day, and found that the suspicion that was resting on Hooper of being a rebel had no foundation: he was very poor, scarcely able to obtain food for his family. During conversation with Hooper we learned that one Rook, who was a neighbor to Hooper, had a boat which he used to convey deserters and others across the river. On drawing near to Rook's house we saw two horses, apparently belonging to two rebel cavalrymen, standing at the door. After a short time, Rook, with two rebel officers, came out of the house and proceeded to the boat and crossed the river. After a considerable lapse of time they returned, and, on their coming up the bank of the river, we, being in a clump of bushes, heard them say that they had succeeded in seeing and learning all they wished; that, as the Federals had cavalry all along that road, they would take the south side of the river to march on Nashville, which was Van Dorn's plan. Captain Eastham, who was one of the officers, stated that he had been to our picket-line, and he was sure they could march into Nashville and destroy all the Government stores and take the place, and in two or three weeks he would be in his native city. He further stated that the business of Lieutenant King and himself was to find the strength and distribution of the forces in and about Nashville. We heard Rook tell Lieutenant King that he (Rook) had received some articles direct from Nashville which he wanted Lieutenant King to take with him. The parties then moved up towards Rook's house. We fell back to the woods and came upon a blind road, sufficiently wide to move a large body of troops and yet be under cover from the river,— leaving a road unguarded by our pickets on which the enemy can move to a point within six miles of Nashville. Proceeding on our way up this road, we met many scouts of the enemy passing in every direction, closely watching all the by-paths. On the next morning, in endeavoring to cross the river we were captured by a squad of rebel cavalry, who mounted us on mules, and we were taken to Spring Hill, to Van Dorn's head-quarters,—they stating that we would be paroled and sent back home. From our guard on the way we learned that General Van Dorn would soon march over the road before mentioned to Nashville. On arriving at Van Dorn's head-quarters we were immediately questioned as to the strength of Federal forces and the fortifications about Nashville. We stated that we knew nothing, as our regiment was stationed near Murfreesborough. We were questioned very closely, but gave them no information. We were held at Spring Hill but two or three hours, when we were sent on to Columbia, where we were to be paroled.

"We arrived at Columbia and were there paroled, but, at the suggestion of one of the officers, were placed in prison to await the order of General Bragg. There was no force at Columbia but a small provost-guard. Provisions were very scarce, half-rations only being issued. Rations consisted of corn-meal and bacon. There were no fortifications of account,—some small breastworks and rifle-pits. On the 23d, General Forrest with his command passed through Columbia, taking most of the stores in the commissary department: their destination, we learned, was the Tennessee River. The men were all well mounted. In conversation with imprisoned conscripts we gleaned that the farmers were all discouraged about the coming crop; that unless the war was soon closed they would starve, for the draft on them for food was so heavy and frequent that they had barely enough to live upon. The coming crop will be very small. The prison was filled with deserters and conscripts. The prisoners stated that they were tired and discouraged, and they would all leave if it were not for the tyranny exercised over them. We had a conversation with one Wiley George, who was a leader in the burning of the bridge over Duck River; Wm. Sander assisted in the work. The talk of the prisoners was in favor of the Union,—many stating that they had been deceived. We met one Killdare, who stated that he had brought out of Nashville seven hundred dollars' worth of goods. He said his three girls would come to the city 'and carry them to him, and he would bring them to the rebel lines. We were taken from prison and marched to Shelbyville, where we arrived the 5th of May. We saw their batteries within six miles of Shelbyville,—one brigade of infantry and one of cavalry lying on the pike. The fortifications extended one and a half miles in length. There is stationed there one brigade of infantry. General Cheatham commands the post. The prisons there are full of deserters and conscripts, who are dissatisfied and who were poorly fed and clothed. Many stated that they did not wish to fight longer,—that they were compelled to do so, as Bragg was having all deserters shot. We had a little corn-meal and a little bacon for our rations. The whole country, citizens and soldiers, are on half-allowance. Flour was selling at eighty dollars per barrel, corn five dollars per bushel, bacon one dollar and a half per pound. Little of the country we passed through was cultivated. The wheat-fields are badly affected with the rust. We were then sent on to Tullahoma by railroad, where Generals Bragg and Johnston had their head-quarters, but learned that they would soon move to Shelbyville. All goods are enormously high; food very scarce. Morgan's and McCown's forces were reported to hold themselves in readiness to go into Kentucky. We were charged at Tullahoma with being spies; but, there being no testimony, we were sent to Chattanooga, where we lay in prison three days. There are but few troops there,—perhaps two thousand. The crops are very poor and scant, and all along the route we were questioned concerning the police of Nashville, and many swore that they would hang every one they captured without a trial; and as for 'old Truesdail,' they wished to have him once in their power, and they would teach him what it was to arrest women and children. Some Texas Rangers said that they were watching a chance to shoot Generals Rosecrans and Rousseau, and when that was done they could manage the rest.

"When we arrived at Chattanooga we were put in the guard-house: the prison was filled with conscripts. With few exceptions, they were in favor of deserting and coming over to the Federal army. Many said that they never fired a gun against the Federal army, and never would. The Tennesseeans are tired of the war, and if allowed to go home would go.

"We were then ordered to Knoxville, leaving Chattanooga on the 25th and arriving at Knoxville the 26th. The line of the railroad is guarded; stockades are being erected, and, where the railroad crosses the Tennessee River, fortifications are being made. Here there are three regiments of infantry and one battery of eight guns stationed. The jail at Knoxville is filled to overflowing, prisoners being mostly Union men and Federal officers,— the only charges against them being disloyalty to the Southern Confederacy. All the way from Knoxville to Richmond, to which place we were carried for exchange, provisions are very scarce. Provisions about Knoxville are not plenty; all parties complain of the scarcity. The pedlars along the line of railroad would call out, ' Three dollars Confederate for one greenback. We fell in with three men on the cars: they said they were Eastern men, and shoemakers by occupation; they said there were many Union men in the city who have the ' Stars and Stripes,' and who were only waiting for an opportunity to hoist it as soon as the army made its appearance. They said that it would be almost impossible to take Richmond, the fortifications being immense, and forts at every available point. At Knoxville we passed one company of Indians, whose business was to hunt up Union men in the mountains. At Richmond three Merrimacs were building, and one was ready for service: the others would not be completed for several months. Two were on the stocks, and looked like rough customers. The city was in a great fever of excitement consequent upon the raid of General Stoneman; and if General Stoneman had only gone ahead he could have taken Richmond. At Richmond our prisoners were placed in rooms, so many in one room that it was difficult for them to move, and were fed on half-rations, and when we were marching through the streets were not allowed the privilege of buying any thing to eat. Pedlars were denied the right of coming into prisons to sell their goods. We learned nothing as to the fortifications about Richmond in particular. We heard it said that there was considerable smuggling going on between Maryland and Virginia. At Tullahoma we found Ricketts, a scout sent out from this office, in chains, sentenced to be shot as a spy; another, by name Kelley, was shot there some days since as a spy."

The Misses Elliott.

ONLY excepting Charleston, perhaps no more determined, fanatical lady rebels can be found than in the city of Nashville. The following is a case where two stylish young ladies of that city were dealt with.

"OFFICE CHIEF OF ARMY POLICE, NASHVILLE, May 2, 1863.

"GENERAL:—

"I herewith submit you the papers in the case of Misses Susie and Mary Elliott, daughters of Dr. Elliott, a chaplain in the so-called Confederate army. These young ladies reside with their mother in this city. Their father and two brothers are in the rebel army. They returned to this city on Thursday afternoon, contrary to orders (see pass), and were arrested. After having their baggage examined (finding amongst it a large number of letters to parties residing in this city and elsewhere), they were placed under guard. Both and each of them stated that their sympathies were with those in rebellion. They are extreme Southern sympathizers. They contemplated returning South. When asked whether they visited the rebel camps, they declined answering; and to all questions relative to the Confederate army they refused giving answers. Miss Susie Elliott had a Federal officer's belt in her possession, which she stated was worn by a rebel officer at the battle of Stone River last December. They are young women of education, and, judging from their abilities, if allowed to remain in this city are capable of doing injury to the cause for which we are so earnestly striving. I would especially call your attention to the conditions of the pass on which they left this city; further, to the letter of their father (C. D. Elliott), in which he states that his family 'will take no oath and give no parole.' The sympathies of the whole family are extremely Southern.

"I am, general, your obedient servant,

"WILLIAM TRUESDAIL,

"*Chief of Army Police.*"

The following is a copy of the pass in question:—

"HEAD-QUARTERS, NASHVILLE, March 24, 1863.

"The guards and pickets will pass Miss Mary and Susan Elliott through our lines on the Hardin pike, with carriage, driver, and private baggage, not to return without permission from these head-quarters.

"Good for three days.

"ROBERT B. MITCHELL,

"*Brigadier-General commanding Post.*"

One of the Misses Elliott made the following statement, in which the other concurred upon being requested to do so, at the army police office at Nashville:—

37

"I am a resident of Nashville. On or about the 23d of March, I, with my sister Mary, obtained, through the influence of our uncle, Lieutenant-Colonel G. F. Elliott, late of the 69th Regiment Ohio Volunteers, a pass to go out on the Hardin pike. The said pass was marked 'good for three days,' by special request made by my sister. We went out on the Hardin pike on the 26th of March, and proceeded to Shelbyville to see my father and brother and to obtain some money. These facts we stated to General Mitchell before obtaining our pass. We arrived at Shelbyville on Wednesday evening, April 2, and went to the residence of Mr. John Cowan, where my father was stopping. We remained at Shelbyville quite a number of days, and then proceeded, in company with my father, to Fayetteville to visit a brother (ten years of age), then lying sick. We stopped at Fayetteville some days, returned to Shelbyville, remained there a few days, and then proceeded to return to Nashville, where we arrived this afternoon. Whether I went through the camps of the so-called Confederate army or not I do not feel inclined to state. Neither is it agreeable for me ·to state any thing about the rebel army in any particular. I decline to make any statement as to any of the generals. I obtained the belt that was taken from me by Colonel Truesdail from a cousin of mine, at Shelbyville. His name is Bright Morgan. It was worn at the battle of Murfreesborough by a young man by the name of John Morgan.

"Susie R. Elliott.

"I subscribe to this statement.　　　　　　"Mary Elliott."

Among the papers of the Misses Elliott were found the passes they had used in Dixie. Let us preserve them in the "Annals."

"Days ———.
"No. ———.
　　　"Provost-Marshal's Office, Shelbyville, Tenn., April 6, 1863.
"Pass Dr. Elliott and two daughters to Fayetteville, Tennessee, upon honor not to communicate any thing that may prove detrimental to the Confederate States.

"(Signed)　Wm. B. Dallas, for J. M. Hawkins,
"Major and Provost-Marshal."

"Shelbyville, April 26, 1863.

"Confederate States of America.—Guards and pickets will pass Miss Susie Elliott to Nashville and return. Baggage not to be searched.

"C. A. Thompson,
" Colonel Confederate Army."

As usual, the letters found with these young ladies were mainly of a domestic, melancholy character. We subjoin the following extract from a letter—writer unknown to us—to Mark Cockrill, Esq., of Nashville :—

"We are all doing well,—doing extremely well, considering that we are confined to the limits of the army, and are dieted—from necessity—to oven beans and corn bread,—all of which we get in greatest plenty. The rumor which you all have afloat about the rations of our army being short is not true. As yet we have plenty; and there seems to be very *good* prospect of the continuation of that abundance. The South is full of corn, and the wheat-crop in the portion of Tennessee which we hold is very fine. . . . Provisions. South are all purchased by the army, and 'tis very difficult for families to procure the necessaries of life; and I would advise you all not to come unless you are unsufferably oppressed."

The subjoined letter is also readable. Our readers in Nashville will know to whom it is addressed:—

"SHELBYVILLE, April 26, 1863.
"DEAR NIECE:—

"Tell Dewess that I am happy and proud to know that he is still faithful to the cause of the South, and that it is my sincerest prayer and firmest belief that he will remain so. Tell him that his old friends in the army understand his position, appreciate his feelings, and sympathize with him; and tell him, above all, that if necessary he must sacrifice his own happiness to that of his mother, and in the end all will be well. Now comes the secret and equally foolish part. Tell Mary—I can't say Miss Mary— that I still love, but without hope; and I can only hope that she will think of me as a friend and as the friend of her brother. Do you think she would correspond with me?—as a friend, I mean. Write to me about all these things as soon as you can. I enclose a very brief note for Miss Bessie Thompson. Be certain to let no one see it, and give it to her the first opportunity you have. Tell grandma that I would write now, but that you can tell her every thing, and that it is unsafe for you to carry letters, and that I will write the first chance I have. The rebels will be in Nashville this summer; but you must not wait for them, but come out as soon as you can. Give my best love to grandma, Aunt Lizzie, Julia, Lizzie, Uncle Frank, and all my friends in Nashville. Remember me to Ellen, Ann, and all the servants, *if they are there.* But I must close. My very best love to Mary and yourself. PORTER."

Attached to this epistle is the following order for "something to wear," &c., for which the valiant "Porter," it seems, has to look to the miserable Yankee mudsills:—

ORDER FOR BILL OF GOODS FOR SUMMER.

"Socks, drawers, and other summer clothes, with my black suit, soft hat, shoes, and two pair kid gloves, pants suitable for summer; a suit of summer clothes: let the clothes be a dark gray; two tooth-brushes, and three fine combs."

List of prices of different articles in the South, contained in one of the letters found with the Misses Elliott.

Ginger-cakes, 50 cents to $1.

Candy, $10 per pound, 25 cents per stick.

Tobacco, $3 to $4 per pound.

    "   smoking, $3.50 to $4 per pound.

Whiskey, $40 to $50 per gallon,—all taken at that.

Sardines, $4 to $5 per box, 50 cents each retail.

Wine, $8 to $10 per bottle,—$100 to get tight.

Cigars, 12½ cents, 15 cents, and 25 cents each. Sticking-plaster, to draw on back of neck, thrown in.

Pocket-knives, $12, $15, and $20 each,—prices sharp as razors.

Oysters, $1 per dozen, $6 per can,—three years old.

Breakfast at restaurant, $16; wine extra.

Eggs, $1.50, $2, and $3 per dozen; chickens thrown in.

Butter, $2 and $3 per pound. "Whistle and it comes to you."

Pan-cakes, 50 cents each. "One lasts all day."

The Misses Elliott were sent South speedily, to revel in the full enjoyment of all their "rights," where it is to be hoped they will ere long become wiser and better women.

Killdare, the Scout.

ONE of the most active and efficient men in the secret service is Killdare, the scout. For prudential reasons, we withhold his real name. The circumstances attending his first introduction to the Chief of Police and leading to his subsequent employment by that official have already been related in a preceding sketch,—"A Nest of Nashville Smugglers,"—and need not be repeated here. Whatever it is necessary to know of his personal history, too, is there told; and all that the author proposes in this notice is to give, as nearly in his own words as possible, the report of two trips which he made into the rebel lines. In themselves interesting narratives, affording an inside view of rebeldom, they become still more so as a descriptive revelation of some of the devices and subterfuges necessarily resorted to by this class of men in the prosecution of their dangerous and most important enterprises.

In March last, Killdare left Nashville on horseback with a small stock of goods, of less than a hundred dollars in value, with the purpose of making his way into and through a certain portion of the Confederacy. Swimming his horse across Harpeth Creek, and himself crossing in a canoe, he journeyed on, and passed the night at a house some six miles beyond Columbia, having previously fallen in with some of Forrest's men going to Columbia. The next morning he started for Shelbyville, where he arrived in due season. What there, and in the subsequent portions of his trip, occurred, we will let him tell in his own words.

"When I arrived, I could find stabling, but no feed, for my horse. I put the animal in the kitchen of a house, and gave a boy five dollars to get me a half-bushel of corn, there being none in the town. I sold the little stock of goods to the firm of James Carr & Co., of Nashville, who gave me eight hundred dollars for the lot, and then went to visit General Frank Cheatham, General Maney, and General Bates, whom I saw at the house where I stopped. At the head-quarters of General Cheatham, Colonel A—— arrived from the front, and stated in my presence that the whole Federal line had fallen back; and I further understood from the generals present and Colonel A—— that there would be no fight at Shelbyville. They said that probably there would be some skirmishing by the Federals, but that the battle would be fought at Tullahoma, and they had not more than one corps at Shelbyville, which is under General Polk.

"Forage and provisions for man and beast it is utterly impossible to obtain in the vicinity of Shelbyville. The forage-trains go as far as Lewisport, in Giles county, and the forage is then shipped to Tullahoma, and even farther back, for safe keeping,—as far as Bridgeport. Confederate money is two for one of Georgia; Tennessee, two and one-half for one.

"I next went to Tullahoma; and there I met on the cars a major on Bragg's staff, and scraped an acquaintance through the introduction of a Nashville gentleman. When we arrived within a few miles of Tullahoma, he made a short statement to me, called me to the platform, and pointed out the rifle-pits and breastworks, which extended on each side of the railroad about a mile, in not quite a right angle. The whole force of Bragg's army is composed of fifty-five thousand men, well disciplined: twenty thousand of them are cavalry. When I left Tullahoma, I could not buy meat nor bread. When I arrived at Chattanooga, I gave a nigger one dollar for a drink of whiskey, one dollar for a small cake, and fifty cents for two eggs, which I took for subsistence and started for Atlanta. I met, going thitherward, a good many acquaintances on the trains. When I arrived at Atlanta, I found a perfect panic in money-matters. Georgia money was at seventy-five cents premium, and going up; gold, four and five dollars for one. I remained at Atlanta three days. Full one-half of those I met were from Nashville: they were glad to see me.

"I commenced my return to Tullahoma with a captain from Nashville, who also showed me the rifle-pits, as I before stated. I made my way on to Shelbyville, and then I got a pass from the provost-marshal—a Major Hawkins—to Columbia, where I arrived on Sunday morning. There I found Forrest and his command had crossed Duck River on their way to Franklin. As I started from the Nelson Hotel to the provost-marshal's office, I was arrested on the square as a straggling soldier; but I proved myself the contrary, and started without a pass to Williamsport. There some fool asked me if I had a pass. I told him 'yes,' and showed him the pass l had from Shelbyville to Columbia and the documents I had in my possession, which he could not read. I gave the ferryman a five-dollar piece to take me across the river, and he vouched for my pass,—when I safely arrived at the Federal pickets."

About a month after this, Killdare made another, and his last, trip, the full report of which is subjoined. It will be seen that he was watched and several times arrested. Though he finally escaped, his usefulness as a spy was totally destroyed, his name, appearance, and business having been betrayed to the enemy. He has consequently retired from the business. On his return he made the following report:—

"1 left the city of Nashville on Tuesday, the 14th instant, to go South, taking with me a few goods to peddle. I passed down the Charlotte pike, and travelled two miles up the Richland Creek, then crossed over to the Hardin pike, following that road to Harpeth Creek, and crossed below De Morse's mill. At the mill I met —— De Morse, who said to me, 'Killdare, do you make another trip?' I replied, 'I do not know.' De Morse then said, 'If you get below the meeting-house you are saved,' and smiled. I proceeded on my way until I came to a blacksmith-shop on the pike, at which a gentleman by the name of Marlin came out and asked if I had heard any thing of Sanford being killed on the evening of the 13th instant. I told Marlin I did not know any thing about it, and proceeded on to South Harper to Squire Allison's, which is seventeen miles from Nashville. I then fed my mules, stopped about one hour, and proceeded across South Harper towards Williamsport.

"About one mile the other side of South Harper, two rebel scouts came galloping up, and asked me what I had for sale. I told them needles, pins, and playing-cards. They then inquired, 'Have you any papers to go South?' I replied I had, and showed them some recommendations. They asked me to get down from my carryall, as they wanted to talk with me. This I did; and they then asked,—

"'Have you any pistols?'

"'No,' I replied.

"Stepping back a few paces, and each drawing a pistol, one of them said, 'You —— scoundrel, you are our prisoner: you are a Yankee spy, and you carry letters from the South, and at the dead hour of night you carry these letters to Truesdail's office. We lost a very valuable man on Monday while attempting to arrest you at your house: his name was Sanford, and he was a great deal thought of by General Van Dorn. So now we've got you, —— you, turn your wagon round and go back.'

"We turned and went to Squire Allison's again, at which place I met Dr. Morton, from Nashville, whom I requested to assist in getting me released. Dr. Morton spoke to the men, who, in reply, said, 'We have orders to arrest him as a spy, for carrying letters to Truesdail's head-quarters.' They then turned back to South Harper Creek, and took me up the creek about one mile, where we met about eight more of these scouts and Colonel McNairy, of Nashville, who was riding along in a buggy. The lieutenant in command of the squad wrote a despatch to Van Dorn, and gave it to one of the men, by the name of Thompson, who had me in custody, and we then proceeded up the creek to Spring Hill, towards the head-quarters of General

Van Dorn. About six miles up the creek, Thompson learned I had some whiskey, which I gave him, and of which he drank until he got pretty well intoxicated. In the neighborhood of Ivy we stopped until about six o'clock in the evening. About one mile from Ivy the wheel of my carryall broke. A neighbor came to us with an axe and put a pole under the axletree, and we proceeded on our way. We had gone but a few hundred yards when the wagon turned over: we righted it, and Thompson took a carpet-sack full of goods, filled his pockets, and then told me ' to go to ———: he would not take me to head-quarters.' Changing his mind, however, he said he *would*, as he had orders so to do, and showed me the despatch written by Lieutenant Johnson to General Van Dorn. It read as follows:—

"'I have succeeded in capturing Mr. Killdare. Archy Cheatham, of Nashville, says Killdare is not loyal to the Confederacy. The Federals have mounted five hundred light infantry. Sanford's being killed is confirmed. (Signed) LIEUT. JOHNSON.'

"Thompson, being very drunk, left me, taking the goods he stole. Two citizens came up shortly and told me to turn round, and stop all night at Isaac Ivy's, 1st District, Williamson county. There we took the remainder of the goods into the house. At three o'clock in the morning a negro woman came and knocked at the door.

"Mr. Ivy says, 'What do you want?'

"'A soldier is down at the creek, and wants to know where his prisoner is,' was the reply.

"'What has he done with the goods he took from that man?'

"'He has left them at our house, and has just started up the creek as I came up.'

"'That will do. Go on.'

"I was awake, and tried to make my escape, asking Mr. Ivy if he had a couple of saddles to loan me. He said he had; and I borrowed from him seven dollars, as Thompson took all my money (fifty dollars in Georgia currency). He (Ivy) then told me the route I should take,—going a few miles towards Franklin, and then turn towards my home in Nashville. Taking Ivy's advice, we proceeded on our way towards Franklin. About eight miles from Franklin, four guerrillas came up to me and fired two pistols. 'Halt!' said they: 'you want to make your way to the Yankees. We have a notion to kill you, any way.'

"They then ordered me to turn, which I did,—two going behind, whipping the mules, and hooting and hallooing at a great rate. We then turned back to Ivy's. When we got there, I said,—

"'Where is Thompson, my guard, who told me to go on?'

"'He was here early this morning, and has gone up the hill hunting you, after borrowing my shot-gun,' was the answer.

"Some conversation ensued between the parties, when Ivy wrote a note to General Van Dorn and gave it to Thompson. Ivy then gave us our equipage, and we went towards Spring Hill. On the way we met, on Carter's Creek pike, a camp of four hundred Texan Rangers. We arrived at Spring Hill at sundown of the day following. At Van Dorn's head-quarters I asked for an interview with the general, which was not allowed, but was ordered to Columbia to prison until further orders.

"On Friday evening a Nashville soldier who stood sentinel let me out, and said, 'You have no business here.' I made my way towards Shelbyville, crossed over Duck Creek; made my way to the Louisburg and Franklin pike, and started towards Franklin. Before we got to the pickets we took to the woods, and thus got round the pickets. A farmer reported having seen me to the guard, and I was taken again towards Van Dorn's head-quarters, six miles distant. I had gone about one mile, when I fell in with Colonel Lewis's command, and was turned over to an orderly-sergeant with whom I was acquainted and by whom I was taken to the headquarters of Colonel Lewis. There I was discharged from arrest, and was told by the colonel what route I should take in order to avoid the scouts. I then started towards Columbia, and thence towards Hillsborough. At Hillsborough I met a friend by the name of Parkham, who guided me within five miles of Franklin, where I arrived at daylight this morning. On Friday last Colonel Forrest passed through Columbia with his force (three thousand strong), and six pieces of artillery, to Decatur, Alabama. One regiment went to Florence. The whole force under Van Dorn at Spring Hill does not exceed four thousand; and they are poorly clothed. I understood that the force was moving towards Tennessee River, in order to intercept forces that were being sent out by General Grant.

"SAM. KILLDARE."

This Archy Cheatham, who it appears had informed upon Killdare, was a Government contractor, and professed to be loyal. The manner in which he obtained his information was in this wise.

One day a genteel, well-dressed young man came to the police office and inquired for Judge Brien, an employé of the office. The two, it seems, were old acquaintances, and for some time maintained a friendly conversation in the presence of Colonel Truesdail. The visitor, whose name was Stewart, having taken his leave, Brien remarked to the colonel,—

"There is a young man who can do us a great deal of good."

"Do you know him?" said the colonel.

"Very well. He talks right."

The result was that Stewart and Colonel Truesdail soon afterwards had a private conversation in reference to the matter. Stewart stated that he lived about two miles from the city upon his plantation, that he was intimate with many prominent secessionists, was regarded as a good Southern man, and could go anywhere within the lines of the Confederacy. The colonel replied that he was in want of just such a man, and that he could be the means of accomplishing great good. It was an office, however, of vast responsibility, and, if he should be employed, he would be required to take a very stringent and solemn oath, which was read to him. To all this Stewart assented, and took the oath, only stipulating that he should never be mentioned as having any connection with the police office. He was consequently employed, and told to go to work at once.

For a time all seemed well enough. One or two minor cases of smuggling were developed by him. He subsequently reported that he had become acquainted with the cashier of the Planters' Bank and a Mrs. Bradford, who lived five miles from the city and made herself very busy in carrying letters, in which she was aided by Cantrell, the cashier. He was also in the habit of meeting large numbers of secessionists, among whom was Archy Cheatham. He also was a member of a club or association which met every Saturday to devise ways and means for aiding the rebellion, and at which Mrs. Bradford and Cantrell were constant attendants. One day he reported that Mrs. Bradford was just going to carry out what was ostensibly a barrel of flour, but really a barrel of contraband goods covered over with flour at each end. And so it went on from week to week. Somebody was just going to do something, but never did it, or was never detected; and, despite the many fair promises of Stewart, the results of his labors were not deemed satisfactory.

On the night that Killdare came in from his last trip, Stewart was at the office. Something was evidently wrong, and Stewart soon left. To some natural inquiries of the colonel, Killdare answered, excitedly,—

" Somebody has nearly ruined me, colonel !"

" How is that, and who can it be ?"

" Well, I am sure that it is a man by the name of Stewart and Archy Cheatham who have done the mischief. Cheatham has been out in the country some fourteen miles, and there he met Lieutenant Johnson, whom he told that I was disloyal to the Confederacy and one of your spies. The result was that I was arrested, and came near—altogether too near hanging for comfort. Johnson telegraphed to Van Dorn that he had caught me; but I got away, and, to make a long story short, have been arrested and have escaped three times."

This opened the colonel's eyes somewhat, and inquiries were at once set on foot, which disclosed the fact that Stewart was a rebel of the deepest dye and had been " playing off" all the time. It was found that he had not only informed Cheatham of Killdare's business and position, but had himself been out in the country some fourteen miles, and had told the neighbors that Killdare had gone South in Truesdail's employ. He told the same thing to two guerrillas whom he met, and even taunted Killdare's children by saying that he knew where their father had gone. The colonel, for once, had been thoroughly deceived by appearances; but it was the first and last time. After a month or six weeks' search, Stewart was found and committed to the penitentiary; and before he leaves that institution it is by no means improbable that he will have ample time and opportunity to conclude that his operations, though sharp and skilful, were not of the most profitable character.

Death of a Rebel General and Villain.

THE name of the rebel General Earl Van Dorn will figure largely in the history of the rebellion in the Southwest. A bold, bad, brave man, his sudden and tragic death is a fit ending of his earthly career. A betrayer of his country, of his own home and fireside, and of the honor and peace of another once loved and happy family, the penalty he paid for his crimes was merited, if not lawful. The several newspaper versions of the affair heretofore published are grossly incorrect; and to the records of the police of the Army of the Cumberland we can appeal with confidence in the truthfulness of their revelations.

Upon the escape of Dr. George B. Peters and his arrival within the lines of the Federal army, Colonel Truesdail, then at Murfreesborough, learning of his arrival, ordered him to be held, that he might be examined as to the facts touching his killing of Earl Van Dorn, and also as to his political sentiments, whereupon he was arrested and held until Colonel Truesdail's return, and the following narrative of facts obtained, as well as conclusive evidence that he was and had been a loyal citizen to the United States Government.

"OFFICE OF ARMY POLICE, NASHVILLE, May 23, 1863.

"VOLUNTARY STATEMENT OF DR. GEORGE B. PETERS.

" I was born in the State of North Carolina, and raised in Murray county, Tennessee, where I now reside. I have practised medicine twenty-three years in Bolivar, Hardeman county, Tennessee. I was State Senator from the Twenty-First Senatorial District of Tennessee in the years 1859–60–61. For some years past I have been planting in Philips county, Arkansas, where I have been constantly during the last twelve months. After the Federal troops reached Helena, Arkansas, and had possession of the Mississippi River to that point, I went to Memphis and took the oath of allegiance to the United States Government. This was in the summer of 1862. After that time I dealt in cotton and carried supplies to my neighbors by consent of the military authorities there commanding, and never went beyond the Federal lines until recently. I have in my possession safeguards from Rear-Admiral Porter, commanding gunboat flotilla, and Major-General U. S. Grant, commanding Department of Mississippi, for the protection of my property. About the 4th day of April, 1863, I came to Memphis and obtained a pass to go to Bolivar, Tennessee, at which place I received a pass from General Brannan, commanding post, to pass out of the Federal lines, my intention being to go to Spring Hill, Murray county, where my wife and family were staying. I arrived at my home on the 12th of April, and was alarmed at the distressing rumors which prevailed in the neighborhood in relation to the attentions paid by General Van Dorn to my wife. I was soon convinced of his intentional guilt,—although a doubt still lingered on my mind as to the guilt of my wife. After witnessing many incidents too numerous and unpleasant to relate, and which confirmed the guilt of General Van Dorn, on one occasion, when a servant brought a note to my house, I distinctly told him I would blow his brains out if he ever entered the premises again, and to tell his whiskey-headed master, General Van Dorn, that I would blow his brains out, or any of his staff that stepped their foot inside of the lawn, and I wanted them to distinctly understand it. My wife did not hear this order.

"Notwithstanding all this, I came to Nashville on the 22d of April, and was exceedingly mortified on my return home to hear that Van Dorn had visited my house every night by himself during my absence, my wife having no company but her little children. I then determined to catch the villain at his tricks: so I feigned a trip to Shelbyville, but really did not leave the premises. The second night after my supposed and pretended absence, I came upon the creature, about half-past two o'clock at night, where I expected to find him. He readily acknowledged my right to kill him, and I fully intended to do so,—gave him a few moments to make certain declarations,—in which he intended to exonerate my wife from dishonor and to inculpate himself completely,—and, upon his agreeing to make certain acknowledgments over his own signature, I agreed to give his life to his wife and children. He readily, upon the honor of a soldier, accepted the proposition, but stated that he cared but little for his wife. I then ordered him off, and we parted about three o'clock. Next day, being sick in bed, I was unable to call upon him as agreed upon between us; but the second morning, after having recruited my health sufficiently, I called upon him and notified him that I was ready to receive that written acknowledgment,—when he attempted to evade it by springing a discussion as to its propriety. I unhesitatingly told him I would give him one half-hour, and further told him that he knew what the consequence would be in case of a refusal to comply. I then went up through the village to communicate to a friend these facts, inasmuch as no one else was privy to them. At the expiration of the time, I returned to Van Dorn's head-quarters, and found him engaged in writing. He stopped and read to me what he had written. The first proposition was written out in accordance with the previous interview; the second was a misrepresentation and lie; the remaining two he utterly refused to comply with. I then denounced him for his bad faith; and he in reply said it would injure the cause, the service, and his reputation for that thing to be made public. I answered, 'You did not think so thirty hours ago, when your life was in my hands: you were then ready to promise any thing. Now you think I am in your power, and you will do nothing; but, sir, if you don't comply with my demands I will instantly blow your brains out.' He replied, scowlingly, 'You d—d cowardly dog, take that door, or I will kick you out of it.' I immediately drew my pistol, aiming to shoot him in the forehead, when, by a convulsive movement of his head, he received the shot in the left side of his head just above the ear, killing him instantly. I picked up the scroll he had written, for evidence. I then went to Shelbyville to surrender myself to General Polk. believing they would not arrest me. Finding out, however, that they intended arresting and incarcerating me, I came around by McMinnville, thence by Gallatin to Nashville, within the Federal lines. I shot him about eight o'clock in the morning. Van Dorn was seated at his desk. When I arrived at Spring Hill first, Van Dorn immediately had me paroled. When I reached Nashville, having left my certificate of having taken the oath of allegiance at Memphis, I renewed the oath and gave security.

"GEORGE B. PETERS."

Prison-Experience of a Union Spy.

As an illustration of the cruelty of the Southern rebels, the following narrative of James Pike, a member of Company A, 4th Ohio Cavalry, is given in his own words. Upon leaving Macon, Georgia, he came to Richmond, and after considerable delay he was exchanged and went to Ohio, where he was ordered to report to Governor Tod, who sent him to his command at Murfreesborough. Much of Pike's statement has been fully corroborated by other testimony. The spirit which could prompt such treatment towards helpless prisoners needs no comment. It exhibits a phase of Southern character which should call to the cheek of every friend of humanity a flush of indignation, and inspire within his breast a determination to visit upon the heads of these violators of the laws of humanity and civilization well-merited retribution.

" MURFREESBOROUGH, March 22, 1863.

" On the 24th of April, 1862, I was taken prisoner near the town of Bridgeport, Tennessee, by a battalion of rebel cavalry under command of a Colonel Starns. I was alone on a scout at the time, and fell in with nine of the enemy's pickets. I got the first shot, and killed the sergeant (so I was told by Captain Poe, who had command of the pickets). I was pursued by five companies of cavalry. After running several miles, I was obliged to stop and dismount at a house to get something to eat, and while there was surrounded by one of the pursuing companies and captured. I was then tied on a horse and carried over a mountain to where the battalion was camped, arriving there about nine o'clock P.M. When we got there, I was immediately surrounded by about two hundred men, some crying, 'Hang him!' 'Shoot him!' 'Shoot the d——d Yankee!' and several levelled their guns on me, some of them being cocked. A Captain Haines told them that I was his prisoner and under his protection, and he detailed twenty-four men to guard me, placing two men at each corner of my blanket. When we went to bed, the captain lay down on one side of me and his first lieutenant on the other; and in this way I was preserved from assassination.

" The next day I was taken to Bridgeport. I fared very well at that place; but the day following I was taken to Chattanooga and confined in the jail, a two-story building. The upper story, where I was confined, was about twelve feet square. Here were confined nineteen Tennesseeans, a negro, and myself. In the dungeon, which was only ten feet square, were confined twenty-one men belonging to the 2d, the 31st, and 33d Ohio Infantry, who were charged with being *spies*. They were under command of a Captain Andrews, who was then under sentence of death by a court-martial recently held at Chattanooga. They were waiting for the Secretary of War at Richmond to ratify the proceedings of the court-martial previous to executing the captain, and they said if they were ratified that the rest would certainly be hung. I was afterwards informed by the rebels that Andrews and eight of the men were hung at Atlanta, Georgia. I was told subsequently by rebel citizens that they hung Andrews and seventeen men. I once went into the dungeon where these men were, and found them handcuffed, and chained in pairs by the neck with a heavy chain, which was locked around each man's neck with a padlock that would weigh two pounds. These padlocks were larger than a man's hand. We were fed twice a day on tolerably good bread, spoiled beef, and coffee made of cane-seed. There was no sink in the jail; and our offal stood in a bucket in the room where we were confined, day and night, and was only emptied twice a day, and of course the stench was intolerable. We were denied the privilege of washing our clothes, or having it done. The jail was literally swarming with vermin, nor was it ever cleaned out.

"From Chattanooga I was taken to Knoxville to another jail, and confined in an iron cage. Here I was told by a man named Fox, the jailer, that I was brought to Knoxville to be tried by a court-martial as a spy, and that if I was tried I would no doubt be hung. This court-martial adjourned without bringing me to a trial, as did the one at Chattanooga. From there I was sent to Mobile, where another court-martial was in session. After keeping me about eight days at this place, I was next sent to Tuscaloosa, Alabama. From this city I was taken, in company with all the prisoners at that post, to Montgomery, Alabama. The first day out I was taken ill with pneumonia and typhoid fever; but the rebel surgeons refused me any medicines, and even a bed, and I was left for twelve days lying on the deck of the boat, with nothing to eat but corn-bread and beef, which latter, the rebels said, had been packed five years. At Tuscaloosa they shot a Federal soldier for looking out of a window, and wounded another in the face for the same offence. At Montgomery they refused to let me go to a hospital, although in an utterly helpless condition. Here they shot a Federal lieutenant under the following circumstances: he had been allowed to go out for milk, accompanied by a guard, and he was waiting for a woman to hand the milk out through a window, when the guard gave the order to 'come on.' 'Wait a moment till I get my milk,' said the lieutenant. The guard made no reply, but instantly shot him in the breast with a shot-gun, killing him forthwith.

"From Montgomery I was taken to Macon, Georgia, in company with twelve hundred others. Here we were allowed seven pounds of corn-meal and two and a half pounds of bacon of bad quality for seven days. We were allowed two surgeons and but very little medicine. Our men fared badly here, being punished severely for the most trifling offences. One man, named Cora, was kept tied up three days by the wrists to a tree, so that his toes just touched the ground, because he helped kill a yearling calf that got into the camp. A Floridian and two Kentuckians, political prisoners, were confined in the jail of Macon on quarter-rations for twenty-two days. The only offence they had committed was to attempt to escape from the prison-lot. Our men were pegged down on the ground for any misdemeanor. This was done by stretching out the limbs and driving a forked stick down over them, and the operation was completed by driving one down over the neck. It would be impossible to tell all of the hardships to which we were subjected; but I have endeavored to portray a few of them. They may be summed up thus :—

"We were confined in bad quarters, and many were without any quarters. Our dead were left unburied for days together, and some entirely so,—at least to our knowledge. We were denied medical attendance. Our chaplains were forbid preaching to us or praying for us (*by order of Major Rylander*). Our men and officers were shot without cause. An insane Federal was shot at Macon, Georgia, for no offence. We were compelled to bury our dead in the river-banks where their bodies were liable to be washed out. We were beaten with clubs while on board the steamer *en route* for Montgomery, Alabama. We were fed on foul and unwholesome diet, and frequently left without any rations for two or three days at a time. Our exchange was delayed as long as possible, and we were confined in camps surrounded by swamps, as the rebels said, that we all might die. I find it impossible to enumerate all the hardships put upon us, but have enumerated such as were the most intolerable.

"JAMES PIKE,

" *Co. A, 4th O. V. C.*"

Having thus been imprisoned in several of the Southern States, our spy was finally exchanged in Virginia, and returned to our army in March last, after eleven months of absence, and mostly of captivity.

A Nameless Spy.

WE have a difficult task to perform in this chapter,—to describe the operations of one of the most daring and valuable spies of the Army of the Cumberland, and yet to so protect him as regards identity that he may not incur the risk of future injury, and perhaps of assassination, at the hands of rebels or their sympathizers in the South. We are about to speak of a spy who went into and came out from Bragg's army at Murfreesborough three times during the week of battles at Stone River,—who even dined at the table of Bragg and of his other generals,—who brought us correct information as to the force and position of the rebel army, and of the boasts of its head-officers. This spy was the first to assure us positively that Bragg would fight at Stone River, telling us of that general's boast that "he would whip Rosecrans back to Nashville if it cost ten thousand men." For the four days' service thus rendered by our spy he was paid five thousand dollars by order of our general, and the author saw the money passed to him.

In 1862 there lived in the State of ——— a Union man, with wife and children. He was a friend of the Union, and an anti-slavery man upon principle. After the rebellion broke out, and when the "Southern heart" had become fired, this man, living in a strong pro-slavery region and surrounded by opulent slaveholders, his own family connections and those of his wife being also wealthy and bitter secessionists, very prudently held his peace, feeling his utter inability to stem the tide of the rebellion in his section. This reticence, together with his known Southern birth and relations, enabled him to pass unsuspected, and almost unobserved, at a time when Breckinridge, Marshall, Preston, and Buckner, and other ardent politicians of Kentucky chose the rebellion as their portion and endeavored to carry with them the State amidst a blaze of excitement. Thus, without tacit admissions or any direct action upon his part, the gentleman of whom we write was classed by the people of his section as a secessionist.

Circumstances occurred during that year by which this person was brought into contact with a Federal commander in Kentucky, General Nelson. Their meeting and acquaintance was accidental. Mutual Union sentiments begat personal sympathy and friendship. Nelson wished a certain service performed in the rebel territory, and he persuaded the citizen to undertake it,—which the latter finally did as a matter of duty, we are assured, rather than of gain, for he made no charge for the service after its speedy and successful performance. Soon after, a similar work was necessary; and again was the citizen importuned, and he again consented, but not considering himself as a professional spy.

During this or a similar trip, and while at Chattanooga, our man heard of the sudden death of General Nelson. He was now at a loss what to do. Finally he determined to return and report his business to Major-General Rosecrans, who had assumed command of the Federal army. Thus resolved, he proceeded to finish his mission. After ascertaining the position of military affairs at Chattanooga, he came to Murfreesborough, where Bragg's army was then collecting. Staying here several days, he was urged by his Southern army friends to act as their spy in Kentucky. The better to conceal his own feelings and position, he consented to do so, and he left General Bragg's head-quarters to go to that State by way of Nashville, feigning important business, and from thence to go to his home, passing by and through Rosecrans's army as it lay stretched out between Nashville and Louisville.

The nameless man now makes his way to the Federal head-quarters, seeks a private interview with General Rosecrans, and states his case fully as we have just related. Here was something remarkable, surely,—a spy in the confidence of the commanders of two great opposing armies! Our general took much pains to satisfy himself of the honesty and soundness of the stranger. He was pleased with the man's candid manner, and his story bore an air of consistency and truth. Yet he was a Southerner, surrounded by rebellious influences, and enjoyed Bragg's confidence; and what guarantee could be given that he was a Union man at heart? None; and our general, in great perplexity, held council with his Chief of Police, and requested the latter to "dig up" the case to its very root. This was done; but in what manner we need not specially state. Satisfied that it would do to trust the spy, to a certain extent at least, he was now sent on his way to perform his mission for Bragg. At all events, that scheming general so supposed when our man's report was made at the rebel head-quarters a few days afterwards. His information was very acceptable to Bragg; but we strongly question its value to rebeldom, as the spy reported only what he was told by that old fox Colonel Truesdail.

Perhaps the reader will inquire, how can we answer for the report thus made to Bragg? it may have been more true and valuable than we supposed. Well, there is force in the query. We are fallen upon strange times, when honesty, virtue, and patriotism are at heavy discount in rebeldom, and the Indian's idea of the uncertainty of white men is by no means a myth. However, we were then quite confident of the worthlessness of the report of our spy to Bragg, because *he had nothing else* to tell him. For five days did our spy keep himself locked in a private room in the police building at Nashville. His meals were carried to him by a trusty servant. His door was ".shadowed" constantly by our best detectives, and so were his steps if he ventured upon the street for a few moments after dark. It was cold and bleak winter weather, and he toasted himself before his comfortable fire, read books and papers, and conferred often with the Chief of Police and his assistant, affording them, strangers as they were to that region of country, a fund of valuable information respecting the rebels of Kentucky and Tennessee. He was a man of fine address and good intellectual attainments. When our man concluded it was about time for his return to Bragg's army, he was politely escorted by our mounted police to a proper point beyond our lines, and by a route where he would see nothing of our forces. The reader will now appreciate the grounds of our confidence, we doubt not, in the worthlessness of at least one of General Braxton Bragg's spy reports.

In due time this nameless gentleman again enters our lines, and is escorted in by our pickets to the general commanding, to whom he reports in person concerning all that is transpiring in Bragg's army at Murfreesborough, and then he resumes his pleasant private quarters at the army police building.

How little could the rebel general Zollicoffer have thought, or have imagined as the wildest dream, while building his elegant house in High Street, Nashville, that its gorgeous rooms should ever be devoted to such purposes! After a brief stay, another trip was made by our man to Bragg's head-quarters, we using the same precautions as previously. In fact, our spy desired, and even demanded, such attention at the hands of the Chief of Police. Said he,—

"I am a stranger to you all. I can give you no guarantee whatever of my good faith. It is alike due to you and to myself that I be allowed no opportunities for deceiving you."

The report he carried to Bragg on his second trip delighted the latter. His officers talked with our man freely, and, after staying at Murfreesborough two or three days and riding and walking all about in the most innocent and unconcerned manner, he was again sent back to Nashville to "fool that slow Dutchman, Rosecrans," as one of the rebel officers remarked. Of the importance of the report now brought to the "slow Dutchman" we need not state further than that it contributed its due weight to a decision fraught with tremendous consequences to the army and to the country. Marching-orders were soon after issued for the advance of the Army of the Cumberland upon Murfreesborough.

Now commenced a period of excessive labor and peril for the nameless spy. Generals Rosecrans and Bragg each wanted instant and constant information as the armies approached. The minutiæ of this man's work for four or five days we need not stop to relate: it is easily imagined. Within that time he entered the rebel lines and returned three times. He gave the outline of Bragg's line of battle, a close estimate of his force, an accurate account of his artillery and his earthworks, the movements of the rebel wagon and railroad trains, &c. &c. He was very earnest in assuring Rosecrans that Bragg intended to give severe battle with superior numbers.

This information proved true in all essentials, and its value to the country was inestimable. We had other spies piercing the rebel lines at this time, but they did not enjoy the facilities possessed by the nameless one. Almost with anguish did he exclaim against himself, in the presence of the author, for the severe manner in which he was deceiving the rebel general and involving the lives of his thousands of brave but deluded followers.

After the first great battle the work of such a spy is ended, or, rather, it ceases when the shock of arms comes on. Thenceforth the armies are moved upon the instant, as circumstances may require. Our man, who during the four days had been almost incessantly in the saddle, or with his ears and eyes painfully observant while in the camps, took leave of our army upon the battle-field, and retired to a place of rest.

One incident occurred during his last visit to Bragg which is worthy of mention. That general took alarm in consequence of his report, and at once started a special messenger to General John H. Morgan—who was then absent with his cavalry in Kentucky to destroy Rosecrans's railroad-communications (in which Morgan succeeded)—to return instantly with his command by forced marches to Murfreesborough. That same night our man reported this fact to the Federal commander, described the messenger and what route he would take, &c. The information was telegraphed at once to Nashville, Gallatin, and Bowling Green, and a force was sent from each of those posts to intercept the messenger. They failed to apprehend him,—which, however, proved of no consequence, as the battles of Stone River were fought and Bragg was on his retreat from Murfreesborough by the time Morgan could have received the orders.

Our spy was a brave man: yet during the last three days of his service he was most sensible of its peril. To pass between hostile lines in the lone hours of the night,—for he did not wait for daylight,—to be halted by guerrillas and scouts and pickets, with guns aimed at him, and, finally, to meet and satisfy the anxious, keen-eyed, heart-searching rebel officers as well as our own, was a mental as well as physical demand that could not long be sustained. While proceeding upon his last expedition, the author met the nameless one upon a by-road. We halted our horses, drew near, and conversed a few seconds in private, while our attendants and companions moved on. He was greatly exhausted and soiled in appearance,—his clothing having been rained upon and splashed by muddy water, caused by hard riding, and which had dried upon him. He said he was about to try it once more, and, though he had been so often and so successfully, yet he feared detection and its sure result, the bullet or the halter. He had been unable, amid the hurry and excitement, to make some final disposition of his affairs. He gave us a last message to send to his wife and children in case it became necessary ; and he also desired a promise— most freely given—that we would attend to the settlement of his account with our general for services recently rendered. Thus concluding, he wrung our hand most earnestly, and, putting spurs to his fresh and spirited animal, dashed off upon his mission. Twenty hours afterwards we were relieved of our anxious forebodings by his safe and successful return. We have stated the price paid him for his labors: it was well earned, and to our cause was a most profitable investment.

Nashville as a Type of the Rebellion.

THE disorders which afflict a nation are most perceptible in a large city. Congregated iniquity there spawns its mass of corruption, to fatten, fester, and decay, and to reproduce itself in succeeding generations. The polluting tide floods in, increasing wave upon wave, threatening society with its utter contamination, and almost denying an expectation or hope that more of good than evil can emanate from such a Nazareth.

Reasonable fears are entertained, by many citizens, that, in some of the larger cities of the United States, virtue and religion have lost their power as controlling political forces,—that the true principles of government, upon which alone a republic can be founded and maintained, are displaced by those resulting from passion and vice,—and that it is already written that Rome and her degenerate people, who were the sport and the prey of party leaders and were lost two thousand years ago, will find a parallel in the cities of the great Republic of the nineteenth century. But, happily, our country is not all Rome. THE PEOPLE, who dwell in mountain, valley, and plain, are yet pure; and through them the reigning vices of the city stews are yet controlled and controllable. And when the present purification by fire and the sword shall be complete, these rural virtues, shining all the brighter, will blazon forth to the world, still higher and grander evidences of man's capability of self-government.

The present rebellion was hatched in the cities of the South, by her partisan leaders. From these centres of political influence there were sent forth false doctrines during many years, intended as firebrands to enkindle a terrible conflagration in "the Southern heart." To the Southern leaders political power and place—only truly honorable when unsolicited—became an all-absorbing passion. The natural growth of the free States, and the consequent loss of political ascendency to the hitherto dominant South, disturbed her politicians in their present desires and alarmed them respecting the future: hence their rebellion, and their appeal to that "last argument of kings," *ultima ratio regum*,—the musket and the sword.

In the Revolution of '76 the loyal people of our country sprang alike to arms and achieved their independence as a republic. The rebellion of 1861 culminated in Southern cities,—among the wealthy, the aristocratic, and the ambitious. It first broke forth at a point where the seeds of social dissolution of the republic had taken earliest and deepest root. The rural population of the Southern States were not prepared for such a step: they held back, appalled at the course of the leaders and their mobs in Charleston, New Orleans, Mobile, and Nashville. By means and appliances the most artful and the most violent,—which will fully test the patience and research of the future historian to solve and portray,—the reluctant and protesting rural population of the South, urged with all the mock philosophy of an Antony, watched with the myriad prying eyes of an Argus, and forced as by the hundred bloody hands of a Briareus, were launched into a hapless sea of rebellion; and thus were a great, happy, prosperous people seduced into a causeless and destroying civil war.

We write of Nashville,—the gem and the boast of Tennessee,—the Western queen of the vaunted Southern Confederacy,—where centred the wealth, the aristocratic refinement, the talent, and the political influence of the State. We charge it boldly upon that city that, by the grandest sublimation of political finesse upon the part of her party leaders, rebellion was inaugurated in old Tennessee,—the most populous and fertile and, as regards war-*material*, the most valuable of all the slave States. For this reason have we chosen Nashville as a text for this chapter; for truly her past history and position, contrasted with her present prostrate condition, present her as a memorable and pitiable type of the pending rebellion. The thousands of desecrated and burning homes of Tennessee are reflected from her domes, and the countless graves of her lost and dishonored sons have no monument save the profaned temples of this proud and ruined city.

Previous to 1861, Nashville was one of the most beautiful, gay, and prosperous cities of the Union. Her inhabitants numbered thirty thousand, and were rapidly increasing. She was the wealthiest place of her class in the country. Her public buildings and private edifices were of the grandest and most costly character. The State Capitol rose from a rock one hundred and seventy-five feet above the Cumberland River,—is said to be the finest structure of its kind in America, and cost over a million of dollars. Church-edifices reared their tall spires upon every hand. An extensive State penitentiary, a medical college with three hundred students, and a university, styled the "Western Military Institute" and boasting of three hundred scholars, were here located. At one period twelve newspapers were published in this city,—five of them being dailies. She possessed a banking-capital of $5,181,000. Her suspension bridge, spanning the Cumberland River, was a glory in architecture and popular estimation, erected at a cost of upwards of $100,000. Her public water and gas works were ample, and built at great expense; and she boasted of eight elegant stone (Macadam) turnpikes leading to the interior in various directions and to adjoining States. At her feet was poured the traffic from three extensive railroad-thoroughfares, which extended hundreds of miles to Alabama, to Georgia, and East Tennessee, and through Kentucky to Louisville. She lay at the head of navigation of the Cumberland River,—a fine boating-stream during two-thirds of the year and navigable for small craft the year round. Her merchants controlled a vast cotton and tobacco trade, and supplied the Southern interior, hundreds of miles in extent, with dry-goods, hardware, and the thousand articles of American and foreign manufacture. Her business streets were lined with monster mercantile concerns, and her suburbs were resplendent with beautiful cottages and almost palatial mansions, and delightful groves of aged forest-trees. A visitor to this fair city previous to the rebellion, when viewing all that we have just described, and witnessing in addition the fleet of steamers at the levee, the rush of business upon the streets, and the sweeping by of dashing carriages and gayly-arrayed riding-parties mounted on blooded horses, might safely conclude that Nashville was one of the favored cities of the world.

The boom of the cannon that first opened upon Sumter proved the funeral knell of all this peace and happiness. Intoxicated with prosperity, its votaries abandoned the principles of government which alone had created and secured it. Spoiled by a pernicious social system, they launched forth upon an ocean of false doctrines which were repudiated by all civilized nations. The story of the political storms in Tennessee,—of the persistent efforts of the Nashville secession leaders,—of the several votes forced upon the people before secession could be invested with a legal semblance,—of the distrust and reluctance of the masses,—we need not pause to relate: it is history.

Once fully committed to the rebellion, the rebel leaders at Richmond deigned to throw some sops to their Western "metropolis," and extensive military depots were created, shops and foundries were set in motion, cannon were cast, gunboats were put in process of construction, percussion-caps, soldiers' clothing, &c. were manufactured by the million, and thousands of hogs were packed for the use of the Confederate armies. Verily, it was asserted that Nashville would speedily eclipse Louisville, Cincinnati, and St. Louis,—that her prospects were excellent for becoming, in fact, the capital of the great Southern Confederation.

Thus for a season affairs went on swimmingly in Nashville, and until the fall of Fort Donelson occurred. Up to that period, almost, there had existed a strong Union element in the city; but the secessionists had taken measures to root it out effectually, the prominent Union men being driven from their homes to the North. A "vigilance committee" had been formed, its avowed object being to "spot" every adherent to the old Government, and to notify him to take the oath of allegiance to rebellion, to enter its ranks as a soldier, or contribute visibly and liberally to its support, or to choose the alternative, banishment from the place. Such a notice was served upon the venerable patriot, Judge Catron, of the Supreme Court of the United States, who was a resident of that city. He scornfully cast the dust of the rebellious city from his feet, and left his home and property to their fate. Upon the evening of the day preceding the surrender of Fort Donelson, the rebel citizens of Nashville held high carnival. They met in a public place, indulged in wild, vociferous speechification and shouts, and improvised a torchlight procession, carrying secession flags, emblems, and transparencies, bearing aloft huge, rough iron pikes,—which latter invention signified utter demolition of the invading Yankees. The orgies were under the management of little Dick Cheatham, the mayor of the city. Speeches were made of an extravagant character,—a liberal portion of them being devoted to denunciation of the Unionists of that city and State.

"Yes," quoth Cheatham, "drive 'em out from among us. Let me deal with these traitors, and I will hang them first and try them afterwards!"

But there was a fate in store for the rebels of Nashville of which they little dreamed. Up to the time above mentioned, all had gone well at Donelson. Hourly reports came up that the Federal army was kept at bay and their gunboats were repulsed. Steamers were plying busily between the city and the fort, forwarding supplies and reinforcements. The weather was extremely inclement, the late snows and rain-storms of winter being at hand, and the men of both armies were suffering almost incredible hardships, standing ankle-deep in the frozen slush and mud of the trenches. During the week previous, the ladies of Nashville, with a devotion worthy of a better cause, had loaded a steamboat with carpets taken from their floors, and spare bedding and warm clothing of all kinds, for their suffering soldiers. Upon the surrender these carpets were found cut into strips, with a hole in the centre, hanging over the shoulders of the half-frozen rebel soldiers.

The Sabbath of February 16, 1862, is an epoch in the history of Nashville and of Tennessee. Until ten o'clock that morning all was well with the rebellion. The last boat up from Donelson, arriving several hours previous, reported still stronger evidences of the defeat of the Federals. At the usual hour the church-bells of the city called its people forth to public worship. It was a beautiful Sabbath morning, bright sunshine succeeding many days of winter darkness and storm, and there was a general attendance. The clergy of Nashville had offered their prayers for the rebellion,— for they were wild secessionists to a man,—and had taken their texts, when, lo! a hum of excitement and commotion began to be manifest in the streets. Soon notices were handed in at the doors and were carried to the sacred desks. The ministers paused, and clutched eagerly at what they supposed was welcome intelligence. They read it aloud with ashen cheek and faltering tongue. Donelson had surrendered!—the Confederate army was captured!—the Federal gunboats were now on their way up the river to destroy the city!

The people rushed from the churches, to find confusion and dismay visible in the streets upon every hand. There was now a gathering-up of valuables and a pressing of teams of every description. Wagons, carts, drays, and every animal that could be found were at once put in requisition. The city authorities were palsied. The rebel army stores were opened, and the citizens urged to aid in removing the vast amounts of pork, sugar, &c. to the railroad depot and to the interior. But the people had their personal safety nearest at heart, and the invitation was disregarded. A crowd of the poorer classes swarmed around the commissary and quartermaster depots, and began an indiscriminate appropriation of hams, shoulders, sugar, clothing, and goods of every description. The wholesale stores, and even dry-goods and silk houses, were burst open, or purposely thrown open, and whole bolts of cloth, entire pieces of costly fabrics, arms-full of boots and shoes, and rolls of new carpeting, were thrown pell-mell into the street, or lay loose upon the floors and walks, awaiting the disposal of the mob. Squads of soldiers assailed the beautiful suspension bridge with axes, saws, and cold chisels, and, after hours of cursing and exertion, succeeded in utterly destroying it. The elegant railroad-bridge was given to the flames. At the State-House were to be seen gangs of excited men in shirt-sleeves, rushing out with the archives and other valuable public property and tossing them loosely into wagons, to be carried to the Chattanooga depot for instant shipment to the South. Ere long the hegira of Nashville secessionism was under full headway. Families were hurried off in every possible manner, the turnpikes leading southward being lined with the fugitives. By sunset all had gone who could go; and these kept going all night, many of them not stopping until they reached Shelbyville, Fayetteville, and even Huntsville, Alabama.

This frantic evacuation was in character with the preceding features of the rebellion,—as wild and as causeless. Vast amounts of property were needlessly destroyed, and the boastful secessionists who had so valiantly carried the pikes in procession the night previous, and had cheered at the spectacle, had shown the world that their courage was of words rather than of deeds. No gunboats came up the river; and not until a full week afterwards—the following Sabbath—did the Federal army arrive opposite Nashville. The rebels thus had ample time to move off their stores and goods. Lest this account of the rebel flight from Nashville be considered overdrawn, we insert the following description of the event from a rebel source,—Pollard's " Southern History of the War," published at Richmond, Virginia, 1862.

" The fall of Fort Donelson developed the crisis in the West, which had long existed. The evacuation of Bowling Green had become imperatively necessary, and was ordered before and executed while the battle was being fought at Donelson. General Johnston awaited the event opposite Nashville. The result of the conflict each day was announced as favorable. At midnight on the 15th of February, General Johnston received news of a glorious victory,—at dawn, of a defeat.

" The blow was most disastrous. It involved the surrender of Nashville, which was incapable of defence from its position, and was threatened not only by the enemy's ascent of the Cumberland, but by the advance of his forces from Bowling Green. Not more than eleven thousand effective men had been left under General Johnston's command to oppose a column of General Buell of not less than forty thousand troops, while the army from Fort Donelson, with the gunboats and transports, had it in their power to ascend the Cumberland, so as to intercept all communication with the South. No alternative was left but to evacuate Nashville or sacrifice the army.

" The evacuation of Nashville was attended by scenes of panic and distress on the part of the population unparalleled in the annals of any American city. The excitement was intensified by the action of the authorities. Governor Harris mounted a horse and galloped through the streets, proclaiming to everybody the news that Donelson had fallen,—that the enemy were coming and might be expected hourly, and that all who wished to leave had better do so at once. He next hastily convened the Legislature, adjourned it to Memphis, and, with the legislators and the State archives, left the town.

" An earthquake could not have shocked the city more. The congregations at the churches were broken up in confusion and dismay; women and children rushed into the streets, wailing with terror; trunks were thrown from three-story windows in the haste of the fugitives; and thousands hastened to leave their beautiful city in the midst of the most distressing scenes of terror and confusion, and of plunder by the mob.

" General Johnston had moved the main body of his command to Murfreesborough,—a rear-guard being left in Nashville under General Floyd, who had arrived from Donelson, to secure the stores and provisions. In the first wild excitement of the panic, the store-houses had been thrown open to the poor. They were besieged by a mob ravenous for spoils, and who had to be dispersed from the commissariat by jets of water from a steam fire-engine. Women and children, even, were seen scudding through the streets under loads of greasy pork, which they had taken as prizes from the store-houses. It is believed that hundreds of families, among the lower orders of the population, secured and secreted Government stores enough to open respectable groceries. It was with the greatest difficulty that General Floyd could restore order and get his martial law into any thing like an effective system. Blacks and whites had to be chased and captured and forced to help the movement of Government stores. One man, who, after a long chase, was captured, offered fight, and was in consequence shot and badly wounded. Not less than one million of dollars in stores was lost through the acts of the cowardly and ravenous mob of Nashville. General Floyd and Colonel Forrest exhibited extraordinary energy and efficiency in getting off Government stores. Colonel Forrest remained in the city about twenty-four hours, with only forty men, after the arrival of the enemy at Edgefield. These officers were assisted by the voluntary efforts of several patriotic citizens of Nashville, who rendered them great assistance.

"These shameful scenes, enacted in the evacuation of Nashville, were nothing more than the disgusting exhibitions of any mob brutalized by its fears or excited by rapine. At any rate, the city speedily repaired the injury done its reputation by a temporary panic, in the spirit of defiance that its best citizens, and especially its ladies, offered to the enemy. We discover, in fact, the most abundant evidence in the Northern newspapers that the Federals did not find the 'Union' sentiment that they expected to meet with in the capital of Tennessee, and that, if there were any indications whatever of such sentiment, they were 'found only among the mechanics and laboring-classes of the city.' The merchants and business-men of Nashville, as a class, showed a firm, unwavering, and loyal attachment to the cause of the South. The ladies gave instances of patriotism that were noble testimonies to their sex. They refused the visits of Federal officers, and disdained their recognition ; they collected a fund of money for the especial purpose of contributing to the needs of our prisoners ; and, says a recipient of the bounty of these noble women, as soon as a Confederate prisoner was paroled and passed into the next room, he found pressed in his hands there a sum of money given him by the ladies of Nashville. Many of the most respectable of the people had been constrained to leave their homes rather than endure the presence of the enemy. The streets, which, to confirm the predictions of Northern newspapers of the welcomes that awaited the 'Union' army in the South, should have been gay and decorated, presented to the enemy nothing but sad and gloomy aspects. Whole rows of houses, which but a short while ago were occupied by families of wealth and respectability, surrounded by all the circumstances that make homes happy and prosperous, stood vacant, and the gaze of the passer-by was met, instead of, as in former days, with fine tapestry window-curtains and neatly polished marble steps with panes of dust-dimmed glass."

After a day or two, the valorous rebel citizens recovered from their fright, began to realize the value and comforts of home, and commenced their return to the city. During the entire week after the flight, Mayor Cheatham was anxiously casting about for some appearing Federal force, to whom he could perform the farce of a formal surrender of the city. Upon the succeeding Sabbath, the Federal army appeared across the river, and Cheatham and one or two other city dignitaries crossed in "a dug-out," and, in terms and manner very different from the week before, he tendered the submission of the helpless and prostrate city.

As is related by the Southern historian above quoted, the Federal army met with a chilling reception upon its entering Nashville. The streets were almost deserted ; the stores and shops were entirely closed ; there was not a hotel open.   Where but a few days before rebel flags had waved defiantly upon hundreds of house-tops, now not one could be seen to greet the presence of national Government.   If there were a few Unionists present, they were as yet too greatly cowed, and the Federal power was as yet too recently asserted, to permit a demonstration in the midst of such universal hatred.

Matters thus remained during Buell's campaign in the South.   Upon his retreat to Kentucky in pursuit of Bragg, the rebel citizens of Nashville were greatly emboldened.   And when Bragg again retreated from Kentucky and moved up to Murfreesborough, they were still confident of his victory over the Federal forces; for up to this time they had not lost confidence in the ultimate success of the rebel armies and leaders.   But when General Rosecrans entered Nashville with his army, matters began to wear a different aspect.   Other causes also contributed to this result.   New Orleans was conquered and firmly held; the national Government was beginning to put forth its power in earnestness,—its vast armies and fleets assailing the rebels upon every quarter; and we had commenced undermining them in their most vital point, by operating against them with their slaves.   The vast fortifications now being erected by the Federals around the city assured them that they were conquered; and the influence of all this upon such a people was plainly visible.   Still they clung feebly to hope, until after the final defeat of Bragg before Murfreesborough.

Oh, the anxiety, the agony, of the rebellious people of Nashville during that week of battle!   Their fathers, brothers, and sons were mingling in that conflict.   Upon its result hung the issue of their cause.   The boldest of the men gathered in knots at their door-steps to discuss the probabilities, while the women met in parlor groups, prepared lint and bandages, and eagerly hoped for good tidings.   When the report of the first day of heavy battle came in, announcing the defeat of Rosecrans's right wing, there was intense joy and renewed hope in many a Nashville home.   Rebels clustered in the streets and flitted about their houses during all that eventful New Year night.   The next day they still had faith and hope; and, as several hundred rebel prisoners, taken in battle, were marched through the city to the State-House, smiles and the waving of handkerchiefs greeted their passage up the streets.   The bitter truth came at last,—too bitter for ready belief.   Its realization was the death-knell of their hopes.   From that day to the present the leading rebels of Nashville and of all Tennessee have despaired, and, as time has rolled away, they have gradually become more disheartened in their own bad cause and more ready and desirous to make their peace with the Federal Government.

The police record of the Army of the Cumberland is fraught with interesting items pertaining to the rebel citizens of Nashville.   That record is before us; and it is due to history, to the cause of the Union, to our army, and to the memory of the two thousand of our brave Northmen who laid down their lives upon the battle-fields of Stone River, that this people, who have been mainly instrumental in bringing on the war in Tennessee, should now be held responsib.e to public opinion and to the law of the land for their outrageous "deeds done in the body."

Andrew Ewing was one of the most prominent rebels of Tennessee. He was a lawyer and a politician,—a man of notoriety and influence. He lived upon a beautiful place in the suburbs of Nashville, the mansion standing amid a grove of noble forest oaks and hickories which were valuable beyond price. He was reputed to be worth one hundred and fifty thousand dollars, most of which he inherited from his father. He was one of the first and wildest of secessionists. The Union had been a good thing for Andrew, and for his father, and for his father's father. He was rich and influential, lived in a prospering country, and was threatened by no violence, present or prospective. He turned rebel solely to be President of the rebels, or for something of that sort. At least we can conceive of no other possible reason. Ewing was severe upon Union men before the fall of Fort Donelson. He walked at the head of the torchlight procession at Nashville which we have referred to above; he made a speech to the mob during that evening, urging that every Union man be "spotted" and be forced to join them or to leave. He carried a pike in that procession. He fled with his family from Nashville during the general panic and evacuation, and has since abode in the far South. His son is in the rebel army. He was with Forrest's men when they attacked Nashville last fall and were repulsed by General Negley. The day previous to that event, he made a speech in Franklin, twenty miles below, in which he declared the true policy to be to attack the city, and, if necessary, "to make Nashville ash-ville." During that battle he stood where he could witness the cannon firing about his home and the premises of his neighbors. Our troops found his great house deserted, and made use of it all winter. His beautiful grove has been felled for fortification-timber and fuel,—not a shade-tree left standing upon the place. Ewing is ruined. Truly, his case may be cited as a faithful type of the results of this rebellion.

John Overton, living four miles south of Nashville, on the Franklin pike, is noted upon the police records as one of the rank, original secessionists of Nashville. He is said to be the richest man in Tennessee,—worth five millions of dollars. He has given, or boasted of having given, a large sum of money to aid the Southern cause. He was at the battle of Shiloh, acting as an adviser and sympathizer. His only grown son is in the rebel army. The immense new hotel at Nashville, covering a block of ground, was his project, the citizens also contributing one hundred thousand dollars to aid in its erection. The walls were laid, and the roof put on, when Overton turned his attention to rebellion, and the work stopped. He ran off at the time of the general "skedaddle," and is now a fugitive. The great hotel has been used for military barracks and hospital purposes. He was not a notable man at all, save as a money-jug; and that trait will not constitute him a specialty hereafter, we apprehend.

The records state that John M. Bass was another very active leader in the Tennessee rebellion. He lived in a fine mansion on Church Street, Nashville,—became uneasy at the proximity of Yankee bayonets before the fall of Donelson, and went to Louisiana and Arkansas to look after his plantations. His wealth is reputed at a million of dollars. His eldest son, a Dr. Bass, was killed, while among a guerrilla-band, by our troops under General Negley. Bass is a ruined man. A single grown-up daughter, and one or two house-servants, have had charge of his house, &c., and have not as yet been disturbed, we presume.

Thomas Acklin, a hearty secessionist, very wealthy, and residing on a most gaudy, showy place near Nashville, was a lawyer from Huntsville, Alabama. He married a widow Franklin, whose first husband was immensely wealthy. She had two children by her former marriage, to whom the property was mainly devised. They both died, and the property descends to the second tier of children. The police record contains a description of Acklin's premises; for they are rather a specialty in the way of extravagance. The place is situated two miles out from the city, and comprises about one hundred acres of land. His buildings are gothic-ified and starched and bedizened to perfection. Serpentine walks, shrubbery, and all of that sort of thing, abound in great quantity and profusion. A tower, one hundred and five feet high, is built near a spring a fourth of a mile distant from the buildings, and a steam-engine within its base forces water to its top, whence it is piped in every direction over the grounds. The improvements upon this place, such as the buildings, statuary, walls, &c., cost over a quarter of a million of dollars. Looking over upon it from adjacent high grounds, the white marble fountains, emblems, and statues cause the place to resemble somewhat a fashionable first-class cemetery. The Acklin place exhibits a vast outlay of money, and but little artistic skill in its expenditure. Its proprietor, not satisfied with all this wealth, must needs dabble in secession; and he, too, is off with the rebel army. His wife, however, well fills his place, says our report, so far as rebellion sympathies and hate can extend. With such a record of Thomas Acklin, the author simply puts the question to the country, what is to be done?

General Hardin is one of the notable rebel citizens of Nashville, possessing great wealth and descending from an old and influential family. He was an ardent, original secessionist. The old Government was quite too oppressive upon him to be longer content. Let us endeavor to ascertain the particular *oppression* under which this man groaned. He lived six miles west from the city, on the Hardin pike. He had a little farm of some five thousand acres. His mansion and all its appurtenances would, in many respects, vie with those of the old manorial estates of the English barons. His buildings were very extensive,—great barns, and outlying tenements for his tenants and his slaves. He was reputed to be worth two and a half millions of dollars. He was not only a millionnaire: he was also a great stock fancier and breeder. His stables were filled with the most beautiful and valuable horses and horned cattle, many of them imported. He kept two or three celebrated blooded stallions. A herd of elegant deer tossed their antlers in his park, unmolested, and a herd of buffalo—the genuine article, from the plains of the far West—bellowed and butted over his great pastures in half-civilized mood. A flock of imported Cashmere goats were also here upon exhibition,—possibly divers other quadrupeds, too numerous to mention,—and also barn-yard fowls of all the ordinary and fanciful varieties. Added to all this, Hardin was a man of social note: he was a live general. Happily, too, he had acquired the title without wading through any extensive ocean of blood. How he became a general is immaterial; and we must pass on. As he was a judge of horse-flesh and of short-horns, he usually sat in the judge's stand at the prominent races; and his knowing pinch of a prize steer's rib, or rump, at a country fair, was highly prized. Last, but certainly not least, the general has an interesting family of wife and daughters, who are highly esteemed by all, and against whom the police records contain not one word of reproach.

Such being the social and the pecuniary status of General Hardin, the reader will inquire where comes in the unbearable oppression which drove such a man into rebellion. We cannot explain. Our records, usually so suggestive, are here silent, and the hiatus must pass with the history into the womb of time. All we can say upon this head is soon said. Hardin had wealth and family position,—which latter means something among the Southern aristocracy,—but he was not eminently a man of brains, and had no reputation as a speaker or writer. His ideas hardly rose above the eaves of his stables, and his tastes were upon a level with the roll of his grazing-lands. He had just sufficient ability to conceive that horses and negroes are the *summum bonum* of this life, and that a separate and distinct Southern Confederacy was the best form of government for rich men of his ilk. Hence, we repeat, he was an *original* secessionist, one who upheld the firing upon Fort Sumter, and gloried in the pluck of the little man in large leathers, South Carolina. When the secession of Tennessee was advocated, he was quite conspicuous, but principally as a tool of the Ewings, Isham Harris, and others; and he gave—at least it was so reported at the time, for political effect—half a million of dollars to aid that cause.

General Hardin was bitterly opposed to the North from education, aristocratic affinities, and supposed personal interests. Formerly he was in the habit of travelling to the North in the summer-season on trips of pleasure. A circumstance occurred during one of these excursions which, we are assured by Nashville citizens, had a strong tendency to further embitter Hardin's mind against Northern institutions. Some years ago he visited Cape May, a notable sea-shore rendezvous of the fashionables of our country. He was accompanied by the two young McGavocks, his nephews, scions of rich Tennessee stock, and a group of ladies. The McGavocks had a difficulty with the colored servants at the Cape, and a regular pitched battle ensued, we believe, which resulted in the triumph of the negroes, the discomfited Southrons retiring from the field in disorder. Hardin remembered the affront, and from that time was more than ever opposed to the "nigger-equality" doctrines of the North.

When the Federal troops entered Nashville, General Hardin did not evacuate. He was summoned before the military authorities, and, with General Barrow, was sent to Fort Mackinaw, Lake Michigan, where he remained as a prisoner of war from the 6th day of April until about the last of September, 1862, when he was released upon a bond of twenty thousand dollars to appear and answer before the United States District Court of Tennessee to the charge of treason, and the trial is still in abeyance. We must briefly conclude with the statement that civil war has well performed its mournful task in the case of Hardin. A portion of our army was quartered on or near his place during many weeks. There was grand hunting after those deer and buffalo. The goats were ruthlessly taken "in the wool." The stables were confiscated,—what were left of the stud, the rebels having taken the best of the serviceable blooded nags. Hundreds of tons of his hay and thousands of bushels of his grain were hauled into our camps. Miles of his fencing were burned. His men negroes kept company with his departed stock. We recollect the trouble the general had concerning his old imported gray stallion: it was taken—we might as well say stolen—from him three or four times. The general commanding had given him a protection document, and the army police had upon several occasions discovered and restored the noble animal, which was really fit for breeding-purposes only. The last time the old horse was seized he was found in a solitary place, a forest, where he had been placed for security. Some negroes reported the fact to a squad of Federal cavalry, and the commander of the latter, unaware of the peculiar circumstances attending the ownership, gobbled the animal forthwith. Hardin once more visits head-quarters, then at Murfreesborough, finds his horse, upon which is mounted a Federal officer of the first degree, and the latter, to his intense disgust, is compelled to surrender the beast. This account of General Hardin is gathered from many sources, and may be incorrect in minor points. But it portrays the general character and position of the man; and that is the sole aim of the author. May we not safely conclude this sketch by classing its subject, after contrasting his former prosperity with his present misfortunes, as another eminent type of the rebellion?

General Washington Barrow, the companion of Hardin in his imprisonment at the North, was also a prominent citizen of Nashville, or, rather, he resided at Edgefield, on the opposite side of the river. He was a member of the rebel State Senate. His wife's father was a very rich man. He gave no bond, but was finally paroled from prison and exchanged, and has since remained in rebeldom. A few weeks since a party of Tennessee rebel politicians met at Winchester, where was located a portion of General Bragg's army, and performed the farce of a State Convention; and then and there General Barrow was nominated as the secession candidate for Governor. Since then Bragg's army has been driven entirely from the State, excepting a little nook at Chattanooga; and how to make his "calling and election sure" must be a puzzler indeed to the secession candidate, as none but Union candidates and Union voters will ever again be tolerated in the old Mountain State.

Richard Cheatham, Esq., Mayor, &c. of the rebel city of Nashville, was a very rabid secessionist. He was not wealthy, nor was he a man of any especial talent. A few years since he was a dealer at faro-tables, and was one of the fast, rattling young men of the day, who occasionally are thrown to the surface by the rolling waves of violent times. Cheatham's ability was about equal to the task of hounding down Union men, of managing vigilance committees, and of the superintendènce of torchlight processions. The patriotism, or rebelism, or call it what you will, of such men, rarely carries them up to the cannon's mouth, or to a severe death in that "last ditch." He has taken excellent care of his individual bacon, while hundreds of the poor youth of Tennessee, goaded on by his and kindred efforts, now fill unknown graves. Since the battle of Stone River and the abandonment of rebel hopes, Cheatham has become quite moderate and affable, and has even ventured slightly into Federal army contracts, we hear it asserted. Good for Richard! He will make just as good a Union man as he was a bad rebel; for circumstances control such men. Major-General Cheatham, of the rebel army, is his cousin.

John Weaver, Esq., president of the Planters' Bank, wealthy and influential, resides upon an elegant place five miles south of Nashville, near the State Lunatic Asylum. He was an original secessionist. Persons coming into his bank during the few bright days of the rebellion would hear his earnest and honeyed argument, which ran thus:—"The true policy of the South is to set up for herself. At any rate, now that she has done so, Tennessee must go with her. As for our city, it will be the making of us. The North will get no more of our cotton and tobacco: we will ship from here direct to Europe via New Orleans, with free trade as our great lever. Nashville stands by far the best chance of being the capital of the Confederacy, in which case our real estate will advance in value two hundred per cent. In any event, we will eclipse Louisville, Cincinnati, and St. Louis, if Missouri don't come in with us, and thus we will knock those cities cold as a wedge." Mr. Weaver was a fair, earnest secessionist, really one of the most respectable and dangerous in the South. He has not been damaged greatly by the war as yet, we believe; and what will be done in his case is involved in the great question of the final adjustment of the rebellion. That such cool, clear, cautious men as Weaver will entirely escape the calamities which he and his class have been greatly instrumental in bringing upon the thousands of ruined families of Tennessee, is too monstrous an idea to be entertained.

John Kirkman, Esq., of the Union Bank, Nashville, also occupies a page in the police record of the Army of the Cumberland. He was rich, influential, and lived in the finest style. He was a secessionist, cautious, but of unquestionable fulness and ripeness. His only son was in the rebel army, and was killed at the last battle of Fort Donelson. Like Weaver, Mr. Kirkman was a secessionist in a financial point of view. He argued in this wise:—"The wealth of the South is in cotton. We cannot produce cotton without slaves. The North is growing ahead of us, and threatens slavery with extermination, and the only safety of the South is a separate government and her taking her half of all the new territory." He opined, with Weaver, that Nashville would prove the Western star of the Southern Confederacy. Last winter he was called upon by our army officials to explain certain transactions of his bank which were deemed suspicious. The Nashville banks were then issuing large amounts of new paper money to the people and to the army. Some of it was got up in "greenback" style. The new notes were of small denominations,—one and two dollar bills. For banks to be issuing new money at such a time, when it was notorious that they had not a dollar of gold in their vaults to redeem with, was a circumstance that demanded attention. Mr. Kirkman explained that these banks were simply issuing this small-bill money for public convenience, they retiring in its place, and to its precise extent, bills of large amounts, as twenty, fifty, and one hundred dollar notes. The explanation was satisfactory, as these banks were permitted thus to change their currency by legislative enactment, and there had been a great want of bills under five dollars up to that time, the army having been paid off in fives, this being before the day of abundance of small United States ones and twos, and of postage currency. Incidentally the conversation turned upon banking-affairs. Kirkman assured the official that the bullion of his bank had been sent to the North for security in the early days of the rebellion. This is not believed by the Union men of Tennessee, they being positive that the specie of not only the Nashville banks, but of all the banks in the South, has been sent to Europe, and has formed the fund from which ships, arms, and munitions of war have thus far been furnished to maintain the Southern rebellion. At all events, Mr. Kirkman freely admitted that the deposits of the Southern banks would not cover a tithe of their circulation, even if secure,—that the securities of the banks for the redemption of their issues were mainly in notes, stocks, bonds, and judgments,—and that if the Southern revolution was unsuccessful all the banks would be ruined.

"For," said he, "if the people are impoverished, if they cannot pay their notes, if the stock of our corporations, such as gas-works, turnpikes, railroads, &c., become worthless, if State stocks fall to a mere nominal value, and if our judgments are not liens upon real estate, hereafter, because of confiscation, &c., then the entire banking-system of the South is exploded."

There lives a lady in Nashville who figures slightly upon our records,—a lady who is extensively known in city and general circles,—Mrs. Ex-President Polk. She is a woman of note,—wealthy, smart (that is a better term than "talented" in this instance), and was rather at the head of the female sex of that region as regards all the social bearings. Mrs. Polk was a true rebel. She was too shrewd to be violent, however, and too well-bred to evince her dislike openly to even the humblest member of our army. Severely cool and reticent, she was unmolested, and, when necessary for her to approach the military authorities for a pass or other requisites, she was sufficiently bending and gracious to gain her point. She has no children: she took to nursing the rebellion of the Southern aristocracy. Her influence upon the wealthy females of her city must have been almost unbounded. She was the President of the Nashville Ladies' Southern Aid Society, and occupied much of her time in duties pertaining to that position. The society met at her house occasionally, and at other private houses upon special occasions; but its general place of meeting was at the Masonic Hall. It is stated upon good authority that Mrs. Polk was greatly intent upon urging the men of Nashville to enter the rebel army, and that she advised the young ladies of that city to send petticoats and hoop-skirts to young men who had proved backward in volunteering. Since the permanent occupation of Tennessee by our army, this lady has been entirely unmolested in person and property. When the stables of the town were swept of every serviceable horse for army use, General Rosecrans ordered hers to be exempted, from a proper respect to the past. She now reposes amid comfort and elegance, while desolation sits brooding around her over the face of a once happy and prospering country. There is a wisdom in the ordering of earthly things past all human comprehension, and the fiat of Heaven alone can right many of the wrongs of erring mortals.

We might pass on through this police record, filling a volume with its gleaming and bristling facts; but our space is limited, and we must forbear. We have commented upon several of the prominent characters; and yet upon how small a portion of the ground have we trenched! To pass by such men as Bird Douglass,—rich, prosperous, and who ought to have been contented' and thankful,—and French, and McNairy, and Evans, and the Strattons, *et id genus omnes*, is gross injustice. Douglass, a rich merchant, made wealthy by extensions granted him by his Northern creditors, now repudiates by rebellion, and advertises in the public newspapers that he has one thousand dollars to give as his first offering to secession, and has two sons for its army, and that if they are killed he has two negro servants, each of whom can pick off a squirrel from a tree-top at two hundred yards, to take their place. R. C. McNairy was an active member of their vigilance committee, &c.: now he sees matters in a different light: the cannon has become a telescope, and he sighs for a return of the old order of things. He is a fair sort of a man, and was rather forced along by the all-powerful current. God has given to some men pluck and denied it to others, and is merciful. Henry S. French was a rebel, and then played the Union card to subserve rebelism. Reporting himself as an impoverished Union refugee, he obtained a permit to pass three thousand eight hundred barrels of salt from Louisville, through the canal, to a point on the Ohio River where he could pack some meat for the United States Government or for sale. At that time it was policy to prevent salt being sold to rebels, and the river salt-traffic was closely guarded. French takes his salt down to a point near the mouth of the Cumberland, whence it was engineered up that river, past the military authorities, gunboats, &c., in some way not explained in our records, was brought to Nashville, and there sold to the Confederate Government at forty dollars per barrel, it costing Mr. French but three dollars per barrel. With the aid of this salt, the rebels packed one hundred and fifty thousand head of hogs, at Nashville, for their army that season. This statement is vouched for by several Union citizens of Nashville. Meanwhile, Mr. French passes as one of the peaceable, quiet, non-committal do-nothings of the rebellion.

One other case we cannot pass by,—that of Mark R. Cockrill,—an old man of great wealth, living near Nashville. He was reputed to be worth two million dollars, and owned twelve miles of land lying on the Cumberland River. It was reported to the Chief of Army Police that this Mr. Cockrill had induced guerrillas to lie in wait near his place for the purpose of seizing upon and destroying our forage-trains, &c., and that he was still a very bitter rebel. Having been ordered to appear at the office of the Chief of Police, he made the subjoined statement:—

"I am upwards of seventy-four years of age, and have six children, —three of them being sons, and one of them is in the Confederate army. I was born near this city. I had about ninety-eight slaves, but most all have left me. My son has been in the Confederate service since the war began; is twenty-two years old; was captain in that service; think he is now in the Commissary Department. I voted for separation every time; was not a member of any public committee; have had nothing to do with getting up companies or any thing else connected with the army. Have talked a good deal: was opposed to guerrillaism; have ordered them away from my house. I have lost twenty thousand bushels of corn, thirty-six head of horses and mules, sixty head of Durham cattle, two hundred and twenty sheep,— very fine ones, valued at one hundred dollars each,—two hundred tons of hay. The Federals have taken all this. I have two thousand sheep left, and I have a few milch-cows and five or six heifers. I was worth about two million dollars before the war commenced. The Confederates have taken three horses from me only. I have loaned the Confederates twenty-five thousand dollars in gold. They have pressed from me no other property. I have their bonds at eight per cent. interest, payable semi-annually in gold, for this twenty-five thousand dollars. I thought when I loaned this money that the South would succeed, and I think so now. I do not think that the two sections can ever be brought together. The Federals also took two thousand pounds of bacon from me; also two thousand bushels of oats. Some twenty-five or thirty of my men negroes ran away,—six of them, however, being pressed. I have about five thousand six hundred acres of land. My son James R. is with the South; lives on a place belonging to me; but he has never taken any active part. The Federals have taken over three thousand dollars' worth of wood from me. I have never received any pay for any thing taken from me. I came in yesterday to get a negro black-smith of mine to go out with me: he consented to go if I could get a pass for him; have not been in town before for four months. I paid one thousand dollars as an assessment by General Negley about four months since to the United States Government, as a loan. I have been very much aggravated by the taking of my property, and have been very harsh in my expressions towards those who have visited my place for such purposes. I will not give bond for loyal conduct, or that I will not aid or abet by word or deed the Southern cause. The loan to the South was made voluntarily, and supposing it to be a good investment. While I was loaning to individuals the loan was made to the Southern Government just as I would have loaned to any other party.
"(Signed)   M. R. COCKRILL"

There is Mr. Cockrill's case, in his own language. Need we add a word to it? When brought into the police-office, the poor old man was almost beside himself with passion. The language he used respecting the Federal troops was, "Kill 'em! Plant 'em out! Manure the soil with em! ——

39

—— 'em !'" &c. He utterly refused to give the non-combatant's oath and bond; and when assured by General Rosecrans that he must do so or he would be sent out of the state, and perhaps to a Northern prison, he struck his hands against his breast, and exclaimed,—

"Take my heart out,—kill me, if you will: I will not give any bond by which enemies here can swear falsely and I be prosecuted for its forfeiture."

The general assured him that he had but a choice of two evils,—to give the bond, or be sent away. He preferred the former.

We must pass over an interesting police case where a rebel family of Nashville were called upon to answer for exhibiting "a Yankee bone" upon their parlor-table,—which bone was declared by them to be a relic from the Bull Run battle-field. Also of several female rebel smugglers, upon one of whom was found divers articles, and among them a piece of fine gray cloth, in extent twenty-one yards, to be used for rebel officers' uniforms, which she had tucked together and hung upon her as a skirt. We regret that our space for such mention is entirely exhausted.

The rebel people of Nashville have been rigorously dealt with in consequence of their wild conduct. Brigadier-General Mitchell, commandant of that post during last winter and spring, and Lieutenant Osgood, his aide and pass-officer, were very strict and inflexible in their administration of city affairs. These people were not allowed to travel or to do business; and the most wealthy have been troubled at times to get fuel, food, and clothing.

The rebel ladies made such an ado over wounded Confederate soldiers as to give rise to the following military order:—

"HEAD-QUARTERS U. S. FORCES, NASHVILLE, TENN., February 1, 1863.

" *Orders.*—The general commanding at this post desires to express his admiration of the zeal evinced by certain secession families in administering to the wants and alleviating the sufferings of the Confederate wounded to-day brought to this city. Great praise should be awarded them for their devotion for the suffering soldiers of that cause to which they are so enthusiastically allied.

"Desiring to give them still greater facilities for the exercise of that devotion which to-day led them through the mud of the public streets of this city unmindful of the inclemency of the weather, and desiring further to obviate the necessity of that public and flaunting display which must be repugnant to the retiring dispositions of the softer sex, the general commanding directs as follows:—

"Surgeon Thruston, medical director, will select forty-five of the wounded and sick Confederate soldiers this day brought from the front, to be quartered as follows:—Fifteen at the house of Mrs. McCall, fifteen at the house of Dr. Buchanan, and fifteen at the house of Sandy Carter,—all on Cherry Street immediately below Church Street.

"As it is desirable that the sick and wounded should not be agitated by the presence of too many persons, no one will be admitted to the rooms in which the wounded are, except their surgeons, without passes from Surgeon Thruston.

"Each family above named will be held responsible for the safe delivery of the Confederate soldiers thus assigned when called for by proper military authority, under penalty, in failure of such delivery, of forfeiture to the United States of their property and personal liberty.

"By order of Brigadier-General ROBERT B. MITCHELL, Commanding.

"JNO. PRATT, *A. A. G.*"

The labors of Lieutenant Osgood in this connection were handsomely ac knowledged by the mayor of Nashville, in March last, as follows:—

"Lieutenant OSGOOD, *Provost-Marshal, Staff-General Commanding:*—

"Allow me, in behalf of the donors, Union friends of Nashville, to present to you this beautiful and rich sword-belt and sash, as a token of their high esteem for the fidelity and ability with which you have discharged the duties of the position assigned you at the head-quarters of this post, and for the sagacity you have displayed in detecting and circumventing the wiles and plans of rebels, and also the strict observance you have given to the orders of your superiors in command.

"Take them; preserve them; hand them down to your posterity as mementoes of the services you have rendered in crushing out this causeless and wicked rebellion.   Yours, truly,   JOHN HUGH SMITH."

The civil power is also beginning to be felt in Tennessee. The Federal Grand Jury, under a charge by Judge Trigg, recently found three hundred indictments, at Nashville, for treason and conspiracy against the leaders of the rebellion in that State; and among the culprits indicted are some prominent clergymen.

Having thus portrayed some of her individual types of the rebellion, we must leave the subject with a brief description of the city of Nashville as she is. We stated that she was one of the brightest, most wealthy and prosperous cities of the Union. Of all this she is now the exact reverse. Her finest buildings, such as her colleges, churches, and elegant stores, are now used as military hospitals and store-houses. Her streets are dirty, and, where main outlets from the city, they have been cut in two,—dug out, as though a canal was being made through them,—the dirt thrown up on each side, as barricades against rebel attack upon the city, when it was invested and threatened last year. Her suburbs are a mournful wreck in many localities,—houses deserted, fences gone, fruit-trees gnawed and disfigured; and the pedestrian is only reminded that he is passing over what was once a smiling garden, by his feet catching against some yet struggling and crushed grape-vine or rose-bush. The groves —the glory of the place—are cut down, and the grounds present the appearance of a new "clearing," a stump-field. St. Cloud Hill, once the fashionable retreat, where children romped amid the lovely shade and where lovers lisped in cooing numbers, is now a bleak, barren, granite mountain, a frowning fortress rising from its summit, with cannon trained upon and about the devoted city. The old, wealthy merchants of the city—those who yet remain—are prostrate in the dust of bankruptcy, and new traders—men from the North—are daily rising up in their places. The several printing-offices are held by the United States authorities as subject to confiscation, and some of them are leased and their material is now being used in battling for free government. The extensive Methodist Book Concern (Church South) has long been closed and in the hands of the United States Marshal, its managers and apostles taking to the rebellion at the very outset as naturally as the young waterfowl seeks its familiar element. As we write, the city of Nashville is stagnant, prostrate, and in the abject position of a subjugated city. She is changing, however; and as the Union is more surely restored and its future guaranteed, she will revive. New men will enter, and new and better times will ensue. She will be purged from the curse that has afflicted her and dragged her down. Slavery will no longer blight and wither her morals, nor will a haughty, unproductive aristocracy prey upon her vitals. Tennessee, with free labor, has the capability of becoming one of the grandest States of the Union; and Nashville is her crown-jewel. May the old State speedily emerge from the mire in which she has been forced to wallow by the wildness of her spoiled leaders, and may her coronal gem, the "Rock City," shine all the brighter for her momentary eclipse,—when, no longer a type of devastating rebellion, her name shall stand as a synonym of prosperity, beauty, and progress!

One more thought, ere we close the Police Record of the Army of the Cumberland. What is there contained is gathered in the line of official duty, irrespective of person and place. For what we publish of it we have no apology to offer. Let it stand as best it may. Call it scandal, or harshness, or what else one may, it is TRUTH, and cannot be successfully travestied or denied. This volume is presented as a *picture* of the Army of the Cumberland and of the war in Tennessee. It would not be a picture if merely an outline. No: it requires the minutiæ, the detail, the tint, the shading, and the drapery of the background, all together, to constitute a harmonious and complete view of the present rebellion. This we have attempted to give, in all candor, earnestness, and charity.

"Charity?" queries some friendly reader. "Why, then, drag names of erring and possibly repentant individual rebels thus into notoriety and embalm them in history?" Ah, friend, the claims of retributive justice are ill satisfied by the infliction of even that penalty upon the heads of these great offenders. We write of the proud, the haughty, the controlling minds of the rebellion. And we live in strange times, and are surrounded by many a wild and saddening scene. We have learned lessons of late in a rude, unvarnished, but truthful school. As we write, we can look out from our window upon a field of newly-heaped soldiers' graves,—the graves of our brothers and sons of the North. Who laid them there? Across yonder swelling field rises a solitary chimney-stack,—a monument of what once was a home of peace and plenty. Who plied the brand? And the faint wailing notes of a far-off martial strain now steal upon the ear, borne to our window upon the wings of a summer zephyr: they come from the distant camp, where thousands have gathered to wage the battle for national existence. Should we refrain from mention of the prime *cause* of all this death, destruction, and privation? We think not. These times and scenes cannot long continue, in the nature of things. Peace must come: it must follow exhaustion, if it does not spring from victory. The future historian will then appear, to weave and create for his day and generation. There will be a Bancroft, in those later times, to round the swelling periods, and a Macaulay, to invest with grace and beauty the historic pages of the slaveholders' rebellion of the nineteenth century. They will search for such lesser lights and shadows as are here recorded with which to gild and tint their complete picture. And beneath that picture they will again write, as was written by the Eternal One, "They have sown the wind, and they shall reap the whirlwind."

INCIDENTS, ANECDOTES, REMINISCENCES, AND POETRY

OF THE

ARMY OF THE CUMBERLAND.

Guerrillas burning Steamers on the Cumberland River.

INCIDENTS AND REMINISCENCES.

BURNING OF STEAMBOATS ON THE CUMBERLAND.—During the month of December, 1862, the water in the Cumberland was at its lowest stage. Only the lightest class of steamers could reach Nashville, and the grounding, delay, and reshipment to cross the Harpeth Shoals, some thirty miles below Nashville, was materially added to by the presence of rebel forces, here and there, along the river-banks in that vicinity. In the early part of that month, four steamers were thus destroyed in one day, and also the small gunboat William H. Sidell, which had been hastily improvised from a little stern-wheel steamboat, the work being done at Nashville during the blockade.

An eye-witness of the event thus describes it:—

"No evidences of danger were seen until, approaching Harpeth Shoals, we beheld the smoking hull of the steamer Charter and several burning houses on the south side of the river. The steamer had been burned by the guerrillas under the notorious Colonel Wade, and the houses by Lieutenant Van Dorn, of the 1st Ohio, in charge of the national gunboat Sidell. A short distance below was a large fleet of Federal steamers engaged in getting over the shoals, under the protection of the gunboat. On passing Van Dorn's fleet, I hailed him, and inquired as to danger below. He replied, 'There is no danger below: I have cleaned them out.' We passed on, the Trio a mile or so in advance. Nearly two miles below the gunboat we caught sight of the Trio lying to in a cove opposite the shoals. Knowing that she was short of fuel, we concluded that she was engaged in taking on a supply of wood. On nearing her, we saw several mounted soldiers drawn up in line along the shore. As many of them had on Federal overcoats, we thought them to be our cavalry. They hailed us, and ordered us to land.

"I at once discovered them to be guerrillas, and ordered Captain Robinson to land. The order was promptly obeyed. The current being strong, the boat did not yield readily to the turn of the pilot, making slow progress in swinging around, causing her to drag slowly down the stream. This caused the guerrillas to think that we were not going to land, and they immediately fired two heavy volleys of musketry, followed by two discharges of six-pound balls, all taking effect on the steamer.

"Your correspondent, in company with Captain Robinson and pilot Kilburn, of Covington, was standing on the hurricane-deck when the firing took place. I hailed them and told them to fire no more, as we were loaded with wounded, and would land as soon as possible. They tried to kill the man at the wheel, who stood bravely at his post amidst all the fire until the boat was tied up. On our near approach to them, I hastened down to

647

still the dreadful confusion that the firing had caused. Several ladies were on board; and, be it said to their praise, they behaved like true heroines,—no fainting or screaming,—all as quiet as could be desired under such circumstances. On my return to the front of the boat I was met by Colonel Wade, who, with a horrible oath, ordered Dr. Waterman, the surgeon in charge of the wounded, to take his d—d wounded Yankees ashore, as he would burn the boat and us too unless the order was obeyed. I instantly appealed to him in behalf of the wounded. During this time his followers had come on board and took full possession of every thing.

"Here I should like, if I could, to picture out to your readers and the world at large the awful scene of pillage and plunder that ensued. All but two or three of them were demoralized by the drink obtained, previous to our arrival, from the bar of the Trio. I will not attempt to pen-picture the scene: language fails and words are beggars in attempting to do so. Nearly one hundred of the thieving, plundering gang were engaged in rifling every thing, from the clerk's office to the chambermaid's room. For a few moments the stoutest hearts were appalled, and consternation had seized upon all. On passing around, appealing to them to desist, I met their assistant adjutant-general, in whom I recognized an old acquaintance, who instantly promised to do all in his power to save the boat and stop the plundering. He spoke to Colonel Wade, and he ordered them off the boat; but, alas! that overshadowing curse of both armies was there, in full possession of human hearts that might have been more humane had not the demon-spirit of rum hardened their natural sympathies and unchained their baser passions. In their maddened thirst for plunder they trampled on and over our poor wounded men, taking their rations, blankets, overcoats, canteens, and even money out of their pockets.

"Another steamer hove in sight,—the Parthenia, on her way to Clarksville. She was ordered ashore, and the same scene was enacted in her cabin, save the fact that she had no sick or wounded of any account, but had several passengers. The rangers at once boarded her, and, for some time, utter 'madness ruled the hour.' The Parthenia was a new steamer, costing thirty-three thousand dollars, finely finished and furnished. While engaged in rifling her and piling up combustibles on different parts of the boat to make her burn rapidly, the gunboat Sidell, spoken of elsewhere, hove in sight. Her appearance was a signal of joy to our men and of alarm to the rebels, who immediately mounted their horses, ready to run. We hailed Van Dorn, and told him to anchor in the middle of the stream, and not come between our boat and the range of the guerrillas' cannon.

"To our utter astonishment, instead of getting ready to cover himself with glory in the saving of so much property and several lives, he simply fired his revolver and then ignominiously and cowardly waved his white handkerchief in token of surrender. The rebels had fired several volleys at him, and did no harm, save the wounding of one of Van Dorn's gunners. He then ordered one of his own men to strike the colors, which order was obeyed. They then crossed over to the rebel side, who, with tremendous yells, took possession of her."

During this time the weather was cold and stormy, and many of our wounded men were left upon the river-bank, without blankets, fire, or attendants, for several hours, until another steamer arrived from Clarksville to their relief. The rebels spared one small steamer to go to Clarksville upon the captain entering into a written agreement that the boat should hereafter carry no other supplies or do any work for the Government other than sanitary work.

An Affecting Scene.—The spirit of the rebellion in Nashville is completely broken. We can say the same truly of all Tennessee. The battle of Stone River, the erection of the vast forts and fortifications at Nashville and Murfreesborough, and the complete occupation of all that country, are tangible and irresistibly converting evidences to that hitherto blind and haughty people.

During the observance of the recent order of Brigadier-General Mitchell, commanding the post of Nashville, which invited all rebel citizens to come forward and take the oath of allegiance who desired to stay there in the full enjoyment of citizens' privileges, several remarkable scenes occurred. Great crowds of rebels assembled before the office of the provost-marshal daily, eager to make their peace with the old Government. One scene is thus related by an eye-witness:—

Two prominent citizens of Edgefield, across the river from Nashville, emerged from the throng, passed into the office, and, with apparent satisfaction, took the oath. An elderly woman, plain in dress and appearance, looked on, greatly agitated. She was a Union woman. Those two prominent citizens were her neighbors. She had two sons, who were at heart Union boys if left to their better judgment and her counsels and prayers. These men had coaxed, wheedled, driven those sons into the rebel army, —where perhaps they now were, if alive. Tears streamed down her cheeks upon this occasion, and soon, quite unable to contain herself, she rushed through the crowd, wringing her hands and shouting as if in the heartiest camp-meeting frame of mind. The scene drew tears from eyes unused to weeping. Was it joy, or sorrow, or pity, or all combined, that then welled up from that poor mother's heart and found utterance?

"Come out, Sammy!"—An expedition from our army, when near New Middleton, Smith county, Tennessee, recently came suddenly upon the premises of one Sam Ellison, a vigorous conscript-agent. Taken short, he descends into a dark, deep, out-of-the-way well, hoping thus to escape. A careful search failed to reveal his hiding-place, until a *dark*-ey hint caused an examination of the well. A poor Union refugee, the pilot of the expedition, and who had been run off into the cedars by the efforts of this same agent, approached, bent over the curb, shaded his face with his hands that he might peer into the darkness below, and soon, espying the crouching object near the water, he blandly remarked,—

"Come out, Sammy; come out. We've come to call on ye: come out, my boy."

Sam came.

A Loss of Supplies.—Mike Ryan, of Company K, 21st Illinois Volunteers, was "marching on" in the line of his duty, on Tuesday evening, upon the battle-field of Stone River, when a grape-shot swept past him and tore away his haversack, which was filled with three days' rations. Without halting an instant, or changing countenance, he remarked,—

"Och, an' be jabers, if the inemy hasn't flanked me an' cut off me supplies !"

LIFE A DRAG.—Long after midnight,—perhaps two o'clock in the morning, —while in camp at Murfreesborough, the author was at General Rosecrans's head-quarters, when there seemed to be a momentary cessation of business and conversation in his room. The general leaned back in his chair, shaded the light from his face with one hand, and not only looked, but seemed to *feel* himself, the picture of weariness.

"General, you are leading a hard life," we remarked. He answered, gently,—

"Yes, rather hard; and, if this life were *all*, it would be a wretched drag."

WELL COME UP WITH.—Anderson Sharp, a well-to-do farmer living seven miles southeast of Shelbyville, owning slaves and cultivating three hundred acres of land, was very careful last fall to crib his corn in a secret place beyond reach of "the Yankees," as he alleged. In fact, however, he was equally careful to preserve it from the rebels; for, although he dearly loved their treason, he doubted the value of their currency. His negroes marvelled at this inconsistency, and betrayed his corn-piles to *both* armies. The rebels were nearest, and got the corn. However, we got the negroes!

A GALLANT CHARGE.—On the 4th day of March last, Colonel Minty, with his cavalry command, the 7th Pennsylvania Cavalry, in the advance, made a dashing charge, sabre in hand, upon a superior rebel force near Unionville, Tennessee. They killed several, and captured fifty-two prisoners. Eight of the rebel dead were found with their heads split open by the sabre. The rebels fled,—their flight, and in fact their fight, being much impeded by their haste to cast off the blue Federal overcoats with which many were clothed. This was after the issue of the order of General Rosecrans declaring that all enemies dressed in our uniform should when taken prisoners be treated as spies.

"DAR !"—The Federal engineers at Nashville resolved upon demolishing the old Blind Asylum building, in the suburbs of that city, it obstructing their works. The walls were massive, and were mined to be blown up with gunpowder. Several holes were dug at various points, the powder placed, fuses prepared, &c., and a negro laborer was stationed over each, with a light, to touch them all at the same instant, upon a given signal. Sambo was very nervous, wondering, and excited,—too much so to succeed.

Impressing the Contrabands at Church in Nashville.

At the signal moment each dashed his light upon the place and broke for shelter "like a quarter-horse." One or two of them had courage to wait and see the fuse begin to burn. "Dar! dar!" shouted they, and away they travelled. The explosion was not at all simultaneous, and the walls were breached only in spots. Two or three times was the attempt repeated, with similar results, occasioning much merriment. Not a single "American of African descent" could be induced to stay until the fuses were surely fired. "Dar! dar!" was the fearful announcement; and the engineers were forced to assume the task. In justice to Sambo, we should state, however, that a very brief acquaintance with prepared saltpetre disarms him of his fears.

THE SOLDIER'S OATH.—At Louisville, Major William H. Sidell, mustering-in officer, had just administered the usual army oath to some new recruits, when a secesh lady (may we call her Mrs. Johnson?) remarked to him, with a smiling air, but considerably impregnated with contempt,—

"Well, major, have you brought your men down to *that* depth of slavery?"

"Madam," answered he, with politest bow and smile, "that same oath your Jeff Davis, and Bragg, and most of your rebel generals, have taken, and," he added, in a low, deep voice, "*have broken!*"

GATHERING IN THE CONTRABANDS.—Our Southern brethren have been sensitive upon the negro-labor question from the commencement of the rebellion up to this time. As a general rule, they preferred losing or lending a horse rather than a slave. They feared army influences upon their chattel,—that he would become "a mean nigger." Of course the same difficulty would not arise in the army education of the horse or mule. For this reason it is—at least, we can conceive of no other—that the rebel planter has often fled, at short notice, with his negroes, leaving wife, children, mules, hogs, and household goods to the mercy of the invading Northmen. At the outset the negroes were crammed with most awful accounts of the ways of the savage Yankees, and many of the poor creatures were equally eager with their masters to fly from us.

Thus premising, we have to relate an amusing affair which occurred at Nashville last fall. Upon the commencement of the fortifications in that city, orders were given to impress all able-bodied male negroes, to be put at work upon the forts. The slaveholders of the city at once began to secrete their negroes in cellars and by-ways. The Federal officers said nothing, but resolved to bide their time,—their gangs upon the works, meanwhile, singing and wheeling away quite merrily. After several days all sensation subsided, and an occasional colored individual would be seen at an open window or shuffling around a street-corner. At length the time for action was at hand. A fine Sabbath evening came, and with it a large congregation of pious negroes, in all their Sunday array and perfumery. They felt in fine feather; for was not the city being fortified and defended, and the day of jubilee for the colored race close at hand? A hymn flowed out in harmonious cadence, equal in volume to the rolling flood of the Cumberland. A prayer was offered with great earnestness and unction, and the preacher had chosen his text, when, lo! an apparition appeared at the door,—yes, several of them! A guard of blue-coated soldiers, with muskets, entered, and announced to the startled brethren that the services of the evening would be concluded at Fort Negley. Out went the lights, as if by magic, and there was a general dive for the windows. Shrieks, howls, and imprecations went forth to the ears of darkness, rendering night truly hideous. Fancy bonnets were mashed, ribbons were rumpled, and the destruction of negro finery was enormous. Some reached the windows and crawled out, and into the hands of guards who were waiting outside. The shepherd of the flock was thus caught, it is said, while making a dive through the window, head first, butting over two "bold soger boys" as he came out. The scene was amusing indeed. And the next morning it was still more comical,—the same crowd being at work at the fort, dressed in their mussed and bedirtied finery of the previous evening, in which they had slept upon the earthworks,—they, meanwhile, being the jeer and sport of their surrounding darkey acquaintances.

It is due to these colored laborers of Nashville to add that by their labor, during some three months' time, Fort Negley and other fortifications were built. They cut the stone, laid the stone wall, wheeled and carted the earth, blasted the rock; and they performed their work cheerfully and zealously, and without any pay, except their daily rations and perhaps some clothing.

A Review of the Chivalry.—A Union prisoner at Shelbyville, on the 8th of March last, was invited by Major Clarence Prentice, commanding some rebel cavalry, to ride with him, while he inspected some regiments under the command of Colonel James Hagan, of Mississippi, acting brigadier-general. The troops were in line,—a motley, ragged set. Old Jack Falstaff, marching with his ragamuffins through Coventry, could not have presented a more tattered picture. As Major Prentice passed along, one man would be particular to hold out conspicuously a foot without boot, shoe, or even stocking; another would call his attention to elbows protruding through holes much too large for them; another would take especial care to render prominent ragged unmentionables and yawning rents therein, "gaping wide as Erebus;" and so on throughout the whole line. One tall, gaunt, long-haired fellow, whose miserable apology for a hat had no top, raised his hand, drew through the hole where the top ought to be a mass of tangled, yellow hair, and held it there at full length. The scene was almost too ridiculous for the maintenance of gravity, and only by an extraordinary effort could the inspector control himself sufficiently to sustain the dignity due the occasion.

In one of these regiments of two hundred and sixty-four men and horses, there were but *four* pair of socks; forty-seven of the men had no guns, and one hundred and forty-seven of the horses were without saddles. In the other,—styled the 8th Confederate Cavalry,—numbering two hundred and seventy-four men, two hundred and four of whom were present at review and seventy on picket-duty, one hundred and twenty-five were without hats and thirty-two without arms. Such a state of affairs seems to have disgusted the major, as in less than a month thereafter he renounced all connection with the rebels and returned to Louisville.

Bragg and his High Private.—The following incident was related to a Union man in Shelbyville, Tennessee, by Major Hunter, of the Confederate army, who formerly resided in Shelbyville, but who latterly resided some twenty miles from Helena, Arkansas. The major was fond of the story, and often repeated it.

While Bragg's troops were on their retreat from Murfreesborough, ragged, hungry, and weary, they straggled along the road for miles, with an eye to their own comfort, but a most unmilitary neglect of rules and regulations. Presently one of them espied, in the woods near by, a miserable broken-down mule, which he at once seized and proceeded to put to his use, by improvising, from stray pieces of rope, a halter and stirrups. This done, he mounted with grim satisfaction, and pursued his way. He was a wild Texas tatterdemalion, bareheaded, barefooted, and wore in lieu of a coat a rusty-looking hunting-skirt. With hair unkempt, beard unshorn, and face unwashed, his appearance was grotesque enough; but, to add to it, he drew from some receptacle his corn-cob pipe, and made perfect his happiness by indulging in a comfortable smoke.

While thus sauntering along, a company of bestarred and bespangled horsemen—General Bragg and staff—rode up, and were about to pass on, when the rather unusual appearance of the man attracted their notice. The object of their attention, however, apparently neither knew nor cared to know them, but looked and smoked ahead with careless indifference.

" Who are you?" asked the major-general.

" Nobody," was the answer.

" Where did you come from ?"

" Nowhere."

" Where are you going?"

" I don't know."

" Where do you belong ?"

"Don't belong anywhere."

" Don't you belong to Bragg's army?"

"Bragg's army! Bragg's army!" replied the chap. "Why, he's got no army! One half of it he shot in Kentucky, and the other half has just been whipped to death at Murfreesborough."

Bragg asked no more questions, but turned and spurred away.

THE UNION LADIES OF SHELBYVILLE.—Shelbyville, Tennessee, has always been known as a Union town; and the following incident shows that its ladies, at least, are willing to make known their faith by their works.

On the 4th of March last, General Van Dorn, with several thousand rebel cavalry and infantry, surprised a brigade of Federal troops below Franklin, and took twelve hundred and six of them prisoners. They were marched to Shelbyville and placed under guard at the court-house. They had scarcely arrived when it became known that they were in a famishing condition, having eaten nothing for a day and a half. Following this report came a stir and bustle in many of the Shelbyville kitchens. Ere long the Union ladies began to throng from their houses into the street, each with her servants carrying baskets, buckets, and bundles. A procession was formed, and away they marched to the court-house. As they passed along, the rebel guards eyed them askance,—some with surly looks, while others asked, "Won't you sell us some?" One or two officers seemed disposed to interfere; but the ladies persisted and prevailed. The court-house was reached and the Union soldiers fed.

It was an animated and beautiful scene, illustrative at once of the courage and the kindness of these noble-hearted women. It was no small matter to brave the taunts and jeers that assailed them on the way; but the thanks which were *looked* rather than spoken, as with bright, happy faces they distributed to the half-starved men the good cheer they had brought with them, more than repaid them for it all. And many a weary captive thanked God that day that there were still left in the old land some "who had not bowed the knee to Baal," and in fervent prayer invoked a blessing upon the heads of the noble Union women of Shelbyville.

Three months later, upon the advance of our army to Shelbyville, these Unionists welcomed us with banners and smiles and many other evidences of their heartfelt joy and gratitude.

REBEL CHARITY.—The heartlessness of the chivalry was well illustrated by a case which recently came to the notice of the Chief of Police. A Mrs. Lucy Brown, living about three miles from McMinnville, Cannon county, Tennessee, came into Nashville on the last day of March, bringing with her three children, the oldest of whom was only seven years of age. Their condition was pitiable in the extreme. Both herself and children were literally covered with rags, and were suffering from hunger and from cold. Some two weeks before, she said, Morgan's men came to her house, and, under the pretence that her husband was in the Union army, carried away every thing she had, leaving only one bed and two pieces of quilts, but not a mouthful of any thing for herself and boys to eat. To save herself from starvation, as well as to search for her husband, who was a Union refugee, she had come to Nashville.

Her wretched plight excited commiseration; and, in the absence of other suitable accommodations, she was sent to the house of Dr. W. A. Cheatham

—a brother-in-law of Morgan—to be clothed and fed,—the Chief of Police at the same time giving her several dollars with which to purchase shoes, &c. Despite the many favors which had been shown to Cheatham's family, and the forgiving courtesy and kindness with which they had been treated, this call upon them for temporary aid was responded to with a very bad grace. Mrs. Brown was left in her rags, turned into a basement room, and forced to eat and sleep with the negroes. She was closely questioned about Morgan and his men, and was told that it was not Morgan's men at all, but Federal soldiers, who had robbed her. There she remained some days, the family having nothing to say to her. Occasionally Mrs. Cheatham would bring some lady friends down to the kitchen to see her and her children, when they would question her and tell her she lied, and, with a spiteful laugh, Mrs. Cheatham would assure her friends that this Mrs. Brown was not what she was trying to palm herself off for, but only "one of old Truesdail's spies."

A SOLDIER'S PLAN OF SETTLEMENT.—The railroad from Murfreesborough to Nashville passes through what was once a fine farming-land; now, however, fences are down and gone, houses burned, and the whole country wears a desolate appearance. Gliding along in the cars, one day, past many fields which were just becoming green with tender grass, the author heard one of a lively group of soldiers remark,—

"I tell you, boys, what should be done all along here. Let Uncle Sam run his surveyor's chain all over this; then let every soldier pre-empt his one hundred and sixty acres, and it will be God's land again."

Possibly it would trouble a wordy politician in a three-hours speech to arrive at a more politic conclusion,—one that would more nearly remunerate the soldier, the sooner build up and beautify that country, and prove a more merited judgment upon a rebellious people.

GIRLS' WIT.—Upon going to the tent of the head-quarters photographer, at Murfreesborough, Tennessee, recently, to have his manly countenance painted by the sunbeams, Brigadier-General Garfield, Chief of Staff, found there a bevy of rebel girls. As he entered, with a number of military friends, they hastily left the premises. Passing out of the door, one of them slyly remarked,—

"Let John Morgan come in here, and he'll take that Yankee general much quicker than the camera can."

FORAGING A MILITARY SCIENCE.—The soldiers of the Army of the Cumberland are "heavy on drill." The manual of arms has become a habit with them, and their quickness in executing commands is a marvel akin to intuition. But especially are they worthy of commendation when foraging, either in the aggregate or upon individual responsibility. Woe unto pigs and sheep and calves and chickens when they are on the march!

Recently a Wisconsin colonel was boasting of his regiment, declaring most roundly that his boys, while marching by the flank in dress and step, could catch, kill, skin, divide, and stow away a half-grown hog unnoticed by the next company, front or rear. An Ohio captain, nothing daunted upon hearing this, said his boys were equally clever. In camp, of nights, they usually had veal or mutton. While slaughtering, they would mount their own guard, and, at the least alarm of an officer approaching, down the butchers would get upon the grass, with a blanket thrown over the carcass, around which they would be sitting demurely, intent upon a very interesting game of "euchre" or "seven-up."

THE PRAYER OF THE WICKED.—During the month of December last, and for many weeks previous, a severe drought prevailed in Tennessee. The Cumberland River was fordable in many places, the smaller streams nearly dry, and in sundry localities water for stock very scarce. During its continuance, a Union man at Shelbyville, while in attendance upon the Methodist church at that place, heard a prayer offered from the pulpit by the officiating minister, in which occurred a sentence somewhat as follows:—

"O Lord, as a nation free and independent, look down upon us in mercy and loving-kindness, and hold us within the hollow of thy hand amidst all our desolation and sorrow. Let the rays of heaven's light smile upon our fields, and the dews of beneficent mercy be shed upon our valleys. Let the rain descend to beautify and fructify the earth and to swell the rivers of waters; but, O Lord, do not raise the Cumberland sufficient to bring upon us the damnable Yankee gunboats!"

This is the correct version: it has been going the rounds of the newspapers mutilated.

REBEL PETTICOAT GOVERNMENT.—The dear ladies of the South are desperately wicked little rebels, as a whole. Very many instances have come to light within the lines of this army where the men would have abstained from and abjured the rebellion had it not been for the determined wildness of the women.

A young man, intelligent and of pleasing demeanor, when taken prisoner by our forces stated that he never was a rebel at heart, nor was his mother. He had determined to keep out of their army, and resolutely did so for a time. He soon found, however, that he was a marked man,—was jeered at and scorned by every young lady in his neighborhood. He braved it for a while; but one day matters came to a crisis. A party of girls came to his house, bringing with them shawls, dresses, and a skeleton hoop-skirt, which they left for him to put on! The dose was overpowering, and he went off at once and joined the rebel army.

The same spirit has pervaded the whole of the benighted South. There, as everywhere, the women are the purest or the worst of the race.

The Misses Smith, residing four miles from Murfreesborough, upon a recent occasion boastingly assured some Federal officers, at their dinner-table, that they, with other young ladies of that vicinity, had formed themselves into a rebel association for the express purpose of forcing every young man of their acquaintance into the army, and that they had been eminently successful in so doing. In several instances they had threatened the backward beaux with petticoat and hoop-skirt presentations.

GENERAL PALMER AND THE HOG.—Two years ago our officers were very strict in respect to foraging upon the individual hook. Chickens and pigs were held sacred, because

> "It is a sin
> To steal a pin," &c.

But a year or so of earnest war taught the nation a lesson, and this strictness has been greatly relaxed. Now it is practically "root, hog, or die" with our soldiers when in the enemy's country.

Early one morning in 1862, while at Farmington, near Corinth, Mississippi, as Brigadier- (now Major-) General Palmer was riding along his lines to inspect some breastworks that had been thrown up during the previous night, he came suddenly upon some of the boys of Company I, 27th Illinois Volunteers, who had just shot a two-hundred-pound hog, and were engaged in the interesting process of skinning it. The soldiers were startled; their chief looked astonished and sorrowful.

"Ah! a body,—a corpse. Some poor fellow gone to his last home. Well, he must be buried with military honors. Sergeant, call the officer of the guard."

The officer was speedily at hand, and received orders to have a grave dug and the body buried forthwith. The grave was soon prepared, and then the company were mustered. Pall-bearers placed the body of the dead upon a stretcher. The order was given to march, and, with reversed arms and funeral tread, the solemn procession of sixty men followed the body to the grave. Not a word passed nor a muscle of the face stirred while the last rites of sepulture were being performed. The ceremony over, the general and his staff waved their *adieux*, and were soon lost in the distance.

The philosophy of the soldier is usually equal to the emergency. He has read and pondered. He now painfully realizes that flesh is as grass, and that life is but a shadow. But he thinks of the *resurrection*, and his gloom passes away. So with the philosophic boys of Company I, 27th Illinois. Ere their general was fairly seated at his own breakfast-table, there was a raising of the dead, and savory pork-steaks were frying in many a camp-pan.

A REBEL "Pow-wow" DENIED.—A day or two after the battle of Stone River, and while burial-parties were yet busy upon the field, a minister of the gospel, of secession proclivities, applied to the general commanding at Murfreesborough for permission to take the body of the rebel General James

40

Rains to Nashville—his former home—for burial.   General Rosecrans, alive to the courtesies of military life, readily consented,—when it was intimated to him that the secessionists of Nashville were intending to make the funeral a rebel ovation.   The idea stung him.   Turning to the applicant in his earnest, brusque manner, he remarked,—

"I wish it to be distinctly understood that there is to be no fuss made over this affair,—none at all, sir.   I won't permit it, sir, in the face of this bleeding army.   My own officers are here, dead and unburied, and the bodies of my brave soldiers are yet on the field, among the rocks and cedars. You may have the corpse, sir; but remember distinctly that you can't have an infernal secession 'pow-wow' over it in Nashville!"

CONQUERING BY STARVATION.—Starving out an enemy may at times be a sure process; but in a country of such vast extent as rebeldom it is certainly a slow one.   However, signs ominous of such a result have been visible, and were the subject of a recent discussion by a party of officers at the head-quarters of Major-General Sheridan, near Murfreesborough.   The general was not as sanguine on the point as many others, and remarked,—

"Gentlemen, don't let us be as mistaken in this as I was once in my Missouri campaigning.   The word went out, all over the State, that there was a great scarcity of salt; there was no salt for meat, nor even for bread. Because of these reports, I was extremely cautious to shut down on the salt-trade in my rear.   Not a bushel of salt would I pass into or beyond my lines.   In this I thought I was doing good service; but imagine my surprise and hearty disgust, on entering Springfield, Missouri, to find that the only article left behind by Price and his men in their hasty flight, and of which I found large quantities there, was—*salt!*"

A REBEL BEECHER.—The Beechers are known throughout the Union as men of talent and of positive views,—many term them extreme, especially on the slavery question.   But this rebellion has even cut in twain the family of the Beechers.   During the battle of Stone River, Dr. Charles Bunce, of Galesburg, Illinois, assistant surgeon of the 59th Illinois Volunteers, remained upon the field, busily engaged in caring for his wounded men, and with them was made a prisoner.   Soon after, while surrounded by a group of rebel officers to whom he had been introduced, he remarked, in the course of conversation, that he was surprised to find even New Yorkers among the officers of the Southern army.

"Worse than that, sir," said a bystander.   "In me you see a man from Massachusetts and Illinois.   My name is Edward A. Beecher, son of Edward Beecher, President of Knox College at Galesburg, Illinois.   Henry Ward Beecher is my uncle."

"Why, Galesburg is my town, and I know your father well," replied the Illinois doctor.

The pleasure of the acquaintance thus formed was mutual, and the doctor soon found that he had met with a genuine Beecher in appearance and manners. This son of Edward the eminent was a quartermaster in General Cheatham's division, and previous to the war had practised law at Memphis, Tennessee. He was not at all bitter in his feelings nor harsh in his views, yet was withal a most determined rebel.

A SOUTHERN "LADY."—A friend visiting the camps near Major-General Sheridan's head-quarters at Murfreesborough, several weeks after the battle of Stone River, heard the following incident of Southern society related by Colonel J. R. Miles, of the 27th Regiment Illinois Volunteers. The topic of discussion was the negro, " as usual."

The colonel said he had been rather sold on one occasion down in Alabama, last year, while the Federal troops were occupying the line of the Memphis & Charleston Railroad. His command was detailed to guard a bridge, near which lay large, rich plantations. On a pleasant Sabbath afternoon, as he reclined listlessly in his tent, a carriage drove up. The horses were of the finest, the coach elegant, and the driver with gloves, &c. *à la mode*. A beautifully-dressed lady was the occupant,—a little dark in feature, perhaps, but still fair. Her hair was in ringlets, a " love of a bonnet" on her head, a large pin glittering upon her breast, and jewelry displayed elsewhere in profusion. The colonel walked to the carriage with due alacrity, saluted the lady most respectfully, and awaited her commands. She said she resided on a plantation near by, and had come to inquire about a straw-cutting machine that had been borrowed or taken by the soldiers. The colonel made due explanation, and said the machine should speedily be returned.

"I hope so," said she; "for Master Mosely needs it sadly."

"What's that? Did you say *Master* Mosely ?"

" Yes, sir, I did."

" You don't say that he is your master,—that you are a slave,—do you ?"

The "lady"—we suppose we must continue to call her a "lady," for consistency's sake—smiled quite charmingly, as she replied, calmly,—

" Yes, sir."

The colonel took a second glance at the carriage, the horses, the silvered harness, the driver, and then at the finely-dressed person within, and was completely astounded, albeit he was born and raised in Kentucky, near the Tennessee line, not more than thirty miles from Nashville.

" Pray," queried he, further, " is your master a married man ?"

" No : he is a widower."

" Well, does he treat you as his wife ?"

She did not answer this question direct, but bade the driver start on, and, as she was driven off, remarked,—

" I live in his house."

Subsequent inquiries revealed the following state of the case. A Virginia planter had sold this girl to go South, upon the express agreement that she was to be handsomely provided for,—the general supposition being that she was his child. The trader brought her to this widower's designedly, and doubled his money in the trade. She was now perhaps thirty years old, and certainly a very handsome woman. Mosely was a rich planter, living on Mallard Creek, about half-way between Courtland and Decatur, and had a family by his first wife, one of whom was a daughter, now some sixteen years of age.

A REBEL STORY.—At the dinner-table of Mrs. Jernigan, a Union lady in Shelbyville, Tennessee, and whose husband is a refugee from his home as we write, the following incident was related, during the month of March, 1863, by a rebel officer of John Morgan's command, latterly in the rebel Quartermaster's Department.

Some months ago, a Federal officer in charge of a small expedition caught two bushwackers and had them hung. They belonged to Morgan's command; and he vowed vengeance on the first prisoners he should capture. Soon afterwards he took seventeen Federal soldiers prisoners, and put his threat into execution. Six he shot, seven he hung, and four were despatched with an axe,—"as you would kill hogs," the narrator said.

The minutiæ of the tale we will suppress, in the name of humanity. The narrator, however, gloated over the manner in which the poor soldiers pleaded for their lives, or for at least an honorable soldier's death, and, in a spirit of bravado, dwelt leisurely upon the horrid details. This evidence has been preserved to fill one of the darkest pages in the history of the accursed rebellion.

SECESH RELIGION.—As two of the army secret police were passing the house of a certain Mrs. Harris, a secession woman of Edgefield, opposite Nashville, Tennessee, whose husband had been arrested and imprisoned the previous week upon the charge of stealing Government horses and running them South, they were espied by her from her window. Stepping to the door, she calls to them and invites them in. They decline the invitation, because, they say, they are in a great hurry. She then inquires about her husband, and is told that he is safe—in jail at Nashville.

"But didn't you tell me that you would help him all you could, when you came to see me about him the other day?" she asked.

"Yes," was the reply; "and we did help him right well. He is where the dogs won't bite him now," was the jeering rejoinder.

The woman was in a rage in a moment. She had been imposed upon; and she burst forth with the angry exclamation,—

"Oh, you thieving Yankee scoundrels! that's the way you serve a poor woman, is it?"—and so on for full three minutes, ending her harangue with the following unanswerable declaration:—"Oh, I never had any religion, and I never expect to have any until you two knaves and that wicked old Truesdail, your master, are all hung. Then I shall have religion. I shall jump and scream for very joy."

The policemen hurriedly "skedaddled," amid a general opening of doors, windows, and ears in the neighborhood.

A PRACTICAL CAMP-JOKE.—The soldier in his best estate is full of fun. In a tent in the camp of the 11th Indiana Battery, near Murfreesborough, in the absence of chairs a rude bench had been constructed by placing a board upon cross-legs. The board was soon found too limber to bear up the crowd which daily enjoyed its comforts, and was, in consequence, strengthened by laying another thick plank over it. A roguish sergeant one day removed this top plank, bored a number of auger-holes nearly through the bottom board, filled them with powder, laid a train from one to another, prepared his fuse, and then replaced the plank. Shortly after, the bench, as usual, was filled with his unsuspecting comrades,—when he reached down and touched the fuse with his lighted cigar. Of course, there was an explosion just about that time, which hoisted the party as would a petard, upsetting the stove and tent-furniture, knocking down the tent, and enveloping all in smoke and dire confusion.

A SOLDIER'S ARMISTICE.—One of the most remarkable features of this war is the absence of vindictiveness among the soldiery of the two sections. When parties have met with flags of truce, the privates will freely converse, drink from each others' canteens, and even have a social game of cards in a fence-corner. Especially upon picket-duty has this friendliness broken in upon discipline,—so much so that in many instances orders have been issued strictly forbidding such intercourse. The following incident is related by a member of the 8th Kentucky:—

"On the 27th of December, our army arrived at Stewart's Creek, ten miles distant from Murfreesborough. The following day, being Sabbath, and our general being devout, nothing was done, except to cross a few companies on the left as skirmishers, our right being watched by the enemy's, as well as ours,—both extending along the creek on opposite sides. Despite of orders, our boys would occasionally shut an eye at the Confederates, who were ever ready to take the hint. This was kept up until evening, when the boys, finding they were effecting nothing at such long range, quit shooting, and concluded they would 'talk it out,'—whereupon the following occurred:—

" *Federal* (at the top of his voice).—' Halloo, boys! what regiment?'

" *Confederate.*—' 8th Confederate.'

" *Federal.*—' Bully for you!'

" *Confederate.*—' What's your regiment?'

" *Federal.*—' 8th and 21st Kentucky.'

" *Confederate.*—' All right.'

" *Federal.*—' Boys, have you got any whiskey?'

" *Confederate.*—' Plenty of her.'

" *Federal.*—' How'll you trade for coffee ?'

" *Confederate.*—' Would like to accommodate you, but never drink it while the worm goes.'

" *Federal.*—' Let's meet at the creek and have a social chat.'

" *Confederate.*—' Will you shoot ?'

" *Federal.*—' Upon the honor of a gentleman, not a man shall. Will you shoot ?'

" *Confederate.*—' I give you as good assurance.'

" *Federal.*—' Enough said. Come on.'

" *Confederate.*—' Leave your arms.'

" *Federal.*—' I have left them. Do you leave yours?'

" *Confederate.*—' I do.'

" Whereupon both parties started for the creek to a point agreed upon. Meeting almost simultaneously, we (the Federals) were, in a modulated tone, addressed in the usual unceremonious style of a soldier, by—

" *Confederate.*—' Halloo, boys ! how do you make it ?'

" *Federal.*—' Oh, bully ! bully !'

" *Confederate.*—' This is rather an unexpected armistice.'

" *Federal.*—' That's so.'

" *Federal.*—' Boys, are you going to make a stand at Murfreesborough ?'

" *Confederate.*—' That is a leading question : notwithstanding, I will venture to say it will be the bloodiest ten miles you ever travelled.'

" Thus the conversation went on for some time, until a Confederate captain (Miller, of General Wheeler's cavalry) came down, requesting an exchange of papers. On being informed we had none, he said he would give us his anyhow, and, wrapping a stone in the paper, threw it across. Some compliments were passed, when the captain suggested that, as it was getting late, we had better quit the conference ; whereupon both parties, about twenty each, began to leave, with, ' Good-bye, boys : if ever I meet you in battle, I'll spare you.' So we met and parted, not realizing that we were enemies."

A VANDAL GENERAL.—Brigadier-General Morton, of the Pioneer Brigade, has a *penchant* for pulling down houses in rebeldom, where they stand in the way of his military operations. The most costly edifice speedily tumbles if obstructing the range of artillery from his fortifications. Two hours' or half a day's notice will be given, and, whether vacated or not, at the expiration of that time off goes the roof. While superintending the building of Fort Negley, at Nashville, General Morton found it necessary to remove many houses in the outskirts of the city. This gave him quite a local reputation,—such as it was,—but of which he was totally regardless. One morning early he rode about the suburbs of Nashville with some friends, to show them the works, pointing, as he rode along, with his hand in divers directions. The inhabitants, now constantly on the *qui vive* for military operations, were terrified,—were sure he was giving orders to his staff to pull down houses and make new streets; and several of them, in a most excited and in some instances quite ludicrous manner, appealed to him and to the city authorities to spare them.

A Foraging-Incident.—During the month of March, 1863, an extensive foraging and reconnoitring expedition, comprising several hundred men and teams of Major-General Reynolds's division, went out from Murfrees-borough towards Lebanon, through a fertile and well-stocked country, the people of which were mainly intensely rebel. The expedition was very successful, bringing back corn, fodder, poultry, pigs, and cattle innumerable,—also some four hundred head of horses and mules, to aid in mounting Colonel Wilder's infantry brigade. While out upon this expedition, the train came to the premises of an active, wealthy, bitter old rebel,—one who had made himself very busy in procuring volunteers for the rebel army, and particularly obnoxious to his Union neighbors by assisting the rebel agents to hunt down conscripts. He looked rather astonished when our advance cavalry was followed off by his horses. The quartermaster came next, with his mules and the contents of his corn-cribs. When the commissary marched by in charge of the gentleman's extra-fat cattle, "secesh," in great alarm, wanted to know if we were not going to pay for his "goods." "We are not paying money at present to any one," blandly replied the quartermaster. "Well, but you will give me a receipt for them?" "Certainly, sir: here are your vouchers already made out." "Secesh" read them, apparently well pleased, until he came to the inexorable words, "to be paid at the close of the war, upon proof of loyalty." "Well, if that is the case," said he, "they may go to the d—l;" and, turning to a couple of his darkies, who were looking on with open mouths, he administered to them a few vigorous kicks *a posteriori*, exclaiming, "—— you, you go too!"

The General at Review.—When the commander-in-chief of the Army of the Cumberland rides out to review his troops, there is usually something of a pleasant as well as instructive character going on. Upon his appearing, the welkin rings with the hearty cheers of the troops. When dressed in line, the general occasionally passes along in front, scanning each man closely and with a skilful and practised eye, noticing in an instant any thing out of place in their dress or accoutrements. He always keeps a sharp look-out for his officers, holding them accountable for the conduct of the men. On review a short time since, he gave a forcible illustration of his ideas on the subject. He noticed a private whose knapsack was very much awry, and drew him from the ranks, calling at the same time for his captain, who approached. "Captain, I am sorry to see you don't know how to strap a knapsack on a soldier's back." "But I didn't do it, general." "Oh, you didn't? Well, hereafter you had better do it yourself, or see that it is done correctly by the private. I have nothing more to say to him. I shall hold you responsible, sir, for the appearance of your men." "But if I can't make them attend to these matters?" said the officer. "Then, if you *can't*, you had better leave the service."

When he finds occasion to "jog" a soldier for some remissness, he will do it effectually, and yet in a manner so genial and kindly that no offence is taken, but rather his men admire him the more. For example, reviewing a brigade recently, he came to a good-looking private whose shoes were quite too much the worse for wear,—albeit there were hundreds of boxes of shoes then in the quartermaster's department of our army. General Rosecrans halted and inquired into the case. The soldier stated that he had applied time and again, but could draw no shoes. The captain came up: he said he had tried his utmost, and *he* could get none. "Bad work, sir! very bad work! It won't do, sir!—it sha'n't do, sir!" remarked the general: "your men must have comfortable clothing. I want all my men to stir up their captains, and I want the captains to stir up their colonels, and I want the colonels to keep at their generals, and then let the generals come to me and stir me up, and keep stirring up, all of you, until these needless evils are remedied. That's the way to do it!"

Upon another occasion, General Rosecrans noticed a private without a canteen, but otherwise quite neatly arrayed. "Ah, here's a good soldier; all right,—first-rate,—with one little exception. Good clothes and good arms: he marches, and drills, and fights, and eats. But he don't drink. That's queer; and I fear he won't hold out on a pinch. March all day in the heat and dust, yet don't want to drink! Rather afraid of a break-down here. Better have the canteens, boys, and well filled, too!" And he passes on, leaving a lesson and a smile.

At the Grave.—Upon the battle-field of Stone River the author saw a Northern father standing with folded arms and clouded yet firm countenance, while assistants were raising the body of his only son, that he might return with it to the home in the land of prairie and lake. What Cato said of his boy fallen in battle might well have been repeated by that father:—

> "Thanks to the gods! my boy has done his duty.
> Welcome, my son! There set him down, my friends,
> Full in my sight, that I may view at leisure
> The bloody corpse, and count those glorious wounds.
> How beautiful is death when earn'd by virtue!
> Who would not be that youth? What pity 'tis
> That we can die but once to save our country!
> Why sits that sadness on your brow, my friends?
> I should have blush'd if Cato's house had stood
> Secure and flourish'd in a civil war."

The Contrabands at Nashville.—The reader will remember that upon the retreat of General Buell's army to Kentucky in pursuit of Bragg, Nashville was left with but a small garrison, and fortifications were at once com-

Impressing Negroes to work on the Nashville Fortifications.

menced with alacrity and vigor by the officer in command. Every able-bodied negro in the city whom he could lay hands upon was "pressed" and put upon the work. Barber-shops and kitchens were visited, and their inmates taken "willy-nilly." The Commercial Hotel was thus cleared of servants one morning: there was no dinner for many an expectant guest, and the house was closed. By such means a force of two thousand negroes were soon at work upon Fort Negley. Every description of vehicle—milk-wagons, coal-carts, express-wagons, open carriages, &c.—was also impressed. Our artist has given the scene on the opposite page.

To the credit of the colored population be it said, they worked manfully and cheerfully, with hardly an exception, and yet lay out upon the works of nights under guard, without blankets, and eating only army-rations. They worked in squads, each gang choosing its own officers; and it was amusing to hear their captains exclaim to the wheelbarrow-men, "Let dem buggies roll, brudder Bones and Felix;" or, "You niggas ovah dah, let dem picks fall easy, or dey'll hurt somefin," &c. &c. When the attack upon the city was threatened, many of these negroes came to the officer of the day and asked for arms to help beat off the rebels,—a request he was unable to grant, but assigned to them their places behind the works, with axes, picks, and spades, in case the enemy should come to close quarters.

WANT OF CONFIDENCE.—A shrewd negro blacksmith in Shelbyville, Tennessee, had accumulated by his labor some seven hundred dollars in Confederate shinplasters. Anxious to invest it in something promising a more certain return for his toil, he recently gave the entire pile for a sorry-looking horse and buggy. A Confederate officer, hearing of the occurrence, remarked to him,—

"Bill Keyes, you are a fool!"

"Perhaps I am, sir," replied Bill; "but I'll be cussed if your Confederate stuff shall die on my hands!"

"KISSING A NIGGER."—A young officer upon the staff of one of our generals, who was temporarily sojourning at head-quarters in the Zollicoffer House, on High Street, Nashville, one day stopped before the door of a neighboring house to admire and caress a beautiful little girl. She was fair, bright, and active; her hair was in ringlets, and she was neatly dressed. Imagine the emotions of our kind-hearted officer when a young lady remarked to him, with a perceptible sneer,—

"You seem to be very fond of kissing niggers."

"Good gracious!" was the startled reply: "you don't call that child a nigger, do you?"

"Yes, I do. She is nothing else."

The officer took another glance at the child, who seemed even more fair than the young lady, and turned away, reflecting upon some of the "peculiarities" of Southern society.

THE IRISH SENTINEL.—A son of the Green Isle, a new member of Colonel Gillam's Middle Tennessee Regiment, while stationed at Nashville recently, was detailed on guard-duty on a prominent street of that city. It was his first experience at guard-mounting, and he strutted along his beat apparently with a full appreciation of the dignity and importance of his position. As a citizen approached, he shouted,—

"Halt! Who comes there?"

"A citizen," was the response.

"Advance, citizen, and give the countersign."

"I haven't the countersign; and, if I had, the demand for it at this time and place is something very strange and unusual," rejoined the citizen.

"An', by the howly Moses, ye don't pass this way at all till ye say Bunker Hill," was Pat's reply.

The citizen, appreciating the "situation," advanced and cautiously whispered in his ear the necessary words.

"Right! Pass on." And the wide-awake sentinel resumed his beat.

A DODGE FOR A PASS.—Our general has ordered that officers' and soldiers' wives shall stay at home, or, at least, advises them that they had better not come out to the army at Murfreesborough. There are no hotels, no nice eatables, none of the comforts of life, here. On the contrary, many ugly sights and smells will be encountered; and, on the whole, home will be a much more agreeable place. Hence the dear ladies can get no passes to come,—sad fact, but very necessary denial.

But an officer's wife is shrewd. If she can circumvent the epaulet and shoulder-straps, 'tis done; and she takes not a little delight in the operation, One of them recently telegraphed from Louisville to General Garfield, Chief of Staff, that her husband, an artillery officer, was very sick,—perhaps dying,— and that she must see him, and requested the general to authorize the issuing to her of a pass to Murfreesborough. The general's heart was touched; but, knowing nothing of the matter, he referred it to Colonel Barnett, Chief of Artillery. The colonel, too, sympathized with the distressed wife, and kindly sent an orderly out to the husband's battery to inquire into his condition, that the devoted wife might be advised thereof. Speedily the husband himself came in, with astonishment depicted in his face. Something's the matter, somewhere or somehow, he doesn't exactly know what.

"How do you do?" asks the Artillery Chief.

"First-rate, sir."

"Where have you been of late?"

"At my battery,—on duty."

"Have you not been sick lately?"

"No, indeed! Never had better health in my life."

"Quite sure of it, are you?"

"Of course I am."

"You have been on duty all the time? Haven't you been absent from your command at all?"

"Not a day."

"Perfectly well now,—no consumption, liver-complaint, fever, spleen, or Tennessee quickstep? eh?"

"Certainly not. Why do you ask?"

In reply to this query the telegram of his anxious wife was handed to him. He read it, looked down and pondered for a moment in silent wonder at the ingenuity of woman, then called for a bottle of wine, and a general "smile" circulated among the bystanders. The loving wife was informed by telegraph that her husband was in no danger,—in fact, was doing remarkably well. Thus she was circumvented for a time. Yet, to "vindicate the truth of history," we must add that she gained her point in some other way,—what Yankee wife will not?—and made her visit successfully.

THE following direction upon a letter which passed through the post-office from Murfreesborough we quote:—

> "Haste away, old engine, thou fiery steed!
> Bear me to *C. E. Haines* with lightning speed:
> You will find him engaged at work on his farm,
> As busy as a bee, and doing no harm,
> While receiving a farmer's hard-earn'd bounty
> From the folks of *Clarksborough, Gloucester county,*
> *New Jersey.*"

THE ROMANCE OF WAR.—The following order is said to have originated at the head-quarters of that correct disciplinarian, Major-General Rosecrans:—

"HEAD-QUARTERS DEPARTMENT OF THE CUMBERLAND, April 17, 1863.

"GENERAL :—The general commanding directs me to call your attention to a flagrant outrage committed in your command,—a person having been admitted inside your lines without a pass and in violation of orders. The case is one which calls for your personal attention, and the general commanding directs that you deal with the offending party or parties according to law.

"The medical director reports that an orderly sergeant in Brigadier-General ——'s division *was to-day delivered of a baby,*—which is in violation of all military law and of the army regulations. No such case has been known since the days of Jupiter.

"You will apply the proper punishment in this case, and a remedy to prevent a repetition of the act."

THE OVERTON FAMILY.—At the breaking-out of the rebellion, John Overton was one of the wealthiest men in Tennessee. His plantation, seven miles south of Nashville, embraced several thousand acres of land, with buildings and improvements exhibiting the finest taste. Although the whole family were known to be violent secessionists, the first blast of war swept by without injury to them. Their crops were untouched, their groves and lawns were unscathed, and, while others felt the iron hand of war, theirs was still the abode of luxury and plenty. The plantation was left nominally in the care of Mrs. Overton, her husband and sons being in the rebel army. This, however, did not prevent her asking and obtaining unlimited protection from the Federal authorities.

Soon after General Negley assumed command of Nashville, information was received that a large amount of rebel stores, consisting of horseshoe iron and nails, was concealed at this place; and a detachment of the 11th Michigan Infantry, under command of Captain Hood, was sent to seize the goods. Arriving at the house, situated in a beautiful grove at some distance from the road, the captain halted his men outside of the door-yard, caused them to order arms and remain in place, and announced himself at the door. The summons was answered by a lady, when the following colloquy ensued:—

"Is Mr. Overton at home, madam?"

"No, sir: he is with the Confederate army," was the lady's answer.

"I presume he is a rebel, then?"

"Yes, sir: he is a rebel all over."

"Well, madam, I wish to see some person who is in charge of the place. I am ordered to search for articles contraband of war."

"I am Mrs. Overton. You can search the place if you wish; but you will not find any thing contraband. I wish, however, you would keep the soldiers away from the house."

The captain assured her that no depredations would be committed by the soldiers, who were still standing at their arms, and added,—

"I will commence by searching under the floor of the meat-house."

The lady opened her eyes with astonishment. Recovering herself, she replied,—

"There is no use of having any words about it. You will find some horseshoes there."

And they were found. About two tons of valuable iron was unearthed and turned over to the Government.

In the fall of 1862 Rosecrans's victorious army relieved Nashville, and remained a few days in the city. Early in December a general advance was made, and the left wing of the army encamped on the Overton place, and it was then known as "Camp Hamilton." The camp-fires of the Union army were lighted on every part of the farm, and the rights of private property gave way to the stern necessities of war. Grove and woodland resounded with the sturdy strokes of the axeman, and disappeared. Fences were destroyed, and the crops and stock were taken for the necessary use of the army, and receipts given, to be paid when the owner should "establish his loyalty." The place which in peaceful days had blossomed as the rose was soon a desolate waste, with its palatial mansion standing "alone in its glory."

The general commanding doubtless chose the camp with reference to its strategic importance in his approach on Murfreesborough; but by the natural course of events its rebel owners learned what it is to "sow the storm and reap the whirlwind."

A REBEL WOMAN NONPLUSSED.—Last winter a forage-train went out of Nashville, and two or three of the Michigan soldiers guarding it called at a house for dinner. The woman, ready to take their money and get their favor, at once prepared it. While they were eating, she thought it a favorable moment for conversation, and propounded the usual question of Secessia :—

"What in the world did all you people come down here to fight us for?"

"The fact is, madam," quickly answered one of her guests, dropping his knife and fork, leaning back in his chair and looking her calmly in the face, "we understood your folks were going to free all your negroes and send them up North, and we don't want them and won't have them. So we've come down here to put a stop to it."

The old lady was silenced by this spiking of her guns.

THE OVERSEER AND THE WATERMELONS.—While marching from Tuscumbia to Courtland, last summer, with a portion of his command, the late Colonel Roberts, of the 42d Illinois Regiment, halted with his escort at a plantation by the roadside, for refreshment of some kind. No white person was about but the overseer, and he was surly and crabbed enough.

"Are there any watermelons about?" asked the colonel.

"I've got none," doggedly answered the overseer.

"Well, if you haven't any, hasn't somebody on the place?"

"I don't know. Shouldn't wonder if the niggers had some. You can find out by asking them."

"Look here, sirrah!" exclaimed the gallant colonel, now somewhat irritated, "these airs you are putting on are about played out in this country. Tell your negroes to bring out some of those melons, and do it quick."

The command was too imperative to be disregarded, and the overseer started off. In a few minutes he returned with the negroes and a number of fine, large melons. The party ate freely of them, and, when all were disposed of, the colonel turned to one of the negroes and asked,—

"Boy, were those your melons?"

"Yeas, sah! I growed 'em."

"All right. What's your charge?"

"Reck'n dey am wuth a dollah, sah."

"Cheap enough! Now, Mr. Overseer, pay that boy a dollar."

"What for?" growled out the overseer.

"Because I tell you to, and because you have acted the dog instead of the gentleman. Hand over the dollar forthwith."

The dollar was paid to Sambo, and the colonel rode off, leaving the overseer standing in the porch, a little wiser, if not a better, man.

NEGRO EQUALITY ILLUSTRATED.—Quite recently, at a Louisville boarding-house, a lady of Northern birth and education, but a bitter rebel, was reading to a mixed company an absurd account of some Northern women landing at Hilton Head, South Carolina, and embracing an old negress, calling her "sister," &c. The lady was triumphantly vindictive, and exclaimed to a Federal captain,—

"What do you think of that? Isn't that a beautiful specimen of your negro equality?"

The captain was annoyed, and hardly knew what to say. He said nothing, in fact, but turned and walked to the window. Glancing out, he saw on the opposite sidewalk a group of negroes enjoying themselves in the sun as only negroes can. They were of all sizes and all shades of color,—some almost white. Smiling at the thought that it was now his turn, he said to the rebel lady,—

"Will you step to the window a moment?"

"Certainly," (suiting the act to the word.)

"Look there. Do you see that?"

"See what, sir?"

"Why, that black-yellow-white group on the other side."

"Certainly I do. What is there strange about it?"

"Oh, nothing, I suppose: only one would think there must have been considerable negro equality practised by the white people of the South, as well as those of the North."

The lady "retired," and thereafter was somewhat less insulting in her demonstrations.

A FIGHTING PARSON.—Colonel Granville Moody, of the 74th Ohio, is a famous Methodist preacher from Cincinnati. He is something over fifty, six feet and two or three inches, of imposing presence, with a fine, genial face and prodigious vocal range. The reverend colonel, who proved himself a fighting parson of the first water, was hit four times at the battle of Murfreesborough, and will carry the marks of battle when he goes back to the altar. His benevolence justifies his military flock in the indulgence of sly humor at his expense; but he never permits them to disturb his equanimity. Several battle-anecdotes of him are well authenticated. Not long ago, General Negley merrily accused him of using heterodox expletives in the ardor of conflict.

"Is it a fact, colonel," inquired the general, "that you told the boys to 'give 'em hell'?"

"How?" replied the colonel, reproachfully: "that's some more of the boys' mischief. I told them to give the rebels 'Hail Columbia;' and they have perverted my language."

The parson, however, had a sly twinkle in the corner of his eye, which left his hearers in considerable doubt.

Our Western circuit-preachers are known as stentors. Where others are emphatic, they roar in the fervor of exhortation, especially when they come in with their huge "Amen." This fact must be borne in mind to appreciate the story. The colonel's mind was saturated with piety and fight. He had already had one bout with the rebels, and given them "Hail Columbia." They were renewing the attack. The colonel braced himself for the shock. Seeing his line in fine order, he thought he would exhort them briefly. The rebels were coming swiftly. Glancing first at the foe, then at the lads, he said, quietly, "Now, my boys, fight for your country and your God," and, raising his voice to thunder-tones, he exclaimed, in the same breath, "AIM LOW!" Says one of his gallant fellows, "I thought for an instant it was a frenzied ejaculation from the profoundest depths of the 'Amen corner.'" Any day now you may hear the lads of the 74th roaring, "Fight for your country and your God—aim low!"

A "NEVER-DID-ANY-THING" REBEL.—Rebels in Tennessee are of as many shades and dyes as are the negroes. Some are in the army, some are dodging about acting as spies, and some stay at home, invite Union soldiers to their houses, treat them kindly, and at night repair to the nearest rebel camps and give an account of Federal movements, strength, and, if possible, destination. Of all classes of rebels, these "I never did any thing"s are regarded by our army as the most contemptible. The following incident well illustrates their character and disposition.

About the middle of April last, as a body of our cavalry, under command of Colonel Minty, were passing a fine country mansion whose owner was known to be one of the heartiest sympathizers with rebellion, the force halted for an hour at this house, and the colonel sent to this man for some forage. As he did so, this gentleman walked over pompously to that officer and presented a "safeguard," showing that he was entitled to the protection of the United States Government and that nothing in his possession was to be molested. Minty, as a good soldier would, called his men back. Matters went on well for about half an hour, and every thing on his premises was held sacred; when, lo! a magazine exploded. A detachment of "Lincoln hirelings" had had the impudence to desecrate the carpeted floor of this hitherto sacred mansion and ruthlessly take therefrom two of "Jeff's boys," who were neatly ensconced in a cupboard. At this discovery the Union troops helped themselves, plentifully, to food for man and beast. The planter now stalked out,—not with a dignified and pompous air, as on the former occasion, but with "solitary step, and slow,"—and approached the colonel, who immediately asked,—

"Well, sir, did you ever do any thing in your life to injure the Government?"

"Wa-all, I reckon not; and, you see, they are taking all my fodder."

"Yes, sir; and I think we'll take you also."

"Wa-all, now, colonel, you see, sir——[Here he was interrupted by Colonel Minty.]

"Yes, sir, I see two rebel soldiers, one of whom I had before in irons, but escaped. The other decoyed one of my sergeants, by pledging his honor that if he went with him across the field, nothing should happen him; and I have not seen that sergeant since, sir."

"Them boys you see, sir, one is my nephew and the other a discharged soldier."

"We'll see about that, sir."

Then, calling up the prisoners, the colonel asked them if they were rebel soldiers. Both acknowledged that they were, and belonged to Dick McCann's band. The planter hung his head, as Colonel Minty resumed,—

"Now, sir, what do you think of yourself? Did you ever 'do any thing' in your life? How can a man of your age have the impudence to tell me, before these officers and men, that you never aided or abetted the rebellion, when you have done every thing in your power to assist McCann, Forrest, Morgan, and Wharton? You have gone further than this, even. You have given up your son and horses to McCann, and boasted that you laid him on the altar of his country. You are a sorry kind of a Spartan, sir; but, before I leave, allow me to give you this wholesome advice. Do you see that railroad?"

"I do, sir."

"Well, sir, should any thing happen to that road within three miles on either side, I will burn your house, and take every thing you have got. Do you mind that?"

The planter looked melancholy, and, after a pause, faintly said,—

"I will try and do every thing I can to prevent any accidents on the road."

"That will do, sir. You may leave." And he did leave, at a double quick.

———————

BEATING THEM AT THEIR OWN GAME.—Colonel Wilder, of the old 17th Indiana Regiment, and now commanding a brigade of mounted infantry, is a terror to the rebels. He roams through the country at will, and is always where they least expect him. Among other good things, he has invented a plan to capture rebel pickets, which is quite original,—certainly new to the present generation.

A dozen resolute men advance nearly within sight of the pickets. All but one conceal themselves. This man dons a butternut dress and advances. He beckons to the pickets. Without suspicion or fear, they come on to meet him. Suddenly the rebel picket sees men concealed behind the rocks on both sides of him. He is quietly told to uncap his rifle and let it full without any noise. Thus he remains in the road, as though nothing had happened, and on comes another and another, until ten or twelve are captured. In this way, on a recent occasion, Wharton's pickets were quietly gobbled up, and an enemy suddenly appeared before him as though they had dropped from the clouds.

A BRAVE BOY IN BATTLE.—During the battle of Friday, at Stone River, General Rousseau rode up to Loomis's battery, and saw there a youth of the battery holding horses, and in the midst of a very tempest of shot and shell. He was so unconscious of fear and so elated and excited, that, being debarred from better occupation than holding horses, his high spirits found vent in shouting out songs and dancing to the music. The general was so pleased with his whole deportment that he rode up to him and said, "Well done, my brave boy! let me shake hands with you." A few days after the fight, General Rousseau visited the camp of the battery, and, mentioning the circumstance to the commanding officer, expressed a desire to see the youth again. "Step out, McIntire," said the officer. The youth came forward, blushing deeply. The general again commended his conduct, and said, "I shook hands with you on the battle-field; and now I wish to do it again, in the presence of your brother soldiers. May you carry the same brave spirit through the war, and come out safely at last, as you are sure to come out honorably." The general then again shook his hand warmly, in the presence of his officers and of his companions.

A PASS TO RAISE GEESE.—An old lady at Nashville, country-raised, from down in Williamson county somewhere, had long been cooped up in that devoted city, and desired to pass the blockade into Dixie. So she seasoned up and roasted a bribe, which she hoped, with a plentiful use of smiles and "soft sawder," would gain her point. In due time she arrived at the headquarters of Lieutenant Osgood.

With a cold roast turkey in her haversack, she made a flank movement upon the sentinels, and advanced through the crowd. After knocking over two or three men present, and treading on the neck of a small dog, she double-quicked into the *boudoir* of the indefatigable lieutenant.

"Well, madam," says he, "what can I do for you to-day?"

"Well, I'm hunting for the colonel."

"Hunting for the colonel?—Colonel who?"

"Why, Colonel Osgood: I reckon you're he." And at this juncture she "slung" the cold roast turkey towards the lieutenant, who was not only much astonished, but slightly injured. He recovered himself, however, and ejaculated,—

"That's a *fowl* blow, madam."

"Yes: I reckoned you'd like it, colonel."

"Yes,"—laughing,—"but I don't like it that way. But what do you want, madam?"

"I want a pass to——"

"Are you a Union lady?"

"Never been nothing else. My old man—I reckon you know the squire—he's been here a heap o' times, and——"

"That's all right, madam. Just tell me about the pass: what do you want of it?"

"Colonel," says she, confidingly, "I want a pass to raise geese."

"To what?" asked the lieutenant.

"To raise geese."

"You have always been a loyal lady?" asked Osgood.

"Colonel, I reckon. You see the old man—I reckon you know old squire——"

"All right, madam. You have never aided the Confederate Government or fed rebel cavalry?"

"Well, I reckon if I did the old man—I reckon the squire has been here —you know the——"

"No matter about the old man, madam. Have you always been a loyal lady?"

"Yes, I reckon I have."

"Well," says Osgood, turning to one of his clerks, "*give this woman a pass to raise geese!*"

"ROUSSEAU OR A RABBIT."—Much sport usually ensued in the camps about Murfreesborough, last spring, when a rabbit—of which there were many—would be started. There is generally much cheering and excitement, too, when Major-General Rousseau, who is universally popular, a splendid horseman, and always elegantly mounted, rides about the camps. Upon hearing a prodigious shout, one evening, near by his head-quarters, General Jefferson C. Davis inquired the cause.

"I can't say exactly, general," replied his aide, after stepping to the tent-door; "but I think it's the boys either after General Rousseau or a rabbit."

WHERE THE DAMAGE WAS DONE.—Russell Houston, Esq., an old and prominent citizen of Nashville, and a Union man, had not long ago built him an elegant residence, in the suburbs of the city. It occupied, unluckily, a knoll, or swell of land, where it was deemed desirable by our engineers to build a fort. When apprized, Mr. Houston made no objection: rather he encouraged and aided them in their plans in the most cheerful and commendable manner. One day some rebel ladies were visiting his family, and attempted consolation, bitterly exclaiming against this "Yankee vandalism."

"Ah, madam," he replied to one of them, "these troops have done me no harm. It was the firing of the first gun of the rebellion at Charleston that destroyed my property!"

Guerrillas destroying a Railroad-Train near Nashville.

A SOLDIER'S IDEA OF THE FIRST DAY'S BATTLE AT STONE RIVER.—"You say 'you can't understand about army wings, they being crushed, falling back, &c.' Well, here it is, in short. .Suppose our army to be like a bird at Stone River, head towards Murfreesborough, its body, Thomas's corps, being the centre, McCook's corps the right wing, spread wide open, and Critten-den's corps, thus spread, the left wing. That will do well enough for illus-tration. Well, Bragg's army pile in on McCook's wing, at its tip, and break off an inch or so by capturing batteries and several hundred of our men. And the feathers fly mightily all along that wing, and it is over-powered, and falls back in retreat, just as the bird would fold its wing, until it laps right up 'longside the centre. That's the way it was done. But they didn't move our head nor centre, though,—nary! Well, the reb cavalry, of which they had a powerful slue during this fight, came round on our rear on the big Nashville road, where were our hundreds of wagons and ambulances. There, we will say, is the bird's tail; and the supply-wagons, and doctors' tools, and niggers, we'll call them the tail-feathers. Now, them feathers flew some, you better believe!"

We are not sure but that such a narration, made by a private to an old hoosier at a street-corner, gives a more forcible idea of the general result of that battle to many minds than would the most elaborate description.

AMUSING INSTANCE OF REBEL DESERTION.—After the recent advance of our army upon Bragg at Tullahoma, and his retreat, the Pioneer Brigade pushed on to Elk River to repair a bridge. While one of its men, a private, was bathing in the river, five of Bragg's soldiers, guns in hand, came to the bank and took aim at the swimmer, one of them shouting,—

"Come in here, you —— Yank, out of the wet!"

The Federal was quite sure that he was "done for," and at once obeyed the order. After dressing himself, he was thus accosted:—

"You surrender, our prisoner, do you?"

"Yes; of course I do."

"That's kind. Now we'll surrender to you!" And the five stacked arms before him, their spokesman adding,—

"We've done with 'em, and have said to old Bragg, 'good-by!' Secesh is played out. Now you surround us and take us into your camp."

This was done accordingly, and is but one of hundreds of instances of wholesale desertion coming to the knowledge of our officers during the past two months—July and August—in Lower Tennessee.

GUERRILLAS UPON THE RAILROADS.—One of the surest means of delay, if not of destruction, to the Federal armies, as the rebel enemy supposed, was the destruction of railroads in the rear of our forces. To maintain such avenues of communication has cost the Army of the Cumberland hundreds of lives and countless days of careful, wearisome guarding and scouting.

As a whole, our success in this regard is really wonderful. But once has Morgan succeeded in damaging the Nashville & Louisville Railroad to any extent: then he required almost an army, which stopped all travel upon that road for some ten days, and delayed the forwarding of stores for about four weeks. Happily, the Cumberland River suddenly rose to a fair stage about that time, and the rebels took nothing by their motion.

Our artist has given, in the foregoing plate, a scene which occurred last winter upon the railroad above named, at a point some forty miles north of Nashville, and at a time when that road was not so systematically and effectually guarded as at present. A band of some sixty rebels, marauders, said to be lawless residents and "independent" cavalry, misplaced a rail near by a sharp curve, and secreted themselves in the edge of the forest near by. The train was coming down at a slow and precautionary rate of speed, as the country thereabout was favorable for guerrilla operations, and the engine, when it arrived at that spot, toppled over upon one side, no very great damage, however, ensuing from the stoppage. The guerrillas were now seen with guns aimed, kneeling in a line, to appear as formidable as possible, and they fired a deafening volley at the train, but killed no one. They probably fired overhead to frighten rather than to hurt the passengers. They then proceeded to rob the passengers indiscriminately. While thus quite leisurely employed, and in burning the cars, a bridge-guard of brave men of our army, stationed a mile below, hastened up on the double-quick, and when within sight the robbers made off at the top of their speed.

Resolved to put a stop to such proceedings, the commander of the post at Gallatin sent up a force and thoroughly scouted through that region, bringing into his camp every male citizen, and keeping them confined for several days. The old town of Gallatin was at once filled with their distressed wives, parents, and daughters. Developments were made convicting several of the men thus arrested: and it was soon after hinted to the writer that those persons were summarily "*sent to the front.*" The "front" to which they were marched is reported as only half a mile, or thereabouts, in the rear of Gallatin, where trees abounded with favorably projecting limbs. At all events, those people were taught a severe lesson, and to apparent good purpose, as a second affair of the kind has not occurred.

A BATTLE-FIELD WAR-COUNCIL.—At Stone River, during the evening of December 31, several of the generals of the Army of the Cumberland assembled at the head-quarters of the commander-in-chief. It was a momentous occasion. Our right wing, comprising more than one-third of our whole force, had been driven back with great loss. The generals arrived after dark at the tent of their commander, near the torn and bloody battle-ground, yet reeking with the dead. Each reported as to the status of his forces, and then, after other brief remarks of a personal character, conversation gradually subsided. General Rosecrans was the most conversational and cheerful, and had a smile and pleasant word for all. Excepting himself and Generals Thomas and Van Cleve, our commanders are young in years, and to most of them this was their first, and to all their greatest, battle. Hence their gravity and reticence—as certainly became them—upon this occasion. It was noticeable that they volunteered no opinions as to the best course for the morrow, whether to attempt to hold the present ground, to advance, or to retreat to Nashville. The supply-trains had been sent back to that city during the day by the general commanding, to relieve himself from the task of guarding them from the horde of rebel cavalry. Thus left almost empty-handed, retreat to Nashville, even during that night if necessary, was a course not entirely beyond reason, the enemy's superior force and nearness to his supplies considered.

If any of our generals at this conference had such thoughts or opinions, they certainly would not have then advanced them. It was a time and occasion—a turning-point—that rarely happens in a lifetime or a century. Even the sage General Thomas, now calm and placid in manner as a summer eve, waited to hear from his chief, and a stiffness pervaded the assembly until General Rosecrans broke the spell.

"Gentlemen," said he,—and the substance of his remarks is given us from recollection,—"we have come out to fight and to win this battle, and WE SHALL DO IT. True, we have been a little mixed up to-day; but we won't mind that. The enemy failed in all his attempts after we found what he was driving at. Our supplies may run short, but we will have out our trains again to-morrow. We will keep right on, and *eat corn for a week but what we win this battle*. WE CAN AND WILL DO IT!"

As the general advanced in his remarks, he became the more warmly in earnest. The effect of his words upon his officers was marked and exhilarating. All restraint was at once removed, now that their course was fully settled, and plans for the morrow soon engaged general attention.

Candor requires us to state that, in all probability, had General Rosecrans determined differently,—had he upon this occasion taken a dark view of the situation, and whispered words of caution and favored a prudential retreat, —our army would have fallen back ingloriously behind the forts at Nashville, and thus, unquestionably, Tennessee and Kentucky would not be as they are to-day, entirely free from rebel armies, and the Gulf States threatened from the West, but, on the contrary, they would now be the strongest sections of the so-called Southern Confederacy. Is there any impropriety, then, we ask, in classing this instance with those recorded in the world's history, where one master-spirit has saved an army and made a successful campaign, and thus proven himself a prominent instrument in solving the destiny of his country?

ARMY POETRY.

THE pensiveness and quiet of camp-life not unfrequently induce a melancholy mood, which finds solace in poetry. Songs and song-books are in every camp, and many a soldier of literary turn gives expression to his pent-up feelings in verse, ranging from the machine order through all the intermediate grades up to the truest and most soul-thrilling poetry. From a quantity of such productions we select the following as specimens of the grave and gay, the sentimental and comical. We do not present them as by any means specimens of a high order of poetry. The number and variety might be indefinitely extended; but these are deemed sufficient to fully represent the Army of the Cumberland in its poetical aspect.

The following lines are said to have been found, in manuscript, in the pocket of a dead rebel on the battle-field of Stone River. All that is known of him is that he was probably a Tennesseean. The lines, we presume, are original:—

DISAPPOINTMENT.

TO MISS —— ——.

My song has fled,
My muse is dead,
And woe beshrouds my way,
And the early crow,
And the herd's deep low,
Betide a gloomy day.

For how could I,
With an endless sigh,
Be ever happy more,
With the hope that's fled,
And the *no* you've said,
Feel as I felt before?

Adieu! fair muse;
Thy charms I lose;
With a tear and a sigh thou'rt gone;
And my hope sinks deep
In the night of sleep,
And yields to thy magic wand.

What good's a light
In a dreary night,
If its rays afford no cheer?
And why pursue
Its golden hue,
If each step is trod in fear?

Oh, woe the thought
That ever brought
On me the fatal blow!
In my restless sleep
I dream and weep,
Because it fail'd me so!

Yet why this chill
My heart should fill
And bow my head with grief?
Doth not the field
More flowers yield
Than's gather'd in the sheaf?

678

Look o'er the plain,
Along the lane,
And on the grassy lawn,
And by the brook,
In the little nook
Where plays the lovely fawn.

The dew-drop there,
So sweet and fair,
Just opening to the gaze:
I'll from it sip,
With my own lip,
The charm where its sweetness lays.

The rose-bud, too,
There brings to view
Its sweet and lovely form;

And as it blows
It gently throws
Its fragrance to the storm.

And though a sting
A thorn may bring,
She's queen of flowers still:
The little pain
Grows sweet again,
And all's a joyous thrill.

Then fare thee well!
My joys foretell
Yon blossom's waiting now;
I'll off to the grove
With my own fond love,
And plant a kiss on her brow.　　M.

A PRIVATE in the Army of the Cumberland thus protests against that slighting spirit of contempt which finds expression in the words, "only a private." Who will say that the author of these lines has not proven himself immensely the superior of many a vain-glorious coxcomb who would no sooner think of comparing himself with a "private" than with a beggar?

"ONLY A PRIVATE."

"ONE man kill'd in the skirmish to-day!"
He was "only a private," they say;
　　He was "only a private"!—Oh, how
Could they dare thus speak of the dead
For our country so nobly who bled,—
　　So deserving a laurell'd brow?

Oh, perhaps we have harden'd our hearts
Until death no impression imparts,
　　Nor the bitter anguish of friends;
He was "only a private;" 'tis sad
That his valor such slight notice had.
　　Now his body with common earth
　　　　blends.

Does a father enfeebled with years,—
Or a mother all trembling in tears,—
　　A dear sister, whose love is a gem
Of the purest,—or brother,—in vain
Keep a watching for him? Ne'er again
　　In this world he'll return unto them.

Are there orphans awaiting neglect?
Does a widow her husband expect?
　　Is it known at his home how he died?—
How he bravely with face to the foe
From a bullet received a fell blow,
　　When life sail'd out on the ebbing red
　　　　tide?

By the river now classical made,
On the Cumberland's banks, he was laid,—
　　By his comrades laid sadly away:
A plain hillock they fashion'd with care,
And then planted an evergreen there
　　To him who fell on that day.

Let us hope in the region above
He enjoyeth that fulness of love
　　Oft grudgingly denied him in this.
May a mercy as tender as great
Ope in heaven the pearliest gate,
　　And admit him an angel to bliss.

As a specimen of the very common article of "machine poetry," the following is passable.

BATTLE OF STONE RIVER.

BY A PRIVATE OF COMPANY F, 27TH REGIMENT ILLINOIS VOLUNTEERS.

COME, freemen all, both great and small,
  And listen to my story,
And, while our country is our theme,
  We'll sing about her glory.
I guess you've heard how Braxton Bragg
Into Kentucky paddled,
And how at Perryville he fought,
  And then he quick "skedaddled."

And how he thought, in Tennessee,
  At Murfreesborough seated,
The rout of all the Union hosts
  Would quickly be completed.
But Rosecrans, the conqueror,
  Had Buell superseded,
And justly thought this boasting Bragg
  A whipping sorely needed.

And so he thought the holidays
  The proper time for action,
To try this boasting rebel's strength
  And drive him from this section.
On Christmas day our orders came,
  And to the general handed.
McCook, a hero known to fame,
  Our gallant corps commanded.

Near Nolensville we met the foe,—
  They thought, securely seated.
Our batteries let a few shell go,
  And fast the rebs retreated.
So on we went, on victory bent,
  To view old Bragg's position:
We brought some pills to cure his ills,
  With Rosey for physician.

At break of day on the next morn,
  While the old year was dying,
The rebel force advanced their hosts
  To where our right was lying.
And now the news is quickly borne,—
  The foe our right is turning!
In countless numbers, on they come,
  All efforts swiftly spurning!

But as the foe appears so soon,
  In full and open view, sirs,

Brave Houghtaling plays them a tune
  Called Yankee-doodle-do, sirs.
And as the enemy bore down
  On Sheridan's division,
We fed them with the best we had,
  Gave bullets for provision.

Now on three sides the foe he rides
  Triumphant, to our grief;
Brave Negley then, with gallant men,
  Quick flies to our relief.
Firm as a rock brave Palmer stands,
  Our centre firm securing,
While Rousseau's men, with steady aim,
  A deadly fire are pouring.

Upon our left bold Crittenden—
  The Union hosts reviving,
As we can hear by cheer on cheer—
  The foe is swiftly driving.
On every hand we make a stand,
  All steady, firm, and true, sirs;
At close of eve rings out the shout!
  This day shall rebels rue, sirs.

But, while that shout is ringing out,
  'Tis mingled with our pain,
To think of our brave gallant men
  Now lying with the slain.
Brave Sill lies there, all cold and bare,
  With Garesché so brave,
And Roberts, Schaeffer,—honored names:
  They fill a hero's grave.

Sad duty this, to mention one
  We intimately knew,—
Our Harrington, beloved by all,
  So gallant, brave, and true.
He fell where brave men wish to fall,
  Where loudest sounds the battle,
Where stoutest hearts might stand appalled,
  Mid thundering cannon's rattle.

And, though his voice is still'd in death,
  We seem to hear his cry,
As cheering on his brave command,—
  "My boys, that flag stand by."

On New-Year's day, as people say,
   Bragg show'd his full intention
To drive us off,—make us the scoff
   Of all this mighty nation.

But Rosey knew a thing or two,
   And made him quick knock under,—
Gave him to feel the true-edged steel,
   Mid storms of Yankee thunder.
Says Bragg, " I'm sad : my cause is bad,
   And so, to save my bacon,
I will retreat, and save defeat ;
   For Rosey can't be taken."

So, while our men were strengthening
   Where we were situated,
To make secure, and victory sure,
   Old Bragg evacuated.

Now let our songs ascend on high
   To the All-Wise as giver,
And Rosey's name we'll crown with fame,
   As hero of Stone River.

When those we love request a sign
   For words as yet unspoken,
That sign shall be, Remember me,
   A ROSEY wreath for token.
And, now, may *roses* crown our land,
   May blissful peace soon come, sirs,
May Bragg-ing traitors soon be damn'd,
   And we in peace at home, sirs.

Then, boys, fill up the brimming cup.
   We'll toast the Union ever:—
Our health, the man that can Bragg tan,
   The hero of Stone River.

WE make room for another excellent jingle of camp-rhymes. Our reader, at his peaceful and comfortable fireside, can but faintly realize the pleasure —yes, " solid enjoyment"—which our soldiers derive from the jovial evening camp-song, at times !

"THE ELEPHANT."

BY TENT No. 1, COMPANY E, 42D INDIANA VOLUNTEERS.

OUR Uncle Samuel keeps a show, most wondrous and most rare,
That's fill'd with every sort of beast to please a man or scare ;
And to find this famous show of his the people came from far,
And march'd down South to see the menagerie of war.
A lot of us raw hoosiers from " The Pocket" thought we'd go
And have a three-years sight at this strangely wondrous show :
So we shoulder'd up our muskets, and, with knapsacks on our backs,
We travell'd in Kentucky, but saw neither beast nor tracks.

At last we heard the show had moved away to Tennessee :
So off we started on some boats, to see what we could see,
And down at Wartrace, in the brush, where Southern sunrays glance,
A few who started in our crowd beheld " the *monkey* dance."
But then the beast we wish'd to see, somehow, we couldn't find,
For 'twas "the Elephant" we search'd, with ever-curious mind ;
So off to Alabama's soil we travell'd for a while,
And trudged and tramp'd and picketed o'er many a Southern mile.

Now Bragg and Buell own'd the beast,—a partnership concern,—
And, as we could not find him South, we thought we would return.
So northward we began to march : at last we sat us down,
To rest a bit and eat a bite, in Louisville's great town.
Then General Buell fix'd the show, and bade us march a while,
And said we'd see " the Elephant" short of a hundred mile.

So off we tramp'd toward Perryville, and when we got down there
We saw the "Baby Elephant" cut capers fit to scare.
Although a *Baby* Elephant, he was a vicious beast,
And never could be tamed by man,—the rebels thought, at least.

But General Buell soon sold out, and General Rosecrans bought,
And then the beast was bound to thrive,—at least, the soldiers thought;
For Bragg and "Rosey," well we knew, would make the *Baby* grow,
And Bragg at last pick'd out a place to have another show.
The place was on Stone River, near Murfreesborough town,
And to see the show the people came from all the country round:
Some forty thousand Federals came, with steady step and slow,
And fifty thousand rebels *stay'd* to see the famous show.

And there they saw "the Elephant." My gracious! how he'd grown
Since first we saw him roaming in Kentucky all alone!
We saw him in the cedar grove, we saw him on the plain,
And some who saw him on that day will see him ne'er again.
And now, whene'er we hear a man talk loud about his might,
And tell about his bravery, and what he'd do in fight,
And tell how many foes he'd whip and make them run and pant,
We simply say, You ne'er have seen the famous "Elephant."

"The Old Union Wagon," written and composed by Rev. John H. Lozier,
chaplain of the 37th Indiana Volunteers, is an admirable specimen of a
popular patriotic army melody. It was written at the head-quarters of
General Negley's division, at Camp Hamilton, on the "Overton Plantation,"
five miles from Nashville, Tennessee. It was originally intended merely as
a camp-song in answer to "The Southern Wagon," which the "Secesh"
damsels are always ready to sing for the "Yankees." It was afterwards
published by John Church, Jr., of Cincinnati, as sheet-music, and was sung
with great *éclat* at Pike's Opera-House, at the immense Union meeting
held there to respond to the resolutions sent by the Army of the Cumberland to the people of the North. It is now having a great run in the West
and the army. The words are as follow:—

THE OLD UNION WAGON.

In Uncle Sam's dominion, in eighteen sixty-one,
The fight between Secession and Union was begun:
The South declared they'd have the "rights" which Uncle Sam denied,
Or in their secesh wagon they'd all take a ride.
          Hurrah for the wagon, the old Union wagon!
          We'll stick to our wagon and all take a ride!

The makers of our wagon were men of solid wit;
They made it out of "Charter Oak," that would not rot or split;
Its wheels are of material the strongest and the best,
And two are named the North and South, and two the East and West.

Our wagon-*bed* is strong enough for any "revolution,"
In fact, 'tis the "*hull*" of the "old Constitution;"
Her coupling's strong, her axle's long, and, anywhere you get her,
No monarch's frown can "back her down," no traitor can *upset* her.

This good old Union wagon the nation all admired;
Her wheels had run for fourscore years and never once been "*tired;*"
Her passengers were happy, as along her way she whirl'd,
For the good old Union wagon was the glory of the world!

But when old Abram took command, the South wheel got displeased,
Because the *public fat* was gone that kept her axle greased;
And when he gather'd up the reins and started on his route,
She plunged into secession and knock'd some "felloes" out!

Now, while in this secession mire the wheel was sticking tightly,
Some tory passengers got mad and cursed the driver slightly;
But Abram "couldn't see it," so he didn't heed their clatter:
"There's too much *black mud* on the wheel," says he:—"*that's what's the matter.*"

So Abram gave them notice that in eighteen sixty-three,
Unless the rebels "dried it up," he'd set their niggers free,
And then the man that led the van to fight against his nation
Would drop his gun, and *home* he'd run, to fight against *starvation.*

When Abram said he'd free the slaves that furnish'd their supplies,
It open'd Northern traitors' *mouths* and Southern traitors' eyes.
"The slaves," said they, "will run away, if you thus rashly free them!"
But Abram "guess'd perhaps they'd best *go home and oversee them.*"

Around our Union wagon, with shoulders to the wheel,
A million soldiers rally, with hearts as true as steel;
And of all the generals, high or low, that help to save the nation,
There's none that strikes a harder blow than *General Emancipation!*
 Hurrah for the wagon, the old Union wagon!
 We'll stick to our wagon and all take a ride!

THE following effusion was found in a rebel mail-package captured upon the person of a Confederate spy and containing some two hundred letters from rebeldom to friends within our lines. Whatever else may be said of it, no one can question its entire originality. The poet seems to be heartily sick of the war, and gives vent in verse to his feelings,—no prose being strong enough to do them justice. We give "his piece," with all its beauties, *verbatim et literatim.* Upon an outer fold of the soiled manuscript is written, "W R Brown to Sally Brown a song composed by me."

UPON; THE, WAR;

THIS is a War of dreadful scourrage	This is a war of great invasion,
OF which it takes a man of courrage	For which there is no good occasion
It is a war of subgugation	It is war of confiscation
OF which there is no cessation	OF which there is no obligation
And we are all on the go down	And we are all on the go down

This is a War of great confusion
OF Yankey foolish vain intrusion
It is a war of vain Ambition
And caused Amerricas bad condition
   And we are all on the go down

This is a War of death and Blood
OF which there cant be any good
It is a War, that's, verry bad
Oh let it cease and all be glad
   Or we are all on the go down

This is a War, that's, long beginding
OF which no man can tell the ending
It is a War that's fast and slow
It brings the high and lofty low
   And we are all on the go down.

This is a War of dreadful horrow
Which causes Weeping griefe and Sorrow
This is a War while womens moarning
Men are seffering dieing groaning
   And we are all on the go down

This is a War we all regret
OF which too many are inclined to fret

You take it easy and be resigned
For in this War we are all confined
   And we are all on the go down

This is a War, the Prophets say
OF which the south shall gain the day
But the Lord hath willed it so to bee
That none hath gainded it yet we seo
   And we are all on the go down

This War has caused the darkest Cloud
And ruined Amerrica that once was proud
And Wrapted a great and mighty crowd
OF once happy Amerrica's sons in shroud
   And we are all on the go down

This is a War we all must know
Thats Rageing Fast and ending slow
While ambition excitement rageing high
Its bringing want starvation nigh
   And we are all on the go down

This War; Oh Lord do let it cease
And this people speak lasting peace
And instead of death sorrow and sin
Religion peace health and life begin
   For we are all on the go down.

BATTLE OF STONE RIVER.

Official Report of Major-General Wm. S. Rosecrans.

HEAD-QUARTERS DEPARTMENT OF THE CUMBERLAND,
MURFREESBOROUGH, TENNESSEE, February 12, 1863.

GENERAL:—As the sub-reports are now nearly all in, I have the honor to submit, for the information of the general-in-chief, the subjoined report, with accompanying sub-reports, maps, and statistical rolls of the battle of Stone River.

To a proper understanding of this battle, it will be necessary to state the

PRELIMINARY MOVEMENTS AND PREPARATIONS

Assuming command of the army, at Louisville, on the 27th day of October, it was found concentrated at Bowling Green and Glasgow, distant about one hundred and thirty miles from Louisville; from whence, after replenishing with ammunition, supplies, and clothing, they moved on to Nashville, the advance-corps reaching that place on the morning of the 7th of November, a distance of one hundred and eighty-three miles from Louisville.

At this distance from my base of supplies, the first thing to be done was to provide for the subsistence of the troops, and open the Louisville & Nashville Railroad. The cars commenced running through on the 26th of November, previous to which time our supplies had been brought by rail to Mitchellsville, thirty-five miles north of Nashville, and from thence, by constant labor, we had been able to haul enough to replenish the exhausted stores for the garrison at Nashville, and subsist the troops of the moving army.

From the 26th of November to the 26th of December, every effort was bent to complete the clothing of the army, to provide it with ammunition, and replenish the depot at Nashville with needful supplies to insure us against want from the largest possible detention likely to occur by the breaking of the Louisville & Nashville Railroad; and, to insure this work, the road was guarded by a heavy force posted at Gallatin.

The enormous superiority in numbers of the rebel cavalry kept our little cavalry force almost within the infantry lines, and gave the enemy control of the entire country around us. It was obvious, from the beginning, that we should be confronted by Bragg's army, recruited by an inexorable conscription, and aided by clouds of mounted men, formed into a guerrilla-like cavalry to avoid the hardships of conscription and infantry service. The evident difficulties and labors of an advance into this country, and against such a force, and at such a distance from our base of operations, with which we were connected by a single precarious thread, made it manifest that our policy was to induce the enemy to travel over as much as possible of the space that separated us,—thus avoiding for us the wear and tear and diminution of our forces, and subjecting the enemy to all these inconveniences, besides increasing for him and diminishing for us the dangerous consequences of a defeat.

The means taken to obtain this end were eminently successful. The enemy, expecting us to go into winter quarters at Nashville, had prepared his own winter quarters at Murfreesborough, with the hope of possibly making them at Nashville, and had sent a large cavalry force into West Tennessee to annoy Grant, and another large force into Kentucky to break up the railroad. In the absence of these forces, and with adequate supplies in Nashville, the movement was judged opportune for an advance on the rebels. Polk's and Kirby Smith's forces were at Murfreesborough, and Hardee's corps on the Shelbyville and Nolensville pike, between Triune and Eagleville, with an advance-guard at Nolensville; while our troops lay in front of Nashville, on the Franklin, Nolensville, and Murfreesborough turnpikes.

THE PLAN OF THE MOVEMENTS

Was as follows:—

McCook, with three divisions, to advance by the Nolensville pike to Triune.

Thomas, with two divisions (Negley's and Rousseau's), to advance on his right, by the Franklin and Wilson pikes, threatening Hardee's right, and then to fall in by the cross-roads to Nolensville.

Crittenden, with Wood's, Palmer's, and Van Cleve's divisions, to advance by the Murfreesborough pike to Lavergne.

With Thomas's two divisions at Nolensville, McCook was to attack Hardee at Triune; and if the enemy reinforced Hardee, Thomas was to support McCook.

If McCook beat Hardee, or Hardee retreated, and the enemy met us at Stewart's Creek, five miles south of Lavergne, Crittenden was to attack him; Thomas was to come in on his left flank, and McCook, after detaching a division to pursue or observe Hardee, if retreating south, was to move, with the remainder of his force, on their rear.

THE MOVEMENT

Began on the morning of the 26th of December. McCook advanced on the Nolensville pike, skirmishing his way all day, meeting with stiff resistance from cavalry and artillery, and closing the day by a brisk fight, which gave him possession of Nolensville and the hills one and a half miles in front, capturing one gun, by the 101st Ohio and 15th Wisconsin Regiments, his loss this day being about seventy-five killed and wounded.

Thomas followed on the right, and closed Negley's division on Nolensville pike, leaving the other (Rousseau's) division on the right flank.

Crittenden advanced to Lavergne, skirmishing heavily on his front, over a rough country, intersected by forests and cedar-brakes, with but slight loss.

On the 26th, General McCook advanced on Triune; but his movement was retarded by a dense fog.

Crittenden had orders to delay his movements until McCook had reached Triune and developed the intentions of the enemy at that point, so that it could be determined which Thomas was to support.

McCook arrived at Triune, and reported that Hardee had retreated, and that he had sent a division in pursuit.

Crittenden began his advance about eleven o'clock A.M., driving before him a brigade of cavalry, supported by Maney's brigade of rebel infantry, and reached Stewart's Creek, the 3d Kentucky gallantly charging the rear-guard of the enemy, and saving the bridge, on which had been placed a pile of rails that had been set on fire. This was Saturday night.

McCook having settled the fact of Hardee's retreat, Thomas moved Negley's division on to join Crittenden at Stewart's Creek, and moved Rousseau's to Nolensville.

On Sunday the troops rested, except Rousseau's division, which was ordered to move on to Stewartsborough, and Willich's brigade, which had pursued Hardee as far as Riggs's Cross-Roads, and had determined the fact that Hardee had gone to Murfreesborough, when they returned to Triune.

On Monday morning McCook was ordered to move from Triune to Wilkerson's Cross-Roads, six miles from Murfreesborough, leaving a brigade at Triune.

Crittenden crossed Stewart's Creek by the Smyrna bridge, on the main Murfreesborough pike, and Negley by the ford, two miles above,—their whole force to advance on Murfreesborough, distant eleven miles.

Rousseau was to remain at Stewart's Creek until his train came up, and prepare himself to follow.

McCook reached Wilkerson's Cross-Roads by evening, with an advance brigade at Overall's Creek, saving and holding the bridge, meeting with but little resistance.

Crittenden's corps advanced, Palmer leading, on the Murfreesborough pike, followed by Negley, of Thomas's corps, to within three miles of Murfreesborough, having had several brisk skirmishes, driving the enemy rapidly, saving two bridges on the route, and forcing the enemy back to his intrenchments.

About three o'clock P.M., a signal-message coming from the front, from General Palmer, said that he was in sight of Murfreesborough, and the enemy were running. An order was sent to General Crittenden to send a division to occupy Murfreesborough.

This led General Crittenden, on reaching the enemy's front, to order Harker's brigade to cross the river at a ford on his left, where he surprised a regiment of Breckinridge's division, and drove it back on its main lines, not more than five hundred yards distant, in considerable confusion; and he held this position until General Crittenden was advised, by prisoners captured by Harker's brigade, that Breckinridge was in force on his front, when, it being dark, he ordered the brigade back across the river, and reported the circumstances to the commanding general on his arrival, to whom he apologized for not having carried out the order to occupy Murfreesborough. The general approved of his action, of course, the order to occupy Murfreesborough having been based on the information received from General Crittenden's advance division that the enemy were retreating from Murfreesborough.

Crittenden's corps, with Negley's division, bivouacked in order of battle, distant seven hundred yards from the enemy's intrenchments, our left extending down the river some five hundred yards. The Pioneer Brigade, bivouacking still lower down, prepared three fords, and covered one of them, while Wood's division covered the other two.

Van Cleve's division being in reserve, on the morning of the 30th Rousseau, with two brigades, was ordered down early from Stewart's Creek, leaving one brigade there and sending another to Smyrna to cover our left and rear, and took his place in reserve in rear of Palmer's right, while General Negley moved on through the cedar-brakes until his right rested on the Wilkerson pike. The Pioneer Corps cut roads through the cedars for his ambulances and ammunition-wagons.

The commanding general remained with the left and centre, examining the ground, while General McCook moved forward from Wilkerson's Cross-Roads, slowly and steadily, meeting with heavy resistance, fighting his way from Overall's Creek until he got into position, with a loss of one hundred and thirty-five killed and wounded.

Our small division of cavalry—say three thousand men—had been divided into three parts, of which General Stanley took two, and accompanied General McCook, fighting his way across from the Wilkerson to the Franklin pike and below it, Colonel Zahn's brigade leading gallantly, and meeting with such heavy resistance that McCook sent two brigades from Johnson's division, which succeeded in fighting their way into position, while the 3d Brigade, which had been left at Triune, moved forward from that place and arrived at nightfall near General McCook's head-quarters. Thus, on the close of the 30th the troops had all got into position.

At four o'clock in the afternoon, General McCook had reported his arrival on the Wilkerson pike, joining Thomas,—the result of the combat in the afternoon, near Grieson's house, and the fact that Sheridan was in position there, that his right was advancing to support the cavalry,—also that Hardee's corps, with two divisions of Polk's, was on his front, extending down towards the Salem pike.

Without any map of the ground, which was to us *terra incognita*, when General McCook informed the general commanding that his corps was facing strongly to the east, the general commanding told him that such a direction to his line did not appear to him a proper one, but that it ought, with the exception of his left, to face much more nearly south, with Johnson's division in reserve, but that this matter must be confided to him, who knew the ground over which he had fought.

At nine o'clock P.M. the corps commanders met at the head-quarters of the general commanding, who explained to them the following

PLAN OF THE BATTLE.

McCook was to occupy the most advantageous position, refusing his right as much as practicable and necessary to secure it, to receive the attack of the enemy, or, if that did not come, to attack himself, sufficient to hold all the force on his front.

Thomas and Palmer to open with skirmishing, and gain the enemy's centre and left as far as the river.

Crittenden to cross Van Cleve's division at the lower ford, covered and supported by the sappers and miners, and to advance on Breckinridge.

Wood's division to follow by brigades, crossing at the upper ford, and, moving on Van Cleve's right, to carry every thing before them into Murfreesborough.

This would have given us two divisions against one, and, as soon as Breckinridge had been dislodged from his position, the batteries of Wood's division, taking position on the heights east of Stone River, in advance, would see the enemy's works in reverse, would dislodge them, and enable Palmer's division to press them back and drive them westward across the river or through the woods, while Thomas, sustaining the movement on the centre, would advance on the right of Palmer, crushing their right, and Crittenden's corps, advancing, would take Murfreesborough, and then, moving westward on the Franklin road, get in their flank and rear, and drive them into the country, towards Salem, with the prospect of cutting off their retreat and probably destroying their army.

It was explained to them that this combination, insuring us a vast superiority on our left, required for its success that General McCook should be able to hold his position for three hours; that, if necessary to recede at all, he should recede as he had advanced on the preceding day, slowly, as steadily, refusing his right, thereby rendering our success certain.

Having thus explained the plan, the general commanding addressed General McCook as follows:—

"You know the ground; you have fought over it; you know its difficulties. Can you hold your present position for three hours?"

To which General McCook responded,—

"Yes; I think I can."

The general commanding then said,—

"I don't like the facing so much to the east, but must confide that to you, who know the ground. If you don't think your present the best position, change it. It is only necessary for you to make things sure."

The officers then returned to their commands.

At daylight on the morning of the 31st, the troops breakfasted, and stood to their arms, and by seven o'clock were preparing for the

BATTLE.

The movement began on the left by Van Cleve, who covered the crossing at the lower fords. Wood prepared to sustain and follow him. The enemy meanwhile had prepared to attack General McCook, and by six and a half o'clock advanced in heavy columns, regimental front, his left attacking Willich's and Kirk's brigades, of Johnson's division, which were, after a sharp but fruitless contest, crumbled to pieces and driven back, leaving Edgarton's and part of Goodspeed's batteries in the hands of the enemy.

The enemy, following up, attacked Davis's division, and speedily dislodged Post's brigade. Carlin's brigade was compelled to follow, as Woodruff's brigade, from the weight of testimony, had previously left its position on his left. Johnson's brigades, in retiring, inclined too far to the west, and were too much scattered to make a combined resistance, though they fought bravely at one or two points before reaching Wilkerson's pike. The reserve brigade of Johnson's division, advancing from its bivouac near Wilkerson's pike towards the right, took a good position, and made a gallant but ineffectual stand, as the whole rebel left was moving up on the ground abandoned by our troops.

Within an hour from the time of the opening of the battle, a staff-officer from General McCook arrived, announcing to me that the right wing was heavily pressed and needed assistance; but I was not advised of the rout of Willich's and Kirby's brigades, nor of the rapid withdrawal of Davis's division, necessitated thereby. Moreover, having supposed his wing posted more compactly, and his right more refused, than it really was, the direction of the noise of battle did not indicate to me the true state of affairs. I consequently directed him to return and direct General McCook to dispose his troops to the best advantage, and to hold his ground obstinately. Soon after, a second officer from General McCook arrived, and stated that the right wing was being driven,—a fact that was but too manifest, by the rapid movement of the noise of battle towards the north.

General Thomas was immediately despatched to order Rousseau—then in reserve—into the cedar-brakes to the right and rear of Sheridan. General Crittenden was ordered to suspend Van Cleve's movement across the river on the left, and to cover the crossing with one brigade and move the other two brigades westward, across the fields towards the railroad, for a reserve. Wood was also directed to suspend his preparations for crossing, and to hold Hascall in reserve.

At this moment fugitives and stragglers from McCook's corps began to make their appearance through the cedar-brakes in such numbers that I became satisfied that McCook's corps was routed. I therefore directed General Crittenden to send Van Cleve in to the right of Rousseau, Wood to send Colonel Harker's brigade farther down the Murfreesborough pike, to go in and attack the enemy on the right of Van Cleve, the Pioneer Brigade meanwhile occupying the knoll of ground west of the Murfreesborough pike, and about four hundred or five hundred yards in the rear of Palmer's centre, supporting Stokes's battery. Sheridan, after sustaining four successive attacks, gradually swung his right round southeasterly to a northwestern direction, repulsing the enemy four times, losing the gallant General Sill of his right and Colonel Roberts of his left brigade, when, having exhausted his ammunition, Negley's division being in the same predicament, and heavily pressed, after desperate fighting they fell back from the position held at the commencement, through the cedar woods, in which Rousseau's division, with a portion of Negley's and Sheridan's, met the advancing enemy, and checked his movements.

The ammunition-train of the right wing, endangered by its sudden discomfiture, was taken charge of by Captain Thruston, of the 1st Ohio Regiment— an ordnance officer, who by his energy and gallantry, aided by a charge of cavalry and such troops as he could pick up, carried it through the woods to the Murfreesborough pike, around to the rear of the left wing, thus enabling the troops of Sheridan's division to replenish their empty cartridge-boxes. During all this time, Palmer's front had likewise been in action, the enemy having made several attempts to advance upon it. At this stage it became necessary to readjust the line of battle to the new state of affairs. Rousseau and Van Cleve's advance having relieved Sheridan's division from the pressure, Negley's division and Cruft's brigade from Palmer's division withdrew from their original position in front of the cedars, and crossed the open field to the east of the Murfreesborough pike, about four hundred yards in rear of our front line, where Negley was ordered to replenish his ammunition and form in close column in reserve.

The right and centre of our line now extended from Hazen to the Murfreesborough pike, in a northwesterly direction, Hascall supporting Hazen, Rousseau filling the interval to the Pioneer Brigade, Negley in reserve, Van Cleve west of the Pioneer Brigade, McCook's corps refused on his right and slightly to the rear on the Murfreesborough pike; the cavalry being still farther to the rear on the Murfreesborough pike and beyond Overall's Creek.

The enemy's infantry and cavalry attack on our extreme right was repulsed by Van Cleve's division, with Harker's brigade and the cavalry. After several attempts of the enemy to advance on this new line, which were thoroughly repulsed, as were also the attempts on the left, the day closed, leaving us masters of the original ground on our left, and our new line advantageously posted, with open ground in front, swept at all points by our artillery. We had lost heavily in killed and wounded, and a considerable number in stragglers and prisoners; also twenty-eight pieces of artillery, the horses having been slain, and our troops being unable to withdraw them, by hand, over the rough ground; but the enemy had been roughly handled and badly damaged at all points, having had no success where we had open ground and our troops were properly posted,— none which did not depend on the original crushing of our right and the superior masses which were, in consequence, brought to bear upon the narrow front of Sheridan's and Negley's divisions and a part of Palmer's, coupled with the scarcity of ammunition, caused by the circuitous road which the train had taken and the inconvenience of getting it from a remote distance through the cedars. Orders were given for the issue of all the spare ammunition; and we found that we had enough for another battle, the only question being where that battle was to be fought.

It was decided, in order to complete our present lines, that the left should be retired some two hundred and fifty yards, to more advantageous ground, the extreme left resting on Stone River, above the lower ford, and extending to Stokes's battery. Starkweather's and Walker's brigades arriving near the close of the evening, the former bivouacked in close column, in reserve, in the rear of McCook's left, and the latter was posted on the left of Sheridan, near the Murfreesborough pike, and next morning relieved Van Cleve, who returned to his position in the left wing.

DISPOSITION FOR JANUARY 1, 1863.

After careful examination, and free consultation with corps commanders, followed by a personal examination of the ground in the rear as far as Overall's Creek, it was determined to await the enemy's attack in that position, to send for the provision-train, and order up fresh supplies of ammunition, on the arrival of which, should the enemy not attack, offensive operations should be resumed.

No demonstration on the morning of the 1st of January: Crittenden was ordered to occupy the points opposite the ford on his left, with a brigade.

About two o'clock in the afternoon, the enemy, who had shown signs of movement and massing on our right, appeared at the extremity of a field a mile and a half from the Murfreesborough pike; but the presence of Gibson's brigade, with a battery occupying the woods near Overall's Creek, and Negley's division, and a portion of Rousseau's, on the Murfreesborough pike, opposite the field, put an end to this demonstration; and the day closed with another demonstration by the enemy, on Walker's brigade, which ended in the same manner.

On Friday morning, the enemy opened four heavy batteries on our centre, and made a strong demonstration of an attack a little farther to the right; but a well-directed fire of artillery soon silenced his batteries, while the guns of Walker and Sheridan put an end to his effort there.

About three o'clock P.M., while the commanding general was examining the position of Crittenden's left, across the river, which was now held by Van Cleve's division, supported by a brigade from Palmer's, a double line of skirmishers were seen to emerge from the woods in a southeasterly direction, advancing across the fields, and were soon followed by heavy columns of infantry, battalion front, with three batteries of artillery.

Our only battery on this side of the river had been withdrawn from an eligible point; but the most available spot was pointed out, and it soon opened here upon the enemy. The line, however, advanced steadily to within one hundred yards of the front of Van Cleve's division, when a short and fierce contest ensued. Van Cleve's division, giving way, retired in considerable confusion across the river, followed closely by the enemy.

General Crittenden immediately directed his chief of artillery to dispose the batteries on the hill, on the west side of the river, so as to open on them, while two brigades of Negley's division, from the reserve, and the Pioneer Brigade, were ordered up to meet the onset.

The firing was terrific, and the havoc terrible. The enemy retreated more rapidly than they had advanced: in forty minutes they lost two thousand men.

General Davis, seeing some stragglers from Van Cleve's division, took one of his brigades and crossed at a ford below, to attack the enemy on his left flank, and, by General McCook's order, the rest of his division was permitted to follow; but, when he arrived, two brigades of Negley's division, and Hazen's brigade of Palmer's division, had pursued the flying enemy well across the field, capturing four pieces of artillery and a stand of colors.

It was now after dark, and raining, or we should have pursued the enemy into Murfreesborough. As it was, Crittenden's corps passed over, and, with Davis, occupied the crests, which were intrenched in a few hours.

Deeming it possible that the enemy might again attack our right and centre, thus weakened, I thought it advisable to make a demonstration on our right by a heavy division of camp-fires, and by laying out a line of battle with torches, which answered the purpose.

SATURDAY, THIRD DAY OF JANUARY.

It rained heavily from three o'clock in the morning: the ploughed ground over which our left would be obliged to advance was impassable for artillery. The ammunition-train did not arrive until ten o'clock: it was, therefore, deemed inadvisable to advance; but batteries were put in position on the left, by which the ground could be swept, and even Murfreesborough reached, by the Parrott shells.

A heavy and constant picket-firing had been kept up on our right and centre and extending to our left, which at last became so annoying that, in the afternoon, I directed the corps commanders to clear their fronts.

Occupying the woods to the left of the Murfreesborough pike with sharpshooters, the enemy had annoyed Rousseau all day, and General Thomas and himself requested permission to dislodge them and their supports, which covered a ford. This was granted, and a sharp fire from four batteries was opened for ten or fifteen minutes, when Rousseau sent two of his regiments, which, with Spear's Tennesseeans and the 85th Illinois Volunteers, that had come out with the wagon-train, charged upon the enemy, and after a sharp contest cleared the woods, and drove the enemy from his trenches, capturing from seventy to eighty prisoners.

Sunday morning, the 4th of January, it was not deemed advisable to commence offensive movements, and news soon reached us that the enemy had fled from Murfreesborough. Burial-parties were sent out to bury the dead, and the cavalry was sent to reconnoitre.

Early Monday morning, General Thomas advanced, driving the rear-guard of the rebel cavalry before him six or seven miles, towards Manchester.

McCook's and Crittenden's corps, following, took position in front of the town, occupying Murfreesborough.

We learned that the enemy's infantry had reached Shelbyville by twelve M. on Sunday; but, owing to the impracticability of bringing up supplies, and the loss of five hundred and fifty-seven artillery horses, further pursuit was deemed inadvisable.

It may be of interest to give the following

GENERAL SUMMARY

Of the operations and results of the series of skirmishes closing with the battle of Stone River and the occupation of Murfreesborough. We moved on the enemy with the following forces:—

Infantry	41,421
Cavalry	3,296
Artillery	2,223
Total	46,940

We fought the battle with the following forces:—

Infantry	37,977
Cavalry	3,200
Artillery	2,223
Total	43,400

We lost in killed:—

Officers	92
Enlisted men	1,441
Total	1,533

We lost in wounded:—

Officers	384
Enlisted men	6,861
Total	7,245
Total killed and wounded	8,778

Being 20.03 per cent. of the entire force in action.

OUR LOSS IN PRISONERS

Is not fully made out; but the Provost-Marshal General says, from present information, they will fall short of two thousand eight hundred.

If there are any more bloody battles on record, considering the newness and inexperience of the troops, both officers and men, or if there have been more fighting-qualities displayed by any people, I should be pleased to know it.

AS TO THE CONDITION OF THE FIGHT,

We may say that we operated over an unknown country, against a position which was fifteen per cent. better than our own, every foot of ground and approaches being well known to the enemy, and that these disadvantages were fatally enhanced by the faulty position of our right wing.

The force we fought is estimated as follows. We have prisoners from one hundred and thirty-two regiments of infantry (consolidations counted as one), averaging from those in General Bushrod Johnson's division four hundred and eleven each,—say, for certain, three hundred and fifty men each, will give

No. men.

	No. men.
132 regiments infantry, say 350 men each	46,200
12 battalions sharpshooters, say 100 men each	1,200
23 battalions of artillery, say 80 men each	1,840
29 regiments cavalry, men each ....400 ⎫	
24 organizations of cavalry, men each .... 70 ⎭	13,280
220	62,520

Their average loss, taken from the statistics of Cleborne, Breckinridge, and Withers's divisions, was about two thousand and eighty each. This, for six divisions of infantry and one of cavalry, will amount to fourteen thousand five hundred and sixty men,—or to ours nearly as one hundred and sixty-five to one hundred.

Of fourteen thousand five hundred and sixty rebels struck by our missiles, it is estimated that twenty thousand rounds of artillery hit seven hundred and twenty-eight men, two million rounds of musketry hit thirteen thousand eight hundred and thirty-two men,—averaging twenty-seven cannon-shots to hit one man, one hundred and forty-five musket-shots to hit one man.

Our loss was as follows:—

					Per cent.
Right wing	15,933.	Musketry and artillery loss			20.72
Centre	10,866.	"	"	"	18.4
Left wing	13,288.	"	"	"	24.6

On the whole, it is evident that we fought superior numbers on unknown ground, inflicting much more injury than we suffered. We were always superior on equal ground with equal numbers, and only failed of a most crushing victory on Wednesday by the extension and direction of our right wing.

This closes the narrative of the movements and seven days' fighting which terminated with the occupation of Murfreesborough. For a detailed history of the parts taken in the battles of the different commands, their obstinate bravery and patient endurance, in which the new regiments vied with those of more experience, I must refer to the accompanying sub-reports of the corps, division, cavalry, and artillery commanders.

Besides the mention which has been already made of the service of *our artillery* by the brigade, division, and corps commanders, I deem it a duty to say that such a marked evidence of skill in handling the batteries, and in firing low with such effect, appears in this battle to deserve special commendation.

Among the lesser commands which deserve special mention for distinguished service in the battle is the Pioneer Corps, a body of seventeen hundred (1700) men, composed of details from the companies of each infantry regiment, organized and instructed by Captain James St. Clair Morton, Corps of Engineers, Chief Engineer of this army, which marched as an infantry brigade with the left wing, made bridges at Stewart's Creek, prepared and guarded the fort at Stone River on the nights of the 29th and 30th, supported Stokes's battery, and fought with valor and determination on the 31st, holding its position until relieved; on the morning of the 2d advancing with the greatest promptitude and gallantry to support Van Cleve's division against the attack on our left; on the evening of the same day constructing a bridge and batteries between that time and Saturday evening; and the efficiency and *esprit de corps* suddenly developed in this command, its gallant behavior in action, the eminent service it is continually rendering the army, entitle both officers and men to special public notice and thanks, while they reflect the highest credit on the distinguished ability and capacity of Captain Morton, who will do honor to his promotion to a brigadier-general, which the President has promised him.

The ability, order, and method exhibited in the management of the wounded elicited the warmest commendation from all our general officers,—in which I most cordially join.

Notwithstanding the numbers to be cared for, through the energy of Dr. Swift, Medical Director, ably assisted by Dr. Weeds and the senior surgeons of the various commands, there was less suffering from delay than I have ever before witnessed.

The 10th Regiment of Ohio Volunteers, at Stewart's Creek, Lieutenant-Colonel J. W. Burke commanding, deserve especial praise for the ability and spirit with which they held their post, defended our trains, secured their guards, chased away Wheeler's rebel cavalry, saving a large wagon-train, and arrested and retained for service some two thousand stragglers from the battle-field.

The 1st Regiment of Michigan Engineers and Mechanics, at Lavergne, under command of Colonel Innes, fighting behind a slight protection of wagons and brush, gallantly repulsed a charge from more than ten times their numbers of Wheeler's cavalry.

For distinguished acts of individual zeal, heroism, gallantry, and good conduct, I refer to the accompanying "*List of Special Mentions and Recommendations for Promotion*," wherein are named some of the many noble men who have distinguished themselves and done honor to their country and the starry symbol of its unity. But those named there are by no means all whose names will be inscribed on the rolls of honor we are preparing and hope to have held in grateful remembrance by our countrymen. To say that such men as Major-General G. H. Thomas, true and prudent, distinguished in council and on many battle-fields for his courage, or Major-General McCook, a tried, faithful, and loyal soldier, who bravely breasted battle at Shiloh and at Perryville, and as bravely on the bloody field of Stone River, and Major-General Thomas L. Crittenden, whose heart is that of a true soldier and patriot, and whose gallantry, often attested by his companions-in-arms in other fields, witnessed many times by this army long before I had the honor to command it, never more conspicuously than in this combat, maintained their high character throughout this action, would but feebly express my feeling of obligation to them for counsel and support from the time of my arrival to the present hour. I doubly thank them, as well as the gallant, ever-ready Major-General Rousseau, for their support in this battle.

Brigadier-General Stanley, already distinguished for four successful battles,—Island No. 10, May 27, before Corinth, Iuka, and the battle of Corinth,—at this time in command of our ten regiments of cavalry, fought the enemy's forty regiments of cavalry, and held them at bay, and beat them wherever he could meet them. He ought to be made a major-general for his services, and also for the good of the service.

As for such brigadiers as Negley, Jefferson C. Davis, Johnson, Palmer, Hascall, Van Cleve, Wood, Mitchell, Cruft, and Sheridan, they ought to be made major-generals in our service. In such brigade commanders as Colonels Carlin, Miller, Hazen, Samuel Beatty of the 19th Ohio, Gibson, Grose, Wagner, John Beatty of the 3d Ohio, Harker, Starkweather, Stanley, and others whose names are mentioned in the accompanying report, the Government may well confide. They are the men from whom our troops should be at once supplied with brigadier-generals; and justice to the brave men and officers of the regiments equally demands their promotion, to give them and their regiments their proper leaders. Many captains and subalterns also showed great gallantry and capacity for superior commands. But, above all, the steady rank and file showed invincible fighting courage and stamina worthy of a great and free nation, requiring only good officers, discipline, and instruction to make them equal, if not superior, to any troops in ancient or modern times. To them I offer my most heartfelt thanks and good wishes.

Words of my own cannot add to the renown of our brave and patriotic officers and soldiers who fell on the field of honor, nor increase respect for their memory in the hearts of our countrymen. The names of such men as Lieutenant-Colonel J. P. Garesché, the pure and noble Christian gentleman and chivalric officer, who gave his life an early offering on the altar of his country's freedom,—the gentle, true, and accomplished General Sill,—the brave, ingenious, and able Colonels Roberts, Millikin, Shaeffer, McKee, Reed, Forman, Fred. Jones, Hawkins, Kell, and the gallant and faithful Major Carpenter, of the 19th Regulars, and many other field officers,—will live in our country's history, as well as those of many others of inferior rank, whose soldierly deeds on this memorable battle-field won for them the admiration of their companions, and will dwell in our memories in long future years after God in his mercy shall have given us peace and restored us to the bosom of our homes and families. Simple justice to the officers of my staff requires their special mention:—the noble and lamented Lieutenant-Colonel Garesché, Chief of Staff; Lieutenant-Colonel Taylor, Chief Quartermaster; Lieutenant-Colonel Simmons, Chief Commissary; Major C. Goddard, senior aide-de-camp; Major Ralston Skinner, Judge-Advocate General; Lieutenant Frank S. Bond, aide-de-camp of General Tyler; Captain Charles R. Thompson, my aide-de-camp; Lieutenant Byron Kirby, 6th United States Infantry, aide-de-camp, who was wounded on December 31; R. S. Thoms, Esq., a member of the Cincinnati bar, who acted as volunteer aide-de-camp, and behaved with distinguished gallantry; Captain William D. Bickham, volunteer aide-de-camp, rendered efficient services on the field; Colonel Barnett, Chief of Artillery and Ordnance; Captain J. H. Gilman, 19th United States Infantry, Inspector of Artillery; Captain James Curtis, 15th United States Infantry, Assistant Inspector-General; Captain Wiles, 22d Indiana, Provost-Marshal General; Captain Mitchler, Topographical Engineer; Captain Jesse Merrill, Signal Corps, whose corps behaved well; Captain Elmer Otis, 4th Regular Cavalry, who commanded the Courier Line, connecting the various head-quarters most successfully, and who made a most successful, opportune, and brilliant charge on Wheeler's cavalry, routing the brigade, and recapturing three hundred of our prisoners. Lieutenant Edson, United States Ordnance Officer, who during the battle of Wednesday distributed ammunition under the fire of the enemy's batteries and behaved bravely. Captain Hubbard and Lieutenant Newberry, who joined my staff on the field, acting as aides, rendered valuable service in carrying orders on the field. Lieutenant Royse, 4th United States Cavalry, commanded the escort of the head-quarters train, and distinguished himself with gallantry and efficiency. All performed their appropriate duties to my entire satisfaction, accompanying me everywhere, and carrying orders through the thickest of the fight, watching while others slept, never weary when duty called, and deserve my public thanks and the respect and gratitude of the army.

With all the facts of the battle fully before me, the relative numbers and positions of our troops and those of the rebels, the gallantry and obstinacy of the contest, and the final result, I say, from conviction, and as public acknowledgment due to Almighty God, in closing this report, "*Non nobis, Domine, non nobis, sed nomine tui da gloriam.*"

(Signed),   WM. S. ROSECRANS,
Major-General Commanding.

BRIGADIER-GENERAL THOMAS.
Adjutant-General United States Army.

Official Report of General Braxton Bragg.

HEAD-QUARTERS ARMY OF TENNESSEE, TULLAHOMA, February 23, 1863.

SIR:—On the 26th of December last the enemy advanced in force from Nashville to attack us at Murfreesborough. It had been well ascertained that his effective force was over sixty thousand effective men. Before night on that day, the object of the movement was developed, by our dispositions in front, and orders were given for the necessary concentration of our forces there distributed, as follows:—

Polk's corps and three brigades of Breckinridge's division, Hardee's corps, at Murfreesborough; the balance of Hardee's corps, near Eagleville, about twenty miles west of Murfreesborough; McCown's division (which, with Stevenson's division removed, constituted Smith's corps) at Readyville, twelve miles east of Murfreesborough; the three cavalry brigades of Wheeler, Wharton, and Pegram, occupying the entire front of our infantry, and covering all approaches to within ten miles of Nashville; Buford's small cavalry brigade, of about six hundred, at McMinnville. The brigades of Forrest and Morgan, about five thousand effective cavalry, were absent, on special service, in West Tennessee and Northern Kentucky, as will be more fully noted hereafter. Jackson's small infantry brigade was in the rear, guarding the railroad from Bridgeport, Alabama, to the mountains. On Sunday, the 28th, our main force of infantry and artillery was concentrated in front of Murfreesborough; while the cavalry, supported by three brigades of infantry and three batteries of artillery, impeded the advance of the enemy by constant skirmishing and sudden and unexpected attacks. To the skilful manner in which the cavalry, thus ably supported, was handled, and to the exceeding gallantry of its officers and men, must be attributed the four days' time consumed by the enemy in reaching the battle-field, a distance of only twenty miles from his encampment, over fine macadamized roads.

Fully aware of the greatly superior numbers of the enemy, as indicated in my early reports from this quarter, it 'was our policy to await attack. The position was selected and line developed with this intention. Owing to the convergence upon our depot of so many fine roads by which the enemy could approach, we were confined in our selection to a line near enough to the point of juncture to enable us to successfully cover them all until the real point of attack should be developed.

On Monday, the 29th, it was reported that heavy columns moved on both the direct road from Lavergne and on the one leading into the Lebanon road by way of Jefferson. But on Tuesday, the 30th, it was ascertained that the Jefferson pike was abandoned by a countermarch, and the whole forces of the enemy were concentrated on and near the direct road on the west of Stone River.

Our arrangements were all completed before the enemy crossed Stewart's Creek, nine miles out, and the infantry brigades were at once called in; and the cavalry was ordered to fall back more rapidly, having most gallantly discharged its duty and fully accomplished the objects desired. Late on Monday it became apparent the enemy was extending to his right to flank us on the left. McCown's division, in reserve, was promptly thrown to that flank, and added to the command of Lieutenant-General Polk. The enemy not meeting our expectations of making an attack on Tuesday,—which was consumed in artillery firing and heavy skirmishing, with the exception of a dash late in the evening on the left of Withers's division, which was repulsed and severely punished,—it was determined to assail him on Wednesday morning, the 31st.

For this purpose Cleborne's division, Hardee's corps, was moved from the second line on the right to the corresponding position on the left, and Lieutenant-General Hardee was ordered to that point, and assigned to the command of that and McCown's division. This disposition, the result of necessity, left me no reserve; but Breckinridge's command on the right, not now threatened, was regarded as a source of supply for any reinforcements absolutely necessary to other parts of the field. Stone River, at its low stage, was fordable at any point for infantry, and, at short intervals, perfectly practicable for artillery.

These dispositions completed, General Hardee was ordered to assail the enemy at daylight on Wednesday, the 31st, the attack to be taken up by Polk's command in succession, to the right flank; the move to be made by a constant wheel to the right,—on Polk's right, as a point; the object being to force the enemy back on Stone River, and, if practicable, by the aid of cavalry, cut him off from his base of operations and supplies by the Nashville pike.

The lines were now bivouacked at a distance, in places, of not more than five hundred yards, the camp-fires of the two being within distinct view. General Wharton's cavalry brigade had been kept on our left, to watch and check the movements of the enemy in that direction, and to prevent his gaining the railroad in our rear, the preservation of which was of vital importance. In this he was aided by Brigadier-General A. Buford, who had a small command of six hundred new cavalry. The duty was most ably, gallantly, and successfully performed.

On Monday night Brigadier-General Wheeler proceeded with his cavalry brigade and one regiment from Pegram's, as ordered, to gain the enemy's rear. By Tuesday morning, moving on the Jefferson pike, around the enemy's left flank, he had gained the rear of their whole army, and soon attacked their trains, their guards, and the numerous stragglers.

He succeeded in capturing several hundred prisoners and destroying hundreds of wagons loaded with supplies and baggage. After clearing the road, he made his way entirely around, and joined the cavalry on our left.

The failure of General McCown to execute, during the night, an order for a slight change in the line of his division, and which had to be done the next morning, caused some delay in the general and vigorous assault by Lieutenant-General Hardee. But about seven o'clock the rattle of musketry and the roar of artillery announced the beginning of the conflict. The enemy was taken completely by surprise: general and staff officers were not mounted, artillery horses not hitched, and infantry not formed. A hot and inviting breakfast of coffee and other luxuries, to which our gallant and hardy men had long been strangers, was found upon the fire, unserved, and was left while we pushed on to a more inviting feast,—that of captured artillery, flying battalions, and hosts of craven prisoners, begging for their lives they had forfeited by their acts of brutality and atrocity. While thus routing and pushing the enemy on his front, Lieutenant-General Hardee announced to me, by a messenger, that the movement was not being as promptly executed by Major-General Cheatham's command on his right—the left of General Polk's corps—as he expected, and that his line was consequently exposed to an enfilading fire from the enemy's artillery in that front. The necessary instructions for prompt movement at that point were immediately despatched, and in a short time our whole line, except Breckinridge's command, was warmly engaged. From this time we continued to drive the enemy more or less rapidly, until his line was thrown entirely back at right angles to his first position and occupied the cut of the railroad, along which he had massed his reserves and posted very strong batteries. The enemy's loss was very heavy in killed and wounded,—far exceeding our own, as appeared from a critical examination of the field, now almost entirely in our possession. Of artillery alone we had secured more than twenty-five pieces.

While the infantry and artillery were engaged in this successful work,

Brigadier-General Wharton, with his cavalry command, was most actively and gallantly engaged on the enemy's right and rear, where he inflicted a heavy loss in killed and wounded, captured a full battery of artillery attempting to escape, and secured and sent in near two thousand prisoners.

These important successes and results had not been achieved without heavy sacrifices on our part, as the resistance of the enemy, after the first surprise, was most gallant and obstinate.

Finding Lieutenant-General Hardee so formidably opposed by the movement of the enemy on his front, reinforcements for him were ordered from Major-General Breckinridge; but the orders were countermanded, as will hereafter appear, and Polk's corps was pressed forward with vigor, hoping to draw the enemy back or rout him on the right, as he had already been on the left. We succeeded in driving him from every position except the strong one held by his extreme left flank, resting on Stone River, and covered by a concentration of artillery of superior range and calibre, which seemed to bid us defiance. The difficulties of our general advance had been greatly enhanced by the topography of the country. All parts of our line had to pass in their progress over ground of the roughest character, covered with huge stones and studded with the densest growth of cedar, the branches reaching the ground and forming an almost impassable "brake." Our artillery could rarely be used ; while the enemy, holding defensive lines, had selected formidable positions for his batteries, and this dense cover for his infantry, from both of which he had to be dislodged by our infantry alone. The determined and unvarying gallantry of our troops, and the uninterrupted success which attended their repeated charges against these strongholds, defended by double their numbers, fully justified the unbounded confidence I had ever reposed in them and have so often expressed.

To meet our successful advances, and to retrieve his hopes in the front of his left, the enemy early transferred a portion of his reserve from his left to that flank, and by two o'clock had succeeded in concentrating such a force in Lieutenant-General Hardee's front as to check his further progress. Our two lines had by this time become almost blended, so weakened were they by losses, exhaustion, and extension to cover the enemy's whole front.

As early as ten o'clock A.M., Major-General Breckinridge was called on for one brigade, and soon after for a second, to reinforce or act as a reserve to Lieutenant-General Hardee. His reply to the first call represented the enemy crossing Stone River in heavy force in his immediate front ; and on receiving the second order he informed me that they had already crossed in heavy force, and were advancing to attack his lines. He was immediately ordered not to await attack, but to advance and meet them. About this same time a report reached me that a heavy force of the enemy's infantry was advancing on the Lebanon road, about five miles in Breckinridge's front. Brigadier-General Pegram, who had been sent to that road to cover the flank of the infantry with his cavalry brigade,—save two regiments detached with Wheeler and Wharton, —was ordered forward immediately to develop any such movement. The orders for the two brigades from Breckinridge were countermanded, while dispositions were made, at his request, to reinforce him. Before they could be carried out, the movement ordered disclosed the fact that no force had crossed Stone River, that the only enemy in our immediate front there was a small body of sharp-shooters, and that there was no advance on the Lebanon road. These unfortunate misapprehensions on that part of the field, which, with proper precaution, could not have existed, withheld from active operations three fine brigades until the enemy had succeeded in checking our progress, had re-established his lines, and had collected many of his broken battalions.

Having now settled the question that no movement was being made against our right, and none even to be apprehended, Breckinridge was ordered to leave two brigades to support the batteries at "A," on his side of Stone River, and with the balance of the force to cross to the left and report to Lieutenant-General Polk. By the time this could be accomplished, it was too late to send this force to Lieutenant-General Hardee's support, who was unable to make further progress, and he was directed to maintain his position. Polk was directed, with these reinforcements, to throw all the force he could collect upon the enemy's extreme left, and thereby either carry that strong point, which had so far resisted us successfully, or, failing in that, at least to draw off from Hardee's front the formidable opposition there concentrated.

The three brigades of Jackson, Preston, and Adams were successively reported for this work. How gallantly they moved to their work, and how much they suffered in the determined effort to accomplish it, will best appear from the reports of subordinate commanders and the statement of losses therewith. Upon this flank—their strongest defensive position resting on the river-bank—the enemy had concentrated not less than twenty pieces of artillery, masked almost entirely from view, but covering an open space in front of several hundred yards, supported, right, left, and rear, by heavy masses of infantry.

The position proved impenetrable, and, after two unsuccessful efforts, the attempt to carry it by infantry was abandoned. Our heaviest batteries of artillery and rifled guns of long range were now concentrated in front, and their fires opened on this position. After a cannonade of some time, the enemy's fire slackened, and finally closed near nightfall. Lieutenant-General Hardee had slightly retired his line from the farthest point he had attained, for better position and cover, without molestation from the enemy.

Lieutenant-General Polk's infantry, including the three reinforced brigades, uniting their front with Hardee's right, and extending to our extreme right flank, formed a continuous line, very nearly perpendicular to the original line of battle, thus leaving nearly the whole field, with all its trophies, the enemy's dead and many of his wounded, his hospitals and stores, in our possession. The body of Brigadier-General Sill, one of their division commanders, was found where he had fallen, and was sent to town and decently interred, although he had forfeited all claim to such consideration by the acts of cruelty, barbarity, and atrocity but a few days before committed, under his authority, on the women and children and old men living near the road on which he had made a reconnoissance.

During the afternoon, Brigadier-General Pegram, discovering a hospital and large numbers of stragglers in the rear of the enemy's lines and across Stone River, charged them with his cavalry, and captured about one hundred and seventy prisoners.

Both armies, exhausted by a conflict of full ten hours' duration, rarely surpassed for its continued intensity and heavy losses sustained, sank to rest with the sun, and perfect quiet prevailed for the night.

At dawn on Thursday morning, the 1st of January, orders were sent to the several commanders to press forward their skirmishers, feel the enemy, and report any change in his position. Major-General Breckinridge had been transferred to the right of Stone River to resume the command of that position, now held by two of his brigades. It was soon reported that no change had occurred, except the withdrawal of the enemy from the advanced position occupied by his left flank. Finding, upon further examination, that this was the case, the right flank of Lieutenant-General Polk's corps was thrown forward to occupy the ground for which we had so obstinately contended the evening before. This shortened our lines considerably, and gave us possession of the centre battle-field, from which we gleaned the spoils and trophies throughout the day, and transferred them rapidly to the rear.

A careful reconnoissance of the enemy's position was ordered, and the most of the cavalry was put in motion for the roads in his rear, to cut off his trains and develop any movement. It was soon ascertained that he was still in very heavy force all along our front, occupying a position strong by nature and improved by such work as could be done by night by his reserves.

In a short time, reports from the cavalry informed me that heavy trains were moving towards Nashville, some of the wagons loaded, and all the ambulances filled with wounded. These were attacked at different places, many wagons destroyed, and hundreds of prisoners paroled. No doubt this induced the enemy to send large escorts of cavalry and artillery and infantry with later trains; and thus the impression was made on our ablest commanders that a retrograde movement was going on.

Our forces, greatly wearied and much reduced by heavy losses, were held ready to avail themselves of any change in the enemy's position; but it was deemed unadvisable 'to assail him as there established. The whole day, after these dispositions, was passed without an important movement on either side, and was consumed by us in gleaning the battle-field, burying the dead, and replenishing ammunition.

At daylight on Friday, the 2d, orders to feel the enemy and ascertain his position were repeated, with the same result. The cavalry brigades of Wheeler and Wharton had returned during the night, greatly exhausted from long-continued service, with but little rest or food for either man or horse. Both the commanders reported the indications from the enemy's movements the same. Allowing them only a few hours to feed and rest, and sending the two detached regiments back to Pegram's brigade, Wharton was ordered to the right bank across Stone River, immediately in Breckinridge's front. Reconnoissances by several staff-officers soon developed the fact that a division had quietly crossed unopposed and established themselves on and under cover of an eminence from which Lieutenant-General Polk's line was commanded and enfiladed. The dislodgment of this force or the withdrawal of Polk's line was an evident necessity. The latter involved consequences not to be entertained. Orders were consequently given for the concentration of the whole of General Breckinridge's division in front of the position to be taken, the addition to his command of the ten Napoleon guns, twelve-pounders, under Captain F. H. Robertson, an able and accomplished artillery officer, and for the cavalry forces of Wharton and Pegram, about two thousand men, to join in his attack on the right. Major-General Breckinridge was sent for, and advised of the movement and its objects, the securing and holding the position which protected Polk's flank and gave us command of the enemy's, by which to enfilade him. He was informed of the disposition of the forces placed at his disposal, and instructed with them to drive the enemy back, crown the hill, intrench his artillery, and hold the position.

To distract their attention from our real object, a heavy fire was ordered to be opened from Polk's front at the exact hour at which the movement was to begin. At other points, throughout both lines, all was quiet. General Breckinridge, at three P.M., reported he would advance at four. Polk's batteries promptly opened fire, and were soon answered by the enemy. A heavy cannonade of some fifteen minutes was succeeded by the musketry, which soon became general. The contest was short and severe; the enemy was driven back, and the eminence gained; but the movement, as a whole, was a failure, and the position was again yielded. Our forces were moved, unfortunately, to the left so far as to throw a portion of them into and over Stone River, where they encountered heavy masses of the enemy, while those against whom they were intended to operate on our side of the river had a destructive enfilade on our whole line. Our reserved line was so close to the front as to receive the enemy's fire, and, returning it, took their friends in the rear. The cavalry force was left entirely out of the action.

Learning from my own staff-officers, sent to the scene, of the disorderly retreat being made by General Breckinridge's division, Brigadier-General Patton Anderson's fine brigade of Mississippians, the nearest body of troops, was promptly ordered to the relief. On reaching the field and moving forward, Anderson found himself in front of Breckinridge's infantry, and soon encountered the enemy's light troops close upon our artillery, which had been left without support. This noble brigade, under its cool and gallant chief, drove the enemy back, and saved all the guns not captured before its arrival. Captain F. H. Robertson, after the disabling wound received by Major Graves, General Breckinridge's gallant and efficient Chief of Artillery, took the entire charge of the artillery of the division, in addition to his own. To his gallantry, energy, and fearlessness is due the smallness of our loss sustained before the arrival of support,—only three guns. His report will show the important part he played in this attack and repulse. Before the end of the whole movement, it was quite dark. Anderson's command held a position next the enemy, corresponding nearly with our original line, while Breckinridge's brigade commanders collected their men, as far as practicable in the darkness, and took irregular positions on Anderson's left and rear. At daylight in the morning they were moved forward to the front, and the whole line was re-established without opposition. During the night, Major-General Cleborne's division was re-transferred to its original position on the right, and Lieutenant-General Hardee directed to resume his command there and restore our line.

On Saturday morning, the 3d, our forces had been in line of battle five days and nights, with but little rest. Having no reserves, their baggage and tents had been loaded, and the wagons were four miles off; their provisions, if cooked at all, were most improperly prepared with scanty means; the weather had been severe from cold and almost constant rain, and we had no change of clothing, and in many places could not have fire. The necessary consequence was the great exhaustion of both officers and men, many having to be sent to the hospitals in the rear, and more still were beginning to straggle from their commands,—an evil from which we had so far suffered but little. During the whole of this day the rain continued to fall with little intermission, and the rapid rise in Stone River indicated that it soon would be unfordable. Late on Tuesday night I had received the captured papers of Major-General McCook, commanding one *corps d'armée* of the enemy, showing their effective strength to have been very nearly, if not quite, seventy thousand men. Before noon, reports from Brigadier-General Wheeler satisfied me that the enemy, instead of retiring, was receiving reinforcements.

Common prudence and the safety of my army, upon which even the safety of our cause depended, left no doubt in my mind as to the necessity of my withdrawal from so unequal a contest. My orders were accordingly given about noon for the movement of the trains and for the necessary preparations of troops.

Under the efficient management of the different staff departments, every thing had been secured and transferred to the rear, including prisoners, captured artillery, small arms, subsistence, means of transportation, and nearly all of our wounded able to bear moving. No movements were made by the troops on either side during this most inclement day, save just at night, when a sharp skirmish occurred between Polk's right and the enemy's left flank, resulting in nothing decisive. The only question with me was, whether the movements should be made at once or delayed twenty-four hours to save a few of our wounded. As it was probable we should lose by exhaustion as many as we should remove of the wounded, my inclination to remain was yielded. The whole force, except the cavalry, was put in motion at eleven o'clock P.M., and the army retired in perfect order to its present position, behind Duck River, without receiving or giving a shot. Our cavalry held the position before Murfreesborough until Monday morning, the 5th, when it quietly retired, as ordered, to cover our front.

We left about one thousand two hundred badly wounded, one-half of whom, we learn, have since died from the severity of their injuries; about three hundred sick, too feeble to bear transportation; and about two hundred well men and medical officers as their attendants. [The real number was two thousand eight hundred.—Author of the "Annals."] In addition to this, the enemy had captured about eight hundred prisoners from us. As the one thousand two hundred wounded are counted once under that head among our losses, they should be excluded from the general total.

As an offset to this loss, we had secured, as will appear from the report of my inspector-general, considerably over six thousand prisoners; had captured over thirty pieces of artillery, six thousand stands of small arms, ambulances, mules, and harness, with a large amount of valuable property, all of which was secured and appropriated to proper uses. Besides all this secured, we had burned not less than eight hundred wagons, mostly laden with various articles, such as arms, ammunition, provisions, baggage, clothing, medicines, and hospital stores. We had lost three pieces of artillery only, all in Breckinridge's repulse. A number of stands of colors—nine of which are forwarded with this report—were also captured on the field. Others known to have been taken were not sent in.

The number of fighting-men we had on the field on the morning of the 31st
of December was less than thirty-five thousand, of which about thirty thousand
were infantry and artillery.

Among the gallant dead the nation is called to mourn, none could have fallen
more honored or regretted than Brigadier-Generals James E. Rains and R. W.
Hanson. They yielded their lives in the heroic discharge of duty, and leave
their honored names as a rich legacy to their descendants. Brigadier-Generals
James R. Chalmers and D. W. Adams received disabling wounds on Wednesday,
I am happy to say not serious, but which deprived us of their valuable services.
Having been under my immediate command since the beginning of the war, I
can bear evidence to their devotion and to the conspicuous gallantry which has
marked their services on every field.

For the sacred names of other heroes and patriots of lower grades, who gave
their lives, illustrating the character of the Confederate soldier on this bloody
field, I must refer to the reports of subordinate commanders, and to the list
which will be submitted. *Our loss, it will be seen, exceeded ten thousand, nine
thousand of whom were killed and wounded.*

The enemy's loss we have no means of knowing with certainty. One corps,
commanded by Major-General Thomas J. Crittenden, which was least exposed
in the engagement, reports over five thousand killed and wounded. As they
had two other corps and a separate division, third of a corps, and their
cavalry, it is safely estimated at three thousand killed and sixteen thousand
wounded; adding six thousand two hundred and seventy-three prisoners, and
we have a total of twenty-five thousand two hundred and seventy-three.

Lieutenant-Generals L. Polk and W. J. Hardee, commanding corps, Major-
Generals J. M. Withers and P. R. Cleborne, commanding divisions, are especially commended to the Government for the valor, skill, and ability displayed
by them throughout the engagement.

Brigadier-General J. Patton Anderson, for the coolness, judgment, and
courage with which he interposed his brigade between our retreating forces
and the enemy, largely superior to him, on Friday evening, and saved our
artillery, is justly entitled to special mention.

Brigadier-Generals Joseph Wheeler and John H. Wharton, commanding
cavalry brigades, were pre-eminently distinguished throughout the action, as
they had been for a month previous in many successive actions with the enemy.
Under their skilful and gallant lead, the reputation of our cavalry has been
greatly enhanced.

For the just commendation of many other officers, many of whom were pre-
eminently distinguished, I must refer to the reports of their more immediate
commanders.

To the private soldier a fair meed of praise is due; and, though it is seldom
given, and so rarely expected that it may be considered out of place, I cannot, in justice to myself, withhold the opinion ever entertained, and so often
expressed, during our struggle for independence. In the absence of the
instruction and discipline of old armies, and of the confidence which long
association produces between veterans, we have, in a great measure, to trust to
the individuality and self-reliance of the private soldier. Without the incentive
or the motive which controls the officer, who hopes to live in history, without
the hope of reward, and actuated only by a sense of duty and patriotism, he
has, in this great contest, justly judged that the cause was his own, and gone
into it with a determination to conquer or die, to be free or not to be at all. No
encomium is too high, no honor too great, for such a soldiery. However much
of credit and glory may be given, and probably justly given, to the leaders in
our struggle, history will yet award the main honor where it is due,—to the
private soldier, who, without hope of reward, and with no other incentive than
a consciousness of rectitude, has encountered all the hardships and suffered all
the privations. Well has it been said, "The first monument our Confederacy
rears, when our independence shall have been won, should be a lofty shaft,
pure and spotless, bearing this inscription:—'To the unknown and unrecorded
dead.'"

The members of my staff, arduously engaged in their several duties before, during, and since the prolonged engagement, are deserving a mention in this report.

Lieutenant-Colonels George G. Gardner and G. W. Brent and Captain P. Thompson, Adjutant Inspector-General's Department; 1st Lieutenants Towson Ellis and F. S. Parker, regular aide-de-camps; Lieutenant-Colonel Beard, Inspector-General; Lieutenant-Colonels A. J. Hays and P. A. May; Major James Stainbridge, Louisiana Infantry, and Major Wm. Clarelate, 7th Alabama Volunteers, Adjutant Assistant Inspector-Generals; Lieutenant-Colonel L. W. O'Bannow, Chief Quartermaster; Major J. J. Walker, Chief Commissary; Majors F. Molloy and G. M. Hillyer, Assistants; Lieutenant-Colonel H. Aladowski, Chief of Ordnance; Captains W. H. Warren and O. T. Gibbs and Lieutenant W. F. Johnson, Assistants; Captain S. W. Steele, Assistant Chief Engineer, and Lieutenants H. C. Forie, and H. H. Buchanan, and J. R. P. McFall; Lieutenant-Colonel J. H. Hollinquist, Acting Chief of Artillery; First Lieutenant R. H. Thompson, Assistant Surgeon; A. J. Foard, Medical Director; Surgeon E. A. Llewellen, Assistant Medical Director; Acting Surgeon T. G. Richardson, attendant on myself, staff, and escort; Colonel David Urquhart, of Louisiana; J. Stoddard Johnston, of Kentucky; and St. Leger Grenfel, of England, the two former volunteer aides, long on my staff, serving me most effectively; Major E. W. Baylor, Assistant Quartermaster; Major B. O. Kennedy, Assistant Commissary of Subsistence, and Lieutenant William M. Bridges, aide-de-camp to the late Brigadier-General Duncan, reported just before the engagement, and joined my staff, on which they served through the battle; Colonel M. L. Clark, of the Artillery P. A., did me the favor to join and serve on my staff during the engagement.

His Excellency Isham G. Harris, Governor of Tennessee, and the Hon. Andrew Ewing, member of the Military Court, volunteered their services and rendered me efficient aid, especially with the Tennessee troops, *largely in the ascendant in the army*. It is but due to a zealous and efficient laborer in our cause that I here bear testimony to the cordial support given me at all times, since meeting him a year ago in West Tennessee, by his Excellency Governor Harris. From the field of Shiloh, where he received in his arms the dying form of the lamented Johnston, to the last struggle at Murfreesborough, he has been one of us, and has shared all our privations and dangers, while giving us his personal and political influence with all the power he possessed at the head of the State Government. To the medical department of the army, under the able administration of Surgeon Foard, great credit is due for the success which attended their labors. Sharing none of the excitement and glory of the field, these officers, in their labor of love, devoted themselves assiduously in attending the sufferings of their brother soldiers at war, when others are seeking repose. The reports of subordinate commanders have been especially called for, and are soon expected, when they will be promptly forwarded.

During the time the operations at Murfreesborough were being conducted, important expeditions under Brigadier-Generals Forrest and Morgan were absent in West Tennessee and Northern Kentucky. The reports already forwarded show the complete success which attended these gallant brigadiers, and commend them to the confidence of the Government and gratitude of the country.

I am, sir, very respectfully, your obedient servant,

BRAXTON BRAGG,
General Commanding.

General S. Cooper, *Adjutant-General, Richmond, Va.*

THE END.

General Rosecrans's Report of the Chickamauga Campaign.

HEAD-QUARTERS ARMY OF THE CUMBERLAND, October 12, 1863.

REPORT OF THE OPERATIONS OF THE ARMY OF THE CUMBERLAND—THE OCCUPATION OF MIDDLE TENNESSEE, AND PASSAGE OVER THE CUMBERLAND MOUNTAINS.

The rebel army, after its expulsion from Middle Tennessee, crossed the Cumberland Mountains, by way of the Tantallon and University Roads, then moved down Battle Creek and crossed the Tennessee River, on bridges, it is said, near the mouth of Battle Creek, and at Belly's Ferry, and on the railroad bridge, at Bridgeport. They destroyed a part of the latter, after having passed over it, and retired to Chattanooga and Tyner Station, leaving guards along the river. On their arrival at Chattanooga, they commenced immediately to throw up some defensive field-works at that place, and also at each of the crossings of the Tennessee, as far up as Blythe's Ferry.

Our troops, having pursued the rebels as far as supplies and the state of the roads rendered it practicable, took position from McMinnville to Winchester, with advances at Pelham and Stevenson. The latter soon after moved to Bridgeport, in time to save from total destruction a saw-mill there, but not in time to prevent the destruction of the railroad bridge.

After the expulsion of Bragg's forces from Middle Tennessee, the next objective point of this army was Chattanooga. It commands the southern entrance into East Tennessee, the most valuable, if not the chief, sources of supplies of coal for the manufactories and machine-shops of the Southern States, and is one of the great gateways through the mountains to the campaign counties of Georgia and Alabama.

For the better understanding of the campaign, I submit a brief outline of the topography of the country from the barrens of the northwestern base of the Cumberland Range, to Chattanooga and its vicinity.

The Cumberland Range is a lofty mass of rocks separating the waters which flow into the Cumberland from those which flow into the Tennessee, and extending from beyond the Kentucky line in a southwesterly direction nearly to Athens, Alabama. Its northwestern slopes are steep and rocky and scalloped in coves, in which are the heads of numerous streams that water Middle Tennessee. Its top is undulating or rough, covered with timber, soil comparatively barren, and in dry seasons scantily supplied with water. Its southeastern slope above Chattanooga for many miles is precipitous, rough, and difficult all the way up to Kingston. The valley between the foot of this slope and the river seldom exceeds four or five miles in width, and, with the exception of a narrow border along the banks, is undulating or hilly.

The Sequatchie Valley is along the river of that name, and is a cañon or deep cut splitting the Cumberland Range, parallel to its length. It is only three or four miles in breadth, and fifty miles in length. The sides of this valley are even more precipitous than the great eastern-and-western slopes of the Cumberland, which have just been described. To reach Chattanooga from McMinnville, or north of the Tennessee, it is necessary to turn the head of this Valley of the Tennessee, or to cross it by Dunlap or Thurman.

That part of the Cumberland Range between Sequatchie and the Tennessee, called Walden's Ridge, abuts on the Tennessee in high rocky bluffs, having no practicable space sufficient for a good wagon-road along the river. The Nashville & Chattanooga Railroad crosses that branch of the Cumberland Range west of the Sequatchie, through a low gap, by a tunnel east of Cowan, down the gorge of Big Crow Creek to Stevenson, at the foot of the mountain, on the Memphis & Charleston Railroad, three miles from the Tennessee and ten miles from Bridgeport.

Between Stevenson and Chattanooga, on the south of the Tennessee, are two ranges of mountains, the Tennessee River separating them from the Cumberland, its channel a great chasm cut through the mountain-masses, which, in those places, abut directly on the river. These two ranges are separated by a narrow valley, through which runs Lookout Creek.

The Sand Mountains are next to the Tennessee, and their southern extremity is called Raccoon Mountain. Its sides are precipitous, and its top barren oak ridges, nearly destitute of water. There are but few, and these very difficult, wagon-roads by which to ascend and descend the slopes of this mountain.

East of Lookout Valley is Lookout Mountain, a vast palisade of rocks, rising twenty-four hundred feet above the level of the sea, in abrupt rocky cliffs, from a steep, wooded base. Its eastern sides are no less precipitous. Its top varies from one to six or seven miles in breadth, is heavily timbered, sparsely settled, and poorly watered. It terminates abruptly upon the Tennessee, two miles below Chattanooga, and the only practicable roads across it are one over the nose of the mountain at this point, one at Johnson's Crook, twenty-six miles distant, and one at Winston's Gap, forty-two miles distant from Chattanooga.

Between the eastern base of this range and the line of the Chattanooga & Atlanta or Georgia State Railroad, are a series of narrow valleys, separated by smaller ranges of hills or low mountains, over which there are quite a number of practicable wagon-roads running eastward towards the railroad. The first of these ranges is Mission Ridge, separating the waters of Chickamauga from Chattanooga Creek. A higher range, with fewer gaps, on the southeast side of the Chickamauga, is Pigeon Mountain, branching from Lookout, near Dougherty's Gap, some forty miles south from Chattanooga. It extends in a northerly direction, bearing eastward, until it is lost in the general level of the country, near the line of the Chattanooga & Lafayette Road.

East of these two ranges and of the Chickamauga, starting from Ottawah and passing by Ringgold to the west of Dalton, is Taylor's Ridge, a rough, rocky range, traversable by wagon-roads only through gaps, generally several miles apart.

Mission Ridge passes about three miles east of Chattanooga, ending near the Tennessee, at the mouth of the Chickamauga. Taylor's Ridge separates the East Tennessee & Georgia Railroad from the Chattanooga & Atlanta Railroad.

The junction of these roads is at Dalton, in a valley east of Taylor's Ridge and west of the rough mountain-region in which are the sources of the Coosa River. This valley, only about nine or ten miles wide, is the natural southern gateway into East Tennessee, while the other valleys just mentioned terminate northwardly on the Tennessee to the west of it, and extend in a southwardly direction towards the line of the Coosa, the general direction of which, from the crossing of the Atlanta road to Rome and thence to Gadsden, is southwest.

From the position of our army at McMinnville, Tullahoma, Decherd, and Winchester, to reach Chattanooga, crossing the Tennessee above it, it was necessary either to pass north of the Sequatchie Valley by Pikeville or Kingston, or to cross the main Cumberland and the Sequatchie Valley by Dunlap or Thurman and Walden's Ridge, by the routes passing through these places, a distance of sixty-five or seventy miles, over a country destitute of forage and poorly supplied with water, by narrow and difficult wagon-roads.

The main Cumberland range could also have been passed on an inferior road by Pelham and Tracy City, to Thurman. The most southerly route on which to move troops and transportation to the Tennessee, above Chattanooga, was by Cowan University, Battle Creek, and Jasper, or by Tantallon, Anderson,

Stevenson, or Bridgeport and the mouth of Battle Creek, to same point, and thence by Thurman or Dunlap and Poe's Tavern, across Walden's Ridge. The University road, though difficult, was the best of these two; that by Cowan, Tantallon, and Stevenson being very rough between Cowan and Anderson, and much longer.

There were, also, three roads across to the Tennessee River below Stevenson,— the best, but much the longest, by Fayetteville and Athens, a distance of seventy miles; the next, a very rough wagon-road from Winchester, by Salem, to Larkinsville; and an exceedingly rough road by way of Mount Top, one branch leading thence to Bellefont, and the other to Stevenson.

On these latter routes little or no forage was to be found, except at the extremities of the lines, and they were also scarce of water. The one by Athens has both forage and water in abundance.

It is evident, from this description of the topography, that to reach Chattanooga or penetrate the country south of it, on the railroad, by crossing the Tennessee below Chattanooga, was a difficult task. It was necessary to cross the Cumberland Mountains with subsistence, ammunition, at least a limited supply of forage, and a bridge-train, to cross Sand or Raccoon Mountains into Lookout Valley, then Lookout Mountain, and finally the lesser ranges of Mission Ridge, if we went directly to Chattanooga, or Mission Ridge, Pigeon Mountain, and Taylor's Ridge, if we struck the railroad at Dalton or south of it. The valley of the Tennessee River, though several miles in breadth between the bases of the mountains below Bridgeport, is not a broad alluvial farming-country, but full of barren oak ridges, sparsely settled, and but a small part of it under cultivation.

The first step was to repair the Nashville & Chattanooga Railroad, to bring forward to Tullahoma, McMinnville, Decherd, and Winchester needful forage and subsistence, which it was impossible to transport from Murfreesborough to those points over the horrible roads which we encountered on our advance to Tullahoma. The next was to extend the repairs of the main stem to Stevenson and Bridgeport, and the Tracy City Branch, so that we could place supplies in the depots at those points, from which to draw after we had crossed the mountains.

Through Colonel Innis and his regiment of Michigan Engineers, the main road was opened to the Elk River bridge by the 13th of July, and Elk River bridge and the main stem to Bridgeport by the 25th, and the branch to Tracy City by the 13th of August.

As soon as the main stem was finished to Stevenson, Sheridan's division was advanced, two brigades, to Bridgeport, and one to Stevenson, and quartermaster and commissary stores pushed forward to the latter place with all practicable speed. These supplies began to be accumulated at this point in sufficient quantities by the 8th of August, and corps commanders were that day directed to supply their troops, as soon as possible, with rations and forage sufficient for a general movement.

The Tracy City Branch, built for bringing the coal down the mountains, has such high grades and sharp curves as to require a peculiar engine. The only one we had answering the purpose, having been broken on its way from Nashville, was not repaired until about the 12th of August. It was deemed best, therefore, to delay the movement of the troops until that road was completely available for transporting stores to Tracy City.

The movement over the Cumberland Mountains began on the morning of the 16th of August, as follows:—

General Crittenden's corps, in three columns: General Wood, from Hillsborough, by Pelham, to Thurman, in Sequatchie Valley.

General Palmer, from Manchester, by the most practicable route, to Dunlap.

General Van Cleve, with two brigades from McMinnville, the third being left in garrison there, by the most practicable route, to Pikeville, the head of Sequatchie Valley.

Colonel Minty's cavalry to move on the left by Sparta, to drive back Detrel's cavalry towards Kingston, where the enemy's mounted troops under Forrest were concentrated, and then, covering the left flank of Van Cleve's column, to proceed to Pikeville.

The 14th army Corps, Major-General George H. Thomas commanding, moved as follows:—

General Reynolds, from University, by way of Battle Creek, to take post concealed near its mouth.

General Brannan to follow him.

General Negley to go by Tantallon, and halt on Crow Creek, between Anderson and Stevenson.

General Baird to follow him and camp near Anderson.

The 20th Corps, Major-General A. McD. McCook commanding, moved as follows:—

General Johnson by Salem and Larkin's Ford to Bellefont.

General Davis by Mount Top and Crow Creek to near Stevenson.

The three brigades of cavalry by Fayetteville and Athens, to cover the line of the Tennessee from Whitesburg up.

On his arrival in the Sequatchie Valley, General Crittenden was to send a brigade of infantry to reconnoitre the Tennessee, near Harrison's Landing, and take post at Poe's Cross-Roads; Minty was to reconnoitre from Washington down and take post at Smith's Cross-Roads; and Wilder's brigade of mounted infantry was to reconnoitre from Harrison's Landing to Chattanooga, and be supported by a brigade of infantry which General Crittenden was to send from Thurman to the foot of the eastern slope of Walden's Ridge, in front of Chattanooga.

These movements were completed by the evening of the 20th of August. Hazen's brigade made the reconnoissance on Harrison's Landing, and reported the enemy throwing up works there, and took post at Poe's Cross-Roads on the 21st. Wagner, with his brigade, supported Wilder in his reconnoissance on Chattanooga, which they surprised and shelled from across the river, creating no little agitation. Thus the army passed the first great barrier between it and the objective point, and arrived opposite the enemy on the banks of the Tennessee.

The crossing of the river required that the best points should be chosen, and means provided for the crossing. The river was reconnoitred; the pontoons and trains were ordered forward as rapidly as possible, hidden from view in the rear of Stevenson, and prepared for use. By the time they were ready, the places of crossing had been selected, and dispositions made to begin the operation. It was very desirable to conceal to the last moment the points of crossing; but, as the mountains on the south side of the Tennessee rise in precipitous, rocky bluffs, to the height of eight hundred or a thousand feet, completely overlooking the whole valley and its coves, this was next to impossible.

Not having pontoons for two bridges across the river, General Sheridan began trestle-work for parts of one at Bridgeport, while General Reynolds's division seized Shellmound, captured some boats, and from these, and material picked up, prepared the means of crossing at that point, and General Brannan prepared rafts for crossing his troops at the mouth of Battle Creek.

The laying of the pontoon-bridge at Caperton's Ferry was very handsomely done by the troops of General Davis, under the direction of General McCook, who crossed his advance in pontoons at daylight, driving the enemy's cavalry from the opposite side. The bridge at Bridgeport was finished on the 29th of August; but an accident occurred which delayed its final completion until September 2.

The movement across the river was commenced August 29, and completed on the 4th of September, leaving the regular brigade in charge of the railroad and depot at Stevenson until relieved by Major-General Granger, who was directed, as soon as practicable, to relieve it and take charge of the rear.

General Thomas's corps was to cross as follows: one division at Caperton's, one at Bridgeport, Reynolds's at Shellmound, in boats, and one division at Battle Creek, on rafts. All were to use the bridge at Bridgeport for such portions of their trains as they might find necessary, and to concentrate near Trenton, and send an advance to Frick's, Cooper's, and Stevens's Gaps on the

Lookout Mountain—the only practicable routes leading down the mountains into the valley called McLemore's Cove, which lies at its base and stretches northeast-wardly towards Chattanooga. General McCook's corps was to cross,—two divisions at Caperton's Ferry,—move to the valley head and seize Winston's Gap, while Sheridan was to cross at Bridgeport as soon as the bridge was laid, and join the rest of his corps near Winston's, by way of Trenton.

General Crittenden was ordered down the Sequatchie, leaving two advance brigades, under Hazen and Wagner, with Minty's cavalry and Wilder's mounted infantry, to watch and annoy the enemy. He was to cross the river, following Thomas's corps at the crossing, and to take post on the Murphy's Hollow Road, pushing an advance brigade to reconnoitre the enemy at the foot of Lookout, and take post at Wauhatchie, communicating from its main body with Thomas on the right, up the Trenton Valley and threatening Chattanooga by passing over the point of Lookout.

The cavalry, crossing at Caperton's and a ford near Island Creek, were to unite in Lookout Valley, take post at Rawlingsville and reconnoitre boldly towards Rome and Alpine.

These movements were completed by McCook's and Crittenden's corps on the 6th, and by Thomas's corps on the 8th of September. The cavalry, for some reason, was not pushed with the vigor nor to the extent which orders and the necessities of the campaign required. Its continual movement since that period, and the absence of Major-General Stanley, Chief of Cavalry, have prevented the report which may throw some light on the subject.

The first barriers south of the Tennessee being crossed, the enemy was found firmly holding the point of Lookout Mountain with infantry and artillery, while our forces on the north side of the river reported the movements of the rebel forces from East Tennessee and their concentration at Chattanooga. To dislodge him from that place, it was necessary to carry Lookout Mountain, or so to move as to compel him to quit his position by endangering his line of communication. The latter plan was chosen.

The cavalry were ordered to advance on our extreme right to Summerville, in Broomtown Valley, and General McCook was ordered to support the movement by a division of infantry thrown forward to the vicinity of Alpine. It was executed on the 8th and 9th of September.

General Thomas was ordered to cross his corps by Frick's, Cooper's, and Stevens's Gaps, and occupy the head of McLemore's Cove. General Crittenden was ordered to reconnoitre the front of Lookout Mountain, sending a brigade up an almost impracticable path, called Nickajack Trace, to Summertown, a hamlet on the summit of the mountain, overlooking Chattanooga, and holding the main body of his corps either to support these reconnoissances, to prevent a sortie of the enemy over the nose of Lookout, or to enter Chattanooga in case the enemy should evacuate it or make but a feeble resistance. Simultaneously with this movement, the cavalry were ordered to push by way of Alpine and Broom-town Valley and strike the enemy's railroad-communication between Resaca Bridge and Dalton.

This movement was promptly begun on the 8th and 9th of September. The reconnoissance of General Crittenden on the 9th developed the fact that the enemy had evacuated Chattanooga the day and night previous; and his advance took peaceable possession at one o'clock P.M. His whole corps, with its trains, passed around the point of Lookout Mountain on the 10th, and camped for the night at Rossville, five miles south of Chattanooga.

During these operations, General Thomas pushed his corps over the moun-tains at the designated points. Each division consumed two days in the pass-age. The weight of evidence gathered from all sources was, that Bragg was moving on Rome, and that his movements began on the 6th of September. General Crittenden was therefore directed to hold Chattanooga with one bri-gade, calling all the forces on the north side of the Tennessee across, and to follow the enemy's retreat vigorously, anticipating that the main body had retired by Ringgold and Dalton. Additional information obtained during the afternoon and evening of the 10th of September rendered it certain that his main body retired by the Lafayette road, but uncertain whether he had gone far. General Crittenden was ordered, at one o'clock A.M. on the 11th, to proceed to the front, and report, directing his command to advance only as far as Ringgold and order a reconnoissance to Gordon's Mills. His report, and further evidence, satisfied me that the main body of the rebel army were in the vicinity of Lafayette. General Crittenden was therefore ordered to move his corps, with all possible despatch, from Ringgold to Gordon's Mills, and communicate with General Thomas, who had by that time reached the eastern foot of Lookout Mountain. General Crittenden occupied Ringgold on the 11th, pushing Wilder's mounted infantry as far as Tunnel Hill, skirmishing heavily with the enemy's cavalry. Hazen joined him near Ringgold on the 11th, and the whole corps moved rapidly and successfully across to Gordon's Mills on the 12th. Wilder, following, and covering the movement, had a severe fight with the enemy at Sill's Tan-Yard.

During the same day the 4th U.S. Cavalry were ordered to move past the Dry Valley road to discover if the enemy was in proximity to that road on Crittenden's right, and open communication with Thomas's command, which, passing over the mountain, was debouching from Stevens's and Cooper's Gaps, and moving on Lafayette through Dry Gap of the Pigeon Mountain. On the 10th, Negley's division advanced to within a mile of Dry Gap, which they heavily obstructed, and Baird's division came up to his support on the morning of the 11th. Negley became satisfied that the enemy was advancing upon him in heavy force, and, perceiving that if he accepted battle in that position he would probably be cut off, he fell back, after a sharp skirmish in which General Baird's division participated, skilfully covering and securing their trains, to a strong position in front of Stevens's Gap.

On the 12th, Reynolds and Brannan, under orders to move, promptly closed up to the support of these two advance divisions. During the same day, General McCook had reached the vicinity of Alpine, and, with infantry and cavalry, had reconnoitred the Broomtown Valley to Summerville, and ascertained that the enemy had not retreated on Rome, but was concentrating at Lafayette. There it was ascertained that the enemy was concentrating all his forces, both infantry and cavalry, upon the Pigeon Mountain, in the vicinity of Lafayette, while two corps of this army were at Gordon's Mills, Bailey's Cross-Roads at the foot of Stevens's Gap, and at Alpine, a distance of fifty miles from flank to flank by the nearest practicable roads, and fifty-seven miles by the route subsequently taken by the 20th Corps. It had already been ascertained that the main body of Johnston's army had joined Bragg, and an accumulation of evidence showed that the troops from Virginia had reached Atlanta on the 1st of the month, and that reinforcements were expected soon to arrive from that quarter. It was, therefore, a matter of life and death to effect a concentration of the army.

General McCook had already been directed to support General Thomas, and was now ordered to send two brigades to hold Dougherty's Gap, and to join General Thomas, with the remainder of his command, with the utmost celerity, directing his march over the road on the top of the mountain. He had already, with great prudence, moved his trains back to the rear of Little River, on the mountain, but, unfortunately, being ignorant of the mountain-road, moved down the mountain at Winston's Gap, down Lookout Valley and Cooper's Gap, up the mountain and down again, closing up with General Thomas on the 17th, and having posted Davis at Brooks's, in front of Dug Gap, Johnson at Pound Spring, in front of Catlett's Gap, and Sheridan at the foot of Stevens's Gap.

As soon as General McCook's corps arrived, General Thomas moved down the Chickamauga, towards Gordon's Mills. Meanwhile, to bring General Crittenden within reach of General Thomas and beyond the danger of separation, he was withdrawn from Gordon's Mills on the 14th, and ordered to take post on the southern spur of Mission Ridge, his right communicating with General Thomas, where he remained until General McCook had effected a junction with General Thomas.

Minty, with his cavalry, reconnoitred the enemy on the 15th, and repulsed him in force at Dalton, Ringgold, Letts, and Rockspring Church. The head of General McCook's column near the same place, General Crittenden was ordered to return to hold possession at Gordon's Mills, his line resting along the Chickamauga, by way of Crawfish Springs.

Thus, on the evening of the 17th, the troops were substantially within supporting distance. Orders were given at once to move the whole line, in the order of battle, down the Chickamauga, with a view of covering the Lafayette road towards Chattanooga, and facing the most practicable route to the enemy's front. The position of our troops and the narrowness of the roads retarded our movements. During the day, while they were in progress, our cavalry, under Colonel Minty, was attacked on the left in the road. It became apparent that the enemy was massing heavily on our left, crossing Reed's and Alexander's bridges in force, while he had threatened Gordon's Mills. Orders were, therefore, promptly given to General Thomas to relieve General Crittenden's corps, posting one division near Crawfish Springs, and to move with the remainder of his corps by the Widow Glenn's house to Rossville and the Lafayette road, his left extending obliquely across it near Kelley's house. General Crittenden was ordered to proceed with Van Cleve and Palmer's divisions to draw the enemy from the Rossville road and form on the left of General Wood, then at Gordon's Mills.

General McCook's corps was to close up to General Thomas, keep the position at Crawfish Springs, and protect General Crittenden's right, while holding his corps mainly in reserve. The main cavalry force was ordered to close in on General McCook's right, watch the crossing of the Chickamauga, and act under his orders. The movement for the concentration of the corps more compactly towards Crawfish Springs was begun on the morning of the 18th under orders to conduct it very secretly, and was executed so slowly that McCook's corps only reached Pound Spring at dark, and bivouacked, resting on their arms during the night. Crittenden's corps reached its position on the Rossville road near midnight.

Evidence accumulated, during the day of the 18th, that the enemy was moving to our left. Minty's cavalry and Wilder's mounted brigade encountered the enemy's cavalry at Reed's and Alexander's bridges towards evening, and were driven in to the Rossville road. At the same time, the enemy had been demonstrating for three miles up the Chickamauga. Heavy clouds of dust had been observed three or four miles beyond the Chickamauga, sweeping to the northwest.

In view of all these facts, the necessity became apparent that General Thomas must use all possible despatch in moving his corps to the position assigned him. He was therefore directed to proceed with all despatch, and General McCook to close up to Crawfish Springs as soon as Thomas's column was out of the way. Thomas pushed forward uninterruptedly during the night, and by daylight the head of his column had reached Kelley's house, on the Lafayette road, where Baird's division was posted. Brannan followed, and was posted on Baird's left, crossing the road leading to Reed's and Alexander's bridges.

At this point, Colonel McCook, of General Grangers corps, who had made a reconnoissance to the Chickamauga the evening before and had burned Reed's bridge, met General Thomas, and reported that an isolated brigade of the enemy was this side of the Chickamauga, and, the bridge being destroyed, a rapid movement in that direction might result in the capture of the force thus isolated. General Thomas ordered Brannan, with two brigades, to reconnoiter in that direction and attack any small force he should meet. The advance brigade, supported by the rest of the division, soon encountered a strong body of the enemy, attacked it vigorously, and drove it back more than half a mile, where a very strong column of the enemy was found, with the evident intention of turning our left and gaining possession of the Lafayette road between us and Chattanooga. This vigorous movement disconcerted the plan of the enemy to move on our left, and opened the battle of the 19th of September.

The leading brigade became engaged at about ten o'clock A.M. on the 19th, on our extreme left, extending to the right, where the enemy combined to move in heavy masses. Apprehending this movement, I had ordered General McCook to send Johnson's division to Thomas's assistance; and he arrived opportunely.

General Crittenden, with great good sense, had already despatched Palmer's division, reporting the fact to me, and receiving my approval. The enemy returned our attack, and was driving back Baird's right in disorder, when Johnson struck the attacking column in flank, and drove it back more than half a mile, until his own right was overlapped and in imminent danger of being turned, when Palmer, coming in on Johnson's right, threw his division against the enemy and drove back his advancing columns. Palmer's right was soon overlapped, when Van Cleve's division came to his support, but was beaten back, when Reynolds's division came in, and was, in turn, overpowered. Davis's division came into the fight then most opportunely, and drove the enemy, who soon, however, developed superior force against his line, and pressed him so heavily that he was giving ground, when Wood's division came, and turned the tide of battle the other way.

About three P.M., General McCook was ordered to send Sheridan's division to the support of our line near Wood and Davis, directing Lytle's brigade to hold Gordon's Mills, our extreme right. Sheridan also arrived opportunely to save Wood from disaster, and the rebel tide was thoroughly stayed in that quarter.

Meanwhile, the roar of musketry on our centre grew louder, and the battle approached head-quarters at Widow Glenn's house, until musket-balls came near and shells burst about it. Our centre was being driven. Orders were sent to General Negley to move his division from Crawfish Springs and above, where be had been holding the line of the Chickamauga, to Widow Glenn's, to be held in reserve, to give support wherever it might be required. At half-past four P.M. he reported with his division; and, as the indications that our centre was being driven became clearer, he was despatched in that direction, and soon found the enemy had dislodged Van Cleve from the line, and was forming there even while Thomas was driving their right. Orders were promptly given Negley to attack him, which he soon did, driving him steadily until night closed the combat.

General Brannan, having repulsed the enemy on the extreme left, was sent by General Thomas to support the centre and at night assume the position on the right of Reynolds. Colonel Wilder's brigade of mounted infantry occupied during the day a position on the Lafayette road, one mile north of Gordon's Mills, where he had taken position on the afternoon previous,—when, contesting the ground step by step, he had been driven by the enemy's advance from Alexander's bridge. Minty's cavalry had been ordered from the same position about noon of the 19th, to report to General Granger at Rossville, which he did at daylight on the 20th, and was posted near Mission Mills to hold in check the enemy's cavalry on their right, from the direction of Ringgold and Graysville.

The reserve corps covered the approaches from the Chickamauga towards Rossville on our left. The roar of battle hushed in the darkness of night, and our troops, weary with a night of marching and a day of fighting, rested on their arms, having everywhere maintained their positions, developed the enemy, and gained thorough command of the Rossville and Dry Valley roads to Chattanooga,—the great object of the battle of the 19th of September. The battle had secured us these objects; our flank covered the Dry Valley and Rossville roads, while our cavalry covered the Mission Ridge and the valley of Chickamauga Creek, into which latter place our spare trains had been sent on Friday, the 18th.

We also had indubitable evidence of the presence of Longstreet's corps and Johnston's forces by the capture of prisoners from each; and the fact that at the close of the day we had present but two brigades which had not been in action, opposed to the superior numbers of the enemy, assured us that we were greatly outnumbered, and that the battle of the next day must be for the safety of the army and the possession of Chattanooga.

During the evening of the 19th, the corps commanders were assembled at head-quarters at Widow Glenn's house. The reports of the position and condition of their commands were heard, and orders given for the disposition of the troops on the following day. Thomas's corps, with the troops which had reinforced him, was to maintain, substantially, its present line with Brannan in reserve. McCook, maintaining his picket-line until it was driven in, was to close on Thomas, his right refused, and covering the position at Widow Glenn's house; and Crittenden to have two divisions in reserve near the junction of McCook's and Thomas's lines, to be able to support either. Plans having been explained and written, advice given to each and read in the presence of all, the weary corps commanders returned about midnight to their commands. No firing took place during the night, and the troops had assumed position when day dawned. The sky was red and sultry, and the atmosphere of the woods enveloped in fog and smoke. As soon as it was sufficiently light, I proceeded, accompanied by General Garfield and some aides, to inspect the lines.

I found General McCook's right too far upon the crest, and General Davis in reserve upon a hillside west of and parallel to the Dry Valley road. I mentioned these defects to the general, desiring Davis's division to be brought down at once, moved more to the left, and placed in close column, by division doubled on the centre, in a sheltered position.

I found General Crittenden's two divisions massed at the foot of the same hill, in the valley, and called his attention to it, desiring them to be moved farther to the left.

General Thomas's troops were in the position indicated, except Palmer's line, which was to be closed more compactly.

Satisfied that the enemy's first attempt would be on our left, orders were despatched to General Negley to join General Thomas, and to General McCook to relieve Negley. Returning to the right, I found Negley had not moved, nor were McCook's troops coming in to relieve him. Negley was preparing to withdraw his two brigades from the line. He was ordered to send his reserve brigade immediately, and follow it with the others only when relieved in line of battle. General Crittenden, whose troops were nearest, was ordered to fill General Negley's place at once, and General McCook was notified of this order, growing out of the necessity of promptly sending Negley to Thomas. Proceeding to the extreme right, I felt the disadvantages of its position, mentioned them to General McCook, and, when I left him, enjoined on him that it was an indispensable necessity that we should keep closed to the left, and that we must do so at all hazards. On my return to the position of General Negley, I found, to my astonishment, that General Crittenden had not relieved him, Wood's division having reached the position of Negley's reserve. Peremptory orders were given to repair this, and Wood's troops moved into position; but this delay subsequently proved of serious consequence. The battle began on the extreme left at half-past eight A.M., and it was half-past nine o'clock when Negley was relieved.

An aide arriving from General Thomas, requesting that Negley's remaining brigades be sent forward as speedily as possible to succor the left, General Crittenden was ordered to move Van Cleve with all possible despatch to a position in the rear of Wood, who closed in on Brannan's right. General McCook was ordered to move Davis up to close in on Wood and fill an opening in the line.

On my return from an examination of the ground in the rear of our right and left centre, I found, to my surprise, that General Van Cleve was posted in line of battle on a high ridge, much too far to the rear to give immediate support to the main line of battle, and General Davis in line of battle in rear of the ridge occupied by Negley's reserve in the morning. General Crittenden was ordered to move Van Cleve at once down the hill to a better position, and General Davis was also ordered to close up to the support of the line near Wood's right. The battle in the mean time roared with increasing fury and approached from the left to the centre. Two aids arrived successively within a few minutes from General Thomas, asking for reinforcements. The first was directed to say that General Negley had already gone, and should be nearly at hand at that time, and that Brannan's reserve brigade was available. The other was directed to say that General Van Cleve would at once be sent to his assistance, which was accordingly done.

A message from General Thomas soon followed, that he was heavily pressed, Captain Kellog, A.D.C., the bearer, informing me at the same time that General Brannan was out of line and General Reynolds's right was exposed. Orders were despatched to General Wood to close up on Reynolds, and word was sent to General Thomas that he should be supported even if it took away the whole corps of Crittenden and McCook.

General Davis was ordered to close on General Wood, and General McCook was advised of the state of affairs, and ordered to close his whole command to the left with all despatch.

General Wood, overlooking the direction to "close up" on General Reynolds, supposed he was to support him by withdrawing from the line and passing to the rear of General Brannan, who, it appears, was not out of line, but was in échélon and slightly in rear of Reynolds's right. By this unfortunate mistake a gap was opened in the line of battle, of which the enemy took instant advantage, and, striking Davis in flank and rear as well as in front, threw his whole division into confusion. The same attack shattered the right brigade of Wood before it had cleared the space. The right of Brannan was thrown back, and two of his batteries then in movement to a new position were taken in flank and thrown back through two brigades of Van Cleve, then on the march to the left, throwing his division into confusion, from which it never recovered until it reached Rossville.

While the enemy poured in through this breach, a long line, stretching beyond Sheridan's right, was advancing. Laibold's brigade shared in the rout of Davis. Sheridan's other two brigades, in movement towards the left, under orders to support Thomas, made a gallant charge against the enemy's advancing column, but were thrown into disorder by the enemy's line advancing on their flank, and were likewise compelled to fall back, rallying in the Dry Valley road and repulsing the enemy, but were again compelled to yield to superior numbers, and retired westward of the Dry Valley, and, by a circuitous route, reached Rossville, from which they advanced, by the Lafayette road, to support our left.

Thus, Davis's two brigades, one of Van Cleve's, and Sheridan's entire division, were driven from the field, and the remainder, consisting of Baird, Johnson, Palmer, Reynolds, Brannan, and Wood, two of Negley's brigades, and one of Van Cleve's, were left to sustain the conflict against the whole power of the rebel army, which, desisting from pursuit on the right, concentrated their whole efforts to destroy them.

At the moment of the repulse of Davis's division, I was standing in rear of his right, waiting the completion of the closing of McCook to the left. Seeing confusion among Van Cleve's troops, and the distance Davis's men were falling back, and the tide of battle surging towards us, the urgency for Sheridan's troops to intervene became imminent, and I hastened in person to the extreme right, to direct Sheridan's movement on the flank of the advancing rebels. It was too late. The crowd of returning troops rolled back, and the enemy advanced. Giving the troops direction to rally behind the ridge west of the Dry Valley road, I passed down it, accompanied by General Garfield, Major McMichael, and Major Bond, of my staff, and a few of the escort, under a shower of grape and canister and musketry, for two or three hundred yards, and attempted to rejoin General Thomas and the troops sent to his support by passing to the rear of the broken portion of our lines, but found the routed troops far towards the left; and, hearing the enemy's advancing musketry and cheers, I became doubtful whether the left had held its ground, and started for Rossville. On consultation and further reflection, however, I determined to send General Garfield there, while I went to Chattanooga to give orders for the security of the pontoon-bridges at Battle Creek and Bridgeport, and to make preliminary dispositions either to forward ammunition and supplies should we hold our ground, or to withdraw the troops into good position.

General Garfield despatched me from Rossville that the left and centre still held its ground. General Granger had gone to its support. General Sheridan had rallied his division, and was advancing towards the same point, and General Davis was going up the Dry Valley road, to our right. General Garfield proceeded to the front, remained there until the close of the fight, and despatched me the triumphant defence our troops there made against the assaults of the enemy.

The fight on the left, after two P.M. was that of the army. Never, in the history of this war at least, have troops fought with greater energy and determination. Bayonet-charges, often heard of, but seldom seen, were repeatedly made by brigades and regiments, in several of our divisions.

After the yielding and severance of the divisions on the right, the enemy made all efforts to break the solid portions of our line. Under the pressure of the rebel onset, the flanks of the line were gradually retired until they occupied strong advantageous ground.

From one to half-past three o'clock, the unequal contest was sustained throughout our line. Then the enemy, in overpowering numbers, flanked around our right, held by General Brannan, and occupied a low gap in the ridge of our defensive position, which commanded our rear. The moment was critical. Twenty minutes more, and our right would have been turned, our position taken in reverse, and, probably, the army routed.

Fortunately, Major-General Granger, whose troops had been posted to cover our left and rear, with the instinct of a true soldier and general, hearing the roar of battle on our left, and being beyond the reach of orders from the general commanding, determined to move to its assistance. He advanced, and soon encountered the enemy's skirmishers, whom he disregarded, well knowing that at that stage of the conflict the battle was not there. Posting Colonel Dan. C. McCook's brigade to take care of any thing in the vicinity and beyond the left of our lines, he moved the remainder to the scene of action, reporting to General Thomas, who directed him to our suffering right.

Arrived in sight, General Granger discovered at once the peril and point of danger, the Gap; and quick as thought he directed his advance-brigade upon the enemy. General Steedman, taking a regimental color, led the column. Swift was the charge and terrible the conflict, but the enemy was broken. A thousand of our brave men killed and wounded paid for its possession, but we held the Gap.

Two divisions of Longstreet's corps confronted the position. Determined to take it, they successively came to the assault. A battery of six guns, placed in the gorge, poured death and slaughter into them. They charged to within a few yards of our pieces; but our grape and canister, and the leaden hail of our musketry, delivered in sparing but terrible volleys, from cartridges taken in many instances from their fallen companions, was too much even for Longstreet's men. About sunset they made their last charge, when our men, being out of ammunition, rushed on them with the bayonet, and they gave way to return no more.

The fury of the conflict was nearly as great on the fronts of Brannan and Wood, being less furious towards the left. But a column of the enemy had made its way to near our left, and to the right of Colonel McCook's position. Apprized of this, General Thomas directed Reynolds to move his division from its position, and, pointing out the rebels, told him to go in there.

To save time, the troops of Reynolds were formed by the rear rank, and, moving with the bayonet at a double-quick with a shout, walked over the rebels, capturing some five hundred. This closed the battle of the 20th. At nightfall the enemy had been repulsed along the whole line, and sank into quietude without attempting to renew the combat.

General Thomas, considering the excessive labors of the troops, the scarcity of ammunition, food, and water, and having orders from the general commanding to use his discretion, determined to retire on Rossville, where they arrived in good order and took post before morning, receiving supplies from Chattanooga, and offering the enemy battle during all the next day and repulsing his reconnoissance. On the night of the 21st, we withdrew from Rossville, took firm possession of the objective point of our campaign,—Chattanooga,—and prepared to hold it.

The operations of the cavalry during the battle of the 19th were very important. General Mitchell, with three brigades, covered our right flank along the line of the Chickamauga above Crawfish Springs, against the combined efforts of the great body of the rebel cavalry, whose attempts to cross the stream they several times repulsed.

Wilder fought, dismounted, near the centre, intervening, two or three times, with mountain-howitzers and Spencer rifles very opportunely.

On the 20th, Minty covered our left and rear at Mission Mills, and later in the day on the Ringgold road.

General Mitchell with his three brigades covered our extreme right, and with Wilder's, after its repulse, extended over Mission Ridge, held the whole country to the base of Lookout Mountain, and all our trains, artillery, caissons, and spare wagons, sent there for renter safety, retiring from the field. He was joined by Post's brigade of Davis's division, which had not closed on the army and was not in action.

On the 21st the cavalry still covered our right as securely as before, fighting and holding at bay very superior numbers. The number of cavalry combats during the whole campaign have been numerous, the successes as numerous; but the army could not have dispensed with those of the 19th, 20th, and 21st.

Our artillery fired fewer rounds than at Stone River, but with even greater effect. I cannot but congratulate the country on the rapid improvement evinced in this part of the service. Our loss of pieces is in part attributable to the rough wooded ground in which we fought, and to want of experience in posting artillery, and partly to the unequal nature of the contest, our infantry being heavily outnumbered.

For the details of these actions, the innumerable instances of distinguished bravery, skill, and gallantry displayed by officers of every rank, and, above all, for self-reliant, cool, and steady courage displayed by the soldiers of the army of all arms, in many instances even shining above that of their officers, I must refer to the accompanying reports of corps, division, brigade, regimental, and battery commanders. The reports of the cavalry commands are not in, for the best of all reasons,—that they have been out nearly ever since, writing with their sabres on the heads and backs of the enemy.

The Signal Corps has been growing into usefulness and favor daily for the last four months, and now bids fair to become one of the most esteemed of the staff services. It rendered very important service from the time we reached the Valley of the Tennessee. For its operations I refer to the report of Captain Jesse Merrill, Chief Signal Officer.

Our Medical Corps proved very efficient during the whole campaign, and especially during and subsequent to the battle. A full share of praise is due to Dr. Glover Perin, the Medical Director of the department, ably assisted by Drs. Grose, Medical Director 14th, Perkins, 20th, and Phelps, 21st Army Corps. A very great meed of praise is due Captain Horace Porter, of the Ordnance Department, for the wise system of arming each regiment with arms of the same calibre, and having the ammunition wagons properly marked, by which most of the difficulties in supplying ammunition, when troops had exhausted it in battle, were obviated. From his report it will be seen that we expended 2,650,000 rounds of musket-cartridges, and 7325 rounds of cannon-ammunition, being 12,675 rounds less of artillery, and 650,000 rounds more of musketry, than at Stone River.

We lost 36 pieces of artillery, 20 caissons, 5834 infantry accoutrements, 8450 stand of small arms.

From the report of Lieutenant-Colonel Wiles, Provost-Marshal General, it will be seen that we took 2003 prisoners. We have 1300 missing, of which some 600 have escaped and come in, and probably 700 or 800 are among the killed and wounded. Of our wounded, some 2500 fell into the hands of the enemy, swelling the balance of prisoners against us to about 5500.

It is proper to observe that the battle of Chickamauga was absolutely necessary to secure our concentration and cover Chattanooga. It was fought in a country covered with woods and undergrowth and wholly unknown to us. Every division came into action opportunely and fought squarely on the 19th. We were largely outnumbered, yet foiled the enemy's flank movement on our left, and secured our own position on the road to Chattanooga. The battle of the 20th was fought with all the troops we had, and, but for the extension and delay in closing our right, we should probably have driven the enemy, whom we really beat on the field. I am fully satisfied that the enemy's loss largely exceeds ours.

It is my duty to notice the services of those faithful officers who have none but myself to notice them.

To Major-General Thomas, the true soldier, the prudent and undaunted commander, the modest and incorruptible patriot, the thanks and the gratitude of the country are due for his conduct at the battle of Chickamauga.

Major-General Granger, by his promptitude, arrived and carried his troops into action in time to save the day. He deserves the highest praise. Major-General McCook, for the care of his command, prompt and willing execution of orders, to the best of his ability, deserves this testimonial of my approbation.

I bear testimony likewise to the high hearted, noble Major-General Crittenden. Prompt in the moving and reporting the position of his troops, always fearless on the field of battle, I return my thanks for the promptness and military good sense with which I sent his division towards the noise of battle on the 19th.

To Brigadier-General James A. Garfield, Chief of Staff, I am especially indebted for the clear and ready manner in which he seized the points of action and movement, and expressed in orders the ideas of the general commanding.

Colonel J. C. McKibben, A.D.C., always efficient, gallant, and untiring, and fearless in battle.

Lieutenant-Colonel A.C. Ducat, brave, prompt, and energetic in action. Major Frank S. Bond, senior A.D.C., Captain J. P. Drouillard, A.D.C., and Captain R. S. Thoms, A.D.C., deserve my honorable mention for the faithful and efficient discharge of their appropriate duties always, and especially during the battle.

Colonel Jas. Barnett, Chief of Artillery; Lieutenant-Colonel Simmons, Chief Commissary; Lieutenant-Colonel H. C. Hodges, Chief Quartermaster; Dr. G. Perin, Medical Director; Captain Horace Porter, Chief of Ordnance; Captain Wm. E. Merrill, Chief Topographical Engineer; Brigadier General J. St. Clair Morton, were all in the battle, and discharged their duties with ability and to my entire satisfaction.

Colonel Wm. J. Palmer, 15th Pennsylvania Cavalry, and his command, have rendered very valuable services in keeping open communications and watching the movements of the enemy, which deserve my warmest thanks.

Lieutenant-Colonel W. M. Ward, with the 10th Ohio Provost and Head-Quarters Guard, rendered efficient and valuable services, especially on the 20th, in covering the movement of retiring trains on the Dry Valley road, and stopping the stragglers from the fight. Captain Garner and the escort deserve mention for untiring energy in carrying orders.

Lieutenant-Colonel C. Goddard, Assistant Adjutant-General; Lieutenant Colonel Wm. M. Wiles, Provost-Marshal General; Major Wm. McMichael, Assistant Adjutant-General; Surgeon H. H. Seyes. Medical Inspector; Captain D. G. Swain, Assistant Adjutant-General and Chief of the Secret Service; Captain William Farrar, Aide-de-Camp; Captain J. H. Young, General Commissary of Musters; Captain A. S. Burt, Acting Assistant Inspector-General; Captain H. Brooke, Acting Judge-Advocate; Captain W. C. Morgendant, Acting Topographical Engineer; Lieutenant George Burroughs, Topographical Engineer; Lieutenant Wm. Porter, Acting Aide-de-Camp; Lieutenant James Reynolds, Acting Aide-de-Camp; Lieutenant M. J. Kelly, Chief of Couriers; and Assistant Surgeon D. Bache, were on the field of battle, and there and elsewhere discharged their duties with zeal and ability.

I must not omit Colonel J. P. Sanderson, of the regular infantry, who, having lately joined us, on those two days of battle acted as aide-de-camp, and carried orders to the hottest part of the field.

Of those division and brigade commanders whose gallantry, skill, and services are prominent, individual special mention accompanies this report. A list of the names of those, and others, of every grade, whose conduct, according to the reports of their respective commanders, deserves special mention, is also herewith sent.

MAJOR-GENERAL W. S. ROSECRANS.

INDEX.